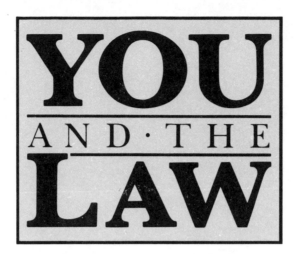

YOU
AND · THE
LAW

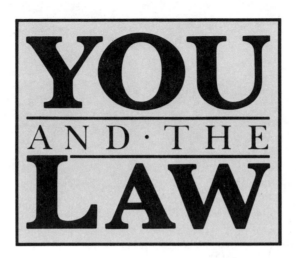

YOU AND·THE LAW

PROFESSOR MICHAEL FURMSTON
T.D., M.A., B.C.L., LL.M.

DR. VINCENT POWELL-SMITH
LL.B., LL.M., D.Litt., F.C.I. Arb.

CONTRIBUTORS

SECTION 1: The Law in Action .... Stephen Jones
SECTION 2: The Law and Your Home .... Richard Whish
SECTION 3: The Law and Your Job .... Vincent Powell-Smith
SECTION 4: The Law and Your Money .... Vincent Powell-Smith
SECTION 5: The Law and Your Business .... John Parkinson
SECTION 6: The Law and Your Family .... Michael Furmston
SECTION 7: Motoring and the Law .... David Feldman
SECTION 8: The Law and Your Leisure
            Gambling .... David Clarke
            Holidays .... John Parkinson
            Sports and Pastimes .... Richard Townshend-Smith
            Using the Countryside .... Christine Willmore
SECTION 9: Criminal Law and You .... Stephen Jones

This edition published 1987 by
Book Club Associates
by arrangement with
The Hamlyn Publishing Group Limited

Typesetting by Phoenix Photosetting, Chatham, Kent
The publishers would like to thank Jonathan Abnett
at Phoenix for his help on this book.

Printed in England

CONTENTS

BIOGRAPHIES viii

INTRODUCTION ix

SECTION 1
THE LAW IN ACTION

INTRODUCTION 2
LEGAL ADVICE 3
Sources of legal advice 3
Funding of legal advice and representation . . . 5
Duty solicitor schemes 14
Complaints against lawyers 15

SETTLEMENT OF DISPUTES 17
The Courts 17

SECTION 2
THE LAW AND YOUR HOME

HOUSE PURCHASE 38
Introduction 38
Choosing the property 38
Financing the purchase 45
Exchanging contracts 52
Completing the transaction 58
Insuring the property 68
Selling 69

RENTING A HOUSE OR FLAT 71
Introduction 71
Private sector tenancies 72
Housing association tenancies 96
Council housing 97
Long leases 103

RIGHTS AND DUTIES OF OWNERS
   AND OCCUPIERS 106
Introduction 106
Neighbours 106
Planning and compulsory purchase 117

SECTION 3
THE LAW AND YOUR JOB

THE CONTRACT OF EMPLOYMENT   122
Employee's duties 122
Employer's duties 123
Written particulars of employment 125
Change of employer 128
Terms and conditions of employment 128

Varying the terms 130
Wages and other benefits 130
Hours of work 133
Holidays 133
Time off work for public duties 133
Maternity rights 133
Disciplinary rules 136
Ending the contract of employment 137

SAFETY, HEALTH AND WELFARE . . 139
Introduction 139
Common law duties 139
Health and Safety at Work etc Act 1974 140
Other legislation 142
Suspension on medical grounds 144

TRADE UNION MEMBERSHIP 145
The legal right to join an independent trade
   union and to take part in its activities 145
The legal right not to belong to a trade union . 146
Exclusion or expulsion by the union 147
Making a complaint 148
Action short of dismissal 148
Union recognition 148
Membership of a trade union 149

DISMISSAL 151
Introduction . . . . , , , . 151
What is dismissal? 151
Fair and unfair dismissal 153
Grounds for dismissal 153
Disciplinary rules and procedures 156

REDUNDANCY 158
Introduction 158
Who qualifies for redundancy pay? 158
What is dismissal for redundancy? 158
Offer of a new job 159
Calculating redundancy pay 161
Lay-off and short-time working 161

DISCRIMINATION IN
   EMPLOYMENT 163
Introduction 163
Discrimination prohibited 163
Equal pay 164
Remedies 165
Racial discrimination 165
Victimisation 166
Segregation 166

GOING TO AN INDUSTRIAL
   TRIBUNAL 167
Industrial tribunals 167

CONTENTS

Reviews and appeals 174
Remedies 174

SECTION 4
THE LAW AND YOUR MONEY

BUYING AND SELLING GOODS 178
Introduction 178
Contractual liability 178
Liability in negligence – direct claims against
    manufacturers 181
Statutory protection 182
Sales between private individuals 184
Auction sales 184
Buying through mail order 185
Unsolicited goods 186
Buying on the doorstep 187

REPAIRS AND SERVICES 188
The contractor's obligations 188
Price of repairs 189
Uncollected goods 189

HIRING GOODS 191
Owner's obligations 192
Hirer's obligations 192

BUYING ON LONG-TERM CREDIT . . 194
Hire purchase 195
Credit sale agreements 200
Other forms of retail credit 201
Regulation of credit business 205
Credit rating and refusal of credit 205
Extortionate credit bargains 206
Rates of interest – calculating the annual
    percentage rate 207

BANK ACCOUNTS 208
Types of account 208
Bank giro 212

DEBTS AND FINANCIAL PROBLEMS 213
Debt collecting agencies 213
County Court proceedings 213
Enforcing a judgment 215
Administration order 216
Bankruptcy 216

SECTION 5
THE LAW AND YOUR BUSINESS

DIFFERENT TYPES OF BUSINESS . . . 218
Sole traders 218
Partnerships 218
Limited companies 222
Business names 262

FINANCING YOUR BUSINESS 264
Different ways of raising capital 264
Problems of getting paid 268

TAX AND YOUR BUSINESS 273
Income tax 273
Corporation tax 277
Capital gains tax 279
Inheritance tax 280
Transfer of a business to a company 280
Sole trader/partnership versus company 281
Value added tax 283
National insurance contributions 284
Taking on employees 285

PROTECTING YOUR BUSINESS'S
    ASSETS 286
Insurance 286
Copyrights, patents, designs and trade marks . 287

ADVERTISING 291

SECTION 6
THE LAW AND YOUR FAMILY

MARRIAGE 296
Introduction 296
Formalities 297
Capacity to marry 300
Effects of a nullity decree 302
Marriages abroad 303
Polygamous marriages 303
Unmarried unions 304

PARENTS AND CHILDREN 305
Parental rights and obligations 305
Who is entitled to exercise parental rights? . . . 306
Adoption 311
Child care 315
Fostering 318
Education 318
Unmarried parents and their children 320
Coming of age 325

FAMILY ASSETS 327
Property rights 327
Position on death of one partner 334
Insurance and pensions 344
Covenants 350
Bankruptcy 351

ENDING A MARRIAGE 353
Introduction 353
Divorce 353
Judicial separation 360
Disputes about children 360
Property and financial questions 360

SECTION 7
MOTORING AND THE LAW

INTRODUCTION: THE LAW, THE HIGHWAY CODE AND SOME DEFINITIONS 370

REQUIREMENTS FOR DRIVING 372
The driver: licensing and learning 372
Motor insurance 377
Vehicle licensing and registration 386
The condition of the vehicle 387

CRIMINAL OFFENCES AND POLICE POWERS 390
Offences connected with motoring 390
Offences and police powers in relation to drink and drugs 392
Other specific moving traffic offences 395
Penalties 395

BREAKDOWNS AND ACCIDENTS ... 397
What to do in the event of a breakdown 397
What to do in the event of an accident 397

CLAIMS AND LIABILITIES 399
Liability for personal injury 399
Liability for damage to property 400
Liability of highway authorities 400
Making claims on the insurer 401
Uninsured drivers 401
Disputes with insurers 401

SPECIAL RULES RELATING TO CARAVANS AND TRAILERS 402

TRAVELLING ABROAD 403

SECTION 8
THE LAW AND YOUR LEISURE

GAMBLING 406
Introduction 406
Some basic principles 406
Betting 408
Gaming 411
Lotteries 414
Taxation on gambling 417

HOLIDAYS 418
Travelling by train 418
Travelling by coach 418

Travelling by air 419
Passports and travelling abroad 419
Problems with travel agents and tour operators 420
Hotels 423
Restaurants 425
Public houses 427

SPORTS AND PASTIMES 429
Introduction 429
The criminal liability of participants 429
The civil liability of participants 431
The criminal liability of organisers 433
The civil liability of organisers 433
The need for insurance 438
Clubs and their members 438

USING THE COUNTRYSIDE 440
Rights of way 440
Other places to use in the countryside 443
What can be done in the countryside 444
At the seaside 445
Protecting the countryside 446

SECTION 9
CRIMINAL LAW AND YOU

INTRODUCTION 452

THE LAW AND THE VICTIM OF CRIME 453
Has a crime been committed? 453
Reasons why the offender may not be convicted in Court 466
What to do if you are a victim 469
Are you entitled to compensation? 470

THE LAW AND THE ACCUSED 474
Summons or arrest? 474
Trial on indictment at the Crown Court 479
Sentence 481
Rights of appeal 483
Disqualifications 485
Controlling stigma 488

BIBLIOGRAPHY 490

INDEX 491

BIOGRAPHIES

MICHAEL FURMSTON read Law at Oxford from 1953 to 1957 and was called to the Bar in 1960. He taught at Birmingham and Belfast before becoming a Fellow of Lincoln College, Oxford in 1974. Since 1978 he has been Professor of Law at the University of Bristol. He was Dean of the Law Faculty from 1980 to 1984, and in 1986 was appointed a Pro Vice-Chancellor of the University. He lives in the Mendips with his wife and their ten children. In his spare time he likes to watch cricket and play chess by post, at which he has represented England in two Olympiads.

VINCENT POWELL-SMITH read Law at Birmingham and taught at the University of Aston before taking up a career as an Arbitrator. He is also a well-known speaker at conferences, a legal journalist and has written a number of books, mainly on the construction industry. He lives in Portugal.

STEPHEN JONES studied Law at Durham, was called to the Bar and then studied Criminology at Cambridge. He has been a Lecturer in the Faculty of Law, University of Bristol since 1974. He is married to the painter, Filomena van Jole.

RICHARD WHISH read Law at Oxford and qualified as a solicitor in 1977. He has been a Lecturer in the Law Faculty of Bristol University since 1978. His interests include opera, gardening and travel.

JOHN PARKINSON read Law at Oxford and qualified as a solicitor before practising with a leading firm in the City of London. He has been a Lecturer in Law at Bristol University since 1980. His interests include architecture, pot-holing, deep sea diving and photography.

DAVID FELDMAN read Law at Oxford and has been a Lecturer in Law at the University of Bristol since 1976. He is married with a daughter and his hobbies include music, cricket, soccer and cooking.

RICHARD TOWNSHEND-SMITH read Law at Oxford and taught at the University of Illinois before becoming a Lecturer in the Faculty of Law at Bristol in 1973. He is married and has two children. In his spare time he like to play cricket, tennis and squash.

CHRISTINE WILLMORE read Law at the University of Bristol before being called to the Bar. She has been a Lecturer at the Faculty of Law, University of Bristol since 1980. She is a Councillor on the North Avon District Council and is Secretary of the Association of Local Councillors. She is Legal Consultant to the Countryside Commission on access issues and Legal Advisor on the preparation of the Access Charter. She is on the National Executive of the Byways and Bridleways Trust.

DAVID CLARKE read Law at Cambridge before qualifying as a solicitor and practising in Lincoln. He has been a Lecturer in Law at Bristol University since 1977 and was recently a visiting Lecturer in the University of Canterbury, Christchurch, New Zealand. He is married with two daughters.

INTRODUCTION

It is a curious paradox about the British that they regard themselves as a law-abiding race but are deeply suspicious of lawyers. This can often mean that the citizen can be vague about the details of the law by which he is trying to abide! With an increasingly complex society, in which governments of all political complexions add inexorably to the body of laws which govern us, this can be very dangerous.

Any attempt to compress so much material into the covers of a single book obviously involves many difficult problems of selection. This book is designed to introduce the reader to those aspects of the law which are most likely to be encountered in everyday life. We have tried to write the sections so that they read as a whole, though obviously some readers will prefer to keep the book primarily as a work of reference. In the choice of topics we have concentrated on those which are most practically relevant, omitting the subtle refinements of which lawyers are perhaps over-fond.

Law is of interest not only to those who have legal problems but all who take an interest in what goes on around them. We have tried therefore to draw a map of the law which will help those who are puzzled by the legal implications of matters that they encounter in the papers or see on TV or hear on the radio.

Lawyers have a saying, 'A man who is his own lawyer has a fool for a client'. It is worth emphasising that this book is not intended to equip the reader to act as his own lawyer. We hope that readers confronted with a personal problem will find here some indications of the way in which the law is likely to handle it, so that they will be better able to seek out a lawyer and take his advice. We hope it may help to make co-operation between lawyers and clients more fruitful.

No reader should attempt to act as his own lawyer on the strength of the information contained herein, and for that reason the Editor, Contributors and Publishers cannot accept responsibility.

The laws described in this book are those of England and Wales as at 1 November 1986.

Michael Furmston

SECTION 1
THE LAW IN ACTION

1.1 INTRODUCTION

People experience all sorts of problems in everyday life and in many cases they look to the law to provide a remedy. In the other sections of this book we shall look at the extent to which these expectations are met. In this first section, however, we shall consider how a person is able to discover if the law can help him; if he can afford the help that is available; and the Court in which his problem can be dealt with. We shall be dealing throughout the book with the legal system and laws of England and Wales: Scotland, Northern Ireland, the Isle of Man and the Channel Islands have their own systems and laws. The reasons for this are historical. It is interesting to note, for example, that Scottish law is largely based on the continental system because Scotland formerly had close trading links with Flanders. On the other hand, English law has strongly influenced the laws of countries which have been under British jurisdiction, such as the USA, Canada, Australia and New Zealand.

'The Law' is usually broken down into divisions which will vary among different legal systems. There is one crucial division, however, which is common to most developed legal systems, including the English, and that is between criminal law and civil law. Many people, no doubt influenced by the large number of crime reports in the newspapers, and television series ranging from 'Perry Mason' to 'Petrocelli', seem to identify 'law' with 'criminal law'. Yet civil law is not only far more voluminous and wide-ranging than criminal law, but it is also far more important for an individual who has a problem which he wants the law to deal with. How does a crime differ from a civil wrong? One way of illustrating the distinction is by looking at the legal consequences that may follow. If a person is convicted of a criminal offence, he will probably be punished. If the punishment should involve the payment of a sum of money – a fine – this would go to the State and not to the victim. It is possible that a Criminal Court may order an accused to pay some compensation to his victim, but this is very unlikely to be adequate. (This is discussed more fully in Section 9.) In any case, compensation is certainly not the main purpose of criminal proceedings. However, if a person were successfully to sue someone – say for a breach of contract or negligence – compensation in the form of a sum of money (known as 'damages') would probably be ordered to cover the loss. Alternatively, a court might order a person to do something or refrain from doing something: this is know as an 'injunction'. Not only is the terminology used in criminal and civil proceedings different (for example, the terms 'prosecute' and 'sue') but the cases will start in different Courts and follow completely different procedures.

1. SOURCES OF LEGAL ADVICE

There are three main sources of legal advice in this country: lawyers, Law Centres and Citizens' Advice Bureaux.

(i) Lawyers

(A) Solicitors. The legal profession is divided into two branches, solicitors and barristers. It is to solicitors that members of the public must turn – there is generally no direct right of access to a barrister. There are more than 45,000 practising solicitors divided among some 6,500 firms. Their operation is controlled by the Law Society with its seat in Central London and local law societies. The Royal Commission on Legal Services, which reported in 1979, found that nearly 60% of people over eighteen had seen a solicitor concerning a personal difficulty. Solicitors provide general legal advice, although there are many firms which specialise in certain types of work, whether it be Legal Aid work in the provinces or commercial work in the City of London. A survey commissioned by the Law Society in 1975–6 shows how solicitors derive their income: conveyancing 47.4%, probate 13.5%, company 12.5%, matrimonial 5.4%, crime 4.5%, personal injury 3.3% and other work 13.4%. There is no precise information, but it is generally accepted that conveyancing work is more profitable than other types of work except commercial and company. This heavy reliance on conveyancing and the fact that the number of solicitors has dramatically increased since the war (more than doubling in the decade from 1970 to 1980) are not unrelated. Solicitors have been assisted in two important respects; (a) by their near-monopoly of conveyancing, and (b) by the steadily increasing number of people who own their own homes. The latter is likely to continue but – in one of the most surprising legal developments in years – the conveyancing monopoly is to be abolished.

The end of the solicitors' conveyancing monopoly. The monopoly, which has existed since 1804, is now contained in section 22 of the Solicitors Act 1974. It is illegal for an unqualified person to draw or prepare any instrument of transfer or conveyance on the sale of land if he does so 'in the expectation of any fee, gain or reward'. Thus, it has always been open to a person to carry out his own conveyancing and several books have been published in recent years to assist a person in doing this. Nor does the prohibition apply to the earlier stages of the transaction and cut-price conveyancing firms have sought to take advantage of this by doing the preliminary work themselves and using a solicitor only to draft the important documents. The Law Society has brought a number of prosecutions under section 22: although the maximum penalty is low (a £50 fine), the pressure seemed to pay off as these firms were never able to offer a serious threat to solicitors.

When the Royal Commission on Legal Services decided by ten votes to five that the conveyancing monopoly should be retained, most people thought that the issue was closed for the foreseeable future. However, a private members' bill in 1983 calling for its abolition was adopted by the Government and a committee was set up to suggest ways in which conveyancing could be carried out by people other than solicitors. The main recommendations adopted are contained in the Administration of Justice Act 1985. A system of licensed conveyancers is to be established. Its operation is to be controlled by a Council for Licensed Conveyancers. The Council will arrange for tests to assess the competence of licensed conveyancers. A person who passes the tests will be eligible for a licence. Each licence will last for twelve months. Obviously, solicitors will not have to obtain these licences. 'Do-it-yourself' conveyancing will still be allowed to continue. At the time of writing the Council for Licensed Conveyancers has been set up, but the system of licensed conveyancers has not been introduced.

Solicitors in general no longer fear competition from licensed conveyancers. What they are far more concerned about is competition in this sphere from building societies and banks. The Building Societies Bill 1985, which at the time of writing is still proceeding through Parliament, enables building societies and banks to offer a conveyancing service. However, in its present form, the Bill does not allow these services to be offered to customers for whom a loan is being provided as part of a 'home-buyer's package'.

The Government apparently takes the view that this would create a conflict of interests for the lending institution. If this restriction should remain in the Bill, banks and building societies would not be interested in conveyancing and solicitors throughout the country would breathe a sigh of relief.

Other monopolies.
(a) Commencing proceedings in Court. Under the Solicitors Act 1974, it is an offence for a non-lawyer to prepare 'any instrument relating to any legal proceeding' if it is done for any 'fee, gain or reward'. There is a maximum fine of £50. Once again, no offence is committed if no fee is charged. This is how voluntary organisations, such as Citizens' Advice Bureaux, manage to complete forms for their clients without breaking the law.

(b) Rights of audience in the Courts. It is widely believed that solicitors and barristers have a monopoly over rights of audience in the lower Courts, with barristers alone having a monopoly in the higher Courts. The position concerning barristers is explained below. Solicitors have rights of audience in Magistrates' Courts and County Courts but it is not the case that they have an absolute monopoly:

(1) Section 122 of the Magistrates' Courts Act 1980 states 'A party to any proceedings before a Magistrates' Court may be represented by counsel or solicitor'. The section does not say that no-one else has rights of audience and Magistrates' Courts commonly allow police officers to represent the prosecution.
(2) Section 60 of the County Courts Act 1984 provides that a party to the proceedings, a barrister or a solicitor may address the Court, and also 'any other person allowed by leave of the Court to appear instead of any party'. However, it is unlikely that a County Court would allow lay representation without a very good reason.
(3) A litigant has always been allowed to represent himself in any Court. He is also allowed to have a friend sitting alongside him to provide help. Such a person is often referred to as a 'McKenzie man', as this right was re-affirmed in the case *McKenzie v McKenzie* (1970).

McKenzie v McKenzie
McKenzie was seeking to divorce his wife. He did not have Legal Aid and was appearing in person. His former solicitors sent a clerk to sit next to him and provide assistance. When the judge discovered this, he told the clerk that he must not participate in the proceedings. The Court of Appeal held that there was a long-established right for a litigant in person to have such a helper. It approved the view expressed in a case decided in 1831: 'Any person, whether he be a professional man or not, may attend as a friend of either party, may take notes, may quietly make suggestions, and give advice; but no one can demand to take part in the proceedings as an advocate . . .'

Advertising. Solicitors are subject to a number of professional restrictions. For example, they are not allowed to tout for business or share their offices with people who are not lawyers. Until 1984, they were not allowed to advertise. However, following pressure from various sources, the Law Society decided to allow advertising from October 1st of that year. Solicitors are now allowed to advertise in the newspapers and on the radio. Unlike their brethren in Scotland, they are not allowed to advertise on television. Nor are they allowed to mail advertisements. The advertisements must not be in bad taste or suggest that their firm is better than others. Solicitors can state the type of work they are prepared to carry out and how much they would charge for it.

It seems that, after some early enthusiasm, few solicitors now make use of advertising. In December 1985 it was announced that solicitors had voted in favour of keeping the right to advertise – but only by a fairly small majority.

(B) Barristers. Although the public perception of a barrister is of a man who spends his working life in Court, in reality barristers – like many solicitors – divide their time between Court work and paperwork in their office (known as 'chambers'). The paperwork comprises writing opinions on different points of law for solicitors and drafting documents in relation to Court cases. Barristers generally have sole rights of audience (other than a litigant himself) in the Crown Court, the High Court, the Court of Appeal and the House of Lords. As they only receive instructions from solicitors, they have little professional contact with laymen. Unlike solicitors, they are not allowed to form partnerships, but they share chambers, clerical staff and a clerk. A barrister's clerk is a very important individual. He deals with solicitors and negotiates the barrister's fees. He usually takes a commission from the fees as his own remuneration; this may be as much as 10%.

The number of practising barristers has greatly increased in the last 30 years. In the 1950s the figure was about 2,000 but by the end of 1982 it had risen to 4,864. There are now over 5,000 practising barristers. We have already seen a similar development in relation to solicitors but the reason for the Bar's increase is the considerable extension of Legal Aid in criminal and divorce work. Around 10% of barristers are 'Queen's Counsel' (QCs). They are sometimes referred to as 'silks' because of the silk gowns they wear. A QC will deal with more important cases and, consequently, charge higher fees. He is no longer involved in much of the paperwork, such as the drafting of statements of claim and defences. There is a risk in applying to 'take silk' because there are not so many important cases about and there is always the danger that a QC will find himself without any work. Formerly, a QC always had to appear in Court with another barrister, known as a 'junior'. (The 'junior' could be older than the QC!) The Monopolies and Mergers Commission considered the rule to be against the public interest and in 1977 it was revised. A QC now has the right to appear in Court without a junior, but he can expect that a junior has been instructed unless he is told to the contrary. He can also refuse to appear without a junior if he feels it would affect his ability to conduct the case or any other case, or to 'fulfil his professional or semi-professional commitments'. As QCs in practice only appear in big cases, it is unusual to find one in Court without a junior.

(ii) Law Centres and Advice Centres
The first Law Centre opened at North Kensington in 1970. The Royal Commission on Legal Services carried out a survey of Law Centres in 1978. At that time there were 27, with 17 in Greater London and the rest in Belfast, Birmingham, Cardiff, Coventry, Liverpool, Manchester, Merthyr Tydfil and Newcastle. By 1984 the number had risen to 45. Law Centres provide free legal advice and tend to specialise in the sorts of problems typically experienced by residents of the inner city areas in which they are usually situated, such as tenants' rights and welfare law. They are staffed by qualified lawyers and are heavily reliant for financial support on local authority funding and charitable sources. Cutbacks in local authority expenditure in recent years have resulted in the future of many Centres being placed in jeopardy and it seems likely that a number will be forced to close.

Advice Centres are run on a part-time basis, usually in the evenings. They are staffed by local solicitors, giving their services free. There is no charge to the client, but unlike a Law Centre, a solicitor in an Advice Centre cannot start Court proceedings on a client's behalf. He would have to see the client privately in his office.

(iii) Citizens' Advice Bureaux
There are about 840 Citizens' Advice Bureaux throughout the country. They are mostly staffed by volunteers but about 10% of the workers are paid. They are usually financed by local authorities and provide free advice. A survey carried out for the Royal Commission on Legal Services in 1976 indicated that about a third of the inquiries dealt with by Bureaux had some legal content. In nearly half the Bureaux there are schemes whereby local solicitors turn up on a rota basis to offer free advice. Citizens' Advice Bureaux are also very useful in directing clients to sources of specialist advice such as solicitors (they keep lists of all the local firms), Law Centres or Advice Centres.

2. FUNDING OF LEGAL ADVICE AND REPRESENTATION

(i) The Legal Advice and Assistance Scheme
Many people get their initial advice either from an agency such as the Citizens' Advice Bureau or from their trade union. Such bodies may advise that the problem needs specialist advice. However, a person may be deterred from obtaining this by the thought that he would have to pay for the services provided. But this is not necessarily the case. If the individual is eligible under the Legal Advice and Assistance Scheme, he may only have to pay a reduced fee, or possibly no fee at all.

The first step to take is to find a solicitors' firm which participates in the Legal Aid Scheme. Most firms (with the exception of large commercial practices) will take legal aid work and it is usually possible to see this from a sign in the solicitors' office window. The Legal Advice and Assistance Scheme, which was introduced in April 1973, is usually referred to as the 'Green Form Scheme' because of the colour of the claim form. An example of a completed form is shown opposite. An individual may obtain advice or assistance either orally or in writing. The sort of help provided by the solicitor includes writing letters, carrying out negotiations, drafting documents (including a will and a conveyance) and helping to draft Court forms or prepare an argument for the client to present in Court. The client can also be helped to complete a form applying for full legal aid and, in practice, the green form is often used for this purpose. The only occasions when the Green Form Scheme can be used to provide legal representation are for domestic proceedings in Magistrates' Courts (for example, an application for maintenance) or before the Mental Health Review Tribunal.

(A) Financial eligibility. The client will only be eligible under the scheme if he satisfies the means test. For this purpose, the client's resources are divided into 'disposable income' and 'disposable capital'.

'Disposable income' is the clients actual income less tax, national insurance contributions and an allowance for each dependant. The dependant's allowances are shown on the Green Form Key Card (see page 9).

'Disposable capital' refers to the value of the client's possessions, excluding his house, his furniture, his clothes and the tools of his trade. The client has a free limit at £800 with allowances for dependants (see page 9). For cases where representation is allowed the disposable capital limit is £3,000. There is no contribution payable on disposable capital. If the client is married, the income and capital of the spouse are taken into account unless they are separated, or have a 'contrary interest' (are in dispute with each other, as in a divorce case). A cohabitee's finances are not taken into account. If a child is suing through its parents, the finances of the parents will be considered jointly; but if a child is suing one of its parents (for example, to recover money from his father's insurers after a car accident), that parent's finances would not be taken into account as he would have a 'contrary interest'.

(B) How much advice can be obtained under the scheme? When the scheme was introduced, the limit was £25 worth of work and the scheme is still sometimes referred to as the '£25 scheme'. The limit now stands at £50 (or £90 for undefended divorce cases). At present, solicitors are paid £28.50 an hour for providing advice under the scheme (there are additional payments for writing letters and making telephone calls). It is possible for a solicitor to apply to the Law Society's Legal Aid Office to have the limit raised in any particular case and permission can be given over the telephone. The client's contribution is not affected by this. The £50 limit does not apply in the cases where representation is allowed.

(C) The statutory charge. One of the biggest difficulties concerning the Green Form Scheme is the existence of the 'statutory charge'. If the solicitor's fees are more than the contribution he receives from the client (and in some cases there will be no contribution at all) he can claim the difference from any money he recovers on his client's behalf. The effect of this is that it is worthless to use the Green Form Scheme to pursue small claims. Suppose that a solicitor writes letters for A, who pays no contribution, to help him recover £25 which A is owed and the amount is paid. The solicitor's fee is £20. He can deduct this from the money which he has recovered for A, so A only receives £5.

The statutory charge does not always apply. If no property or money is recovered, there is nothing on which to impose the charge. The charge cannot be deducted from money recovered for maintenance payments or from a number of benefits including maternity benefit, child benefit, family income supplement, industrial injury benefits, rent allowances and rebates, retirement pension, supplementary benefit, unemployment benefit, and from only half the payments received from redundancies. Moreover, the charge can be waived in any case where it 'would cause grave hardship or distress to the client to enforce' it or where its enforcement would cause 'unreasonable difficulty because of the nature of the property'. The moral here is that any client who thinks he might come under one of the exceptions should raise the matter with the solicitor, who can then ask the Legal Aid Office to waive the charge.

LA/Rep/6A
GREEN FORM

THE LAW SOCIETY

LEGAL AID
ENGLAND and WALES

Key Card →

SOLICITOR'S REPORT ON LEGAL ADVICE AND ASSISTANCE GIVEN UNDER
THE LEGAL AID ACT 1974

PLEASE USE BLOCK CAPITALS		
Surname SMITH	Forenames WILLIAM	Male/~~Female~~	AREA REF. No.

Address 1 ACACIA AVENUE, CLIFTON, BRISTOL 8

Full name and address of applicant

CAPITAL	CLIENT	£ 750
TOTAL SAVINGS and OTHER CAPITAL	SPOUSE	£ 200
	TOTAL	£ 950

Ⓐ *Applicant's capital*

INCOME
State whether in receipt of Supplementary Benefit or Family Income Supplement.
~~YES~~/NO   If the answer is YES ignore the rest of this Section.

Ⓑ

Total weekly Gross Income

Client	£ 120.00
Spouse	£ NIL
TOTAL	£ 120.00

Applicant's income

Allowances and Deductions from Income

Income tax	£ 14.40
National Health Contributions, etc.	£ 11.25
Spouse	£ 28.75

Ⓒ Ⓓ Ⓔ

Dependent children and/or other dependants	Number	
Under 5		£
5 but under 11	I	£ 12.65
11 ,, ,, 13		£
13 ,, ,, 16		£
16 ,, ,, 18		£
18 and over		£

Ⓕ

LESS TOTAL DEDUCTIONS	→ £ 67.05
TOTAL WEEKLY DISPOSABLE INCOME	£ 52.95

TO BE COMPLETED AND SIGNED BY CLIENT

I am over the compulsory school-leaving age.

I ~~have~~/have not previously received help from a solicitor about this matter under the Legal Aid and Advice Schemes.

I am liable to pay a contribution not exceeding .. .. £ NIL   Ⓖ

I understand that any money or property which is recovered or preserved for me may be subject to a deduction if my contribution (if any) is less than my Solicitor's charges.

The information on this page is to the best of my knowledge correct and complete.   I understand that dishonesty in providing such information may lead to a prosecution.

Date...................   Signature *William Smith*............................

Applicant's signature

CLAIM FOR PAYMENT TO ACCOMPANY FORM LA/ACC/8B

Name of Client

Where appropriate did the Court give approval to assistance under Section 2 (4) of the Legal Aid Act 1974?   Yes/No.

Has a Legal Aid Order been made?   Yes/No.

If so, give date

PLEASE ATTACH ANY AUTHORITIES GIVEN BY THE AREA COMMITTEE

TICK THE APPROPRIATE LETTER TO INDICATE THE NATURE OF THE PROBLEM

A. Divorce or judicial separation (see note on page 1)

B. Other family matters (Specify in Summary)

C. Crime

D. Landlord/tenant/housing

E. H.P. and Debt

F. Employment

G. Accident/injuries

H. Welfare benefits/tribunals

J. Immigration/Nationality

K. Consumer problems

L. Other matters (Specify in Summary)

Has any money or property been recovered? If so, give details.

No. of letters written	
No. of telephone calls Made Received	
Time otherwise spent: Specify in Summary	

Summary of work done:

Has a legal aid certificate or order been granted? Yes/No.

If not, is one being applied for? Yes/No.

Certificate or Order No. if appropriate:

PARTICULARS OF COSTS

	£		£
1. Profit costs		Details of disbursements:—	
2. Disbursements (including Counsel's fees)		Counsel's fees (if any)	
3. Add VAT as appropriate		Other disbursements (listed)	
TOTAL CLAIM			
4. Deduct maximum contribution (if any)			
NET CLAIM			

Have you previously made a claim for legal advice and assistance for your client in respect of divorce or judicial separation proceedings or matters connected therewith.   YES/NO   If Yes, how much was allowed £

Signed   Solicitor   Date   Solicitor's ref.

Firm name (in full)

Address

Date

NOTICE OF PROVISIONAL ASSESSMENT

The Area Committee have assessed your costs in this matter as set out below. In view of the fact that the sum assessed is less than that claimed, you may make written representations to the Committee in support of your claim as originally submitted or on any item in it, if you wish. These representations must be received within 14 days of the date hereof. I have deleted this matter from the consolidated claim form LA/ACC/8B with which it was sent and I should be obliged if you would do the same. If you accept the provisional assessment, please include this matter on your next consolidated claim form as assessed below AND RE-SUBMIT THIS FORM WITH IT.

Area Secretary.

£

1. Profit costs

2. Disbursements

3. Add VAT as appropriate

TOTAL CLAIM

4. Deduct maximum contribution (if any)

NET CLAIM

NOTE.—You are advised to keep a copy of this page because if in the same matter your client obtains a L.A. Certificate or Order, you may on taxation of your costs and disbursements be required to produce to the Taxing Officer a copy of this form indicating work done and quantum of payment. You may also require a copy of this page if after submitting your claim for payment you apply to the Area Committee for a financial extension to enable you to give further advice and assistance to your Client.

APRIL 1977

LEGAL AID
ENGLAND and WALES

THE LAW SOCIETY

Please see over for
explanatory notes.

GREEN FORM KEY CARD
(No. 17)
Effective from 12th March 1986

Green Form

N.B. The green form (LA/Rep/6A)
should not be used for advice to suspects
at police stations from 1st January 1986.
Such cases will be covered by forms
LA/Rep/12 and LA/Acc 10 which were
supplied to the profession during
December 1985.

CAPITAL means the amount or value of every resource of a capital nature
In computing Disposable Capital disregard
(i) the value of the main or only dwelling house in which the client resides, and
(ii) the value of household furniture and effects, articles of personal clothing and tools or
implements of the client's trade, and
(iii) the subject matter of the advice and assistance.

Maximum Disposable Capital for Financial Eligibility (dependant = spouse, child or relative)

Advice and Assistance	Assistance by way of representation
£ 800 – client with no dependants	£3000 – client with no dependants
£1000 – client with 1 dependant	£3200 – client with 1 dependant
£1120 – client with 2 dependants	£3320 – client with 2 dependants
Add £60 for each additional dependant	

The capital and weekly income of both
husband and wife must be taken into
account, unless:
(a) they have a contrary interest;
(b) they live apart; or
(c) it is inequitable or impracticable
to aggregate their means.
If a housewife living with her husband
is seeking advice in connection with a
matter in which he has a contrary
interest, the money which she receives
from him for normal household expenses
should not be included as part of her own
separate income.

INCOME means the total income from all sources which the client received or became entitled to during
or in respect of the seven days up to and including the date of this application.

Note – a client in receipt of supplementary benefit or family income supplement is entitled to advice
and assistance without contribution provided that his disposable capital is within the limits
set out in **A** above.

In computing Disposable Income deduct:-
(i) Income Tax

(ii) Payments under the Social Security Acts 1975-80

These deductions also apply to the
spouse's income if there is aggregation.

(iii) £28.75 in respect of either husband or wife (if living together) whether or not their means
are aggregated. Where they are separated or divorced, the allowance will be the actual
maintenance paid by the client in respect of the previous 7 days.

(iv) £12.65 for each dependent child or dependent relative of the household under 11
years of age
£18.90 for each dependent child or dependent relative of the household of 11 but
under 16 years of age
£22.75 for each dependent child or dependent relative of the household of 16 and 17
years of age
£29.50 for each dependent child or dependent relative of the household of 18 years
of age or over

There is no deduction in relation to a
foster child.

Client's Contributions

Disposable Income		Maximum Contribution	Disposable Income		Maximum Contribution
Not exceeding £54 a week		nil	Not exceeding £83 a week		£29
,,	£62 ,,	£5	,,	£87 ,,	£34
,,	£67 ,,	£11	,,	£91 ,,	£38
,,	£71 ,,	£16	,,	£95 ,,	£42
,,	£75 ,,	£21	,,	£99 ,,	£47
,,	£79 ,,	£25	,,	£104 ,,	£52
			,,	£108 ,,	£57
			,,	£114 ,,	£62

Where the initial green form limit is £50 client's contribution in excess of this amount can only be called
for if a financial extension has been obtained from the general committee.

Note

The green form must be signed by the client at the initial interview as soon as his eligibility has been
determined except in the case of an authorised postal application.

9

GREEN FORM KEY CARD (No. 17)
EXPLANATORY NOTES

1. General

Your attention is particularly drawn to the *Legal Advice and Assistance Regulations (No. 2) 1980* ("the regulations") *pp. 107-123 Legal Aid Handbook 1984* and the *Notes for Guidance on Advice and Assistance* issued by the Council of The Law Society which appear in the *Handbook pp. 199-209.*

2. Financial Eligibility

(a) The responsibility for determining eligibility is placed upon the solicitor (*reg. 7*).

(b) *Schedule 2* of the regulations sets out the method of assessment of resources of the client. The only deductions and allowances which can be made are those referred to in *schedule 2*. Built-in deductions have already been made for miscellaneous expenditure such as rent, mortgage repayments and hire-purchase repayments etc.

(c) When considering a client's means it may be useful to have the following points in mind –

(i) If part of the main dwelling is let and the client lives in the remaining part, although the capital value of the main dwelling house should be left out of account in computing capital, the rent should be included in computing income.

(ii) Capital means the amount or value of every resource of a capital nature so that capital derived from a bank loan or borrowing facilities should be taken into account.

(iii) There is no power to disregard income in self-employed cases merely because the client may have incurred unspecified expenses at an earlier date.

(iv) A cohabitee cannot be included within the definitions of a spouse or dependant. No allowances can therefore be made in respect of a cohabitee nor can his/her income be aggregated with that of the client seeking advice or assistance.

(v) Income means the total income from all sources which the client received or became entitled to during or in respect of the seven days up to and including the date of application. It will include child benefit.

(vi) Fostering allowances received in respect of fostered children should not be taken into account in assessing the financial eligibility of the client.

3. Solicitor and Client relationship

(a) A solicitor for reasonable cause may either refuse to accept an application for legal advice and assistance or having accepted it, decline to give advice and assistance without giving reasons to the client. He may however be required to give reasons to the general committee.

(b) Once financial eligibility has been established, a client should be told of the amount of the contribution due (if any), and arrangements should be made for payment either outright or by instalments. Any contribution paid should be retained on client's account until the matter for which advice and assistance has been given has been concluded.

(c) When the contribution exceeds the costs payable and VAT, the excess should be returned to the client.

4. Remuneration

(a) No VAT is payable on the client's contribution but VAT is of course, payable upon the solicitors costs whether paid out of the legal aid fund or from the contribution paid by the client.

(b) The initial financial limit of expenditure (at present £50, or in the case of an undefended divorce or judicial separation petition case £90) is exclusive of VAT as is any financial extention granted.

(c) The financial limit of £90 in undefended divorce or judicial separation cases is only applicable where a petition has been drafted. It need not however have been filed.

(d) The legal aid fund is only responsible for paying to solicitor and counsel such of their costs as are not covered by the client's contribution (if any) party and party costs awarded and the charge which arises in the solicitors favour on any property recovered or preserved. *Schedule 5* of the regulations sets out the circumstances when the charge does not apply. Application may be made to the area committee for authority not to enforce the charge where (a) it would cause grave hardship or distress to the client, or (b) it could be enforced only with unreasonable difficulty – *(reg 26.)*

5. Authorities

A solicitor may not take steps in court proceedings unless either approval is given by the general committee for assistance by way of representation in a magistrates' court or the court has made a request under *reg 19* of the regulations. It should be noted that the financial limit prescribed by *section 3(2) of the Legal Aid Act 1974* (at present £50) cannot be exceeded when a request has been made under *reg 19* and the solicitor has represented the client.

(a) The authority of the general committee is required before accepting an application from a child *(reg 8(1))*, a person on behalf of a child or patient, such person not falling with the categories referred to in reg 8(2)(a) (b) or (c) *(reg 8(2)(d))*, a person residing outside England and Wales *(reg 9)* and a person who has already received advice and assistance from another solicitor on the same matter *(reg 10)*.

(b) Approval of the general committee is required for assistance by way of representation *(reg 17(1))*. Even if approval is given the prior permission of the general committee is required to obtain a report, or opinion of an expert to tender expert evidence and to perform an act which is either unusual in its nature or involves unusually large expenditure *(reg 17(4).)* Thus the prior permission of the general committee would be required before obtaining a blood test in affiliation proceedings.

MARCH 1986

Printed by Oakley Press Limited

(ii) The Fixed Fee Scheme

It is not commonly realised that the Law Society operate a scheme whereby a solicitor can give half an hour's legal advice for a flat fee of £5. Anyone can use this scheme; there is no means test. Most solicitors who participate in the Legal Aid Scheme offer this service, but a client should make it clear to the solicitor from the outset if he wishes to use the Fixed Fee Scheme or he is likely to find himself being charged the full commercial rate! Solicitors have been told by the Law Society that they can refuse to give an interview 'in appropriate circumstances' so a client cannot insist on his half-hour's advice.

(iii) Legal Aid

The two schemes discussed above both deal with the funding of legal advice. However, an individual may find himself having to appear in Court and the costs involved here could be far higher than for simply consulting a solicitor. The state also provides subsidised or, in some cases, free legal representation. Two separate schemes operate, one for civil cases and the other for criminal cases.

(A) Legal aid in civil cases. The appropriate form for civil legal aid, Legal Aid Form No 1, can be obtained from solicitors and certain other places, such as Citizens' Advice Bureaux. It is important that the form is filled in properly, so it is worthwhile obtaining a solicitor's advice. The Fixed Fee Scheme can be used for this purpose, as can the Green Form Scheme, and some solicitors will provide free assistance on the basis that they are likely to receive the custom if legal aid is granted. Before an individual can be granted civil legal aid, he has to satisfy two requirements:

(a) The merits test. Under section 7(5) of the Legal Aid Act 1974, 'a person shall not be given legal aid in connection with any proceedings unless he shows that he has reasonable grounds for taking, defending, or being a party thereto, and may also be refused legal aid if it appears unreasonable that he should receive it in the particular circumstances of the case'. The Act does not provide any guidelines as to how these tests should be applied, but consideration has usually been given as to whether the average solicitor would advise a client to spend his own money on the case, if he had the means available. The result of this is that legal aid has rarely been granted for small claims. The Law Society's Notes for Guidance now say that the value of the claim to the applicant

himself should be taken into account in making the decision.

If the Legal Aid Committee has doubts about the case, they can give a 'limited certificate' which will allow legal aid up to a certain stage of the proceedings. Before any additional funding can be given, the Committee must look at the case again.

(b) The means test. Satisfying the merits test alone is not sufficient. The applicant must fall within the financial limits.

Applicants can be divided into three groups:

(a) those who can receive free legal aid (their disposable income does not exceed £2,255 and their disposable capital does not exceed £3,000);

(b) those who can receive legal aid subject to a contribution (their disposable income exceeds £2,255 but is less that £5,415 or their disposable capital is between £3,000 and £4,710);

(c) those who cannot receive legal aid (either their disposable income exceeds £5,415 or their disposable capital exceeds £4,710).

'Disposable income' is assessed in accordance with the applicant's projected income over the next twelve months. From this are deducted tax, national insurance contributions, work-related expenses (such as fares and essential equipment) and rent or mortgage payments. At the time of writing, the dependant allowance is a figure of 50% above the supplementary benefit rate, but it has recently been announced that this figure is soon to be reduced to 25%.

'Disposable capital' refers to the value of the applicant's possessions including savings and the amount that could be borrowed on insurance policies, with allowances for certain items. These include value of the house, furniture, clothes, car, tools and trade equipment, and the subject matter of the proceedings (for example, if a couple in divorce proceedings could not agree on how to divide their possessions, the value of the possessions would be ignored).

At present, the dependants' allowances are as follows:

Husband or Wife	£1,794
Each dependant child or dependant relative:	
Under 11	£ 788
11–15	£1,178
16–17	£1,420
18 and over	£1,841

The Law Society has produced an illustrative table based on these figures (see below). The husband's and wife's resources will be added together in the same way as under the Green Form Scheme.

Where a contribution is payable, it is in the case of income assessed by taking the excess over the free limit (£2,255) and dividing it by 4. For capital, the contribution is usually any excess over the free limit (£3,000) but some discretion is allowed.

Nowadays, it can take two or three months before a civil legal aid application is processed. In emergencies, however, it is possible for a solicitor to telephone the Legal Aid Office and ask for legal aid to be granted at once. The office may request that the completed form be delivered so that it can be considered immediately or it might even be prepared to grant permission over the phone. In this case, the means testing would be carried out later. The emergency procedure is very useful if the solicitor needs to obtain an injunction quickly and is often used in the case of wrongfully-evicted tenants or for the exclusion of violent spouses or partners from the home.

(B) Legal aid – the actual cost to the litigant. It is only at the end of the case that the final position on costs becomes clear. It is possible that, even if a legally-aided litigant wins the case, he may be required to pay a further sum for, once again, we come upon the problem of the statutory charge.

Type of Applicant	Income from all sources before deduction of income tax, NI contributions and rent	
	Maximum permitting free legal aid	Minimum which makes applicant ineligible for legal aid
	(D I £2255)	(D I £5416)
	Gross income including child benefit	Gross income including child benefit
1. Single person	£4181 (£80.40 pw)	£9500 (£182.69 pw)
2. Married couple	£6644 (£127.76 pw)	£11,825 (£227.40 pw)
3. Married couple with one child aged 6	£7702 (£148.11 pw)	£12,885 (£247.78 pw)
4. Married couple with two children aged 4 and 8	£8761 (£168.48 pw)	£13,943 (£268.13 pw)
5. Married couple and three children aged 4, 8 and 13	£10,460 (£201.15 pw)	£15,543 (£298.90 pw)
6. Married couple and four children aged 4, 8, 13 and 15	£12,158 (£233.80 pw)	£17,070 (£328.26pw)
7. Married man apart from wife paying court order of £1200 pa	£5694 (£109.50 pw)	£10,876 (£209.15 pw)
8. Single parent with two children aged 4 and 8	£5669 (£109.01 pw)	£10,851 (£208.67 pw)
9. Single parent with three children aged 4, 8 and 13	£7368 (£141.69 pw)	£12,550 (£241.34 pw)

This operates in a similar way as under the Green Form Scheme but, owing to the higher costs involved in litigation, the effect has often been far more devastating. However, following the introduction of an important change in the costs rules in April 1986, it is now being predicted that the impact of the statutory charge will be reduced.

(a) The winner receives legal aid. The basic rule in English civil cases is that the loser pays the winner's costs, irrespective of whether either party received legal aid. If the loser is ordered to pay damages, these will go to the winner's solicitor. He will then pass them on to the Legal Aid Office and they will not be paid to the winner himself until all the legal costs have been settled. The solicitor will then work out his own fees. The problem that arose in the past was that the method of calculating the amount of costs the loser paid to the winner (which was known as the party-and-party basis) was less generous than the method of calculating the amount of costs the solicitor would obtain from the Legal Aid Fund (this was known as the 'common fund' basis). Therefore, a shortfall could arise. If this happened, the solicitor could look for the balance to his client's contribution. But his client might not have made a contribution, or the contribution might not be big enough to meet the shortfall. In this case, the solicitor could claim the balance out of the damages awarded to his client.

This problem is now less likely to arise because the party-and-party basis of assessing costs has been replaced by the 'standard basis'. This is a more generous test: whereas the party-and-party basis only allowed costs which were 'necessary to enable the adverse party to conduct the litigation and no more', the standard basis will allow 'a reasonable amount in respect of all costs reasonably incurred'. Legal aid costs are also now assessed on the standard basis so, unless a litigant employs particularly extravagant lawyers, the discrepancy between two sets of costs should be considerably reduced or even disappear.

Unfortunately, this does not mean the end of the statutory charge. The loser may be ordered to pay the winner's costs but be unable to do so, or he may disappear. Alternatively, the loser may not be ordered to pay the winner's costs. (The situations when this can happen are discussed below.) In these circumstances, the shortfall between what is received by the Legal Aid Office and the money it pays the solicitor could be large and the winner could end up losing all his damages.

Just as with the Green Form Scheme, some awards are exempt from the statutory charge. These include maintenance payments to a wife or child, the first £2,500 of a settlement in a matrimonial case (where property has been transferred from one spouse to the other) and a number of social security benefits. The Legal Aid Office cannot waive the charge completely, but it can postpone its payment. In the case *Hanlon v The Law Society* in 1980, the House of Lords held that the Law Society could delay enforcing the charge where property is transferred in matrimonial proceedings. This will prevent the matrimonial home having to be sold to pay for the costs. The charge will be attached to the home and be enforced if the home is sold. There is still a problem, however, when a transfer of money is ordered to one spouse in order to buy a new matrimonial home.

(b) The loser receives legal aid. If a legally-aided person loses his case, he is liable to pay his costs up to the limit of his contribution. He is also required to pay a reasonable amount towards the winner's costs and this has usually been assessed as an amount equivalent to his contribution. The balance is paid by the Legal Aid fund.

(C) Legal aid in criminal cases. The initial decision to grant legal aid in a Magistrates' Court is made by the Court clerk. If he feels unable to make the order, the Court must make the decision. Legal aid in the Crown Court can be granted either by the magistrates, on committal for trial, or by the Crown Court itself. The accused can challenge a refusal to grant legal aid by the Court by applying to a Criminal Legal Aid Committee, which comprises barristers and solicitors. As with civil legal aid, the accused has to satisfy both a merits test and a means test.

(a) The merits test. Under the Legal Aid Act 1974 section 29(1), the merits test is whether the granting of legal aid is in the interests of justice. The Courts have usually decided this by applying criteria recommended by the Widgery Committee in 1966. Subject to the means test, Legal Aid should be granted where a Court considers:

(a) That the charge is a grave one in the sense that the accused is in real jeopardy of losing his liberty or suffering serious damage to his reputation;

(b) that the charge raises a substantial question of law;

(c) that the accused is unable to follow the proceedings and state his own case because of his inadequate knowledge of English, mental illness or other mental or physical disability;

(d) that the nature of the defence involves the tracing and interviewing of witnesses or expert cross-examination of a witness for the prosecution;

(e) that legal representation is desirable in the interest of someone other than the accused as, for example, in the case of sexual offences against young children where it is undesirable that the accused should cross-examine the witness in person.

In practice, there is no difficulty in these criteria being satisfied for trial at the Crown Court – in 1984, 98% of Crown Court defendants received criminal legal aid. However, in Magistrates' Courts the position is very different. In 1984, 2% of defendants in summary trials (ie cases that can only be tried by magistrates) received legal aid, whereas the figure was 67% for defendants in trials of either-way offences (ie cases where the defendant could have chosen to be tried by the Crown Court but has elected trial by magistrates). Wide discrepancies have been shown in the rates of granting legal aid between different Magistrates' Courts and the overall situation has not been helped by directives from the Government encouraging the saving of costs.

(b) The means test. Formerly, means testing was operated on a rather vague basis, but it has been much stricter since 1 March 1984, under the provisions of the Legal Aid Act 1982. The object was to increase contributions from defendants and a system of means testing similar to that used for civil legal aid was introduced. The Court now ascertains the applicant's disposable income and capital by means of a questionnaire. The contribution is one-quarter of any disposable income over the free limit of £46 a week and all the applicant's capital in excess of £3,000. There are allowances against income for living expenses and dependants, but no allowances against capital. The spouses' resources are usually added together for these calculations. Contributions are payable in weekly instalments and payment should start seven days after the order. The Court has a certain amount of discretion including the power to remit the contribution if the defendant is subsequently acquitted or his appeal allowed.

3. DUTY SOLICITOR SCHEMES

The first scheme was set up by the Bristol Law Society in 1972 with a view to providing legal advice to unrepresented defendants at Magistrates' Courts. Solicitors working voluntarily on a rota basis visited the defendants in the cells and offered their help. Advice was given on such matters as plea, the question of bail, the availability of legal aid and the desirability of an adjournment. In the early years, the development of the scheme in other parts of the country was uneven; by 1975 there were only 29 Duty Solicitor Schemes in operation. Nevertheless, by 1984 there were over 130 schemes, and duty solicitors, with the blessing of the Royal Commission on Legal Services, are now officially recognised as providing an indispensable part of our legal services. This was reflected in the Legal Aid Act 1982 which, in section 1, provided for the creation of a nationwide Duty Solicitor Scheme with remuneration for the participating solicitors. In October 1983 the Legal Aid (Duty Solicitor) Scheme 1983 was set up. Twenty four regional duty solicitor committees have been established and in each of these there are local duty solicitor committees. Each local committee must include at least three solicitors who have 'considerable current experience of advocacy in criminal cases in magistrates courts'. The duty solicitor must tell each defendant he sees that the defendant can instruct any solicitor he wishes and that the duty solicitor should not act if the defendant has his own solicitor. However, the duty solicitor can still act if the defendant's own solicitor is unavailable, or if the defendant gives him written permission to do so.

If no advice or representation has been given on the same charge(s), the duty solicitor can give advice to a defendant in custody and make a bail application for him. Unless the duty solicitor considers that an adjournment is necessary in the interests of justice, or of the defendant, he must represent the defendant if he is pleading guilty and wants the case to be concluded on that Court appearance. He should also help the defendant apply for legal aid in respect of any later appearance.

Under the provisions of the Police and Criminal Evidence Act 1984, a 24 hour Duty Solicitor Scheme in police stations has been established. This is being run in association with the Magistrates' Courts scheme: indeed, any solicitor who wishes to take part in the Magistrates' Court scheme must be prepared to participate in the police stations scheme as well. The scheme came into operation on 1 January 1986.

4. COMPLAINTS AGAINST LAWYERS

(i) Solicitors

There are two ways of pursuing complaints against a solicitor: raising the matter with the Law Society, the solicitors' professional body, and suing the solicitor for negligence. The former method has always been the easier, but it has suffered from the disadvantage of carrying no form of compensation for the client – unless the knowledge that the solicitor has been disciplined can be said to amount to compensation. However, Part 1 of the Administration of Justice Act 1985 provides new powers for the Law Society to deal with complaints against solicitors. These new powers for the Law Society came into operation in September 1986.

The Council of the Law Society will be able to order a solicitor to remit or repay part or all of his costs to the client or to take any action that the Council specifies to be in the client's interest to rectify the matter that gave rise to the complaint. These powers can be used whenever the Council considers that the solicitor's professional services 'were in any respect not of the quality that could reasonably have been expected of him as a solicitor'. The Council will not exercise any of these powers unless it considers that, in all the circumstances, it would be appropriate to do so and, in determining this, the Council may consider the existence of any civil remedy (such as an action for negligence) and whether it would be reasonable to expect the client to start such proceedings. The Solicitors' Disciplinary Tribunal, an independent body set up under the Legal Aid Act 1974 to deal with serious disciplinary cases, can also use these new powers in cases which come before it and involve both professional misconduct and inadequate services. The Lay Observer, a layman whose job is to consider allegations that the Law Society has not dealt with complaints properly, will be able to refer such cases to the Tribunal.

Until these new powers come into effect, it is impossible to predict whether they will provide a significantly better remedy for the disgruntled client than the existing complaints procedure. Much will depend on how the Law Society and the Solicitors' Disciplinary Tribunal choose to interpret the new provisions. If the Council or the Tribunal orders that a refund of costs should be made, the client need not worry about the solicitor's ability to pay. All practising solicitors are insured to meet claims by clients and, if for any reason the insurance were ineffective or insufficient, the Law Society would provide the money from its compensation fund which is made up of contributions from all practising solicitors.

If a client wishes the Law Society to investigate a complaint against a solicitor, he should write to The Secretary, Professional Purposes, The Law Society, 113 Chancery Lane, London WC2A 1LP.

The alternative remedy of suing a solicitor for negligence would involve all the difficulties of Legal Aid, which are discussed above. In claims of less than £500, the matter should be far simpler on account of the County Court arbitration scheme (see page 17). Certainly, there is plenty of authority for solicitors' being found liable for negligence. Proof that the solicitor's performance was 'in any respect not of the quality that could reasonably have been expected of him as a solicitor' (the new test in disciplinary proceedings) would probably suffice. It is important to note, however, that to succeed in such an action, the client must show (a) that he has suffered a loss *and* (b) that the loss was caused by the solicitor's negligence.

Once again, impecunious solicitors should not cause any difficulty because of the compulsory insurance and the Law Society's compensation scheme.

(ii) Barristers

The Bar has not carried out any reform to its complaints procedure so – as the situation has hitherto been with solicitors – there is not much for the litigant to gain except the satisfaction of seeing a barrister made the subject of disciplinary proceedings. Barristers are subject to a fairly strict code of professional ethics but most of these relate to their general behaviour rather than the quality of their work. In any case, most of a barrister's dealings are with solicitors rather than litigants. Complaints against barristers are dealt with by the Professional Conduct Committee of the Senate. (The Senate is formed from representatives of each of the four Inns of Court and the Bar Council. Every barrister has to belong to an Inn of Court.)

Barristers cannot be sued for negligence in respect of their advocacy in Court. This was established by the House of Lords in the case *Rondel v Worsley* in 1967.

Rondel v Worsley

Rondel chose Michael Worsley, a barrister, to defend him at his trial. After he was convicted, he claimed that Worsley had presented his case negligently and sued him. Worsley sought to have the statement of claim struck out as disclosing no cause of action. The House of Lords held that barristers should be immune from being sued in respect of their performance in Court on the grounds of public policy.

Lord Denning in the Court of Appeal had outlined four reasons to justify this immunity: (1) that a barrister should be able to work 'fearlessly and independently' without being threatened with negligence actions, (2) 'a barrister cannot pick and choose his clients', (3) a barrister's duty to the Court – 'he must disregard the most specific instructions of his client, if they conflict with his duty to the Court', and (4) the 'floodgates' argument – 'if this action is to go to trial, it will lead to dozens of like cases'.

These justifications have been criticised, but they represent the law. In another House of Lords decision, *Saif Ali v Sydney Mitchell & Co* (1978), consideration was given to whether a barrister's immunity extended to work done out of Court.

Saif Ali v Sydney Mitchell & Co

Saif Ali suffered injuries in a car accident. He went to the defendant firm of solicitors and they sought a barrister's opinion. The barrister gave negligent advice as a result of which Saif Ali was unable to sue the other motorist within the permitted time limits. Saif Ali sued the solicitors for negligence and they sued the barrister. The House of Lords held that the immunity could only apply to work out of Court if it was 'so intimately connected with the conduct of the cause in Court that it can fairly be said to be a preliminary decision affecting the way that cause is to be conducted when it comes to a hearing'.

In the absence of further guidance from the Courts it is difficult to say what precise aspects of a barrister's work are not covered by the immunity but it seems clear that barristers could be liable for acting negligently in giving advice. Solicitors are covered by the same immunity when they appear as advocates.

Barristers also have to be insured against claims for negligence.

THE COURTS

The Courts in England and Wales are arranged in a hierarchical structure and there are rules which provide that certain cases have to be heard in certain Courts. Broadly speaking, Courts can be divided in two ways: between Courts which deal with civil cases and those which deal with criminal cases; and between trial Courts and appeal Courts. Neither classification is logically adhered to so that some Courts (such as Magistrates' Courts) deal with both civil and criminal cases, and some Courts (such as Crown Courts) hear both trials and appeals. In this analysis, we shall consider each Court in respect of its main function.

(i) Civil Courts

(A) County Courts. There are two main levels of trial Court in civil cases, the County Court and the High Court. County Courts deal with cases involving smaller sums of money than the High Court. Almost the entire range of civil proceedings is dealt with in County Courts and they can hear the following actions:

(a) A breach of contract or tort (a tort is a civil wrong for which a person may be ordered to pay damages, such as negligence, libel or trespass) where the amount in dispute does not exceed £5,000. However, actions for libel or slander must be heard in the High Court, whatever the amount claimed. If a plaintiff is prepared to abandon the excess above £5,000, or if the defendant agrees in any case, the action can be heard in a County Court. If a person brings an action in the High Court which he could have brought in a County Court, he will be penalised in costs (see below).

(b) Actions involving land, houses or buildings, provided the rateable value does not exceed £1,000 (or £1,500 in Greater London). If it does, the case will have to be heard in the High Court.

(c) 'Equity Proceedings'. Typical cases include building society repossessions after failure to keep up mortgage payments, and arguments about the provisions of a trust fund or the administration of a deceased person's estate. The County Court limit here is £30,000 (or £15,000 in the case of disputes about wills).

(d) Matrimonial causes. Actions for divorce, nullity or judicial separation are started in certain designated County Courts. If the petition is defended, it will be heard in the High Court. When dealing with the divorce, the County Court can deal with questions involving family property, custody and maintenance. Adoption and guardianship cases can be heard either in a County Court or a Magistrates' Court.

(e) Other areas where County Courts have jurisdiction include landlord and tenant, hire purchase, consumer credit, partnership and the winding-up of companies with a paid-up capital not exceeding £120,000. Some County Courts also deal with bankruptcies.

County Court procedure. In recent years County Court procedure has been amended to make it easier for an individual to conduct his own case. When County Courts were created in 1846, it was envisaged that they would provide an accessible forum for the settlement of small claims. However, by the 1960s County Courts were mostly used as debt-collecting agencies for finance companies and mail order firms. The changes were designed to simplify the forms, make the procedure more informal and discourage the use of legal representation.

There are two types of County Court action: (a) fixed date action – any claim other than for the payment of money is a fixed date action; (b) default action – any claim for a payment of money is a default action.

The plaintiff (the name given to the person who brings the action) must ascertain precisely whom he wants to sue. He must be careful to ascertain the correct name and address. A partnership should be sued in the name of the firm or, alternatively, in the names of all the partners (any unnamed partner will not be liable). A company should be sued in its name. The plaintiff does not have a free choice of the Court he wants to sue in. He must sue either in the Court in the area where the defendant lives or carries on his business; or the Court in the area where the action arose.

PARTICULARS OF CLAIM (GENERAL)

Full name of plaintiff

IN THE BRISTOL COUNTY COURT

Case No:

Plaintiff
(Your name)

WILLIAM SMITH

Defendant
(Name of person(s)
or company you
wish to sue)

JOHN EVANS

Full name of defendant

State the nature of
your claim

DAMAGE TO CAR AND
TRAVELLING EXPENSES

A brief description is
sufficient

Amount claimed

£247 50

If the amount of your claim exceeds £500
State whether, if the claim is disputed,
you want it heard by an arbitrator.

GROUNDS FOR CLAIM

(State briefly why you consider that the defendant is liable for the amount
that you are claiming)

On January 5th 1986 I was driving my Ford Escort motor
car, registration number ABC 123, in Acacia Avenue, Clifton,
Bristol 8. The defendant drove his motor car, a Vauxhall
Cavalier registration number DEF 456, into Acacia Avenue
when it was not safe to do so. There was a collision between
the two vehicles and it cost me £200 to repair the damage
to mine it has also cost me £47 50 to hire another car
while mine was being repaired.

A concise statement of
the facts of the case and
the reasons why the
plaintiff considers that
the defendant is liable

Signature: William Smith.

Signature of plaintiff

Date: _____

continue over page if necessary

j General
HMSO Btl 405420/1

BR 19

18

PARTICULARS OF CLAIM (ACCIDENT: REPAIRS TO VEHICLE (AND DAMAGES))

Full name of plaintiff

IN THE BRISTOL COUNTY COURT.

Plaint No.

Plaintiff
(Your name)

WILLIAM SMITH

Defendant
(Name of person(s)
or company you
wish to sue)

JOHN EVANS

Full name of defendant

Nature of claim

Expenses arising out of a road
accident caused by the defendant's
negligence

Date of accident

5 | 1 | 86

Place   (street or road and
locality)

ACACIA AVENUE, CLIFTON. BRISTOL 8

Description of your vehicle
and index number

FORD ESCORT, ABC 123

Description of defendant's
vehicle and index number

VAUXHALL CAVALIER. DEF 456

Name of driver of defendant's
vehicle, if not defendant

Cost of repairs to your
vehicle

£200

Cost of hiring another
vehicle or travelling expenses
while your vehicle was being
repaired

£47 50

Total of claim

£247.50

If the amount of your claim exceeds £500
state whether, if the claim is
disputed, you want it heard by an
arbitrator

GROUNDS FOR CLAIM
(State briefly what happened and why you say that the defendant was to blame)

The defendant drove his car from Holly Crescent into
Acacia Avenue when it was not safe to do so. There was a
collision between the two cars and it cost me £200 to repair
the damage to mine.

A brief description is
sufficient

continue over page if necessary

Signature: William Smith.

Date:_____

Signature of plaintiff

h Accident: repairs to vehicle (and damages)

19

The following steps should then be taken:

1. Efforts should be made to reach a settlement. The defendant should be written to and a reasonable time allowed for him to reply. It is a good idea to send the letter by recorded delivery.

2. If there is no reply to the letter, or it seems unlikely that the claim will be met, it is advisable to give the defendant warning that the plaintiff intends to sue him in the County Court.

3. The plaintiff should then draw up a document called a 'Particulars of Claim'. The purpose of this is to set out briefly the nature of the plaintiff's claim and why it is alleged that the defendant is liable. It is customary for the claim to be set out in numbered paragraphs and written in the third person (i e refer to 'the plaintiff' rather than 'I'). Nowadays, a number of County Courts have a general particulars of claim form, and special forms to deal with common 'small claims' problems which a plaintiff can use if he wishes (see pages 18 and 19). Otherwise, he must draft the document himself (see illustration opposite).

It is worthwhile for the plaintiff to consider at this stage whether it is advisable to limit the claim to £500 to bring it within the arbitration procedure (see below).

4. The next stage is for the plaintiff to take or send the following documents to the Court.
(a) A 'Praecipe' or form requesting that proceedings should start. There are different forms to cover different types of claim: the Court will supply the appropriate one (see page 22). The form provides the option for the documents to be served by post and in most cases this will be sufficient.
(b) Two copies of the Particulars of Claim.
(c) The Court fee

Sum claimed	Fee
Up to £300	10p per £ (minimum £7)
Over £300–£500	£37
Over £500 or unlimited	£43

5. The Court will send a 'plaint note' to the plaintiff stating that proceedings have commenced (see page 24). In a 'fixed date' action the Court will arrange a date for a preliminary hearing. A summons and a copy of the particulars of claims are then sent to the plaintiff.

6. The next step depends on the nature of the case:

Fixed date action. The defendant can complete one of three forms sent to him by the Court (see page 25). If he admits the claim he can fill in the Admission Form. Alternatively, if he feels he has a defence, he should complete the Defence Form, and the Counterclaim Form if he wants to make his own claim against the plaintiff. The defendant may defend the claim but make a 'payment into Court' (i e pay a lesser sum to the Court as a settlement). If the plaintiff refuses this payment and subsequently is awarded a lesser amount, he will have to pay all the costs from the date the payment was made.

Default action. If the defendant does not respond to the claim within fourteen days, the plaintiff can obtain judgment in default. To do this, the plaintiff must return a special form (see page 27) and the plaint note to the Court. The plaintiff can ask for the whole amount which is owing, or accept instalments. If the defendant admits the claim, he will return the Admission Form to the Court. Once again, instalments might be offered but the plaintiff does not have to accept payment in this way. The defendant can, of course, deny liability. In this case, a pre-trial review will be arranged and the case will proceed as if it were a fixed date action.

7. For the pre-trial review the plaintiff must attend the Court with any evidence (such as letters and receipts) which could help him prove his case. If the defendant does not appear, the plaintiff can ask for judgment in default. If the defendant appears, the review will take place. The pre-trial review was introduced in 1972 to encourage the settlement of small claims. The parties get together before a County Court registrar who is authorised to '. . . give all such directions as appear to him necessary or desirable for securing the just, expeditious and economical disposal of the action' and '. . . endeavour to secure that the parties make all such admissions and agreements as ought reasonably to be made' (County Court Rules, Order 17). For example, either side can ask for 'further and better particulars', or more information about the other side's case; or copies of documents that are referred to in the pleadings.

Arbitration. If the plaintiff's claim does not exceed £500, the case will usually be referred to arbitration. Either party can ask for an ordinary trial instead, but this will not be allowed unless the registrar considers that complicated questions of

PARTICULARS OF CLAIM

In the Bristol County Court   Plaint No.

Between

    WILLIAM SMITH   Plaintiff

    and

    JOHN EVANS   Defendant

Particulars of Claim

1.   On January 5th 1986 the Plaintiff was driving his Ford Escort motor car registration number ABC 123 in Acacia Road, Clifton, Bristol 8, when he was involved in a collision with a Vauxhall Cavalier motor car, registration number DEF 456, driven by the Defendant.

2.   The collision was caused by the negligence of the Defendant who drove out of a minor road on to a major road when it was not safe to do so.

3.   The Plaintiff claims £200, the cost of repairing his motor car and £47.50, the cost of hiring a motor car while his own motor car was being repaired.

Dated this   day of   1986

                    Davies, Brown & Co., 10 North Street, Clifton, Bristol 8, Solicitors to the Plaintiff who will accept service of all proceedings on behalf of the Plaintiff at such address.

To the Registrar of the Court
and to the Defendant

Full name of plaintiff

Full name of defendant

The facts of the case are stated

It is alleged that the accident was caused by the defendant's negligence

Details are given of the plaintiff's claim

REQUEST FOR DEFAULT SUMMONS

IN THE   BRISTOL   **COUNTY COURT**

CASE No.

THIS SECTION TO BE COMPLETED BY THE COURT

Summons in form: N.1 Fixed Amount ☐   N.2 Unliquidated ☐

Service by: Bailiff ☐   Plaintiff('s solicitors) ☐   Post (Certificate (overleaf) ☐   Post (At defendant (company's R.O.) ☐   Date issued ☐

Statement of Parties   **Please use block capitals**

1. PLAINTIFF'S names in full, and residence or place of business.
2. If suing in a representative capacity, state in what capacity.
3. If a minor required to sue by a next friend, state that fact, and names in full, residence or place of business, and occupation of next friend.
4. If an assignee, state that fact, and name, address and occupation of assignor.
5. If co-partners suing in the name of their firm, add "(A Firm)".
6. If a company registered under the Companies Act, 1948, state the address of registered office and describe it as such.

WILLIAM SMITH
1, ACACIA AVENUE
CLIFTON
BRISTOL 8

→ Full name and address of plaintiff

Plaintiff's solicitors name and address for service

Solicitor's reference

7. DEFENDANT'S surname, and (where known) his or her initials or forenames in full; defendant's residence or place of business (if a proprietor of the business).
8. Whether male or female.
9. Whether a minor (where known).
10. Occupation (where known).
11. If sued in a representative capacity, state in what capacity.
12. If co-partners are sued in the name of their firm, add "(A Firm)" or if a person carrying on business in a name other than his own name is sued in such name, add "(A trading name)".
13. If a company registered under the Companies Act, 1948 is sued the address given must be the registered office of the company, and must be so described.

JOHN EVANS
2, RAILWAY CUTTINGS
REDLAND
BRISTOL 6

→ Full name and address of defendant

WHAT THE CLAIM IS FOR

DAMAGE TO CAR AND
TRAVELLING EXPENSES

AMOUNT CLAIMED	247	50
ISSUE FEE	24	80
SOLICITOR'S COSTS		
TOTAL	272	30

→ Total of original claim

→ The court fee is on a sliding scale. Its amount depends on the sum claimed

→ A brief description is sufficient

[Strike out if inappropriate:- I apply for this action, if defended to be referred to arbitration].

NOTES:

1. Two copies of the plaintiff's particulars of claim are required before a summons can be issued, and if there are two or more defendants to be served, an additional copy for each additional defendant.
2. Any claim for £500 or less which is defended will be referred to arbitration automatically, but the reference may be rescinded on application.
3. When a defended claim is arbitrated the right of appeal against the arbitrator's award is very limited.
4. If the defendant's address is outside the district of the court you must complete Section A overleaf.
5. The certificate in Section B overleaf should be completed and signed if service by post is required.

N.201   Request for default summons (single case) Order 3 Rule 3(1)

SECTION A

This section must be completed by the plaintiff to show that the court has jurisdiction under Order 4 Rule 2 of the County Court Rules, 1981.

NOTES:-

(i)   Where the claim is for the amount of any instalment or instalments due and unpaid under a hire-purchase agreement Question 3 must be answered.

(ii) Where the claim is founded on a contract for the sale or hire of goods Question 2 must be answered and if the answer is "No" Question 3 must be answered.

(iii) Where the claim is founded on contract but neither of the foregoing descriptions applies such of Questions 1, 4 and 5 as are applicable should be answered, or, if none of these are applicable Question 6 must be answered.

(iv) Where the claim is not founded on contract, Question 6 only, is applicable and must be answered.

1. Was the contract made in the district of the court, and, if so where? .... (If the address given is within the district of the court no further questions need be answered)	
2. Was the purchase price or rental payable in one sum?	
3. Did the defendant reside or carry on business in the district of the court at the time when the contract was made and, if so, where?	
4. Where, and how, was the order for the goods [*or* given by the defendant to the plaintiff [*or* assignor]?	
5. Where was payment to be made by the defendant under the contract?	

6. What are the facts upon which the plaintiff relies as showing that the cause of action arose wholly, or in part, in the district of the court?

SIGNED .... **PLAINTIFF**   DATED ....

NOTE:- If the action is wrongly issued in this court because this section has been wrongly answered the court may transfer the action or order it to be struck out, and may order the plaintiff to pay the defendant's costs.

→ This section only applies where the defendant's address is outside the district of the court

SECTION B

(1) State surname and where known initial(s) or fore-names.

I request that the defendant(s) (1)   JOHN EVANS

be served with the summons by post. I certify that I have reason to believe that the summons, if sent to the defendant(s) at the address(es) stated overleaf will come to his/~~their~~ knowledge in time for him/~~them~~ to comply with the requirements of it.

I/~~The plaintiff~~ understand(s) that if judgment is obtained as a result of postal service and is afterwards set aside on the ground that the service did not give the defendant(s) adequate notice of the proceedings, I/~~the plaintiff~~ may be ordered to pay the cost of setting aside the judgment.

DATED

Signed
Plaintiff('s solicitor)   William Smith.

→ The plaintiff requests that the summons be served by post

→ Signature of plaintiff

Certificate for postal service Order 7 Rule 10(2)   Printed in the U.K. for H.M.S.O.   Dd 8419715 11/83 G617

23

PLAINT NOTE (DEFAULT SUMMONS)

In the BRISTOL County Court

BETWEEN .... WILLIAM SMITH == PLAINTIFF

AND

CASE No.	DEFENDANT	ISSUE FEE	DATE OF POSTAL SERVICE	JUDGMENT
	JOHN EVANS	£24.80	3 JUNE '86	

To the Plaintiff

The above action(s) was/were issued today and you will be entitled to judgment 14 days after the date of service of the summons, unless within that time the defendant pays into court the total amount of the claim and costs or delivers at the court office a defence, an admission with an offer of payment or a counterclaim. If payment is made you will be notified. If a defence, or counterclaim is delivered you will be sent a copy. If the defendant does not reply to the summons or if he delivers an admission without an offer of payment you must apply for judgment to be entered.(1) If you do not, the action will be struck out twelve months after the date of service.

The summons must be served within twelve months from today. You may apply for this period to be extended provided your application is made before the summons expires.(2)

Always bring this plaint note with you when you come to the court office for any purpose connected with these proceedings.

If judgment is entered then, unless otherwise directed the defendant will be ordered to make payments into the court. The court will send the money to you. If you receive any money from the defendant you must notify the court.

(1) Order 9 Rule 10
(2) Order 7 Rule 20

DATED   3/6/86

Address all communications to the Chief Clerk AND QUOTE THE ABOVE CASE NUMBER(S)

THE COURT OFFICE AT

GREYFRIARS, LEWINS MEAD, BRISTOL, BS1 2NR,

is open from 10 a.m. to 4 p.m. Monday to Friday.

N.205—Plaint note (default summons). Order 3 Rule 3(2)(d)(I).

MCR 345285/1/F24840 20m 8/85 TL

Full name of plaintiff

Full name of defendant

In this case the summons has been served by post

The court fee is on a sliding scale. Its amount depends on the sum claimed

WARRANT No.	AGAINST DEFENDANT	ISSUE FEE	WARRANT No.	AGAINST DEFENDANT	ISSUE FEE

No. OF OTHER PROCESS	AGAINST DEFENDANT	ISSUE FEE	DATE, TIME AND PLACE OF HEARING

FORM OF ADMISSION, DEFENCE AND COUNTERCLAIM

Full name of plaintiff

Full name of defendant

In the BRISTOL County Court.

CASE No.

WILLIAM SMITH v JOHN EVANS

ADMISSION

Read the instructions on the back of the summons carefully before completing this form. Immediately after you have filled in this form send it by post or take it to the Court Office as stated on the summons. PLEASE USE BLACK INK.

1. Do you admit the plaintiff's claim in full   YES/NO

2. Do you admit part of the plaintiff's claim   YES/NO
   If so, how much do you admit?   £ 147.50
   (Put your reasons for disputing the balance overleaf)

3. If you wish the court to consider whether to make an instalment order answer the following questions:—

PAY AND MEANS

(a) What is your occupation   Electrician

(b) What is the name and address of your employer?

   Self-employed

(c) What is your pay before deductions?   £ 750 per week/month

(d) What overtime, bonuses, fees, allowances or commissions do you receive?   £ NONE per week/month

(e) What is your usual take home pay?   £ 500 per week/month

(f) Do you receive
   (i) a pension?   £ NO per week/month
   (ii) any state benefits?   £ NO per week/month
   (iii) any other income?   £ NO per week/month

(g) What contributions, if any, are made by any member of your household?

   NONE

LIABILITIES

(a) What persons, if any, are financially dependent on you? Please give details including the ages of any dependent children:—

   Wife

(b) What rent or mortgage instalments are you liable to pay?   £ 145.50 per week/month

   What amount do you actually pay?   £ 145.50 per week/month

(c) What rates are you liable to pay?   £ 42.18 per week/month

   What amount do you actually pay?   £ 42.18 per week/month

(d) Do you have to pay under any Court Orders? Please give details including name of court and case number

   NO

(e) What other regular payments do you have to make?

   NONE

(f) Have you any other liabilities which you would like the Court to take into account? Please give details:—

   NONE

This is the amount the defendant admits he owes the plaintiff

Defendant's occupation

Details of defendant's income

Defendant's full address

Signature of defendant

In this case the defendant is offering to pay £10 a month

WHAT OFFER OF PAYMENT DO YOU MAKE?

Payment in full on the   day of   19   OR by instalments of £ 10.00 per month

Address to which notices about this case should be sent to you   2, RAILWAY CUTTINGS REDLAND BRISTOL 6

SIGN HERE   John Evans

DATE

N9   Form of Admission, Defence and Counterclaim to accompany form N1, 2, 3 and 4
Order 3 Rule 3(2)(c)

MCR 337702/1/F24340 50m 9/84 TL

25

FORM OF ADMISSION, DEFENCE AND COUNTERCLAIM – *continued*

Full name of plaintiff

Full name of defendant

In the BRISTOL County Court.

CASE No.

WILLIAM SMITH v JOHN EVANS

DEFENCE	COUNTERCLAIM
1. Do you dispute the plaintiff's claim or any part of it? YES/~~NO~~	1. Do you wish to make a claim against the plaintiff? ~~YES~~/NO
2. If so, how much do you dispute and what are your reasons?	2. If so, for how much? £ ....
	3. What is the nature of the claim?

The defendant can make his own claim against the plaintiff. In this case he does not wish to do so

I admit that the collision was my fault but the amount of damage I caused would not have cost £200 to repair

The defendant admits that he caused the accident but disputes the amount of damage caused

TO BE COMPLETED WHERE THE SUM CLAIMED OR AMOUNT INVOLVED EXCEEDS £500

If you dispute the plaintiff's claim or wish to make a claim against him do you want the proceedings referred to arbitration? YES/NO

NOTES:

1. Any claim for £500 or less which is defended will be referred to arbitration automatically, but the reference may be rescinded on application.

2. When a defended claim is arbitrated the right of appeal against the arbitrator's award is very limited.

3. If your claim against the plaintiff is bigger than his claim against you, you may have to pay a fee before it can be dealt with. You can find out whether a fee is payable by enquiring at any county court office.

Address to which notices about this case should be sent to you ⎰ 2, RAILWAY CUTTINGS REDLAND BRISTOL 6

SIGN HERE ...... John Evans ——— Signature of defendant

DATE ....

Defendant's full address

N9 Form of Admission, Defence and Counterclaim to accompany forms N1, 2, 3 and 4 Order 3 Rule 3(2)(c)

26

REQUEST FOR ENTRY OF JUDGMENT IN DEFAULT ACTION

IN THE   BRISTOL   COUNTY COURT

BETWEEN   WILLIAM SMITH .... PLAINTIFF

Full name of plaintiff

AND   JOHN EVANS ==================   CASE No.
.... DEFENDANT

Full name of defendant

To the Court
I request you to enter judgment by default against   JOHN EVANS
.... defendant(s)

Delete as appropriate

(Payable forthwith,) ========
(Payable on the ....)
(Payable by instalments of £ .... per .... commencing on ....)

In this case the plaintiff wants the whole amount paid immediately

	£	
Amount of claim as stated in summons	247	50

Total of original claim

	£	
Court fees entered on summons	24	80
Solicitor's charge (if any) entered on summons		
Solicitor's charge (if any) on entering judgment		

The court fee is on a sliding scale. Its amount depends on the sum claimed

SUB-TOTAL	272	30
Deduct amount (if any) paid into court by defendant	147	50
Deduct amount (if any) paid to plaintiff direct since issue		
Balance payable by defendant and for which judgment is to be entered	124	80

This is the amount that the defendant admits he owes the plaintiff

Balance of plaintiff's claim

TAKE NOTICE—This form must not be used in respect of:—
(a) a claim for money secured by a mortgage or
(b) a claim for unliquidated damages (use form N.234)

N.14.   Request for entry of judgment in default action Order 9, Rule 6(1)

DATED

Plaintiff (or Plaintiff's Solicitor)

Printed in the UK for HMSO Dd.8868501 7/84 (11037)

27

law or extremely complicated questions of fact are involved; that the plaintiff is alleging fraud; or that the subject matter of the case, the circumstances of the parties, or the interests of other persons affected by the claim make arbitration inappropriate. Moreover, if both parties want a trial, a trial will be held. If the claim exceeds £500, either party can request the registrar to order arbitration.

The reason arbitration is used in County Courts is to encourage litigants to appear in person without having to worry about procedural considerations or their ability as advocates. The arbitration is supposed to be informal. The rules of evidence are not strictly enforced and the arbitrator is expected to see that all the relevant arguments are considered and, in general, play a far more active role than would a judge in an ordinary adversarial trial. Legal representation is not prohibited but (where the claim is for not more than £500) solicitors' costs cannot be recovered from one's losing opponent, except for those stated on the summons (i e the costs involved in preparing the case), those incurred from the enforcing of the judgment and those incurred through the unreasonable conduct of the opposing party (see below). Generally, it is not possible to appeal against the arbitrator's decision.

If there is no arbitration, the case will go to trial. The plaintiff will give evidence, together with his witnesses. The defendant can cross-examine the plaintiff and the witnesses. The process is then reversed. The plaintiff and defendant can make a closing speech and judgment will then be delivered. The winner should ask for his costs. It is worth remembering that a 'McKenzie man' can be used by either side at the trial.

Enforcement of County Court judgments.

The obtaining of a judgment is only the first step for the plaintiff in his quest to receive compensation. His next problem is obtaining the money from the defendant. In some cases, the defendant may have no money at all, but defendants who can afford may try and delay, or even avoid making payment. If this is the case, there are various ways in which the judgment can be enforced.

The first stage, however, is for the creditor to request the Court to conduct an inquiry into the debtor's means. If the Court agrees, the debtor will be ordered to attend an oral hearing. The creditor will also have to attend. The debtor will be closely questioned as to both his means and his property. His answer will be written down, read back to him and he will be required to sign a copy. The debtor may also have to produce any relevant documents. If the debtor fails to attend the hearing, the Court will arrange a new date and notify the debtor that he risks being committed to prison if he does not attend on this occasion.

The following are possible ways of enforcing the judgment:

(a) A charging order on the debtor's home. This device can only be used if the debtor owns his own home. The creditor can apply to the Court for a charge to be put on the property. This means that, if the debt remains unpaid, the Court can order the house or flat to be sold so that the debt can be paid out of the proceeds. The Court will in practice be unwilling to order a sale but the possibility can often make the recalcitrant debtor take some action.

(b) Execution. The Court can be asked to send a bailiff to take possession of the debtor's belongings and then sell them at an auction to meet the debt. No Court hearing takes place. The bailiff is allowed to enter the debtor's home (but not break in) and seize any of his belongings except his clothes and the tools of his trade. The bailiff cannot seize goods belonging to another person (such as a spouse or a finance company).

(c) Attachment of earnings order. An order can be made by the Court requiring an employer to make regular deductions from the debtor's pay. This is a useful device if the debtor has regular employment but otherwise is of very limited value.

(d) Garnishee order. The creditor can ask the Court to order that debts owing to the debtor should be paid to the creditor. This could be of particular value where the debtor is known to have money in a bank account. In fact, this order is used infrequently, partly because of the difficulty of ascertaining such information. When the order is used, it tends to be against companies and businesses.

(e) Bankruptcy. This step is very rarely used for small claims and should not be undertaken by a layman. The creditor must be owed over £200. Its only real value is that the initiation of proceedings might provide such a shock to the debtor that he immediately makes payment – if he has the money to pay.

(f) Administration order. Here, the debtor must take the initiative. He can apply to the Court for assistance in sorting out all his debts. The advantage to him is that the Court will stop any actions to recover money from him. The debtor is then allowed to pay off his debts by instalments.

(B) The High Court. The High Court hears the civil cases that are outside the County Courts' financial limits (although, as we have seen, if both parties agree, these cases could be tried in the County Courts). It also hears certain types of appeal in criminal cases. There are three divisions in the High Court:

(a) Queen's Bench Division. This is the busiest Division. It hears contract and tort cases as well as actions for recovering land. The division also encompasses the Commercial Court, which deals with big commercial cases, and the Admiralty Court which deals with maritime cases.

(b) Chancery Division. Equity cases are dealt with in this Division. These are mainly the same matters as were outlined above under the equity jurisdiction of the County Court. The Chancery Division also deals with tax cases, probate and the interpretation of wills, bankruptcy and partnership cases.

(c) Family Division. This Division hears disputes in family cases. Most of these are defended divorce cases but separation, custody, adoption, maintenance and wardship cases are also dealt with, as well as the division of family property on the breakdown of a marriage.

Divisional Courts. Each Division has a 'Divisional Court' which comprises the same judges as in the hearings outlined above. The Divisional Courts are the parts of the High Court that deal with appeals:

(a) Queen's Bench Division. The Divisional Court deals with points of law that arise in criminal cases in Magistrates' Courts. It also has an important function in 'supervising' the activities of inferior Courts or tribunals. If a person wants to complain about the actions of such a Court or tribunal, he can apply to the Divisional Court for judicial review.

(b) Chancery Division. Appeals from County Courts in bankruptcy cases are heard.

(c) Family Division. Consideration is given to appeals from Magistrates' Courts in matrimonial cases.

(C) The Court of Appeal. This court hears appeals from the County Court, civil cases in the High Court, and a number of tribunals including the Employment Appeals Tribunal, the Lands Tribunal and the Restrictive Practices Court. No permission is needed to appeal to the Court. The Court of Appeal is presided over by the Master of the Rolls. The present incumbent is Sir John Donaldson. The judges are called Lords Justice of Appeal.

(D) The House of Lords. The House of Lords is the final Appeal Court in this country in both civil and criminal cases. It will only hear an appeal if permission has been granted either by the Court of Appeal or the Appeals Committee of the House. Usually the case must involve a point of law of general public importance (this is a formal requirement in criminal cases). Most cases in the House of Lords have come from the Court of Appeal but, in 1969, a 'leap-frog' procedure was introduced so that appeals could pass straight from the High Court to the House of Lords. This procedure is used infrequently as it must be apparent that an important point of law is involved at a fairly early stage of the proceedings and that either the case involves the interpretation of a statutory provision, or that a decision of the Court of Appeal or House of Lords requires reconsidering.

The official title of judges in the House of Lords is 'Lord of Appeal in Ordinary', but they are commonly referred to as Law Lords. They are judges who are given life peerages and have usually been promoted through the Court system. The Lord Chancellor and other peers who have held high judicial office (for example, former Lord Chancellors) are also entitled to sit. Historically, the House of Lords as a judicial body and as a legislative body was made up of exactly the same people. Today, however, the non-lawyers take no part in the judicial proceedings of the House of Lords; the Law Lords are members of the legislative body and do sometimes speak in debates which have no party-political content (such as capital punishment).

(ii) Criminal Courts

(A) Magistrates' Courts. As we have seen, Magistrates' Courts have civil jurisdiction in matrimonial cases. They also deal with a number of other civil matters such as failure to pay income tax, national insurance or rates. In addition, they have jurisdiction over alcohol or betting licence applications. Nevertheless, most of the work in Magistrates' Courts involves criminal cases and the Courts deal with 98% of all such cases. Criminal cases can be subdivided into three categories:

(a) Summary offences, which can only be heard in Magistrates' Courts;

(b) Indictable offences, which can only be heard at the Crown Court;

(c) Offences triable either way, where either the prosecution or defence can demand that the case is heard at the Crown Court.

Magistrates' Courts try summary offences and either-way offences where trial by magistrates has been opted for. They also conduct committal proceedings to ascertain if a charge concerning an indictable offence is strong enough to go to trial at the Crown Court. (For more details on this, see Criminal Law and You: Section 9.) Therefore, all criminal cases start in a Magistrates' Court.

Magistrates are laymen, receiving no pay but expenses and a subsistence allowance. In certain large cities, including London, the bench of lay magistrates is replaced by a single professional 'stipendiary' magistrate (in London they are referred to as 'metropolitan magistrates'). A stipendiary has the full powers of a bench of lay magistrates. A bench itself requires at least two magistrates to conduct its full range of business, although usually three or five sit.

(B) The Crown Court. There is technically only one Crown Court which sits in different parts of the country (hence 'The Crown Court at Bristol'). They were introduced under the Courts Act 1971 to replace quarter sessions and assizes. They try indictable offences and offences triable either way where trial at the Crown Court has been chosen. The trial is conducted before a judge and jury. The Crown Court also hears appeals from Magistrates' Courts. The defendant only can appeal and the case is reheard before a judge and two magistrates, but without a jury.

(C) The Court of Appeal, Criminal Division. Appeals from the Crown Court are heard by the Court of Appeal, Criminal Division. Only the defendant can appeal; there is no prosecution appeal against an acquittal (The prosecution can ask the Court to consider a point of law following an acquittal but, whatever the Court decides, it does not affect the accused's acquittal). If the

Court allows an appeal, it can quash the conviction or impose a conviction for another offence. The accused can also appeal against his sentence. Leave to appeal to the Court of Appeal (Criminal Division) is required except when the appeal is simply on a point of law. (More information is given in Criminal Law and You: Section 9.)

(D) The House of Lords. The final Court that can hear appeals in criminal cases is the House of Lords (see above).

(iii) Other Courts

(A) The European Court of Justice. This is the court of law for the European Communities and, since the United Kingdom became a member on 1 January 1973, it stands above the House of Lords at the top of our Court hierarchy. However, as its jurisdiction does not cover internal disagreements between subjects of member states, the great majority of legal disputes in this country can still go no higher than the House of Lords. The Court deals with allegations that a member state has not carried out its obligations under the Treaties; considers disagreements between member states concerning provisions of the Treaties; and judges the legality of the conduct of the Communities' institutions. See for example the ways in which the rights to equal pay have been affected by Article 119 of the Treaty as interpreted by the European Court of Justice (page 164). In addition, under Article 177 of the EEC Treaty, the courts or tribunals of member states may refer cases concerning the Treaty or the EEC institutions to the Court. If the Court is one of final appeal – such as the House of Lords – the case must be referred.

(B) The European Court of Human Rights. The British Government has agreed to comply with the provisions of the European Convention for the Protection of Human Rights and Fundamental Freedoms. Individuals can raise a matter with the European Commission on Human Rights in Strasbourg. This can then be heard by either the Court of Human Rights or the Committee of Ministers at the Council of Europe. However, an applicant must have exhausted all possible legal remedies in the United Kingdom, and the application must be made within six months of the decision from which the appeal is being brought.

The case will only come before the European Court if the Commission has failed to settle the matter to the satisfaction of the parties. Either the Commission or the government concerned can request that the case be heard by the Court. The decisions of the Commission and the Court are unenforceable in the English Courts, but the British Government usually takes steps to give effect to the decisions. For instance, the Court recently decided that it was a breach of the convention for children to receive corporal punishment at school without their parents' consent.

People sometimes confuse the European Court of Human Rights with the European Court of Justice, but the two are totally separate.

(C) The Judicial Committee of the Privy Council. The Judicial Committee has been the final court of appeal from the British Empire since 1833. As there is not much of the Empire left and many of the newly independent countries do not wish to use it, the Committee now hears cases from our remaining colonies and a number of Commonwealth countries such as Australia, New Zealand, parts of the West Indies, Malaysia and Singapore. The Judicial Committee consists of the same judges who sit in the House of Lords and also lawyers who are Privy Councillors (eg Lords Justice of the Court of Appeal and distinguished Dominions judges). Its decisions do not strictly need to be followed by English Courts but they are considered very authoritative.

(iv) Tribunals

Technically, tribunals are not Courts but, in their own areas, they are just as important. They are bodies that have been mainly established this century to deal with newly-developing areas such as supplementary benefit, disputes concerning rent, problems of employment and national insurance. The advantages of tribunals are said to be cheapness, informality, quickness and the provision of specialised assessors. Legal Aid is generally unavailable in tribunals. The procedures vary enormously, from those where an individual could easily present his own case to those where he would experience some difficulty. Many tribunals allow representation by other people, such as friends or trade union officials. Tribunals, although not Courts, are subject to control by the Courts in the form of judicial review by the Divisional Court of the Queen's Bench Division (see page 29).

An important example of a tribunal is an industrial tribunal (see The Law and Your Job: Section 3.7).

(v) Arbitration

We have already considered arbitration in the County Courts but arbitration is often used in other cases – especially in areas of commerce – to enable two parties to have their dispute settled out of Court by an expert arbitrator. The basis of an arbitration agreement is contractual and therefore governed by the general law of contract.

(vi) Costs in Legal Cases

In effect, 'costs' from a client's view refers to the amount he has to pay his solicitor for work that has been done. A solicitor's bill will comprise 'disbursements', 'profit costs' and VAT. Disbursements are the actual expenses the solicitor has incurred, such as search fees in conveyancing. 'Profit costs' refer to the solicitor's fee for doing the work. The term is misleading, as it will certainly not be all profit. There are three main ways in which a solicitor's costs can be controlled:

(a) Where a fixed fee is charged. This can apply, for example, in undefended divorce cases.

(b) If scale fees exist. In this case, the fee will increase in relation to the value of a particular object. Solicitors dealing with a client's building society on the purchase of a property often use scale fees.

(c) The Law Society and the Court can look at a solicitor's bill. In 'contentious cases' (Court cases) the Court will review the bill. In 'non-contentious cases' (non-Court cases) the bill can be sent to the Law Society. They will decide if it is 'fair and reasonable', and issue a remuneration certificate. This will state the correct fee.

The way a solicitor works out his bill will vary depending on whether he is dealing with non-contentious or contentious work.

(A) Non-contentious work. As we have seen, the bill should contain a statement of disbursements, profit costs and VAT. Each should be separately itemised. If the client considers that the bill is not 'fair and reasonable', he should in the first instance raise the matter with the solicitor. If the solicitor is not prepared to reduce the bill, the client can withhold payment and ask the solicitor to refer the bill to the Law Society for a remuneration certificate to be issued, or simply withhold payment. If the solicitor wishes to sue for payment, he will first have to tell the client of his right to ask for a remuneration certificate.

Remuneration certificates are not requested very frequently and this appears to be because they are not widely known about. They are certainly a useful way of challenging a solicitor's bill, especially as the bill cannot be increased by the Law Society, and there is no charge to the client. If the solicitor provides formal notice of the right to request a certificate, the client must act within 28 days. One of the problems that arises in practice is that a client does not become aware of the existence of remuneration certificates until he has paid his solicitor and, by then, he has lost his right to obtain one.

(B) Contentious work. This area has already been discussed in some detail in our consideration of legal aid. We have seen that, generally, the loser has to pay the winner's costs in a civil case, but that the winner can still end up not fully compensated or even out of pocket. The old bases of working out what costs should be allowed have recently been altered and the situation now is as follows:

(a) The standard basis. This is now the normal basis on which a judge will order the loser to pay the winner's costs. The new rule states 'on a taxation of costs on the standard basis there shall be allowed a reasonable amount in respect of all costs reasonably incurred and any doubts which the taxing officer may have as to whether the costs were reasonably incurred or were reasonable in amount shall be resolved in favour of the paying party . . .' This is a more generous test than the old 'party-and-party' basis.

(b) The solicitor and own client basis. On this basis, a client must pay all his own solicitor's fees unless they were 'unreasonably incurred'. The basis is now also used for the taxation of costs in cases involving infants, the idea being that the infant should not have to use any of the damages awarded to him to pay his costs.

(c) The indemnity basis. This is another recent innovation. The rule states 'On a taxation on the indemnity basis all costs shall be allowed except insofar as they are of an unreasonable amount or have been unreasonably incurred . . .' (it goes on to provide that any doubts 'should be resolved in favour of the receiving party'). The indemnity basis will operate in taxation of a trustee's or personal representative's costs in cases concerning the trust fund or the estate. A judge, however, could always make an order on this basis if he felt the circumstances warranted it.

The Courts retain a discretion not to award the winner his costs. This discretion will be exercised in cases where:

(1) The Court did not think that the winner should have brought the action. This sometimes happens in defamation cases.
(2) A payment into Court has been rejected, and the winner is subsequently awarded a lesser amount than was offered.
(3) The plaintiff brought an action in the High Court which he could have brought in the County Court. If the plaintiff is awarded less than £600, he recovers no costs at all: if he is awarded £600 but less than £3,000 he will probably only receive costs at the County Court level.

After a Court case, the solicitors from either side will usually try to agree on the costs that should be paid by the loser to the winner. If the solicitors are unable to agree, the Court will have to 'tax' (work out) the costs. Certain items will be fixed but overall the Court will adopt the standard basis referred to above. Both the winner and the loser can ask the Court to tax his solicitor's costs in a contentious case. This right is not widely known about, so requests are made very infrequently.

(C) Costs of litigants in person. The Litigants in Person (Cost and Expenses) Act 1975 enables a litigant in person to recover up to two-thirds of the rate that a solicitor would have been allowed for representing him in Court. The sum allowed can cover general disbursements but the purchase of books is not covered, nor are any fees that would have been incurred in briefing counsel. The amount paid must not exceed the litigant's actual loss of wages. A very small allowance is made in respect of time and effort spent in preparing the case. The Act does not apply to claims of £500 or less.

(D) Costs in criminal cases.
(a) If the defendant is convicted. The defendant can be required to make a contribution towards the prosecution's costs. There appears to be a wide discrepancy among Courts as to whether or not they grant costs.

(b) If the defendant is acquitted. The defendant may either be awarded no costs at all, be awarded costs to be paid by the prosecution or be awarded costs to be paid out of public funds. If the pros-

✂

FAMILY LEGAL BENEFITS INSURANCE
PROPOSAL FORM

(Please provide answers to all questions in BLOCK CAPITALS)

1. Name of Proposer   (*Mr/~~Mrs/Miss~~)   JOHN EVANS

2. Address   2, RAILWAY CUTTINGS,

   REDLAND

   BRISTOL 6   Telephone No. 7878-1231

3.

4. Are you self-employed? ~~Yes~~/No.

5. Marital Status   *Single/Married/Separated/Divorced/Widowed

6. No. in household

7. No. of properties owned/rented.   *Note:* If over two and under four properties an additional charge of £25 per property will apply.   Cover is not available for Assureds with more than four properties.   If more than one property, please advise addresses of each.

8. How many days do you spend outside the U.K. in any one year?   15   (approx.)

   Occupation Architectural Draftsman

9. Please give details of any claims of legal proceedings involving any member of the household which have taken place within the last three years. (If none—please state 'None'.)

   NONE

*Delete as applicable

P.T.O.

10. Please indicate cover required and payment details.

INDEMNITY LIMIT	Annual Payment Premium	Please tick	Office use	Monthly Payment Premium	Please tick	Office use
£5,000	£80	☐		£90	☐	
£10,000	£100	☐		£114	☐	
£25,000	£120	☑		£132	☐	
Worldwide extension @ 25% of above +25%		☐		+25%	☐	
Loss assessor cover @ £24 p.a. +£24		☑		£24	☐	
Additional properties @ £25 per property						
		Total premium		Monthly Payments	Total premium	

Annual payments

I wish to pay by:
Through my Broker ☐
By cheque ☑ (to be enclosed with form)   I attach completed
Credit card ☐ *Access/Barclaycard/Diners Club/American Express   Direct Debit Mandate ☐

Account No. ☐☐☐☐☐☐☐☐☐☐☐☐☐☐☐☐

11. Declaration

I declare that after due enquiry no member of the household is currently contemplating any claim or legal proceedings (including divorce proceedings).
I am not aware of any circumstances which could give rise to a claim or legal proceedings being pursued by or brought against any member of this household.
I agree that this declaration shall form the basis of the contract between me and the underwriters and I am willing to accept the policy in underwriters' usual form for this class of insurance.

Date __1 APRIL 1986__   Signed __John Evans__

Important Notice
1. Answer questions to the best of your knowledge and belief.
2. All material facts must be disclosed and failure to do so may nullify any Policy· or Certificate issued. *NB. A "material fact" is one likely to influence underwriters' acceptance or assessment of this proposal.*

* Delete as applicable.

3. All cheques to be made payable to Legal Benefits Ltd. A copy of the Certificate wording is available on request to Legal Benefits Ltd.

These statements form the basis of the insurance contract

Failure to declare all material facts makes the insurance cover invalid ecution is ordered to pay the costs, this is usually an indication that the Court feels that the case should never have been brought to Court. Payments are therefore generally made from public funds.

Although it is rare for costs to be awarded in Magistrates' Courts, it is now usual for acquitted defendants in the Crown Court to be awarded their costs. However, a Court might not make an award if it considers the defendant brought suspicion on himself by the way he acted and has led the prosecution to think that it has a stronger case against him than it really has, or where the evidence suggests that the defendant is guilty but he was acquitted on a technical irregularity.

(c) The prosecution's costs. If the defendant is convicted, the Court can make no order, or require the defendant to contribute, or order that the costs be paid out of public funds.

(E) Covering legal costs with insurance. As insurance can nowadays be obtained to cover most risks, it is not surprising that schemes are available to cover legal expenses. The Law Society introduced its own scheme, 'Family Legal Expenses Insurance', in 1982, with the backing of the Sun Alliance, General Accident, Royal, Eagle Star and Prudential insurance companies. The policy, which applies to all members of the insured's family, covers a wide range of areas with specific exceptions. The most important areas excluded are matrimonial disputes, problems involving a second home, cases involving rent, rates or social security tribunals, tax and Customs and Excise disputes, defamation, difficulties with business, charges of driving without a licence or insurance, and non-motor criminal cases. The premium is £66 per annum.

Other schemes exist, an example being the 'Family Legal Benefits' policy operated by Legal Benefits Ltd. The minimum premium is £80 per annum for £5,000 cover and the list of exclusions is smaller than in the Law Society scheme, the main ones being the defence of civil cases arising from events which involve third party bodily injury and property damage; criminal defence costs following a conviction for a crime of dishonesty or violence; and fines and/or legal costs awarded against the defendant after any criminal conviction. In addition, matrimonial cases are not covered during the first year of the policy.

SECTION 2
THE LAW AND YOUR HOME

1. INTRODUCTION

For most people, buying a house or flat will be one of the most important and exciting steps that they will ever take. It will almost certainly be the most expensive one. This section will look at some of the typical issues which confront the average house-buyer, such as how to choose the right property, how to finance the purchase and how to make sense of the legal side of things.

There are two distinct stages involved in the normal conveyancing transaction. During the first stage the purchaser finds a property that suits him and then proceeds to satisfy himself about various important issues; for example he needs to know that he really can afford it, that a motorway is not about to be built through the back garden, and that the property is in a reasonable state of repair. Only after he is sure about these and other questions will he enter into a formal agreement with the vendor to go ahead. At that point contracts are said to be exchanged. This marks the end of the first stage, after which both parties are committed to carry the agreement out: neither can back out. The second stage of the transaction now begins. The purchaser or his legal adviser must now check that various legal requirements are satisfied. It is necessary to make sure that the vendor really is the true owner of the property and that there is no risk of a third party claiming that really it belongs to him; similarly a check must be made to ensure that there are no restrictions affecting the property (for example, preventing its use as an office or smallholding) of which the purchaser is unaware. Also during this stage the important legal documents transferring the property to the purchaser (and, usually, immediately afterwards mortgaging it to the bank or building society) are drawn up. If all goes smoothly, the whole process culminates in the day of 'completion' when the vendor is paid and the purchaser becomes owner and can move in.

The house purchaser today is called upon to make an enormous number of different decisions. Not only must he decide what type of property he wants – urban or rural, house or flat, modern or 'old and with character' (crumbling to pieces); he will also find that there are many other important

questions. Should he have a valuation or a full survey? Should he do his own conveyancing or appoint a solicitor? Should he borrow money from a bank or a building society? What advantages do endowment mortgages have over straight capital repayment mortgages? With whom should the property be insured? The range of issues which the purchaser must face is expanding all the time, not least because the whole business of buying and selling property is becoming more and more competitive. Soon licensed conveyancers will appear to compete with solicitors and building societies may be permitted to move into estate agency. Of course, the greater the choice available to the consumer, the better he is able to select a deal particularly suitable to his circumstances. At the same time, the more options there are available, the easier it is to make a bad choice. This makes it vital that a purchaser should have as much information available as possible to enable him to make the most rational decision he can. On page 68 a list of useful publications is provided which should point the reader in the direction of useful additional information.

The house purchaser must also have a clear idea of what the whole business of buying a house is likely to cost him. The answer is nearly always more than he expected. On page 68 an attempt is made to give a rough idea of the typical costs involved in buying a house.

2. CHOOSING THE PROPERTY

The prospective purchaser's first problem is of course to find a property which suits his needs and is within his price range. An obvious starting point is to visit the estate agents in the area in which he would like to live and to be added to their mailing lists. There is no charge to the purchaser for this service (the vendor pays the commission) so that one should not feel bashful about visiting a number of different firms. The local press is another useful source of information, as are various other publications such as *Exchange and Mart* or *Country Life* which always contain property advertisements. New marketing techniques are being developed all the time, and a would-be house buyer may also find a 'computer agency' or a 'property shop' in the area in which he is looking. Alternatively it may be that a vendor decides to sell his house privately by placing an advertisement in a newsagent's window or a placard in the front garden. However the purchaser discovers the property he wants to buy, his legal position will be the same: until he signs a *written* contract, he will not be legally bound to go ahead with the purchase. Having seen the right house and agreed orally with the vendor that he would like to buy, the purchaser remains at liberty to pull out of the deal until the necessary legal formalities are complied with. The same is of course true of the vendor, which is why one comes across the notorious practice of 'gazumping'. A vendor agrees in principle to sell to one purchaser for £30,000 but, before the deal has been clinched in writing, he receives a better offer of £35,000 from someone else. By that time the first purchaser may have incurred considerable costs instructing both a surveyor to inspect the property and a solicitor to commence the legal side of things, but he has no legal remedy against the vendor. In this respect one just has to hope that the moral scruples of the vendor and purchaser are sufficient to persuade them to see the deal through.

When he has found a property which he wishes to buy, there are a number of further steps which the purchaser must take before taking the plunge and entering into a binding contract with the vendor. He must of course sort out the financial side of things (see Financing the Purchase on page 45, which looks at this in greater detail). The rest of this section considers the other issues he must deal with.

Freeholds and leaseholds. The purchaser will need to find out further details about the property itself. To begin with, he will probably have been told that the property is either 'freehold' or 'leasehold' and will wish to understand the significance of these terms. Where the property is freehold, this means that the vendor owns it outright rather than being answerable to some superior landlord. This does not necessarily mean, however, that it is altogether free from restrictions. The law places many limitations upon the way in which even a freehold owner can use his land: planning permission will be needed before a house can be built or a material change of use of the land is made, and neighbours may have rights of way across freehold land or the power to prevent its use except for specific purposes (e g as a private dwelling-house). But at

least the freehold owner is not answerable to a landlord or obliged to pay him rent.

The position where the land is leasehold is rather different, however. A leaseholder is a tenant and must pay rent periodically to his landlord. Leases vary considerably in nature from one case to another. On the one hand a tenant may simply be granted a weekly tenancy which can be terminated by the landlord serving a notice to quit upon him. On the other, a leasehold may be granted for 999 years, in which case the tenant's position is not particularly different from that of a freeholder. Admittedly he will have to pay a rent to the landlord, but this will normally be for a nominal amount (say £5 per year). The fact that the lease will eventually expire is of no real concern to the tenant, since the termination date is so many years away that it is all but illusory.

A purchaser must be careful, however, if he is offered a leasehold interest in a property whose duration is in between the two extremes mentioned above. In some parts of the country, and in particular in London, many properties are held on 99 year leases. If the lease of a flat was granted for 99 years in, say, 1910, it would now (in 1986) have only 23 years left to run. Not only would this be a cause of concern for the purchaser himself, in that the end of the lease is now in sight, it would also be of significance to any bank or building society considering whether to grant a mortgage. The average mortgage runs for 25 years, and the lender (or mortgagee) will want to protect itself by using the property purchased with its money as a security in case the borrower (or mortgagor) defaults on his payments. Of course there is not much security in a leasehold interest which in the relatively near future will have expired. The answer is obvious: the shorter the unexpired period of the lease is, the more cautious a purchaser should be.

To some people it may seem hard to understand why anyone should ever want to grant a lease for as long a period as 999 years at all. The answer is that, for technical legal reasons, there may be advantages in creating leasehold interests. This is particularly true where blocks of flats are concerned or where a large old house is converted into flats, because it is possible to impose positive duties on leaseholders to repair and maintain their own flats and to contribute towards the cost of keeping the common parts of the property such as staircases and passageways in reasonable condition. It is much more difficult to impose *positive* obligations upon freeholders.

39

Where a purchaser buys a flat in a purpose-built block or in a converted house, apart from acquiring a leasehold interest, he may well be asked to buy a share in a management company responsible for running the property and keeping it in decent condition. The management company will often itself be the owner of the freehold of the property and therefore the landlord of the individual leaseholders. The management company system is a good one because it means that each owner of the flats in a particular block has a say in the way in which the property generally is managed. There can of course be problems, for example when the owner of the top flat thinks that the management company should repair the roof that is leaking but the flat-owners on the ground-floor think that action is unnecessary. But the system does mean that problems such as this can be sorted out formally and in accordance with the rules of the management company's constitution. Matters such as this are best regulated in this official kind of way rather than leaving people to sort out issues of maintenance and repair on a purely *ad hoc* basis as and when problems arise.

In some parts of the country, and in particular in Bristol and Manchester, even freehold land may be subject to a kind of rent, known technically as a rentcharge. This means that a sum of money must be paid, normally annually and normally of only a small amount (£3–£5) to the rentcharge owner. Theoretically, if the rentcharge is not paid, the owner could come and reclaim the property itself in order to recover the sum due. In practice this is rarely if ever done, and since 1977 it has become impossible to create new rentcharges except in certain narrowly defined circumstances. It is also possible to 'buy out' the rentcharge by paying the rentcharge owner a sum of money by way of compensation. This is computed according to a statutory formula. In fact it is rarely worth the freeholder's while buying out the rentcharge, since the annual sum payable is so little. If he buys it out he will have to compensate the rentcharge owner *and* pay the legal costs: for this expense he will simply have relieved himself of a tiny, niggling sum. When land is said in estate agents' particulars to be 'freehold and free', this term means that is is free from any rentcharge.

Fixtures and fittings. When a purchaser has found a property which he would like to buy, he must make it quite clear what is and is not included in the sale. It may well be that an estate agent's particulars of sale specify that the carpets are included in the price of the house, or that certain items such as a greenhouse are to be removed. It is as well to be clear about these issues from the outset so as to avoid confusion or misunderstanding later. It is not unusual for disputes to arise between a vendor and purchaser, for example where the purchaser moves in only to discover that an ornamental greenhouse which he had thought was included in the sale has been removed. In this situation, assuming that the parties have not sorted the matter out in advance between themselves, the law says that a purchaser of land is entitled also to all items of property which have become 'fixtures'. However it is not always easy to say in law whether a particular item (or 'chattel' as lawyers say) has become a fixture, and there have been many cases in which a judge has been called upon to have the final say on this issue. When doing so, he will look at two separate matters. Firstly, he will consider whether the chattel in dispute has become physically attached to the land. The point is that, if there is some physical annexation, then the presumption is that the chattel has become part of the land itself. Thus a house itself built on foundations or a marble fire-place set beneath a chimney-breast would be presumed to be fixtures. On the other hand, a free-standing garden-shed or greenhouse would be presumed still to be chattels (and therefore still the property of the vendor after completion of the sale of the land). However, the judge will also consider a second issue, which is the purpose for which a chattel was placed upon the land. If it was intended to enhance the land itself, it could be a fixture, even though not physically annexed to it. For example a dry-stone wall would qualify as a fixture even though it stands by its own weight and is not physically annexed to the land. On the other hand, a beautiful oriental rug tacked to the panelling of an old house would probably be held to have retained its identity as a chattel and not to have become a fixture. The physical annexation is only a way of displaying the rug itself rather than a method of altering or enhancing the land. It is sometimes extremely difficult to tell whether a particular item falls on one side or the other of the fixture-chattel dividing line – it is therefore vital to reach a clear agreement on this before any possibility of a dispute arises. Litigation to sort matters out can be extremely expensive. In *Dean v Andrews* (1985) the plaintiff agreed to sell his house to the defendant. In the garden there was a large prefabricated greenhouse which was bolted to a concrete plinth. After completion, the defendant refused to allow the plaintiff to remove the greenhouse. The plaintiff sued, and the High Court decided that the greenhouse was not a fixture and awarded the plaintiff £1,500 damages for wrongfully depriving him of his property.

A quite different issue that a purchaser must face is whether or not he should have a survey carried out. Properties may suffer from all sorts of defects which are not necessarily visible when he is being shown around by an eager vendor. Furthermore the law imposes no duty upon a vendor to draw the purchaser's attention to physical defects in the property which cannot be seen but of which he is aware. As far as the law is concerned, the principle *caveat emptor* applies – let the buyer beware. However, although the vendor is not under a duty to disclose defects to a purchaser, he must not make any statements about the condition of the property which are misleading. A purchaser who relies upon a misrepresentation by the vendor and enters into a contract as a result may be entitled either to pull out of the transaction when he discovers the truth or to be paid compensation. Furthermore, a vendor who by his own negligence causes a physical defect in a property may have to pay damages to a purchaser who at a later date suffers injury or loss as a direct result.

Generally, however, it is up to the purchaser to find out for himself whether the property is in reasonable condition. Either he or some of his friends or relatives may be sufficiently knowledgeable about property to be able to form an intelligent impression of its physical state. Otherwise serious consideration should be given to the possibility of instructing a qualified surveyor to look at the property, particularly where the property is an old one or is in an area which gives rise to some concern (e g because of the possibility of flooding or because the situation is a very exposed one). Admittedly, having a survey carried out may add considerably to the purchaser's costs (see page 68), but the sum involved may turn out to be small compared with the expense involved later in replacing a roof or underpinning a house.

When the purchaser is buying a property with the help of a loan from a bank or building society, he will be required anyway to pay the mortgagee a fee for having the property valued. The mortgagee will want to be satisfied that the property more than covers the amount of the loan it is being asked to make so that, if the mortgagor defaults on his mortgage payments, the property can be sold and the loan paid off. However, it is very important for the purchaser to appreciate that a *valuation* is not the same thing as a *survey*. A valuation involves a fairly superficial inspection of the property and an estimate of what it is likely to be worth given its location, amenities and facilities etc, but does not involve a detailed or probing analysis of its physical state. Valuations will be riddled with statements by the valuer that he has not looked in the loft-space or inspected the foundations and that he couldn't tell whether the floor below the fitted carpet is infected by woodworm. If a valuation is seriously misleading, the mortgagee whose security is imperilled as a result could sue the valuer, and the law has recently changed so that the purchaser too (who, after all, pays the fee) could bring an action. However, the fact that a valuation does not require a detailed inspection limits the comeback that the purchaser has if the property turns out to be in worse condition than appeared to be the case.

Because of this the purchaser may be well advised in the case of older or more unusual property or of a property about which he feels some apprehension to ask the person carrying out the valuation for the mortgagee to go further and to conduct a full survey. This will be quite a bit more expensive, but will be much more detailed than a valuation. The surveyor will spend much more time about his task (and will make himself much more troublesome to the vendor). He will ask for furniture to be moved, carpets raised and try to get access to the roof. He will also look much more closely at structural problems such as subsidence or interference with foundations from nearby trees. Because his report will be more detailed, a purchaser will have a much clearer idea of what he is letting himself in for; and if the surveyor negligently makes significant errors in his report, the purchaser may well be able to bring an action against him for compensation.

In *Yianni v Evans* (1981) the plaintiffs wished to buy a house for £15,000. They applied for a mortgage and the prospective mortgagees asked the defendants to value the property at the plaintiffs' expense. They valued it at £15,000 and the plaintiffs therefore went ahead. Some years later serious cracks appeared in the building due to subsidence and by 1976 the cost of putting the property into decent repair was £18,000. The plaintiffs claimed damages against the defendants on the basis that they had been negligent in preparing the valuation. The High Court found for the plaintiffs, even though there was never a contract between them and the defendants (the defendants having been instructed by the mortgagees), and even though the plaintiffs never actually saw the report prepared by the defendants.

A purchaser may feel inclined to opt for an inspection which is less superficial than a valuation but also less detailed than a full structural survey. This can now be done by asking for the surveyor in question to produce a 'Home-Buyers' report. In terms of content and detail, it lies midway between these two extremes as, not surprisingly, does its cost. For many purchasers, such a report may be a sensible compromise.

A further issue which will confront the would-be purchaser at this stage is whether or not to instruct a solicitor to look after the legal side of the transaction and, if so, which solicitor to choose. Until very recently, Parliament gave solicitors a monopoly over the drawing-up of conveyances, the only exception being that an individual could draft conveyancing documents (e g for himself or friends) free of charge. In 1985 the law was altered by the Administration of Justice Act so as to allow people to set themselves up as 'licensed conveyancers' in direct competition with the solicitors' profession. It is too early to know whether licensed conveyancers will be able substantially to undercut the charges made by solicitors or whether they will be able to offer a better or more efficient service. What can be said is that the conveyancing market is much more competitive than it was and that the consumer is in a stronger position than he used to be, when solicitors' fees were often disproportionate to the amount of work involved in the average conveyancing transaction.

The enterprising purchaser may decide that he does not wish to pay a solicitor or a licensed conveyancer to do his conveyancing but instead to attempt to do the work himself. On page 68 there is a list of various books that may be of assistance to the do-it-yourself conveyancer. However, a few words of warning should be given to anyone thinking of taking this option. First, anyone who is buying property with the assistance of a mortgage will be required to pay the legal fees of the solicitor appointed to protect the mortgagee's interests. There is no way that this cost can be avoided – the mortgagee would not trust the purchaser himself to look after its position. On the other hand, where the purchaser instructs a solicitor to do his conveyancing, the same solicitor can usually act for the mortgagee as well. Since one person is doing all the legal work, the cost involved in looking after the mortgagee's interests is relatively smaller. Furthermore the purchaser will incur certain costs – local search fees and Land Registry fees – whether he instructs a solicitor or not.

Registered and unregistered land. A second word of warning to the purchaser considering doing his own conveyancing concerns a more technical legal problem. This is that there is a difference between what is called 'registered' and 'unregistered' land. The method of conveying registered land is very different from, and much simpler than, dealing with unregistered land. An intelligent purchaser could probably cope with a registered land transaction without too much trouble, but where the land is unregistered the situation is much more complex and shrouded in mysterious legal doctrines. The difference is this: where land is registered, virtually all the relevant details concerning it (its address, its owner, restrictions affecting it, rights of way across it) are contained in Her Majesty's Land Registry, and the title to the land is guaranteed by the State. This means that a purchaser needs only to check with the Land Registry to be certain that the vendor is the owner of the house he is to purchase and to find out about any other important details about the property. Assuming that the purchaser is satisfied with the situation, all that is needed is that the vendor should sign a simple form (known as a transfer: see pages 60 and 61) in order to pass the property on to him. Legal formalities are kept to a minimum and no complicated documentation is necessary. However, much of the property in the country is not registered in this way. Where land is unregistered the only way that a purchaser can satisfy himself that the vendor is the true owner is by searching back through all the title deeds of the property: he must search back to what is known as a 'good root of title' by which is meant a title deed which is more than fifteen years old and which adequately identifies the land itself and its ownership. If the purchaser is satisfied that the vendor has a good title, he must then draw up a conveyance for the vendor to sign, seal and deliver. This conveyance will need to be much more complicated than the transfer used in the case of registered land, and normally contains much legal jargon. Even the most astute do-it-yourself conveyancer will find the unregistered land system of conveyancing perplexing.

Why, it might be asked, is some land registered and some unregistered? The answer is that in due course it is intended to register all the land in the country: when that happens the whole process of conveyancing will become infinitely simpler. But the process of registering land is a very slow one: the registered land system has been in effect now for 60 years, and yet still only about half the land in the country has been registered. The current position is that the Land Registry is concentrating mainly on registering the title to *urban* land: only when that process is complete will it turn its attention to rural areas. It can be anticipated therefore that there will continue to be unregistered land for many years to come.

One final comment directed to the purchaser considering doing his own conveyancing is that he should seriously ask himself whether the saving he would make is really so great when weighed against the anxieties involved in trying to cope with the legal problems. There are many other problems involved in buying a house – fixing up the mortgage, appointing a surveyor, getting quotations from firms of furniture removers, sorting things out with the gas, electricity and telephone authorities – without having the added headache of making sure that legally everything is in order. Any saving made may be something of a false economy, particularly given that you cannot sue yourself if you make a mistake: a negligent solicitor can be sued for damages.

(i) Instructing a Solicitor

A purchaser who decides to instruct a solicitor will wonder how to set about selecting which firm is to act for him. Obviously word of mouth is important – a recommendation from a friend can be very useful. Since October 1984 solicitors have been allowed to advertise their services, and the local press or radio may carry helpful advertisements. Besides that, the local Law Society and the Yellow Pages will provide names and addresses of many firms of solicitors, and a purchaser should not hesitate to ring up a number of firms and ask for an estimate of their costs. The market is much more competitive than it used to be, and solicitors are anxious to maintain or increase their business by offering lower prices. However, when obtaining an estimate, one should make sure just what the solicitor is offering: is the figure he suggests to be inclusive of

local search fees, VAT, stamp duty, Land Registry fees, etc., or will these items all appear at the end of the bill to be added to the price quoted for his own services? This is an important issue: the extras may end up being larger than the solicitor's own fee (see page 68).

Whoever does the legal work – solicitor, licensed conveyancer or the purchaser himself – there are three particular matters that must be dealt with at this stage of the transaction. These will be considered in turn.

(ii) The Local Search

A 'local search' must be conducted. What this involves is sending a local search form off to the local authority, asking it a series of important questions concerning the property. There is a standard form available for this purpose, and the search fee at the moment is £14.40. The search form should be sent off as soon as possible, as it may take some weeks for the authority to reply.

The local search will elicit a considerable amount of information about the property: whether it is in a clean-air zone, whether it has had the benefit of a home-improvement grant in the past, whether it has ever been suggested that it should be compulsorily purchased and whether it is connected to the main drains. The local search also deals with the important question of town and country planning: the search should indicate what plans there are for developing the area (the purchaser may well be put off buying a house if there are proposals to erect a trading estate nearby), and whether any new roads are planned in the neighbourhood. A home-owner may have great difficulty in selling his house where the local search indicates that the Government is thinking that one day it will build a by-pass which will abut the end of the back garden. The local search should also indicate whether the property itself was built with planning permission and whether there are any restrictions on the way in which it can be used in the future. There is no point in buying a large old house with the intention of running it as a small hotel if the local authority is going to prevent its use for that purpose. If the vendor has himself built on an extension to the house in the last couple of years, it is necessary to check that he had planning permission from the local authority (and also that he complied with the authority's building regulations): theoretically the authority could insist that any recent building done without its permission should be dismantled.

43

Form LLCl. (*Local Land Charges Rules 1977 Schedule 1, Form C*)

Official Number _____ 069205 _____
(*To be completed by the registering authority*)

The duplicate of this form must also be completed:
a carbon copy will suffice

For directions, notes and fees see overleaf

Insert name and address of registering authority in space below

HEMINGWAY DISTRICT COUNCIL
COUNCIL OFFICES
NEWTOWN
BLANKSHIRE

Register of local land charges

Requisition for search and official certificate of search

Requisition for search
(*A separate requisition must be made in respect of each parcel of land except as explained overleaf*)

An official search is required in ~~Part(s)~~ ALL *of* [1]
the register of local land charges kept by the above-named registering authority for subsisting registrations against the land [defined in the attached plan and][2] described below.

Description of land sufficient to enable it to be identified

57 UPPER BRIDGE STREET, NEWTOWN, BLANKSHIRE

Name and address to which certificate is to be sent

Dear and Dear
5 High Street
Littleham
Wiltshire

Signature of applicant (*or his solicitor*)

A. W. Giggleswick

Date
6.3.86

Telephone number
0546-92153

Reference
V/2E

Enclosure
Cheque/~~Money Order/Postal Order/Giro~~

Official certificate of search

To be completed by authorised officer

It is hereby certified that the search requested above reveals ~~no subsisting registrations~~

or the three registrations described in the Schedule hereto[3] up to and including the date of this certificate.

Signed _N. B. Brown_

On behalf of HEMINGWAY DISTRICT COUNCIL

Date
18.3.86

1 Delete if inappropriate. Otherwise insert Part(s) in which search is required.

2 Delete if inappropriate. (A plan should be furnished in duplicate if it is desired that a copy should be returned.)

3 Delete inapplicable words. (The Parts of the Schedule should be securely attached to the certificate and the number of registrations disclosed should be inserted in the space provided. Only Parts which disclose subsisting registrations should be sent.)

4 Insert name of registering authority.

(iii) The Draft Contract

At this stage of the transaction, another thing that happens is that the vendor or his solicitor will prepare a draft contract and send it to the purchaser or his legal adviser. The draft contract will describe the property, state whether it is registered or unregistered land and who the current legal owner is. It will also describe any restrictions or rights which affect the property and record the agreed purchase price. The draft contract will nearly always be contained in a standard form: there are two particular standard forms of contract in use in conveyancing transactions. One is called the National Conditions of Sale (20th edition) and the other is called The Law Society's Contract for Sale (1984 edition). The point about these standard forms is that they contain a large number of terms and conditions which will bind the vendor and purchaser and which can be of great importance if anything goes wrong with the transaction. For example, if the purchaser refuses to hand over the purchase money to the vendor on the day fixed for completion, there will be a standard term requiring him to pay interest to the vendor on the money that should have been paid. Equally the standard terms will explain what is to happen if the vendor refuses to vacate the property when the purchaser turns up with his removal men. The standard terms and conditions are of great practical importance therefore, although the purchaser will have to have great stamina if he is to read and understand them thoroughly. Having received the draft contract, the purchaser may decide to accept it as it is, or he may try to negotiate some alterations in it. The important point is that at *this* stage, the correspondence between the two sides is still 'subject to contract', that is to say the parties are moving towards the point at which they will enter into a binding agreement, but they have not yet reached it. The Rubicon is not crossed until contracts are exchanged, but there are still some issues that have to be sorted out.

(iv) Enquiries Before Contract

In particular, after receipt of the draft contract, a form will be sent off to the vendor's solicitor called 'Enquiries before contract' (see extract from document on page 46). This form asks a large number of questions about the property – for example about who owns the boundaries, which fixtures or fittings will be removed by the vendor and whether there are any other occu-pants of the property who claim to have an interest in it. It has become the custom for solicitors to add numerous extra enquiries to those that appear in the standard form used for this purpose, and great care has to be exercised by the vendor and his solicitor to ensure that they do not give misleading or incorrect replies. If they do, the purchaser may later be able to sue the vendor for misrepresentation: he may be able to claim damages or, in some circumstances, he may be allowed to set the whole contract aside.

3. FINANCING THE PURCHASE

Of course the most important issue of all for the purchaser is to work out the price that he can afford to pay for his house. Very few purchasers have enough cash to buy a house outright: most will need to borrow a considerable amount of money from a bank or building society if they are to go ahead with the deal. The lender will then take a 'mortgage' on the property which is intended to protect its position in case the borrower fails to pay the loan back on the terms agreed. The lender or 'mortgagee' is protected in various ways; in the first place it takes physical possession of the title deeds of the property: this means that the borrower (or 'mortgagor') is unable to sell up and disappear with the proceeds of sale, since no purchaser would hand over the purchase price except in return for the title deeds. But the mortgagee has other important rights as well. In particular, if the mortgagor gets seriously into arrears in paying off the loan, the mortgagee can apply to the court to have him removed from the property and then can proceed to sell it on the open market. It then uses the proceeds of sale to pay off the loan and any interest due and to cover the legal expenses involved in the transaction. Any money left over is then repaid to the mortgagor (unless there is a second mortgagee, who would be entitled in priority to the mortgagor himself). Generally speaking, however, the potential mortgagee will be careful to ensure that it only lends money to borrowers who should have no difficulty in meeting the costs of repayment. This is why building societies and banks need to know the details of potential borrowers' salaries and job prospects.

It is worth pointing out that even the lucky purchaser with enough cash to buy a house outright should look into the possibility of taking a loan on mortgage. Interest payable on the first £30,000 borrowed on mortgage benefits from tax

Short description of the property

re 43 Sheepfair Lane, Coldfield

Parties Dedlock

to Jellyby

These enquiries are copyright and may not be reproduced

ENQUIRIES
BEFORE CONTRACT

In cases of property subject to a tenancy, forms **Con 291** (general business and residential tenancies) *or* **Con 292** (agricultural tenancies) should also be used.

Please strike out enquiries which are not applicable

Replies are requested to the following enquiries.

Dear and Dear

Proposed purchaser's solicitors.

Date 8.3 198 6

GENERAL ENQUIRIES

The replies are as follows.

Grabbit and Co

Proposed vendor's solicitors.

Date 23.3 198 6

REPLIES

These replies, except in the case of any enquiry expressly requiring a reply from the Vendor's solicitors, are given on behalf of the proposed Vendor and without responsibility on the part of his solicitors their partners or employees. They are believed to be correct but the accuracy is not guaranteed and they do not obviate the need to make appropriate searches, enquiries and inspections.

1. Boundaries
(A) To whom do all the boundary walls, fences, hedges and ditches belong?

(B) If no definite indications exist, which has the Vendor maintained or regarded as his responsibility?

1 (A) See the plan attached to the draft contract.

(B) N/A.

2. Disputes
(A) Is the Vendor aware of any past or current disputes regarding boundaries, easements, covenants or other matters relating to the property or its use?

(B) During the last three years, has the Vendor complained or had cause to complain about the state and condition, or the manner of use, of any adjoining or neighbouring property? If so, please give particulars.

2 (A) The Vendor is not aware of any such disputes.

(B) No.

3. Notices
Please give particulars of all notices relating to the property, or to matters likely to affect its use or enjoyment, that the Vendor (or to his knowledge, any predecessor in title) has given or received.

3 There are none to the Vendor's knowledge.

4. Guarantees etc.
(A) Please supply a copy of any of the following of which the Purchaser is to have the benefit:

agreement, covenant, guarantee, warranty, bond, certificate, indemnity and insurance policy,
relating to any of the following matters:

the construction of the property, or any part of it, or of any building of which it forms part;
any repair or replacement of, or treatment or improvement to the fabric of the property;
the maintenance of any accessway;
the construction costs of any road (including lighting, drainage and crossovers) to which the property fronts, and the charges for adopting any such road as maintainable at the public expense;
a defective title;
breach of any restrictive covenant.

(B) (i) What defects or other matters have become apparent, or adverse claims have been made by third parties, which might give rise to a claim under any document mentioned in (A)?
(ii) Has notice of such defect, matter or adverse claim been given? If so, please give particulars.
(iii) Please give particulars of all such claims already made, whether or not already settled.

4 (A) Copy NHBC agreement herewith; there are no other such documents to the Vendor's knowledge.

(B) None so far as the Vendor is aware.

relief. It may be that a purchaser could invest his cash sum somewhere where it will earn *more* than it would cost to borrow money from a building society with the benefit of tax relief. Furthermore, although the initial monthly mortgage repayment on, say, a £30,000 loan may seem enormous, it will probably seem fairly paltry in ten or twenty years' time assuming that the mortgagor's salary has been increasing roughly in line with inflation. Thus the burden of a mortgage may come to feel less and less as time goes by: a purchaser with cash may well consider therefore that he should use it for some other, more pressing, purpose while taking advantage of the mortgage system to pay for his house.

When considering his financial position, the purchaser must look not only at the price of the house itself, but also take into account the many other expenses inevitably involved in the process of moving house. On page 68 an indication is given of some of the likely other costs that will be incurred.

Assuming that the purchaser does need to borrow money on mortgage, he will need to know what sources of loans are available to him. Traditionally the market has mainly belonged to the building societies, and they have abstained from competing with one another to offer better or cheaper deals to their customers. However, the formal cartel operated by the building societies has recently been abandoned, so that the would-be borrower ought to 'shop around' to find out what various societies have to offer. At the same time, the clearing banks in the last few years have decided to move into the mortgage market, somewhat to the discomfort of the building societies. The borrower ought therefore to consider approaching his bank manager to find out what prospects he would have of receiving a bank loan. One slight disadvantage of borrowing from the bank is that they tend to charge an 'arrangement fee' for setting the deal up, which is often in the region of £100–£150. Building societies do not charge an arrangement fee (although, as explained on page 43 a solicitor will be instructed to look after their legal position, and a fee will be charged for that). On the other hand, the banks are sometimes more flexible in their lending habits than building societies, and they may be prepared to advance rather more than a building society would or to be less fussy about the fact that the property in question is in a run-down condition.

Apart from banks and building societies, there are some other sources of loans for house-purchase. Local authorities sometimes lend money, although today they normally only do so where council tenants wish to exercise their 'right to buy' their homes under the Housing Act 1985. Private loans are not unheard of, and life insurance companies may be another source of help (although they are normally involved in conjunction with a bank or building society where an endowment mortgage is created: see page 50). If a borrower is having difficulty in obtaining a loan, a mortgage broker may well be able to assist, as might his solicitor. Sometimes there is an excess of demand for loans over supply, which can be very frustrating for the would-be purchaser who is ready in all other respects to buy a particular house. One way of attracting the sympathy of a building society is to have been a regular saver with it over a substantial period of time. At other times, the lending institutions seem almost to be falling over one another to offer mortgages. The fluctuations in the mortgage market are among the problems with which purchasers have to contend.

Apart from finding an institution willing to lend him money, the borrower must also consider what type of mortgage is best suited to his needs. There are various different kinds of mortgage available, and it is necessary to consider their relative advantages and disadvantages carefully. In particular one should understand the distinction between capital repayment mortgages, endowment mortgages and pension mortgages.

(i) Capital Repayment Mortgages

Under the most common arrangement, the borrower takes a loan over a number of years – often, though not necessarily, 25 – and throughout that period he repays the loan to the lender, together with interest. Some borrowers may be offered a loan at a fixed rate of interest: in particular local authorities in the past have tended to establish a fixed rate. The practice is not common however, and of course involves a certain amount of risk to the borrower if it subsequently transpires that inflation drops and that cheaper loans are available. Much more common is the situation where the mortgagee reserves the power to vary the interest rate from time to time. In recent years, interest rates generally have become much more volatile and it has been known for mortgage rates to be changed three or four times a year. The borrower will find this a considerable nuisance, since he will be required to change his standing order each time the rate changes. Some building societies have changed their practice in this respect however, and simply ask the borrower to alter his monthly repayments once a year, the alteration being calculated to take into account all interest changes within the previous twelve months. The clearing banks already adopt this practice when lending money on mortgages.

As far as interest rates themselves are concerned, it was the case until fairly recently that all the building societies charged the same rate, but in 1984 their formal cartel came to an end so that the potential borrower is advised to 'shop around' to see what deals are on offer. Furthermore, there was a practice at one time whereby larger loans attracted a higher rate of interest than smaller ones: the surcharge would be payable on the entire loan, not just the portion of the loan above the relevant threshold. Some building societies, now that the cartel has been abandoned, have scrapped this practice so that the consumer should make a point of finding out what their policy is in this respect. Banks also have entered the mortgage market, so that the bank manager should also be approached.

The interest payable on the first £30,000 of the loan attracts tax relief. This of course is one of the great attractions of borrowing money when purchasing a house, and although from time to time the whole policy of granting tax relief to people who are, after all, acquiring an asset which will probably increase in value more quickly than the rate of inflation comes into question, it is unlikely that any Government in the foreseeable future would dare to scrap this privilege. A somewhat strange anomaly of the current situation is that a married couple only qualify for tax relief on the first £30,000 they borrow whereas unmarried people buying a house together are *each* entitled to tax relief on that amount. For some reason therefore there is a systematic bias in favour of people living together out of wedlock, who can borrow up to £60,000 with the benefit of tax relief. The way that the tax relief works is that a borrower's taxable income is reduced by the amount of interest he has to pay in a given year; it follows that the amount of tax he pays is reduced fairly considerably. For example, if George buys 12 High Street for £45,000 with a £30,000 mortgage, and the current interest rate is 12%, consider his position with and without mortgage interest relief where his taxable income is otherwise £14,000.

Benefits of mortgage interest relief		
Without a mortgage:		
Taxable income	£14,000	
Tax payable at 29%		£4,060
With a mortgage:		
Taxable income	£14,000	
less mortgage interest relief (i e annual interest payable on £30,000 at 12%)	£3,600	
	£10,400	
Tax payable at 29%		£3,016
Net saving in tax		£1,044

The privilege of tax relief is particularly efficient for the borrower who pays *higher* rates of tax, since the interest can be deducted from the band of income which attracts the *highest* rate of tax.

Suppose therefore that George's taxable income is £20,200. Income between £17,200 and £20,200 is taxable at 40%. The figures would then work out as follows:

Benefits of mortgage interest relief for higher earners		
Without a mortgage:		
Taxable income		£20,200
Tax payable at 29% on £17,200	£4,988	
Tax payable at 40% on £3,000	£1,200	
Total tax payable		£6,188
With a mortgage:		
Taxable income	£20,200	
Less mortgage interest relief	£3,600	
	£16,600	
Total tax payable at 29%		£4,814
Net saving in tax		£1,374

It may be that a future government wanting to change the tax relief position would do so by removing this particular privilege from higher earners and allowing tax relief only at the basic rate of tax.

The actual arrangements by which tax relief is obtained have changed dramatically in recent years. At one time all borrowers paid a gross monthly sum to the mortgagee, but then received tax relief through their tax codings. This system was highly unsatisfactory – particularly when interest rates went through one of their recurrent volatile phases – and it could take a long time for the Inland Revenue to fix the appropriate coding. Clerical errors were not unknown either, so that a borrower was not getting all the relief to which he was entitled. The position changed in 1983 with the introduction of MIRAS (mortgage interest relief at source). As originally introduced, a person borrowing up to £30,000 and only subject to tax at the basic rate was required only to make a *net* monthly payment to his mortgagee, representing the amount of capital and interest due *after* his tax relief has been taken into account. It is, then, for the mortgagee and the Inland Revenue to arrange between themselves for the balance to be accounted for. The great attraction of this scheme to the borrower is that his repayments automatically take account of tax relief and the nagging anxiety of waiting for the Revenue to calculate the proper tax-coding is eliminated. In 1985, the MIRAS scheme was improved further, since it now can apply even where the loan exceeds £30,000 as long as it is less than £60,000. However, a borrower who pays higher rates of tax will only fall within the

MIRAS system in respect of his income taxed at the basic rate.

An important distinction must be made at this point between 'constant net repayment mortgages' and 'gross profile' mortgages. The distinction relates to the way in which the mortgagee calculates the monthly repayment that the borrower has to make. Most building societies adopt the constant net repayment method and banks the gross profile one. Under the constant net repayment system, the building society fixes a monthly repayment rate which will remain constant from the borrower's point of view (except for changes in the interest rate) throughout the period of the loan. In this situation, in the early years of the mortgage the borrower is mainly repaying interest and in the later years mainly capital, but this does not affect his monthly repayment which is constant throughout. Under the gross profile system the position is different. The bank calculates a constant *gross* payment which it must receive throughout the loan; however, the borrower does not himself pay the *gross* amount but only a net one, with the benefit of tax relief. Since more tax relief is available early in the loan than later, it follows that the net repayment is lower at the start of the loan than at the end. The difference in payments is shown in the following table. The would-be borrower must weigh up the pros and cons: lower monthly payments at the start under a gross profile mortgage or a lower overall payment at the end of 25 years under the constant net repayment scheme.

Sylvester borrows £10,000 at an interest rate of 13% to be repaid over 25 years; the table shows (a) the amount of capital repaid at any stage of

Constant net repayment mortgage – example

Year	Capital Repaid		Net Monthly Repayment	
	Gross Profile	Constant Net Repayment	Gross Profile	Constant Net Repayment
1	64.30	117.20	81.20	85.60
2	72.70	127.80	81.40	
3	82.20	139.50	81.60	
4	92.90	152.10	81.90	Constant
5	100.50	166.00	82.20	throughout
10	193.40	256.60	84.40	
15	356.40	396.70	88.50	
20	656.70	613.70	96.00	
25	1209.90	947.80	109.80	85.60
total	26883.50	25679.90		

the term under the gross profile and constant net repayment system and (b) the monthly net cost to Sylvester throughout the loan.

A first-time buyer anxious about the expense involved in taking out a mortgage and saving the money to put down as a deposit on a house would be well-advised to get hold of details of the Government's 'Homeloan Scheme'. Participants in the scheme are required to save with one of the approved institutions (e g building societies or banks) for two years at least. When they do so they will qualify for a cash bonus of up to £110 *and* an extra loan of £600 (above the mortgage itself) interest-free for the first five years. Details of the Homeloan Scheme are available in Post Offices and building societies.

(ii) Endowment Mortgages

These are quite different from capital repayment mortgages. The borrower receives a loan from the mortgagee but instead of repaying capital and interest throughout the loan, the borrower simply pays the interest payable on the loan. At the same time, however, the borrower also takes out a life insurance policy which, on his death or at the date the policy matures, will yield at least a capital sum equivalent to that borrowed. The policy is 'assigned' to the mortgagee, so that when it matures it can take the capital sum owing to it; any surplus will be handed back to the borrower (assuming it is not a security for any further loan).

Until 13 March 1984 endowment policies were particularly attractive to some borrowers, because tax relief was available not only on the amount of interest payable to the mortgagee but also on the monthly premiums payable to the life insurance company. This was somewhat bizarre, in that it meant in effect that the borrower was being given tax relief on his *capital* payments, and the 1984 Budget took this concession away, but only in respect of *new* policies taken out since. Anyone who took out an endowment policy before that date (and effective leaking meant that many new policies were issued just before that Budget) would be very foolish to surrender it and thus forego the benefit of tax relief.

Tax relief on *new* policies having gone, the endowment mortgage is not quite the same attraction that it was. Mortgagees often charge a slightly higher interest rate (to compensate for the fact that they don't receive any capital until the end of the loan) so that the borrower may find such a loan quite expensive. Also, although the

estimate from the life insurance company will tempt the borrower with promises of 'reversionary bonuses' at the maturity of the policy, these should be considered with some scepticism. The company is suggesting that, apart from paying off the mortgagee's loan, there will also be a tax-free sum – quite sizeable – left over for the policyholder. What has to be asked is whether the promise of, say, £12,500 in cash in 25 years time is really such a bonanza, particularly after inflation is taken into account. The added expense now of paying for the mortgage may not be compensated for by a cash sum later. The borrower should ask for quotations from insurance companies or discuss matters with an insurance broker and compare the offers made as well as considering the expense involved in capital repayment mortgages. Shopping-around, though tiring and time-consuming, is worthwhile in today's mortgage market.

(iii) Pension Mortgages

A fairly new type of loan is the pension mortgage. Generally such mortgages are only available to the self-employed. They may be very attractive, particularly to people paying higher rates of tax, because of their tax efficiency. A person who enters into a private pension scheme can normally agree to take a capital sum on retirement in addition to a provision thereafter. A mortgagee may well lend money on the basis that the loan will be repaid out of the capital sum that becomes available. Although it is not possible for the borrower to assign his rights under the pension scheme to the mortgagee (in the way that he can under a life insurance policy), the mortgagee will have a mortgage on the property acquired with the money anyway, and this should be sufficient to protect its interest. The advantages to the borrower of the arrangement are threefold: tax relief on the interest payable on the loan, tax relief on the money paid into the pension plan and the fact that the pension fund *itself* (run by the company in question) is not taxable. Furthermore, the borrower can claim tax relief against his highest band of taxable income. The self-employed should obviously look into such schemes, although they do of course have some disadvantages. The pension will be expensive, as the investor will have to build up a sum sufficient both to repay the mortgage and to earn a pension for life. There may be difficulties where an investor subsequently ceases to be self-employed or suffers a serious reduction of income. But despite these and other drawbacks, such arrangements may be worth serious consideration.

Apart from considering which type of mortgage is suitable to his needs, the borrower will also have to consider how long he should take to repay it. Many mortgages are taken out over a 25 year period, but shorter terms are not unusual. Obviously the shorter the term, the more the monthly repayments will be: but, from the borrower's point of view, the time when he has got the building society 'off his back' is brought much closer. It is worth considering, however, whether being free of the mortgage is really such an advantage. In 20 years time, the monthly repayments will probably seem insignificant to anyone lucky enough to have risen up the salary scale, and wage inflation will probably have outstripped the rise in the monthly amount anyway. Paying more now for this freedom in the future may be a false economy. From the mortgagee's point of view, they will not consider a short-term loan if the effect would be to push the monthly repayment figure above the amount they consider the borrower can pay; while at the same time they will be sceptical of a period which would take the borrower beyond the normal retirement age. The message must be for anyone approaching or just into his forties to consider quite carefully his 'mortgageability' for the future.

A borrower who gets into trouble with his mortgage repayments may be able to persuade the mortgagee to reschedule the loan. If a 20 year mortgage is rearranged on a 25 year basis, it will follow that the monthly repayment is quite a bit smaller and this may just enable the borrower in financial difficulty to make ends meet.

The borrower in search of a mortgage will be keen to know how large a loan he can expect to receive. This issue depends on two different questions: first, what is the property in question worth and secondly, what is the borrower's income?

(iv) The Property

The mortgagee will protect itself by ensuring that the property is worth enough to cover the amount of its loan. Ultimately the main remedies of a mortgagee whose borrower defaults on his mortgage payments is to take possession of the property and sell it. It is of course vital that the sale will yield enough to pay off the mortgage debt. The mortgagee will always have the property valued therefore (at the borrower's expense) and, as a general rule, will only lend up to 90% of the amount fixed by the valuer. The valuation may well come up with a figure lower than the amount being asked by the vendor. That may enable the purchaser to get the vendor to agree to lower his price, but this will depend on the state of the market. The mere fact that the valuation suggests a figure lower than the purchase price ought not unduly to worry the borrower: valuers in such cases tend to be cautious and to go for a figure which leaves no risk at all of their being sued in negligence by the mortgagee. If there is a serious discrepancy between the two figures, however, the borrower may wish to think again about the wisdom of proceeding.

Where the property is old or unusual or in serious disrepair, the mortgagee may only be prepared to lend a lower percentage of the valuation. This is one of the hazards faced by the home-improvement expert: he may need to save cash or raise it in some other way if he is to be able to proceed. Apart from the 'percentage' problem, the mortgagee may also refuse to advance all of the loan until certain repairs or improvements have been carried out: for example a building society may insist on a roof being replaced or on wet or dry-rot being treated. Retentions such as this can cause the borrower acute liquidity problems, as the inevitable shortfall may make it difficult for him to complete the transaction. The bank may be prepared to assist, but probably at quite high interest rates. One further point is that the mortgagee may insist on protecting itself against the risk of the property being an inadequate security for the loan by asking the mortgagor to pay for a mortgage indemnity policy. A single premium will have to be paid before the mortgage money is handed over.

One hundred per cent loans are not unheard of, but generally they are only allowed in respect of very modern properties built by companies with an established reputation. Some builders in recent years have offered first-time buyers complete financial packages including free conveyancing and 100% loans, but some scepticism is called for: the sale tends to include many fixtures and fittings which a purchaser in the future may not want: the question therefore is whether the property itself, stripped of these 'extras', would be worth the amount of the original loan.

(v) The Borrower's Salary

The other important issue in establishing the size of the loan the mortgagee might make is the borrower's salary. Since the market became more competitive, it has become very important to shop around, since policy differs from one lender to another. As a rule of thumb one can expect to be able to borrow up to 2¾ times one's salary: someone earning £10,000 a year should therefore be able to obtain a mortgage of £27,500. Of course, very frequently the house is to be purchased by a couple, and the question then arises whether a second salary can be taken into account. The answer is almost certainly yes, although it does not follow that a loan of 2¾ the combined salary is available. Instead, the mortgagee may offer 2¾ times one salary plus the amount of the second; alternatively, others may offer double the combined salary. So if Dominic earns £18,000 and Theresa £7,000, on a 2¾ plus 1 basis they would qualify for a loan up to £56,500; on a double the combined salary basis, they could qualify for £50,000.

Would-be joint purchasers will not need to be married or even engaged in order to take advantage of a joint mortgage. As long as each of the partners has a salary, the mortgagee will not nowadays be too scrupulous about the relationship of the borrowers. Mortgagees may, however, be more sceptical about loans to more than two people, as the more co-owners there are, the greater the legal complications tend to be.

Potential borrowers who are self-employed tend to have rather more difficulty in obtaining a mortgage than wage-earners, as the mortgagee will wish to examine the borrower's accounts closely to ensure that he will be capable of meeting his monthly repayments. Mortgagees normally require accounts for at least the last three years when making a decision, which obviously causes problems for anyone who has recently started his own business. It may be that a bank, involved in the capitalisation of the business itself, will be more sympathetic to such a person than a building society.

An important matter for the borrower to consider is what will happen to his family should he die before the mortgage is fully repaid. In the case of an endowment mortgage there is of course no problem: on his death the policy will mature and the mortgage will be paid off. In the case of a capital repayment mortgage, this will not happen: the borrower can, however, take out a 'mortgage protection policy'. On death, the mortgage will be discharged by the insurance company. Such policies are relatively cheap, and any borrower with dependants should seriously

consider taking one out. It may be wiser though to buy a more expensive policy which, apart from covering the mortgage loan, also will produce extra capital for the deceased's family.

4. EXCHANGING CONTRACTS

By this stage the purchaser has found a property to his liking, received a draft contract and replies to preliminary enquiries and conducted a local search; he may also have had a survey carried out and have received a mortgage offer. Assuming that he is still happy to proceed he has now reached the stage of exchanging contracts. This is the crucial point for, having exchanged contracts, there is no turning back. The purchaser cannot take possession of the property until the completion date, which is usually about three or four weeks after exchange, but he is now contractually obliged to go through with the transaction. Should he subsequently refuse to, he could be sued for damages by the vendor. Equally if the vendor refuses to complete, he could be compelled by the court to do so. The contract will look like the sample contract reproduced opposite.

The way in which contracts are exchanged is that each party has an identical copy which he must sign. The purchaser then sends his signed copy (together with a cheque for 10% of the purchase price: see below) to the vendor. The vendor then sends his part to the purchaser, and it is at that stage that the contract becomes legally enforceable: the critical moment is the one at which the two copies have been exchanged.

It is customary for the vendor to require the purchaser to hand over 10% of the purchase price at the moment of exchange, the balance of 90% being payable on completion. The reason for this is that it acts as a disincentive to a purchaser considering backing out of the transaction after exchange of contracts. The law allows the vendor in such circumstances to retain the 10%, even where it represents a larger sum than he could have been awarded by the Court in an action for damages. A purchaser is unlikely to want to forfeit such a large sum of money to the vendor. In some circumstances the purchaser may be granted relief against forfeiture by the Court, but such occasions are fairly rare.

House prices have risen enormously in recent years, and this has caused problems, particularly to first time buyers, who have to find 10% of the purchase price on exchange of contracts (before

> **IMPORTANT**
> This is a technical document, designed to create specific legal rights and obligations.
> It is recommended for use only in accordance with the advice of your solicitors.

THE LAW SOCIETY'S CONTRACT FOR SALE (1984 REVISION)

AGREEMENT made the   8th   day of   April   198 6

BETWEEN   JEREMY MONTAGUE DEDLOCK of
         43 SHEEPFAIR LANE   Vendor
         COLDFIELD NEAR LITTLEHAM   WILTSHIRE

         HARRIET ARIADNE JELLYBY of   Purchaser
         BELVISTA
         UPPER THRUBWELL   DEVON

IT is agreed that the Vendor shall sell and the Purchaser shall purchase in accordance with the following special conditions the property described in the particulars below at the price of

---

PARTICULARS—ALL THAT freehold/~~leasehold~~ property Known as 43 Sheepfair Lane
Coldfield Nr Littleham Wiltshire together with the
dwellinghouse garage and outbuildings thereon which property is
shown edged blue on the plan annexed hereto TOGETHER WITH the benefit
of the right of way across the land hatched in blue on the said
plan as described in a deed of grant dated 14th February 1962 a copy
of which has been supplied to the purchaser.

SPECIAL CONDITIONS OF SALE—SEE BACK PAGE

Purchase money	£42000	00	SIGNED
less deposit paid	£ 4200	00	
	£37800	00	*J. M. Dedlock*
Chattels, fittings etc. CARPETS	£ 1000	00	
Balance	£38800	00	Vendor/~~Purchaser~~

Vendor's Solicitors   DEAR and DEAR   Ref.   V/2e
                         5 HIGH STREET, LITTLEHAM, WILTS

Purchaser's Solicitors   GRABBIT and Co   Ref.   JMH/2/HY
                         29 FORE STREET, TAWNMOUTH, DEVON

Local Authorities   THAMESDOWN DISTRICT COUNCIL, WILTSHIRE COUNTY COUNCIL

53

THE LAW SOCIETY'S GENERAL CONDITIONS OF SALE (1984 REVISION)

1 DEFINITIONS

In these conditions—
(*a*) "completion notice" means a notice served under condition 23 (2)
(*b*) "the contract rate" means the rate specified in a special condition or, if none is so specified, the rate prescribed from time to time under section 32 of the Land Compensation Act 1961 for interest payable thereunder
(*c*) "contractual completion date" has the meaning given in condition 21
(*d*) "conveyance" includes an assignment and a transfer under the Land Registration Acts
(*e*) "lease" includes underlease
(*f*) "normal deposit" means the sum which, together with any preliminary deposit paid by the purchaser, amounts to ten per centum of the purchase money (excluding any separate price to be paid for any chattels, fixtures or fittings)
(*g*) "working day" means any day from Monday to Friday (inclusive) other than—
(i) Christmas Day, Good Friday and any statutory bank holiday, and
(ii) any other day specified in a special condition as not a working day
(*h*) a reference to a statute includes any amendment or re-enactment thereof.

2 SERVICE AND DELIVERY

(1) Section 196 of the Law of Property Act 1925 applies to any notice served under the contract, save that—
(*a*) a notice shall also be sufficiently served on a party if served on that party's solicitors
(*b*) a reference to a registered letter shall include a prepaid first class ordinary letter
(*c*) if the time at which a letter containing a notice would in the ordinary course be delivered is not on a working day, the notice shall be deemed to be served on the next following working day
(*d*) a notice shall also be sufficiently served if—
(i) sent by telex or by telegraphic facsimile transmission to the party to be served, and that service shall be deemed to be made on the day of transmission if transmitted before 4 p.m. on a working day, but otherwise on the next following working day
(ii) when the addressee is a member of a document exchange (as to which the inclusion of a reference thereto in the solicitors' letterhead shall be conclusive evidence) delivered to that or any other affiliated exchange, and that service shall be deemed to have been made on the first working day after that on which the document would, in the ordinary course, be available for collection by the addressee.
(2) Sub-condition (1) applies to the delivery of documents as it applies to the service of notices.

3 MATTERS AFFECTING THE PROPERTY

(1) In this condition—
(*a*) "competent authority" means a local authority or other body exercising powers under statute or Royal Charter
(*b*) "requirement" includes (whether or not subject to confirmation) any notice, order or proposal
(*c*) "relevant matter" means any matter specified in sub-condition (2) whenever arising.
(2) The property is sold subject to—
(*a*) all matters registrable by any competent authority pursuant to statute
(*b*) all requirements of any competent authority
(*c*) all matters disclosed or reasonably to be expected to be disclosed by searches and as a result of enquiries formal or informal, and whether made in person, by writing or orally by or for the purchaser or which a prudent purchaser ought to make
(*d*) all notices served by or on behalf of a reversioner, a tenant or sub-tenant, or the owner or occupier of any adjoining or neighbouring property.
(3) (*a*) Notwithstanding sub-condition (2), the vendor warrants that he has informed the purchaser of the contents of any written communication received by, or known to, the vendor on or before the working day preceding the date of the contract relating to any relevant matter. Failure to give such information before the contract is made shall be deemed to be an omission in a statement in the course of the negotiations leading to the contract, but shall give rise to no right to compensation to the extent that the purchaser has a claim for damages against a competent authority
(*b*) In the event of any conflict or variation between information in fact received from any competent authority relating to any relevant matter and any statement made by the vendor in respect of the same matter, the purchaser shall rely on the information received from the competent authority to the exclusion of that given by the vendor
(*c*) The vendor shall forthwith inform the purchaser of the contents of any written communication received by him after the working day preceding the date of the contract and before the day of actual completion which if received on or before the former day would have fallen within paragraph (*a*).
(4) The purchaser (subject to any right or remedy arising under sub-condition (3)) will indemnify the vendor in respect of any liability under any requirement of a competent authority (whether made before or after the date of the contract), including the reasonable cost to the vendor of compliance after reasonable notice to the purchaser of the vendor's intention to comply, such sum to be payable on demand. The provisions of this sub-condition shall prevail in the event of conflict with any other condition.

4 OPPORTUNITY TO RESCIND

(1) This condition only applies if a special condition so provides.
(2) Within such period as is specified in a special condition or, if none is so specified, within twenty working days from the date of the contract (as to which, in either case, time shall be of the essence), the purchaser shall be entitled, notwithstanding condition 3 (2), to rescind the contract by service of notice on the vendor specifying a matter to which this condition applies affecting the property.
(3) This condition applies to any of the following matters of which the purchaser had no knowledge on or before the working day preceding the date of the contract—
(*a*) a financial charge which the vendor cannot or has not at the purchaser's written request agreed to discharge on or before actual completion
(*b*) a statutory provision prohibiting, restricting or imposing adverse conditions upon the use or the continued use of the property for such purpose as is specified in a special condition or, if none is so specified, the purpose for which the vendor used it immediately before the date of the contract
(*c*) a matter which is likely materially to reduce the price which a willing purchaser could otherwise reasonably be expected to pay for the relevant interest in the property in the open market at the date of the contract.
(4) For the purposes of this condition, the purchaser's knowledge—
(*a*) includes everything in writing received in the course of the transaction leading to the contract by a person acting on his behalf from the vendor, a person acting on the vendor's behalf, or a competent authority (as defined in condition 3 (1) (*a*))
(*b*) does not include anything solely because a statute deems that registration of a matter constitutes actual notice of it.

5 EASEMENTS, RESERVATIONS, RIGHTS AND LIABILITIES

(1) The vendor warrants that he has disclosed to the purchaser the existence of all easements, rights, privileges and liabilities affecting the property, of which the vendor knows or ought to know, other than the existence of those known to the purchaser at the date of the contract, or which a prudent purchaser would have discovered by that date.
(2) Without prejudice to the generality of sub-condition (1)—
(*a*) the purchaser shall purchase with full notice of the actual state and condition of the property and shall take it as it stands, save where it is to be constructed or converted by the vendor
(*b*) the property is sold, and will if the vendor so requires be conveyed, subject to all rights of way, water, light, drainage and other easements, rights, privileges and liabilities affecting the same.
(3) (*a*) In this sub-condition "the retained land" means land retained by the vendor—
(i) adjoining the property, or
(ii) near to the property and designated as retained land in a special condition.
(*b*) The conveyance of the property shall contain such reservations in favour of the retained land and the grant of such rights over the retained land as would have been implied had the vendor conveyed both the property and the retained land by simultaneous conveyances to different purchasers.

6 TENANCIES

(1) This condition applies if the property is sold subject to any lease or tenancy and shall have effect notwithstanding any partial, incomplete or inaccurate reference to any lease or tenancy in the special conditions or the particulars of the property.
(2) Copies or full particulars of all leases or tenancies not vested in the purchaser having been furnished to him, he shall be deemed to purchase with full knowledge thereof and shall take the property subject to the rights of the tenants thereunder or by reason thereof. The purchaser shall indemnify the vendor against all claims, demands and liability in respect of such rights, notwithstanding that they may be void against a purchaser for want of registration.
(3) The vendor gives no warranty as to the amount of rent lawfully recoverable from any tenant, as to the effect of any legislation in relation to any lease or tenancy or as to the compliance with any legislation affecting the same.
(4) The vendor shall inform the purchaser of any change in the disclosed terms and conditions of any lease or tenancy.
(5) If a lease or tenancy subject to which the property is sold terminates for any reason, the vendor shall inform the purchaser and, on being indemnified by the purchaser against all consequential loss, expenditure or liability, shall act as the purchaser may direct.

7 ERRORS, OMISSIONS AND MISSTATEMENTS

(1) No error, omission or misstatement herein or in any plan furnished or any statement made in the course of the negotiations leading to the contract shall annul the sale or entitle the purchaser to be discharged from the purchase.
(2) Any such error, omission or misstatement shown to be material shall entitle the purchaser or the vendor, as the case may be, to proper compensation, provided that the purchaser shall not in any event be entitled to compensation for matters falling within conditions 5 (2) or 6 (3).
(3) No immaterial error, omission or misstatement (including a mistake in any plan furnished for identification only) shall entitle either party to compensation.
(4) Sub-condition (1) shall not apply where compensation for any error, omission or misstatement shown to be material cannot be assessed nor enable either party to compel the other to accept or convey property differing substantially (in quantity, quality tenure or otherwise) from the property agreed to be sold if the other party would be prejudiced by the difference.
(5) The purchaser acknowledges that in making the contract he has not relied on any statement made to him save one made or confirmed in writing.

8 LEASEHOLDS

(1) This condition applies if the property is leasehold.
(2) In all cases the immediate title to the property shall begin with the lease. Where the lease, unless registered with absolute title, is dated not more than fifteen years before the date of the contract and was granted for a term exceeding twenty-one years, the freehold title and all other titles superior to the lease shall be deduced for a period beginning not less than fifteen years prior to the date of the contract and ending on the date of the lease.
(3) A copy of the lease and a copy of, sufficient extract from, or abstract of, all superior leases, the contents of which are known to the vendor, having been supplied or made available to the purchaser, he shall be deemed to purchase with full notice of the contents thereof, whether or not he has inspected the same.
(4) Where any consent to assign is necessary—
(*a*) the vendor shall forthwith at his own cost apply for and use his best endeavours to obtain such consent
(*b*) the purchaser shall forthwith supply such information and references as may reasonably be required by the reversioner before granting such consent
(*c*) if any such consent is not granted at least five working days before contractual completion date, or is subject to any condition to which the purchaser reasonably objects, either party may rescind the contract by notice to the other.
(5) Any statutory implied covenant on the part of the vendor shall not extend to any breach of the terms of the lease as to the state and condition of the property and the assignment shall so provide. This sub-condition applies notwithstanding that a special condition provides for the vendor to convey as beneficial owner.
(6) Where the property is sold subject to an apportioned rent specified as such in a special condition, the purchaser shall not require the consent of the reversioner to be obtained, or the rent to be otherwise legally apportioned.
(7) The purchaser shall assume that any receipt for the last payment due for rent under the lease before actual completion was given by the person then entitled to such rent or his duly authorised agent.

9 DEPOSIT

(1) The purchaser shall on or before the date of the contract pay by way of deposit to the vendor's solicitors as stakeholders the normal deposit, or such lesser sum as the vendor shall have agreed in writing. On a sale by private treaty, payment shall be made by banker's draft or by cheque drawn on a solicitors' bank account.
(2) Upon service by the vendor of a completion notice, the purchaser shall pay to the vendor any difference between the normal deposit and any amount actually paid (if less).
(3) If any draft, cheque or other instrument tendered in or towards payment of any sum payable under this condition is dishonoured when first presented the vendor shall have the right by notice to the purchaser within seven working days thereafter to treat the contract as repudiated.

10 OPTIONAL METHODS OF EXCHANGE

(1) Exchange of contracts may be effected by a method authorised by condition 2 for the service of notices. If so effected, the contract shall be made when the last part is, as the case may be, posted or delivered to a document exchange.
(2) Where contracts have not been exchanged, the parties' solicitors may agree by telephone or telex that the contract be immediately effective and thereupon the solicitors holding a part of the contract signed by their client shall hold it irrevocably to the order of the other party.

11 INSURANCE

(1) If the property is destroyed or damaged prior to actual completion and the proceeds of any insurance policy effected by or for the purchaser are reduced by reason of the existence of any policy effected by or for the vendor, the purchase price shall be abated by the amount of such reduction.
(2) Sub-condition (1) shall not apply where the proceeds of the vendor's policy are applied towards the reinstatement of the property pursuant to any statutory or contractual obligation.
(3) This condition takes effect in substitution for section 47 of the Law of Property Act 1925.
(4) The vendor shall be under no duty to the purchaser to maintain any insurance on the property, save where the property is leasehold and the vendor has an obligation to insure.

12 ABSTRACT OF TITLE

(1) Forthwith upon exchange of contracts the vendor shall deliver to the purchaser—
(*a*) where the title is not registered, an abstract of the title to the property or an epitome of the title together with photocopies of the relevant documents
(*b*) where the title is registered—
(i) the documents, particulars and information specified in sub-sections (1) and (2) of section 110 of the Land Registration Act 1925, save that copies of the entries on the register, the filed plan and any documents noted on the register and filed in the registry shall be office copies, and
(ii) such additional authorities to inspect the register as the purchaser shall reasonably require for any sub-purchaser or prospective mortgagee or lessee.
(2) Where the title is not registered, the vendor shall at his own expense produce the relevant documents of title or an abstract, epitome of title or copy thereof (bearing in each case original markings of examination of all relevant documents of title or of examined abstracts thereof).
(3) Where before the date of the contract any abstract, epitome or document has been delivered to the purchaser, he shall not, save as provided by conditions 6 (2) or 8 (3), be deemed to have had notice before the date of the contract of any matter of title thereby disclosed.

13 IDENTITY AND BOUNDARIES

(1) The vendor shall produce such evidence as may be reasonably necessary to establish the identity and extent of the property, but shall not be required to define exact boundaries, or the ownership of fences, ditches, hedges or walls, nor, beyond the evidence afforded by the information in his possession, separately to identify parts of the property held under different titles.
(2) If reasonably required by the purchaser because of the insufficiency of the evidence produced under sub-condition (1), the vendor shall at his own expense provide and hand over on completion a statutory declaration as to the relevant facts, in a form agreed by the purchaser, such agreement not to be unreasonably withheld.

14 MORTGAGES IN FAVOUR OF FRIENDLY AND OTHER SOCIETIES

Where the title includes a mortgage or legal charge in favour of trustees on behalf of a friendly society, a building society or a society registered under the Industrial and Provident Societies Acts, the purchaser shall assume that any receipt given on the discharge of any such mortgage or legal charge and apparently duly executed was in fact duly executed by all proper persons and is valid.

15 REQUISITIONS

(1) In this condition "abstract" means all the documents, particulars and information required to be delivered by the vendor under condition 12.
(2) Subject to sub-condition (4), the purchaser shall deliver any requisitions or objections relating to the title, evidence of title or the abstract, in writing within six working days of receipt of the abstract (or, in the case of an abstract delivered before the date of the contract, within six working days of the date of contract). Within four working days of such delivery the vendor shall deliver his replies in writing.
(3) The purchaser shall deliver any observations on any of the vendor's replies in writing within four working days of their receipt.
(4) Where some but not all parts of the abstract have been delivered, and defects in title are not disclosed by such parts of the abstract as have been delivered, then in respect only of the undelivered parts or undisclosed defects (as the case may be) the abstract shall be deemed to be received for the purpose of sub-condition (2) at the time or respective times when any previously undelivered part is delivered.
(5) Time shall be of the essence for the purposes of this condition.

16 RESCISSION

(1) If the vendor is unable, or on some reasonable ground unwilling, to satisfy any requisition or objection made by the purchaser, the vendor may give the purchaser notice (specifying the reason for his inability or the ground of his unwillingness) to withdraw the same. If the purchaser does not withdraw the same within seven working days of service, either party may thereafter, notwithstanding any intermediate negotiation or litigation, rescind the contract by notice to the other.
(2) Upon rescission under any power given by these conditions or any special condition—
(*a*) the vendor shall repay to the purchaser any sums paid by way of deposit or otherwise under the contract, with interest on such sums at the contract rate from four working days after rescission until payment
(*b*) the purchaser shall forthwith return all documents delivered to him by the vendor and at his own expense procure the cancellation of any entry relating to the contract in any register.

17 PREPARATION OF CONVEYANCE

(1) The purchaser shall deliver the draft conveyance at least twelve working days before contractual completion date, and within four working days of such delivery the vendor shall deliver it back approved or revised.
(2) The purchaser shall deliver the engrossment of the conveyance (first executed by him, where requisite) at least five working days before contractual completion date.
(3) The purchaser shall not, by delivering the draft conveyance or the engrossment, be deemed to accept the vendor's title or to waive any right to raise or maintain requisitions.
(4) Save to the extent that a covenant for indemnity will be implied by statute, the purchaser shall in the conveyance covenant to indemnify the vendor and his estate (and any estate of which the vendor is personal representative or trustee) against all actions, claims and liability for any breach of any covenant, stipulation, provision or other matter subject to which the property is sold and in respect of which the vendor or any such estate will remain liable after completion.
(5) The vendor shall give an acknowledgment for production and, unless in a fiduciary capacity, an undertaking for safe custody of documents of title retained by him. Where any such document is retained by a mortgagee, trustee or personal representative, the vendor shall procure that such person shall give an acknowledgment for production, and the vendor, unless in a fiduciary capacity, shall covenant that if and when he receives any such document he will, at the cost of the person requiring it, give an undertaking for safe custody.
(6) The vendor shall be entitled on reasonable grounds to decline to convey the property to any person other than the purchaser, by more than one conveyance, at more than the contract price or at a price divided between different parts of the property.

18 OCCUPATION BEFORE COMPLETION

(1) This condition applies if the vendor authorises the purchaser to occupy the property before actual completion, except—
(*a*) where the purchaser already lawfully occupies any part of the property, or
(*b*) where the property is a dwellinghouse and the authority for the occupation is only for the purpose of effecting works of decoration, repair or improvement agreed by the vendor.
(2) The purchaser occupies the property as licensee and not as tenant. The purchaser may not transfer his licence or authorise any other person save members of his immediate family to occupy any part of the property.
(3) The purchaser shall not, by taking such occupation, be deemed to accept the vendor's title or to waive any right to raise or maintain requisitions.
(4) While the purchaser is in occupation of the whole or any part of the property under this condition, he shall—
(*a*) pay and indemnify the vendor against all outgoings and any other expenses in respect of the property and pay to the vendor in respect of such occupation a sum calculated at the contract rate on the amount of the purchase money (less any deposit paid)
(*b*) be entitled to receive any rents and profits from any part of the property not occupied by him
(*c*) insure the property in a sum not less than the purchase price against all risks in respect of which premises of the like nature are normally insured.
(5) The purchaser's licence to occupy the property shall end—
(*a*) on contractual completion date, or
(*b*) upon termination of the contract, or
(*c*) upon the expiry of five working days' notice given by either party to the other,
and thereupon the purchaser shall give up occupation of the property and leave the same in as good repair as it was in when he went into occupation.
(6) If the purchaser, after his licence has ended under sub-condition 5(*a*), remains in occupation with the express or implied consent of the vendor, he shall thereafter occupy on the other terms of this condition and on the further term that the vendor's rights under condition 22 shall not thereby be affected.

19 APPORTIONMENTS

(1) In this condition—
(*a*) "the apportionment day" means—
(i) if the property is sold with vacant possession of the whole, the date of actual completion
(ii) in any other case, contractual completion date
(*b*) "payment period" means one of the periods for which a sum payable periodically is payable, whether or not such periods are of equal length.
(2) This condition shall not apply to any sum if—
(*a*) the purchaser cannot, by virtue only of becoming the owner of the property, either enforce payment of it or be obliged to pay it, or
(*b*) it is an outgoing paid in advance, unless the vendor cannot obtain repayment and the purchaser benefits therefrom or is given credit therefor against a sum that would otherwise be his liability.
(3) On completion the income and outgoings of the property shall, subject to sub-condition (2) and conditions 3 and 22(4) and to any adjustment required by condition 18(4), be apportioned as at the apportionment day.
(4) For the purposes of apportionment only, it shall be assumed—
(*a*) that the vendor remains owner of the property until the end of the apportionment day, and
(*b*) that the sum to be apportioned—
(i) accrues from day to day
(ii) is payable throughout the relevant period at the same rate as on the apportionment day.
(5) Sums payable periodically shall be apportioned by charging or allowing—
(*a*) for any payment period entirely attributable to one party, the whole of the instalment payable therefor
(*b*) for any part of a payment period, a proportion on an annual basis.
(6) (*a*) This sub-condition applies to any sum payable in respect of any period falling wholly or partly prior to the apportionment day, the amount of which is not notified to either party before actual completion
(*b*) A provisional apportionment shall be made on the best estimate available. Upon the amount being notified, a final apportionment shall be made and one party shall thereupon make to the other the appropriate balancing payment.

20 ENDORSEMENT OF MEMORANDUM

Where the vendor does not hand over all the documents of his title, he shall at completion endorse a memorandum of the sale to the purchaser on the last such document in each relevant title and thereupon produce the endorsed documents for inspection.

21 COMPLETION

(1) Contractual completion date shall be as stated in the special conditions but if not so stated shall be the twenty-fifth working day after the date of the contract. Completion shall take place in England or Wales either at the office of the vendor's solicitors or, if required by the vendor at least five working days prior to actual completion, at the office of the vendor's mortgagee or his solicitors.
(2) The vendor shall not be obliged to accept payment of the money due on completion otherwise than by one or more of the following methods—
(*a*) legal tender
(*b*) a banker's draft drawn by and upon a settlement bank for the purposes of the Clearing House Automated Payments System or any other bank specified in a special condition
(*c*) an unconditional authority to release any deposit held by a stakeholder
(*d*) otherwise as the vendor shall have agreed before actual completion.
(3) If completion is effected otherwise than by personal attendance the time for completion is when on a working day
(*a*) the money due on completion is paid to the vendor or his solicitors, and
(*b*) the vendor's solicitors hold to the order of the purchaser all the documents to which he is entitled on completion.
(4) For the purposes of this condition money is paid when the vendor receives payment by a method specified in sub-condition (2). Where the parties have agreed upon a direct credit to a bank account at a named branch, payment is made when that branch receives the credit.
(5) (*a*) This sub-condition applies if the money due on completion is not paid by 2.30 p.m. on the day of actual completion or by such other time on that day as is specified in a special condition
(*b*) For the purposes of condition 22 only, completion shall be deemed to be postponed by reason of the purchaser's delay from the day of actual completion until the next working day
(*c*) The purchaser shall not as a result of the deemed postponement of completion be liable to make any payment to the vendor unless the vendor claims such payment by giving notice at completion or within five working days thereafter (as to which period time shall be of the essence). Payment shall be due five working days after receipt of such notice.

22 COMPENSATION FOR LATE COMPLETION

(1) For the purposes of this condition—
(*a*) "delay" means failure to perform or lateness in performing any obligation of the contract which causes or contributes to lateness in completion
(*b*) a party is "in default" if and to the extent that the period, or the aggregate of the periods, of his delay exceeds the period, or the aggregate of the periods, of delay of the other party
(*c*) "the period of default" means the length of the excess defined in paragraph (*b*) or, if shorter, the period from contractual completion date to the date of actual completion.
(2) If the sale shall be completed after contractual completion date, the party in default (if any) shall be liable to compensate the other for loss occasioned to him by reason of that default.
(3) Before actual completion, or within five working days thereafter (as to which period time shall be of the essence), the party entitled to compensation may, by notice to the other party, opt to be paid or allowed a sum calculated at the contract rate on the amount of the purchase money (less any deposit paid) for the period of default as liquidated damages in settlement of his claim for compensation.
(4) If the vendor is entitled to compensation, he may, before actual completion, by notice to the purchaser, opt to take the net income of the property for the period of default in lieu of such compensation.
(5) The right to recover any compensation under this condition shall not be prejudiced by completion of the sale, whether before or after the commencement of proceedings.

23 COMPLETION NOTICE

(1) This condition applies unless a special condition provides that time is of the essence in respect of contractual completion date.
(2) If the sale shall not be completed on contractual completion date, either party, being then himself ready able and willing to complete, may after that date serve on the other party notice to complete the transaction in accordance with this condition. A party shall be deemed to be ready, able and willing to complete—
(*a*) if he could be so but for some default or omission of the other party
(*b*) notwithstanding that any mortgage on the property is unredeemed when the completion notice is served if the aggregate of all sums necessary to redeem all such mortgages (to the extent that they relate to the property) does not exceed the sum payable on completion.
(3) Upon service of a completion notice it shall become a term of the contract that the transaction shall be completed within fifteen working days of service and in respect of such period time shall be of the essence.
(4) If the purchaser does not comply with a completion notice—
(*a*) the purchaser shall forthwith return all documents delivered to him by the vendor and at his own expense procure the cancellation of any entry relating to the contract in any register
(*b*) without prejudice to any other rights or remedies available to him, the vendor may—
(i) forfeit and retain any deposit paid and/or
(ii) re-sell the property by auction, tender or private treaty.
(5) If on any such re-sale contracted within one year after contractual completion date the vendor incurs a loss and so elects by notice to the purchaser within one month after the contract for such re-sale, the purchaser shall pay to the vendor liquidated damages. The amount payable shall be the aggregate of such loss, all costs and expenses reasonably incurred in any such re-sale and any attempted re-sale and interest at the contract rate on such part of the purchase money as is from time to time outstanding (giving credit for all sums received under any re-sale contract on account of the re-sale price) after contractual completion date.
(6) If the vendor does not comply with a completion notice, the purchaser, without prejudice to any other rights or remedies available to him, may give notice to the vendor forthwith to pay to the purchaser any sums paid by way of deposit or otherwise under the contract and interest on such sums at the contract rate from four working days after service of the notice until payment. On compliance with such notice the purchaser shall not be entitled to specific performance of the contract, but shall forthwith return all documents delivered to him by the vendor and at the expense of the vendor procure the cancellation of any entry relating to the contract in any register.
(7) Where after service of a completion notice the time for completion shall have been extended by agreement or implication, either party may again invoke the provisions of this condition which shall then take effect with the substitution of "seven working days" for "fifteen working days" in sub-condition (3).

24 CHATTELS

The property in any chattels agreed to be sold shall pass to the purchaser on actual completion.

25 AUCTIONS

(1) This condition applies if the property is sold by auction.
(2) The sale is subject to a reserve price for the property and, when the property is sold in lots, for each lot.
(3) The vendor reserves the right—
(*a*) to divide the property into lots and to sub-divide, re-arrange or consolidate any lots
(*b*) to bid personally or by his agent up to any reserve price
(*c*) without disclosing any reserve price, to withdraw from the sale any property or lot at any time before it has been sold, whether or not the sale has begun.
(4) The auctioneer may—
(*a*) refuse to accept a bid
(*b*) in the case of a dispute as to any bid, forthwith determine the dispute or again put up the property or lot at the last undisputed bid.
(5) The purchaser shall forthwith complete and sign the contract and pay, but not necessarily by the means specified in condition 9(1), the normal deposit.

SPECIAL CONDITIONS

A. The property is sold subject to The Law Society's General Conditions of Sale (1984 Revision) ("general conditions") printed within so far as they are not varied by or inconsistent with these special conditions but general condition 8(5) shall apply in any event.

B. For the purposes of the following general conditions—
    1(b)   the contract rate is   4   % per annum above the base rate from time to time of

    1(c)   contractual completion date is   8th May   198 6
    21(2)(b) the specified bank is   BANK OF RURITANIA
    21(5)(a) the latest time is   4   am/pm
    ~~1(a)   the following are not working days~~

    ~~5(3)   the retained bank is~~

C. General condition 4 shall not apply. ~~[For the purposes of general condition 4(2) the period shall be from the date hereof and for the purposes of general condition 4(3)(b) the specified use is~~   .]

D. The Vendor shall convey as   BENEFICIAL OWNER

~~E.~~ ~~The Vendor is the registered proprietor   title no.   with title absolute under title No. at the   District Land Registry. The Vendor authorises the Purchaser's solicitors to inspect the register and to obtain office copies thereof.~~

(or) E. The abstract of title shall begin with a conveyance dated 12th September 1947 and made between Marmaduke Villiers of the one part and Gordon Reginald Postlethwaite of the other part

F. The property is sold with vacant possession on completion.

(or) ~~F.~~ ~~The property is sold subject to the following leases or tenancies:~~

      ~~G.~~ ~~The property also is sold subject to~~

Printed by Oyez Press Limited **Oyez**
27 Crimscott Street, London SE1 5TT   F3681 9-84
★ ★

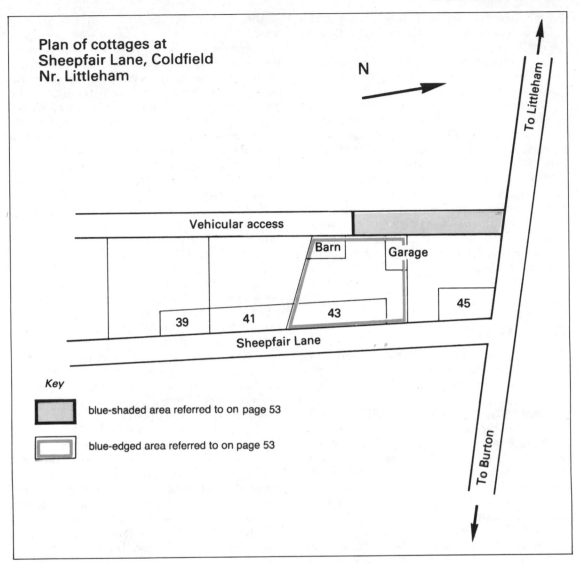

Plan of cottages at
Sheepfair Lane, Coldfield
Nr. Littleham

N

To Littleham

Vehicular access

Barn

Garage

39   41   43   45

Sheepfair Lane

To Burton

Key

blue-shaded area referred to on page 53

blue-edged area referred to on page 53

the mortgage money becomes available: that happens at completion). It may be possible, however, to negotiate with the vendor for the payment of a smaller deposit than is usually given, say of 5%. A 5% deposit on a £40,000 house is £2,000, which would be a lot of money for the purchaser to lose for failing to complete.

When the deposit is handed over to the vendor (or, in the usual case, his solicitor), two things may happen to it. It may be held by the solicitor as a stakeholder: this means that it cannot be released to the vendor until after completion. From the purchaser's point of view this is attractive, since it means that if anything disastrous should go wrong (e g should the vendor die or disappear or go bankrupt) it is an easy matter to

retrieve the money and pull out of the contract. On the other hand, the money may be handed over to the solicitor acting as 'agent for the vendor'. In this case the money can be used for the vendor's purposes (often towards the deposit on the new house which he himself is buying). This is unattractive to the purchaser, who just might find that the vendor breaks the contract and that the deposit cannot be traced, while it is attractive to the vendor who might otherwise have serious liquidity problems in financing his own exchange of contracts. It is impossible to say whether the deposit should or should not be paid to a stakeholder or an agent for the vendor: it depends on whether one is a vendor or purchaser, on the state of the market (in a buyer's market, it will be easier to insist on the money being paid to a stakeholder) and on the degree of trust between the vendor and purchaser. Most important of all is that the purchaser understands what he is doing and the risks involved if he hands the money over to an agent for the vendor.

Now that contracts have been exchanged, both sides are committed to carry out the transaction. When contracts are exchanged, a date will be fixed for completion and each party can begin to make important arrangements about removals etc. One particular point which the purchaser must take into account is that the law considers that, since he is now obliged to complete the transaction, the risk of any damage being caused to the property has passed to him. Therefore insurance cover should be brought into effect the moment that contracts are exchanged.

5. COMPLETING THE TRANSACTION

Once contracts have been exchanged and a date fixed for completion, the purchaser has arrived at the second stage of the transaction during which various legal formalities must be carried out, and important plans laid for the fateful day not far ahead when the property will become his.

On the legal side of things, the purchaser or his legal adviser must check that the vendor really does own the property and that he will be able to pass a 'good title' to the purchaser; also, assuming he is taking a mortgage, the mortgagee will wish to check that all is in order.

If the land is unregistered land (see page 42), the vendor's title is inspected by checking all title deeds affecting the property for at least the last fifteen years. In some cases it is necessary to check back through the deeds for a much longer time. This can be a laborious and complex task and may require considerable technical knowledge of the law of property, which is why it is inadvisable for the purchaser of unregistered land to do his own conveyancing. Having inspected the title deeds, the purchaser's solicitor sends what are called 'requisitions on title' to the vendor's solicitor. These questions are intended to clear up any doubts or problems over the vendor's title, although they also deal with more prosaic issues such as the arrangements for handing over the keys on completion and whether the general and water rates have been paid.

Also at this juncture, if the land is unregistered, the purchaser's solicitor will produce a draft conveyance which is sent to the vendor's side for approval. Once the two sides have agreed on the terms of the conveyance, it will be reproduced in the proper legal form (known as the 'engrossment'). In due course it will be signed and sealed by the vendor and handed over, on completion day, to the purchaser. It will then form one more link in the chain of title deeds which affect the property. The verbal content of conveyances may be somewhat strange to the layman unused to using 'whereas' and 'heretofore' in everyday speech. Such vocabulary is commonplace to conveyancing solicitors however, and the purchaser's conveyance can be expected to look something like the example reproduced opposite.

One further legal formality that must be carried out at this stage where unregistered land is being purchased is to inspect what is called the Land Charges Register. It may be that the vendor's land is affected by restrictions (e g not to use it for commercial purposes) or by a prior contract (e g to sell it to someone else) of which the purchaser is unaware. However, any such incumbrances affecting the vendor will only be enforceable against a purchaser if they are registered at the Land Charges Registry at Plymouth. They must be registered against the name of the owner of the land adversely affected by the right in question, and the purchaser must therefore search the names of all previous owners of the land. If the search reveals no adverse entries, the purchaser can proceed to completion.

If the land is registered land, the purchaser's position is rather simpler. Instead of checking through the title deeds to establish the vendor's title he needs only to inspect the HM Land Registry (not to be confused with the Land *Charges* Registry mentioned in the last paragraph). The purchaser will send requisitions on title to the vendor, one of which will ask for authority to inspect the register (which otherwise is private). The Land Registry will send back an up to date certificate describing what is on the register and who the owner is; provided that the purchaser then completes the transaction and applies to have his name placed on the register within 30 working days, he is fully protected against any subsequent changes in the register. The purchaser's position is also simpler since, instead of having to draft a conveyance with its rather esoteric language, he needs only send the vendor a

THIS CONVEYANCE made the *eighth* day of *October* One thousand nine hundred and eighty six BETWEEN JEREMY MONTAGUE DEDLOCK of 43 Sheepfair Lane Coldfield Near Littleham Wiltshire (hereinafter called "the Vendor") of the one part and HARRIET ARIADNE JELLYBY of Bel Vista Upper Thrubwell Devon (hereinafter called "the Purchaser") of the other part

WHEREAS the Vendor is seised in fee simple in possession of the property hereinafter described and intended to be conveyed free from incumbrances and has agreed to sell the same to the Purchaser for the like estate at the price of Forty Two Thousand Pounds (£42,000)

NOW THIS DEED WITNESSETH as follows:-

In pursuance of the said agreement and in consideration of the sum of Forty Two Thousand Pounds (£42,000) now paid by the Purchaser to the Vendor (the receipt whereof the Vendor hereby acknowledges) the Vendor as beneficial owner Hereby Conveys ALL THOSE pieces or parcels of land situate to the west of Sheepfair Lane Coldfield Near Littleham in the County of Wiltshire Together with the dwellinghouse garage and outbuildings erected thereon or on some part thereof and known as Number 43 Sheepfair Lane aforesaid all which property is for the purpose of identification only edged blue on the plan annexed hereto Together with the benefit of the right of way across the land in solid blue on the said plan which said right is described in a deed of grant dated 14 February 1962 and made between Oswald Wilkie of the one part and Gordon Reginald Postlethwaite of the other part To Hold the same unto the Purchaser in fee simple

IN WITNESS whereof the parties have hereunto set their hands and seals the day and year first before written

SIGNED SEALED and
DELIVERED by the said   *J. M. Dedlock*
JEREMY MONTAGUE DEDLOCK
in the presence of
E.J. Lange
Research Assistant
2 High Street, Newtown
SIGNED SEALED and
DELIVERED by the said   *Harriet A Jellyby*
HARRIET ARIADNE JELLYBY
in the presence of
E.J. Lange

HOUSE PURCHASE

Form 19

HM Land Registry

Land Registration Acts, 1925 to 1971

Stamp pursuant to section 28 of the Finance Act, 1931, to be impressed here.

When the transfer attracts Inland Revenue duty, the stamp should be impressed here before lodging the transfer for registration.

---

(1) For a transfer by a company or corporation form 19(Co) is printed and for a transfer to joint proprietors form 19(JP) is printed.

(')TRANSFER OF WHOLE

(Rule 98 or 115, Land Registration Rules 1925)

County and district (or London borough) }   NEWTOWN, BLANKSHIRE

Title number(s)   BK 10345

Property   12 ACACIA AVENUE

Date   14 May   19 86   In consideration of Forty Eight

Thousand Five Hundred Pounds

(2) Strike out if not required.

pounds (£ 48500   ) *(2) the receipt whereof is hereby acknowledged*

(3) In BLOCK LETTERS, enter full name(s), postal address(es) and occupation(s) of the proprietor(s) of the land.

X̶I̶/We(³)   GAVIN AND LAVINIA GRIGSBY

of 12 ACACIA AVENUE

NEWTOWN, BLANKSHIRE.

(4) If desired or otherwise as the case may be (see rules 76 and 77).

(4) as beneficial owner(s) hereby transfer to:

(5) In BLOCK LETTERS, enter full name, postal address including postcode and occupation of the transferee for entry on the register.

(⁵)

JOHN HILARY STANTON of
THE CHIMES
6 BELL LANE
WRINGTON
CUMBRIA

(6) On a transfer to a Company registered under the Companies Acts, insert here the Company's registration number if entry thereof on the register is desired.

(⁶)(Company registration number   )

the land comprised in the title(s) above mentioned (⁷) (⁸)

(7) Any special clause should be entered here.

(8) A transfer for charitable uses should follow form 36 in the schedule to the Land Registration Rules, 1925 (see rules 121 and 122).

(continued overleaf)

60

(9) If a certificate of value for the purposes of the Stamp Act, 1891, and amending Acts is not required, this paragraph should be deleted.

(9) *It is hereby certified that the transaction hereby effected does not form part of a larger transaction or series of transactions in respect of which the amount or value or aggregate amount or value of the consideration exceeds £*

Signed, sealed and delivered by the said }

    GAVIN GRIGSBY

G. Grigsby

(Seal)

in the presence of

Name   *N. J. Grimaldi*   Signature *NJGrimaldi*

Address   *2 Brown Street, Newtown*

Occupation   *Teacher*

Signed, sealed and delivered by the said }

    LAVINIA GRIGSBY

Lavinia Grigsby

(Seal)

in the presence of

Name   *as above.*   Signature *NJGrimaldi*

Address

Occupation

The Solicitors' Law Stationery Society plc. Oyez House. 27 Crimscott Street, London SE1 5TS   2.86 F6004

5061083

★ ★ ★ ★ ★

standard document known as a 'transfer'. It is a very simple and straightforward document which can be bought from law stationers and will look like the example reproduced on pages 60 and 61.

On completion, the vendor of registered land will hand over the signed transfer to the purchaser. It is then sent to the appropriate Land Registry (there are several in number, distributed throughout England and Wales), and the staff there will simply replace the vendor's name with the purchaser's.

One of the questions in the standard requisitions on title form will ask the vendor (whether of registered or unregistered land) precisely how much money is required to complete the transaction: the 'completion statement' will not necessarily ask for a simple balance of 90% for reasons explained below.

Drawing up a mortgage. While the vendor's title is being checked, the mortgage deed will also be drawn up, assuming the purchaser needs a loan. If the purchaser has instructed a solicitor, it is usual for the same solicitor also to act for the mortgagee. Otherwise, the mortgagee will instruct its own solicitor although the borrower will have to pay the legal costs. The mortgagee's solicitor will check the vendor's title in the same way that the purchaser does; he will also prepare the mortgage deed (more normally today called a legal charge). It will describe the property and name the borrower and contain many terms and conditions which the borrower must observe. Apart from stipulating the amount of the monthly repayments and giving the mortgagee the right to change the interest rate as it sees fit, it will also impose other obligations on the mortgagor, for example not to allow third parties to live in the property and not to let it fall into disrepair. A mortgagor who disobeys these terms may face serious trouble from the mortgagee, which theoretically could claim possession of the property and sell it. The borrower will be required to sign the charge before completion day; it will then come into effect the moment that the vendor hands over the conveyance (in the case of unregistered land) or the transfer (in the case of registered land). For a typical legal charge see opposite.

If the borrower is taking out an endowment mortgage, one further document will also have to be drawn up. This is known as an 'assignment' and it transfers the benefit of the life insurance policy (or policies) from the borrower to the mortgagee. This ensures that when the policy matures, the mortgagee will have the first claim on any money which becomes available.

While these legal documents are being drawn up, the purchaser will need to be making other plans of a more practical nature. Quotations should be obtained from furniture removers, and arrangements should be made with the vendor in respect of issues such as electricity, gas and telephones. Nothing is more irritating than to arrive at the new property only to discover that the telephone line is dead.

Completion statement. Shortly before completion, the purchaser will have to ensure that he (or his solicitor) has enough funds to be able to complete the transaction. It is as well to have thought this issue through well in advance, as it is not unusual to discover at the last moment that the sums do not work out quite as was anticipated. On page 68, an attempt is made to show the costs incurred overall on an average purchase. At this point we are concerned with the problem of the liquidity at the moment of completion. In the ordinary case, the purchaser has already handed over 10% of the price, so that if he is buying for £40,000 he must find the balance of £36,000 on completion. However, for various reasons he may have to find more than he expects.

(a) The vendor may have paid general and water rates in advance, in which case he will demand a credit from the purchaser in respect of the period after completion that has already been paid for. This will be shown in the completion statement sent by the vendor's solicitor in reply to standard requisitions on title.

(b) In the same way the vendor may have paid the ground rent or maintenance charges to the management company of leasehold property in advance.

(c) If the purchase is for more than £30,000, stamp duty of 1% will be payable on completion. The purchaser's solicitor in our example will ask for £400 to cover this cost.

(d) The purchaser's solicitor may also ask his client to make money available at completion to cover disbursements such as Land Registry fees or local search fees; he may even go further and require money to be paid in advance to cover his own costs: in this case the purchaser may well have to find an extra £200 or more at this expensive time.

(e) A further snag is that the purchaser may be banking on having the full mortgage loan of,

HM LAND REGISTRY District Registry: BLANKSHIRE, NEWTOWN Title No: BK 12345

LEGAL CHARGE

Dated   1ST MARCH   1986

Parties   1. The Borrower   CYRIL Q. ALBERY

2. The Chargee   KWIK LOAN COMPANY

The Loan (receipt acknowledged)   TEN THOUSAND POUNDS

Interest Rate   TWELVE   per cent. per annum

Periodic Payment   ONE HUNDRED AND THREE   per MONTH
POUNDS 12 p

Payment Days   FIRST DAY OF THE MONTH

The Property   8 HABERDASHERS ROAD, NEWTOWN

A. Interest shall be calculated in respect of each month/quarter/half-year/year **on the principal** sum outstanding at the beginning of the month/quarter/half-year/year

B. The Charge incorporates the Mortgage Provisions printed overleaf

C. The Charge is not a charge made for securing a current account or further **advances**

Signed, sealed and delivered as follows:—

SIGNATURE	SEAL	WITNESS
Cyril Albery	(LS)	N. Hughes Teacher 16 Haberdashers Rd Newtown
Kwik loan Company	(LS)	Company Secretary

Mortgage Provisions

1 Interpretation

Where the context allows:—

(a) "The Borrower" and "the Chargee" include the persons deriving title under them

(b) Obligations of more than one person are joint and several obligations

(c) Expressions used on the front page of the Charge have the meanings there shown

2 Legal Charge

The Borrower As Beneficial Owner charges the Property by way of legal mortgage with the payment to the Chargee of all the principal money and interest payable by the Borrower to the Chargee

3 Covenants for payment

(a) The Borrower will pay to the Chargee a Periodic Payment on every Payment Day until the whole of the Loan with interest has been fully discharged

(b) If on realisation of the security by the Chargee the net proceeds shall be insufficient to discharge the whole of the moneys outstanding on the security of the Charge then the Borrower will immediately pay the amount of the deficiency with interest until payment

4 Early repayments

The Borrower may at any time or times pay off all or any part of the principal money for the time being outstanding but so that any such partial payment by anticipation shall not interfere with the payment in regular course of the Periodic Payments subsequently payable pursuant to Provision 3 but shall only have the effect of accelerating the ultimate payment of the moneys remaining owing on the security of the Charge

5 Legal Date for redemption

The legal right of redemption ceases on the first of the Payment Days and in favour of a purchaser the statutory power of sale arises on that day

6 Interest

(a) Interest shall be charged by the Chargee at the Interest Rate as well after as before any judgment

(b) Periodic Payments shall be credited in the first place against interest and any balance shall be carried over to reduce the other indebtedness at the end of the period in respect of which interest is calculated

7 Covenants concerning the Property

(a) The Borrower will during the continuance of the Charge keep the Property in good and tenantable repair and insured against loss or damage by fire to the full value thereof in some insurance office or with underwriters of repute to be approved of in writing by the Chargee

(b) The powers of leasing or agreeing to lease or of accepting surrenders of leases conferred on a mortgagor in possession by the Law of Property Act 1925 shall not apply to the Charge

8 Principal money to become payable

The whole of the Loan shall become repayable to the Chargee immediately—

(a) If the Borrower defaults for 21 days or more in making any Periodic Payment

(b) If there is a breach by the Borrower of some obligation of his under the Charge (other than an obligation for the payment of money)

(c) If the Property is compulsorily purchased or acquired or requisitioned

9 Entry to inspect or do works

While the Charge is outstanding the Chargee may enter and inspect the Property at any reasonable time and may also enter and do any work which the Borrower has failed to do

10 Concessions

The Chargee may from time to time by letter or otherwise suspend or vary in favour of the Borrower any payment or repayment of money under the Charge

LEGAL CHARGE

Repayment by instalments

Date	1ST MARCH 1986
Borrower	CYRIL ALBERY
Chargee	KWIK LOAN COMPANY
Property	8 HABERDASHERS ROAD NEWTOWN
Loan	£ 10 000

STATUTORY RECEIPT

I/We

hereby acknowledge that   have this   day of
                  19   received the principal money secured by the within-
written mortgage together with all interest and costs the payment having been
made by

AS WITNESS   hand this   day of
                  19

Signed in the presence of

Con 30A © 1976 **oyez** The Solicitors' Law Stationery Society, plc, Oyez House, 237 Long Lane, London SE1 4PU   F974 1–81
★

say, £35,000 available to meet the sum due at completion. Some mortgagees, however, deduct the first monthly repayment from the actual advance; then the borrower finds himself with, say, £200 less than he anticipated. Also, any premium payable on a mortgage indemnity guarantee (see page 51) will be deducted from the advance. The purchaser must therefore be very careful about his calculations, and discuss them with his professional advisers well before completion.

Assuming that the vendor and purchaser have both appointed solicitors, neither party will usually attend completion. Instead the purchaser's solicitor (or his articled clerk) will go to the office of the vendor's solicitor. What then happens is that the conveyance or transfer is handed over in return for a banker's draft for the balance due. The keys may also be handed over at completion, or else the vendor's solicitor will notify his client or the estate agent concerned that they may now be released to the purchaser. The purchaser's solicitor will also take custody of the title deeds (if the land is unregistered) or the land certificate (if the land is registered). If the registered land is subject to a mortgage which the vendor is going to pay off with the completion money, a charge certificate rather than a land certificate will be handed over, together with a promise to forward the necessary form to have the discharge of the mortgage noted at the Land Registry.

Sometimes the purchaser's solicitor, instead of attending completion personally, will agree with the vendor's to do so postally. This is particularly sensible where the firms in question are some distance from one another. In these cases, the completion money can be transferred telegraphically from the purchaser's solicitor's bank to the vendor's. This normally works well, although anxiety can creep in when the afternoon of completion day is passing by and still the money has not arrived in the hands of the vendor's solicitor's bank. It may be that the money does not arrive within normal banking hours, in which case the vendor's solicitor will advise his client not to part with possession of the property until the following day, after the money has been received. The inconvenience all round is immense, but modern banking methods and the advent of computers will, it is hoped, eliminate this kind of problem.

The transaction having been completed, the purchaser can now move in. On the legal side, there are still a few operations left. If the purchase is for more than £30,000, stamp duty of 1% must be paid to the Inland Revenue. Even if the purchase price was for less than this, the conveyance or transfer must be sent to the Revenue's Stamp Office for it to peruse. The Revenue will impress on the conveyance or transfer a mark which indicates that it has been inspected and that any necessary duty has been paid. Without this mark, the deed is inadmissable in Court should it ever have to be produced as evidence of a person's title. After stamping, if the land is registered, or if it is unregistered but in an area in which registration is now compulsory, the relevant Land Registry must be notified. Fees are payable for this, which vary according to the value of the property and according to whether the land is already registered or not. The Land Registry will bring the register up to date and then, if the property is not subject to a mortgage, send the land certificate to the purchaser's solicitor. The purchaser must decide whether to look after this document himself or have it deposited with his bank or left with his solicitor. If the registered land is subject to a mortgage, then the land certificate remains with the Land Registry and a charge certificate is sent to the solicitor dealing with the conveyance who, in turn, will send it on to the mortgagee. If the land is unregistered, then the question is what to do with the title deeds. If the property is subject to a mortgage, the mortgagee will have them; otherwise it is up to the purchaser whether to take them himself or entrust them to his bank or solicitor.

The purchaser who has instructed a solicitor will now receive a bill (if he hasn't already done so). The bill will be made up partly of the solicitor's own costs, partly of fees which he has had to pay (often termed disbursements) and partly of VAT.

If the purchaser is unhappy about the bill (for example, because it differs considerably from the estimate he was given at the start or because it simply seems excessive in relation to the work done) he should, in the first instance, discuss it with the solicitor himself. If still dissatisfied, the purchaser should apply to the Law Society for a certificate of remuneration. The Law Society cannot raise the bill, but it can lower it. If still unhappy, the purchaser can ask the Court to have the bill 'taxed'. The Court may reduce the bill if it considers it excessive.

This may be an appropriate moment to reflect upon the costs which the purchaser has incurred in the transaction up to this point (and before he has insured the property: see below). Suppose the purchaser has bought a £40,000 house, and has instructed a solicitor to do his conveyancing; the property is registered and quite old so that he has had a Home Buyers' report prepared and has had to pay a mortgage indemnity premium of £50. He also hired a firm of furniture removers to handle that side of things. The costs involved could look like this.

Table of Costs		
Legal Costs		
Solicitors fees	£200.00	
plus VAT	£30.00	
Local Search Fees	£14.40	
Land Charge Search	£0.50	
Land Registry Fees	£98.00	
		£342.90
Stamp Duty		£400.00
Mortgage Indemnity Premium		£50.00
Removal Expenses	£150.00	
plus VAT	£22.50	
		£172.50
Survey (Home Buyers' Report)	£150.00	
plus VAT	£22.50	
		£172.50
Total		£1137.90

This shows how expensive it can be to take the plunge into the property market; this having been said, if the early expense can be got over, house purchase in general tends to be a very sound investment and after the initial shock-waves of moving in have subsided the purchaser will probably not regret his decision.

The following publications may be of interest to anyone considering purchasing a new home.

The Legal Side of Buying a House (Consumers' Association).
Buying a House or Flat (Penguin Handbooks)
Buying a Home (SHAC)
The Conveyancing Fraud (Michael Joseph)
Do It Yourself Conveyancing (David and Charles)
Rights Guide for Home Owners (SHAC)

6. INSURING THE PROPERTY

After purchase of the house or flat, one further important issue is insurance. The matter of life insurance and mortgage protection has already been mentioned above. But the purchaser must also consider insuring the property itself and its contents. These items are customarily dealt with separately, although it is now possible to arrange *combined* cover with some companies which overcomes any arguments when a disaster occurs whether a particular item is covered by the property policy or the contents one.

As far as the property itself is concerned, if the purchaser has taken out a mortgage, he will be required to insure it anyway. This insurance is often effected through the mortgagee's own block insurance policy, although the borrower may be allowed to insure elsewhere should he so wish. The mortgage will stipulate a minimum figure which the borrower must insure for. This figure may well exceed, sometimes quite substantially, the market value of the property, because it may cost more to reinstate, say, an old and unusual cottage than it is actually worth. If the property is a leasehold one, there will often be a covenant requiring the purchaser to keep it insured, and the landlord may dictate which insurance companies the purchaser may insure with. Many policies today are automatically linked to inflation, but any purchaser should reconsider his property insurance position from time to time to ensure that his cover really is adequate. Five years after purchase, with house prices having risen and the purchaser's improvements having 'gentrified' an old terraced-house into a sophisticated, though small, character dwelling, the original insurance figure may well have been overtaken.

As far as contents are concerned, these are purely the concern of the purchaser: the landlord or mortgagee will have no concern with them. But any purchaser would be well-advised to take out a policy, expensive though this tends to be (especially in urban areas renowed for burglaries etc). Even the most impecunious purchaser will be surprised when he stops to consider how much it would cost to replace his clothes, record collection, books and second-hand furniture. He should therefore try to calculate what it would cost to replace his possessions (with a bias towards over- rather than under-valuing) and insure accordingly. He ought to go for a 'new-for-old' policy and to ensure that the policy is linked to inflation. If he has particular valuables which he sometimes takes out with him (for example an expensive camera or a gold watch) he should consider paying an extra premium for 'all-risks' cover: this means that he would be covered if he lost the camera while on holiday in Spain.

7. SELLING

A time will come when the first-time buyer decides that he should take a step up the property ladder, and he will want to know how the mechanics of selling his house differ from what happened when he bought it. Of course, assuming he is selling in order to buy another property, the purchasing side of things will unfold in the same way as has just been described. As far as selling is concerned, the major difference is that the vendor now has the problem of finding a buyer. The question will be whether the vendor should set about this himself, or whether he should appoint a third party to act for him.

If he is to go it alone, the vendor must find out what would be a realistic sale price. Some vendors have an astute knowledge of the property market and may find this an easy matter; others may consider calling in a valuer and paying a fee to have a valuation made. Some valuers will perform this service for nothing, in the hope that they will then be given the selling rights. Having decided on his figure, the vendor can then set about advertising his property in whatever way he sees fit – in newspapers, newsagents' windows or by erecting a placard in the front garden. If he chooses the latter method, he may find himself in trouble with his local authority or with his neighbours who may have the right to prevent such notices. The advantage of selling privately is the avoidance of estate agents' fees. The disadvantage is the time and inconvenience involved in advertising the property and showing would-be buyers around. It is very much a matter of individual circumstances whether this is a wise course to take.

If the vendor decides to look for outside help, he will find that various options are open to him. The traditional marketing method is to appoint an estate agent, who will take a commission as and when a sale is made. The estate agent may be given sole selling rights, in which case he gets his commission even if the vendor fixes up a private deal; a sole agency, in which case he is the only estate agent involved in selling the property; or a joint agency, in which case he and other agents are appointed. Commission rates tend to be higher in joint agency cases than sole ones, making the latter more attractive. Even then though the commission rate may be 2% of the final sale price: a vendor who sells for £45,000 therefore would have to pay £900 plus VAT at 15%. The cost is enormous, but then the estate agent may be able to find a buyer prepared to pay £500 or £1,000 more than the price the vendor could have negotiated privately. It is difficult to advise a vendor in the abstract as to whether he should instruct an estate agent: suffice it to say though that if he is selling *and* buying a new house, he will be faced if he does so with the kind of costs described on page 68, *plus* the legal costs involved in selling the house *plus* his estate agent's fees. Moving house can be a very expensive business.

Some alternative marketing methods are now available. In particular, the vendor should consider using the facilities of computer agencies or property shops which are springing up throughout the country. What happens here is that the vendor pays a fee 'up-front' of say £150–£200. The vendor is responsible for fixing his sale price and for showing potential purchasers around (estate agents will do this themselves). However, the agency or property shop does all the necessary advertising and seeks to find the right type of buyer for any particular vendor. It can be anticipated that this type of selling will become more rather than less common in the future.

If the vendor's property is unusual or difficult to value, he may be advised to sell it at auction rather than by private treaty. A reserve price may be fixed below which the property cannot be sold, and it may be that at auction the price will be bid up beyond the sort of figure that could have been privately negotiated.

A final warning should be given to the vendor. If he is hoping to sell and buy, he will come across the notorious problem of having to synchronise the two transactions. To exchange contracts on a sale before a purchase is arranged will mean that for a period he is homeless; on the other hand to exchange contracts on a purchase before agreeing to sell could be more disastrous still, for he will then have to finance two properties at the same time. It may be that a 'bridging loan' from his bank will tide him over this difficult period, but such loans attract high interest rates and may last for a considerable time if there is much of a problem in finding a purchaser. It follows that when selling and buying, the vendor must inspect his would-be vendor and purchaser as carefully as the property he would like to move on to, so that he can find people whose own personal circumstances are likely to mean that they will be able to fall in with his own plans.

1. INTRODUCTION

Not everyone has the money or the inclination to purchase a house of their own. The natural alternative for such people is normally to rent a house or flat. The law of landlord and tenant is highly complex, and it is very important for both parties to have a full understanding of the rights and obligations which the law imposes upon them.

A relationship of landlord and tenant exists when the landlord grants exclusive possession of his property to a tenant in return for the payment by the tenant of rent. The 'lease' or 'tenancy' so granted may be for whatever period the parties agree: in legal theory a lease could just as well last for a week or for 999 years; and the rent can be payable on whatever basis the parties agree, weekly, monthly, yearly etc. In some circumstances, however, the *amount* of rent payable is controlled by statutory provisions: see below. It may be that the landlord who grants the lease is himself a tenant of someone else. Thus one can end up with a situation in which there is a headlease between the freeholder (see page 39) and his tenant, and a sublease between that tenant and his sub-tenant; in legal theory this 'ladder' could be endlessly prolonged. In each case, the tenant or sub-tenant must pay rent to his immediate landlord.

Leases may be created either for a fixed term or granted on a periodic basis. Where the lease is granted for a term of, say, one year, it will automatically come to an end after twelve months without either party taking any action to terminate it. (Note, however, that even then the tenant may be given statutory protection under the various pieces of legislation entitling him to stay on in the property: see below.) On the other hand the lease may be periodic: it could be granted on a weekly or monthly or yearly basis. In this case, the lease automatically continues at the end of each given period unless and until one of the parties serves a notice to quit on the other indicating an intention to bring it to an end. The amount of notice that has to be given varies according to the type of lease created, but in the case of residential properties, the Protection from Eviction Act 1977 provides that *at least* four weeks' notice must always be given. (Again it

should be noted that even after the notice to quit has expired, the tenant may be given statutory rights to stay in his house.)

Apart from establishing the rent payable and the duration of the lease, the agreement between a landlord and tenant will normally contain many other terms about repairs, decoration, use of the premises, sub-letting and assignment and so forth designed to make sure what the rights and duties of the parties are. Apart from these express terms, the law sometimes implies terms into tenancy agreements, and some Acts of Parliament impose duties upon the parties, and in particular upon the landlord. Some of the more important of these express, implied and statutory terms and conditions will be described below.

During the 1960s and 1970s, Parliament passed various Acts designed to afford greater protection to tenants than the common law allowed them, though legislation of this type can be traced back almost to the start of the century. In particular, the various Rent Acts that were passed attempted to protect tenants from harassment by their landlords, and to prevent landlords evicting them from their houses, unless there was a reasonable ground for doing so; the legislation was also designed to control the amount of rent the landlord could charge. The important aspects of the Rent Acts will be described below. At this point a preliminary matter must be discussed. Generally, the legislation in question protects only *tenants* with *leases* of property. However, it is possible for the owner of the property wishing to rent it to someone to grant him a mere 'licence' to occupy it rather than to confer on him a leasehold interest and to create a relationship of landlord and tenant. The problem with this is that a mere licence to occupy the land does not confer on the licensee Rent Act protection, and so the practice grew up of would-be landlords insisting that they would only grant licences instead of leases. Thus the policy of the legislation, to protect the integrity of the tenant's house, could be easily thwarted.

At one time, the Courts seemed to be perfectly prepared to go along with the device of allowing licences to be used to outflank the Rent Acts. One particular device used was to make an agreement with a licensee which denied him exclusive possession of the property in question: for example the agreement would contain a term entitling the licensor to insist that a third party should be allowed to share the premises. It is an essential requirement of a lease that the tenant should have exclusive possession, and the Courts were content to say that in such a situation no lease had been created, even though the effect of the licensor allowing a third party into occupation would be manifestly absurd. In *Somma v Hazlehurst* (1978) an unmarried couple moved into a bed-sitting room in a property owned by Mrs Somma. They were each asked to enter into separate agreements with her, and Mrs Somma also reserved the right to insist that one other person could move into the bedsitting room with them. The Court of Appeal saw no objection to this arrangement and concluded that there was only a licence not a lease. It saw no reason to object to what some people would regard as an obvious attempt to evade the Rent Act legislation. It did not even object to the situation on moral or public policy grounds.

More recently the House of Lords, the most senior Court in the country, has taken a more realistic approach to this issue. In *Street v Mountford* (1985) Mr Street entered into an agreement with Mrs Mountford whereby she moved into two rooms in a property owned by him at a rent of £37 per week. The agreement was called a 'licence agreement' and Mrs Mountford signed a form expressly stating that she accepted that the Rent Acts could not apply to such an agreement. Later she successfully applied to the Rent Officer to have a fair rent registered, and Mr Street applied to the Court for a declaration that, as there was only a licence, the Rent Officer had no jurisdiction. The County Court found for Mrs Mountford; the Court of Appeal came down on Mr Street's side. The House of Lords, however, unanimously agreed that there was a tenancy protected by the Rent Acts and that the attempt by Mr Street to create a mere licence had failed. The reality of the matter was that Mrs Mountford had been given exclusive possession of the rooms (with her husband) and that the Court should not be misled into thinking there was only a licence simply because of the wording used in the agreement. Interestingly, the House of Lords also went out of its way to *disapprove* of *Somma v Hazlehurst*, considering that the right of the owner to put in a third party was simply a sham which should be disregarded. This case suggests that in future the Courts will be much less inclined to

allow landlords to avoid the legislation by making what in reality are leases appear to be licences, and that many people who at the moment have licence agreements will turn out to be protected by the Rent Acts after all.

This is not to say that every agreement termed a licence will be deemed to be a lease, but that the Courts will be more suspicious of licence agreements than in the past. For example, where someone stays in a hotel or bed and breakfast establishment it would be easy to decide that the parties do not intend to create a relationship of landlord and tenant. Similarly a friend staying in a house or even a lodger in digs would normally be held to be a mere licensee. But in other cases, where the owner of property allows someone to occupy it as a home in return for a commercial rent, the Courts will be very suspicious of any attempt to disguise what is in reality a tenancy by the licence device.

Assuming that a relationship of landlord and tenant does exist between the parties, it is convenient to consider the relevant law under four separate headings. In the next section, the position of private sector tenancies will be considered, then housing association ones and then the particular problems of council housing. Lastly, separate consideration will be given to the position of long leases, which tend to be subject to special rules of their own.

2. PRIVATE SECTOR TENANCIES

The number of private sector tenancies has decreased enormously in recent years. There are various reasons for this: no doubt some landlords have been dissuaded from letting properties because of what they consider to be penal or unfair Rent Act legislation. Since 1979 the Conservative Government has responded to the decline in private sector tenancies by relaxing this legislation in various ways, although it is still not easy to tell what effect this switch in policy will have in the long term.

Three particular problems crop up in disputes between landlords and tenants: can the landlord evict his tenant; can the landlord increase the tenant's rent; and what are the respective rights and obligations of the two parties? We shall consider the law in this order.

(i) Security of Tenure
The basic position is of course that the tenant must give up possession of the property to the

landlord at the end of the time agreed between the parties. In the case of a fixed-term tenancy it will be obvious when this time is reached. If the tenancy is a periodic one, then it ends after one or other party has served a notice to quit. Unless the parties agree otherwise, a weekly tenancy requires a full week's notice to quit; a monthly tenancy needs a month's notice, while a yearly tenancy is ended by giving six months' notice. The notice given must expire at the *end* of a period allowed by the lease. Thus, a monthly tenancy commencing on the first of the month can only be ended by at least a month's notice *ending* on the last day of the month. One further important restriction is imposed upon the landlord: the Protection from Eviction Act 1977 requires that *any* notice to quit residential premises must give not less than one month's notice (i e even if the tenancy is a weekly one). Furthermore the notice to quit will be invalid (and so the tenancy will continue) unless it contains certain 'prescribed information' informing the tenant of the various kinds of rights he may have under the Rent Acts. A typical notice to quit would look like the form on page 74.

Even after the tenancy has expired by effluxion of time or by the service of a notice to quit, the tenant may have a statutory right to stay on in the property if the Rent Act legislation applies (see page 81). Furthermore, even if the tenancy is not protected under the Rent Acts, the landlord is not entitled physically to evict the tenant when the lease comes to an end. The Protection from Eviction Act 1977 requires that landlords wanting to repossess residential premises can only do so by Court action (unless, of course, the tenant voluntarily agrees to go).

In some circumstances the landlord may be entitled to bring the tenancy to an end *before* it has expired, if the tenant has been guilty of some serious breach of covenant. For example, if the tenant fails to pay his rent or uses the property for an improper or immoral purpose, the landlord may take action to 'forfeit' the lease. Generally speaking he can only do so if the lease contains an express provision authorizing him to do so. If he wishes to forfeit because of a failure by the tenant to pay his rent, the tenant can usually redeem the situation (even up to six months after he has actually left the property) by paying off any arrears plus interest that he owes. If the landlord intends to forfeit the lease because of some other misbehaviour by the tenant, he is required by section 146 of the Law of Property Act 1925 to serve a notice on the tenant giving him a reasonable opportunity to remedy the situation. Only if the tenant cannot or will not respond by remedying the breach will the landlord be allowed to proceed to forfeiture. Even then the Court may grant the tenant 'relief against forfeiture' where it appears reasonable to do so. A landlord wanting to forfeit a lease of residential premises is only entitled to do so by taking Court action: it is illegal for him physically to evict the tenant.

Assuming that the tenancy has come to an end, the common law position is that the tenant must go. If he remains in possession, he must pay compensation to the landlord until he actually vacates the property. However, in some circumstances the tenant is given a right to stay on, i e he has what is known as 'security of tenure'. The most important situation is where he has what is termed a 'regulated tenancy' in which case his protection from eviction is considerable. In some circumstances he may have what is called a 'restricted contract' in which case he has some, albeit limited, protection. A new category of protection has recently been introduced for what are termed 'assured tenancies'. These three types of tenancy will be described; thereafter the meaning of a 'shorthold tenancy' will be explained, whereby landlords can now create tenancies which afford tenants no protection against eviction at all.

(A) Regulated tenancies. The basic position of a regulated tenancy is that, when the lease comes to an end, the tenant can remain in the property indefinitely provided that he pays his rent and behaves reasonably. When he dies, his right to remain in the property can be transmitted to his spouse or else to any other member of his family living with him during the six months before his death. When this successor to the original tenant dies, the tenancy can be transmitted again to another successor who will again be a close relative. This means therefore that, where a landlord grants a weekly tenancy to someone and the tenancy turns out to be regulated, the landlord may be unable to recover the property until the tenant, his spouse and one of their children have all died: a weekly tenancy may in fact turn into a lease lasting for 50 or more years. This is why people considering letting a property must take proper legal advice, and why landlords in the past were encouraged to try to create licences rather than leases, since only *leases* qualify for the kind of protection being described.

NOTICE TO QUIT

(BY LANDLORD OF PREMISES LET AS A DWELLING)

Name and Address of Tenant	To Cynthia Rumbold
	of 4 Railway Cuttings, Champlower, Near Harwick
Name and Address of Landlord	[I] [We] [as] [on behalf of] your landlord[s], George Walton
	of 2 Puritan Road, Exeter, Devon
*Me/them or as appropriate	give you **NOTICE TO QUIT** and deliver up possession to* Me
†Address of premises	of† 4 Railway Cuttings aforesaid
‡Date for possession	on‡ 31st March 19 87 , or the day on which a complete period of your tenancy expires next after the end of four weeks from the service of this notice.
Date of notice	Dated 8th October 19 86
	Signed George Walton
Name and Address of Agent if Agent serves notice	N/A

INFORMATION FOR TENANT
(See Note 2 overleaf)

1. If the tenant does not leave the dwelling, the landlord must get an order for possession from the court before the tenant can lawfully be evicted. The landlord cannot apply for such an order before the notice to quit has run out.

2. A tenant who does not know if he has any right to remain in possession after a notice to quit runs out or is otherwise unsure of his rights, can obtain advice from a solicitor. Help with all or part of the cost of legal advice and assistance may be available under the Legal Aid Scheme. He should also be able to obtain information from a Citizens' Advice Bureau, a Housing Aid Centre, a Rent Officer or a Rent Tribunal Office.

[P.T.O.

NOTES

1.   Notice to quit any premises let as a dwelling must be given at least four weeks before it takes effect, and it must be in writing (Protection from Eviction Act 1977, s. 5).

2.   Where a notice to quit is given by a landlord to determine a tenancy of any premises let as a dwelling, the notice must contain this information (The Notices to Quit (Prescribed Information) Regulations 1980).

© **OYEZ** The Solicitors' Law Stationery Society, plc. Oyez House, 237 Long Lane, London SE1 4PU   F1444 6–81
Landlord and Tenant 61

Given the extent of the protection afforded to regulated tenancies, it is of course essential to understand precisely what this term means. The relevant legislation is the Rent Act 1977, to which certain amendments have been made by the Housing Act 1980. The basic definition of a regulated tenancy requires three conditions to be fulfilled:

(a) there must be a lease: it follows therefore that *licences* are not protected (see page 71);

(b) the lease must be of a dwelling-house: it follows that business and agricultural tenancies are not protected by this legislation (but the Landlord and Tenant Act 1954 and the Agricultural Holdings Act 1948 respectively may apply in these situations). The term dwelling-house has been flexibly interpreted by the Courts, and it is possible for maisonettes, flats, single rooms and even beach-huts to qualify as such;

(c) the dwelling-house must be let as a separate dwelling. This means that if the property is let for some other purpose (e g to be used as a shop or office) and the tenant chooses to use it as his residence, he would not be protected by the Act.

It should be noted that, to qualify as a regulated tenancy, it is not necessary for any particular legal formalities to have been complied with: a landlord may orally agree to lease the property, and the terms of the agreement may never have been recorded in writing, but still the tenancy may be a regulated one. Another important point is that the mere fact that the tenant has to share bathroom facilities with other people in the same building does not mean that his tenancy is not regulated; however, to amount to a 'separate dwelling' the tenant must have somewhere to sleep, cook and eat.

Having described a regulated tenancy as a letting of a separate dwelling-house, the Act then proceeds to list a number of exceptions, many of which are of considerable importance in practice. The exceptions are as follows:

(i) Lettings of properties whose rateable value is above a specified threshold. Ascertaining the relevant threshold is a rather complex matter, but basically the policy is to exclude properties in Greater London with a rateable value of more than £1,500 and properties elsewhere with a rateable value of more than £750. It will readily be seen that only very luxurious properties will exceed the relevant threshold, at an end of the market where the tenant is unlikely to be impecunious and in need of protection from the bargaining power of his landlord.

(ii) Lettings of properties at extremely low rents. Generally the rent must be less than ⅔ of the rateable value of the property on 23 March 1965 or later if it only became rated after that date. This exception means that the many long leases (e g of 99 or even 999 years) which are created for technical legal reasons (see page 39) are excluded from the provisions on regulated tenancies. They may, however, benefit from the provisions of other pieces of legislation (see page 103).

(iii) Lettings of a dwelling-house together with other land. The idea of this exception is that, if a letting has the mixed purposes of providing say business or agricultural premises as well as accommodation, then it should not be protected under the Rent Acts. The Act specifically states that, if any land less than two acres in size is let with the dwelling-house, and if it is not to be used for agricultural purposes, then this exception will not apply to take the tenancy outside the Rent Acts.

(iv) Lettings at rents which include payments in respect of board or attendance. For this exception to apply, the amount of the rent attributable to the board or attendance must form a substantial part of the whole. Thus a landlord who provides meals to his tenants or who arranges for the cleaning of a tenant's flat may well satisfy the terms of this exception, provided that the cost of so doing is substantial in relation to the rent as a whole. On the other hand, the mere provision of an early morning cup of tea would not suffice; nor does the provision of services which are equally available to all the tenants in a house or block of flats (such as lighting and cleaning the communal areas or having the gardens maintained).

(v) Lettings to students by certain educational institutions. This exception means that universities and colleges which make accommodation available to their students do not find themselves saddled with obligations under the Rent Acts. Note, however, that a letting by a *private* landlord to a student would *not* fall within this exception.

(vi) Holiday lettings. It would of course be absurd if a holiday letting of a cottage in Cornwall for two weeks in the summer could amount to a regulated tenancy, and so the Rent Act specifically excludes such lettings. The Courts have quite frequently been asked to consider what the true purpose of a letting was, as landlords often insert a term in the lease that the property is let for holiday purposes only. Where the Court considers

this to be a mere device for getting around the Rent Acts, it will not be slow to say so.

(vii) Agricultural holdings. As already noted, tenancies of agricultural holdings are protected under a separate piece of legislation, the Agricultural Holdings Act 1948. They are therefore excluded from the Rent Acts. Farm-workers with tied cottages but without an agricultural holding of their own would not be protected by the 1948 Act; they might, however, be protected under the Rent Act 1977 or else under the Rent (Agriculture) Act 1976.

(viii) Lettings of licensed premises.

(ix) Lettings by a resident landlord. This is an important exception from the Act, intended to enable an owner-occupier to let out rooms within his house without the fear of creating a regulated tenancy. However, even the tenant of a resident landlord is given some protection from eviction, albeit of a much more limited nature than in the case of regulated tenancies, under the provisions dealing with what are called 'restricted contracts' (see page 79). To qualify for this exception, the letting must have commenced after 14 August 1974 and the landlord must be resident in the same building as the tenant; the building, however, must not be a purpose-built block of flats. If the landlord ceases to live in the same building as the tenant, the benefit of the exemption will be lost, although it is possible for short periods of absence to be disregarded.

(x) Lettings by the Crown. This means, for example, that tenants of the Crown Estate Commissioners or of the Duchies of Cornwall and Lancaster do not enjoy protection under the Rent Act.

(xi) Lettings by local authorities. Council tenants have always been outside the protection of the Rent Acts. However, very important new provisions affecting their position were introduced by the Housing Act 1980. In particular this Act introduced security of tenure for them and gave many council tenants the right to buy their homes. The matter is dealt with on page 97.

(xii) Lettings by housing associations. These are dealt with on page 96.

(xiii) Lettings by housing co-operatives.

(xiv) Lettings which qualify as 'assured tenancies'. See page 79.

(xv) Business lettings. They are subject to special provisions of their own, contained in the Landlord and Tenant Act 1954.

(xvi) Lettings to companies.

(xvii) Lettings of parsonage houses by the Church of England.

(xviii) Lettings of dwelling-houses which are, or become, overcrowded.

Assuming that a tenant does in fact have a regulated tenancy, his position is that when his lease comes to an end he is entitled to remain in possession of the property unless and until the landlord succeeds in obtaining a Court order telling him to go. Such an order can only be made in the circumstances described in the Rent Act 1977 which are designed to ensure, generally speaking, that the tenant can only be removed from his home for misbehaviour or because the landlord reasonably requires the property for his own use.

The Act makes a distinction between situations in which the Court has a *discretion* as to whether or not to grant the landlord a possession order, and situations where it is under a *duty* to do so. Obviously the landlord is in a much better position in the latter situation.

(B) Discretionary cases. The Court *may* make an order in the landlord's favour where (a) it would be reasonable in all the circumstances to do so *and* (b) *either* it is satisfied that suitable alternative accommodation for the tenant is available *or* one of the grounds for possession described in the Act is satisfied. These grounds for possession are actually known in the jargon of the legislation as 'Cases', and are numbered from 1 to 10 (but number 7 has been abolished).

The onus of proving reasonableness is on the landlord, and the judge being asked to make the order must take all the relevant circumstances into account including such matters as the conduct of the parties and the nature of the property. It seems to be easier to establish reasonableness where the landlord makes suitable alternative accommodation available than where he is relying on one of the Cases.

Where the landlord is relying upon the availability of suitable alternative accommodation, it is for him to prove that this is so. It is not necessary for him actually to *offer* the accommodation: he may try to prove that in fact alternative accommodation exists. A certificate from the local authority will be conclusive evidence for these purposes. What qualifies as *suitable* alternative accommodation can of course be a highly contentious matter, but it ought to offer the tenant similar security of tenure to that which he already enjoys. Also it should *either* be similar as regards rental and extent to the accommodation afforded by housing authorities to people whose needs are similar to those of the tenant and his family *or* be reasonably suitable to the means of the tenant and to the needs of the tenant and his family as regards extent and character.

If the landlord is not relying upon the availability of suitable alternative accommodation, then he will have to satisfy the Court that one of the grounds for possession is satisfied. The grounds are as follows:

Case 1: that the tenant is in arrears with his rent or is in breach of some obligation under the tenancy. If the rent is paid off before the case comes to Court or if the tenant remedies the breach of obligation (for example by observing a duty to keep the property in reasonable internal condition) the Court will not make an order.

Case 2: that the tenant or any person living with him has been guilty of conduct which is a nuisance or annoyance to adjoining occupiers, or has been convicted of using the dwelling-house, or allowing it to be used, for immoral or illegal purposes.

Case 3: that the condition of the dwelling-house has deteriorated because of actions or omissions on the part of the tenant or any lodger or subtenant of his. In the latter situation, the ground does not apply if the tenant has himself taken reasonable steps to remove the lodger or subtenant.

Case 4: that the condition of any furniture provided for use under the tenancy has deteriorated owing to ill-treatment by the tenant or his lodger or sub-tenant. In the latter situation, the same proviso applies as in Case 3.

Case 5: that the tenant himself has served a notice to quit on the landlord as a result of which the landlord has agreed to sell or let the property to someone else or has taken other steps as a result of which he would be seriously prejudiced if he could not obtain possession. The idea of this is that a tenant who has himself indicated that he intends to vacate the property cannot then be allowed to alter his position and rely on Rent Act protection where to do so would be unfair to the landlord.

Case 6: that the tenant has assigned or sublet the dwelling-house without the consent of the landlord.

Case 7: abolished.

Case 8: that the property is required for an employee of the landlord. This ground only applies where the existing tenant was himself an employee of the landlord, and is designed to ensure that where accommodation is provided along with a job, it is the employee *for the time being* who is entitled to use it.

Case 9: that the dwelling-house is reasonably required by the landlord for occupation as a residence for: (a) himself or (b) any son or daughter of his own over eighteen years of age or (c) his father or mother or (d) his father-in-law or mother-in-law. This ground does *not* apply where the landlord buys a property which is *already* subject to a regulated tenancy: in other words it can only apply where a landlord grants a tenancy of property he already owns to a tenant. The Act goes on to provide that the Court will not grant an order for possession under Case 9 if, after considering all the circumstances, it is satisfied that greater hardship would be caused by making the order than by refusing to do so. There have been many cases under this Case: it is for the landlord to show that he reasonably requires the property as a residence and for the tenant to show that the order would cause him greater hardship than the landlord. It is *very* important to point out that a landlord letting his own home need not rely on Case 9 if he can show that the case is one where possession is *mandatory* under the provisions contained in Case 11 below.

Case 10: that the tenant has sub-let part of the property to someone else at an excessive rent.

(C) Mandatory cases. In some circumstances, a landlord is entitled as of right to an order for possession of his property. In these situations, there is no question of the Court having to consider whether it would be reasonable to make an order: it has a duty to do so provided that one of the grounds is satisfied. A special procedure has been established enabling such cases to be heard very quickly. The grounds for possession are as follows:

Case 11: that the dwelling-house was let by an owner-occupier who, before the commencement of the tenancy, notified the tenant that possession might be recovered under Case 11, and that the landlord or a close relative of his needs the property for his own occupation or needs to sell it in order to buy another one. The idea of this Case is, of course, that a person, say, going abroad to work for a year will be certain that when he returns home he will be able to recover his property. However, the tenant must be served with a Case 11 notice *before* the tenancy begins, so that he will understand precisely what his position is.

Case 12: that the landlord intends, when he retires from regular employment, to occupy the property as his residence and a notice to this effect has been served upon the tenant before the commencement of the tenancy. Thus it is possible to buy a retirement home in Bournemouth and to let it to a tenant for the last couple of years of one's working life secure in the knowledge that the tenant can in due course be removed without any problem.

Case 13: that the tenancy was an out-of-season letting for less than eight months and that the property is used for holiday lettings in-season. Again the tenant must be notified of the situation before the tenancy commences.

Case 14: that the tenancy is for twelve months or less and is of a property normally used as a student letting. Notice must be served on the tenant in advance.

Case 15: that the tenancy is of a property required for a minister of religion, and a notice is served on the tenant that possession may be recovered on this ground.

Cases 16–18: that the property is required for various agricultural employees.

Case 19: that the property is held on a shorthold tenancy. (See page 80.)

Case 20: that the tenancy was granted by a serviceman, and notice of the fact was served on the tenant before the tenancy commenced.

It is often suggested that the law is unduly unfair to landlords and in particular that they are unfairly deprived of the chance of recovering their properties. It will by now have been seen, however, both that there are many exceptions from the category of regulated tenancies and also that there are various grounds on which a landlord may recover possession. In particular, a home-owner who lets his *own* house ought to have no problem over claims to security of tenure by his tenant, provided that he takes proper legal advice and adopts the correct procedure.

(D) Restricted contracts. Even though the tenant does not have a regulated tenancy and so is not entitled to the full measure of protection just described, he may nonetheless have some protection if he has what the legislation calls a 'restricted contract'. The two most important examples of restricted contracts are where a *resident* landlord grants a tenancy of part of the building in which he lives and where a tenancy (or even a licence) is granted at a rent which includes payment for the use of furniture or services. However, the definition of a restricted contract *excludes* regulated tenancies, so that

normally a furnished letting would be entitled to full Rent Act protection in the manner already described. However, we have seen on page 76 that a tenancy is not regulated if it includes the provision by a landlord of services to the tenant. In such a case the tenant must rely on the protection given to restricted contracts.

The protection afforded to a restricted contract differs according to the date of its creation. If it was created before 28 November 1980 the tenant's position is rather better than where it was created after that date.

Pre-28 November 1980 contracts: where the landlord serves a notice to quit on the tenant, the tenant may apply to a Rent Tribunal (*not* the County Court), which has power to postpone the effect of the notice for up to six months after the date on which it would otherwise have expired. Thus the tenant may be able to win himself a bit more time, but only one postponement of up to six months is permitted. Furthermore it should be noted that this protection is not available where a tenancy is for a fixed term and expires by effluxion of time rather than being a periodic tenancy terminable by notice to quit.

Post-28 November 1980 contracts: in such cases, the tenant's position is even weaker; if proceedings take place in the County Court for his eviction, the Court may postpone the date when a possession order is to come into effect for up to three months, but there is no protection beyond this.

(E) Assured tenancies. The Housing Act 1980 created a totally new type of residential tenure known as assured tenancies. The policy of this part of the Act is to encourage the building of new properties in the private sector suitable for letting as opposed to sale. In particular, the rent payable under assured tenancies cannot be controlled at all: the parties are left to negotiate this between themselves. As far as security of tenure is concerned, the tenant does have some protection against eviction, but the relevant provisions are based on the legislation controlling business tenancies rather than on those dealing with regulated tenancies.

To qualify as an assured tenancy, four conditions must be satisfied:

(a) the landlord must not be a private individual but an approved body. Approved bodies so far include various building and property companies, some building societies and some pension funds;

(b) the property in question must be *newly* built:

the policy of the Act is to encourage *new* building;

(c) before the tenant first occupies the property, no-one else must have occupied it except under an assured tenancy;

(d) the tenancy would have had to have qualified as a protected tenancy under the Rent Act 1977 or as a housing association tenancy (see page 96) if it were not an assured tenancy within the terms of the Housing Act 1980.

(F) Security of tenure for assured tenancies.

The procedure whereby the tenant can claim security of tenure is as follows. When the period of the tenancy originally agreed between the parties expires, the tenancy will automatically continue until one of the parties takes steps to bring it to an end. The tenant can himself end it by giving a three months' notice to the landlord in the case of a fixed term tenancy or the appropriate amount of notice needed to terminate a periodic tenancy. Assuming however that the tenant wishes to remain in the property, the landlord and tenant may be able to negotiate a suitable new agreement. Otherwise, if the landlord wishes to remove the tenant he must serve a notice on him in the prescribed form giving him at least six but not more than twelve months' notice. The tenant must then oppose this by applying to the County Court within four months of receipt of the notice. He must also notify the landlord that he is doing so. It will then be for the Court to decide whether to grant the landlord possession, but it can only do so on certain specified grounds namely:

(a) that the property is in disrepair resulting from the tenant not having observed his repairing obligations;

(b) that the tenant has persistently been guilty of delay in paying his rent;

(c) that the tenant has been guilty of other substantial breaches of his obligations under the tenancy agreement;

(d) that suitable alternative accommodation is available for the tenant;

(e) that the landlord intends to demolish or substantially reconstruct the premises. This ground is not available if the tenant offers to provide the landlord with facilities to carry out the proposed work or to take a tenancy of part of the premises unaffected by the work. If the tenant *is* removed under this head, he may be entitled to claim compensation for disturbance from the landlord;

(f) that the landlord wishes to let the property as a whole but the assured tenancy relates only to a part of it;

(g) that the landlord requires the property for his own purposes.

If the landlord cannot satisfy any of these grounds, the Court will grant the tenant a new tenancy which may be for any period up to fourteen years and on such terms and conditions as the Court thinks fit.

(G) Shorthold tenancies.

The Conservative Government which came to office in 1979 was concerned that the law in this area was unduly harsh on landlords and that this had caused the private sector of the landlord-tenant market to shrink to an unacceptable degree. As part of its initiative to remove some of the burden on landlords, it therefore introduced, in the Housing Act 1980, a new form of tenure, known as the shorthold tenancy. As far as security of tenure is concerned, the point of the shorthold tenancy is that, when it expires, the landlord is guaranteed the right to repossess the property provided that all the correct procedures have been followed.

To qualify as a shorthold tenancy at least three, and sometimes four, conditions must be satisfied:

(a) the tenancy must be for not less than one and for not more than five years;

(b) it must not be possible for the landlord to bring the tenancy to an end before the expiry of the tenancy except through forfeiture proceedings for arrears of rent or breach of other obligations in the lease;

(c) before the tenancy commences, a notice in the prescribed form must be served on the tenant stating that it is to be a protected shorthold tenancy;

(d) (*in the case of properties in London only*) a fair rent must be registered before the tenancy begins or an application to have one registered must be lodged within 28 days of the commencement of the tenancy.

An important proviso states that it is not possible to convert a regulated tenancy into a shorthold tenancy: it would be unfair for a landlord to persuade or encourage a tenant to relinquish his protected status under the Rent Act 1977 and to become a mere shorthold tenant. Assuming that the formalities for the creation of a shorthold tenancy have been satisfied, the landlord can bring proceedings when the period expires to have the tenant evicted. There are strict rules as to the form and period of notice which the landlord must give to the tenant should he wish to do so. In particular the notice must be in writing, must give the tenant at least three months' notice of the landlord's intention to institute proceedings, and must indicate that the landlord will be relying (in the jargon of the Act) on 'Case 19'. Having satisfied these formalities, the landlord may commence proceedings and the Court must make an order provided that the landlord has complied with the whole series of formalities just described. Even if they have not been fully complied with, the Court has a discretion to make an order where it is just and equitable to do so. A special procedure is available for this type of case which is intended to provide the landlord with a speedy remedy.

(H) Harassment and unlawful eviction. The various provisions conferring protection upon a tenant when his tenancy expires have now been described. The extent of this protection ranges from the position under a regulated tenancy – where the tenant may be entitled to remain in the property indefinitely and to transmit the tenancy to a successor upon his death – to the position under the shorthold tenancy, where his protection is minimal save that the landlord must observe certain formalities. However, it is very important to draw attention to the Protection from Eviction Act 1977 which contains provisions which relate to any tenancy of premises let for residential purposes. These provisions do *not* confer any security of tenure upon the tenant, but they do attempt to ensure that landlords only repossess the property by taking court proceedings (rather than by taking the law into their own hands) and that landlords do not try to drive the tenant out by what is known as 'harassment'.

Section 1 of the Protection from Eviction Act 1977 establishes two offences. The first is that it is an offence for a landlord unlawfully to deprive a tenant (or, indeed, a licensee) of his occupation of the premises in question; it is a defence that the landlord believes, or has reasonable cause to believe, that the person in question has ceased to reside in the premises. The second offence (known as harassment) is for a landlord to perform acts calculated to interfere with the peace or comfort of the occupant or his family, or persistently to withdraw or withhold services reasonably required for the occupation of the premises as a residence, with the intention of causing the occupant to give up his occupation or

to refrain from exercising his rights in relation to it. Obvious examples of harassment would be the landlord cutting off the electricity to the property, or making threatening telephone calls. A tenant worried about his landlord's behaviour should consult a solicitor or a Citizens Advice Bureau or Legal Advice Centre. Another useful idea is to get in touch with the local authority's Harassment Officer, who will be used to dealing with cases of this nature. A landlord guilty of an offence under section 1 of the Act may be fined or even imprisoned. The maximum penalties if the matter gets to the Crown Court would be an unlimited fine and two years in prison. Furthermore, if in the course of unlawfully depriving the occupant of his home or harassing him the landlord commits a trespass (e g entering the property without permission) he can be sued for compensation, and the Court can award what are known as 'exemplary damages' in such cases in order to indicate the seriousness of the matter. For example, in *Drane v Evangelou* (1977) a tenant successfully applied to the Rent Officer to have his rent reduced. One day he went out and returned home to find that the landlord had forcefully entered the house, bolted the door from the inside and thrown all the tenant's belongings into the back yard. It took the tenant about two months to get a Court order telling the landlord to vacate the property, and to regain possession. By then the house was very dirty and in considerable disorder. The Court ordered the landlord to pay the tenant exemplary damages of £1,000 plus his legal costs. The Court of Appeal upheld this decision.

Sections 2 and 3 of the Protection from Eviction Act 1977 contain further important provisions. Basically they provide that no landlord can recover property let for residential purposes otherwise than through court proceedings. Even some licences benefit from this provision. The idea is to prevent the landlord from evicting the occupant himself; it is much more seemly that such matters should be controlled by the Court itself. Any landlord infringing these provisions can be sued for compensation, and again exemplary damages may be awarded.

(ii) Rent Regulation

When a landlord grants a tenancy to a tenant, the parties will agree on the amount of rent that is to be paid and on the appropriate dates when payment is to be due. The general position in law is that the parties are free to negotiate whatever deal they want, since the law has always been committed to the idea that individuals should be free to strike their own bargains. However, there is often an imbalance between supply and demand in the private sector of rented accommodation, as a result of which Parliament has from time to time legislated to control the amount of rent that a landlord can charge or the frequency with which he may increase it. In the last few years, however, policy in this respect has been undergoing a process of change, and the extent of the tenant's protection has been reduced in some situations. It is best to consider rent regulation separately in relation to regulated tenancies, restricted contracts, assured tenancies and shorthold tenancies. These terms have already been explained in the previous paragraphs.

(A) Regulated tenancies. The Rent Act 1977 establishes a system whereby a 'fair rent' can be registered in respect of any property which is subject to a regulated tenancy. Once a fair rent has been registered, the landlord cannot charge more than the relevant amount, and a tenant who is overcharged can recover the excess. Before describing how the fair rent system works, however, it is necessary to explain the position where *no* fair rent has been fixed.

If no fair rent has been registered for a particular property, then the position is that the landlord and tenant are free to fix whatever rent they can agree upon and the landlord can charge the full amount. It must be noted, however, that if a fair rent has already been registered in the past, the landlord cannot charge a *new* tenant more than he was charging a previous one who has vacated the property. The rent which is fixed attaches to the property *itself*, and not just to the particular tenant living there at the time the rent was registered.

If no fair rent has been registered, it is possible for the landlord to raise the rent from time to time, but there are strict formalities that have to be observed. They are laid down by section 51 of the Rent Act 1977, and if they are not complied with then the excess over the previous rent is irrecoverable by the landlord. A rent agreement must:

(a) be in writing, signed by the landlord and tenant;

(b) contain a statement, in characters not less conspicuous than those used in any other part of the agreement, that (i) the tenant's security of tenure is unaffected by his non-

entry into the agreement and (ii) the agreement will not disable either party from applying for the registration of a fair rent.

Registration of fair rent. Application for the registration of a fair rent may be made to a Rent Officer: a special form is available for this purpose. Rent Officers are appointed by local authorities, although they are independent of them and have security of tenure. The application may be made by the landlord, the tenant, the two of them jointly or by the local authority. The Rent Officer's function is then to determine what would be a fair rent for the property. He is under a duty to hear any representations that the parties may wish to make, and in deciding what would be a fair rent section 70(1) of the Rent Act 1977 requires him to have regard to all the circumstances (other than personal circumstances) and in particular to (a) the age, character, locality and state of repair of the dwelling-house and (b) if any furniture is provided for use under the tenancy the quantity, quality and condition of the furniture.

Section 70(2) of the Act is important, since it specifically provides that the Rent Officer must assume that there is a balance between the supply of housing available in an area and the number of prospective tenants for that housing: in other words he cannot take scarcity of accommodation into account. Section 70(3) provides that in determining what would be a fair rent, he must disregard certain matters such as any deterioration in the property attributable to a breach by the tenant of his obligations under the tenancy or any improvements in it effected by the tenant other than in pursuance of the terms of the tenancy agreement.

Once the Rent Officer has determined the fair rent, it must be entered in the register of fair rents; apart from stating the rent itself, the register must also contain a specification of the property in question, prescribed particulars of the tenancy agreement and (if it is the case) state that the landlord (or a superior landlord) is responsible for the rates. The register is open for public inspection; a fee of £1 is payable. Once a fair rent has been registered, then only that amount is payable. The general position is that, after registration of the rent, it is impossible for it to be increased until two years later. A further application will have to be made to the Rent Officer to increase the rent. However, in some circumstances it is possible to apply to have the registered rent increased within that period, for example if the condition of the property in question or the terms of the tenancy have changed. Either party could apply for the rent to be altered in such circumstances.

Once the fair rent has been registered, the Rent Act 1977 provides that the landlord cannot recover any sum from the tenant in excess of that amount, and the tenant can recover any excess payment he may have made to the landlord.

Either party aggrieved by the decision of the Rent Officer may appeal to a Rent Assessment Committee. Such committees consist of two or three people, many but not all of whom are lawyers. Regulations have established the procedure by which Rent Assessment Committees must conduct their hearings. They may either confirm the Rent Officer's decision or determine a fair rent of their own. In this case the two year period before which the rent may be raised runs from the time of the committee's decision. It is possible to take matters even further, either by applying to the Divisional Court of the High Court to quash the Rent Assessment Committee's decision if it acted outside its jurisdiction, or by appealing to the High Court if it made some error of law.

(B) Restricted contracts. It is possible for the amount of rent payable under 'restricted contracts' to be controlled, although the system is slightly different from the procedure just described in respect of regulated tenancies. It will be recalled from page 79 that the most important example of a restricted contract is the situation in which a landlord is resident in the same property as his tenant. In the case of restricted contracts, the landlord, tenant or local authority may apply to the Rent Tribunal for a rent to be fixed. The Rent Officer is not involved in such cases at all, even though it is he who determines fair rents for regulated tenancies. The Rent Tribunal in fact consists of the same people who sit on Rent Assessment Committees. Unless and until application is made to the Rent Tribunal, whatever amount has been agreed between the parties to the restricted contract is the recoverable sum. When a Rent Tribunal deals with the application, it has power under section 78 of the Rent Act 1977 to (a) approve the rent payable under the contract or (b) reduce or increase the rent to such sum as they may, in all the circumstances, think reasonable or (c) dismiss the reference.

No guidelines are laid down as to the method by which the Rent Tribunal should determine what would be a reasonable rent, although it is assumed that the Tribunal would be guided by much the same considerations as the Rent Officer when he fixes a fair rent for a protected tenancy.

The president of every rent assessment panel has a duty to maintain a register containing various information concerning restricted contracts referred to it. The register is open to the public on payment of a fee. It must contain (a) prescribed particulars of the contract in question; (b) a specification of the property to which the contract relates and (c) the rent as approved, reduced or increased by the Rent Tribunal.

Generally speaking, once a rent has been entered on the register it cannot be changed for two years, although application can be made within that time for a new rent in the circumstances described in section 80(2) of the Rent Act 1977. These are where there has been such a change in:
(a) the condition of the dwelling;
(b) the furniture or services provided;
(c) the terms of the contract or;
(d) any other circumstances taken into consideration when the rent was last considered as to make the registered rent no longer a reasonable rent.

Once a rent has been fixed, it is unlawful for anyone to require an amount in excess of that sum; any excess actually paid is recoverable by the tenant. Furthermore, a local authority can bring proceedings against anyone guilty of overcharging and the court could impose a prison sentence of up to six months upon the guilty party.

(C) Assured tenancies. Where an assured tenancy is created under section 56 of the Housing Act 1980, the policy of the legislation is that the open market rent should be chargeable by the landlord. This means that as long as the original contractual tenancy is still in existence, the tenant must pay whatever sum is stipulated in the agreement. However, if application has to be made to the Court to have the tenancy extended, then the Court has power to fix a new rent. This again, however, should be the open market rent (rather than a 'fair rent' as in the case of regulated tenancies or a 'reasonable rent' as in the case of restricted contracts). The whole idea of the assured tenancy system is to encourage firms to build properties for private lettings, and it is feared that, if the rents could be controlled in such cases, the incentive to build would be lost.

(D) Shorthold tenancies. The advantage to the landlord of shorthold tenancies is that they do not confer any security of tenure on the tenant. Provided that all the proper formalities are complied with, the landlord will be entitled to an order for possession of the property when the tenancy ends (see page 80). As far as rent is concerned, one particularly important point must be made: by section 52 of the Housing Act 1980, any letting of a property within Greater London will only qualify as a shorthold tenancy if a fair rent has been registered before the tenancy commences or if an application for such a registration is made within 28 days of its commencement. This requirement does *not* exist outside the Greater London area, but any shorthold tenant may apply to the Rent Officer for the registration of a fair rent, wherever the property is situate. The same criteria will be applied to determine the fair rent as have already been described (page 82).

(iii) Rights and Obligations of the Parties

Quite apart from the issues of security of tenure and rent regulation, problems frequently arise over the respective rights and obligations of the landlord and tenant under their tenancy agreement. For example, there may be a dispute over who is responsible for the maintenance of the property or as to whether the tenant is allowed to grant a sub-lease to someone else. This section will deal with some of the typical problems that arise in this context, although it is important to stress that this is a very complex area of law and that professional advice ought normally to be taken should a dispute arise.

Many leases will set out, sometimes at great length, the respective rights and duties of the landlord and tenant. A typical lease would look like the example reproduced opposite.

Generally speaking, the 'covenants' in the lease must be observed by both parties, although there are some circumstances in which the law overrides the terms of the lease itself: for example, a landlord has a duty in some circumstances to keep the property he has let in reasonable condition, and he cannot contract out of this duty except in rare circumstances (see below). Even where the lease does not contain *express* covenants, the law will imply some terms and conditions into the agreement between the landlord and tenant: sometimes the Court itself will perform this function, and sometimes an Act of Parliament will do so (see the Housing Act 1961,

the relevant provisions of which were recently re-enacted in the Landlord and Tenant Act 1985). This is very important in practice. A tenancy agreement may be purely oral: the landlord verbally agrees to let the property and the tenant agrees to pay rent. The agreement may never be put into writing, and the parties may not begin to consider what other rights and obligations they intend to undertake. Nevertheless the law will itself impose various terms on them, whether they are happy with them or not.

(A) The landlord's rights. The lease will frequently contain a list of covenants, many of them being imposed by the landlord upon the tenant. Typically these will relate to rent, rates, repairs, alterations and improvements, insurance, rights of entry, assignment and user.

(a) Rent. The basic right of the landlord is, of course, to charge the tenant a rent in return for exclusive possession of the property. Subject to the situations in which the rent can be controlled by the Rent Officer or Rent Tribunal (see page 83), the amount of rent will be fixed between the parties and payable at whatever times they agree. Under some leases, rent is payable in advance and under others in arrears: this is also a matter for agreement. Sometimes a landlord will also charge a 'premium' (also known as 'key-money') before allowing the tenant into possession. However, it is important to note that section 119 of the Rent Act 1977 makes it an offence for anyone to charge a premium as a condition of the grant, renewal or continuance of a protected tenancy. A person guilty under this section can be fined, and any unlawful premium can be recovered by the tenant. Section 128 of the Act provides that a sum payable in advance which is less than 1/6 of the annual rent for the property and which is intended to provide security against any potential liability of the tenant (e g damaging the furniture or property) does not count as a premium.

(b) Landlord's remedies in respect of rent. Where the tenant fails to pay his rent, the landlord has various remedies. First, he may bring a simple action (normally in the County Court) to recover it. Secondly, there is an ancient remedy known as 'levying a distress' whereby the landlord may enter upon the property and seize goods to the value of the rent owed. Today this remedy is severely curtailed: in respect of property occupied residentially, distress may only be levied

This Lease made the SIXTH day of MARCH 1986

Between HARVEY J. RAGWORT of 7 SESAME STREET

BRIDGETOWN CUMBRIA

(hereinafter called "the Lessor " which expression where the context admits includes the persons deriving title under the Lessor) of the one part and JANE PLYMSTOCK of 126A

HIGH STREET BRIDGETOWN aforesaid

(hereinafter called "the Lessee " which expression where the context admits includes the persons deriving title under the Lessee) of the other part: **Witnesses** and it is hereby declared as follows:—

1. **In** consideration of the rent hereinafter reserved and of the covenants by the Lessee hereinafter contained the Lessor hereby demise[s] unto the Lessee :

All THAT PROPERTY known as 14 THE RIDINGS

BADGERLY EDGE DERBYSHIRE

Except and reserved unto the Lessor Full right of passage and running of water and soil from all neighbouring lands and houses of the Lessor through all drains channels and sewers in and under the premises and the right to build on any neighbouring land of the Lessor notwithstanding that the erection of the buildings may interfere with the access of light or air to the property hereby demised:

To hold (except and reserved as aforesaid) unto the Lessee from the TWENTY-NINTH day of SEPTEMBER 1986 for a term of SEVEN years (determinable nevertheless as hereinafter mentioned):

Yielding and Paying therefor during the said term unto the Lessor the yearly rent of ONE THOUSAND FIVE HUNDRED pounds (subject to review as provided in clause 6 hereof) clear of all deductions (except as hereinafter mentioned) by equal quarterly payments on the usual quarter-days in every year the first of such quarterly payments to be made on the 29TH day of SEPTEMBER next and the last to be made in advance on the quarter-day immediately preceding the expiration (or determination under the notice hereinafter provided for) of the said term:

Also Yielding and Paying (by way of further rent) the amount from time to time expended by the Lessor in effecting and maintaining the insurance of the demised premises against loss or damage by fire in a sum not exceeding the full value thereof such further rent to be paid by the Lessee without any deduction on the quarter-day for payment of rent which occurs next after the expenditure by the Lessor .

2. **The** Lessee hereby covenant[s] with the Lessor as follows:—

(1) During the said term to pay the said yearly rent[s] at the times and in manner aforesaid.

(2) To pay all rates taxes charges assessments and outgoings whether parliamentary parochial or otherwise which now are or which at any time hereafter shall be assessed or imposed upon the premises or any part thereof (income tax and tithe redemption annuity only excepted).

[1]

(3) At all times during the said term at the Lessees own cost when and as often as need or occasion shall require well and substantially to repair amend renew uphold support maintain paint grain varnish paper whitewash and cleanse the premises and the drains sewers watercourses walls fences fixtures fittings and appurtenances belonging thereto.

(4) In particular to paint in a good and workmanlike manner twice over with good white lead and oil colour or treat with creosote or tar all the outside wood iron and rough-cast work of the premises (usually painted or tarred) once in every third year during the said term   And in like manner once in every seventh year of the said term to paint with two coats of good white lead and oil colour and paper with suitable papers and grain and varnish all the internal wood metal and cement work which has been or ought to be painted papered grained and varnished.

(5) At the end or other sooner determination of the said term peaceably to surrender and yield up the premises (being so well and substantially repaired amended renewed upheld supported maintained painted tarred papered grained varnished whitewashed and cleansed as aforesaid) unto the Lessor together with all fixtures which at any time during the said term shall have been affixed or shall belong to the premises (tenant's fixtures only excepted).

(6) That the Lessor or any persons authorised by the Lessor may twice or oftener in every year during the said term at all reasonable times in the daytime enter into and upon the premises to view and examine the state and condition thereof and of all defects decays or wants of reparation or amendment (which upon such view shall be found) give or leave notice in writing at or upon the premises for the Lessee to repair and amend the same.

(7) At the Lessees own expense within three months from the giving or leaving of such notice well and sufficiently to repair and amend the same accordingly.

(8) That the Lessee will permit the Lessor and persons authorised by the Lessor at all reasonable hours in the daytime to enter into and upon the demised premises for the purpose of executing alterations or repairs to the adjoining premises or for carrying out upon the demised premises such repairs (if any) as either the Lessor or the Lessee may be liable to effect hereunder or for complying with any statutory obligation imposed on the owner or occupier of the demised premises:

Provided that where the Lessee   is   liable to effect the repairs this power shall not be exercised until the Lessee has made default for thirty days after being required in writing to do the work and in that case the Lessee shall be liable on demand to make good to the Lessor the costs of effecting the repairs with interest at Ten pounds per centum per annum from the date of the demand.

(9) Not during the said term to use exercise or carry on or permit or suffer to be used exercised or carried on in or upon the premises or any part thereof any noisy or offensive trade or business whatsoever without the licence in writing of the Lessor for that purpose first had and obtained but to use the premises only as and for a private dwelling-house.

(10) Not without the consent in writing of the Lessor to make any alteration in or addition to the premises or erect any new building thereon or carry out any operation or institute or continue any use of the premises for which planning permission is required.

(11) Not to assign charge underlet or part with the possession of the premises or any part thereof without the consent in writing of the Lessor provided that such consent shall not be unreasonably withheld in the case of a responsible and desirable person.

(12) Within six months after any assignment charge or underlease of the premises or any part thereof shall have been executed or after the devolution of the said term or any derivative term to produce the disposition or evidence of the devolution to the Lessors solicitors for registration to whom a fee of three pounds shall be paid for each registration:

Provided that no registration shall be required in the case of an underlease for a term of three years or less where the underlessee takes possession.

(13) Not to do or permit to be done in or upon the demised premises or any part thereof any act or thing which may invalidate or render voidable any policies of insurance from time to time effected against loss or damage by fire of the premises or of any fixtures or chattels therein belonging to the Lessor or which may operate to increase the premiums payable in respect of any such policy.

(14) Not to do or permit to be done on the demised premises or any part thereof anything which may be or grow to be a nuisance damage inconvenience or annoyance to the Lessor or to the owners or occupiers of any adjacent premises.

[2]

(15) Not to allow any public meeting or sale by auction to be held on the premises or permit to be placed on the premises any bill signboard placard hoarding or other outward mark or show of business except such reasonable name plates or signs as the Lessor may in writing has previously approved.

(16) Within seven days of the receipt by the Lessee of any notice order or proposal made given or issued to the Lessee by a planning authority under or by virtue of any enactment relating to town and country planning to give full particulars thereof to the Lessor and without delay to take all reasonable or necessary steps to comply with any such notice or order.

(17) To permit the Lessor or the Lessors agents from time to time during the last three months before the expiration or sooner determination of the said term to affix notices upon any conspicuous parts of the premises that the same are to let or to be otherwise disposed of and also at all convenient times in the daytime (by agents or otherwise) to enter into with and show the premises to any person.

3. **Provided** that if any part of the said rents shall be in arrear for Twenty-one days (whether or not lawfully demanded) or if there shall be a breach of any of the covenants by the Lessee herein contained the Lessor may re-enter upon the premises and immediately thereupon the said term shall absolutely determine.

4. **The** Lessor hereby covenants with the Lessee as follows:—

(1) That the Lessee paying the rent hereby reserved and performing and observing all the covenants by the Lessee herein contained shall and may quietly hold and enjoy the premises during the said term without any lawful interruption by the Lessor or any person rightfully claiming through under or in trust for that party.

(2) That the Lessor will during the subsistence of the term hereby granted insure and keep insured against loss or damage by fire all buildings on the premises hereby demised to the full value thereof and will apply all insurance money in or towards reinstating or making good any of the said buildings which may be destroyed or damaged by fire.

5. **Provided** that the Lessee may at the end of the FIFTH year of the said term determine the same upon giving to or leaving at the usual or last-known place of abode in England of the Lessor or to the Lessors solicitors at least THREE months' previous notice in writing of the intention so to do and in such case the said term shall cease at the expiration of the year to which the notice relates as if the same had expired by effluxion of time notwithstanding anything herein contained to the contrary but without prejudice to any rights and remedies under any antecedent breach of covenant or condition.

6. (A) In this clause:

(1) "review date" means the date of the expiration of every THIRD year from 29 SEPTEMBER 1986

(2) "market rent" means the yearly rent which having regard to the terms hereof (other than those relating to the yearly rent) the demised premises would at the review date currently command in the open market there being disregarded any tenant's improvements fixtures or goodwill.

(B) If the machinery of review hereinafter specified is operated in respect of a review date the yearly rent payable hereunder from that review date shall be the market rent.

(C) The machinery of review shall be a written notice expressed to be in respect of a specified review date given to the other party by the party requiring the review and (failing agreement on the amount of the new rent) the fixing of the new rent by an arbitrator agreed or (failing agreement on an arbitrator) appointed on the application of either party by the President of the Royal Institution of Chartered Surveyors.

(D) Time shall not in the first place be of the essence of the machinery of review but the time scale for notice requiring a review shall be three months (so that a three months or longer notice expiring on the review date shall always be effective) and either party may before or after the review date by writing require the other to serve notice or operate any other part of the machinery of review within a reasonable time (which shall become of the essence of the contract accordingly).

(E) Whenever a new yearly rent shall be determined in accordance with this clause a memorandum thereof shall be endorsed on this lease and the counterpart thereof and signed by the parties.

In Witness whereof the parties hereto have hereunto set their hands and seals the day and year first above written.

Signed Sealed and Delivered by the said HARVEY J RAGWORT in the presence of

J. COLES
9 PICKTON STREET
BRIDGETOWN
SIGNED SEALED AND DELIVERED BY JANE PLYMSTOCK IN THE PRESENCE OF
J. COLES (as above)

Harvey J. Ragwort

(L.S.)

J. Plymstock

NOTE.—Leases should be granted by or in the name of the Estate Owner: Law of Property Act 1925, s. 8 (leases under statutory powers), s. 99 (19) (delegation to receiver), Powers of Attorney Act 1971, s. 7 (3) (under power of attorney). If granted to a tenant for life or statutory owner the lease will be a subsidiary vesting deed and must be endorsed with the requisite particulars: Settled Land Act 1925, ss. 10, 53 (2). If the lease is of registered land (whether or not in a compulsory area) it should be granted by or in the name of the registered proprietor. It should be given a Land Registry heading and the parcels should be described by reference to the title number. Where the term granted is for more than 21 years the title thereto must be registered: Land Registration Act 1925, ss. 19 (2), 22 (2); no notice of a lease is to be entered in the charges register if the term does not exceed 21 years and a rent is reserved without taking a fine: *ib*. In a compulsory area the grant of a lease for less than 40 years or the assignment of a lease having less than 40 years to run does not involve first registration of the title: *ib*., s. 123. A Particulars Produced Stamp is required where the lease, granted after August 1931, is for seven years or more: Finance Act 1931, s. 28.

[3]

87

DATED   6TH MARCH   19 86

RAGWORT

– TO –

PLYMSTOCK

Lease

of house known as   14   THE RIDINGS

BADGERLY EDGE   DERBYSHIRE

From   29TH SEPTEMBER   19 86
For Years   SEVEN

Expires   28TH SEPTEMBER   19 93

Determinable as within mentioned.

Rent £ 1500
(variable)

with the authority of the Court, and only the Court's officers actually enter the property. Even then the remedy is not very satisfactory, since some of the tenant's goods (e g those which he needs for work) cannot be taken; nor can chattels being acquired e g on hire purchase or conditional sale. The landlord's third remedy would be to 'forfeit' the lease, i e to bring it to an end. Again this must generally only be done through Court proceedings, and the tenant can stop the forfeiture proceedings by paying off any arrears plus interest. Even *after* the lease has been forfeited, the tenant can apply for relief against forfeiture (i e to have the forfeiture set aside) for up to six months after he vacates the property, provided that he can pay off the arrears. If a tenant remains in possession *after* the lease has ended and has no right to do so, the landlord can then sue for *double* the rent formerly due under the lease.

If the tenant abandons the property *before* the tenancy has come to an end (e g without having served a valid notice to quit or before the expiration of a one year fixed-term), the landlord is entitled to sue for the rent he would have recovered if the tenant was still in possession. Sometimes the landlord may decide not to bother chasing the recalcitrant tenant for his money, but theoretically he is allowed to do so.

(c) Rates. The lease will often specify who is to be responsible for paying the general and water rates. Where this issue is not agreed upon, the normal position is that the tenant as occupier is responsible for their payment rather than the landlord. However, if the tenancy is for less than three months or is a weekly one, section 58 of the General Rate Act 1967 provides that the owner of the property is liable for rates; and by section 55 of that Act general and water rates must be paid by the owner if directed to do so and if the rateable value of the property is less than £200.

(d) Repairs. It is essentially a matter for agreement between the parties as to who should assume responsibility for keeping the property in repair. In some circumstances the law imposes certain obligations upon the landlord (see page 93), and the tenant also has some responsibilities at common law (see page 90); generally, however, the parties are free to negotiate whatever terms they can. The landlord will commonly require a tenant to take responsibility for keeping the interior of the property let in reasonable repair, and may also require the tenant to agree

to keep the exterior of the building in reasonable condition as well. The tenant may of course be in a fairly weak bargaining position, but he should always give some thought to the potential burden of these repairing covenants. Not surprisingly, the landlord is likely to insist on more extensive and onerous covenants on the tenant's part the longer the duration of the lease. The wording of repairing covenants is of very great importance and should be considered very carefully in advance. If a landlord agrees to keep the structure of a building in repair and a tenant the interior, difficult questions can arise as to whether windows, doors or drains fall within the former or the latter sphere of responsibility. Difficulty may also arise as to the meaning of repair: a point may come at which a landlord is attempting to require a tenant to replace rather than merely to repair the property in question.

Even where a landlord requires the tenant to keep the property in repair, it is common for the lease to absolve the tenant from liability for deterioration caused to the property through 'fair wear and tear.' The idea of this exception is that the tenant should not be responsible for disrepair that is attributable simply to the passage of time or to the normal use of the premises in question. However, the fair wear and tear exception tends to be interpreted narrowly by the Courts. In particular, it has been held that where a property is damaged through fair wear and tear, this does not absolve the tenant from liability for *consequential* damage which the original wear and tear would not have produced.

In *Regis Property v Dudley* (1958) the House of Lords was asked to consider the meaning of a fair wear and tear clause in a case concerned with the rent payable by the tenant to the landlord. Lord Denning said:

'I have never understood that in an ordinary house, a fair wear and tear exception reduced the burden of repairs to practically nothing at all. It exempts a tenant from liability for repairs that are decorative and for remedying parts that wear or come adrift in the course of reasonable use, but it does not exempt him from anything else. If further damage is likely to flow from the wear and tear, he must do such repairs as are necessary to stop that further damage. If a slate falls off the roof through wear and tear and in consequence the roof is likely to let through the water, the tenant is not responsible for the slate coming off but he

89

ought to put in another to prevent further damage.'

Where a tenant defaults in his obligation to keep the property in reasonable repair, the landlord has two remedies which he may seek: damages to compensate him for the deterioration in the state of the premises and forfeiture to bring the lease to an end. The landlord is *not* entitled to enter the property and to carry out the repairs himself (though he may be allowed to do so where he is himself liable for repairs: see page 91); nor is he able to ask the Court for an injunction or specific performance compelling the tenant to carry out the repairs.

There are various statutory provisions limiting the landlord's remedies of damages and forfeiture. First, the Landlord and Tenant Act 1927 is important where the landlord seeks damages from the tenant. Section 18 provides that the measure of damages must not exceed the amount by which the value of the reversion (that is to say the landlord's interest in the property when the lease comes to an end) is diminished as a consequence of the breach of covenant. Furthermore the section provides that the landlord cannot recover damages at all for breach of a repairing covenant where it can be shown that the premises are to be demolished or structurally altered in such a way as to make the repairs valueless at or soon after the end of the lease.

Secondly, section 147 of the Law of Property Act 1925 may be of significance where a landlord seeks damages from, or to forfeit the lease of, a tenant for breach of an internal decorating covenant. The tenant in such an action may make an application to the Court, and the Court has power if, having regard to all the circumstances of the case (including in particular the length of the lease) it is satisfied that the landlord's notice requiring the repairs to be carried out is unreasonable, wholly or partially to relieve the lessee from liability for such repairs. However, there are exceptions to this provision: in particular a tenant cannot rely on it where he was required at the beginning of the tenancy to put the property into reasonable condition but never did so. A third provision limiting the landlord's remedies is the Leasehold Property (Repairs) Act 1938. Basically the idea of this Act is that, where a landlord is seeking damages or to forfeit a lease on the grounds of breach by a tenant of his repairing covenant, he can only proceed to do so with the express permission of the court. The court will only grant this permission in the circumstances defined in section 1 of the Act e g that, unless the premises are repaired as a matter of urgency, the value of the landlord's reversion will be substantially diminished.

(e) Alterations and improvements. At common law a tenant is under a duty not to commit what are termed 'acts of waste.' The extent of the tenant's liability varies according to the kind of tenancy he has. Where he is simply a periodic tenant (e g with a weekly or monthly tenancy) he will normally only be liable for what is known as 'voluntary waste' i e deliberate action causing damage to the property such as felling trees or dismantling all or part of the premises in question. However, a periodic tenant must act in a 'tenant-like manner' which means that he must take reasonable care of the property. In *Warren v Keen* (1953) the landlord of a property carried out various repairs necessary to make it fit for human habitation but then claimed the costs of so doing from the tenant. The Court of Appeal held that the tenant only had a duty to behave in a tenant-like manner and was not obliged to go further and carry out the sort of work the landlord had done. Lord Denning gave examples of what sort of things the tenant must do:

'He must, if going away for the winter, turn off the water and empty the boiler. He must clean the chimneys, when necessary, and also the windows. He must mend the electric light when it fuses. He must unstop the sink where it is blocked by waste.'

A tenant for a fixed term of years is under a higher duty, in that he must not commit acts of voluntary *or permissive* waste i e deterioration in the property attributable to negligence or a failure to maintain and repair. A landlord may bring an action for damages against a tenant liable in waste, the measure of damages representing the reduction in the value of the landlord's reversion. For example in *Mancetter Developments v Garmanson and Givertz* (1985) a tenant removed many fixtures from the property he had occupied but, having done so, failed to make good the damage caused as a result (e g by filling in holes). The Court of Appeal agreed that this amounted to waste, and awarded the landlord damages in excess of £1,000. However, this may not be particularly satisfactory from the landlord's point of view. A tenant may alter or improve the premises in a way which does not affect the value of the reversion or which may actually enhance it. In such as case the landlord may find at the end of the lease that he recovers the property in a physical form of which he disapproves and yet that he has no remedy in waste. It is therefore common for the landlord to insist on covenants by the tenant not to alter or improve the property. The precise ambit of such covenants will depend upon the wording used. One important point to note, however, is that they may be *absolute* (prohibiting alterations entirely) or *qualified* (prohibiting alteration without the landlord's consent). The distinction matters because, in the case of qualified covenants, section 19 of the Landlord and Tenant Act 1927 provides that if the alteration would improve the property, the landlord may not refuse his consent to the alteration unreasonably. If the tenancy is a regulated one, the Housing Act 1980 rather than the Landlord and Tenant Act 1927 applies. Sections 81 and 82 of the 1980 Act establish special rules dealing with the issue of alterations and improvements, designed so that the landlord does not act in a capricious or unreasonable way.

(f) Insurance. It is quite normal for the lease to contain a covenant dealing with insurance. Sometimes the landlord agrees to effect the insurance and the tenant to pay the premium. Alternatively the tenant may be required to take out the insurance himself, often with an insurance company stipulated by the landlord. In such cases the landlord can refuse permission to insure with an alternative insurance company without advancing any reasons. If the tenant is under an obligation to insure, he will be in breach of his covenant if the property is at any time uninsured, even if this only happens for a negligible period and even though the property is not actually harmed in any way. The landlord could then insure the property himself and recover an amount equal to the premium paid from the tenant. It is common for the insurance covenant to be coupled with an obligation that any insurance money actually received be spent on reinstating the property. Furthermore, if the property is damaged by fire, the Fires Prevention (Metropolis) Act 1774 enables the landlord to request the insurance company in question to lay out the insurance monies on reinstating the property.

(g) Rights of entry. One question often asked by tenants is whether their landlords have a right to enter the property during the term of the lease. Tenants object to what they consider to be an invasion of their privacy, while landlords tend to feel that they have a vested interest in inspecting the property to see that it is being kept in reasonable condition. The basic legal position is that a lease confers upon the tenant *exclusive possession* of the property in question, so that a landlord has no right to enter it at all. If he does so, he is a trespasser. However, if the landlord has an obligation to repair the property, then he will also be entitled to enter it in order to inspect and repair it. The lease itself may reserve such a power, but even if it does not the law will imply one, whether the landlord's repairing obligation is an express one, one that exists by implication, or one which an Act of Parliament has imposed. Of particular importance in this respect are section 32 of the Housing Act 1961 (now section 11(b) of the Landlord and Tenant Act 1985) and section 148 of the Rent Act 1977, both of which entitle the landlord to enter in connection with repairs. However, it must be noted that this right of the landlord to enter is only exercisable in order to enable him to fulfil his repairing obligations. If he actually enters with some other purpose in mind (eg to harass the tenant or to 'snoop' around the property) he would be acting outside his powers and could theoretically be sued for trespass and convicted of harassment.

(h) Assignment and sub-letting. A tenant may decide that he wishes to assign the remainder of his lease to a third party or to grant a sub-lease to someone. Whether he can do so or not depends upon the terms of the lease. If the lease is silent on this issue, then the tenant is free to assign, sub-let or part with possession of the property as he sees fit and the landlord has no control over the matter at all. In practice, however, it is much more likely that the lease will contain a covenant restraining the tenant from assigning or sub-letting. Sometimes such covenants are absolute in form, which from the tenant's point of view is highly undesirable. More likely, however, is that the covenant provides that there shall be no assignment or sub-letting without the landlord's consent. In this situation, section 19 of the Landlord and Tenant Act 1927 provides that the landlord must not *unreasonably* withhold his consent. Precisely what amounts to 'unreasonableness' in this situation it is hard to define, and the Courts tend to say that each case must be decided on its own facts. On the one hand it has been held reasonable for a landlord to withhold consent where the prospective assignee was financially unsound or would

become a protected tenant under the Rent Acts; on the other it has been held unreasonable to withhold consent simply because the landlord wanted to recover the possession of the property himself. The Race Relations Act 1976 makes it unlawful to withhold consent on grounds of colour, race, nationality or ethnic or national origins (except where the landlord and tenant are residing in the same property). Where a tenant is convinced that a landlord will react unreasonably to a request for consent to assign or sub-let, he must still go through with the process of making the request since otherwise he will be in breach of covenant.

(i) Use of property. If the lease is silent on the matter, the position as between landlord and tenant is that the tenant may use the property for whatever purpose he wishes. However it may be that neighbouring landowners can restrict the way in which the property is used if they have the benefit of any 'restrictive covenants' (see page 110); also the tenant must ensure that he does not infringe the planning laws, for example by setting up a business in property only entitled to be used residentially. This is a matter which must be sorted out with the relevant local authority. In practice most leases will restrict the use for which a tenant may use the property, and a common covenant requires that it only be used as a private dwelling house. In this situation, should the tenant break the covenant the landlord would be able to obtain an injunction ordering him to bring the breach to an end or to bring proceedings to have the lease forfeited.

(B) The tenant's rights. The fundamental right of the tenant is to enjoy exclusive possession of the property in question (subject to the limited rights of the landlord to enter in order to comply with his repairing obligations). However, the law does afford various other rights to tenants. The extent to which the tenant enjoys security of tenure and can have the amount of his rent regulated have already been considered on pages 72–84. The tenant often has various other rights, however, which the law confers upon him whatever the terms of the lease itself.

(a) Quiet enjoyment. In every relationship of landlord and tenant there is a covenant entitling the tenant to what is known as 'quiet enjoyment' of the property. Sometimes the lease contains an express covenant to this effect, but where it does not do so the law implies such a covenant

anyway. Quiet enjoyment does *not* mean that the tenant has a right to enjoy the property free from noise. The term has a more technical meaning than this, and in effect means that the landlord must abstain from acts which physically interfere with the tenant's occupation of the property. The landlord is liable not only for acts committed by himself, but also for lawful acts by third parties deriving title from him (e g a tenant of neighbouring property); also the landlord is liable for acts interfering with the tenant's use of his property, whether those acts are committed on the property itself or not. The significance of the covenant for quiet enjoyment can be better understood with the benefit of a few examples. In *Owen v Gadd* (1956) the tenant recovered damages for loss of custom when his landlord erected scaffolding in front of his shop which barred access to his shop and obscured the windows. This was an example of the acts complained of taking place off the tenant's property. The covenant may also be invoked by the tenant where the landlord behaves in an intolerable way towards the tenant (perhaps with the intention of trying to get him to leave). For example in *Kenny v Preen* (1962) the tenant successfully sued the landlord who had been threatening him and persistently shouting and banging on the front door. In the course of his judgment, Lord Justice Pearson said:

'There was a deliberate and persistent attempt by the landlord to drive the tenant out of her possession of the premises by persecution and intimidation, and [the] intimidation included threats of physical eviction of the tenant and removal of her belongings. In my view that course of conduct by the landlord seriously interfered with the tenant's proper freedom of action in exercising her rights of possession, and tended to deprive her of the full benefit of it, and was an invasion of her rights as tenant to remain in possession undisturbed and so in itself would constitute a breach of the covenant for quiet enjoyment . . .'

In *Perera v Vandiyar* (1953) a landlord who cut off the tenant's gas and electricity supplies was found liable for breach of contract. It is very important to bear in mind that a landlord who behaves in this sort of way with a view to obtaining possession of the property may also be guilty of a criminal offence under the Protection from Eviction Act 1977 (see page 81). It may also be that the landlord is liable in trespass and/or nuisance, in which case the Court has power to award exemplary damages (see page 81). Under the covenant for quiet enjoyment the Court can only award the tenant damages to compensate him for any loss actually suffered.

(b) Non-derogation from grant. There is a general principle of law that, colloquially expressed, requires that a person must not take away with one hand what he has given with the other. In the context of landlord and tenant this means that a landlord cannot let property to a tenant and then commit acts which render it substantially less fit for the purpose for which it was let. To be liable, the landlord must have known at the time of the letting what the tenant's purposes in relation to the property were. In practice, many acts which amount to a derogation from grant will also be actionable by the tenant under the covenant for quiet enjoyment or as a nuisance, but there are some situations where the tenant can rely only on this head of liability. For example in *Aldin v Latimer Clark Muirhead & Co* (1894) land was leased to a timber merchant for the purposes of his business, and the landlord wished to build on his adjoining land in a way which would interrupt the flow of air to the sheds where the timber was dried. It was held that this amounted to a derogation from the landlord's grant, and that the tenant was able to claim damages from his landlord for the harm done to his business as a result.

(c) Warranties as to fitness. Generally speaking, a tenant who takes a lease must take the property as he finds it. It is for him to inspect the property and to satisfy himself that it is suitable for his purpose and in reasonable condition. The law's maxim is *caveat emptor* – let the buyer beware – and this is just as applicable in dealings between landlord and tenant as it is elsewhere in the law. Thus the landlord is not normally required to bring the tenant's attention to defects in the property or under a duty to ensure that it is in a habitable condition. However, there are some exceptions to this general rule. First, where a landlord lets a *furnished* house, he impliedly undertakes that it is fit for human habitation when let. If it transpires that this is not the case (e g because the drains are a health hazard or because the house is infested with bugs) the tenant could repudiate the tenancy and claim damages for any loss suffered. However this liability of the landlord only relates to the condition of the property *at the commencement of the tenancy*: it does not mean that the landlord has a *continuing* duty to keep the property habitable.

Secondly, section 6 of the Housing Act 1957 (recently re-enacted as section 8 of the Landlord and Tenant Act 1985) provides that, where a house is let at a very low rent, there is an implied condition by the landlord that the house is fit for human habitation at the beginning of the tenancy and an implied undertaking that he will keep it in this condition throughout the tenancy. The rent limits are so low however (less than £80 per annum in London and £52 elsewhere) that this Act will not affect the average residential tenant. On the other hand, it may be invoked by tenants with long leases (say 99 years) where the annual rent payable is only nominal.

Thirdly, a landlord who builds an unfurnished property to his own specification may be liable to tenants or their visitors for injury caused by dangerous defects in the property attributable to his own negligence. For example in *Rimmer v Liverpool City Council* (1983) the local authority had designed and built many blocks of flats. In the flats there were internal walls with glass panels quite close to the lounge door. The plaintiff complained to the authority that the arrangement was dangerous as he or his children could easily fall against the panel. The authority replied that the panel was a standard feature and refused to do anything about it. Later the plaintiff fell over some toys of his children and suffered severe injuries from smashing through the glass. The Court of Appeal held that he was entitled to damages, since the local authority, when designing the flats, owed a duty to prospective tenants to see that the property was reasonably safe. In fact it was not safe, and it was irrelevant that the tenant himself knew of the danger presented by the panel.

(d) Repairs. One of the most important issues of all when a tenant takes a lease of a property is the issue of repairs. Who is responsible for looking after the property, making sure, for example, that the roof does not leak and that it is kept in reasonable decorative repair? The issue is a complex one and gives rise to many disputes in practice. It is of course desirable that the parties should expressly allocate their respective repairing obligations between themselves in the original lease in the hope that when problems occur they can be easily resolved. It is quite common for the lease to state that the tenant is to keep the interior of the property in repair and the landlord the

exterior (or the 'structure' or 'fabric' of the building). In certain situations the law imposes repairing obligations on the landlord from which he cannot (normally) escape.

First, as mentioned on page 93, the Housing Act 1957 (now the Landlord and Tenant Act 1985) requires the landlord to keep properties let at a low rent fit for habitation.

Secondly, where a landlord lets a number of flats within a single building to different tenants and the lease is silent as to maintenance and upkeep of the common parts of the building, the Courts may well imply an obligation on the part of the landlord to take responsibility for them. In *Liverpool City Council v Irwin* (1976) the question arose as to who should keep in repair the lifts, staircases, rubbish chutes and passages in a 15 storey tower block owned by the local authority. The 'conditions of tenancy' said nothing about the matter. The House of Lords held that, this being so, the obligation to maintain and repair rested with the landlord, and that the same would be true of a landlord in the private sector. The duty was to keep the common parts in 'reasonable repair.'

Thirdly, the Housing Act 1961 (recently re-enacted in the Landlord and Tenant Act 1985) imposes very important obligations on landlords who grant leases of dwelling-houses for less than seven years. The significance of this piece of legislation cannot be overstated. Section 11 of the 1985 Act implies a covenant by a landlord under such a lease (i) to keep in repair the structure and exterior (including drains, gutters and external pipes) and (ii) to keep in repair and proper working order the installations in the house (a) for the supply of water, gas and electricity and for sanitation (including basins, sinks, baths and sanitary conveniences but not other fixtures, fittings and appliances for making use of water, gas and electricity) and (b) for space heating or heating water. Section 12 of the 1985 Act goes on to provide that it is impossible for the landlord to contract out of these provisions, except to the extent that the County Court considers reasonable. In other words, then, a tenant should not be deterred from asserting his rights under this Act against his landlord simply because a clause in the lease absolves the landlord from liability for repairs or imposes repairing obligations of the type described above upon the tenant. It's important to bear in mind that a tenant has a duty to behave in a 'tenant-like manner' (see page 90). To the extent that disrepair is attributable to the

ble to the tenant's failure to behave in such a way, the landlord will not be liable under the Act.

It is also important to realise that the Act only requires the landlord to *repair and maintain*. In *Quick v Taff-Ely Borough Council* (1985) the local authority let a house to a tenant on a weekly basis. The house was defective in design terms: in particular there was very bad condensation and the tenant's bedding, clothes and other fabrics became mildewed each winter, when the house became virtually uninhabitable. The plaintiff brought an action under section 32 of the Housing Act 1961 (now section 11 of the 1985 Act) and the County Court found in his favour and awarded him damages. The Court of Appeal reversed the decision: the problem was not the defendant's failure to *repair* and *maintain* the building and so the Housing Act did not apply.

When the landlord is under a duty to repair, whether by the terms of the lease itself or because of some implied or statutory covenant, it is a general rule that he will only be liable to the extent that he has notice that the property is in disrepair. It is not necessary that the landlord receives notice from the tenant himself (e g he may find out about the disrepair from a neighbour or a local authority) and in some cases he may even be liable where the Court considers that he *ought* to have known about it (e g because he was in a better position to find out the true position than the tenant). But the guiding principle as far as the tenant is concerned is that he should *always* notify the landlord of any relevant disrepair, preferably in writing and keeping a copy of the letter. Such a letter should be clear and preferably sent by recorded delivery.

Where the landlord is under a repairing obligation, he is entitled to enter the property to inspect and to carry out repairs, although this right must only be exercised for legitimate purposes (see page 51).

(C) Tenant's remedies. Where a landlord is in breach of a repairing covenant, the tenant has various remedies available. The first is to bring an action against the landlord for damages. Suppose that the roof of a house is leaking: the tenant could pay a builder to come and repair the roof and seek reimbursement from the landlord. He would also be able to recover damages for any consequential loss suffered as a result of the landlord's breach, e g where the rain coming through the roof also damages the wallpaper and carpet in the house. The tenant should be able to recover for any consequential damage provided that it is not too 'remote,' that is to say not a reasonably foreseeable consequence of the landlord's breach.

The right to bring an action for damages is often of fairly limited use to a tenant. A tenant may simply be unable to pay a builder to do the work now with a view to bringing an action for damages later because of liquidity problems. Also it may be that the tenant does not have access to the part of the property which has fallen into disrepair e g where the roof which is leaking can only be approached through another tenant's or even the landlord's property. However, other remedies may be available.

(a) Withholding rent. Where a landlord is in breach of a repairing covenant, a tenant is entitled in some circumstances to withhold payment of rent. He can do this where the landlord has been notified of the disrepair and has been given an opportunity to put matters right. If he fails to do so, the tenant is entitled to do the work himself or to instruct someone else to do so and to deduct his expenditure from his payments of rent. There is an element of risk involved in doing this, however, because if a Court were subsequently to decide that the landlord had been given insufficient notice, for example, then the tenant would not be entitled to withhold his rent and would now be in arrears. This in turn might incite the landlord into bringing an action, perhaps not just for the arrears but also for possession. A tenant considering taking this course of action should tread carefully, therefore, and act as reasonably as possible (e g in giving the landlord ample notice, getting two or three estimates for the cost of the repairs etc). Another drawback with this 'self-help' remedy is that the cost of the repairs may be considerably greater than, say, a monthly rent, so that a tenant may only be able to recoup himself over a considerable period of time.

(b) Specific performance. A very useful remedy available to a tenant is to ask the Court to make an order of specific performance, compelling the landlord to carry out his repairing obligations. At one time this remedy could only be granted where the repairs had to be carried out elsewhere than on the tenant's property: for example in *Jeune v Queens Cross Properties Ltd* (1974) the landlord was ordered to reinstate a collapsed balcony to which the tenant did not have access, and in *Francis v Cowlcliffe Ltd* (1976) the landlord was ordered to repair the lifts in a block of flats.

However, section 125 of the Housing Act 1974 (recently re-enacted as section 17 of the Landlord and Tenant Act 1985) now provides that the courts have a general power to grant specific performance requiring a landlord to perform his repairing obligations, whether or not the repairs have to be carried out in the tenant's property.

(c) Local authorities. In some circumstances, it may be more sensible for a tenant to approach his local authority in the hope that it will take action to compel the landlord to carry out necessary repairs. One particular advantage of this, of course, is that the tenant will not then have to incur the risk and cost of instituting Court proceedings. Another is that the landlord may be more inclined to take the necessary action when faced with the power of a local authority rather than with an individual tenant. The local authority has important powers under the Public Health Act 1936 and under the various Housing Acts. Much of the law in this area is now consolidated in the Housing Act 1985. Under the Public Health Act the local authority can take proceedings against a landlord where there is what is known as a 'statutory nuisance.' This means either that the property in question is in such a state that it is a risk to the tenant's health or that there is a defect in the common parts of the building in question which is causing harm in the tenant's property. The local authority can also take action under this Act if the lavatories in a property are insufficient in number or in an unsatisfactory state or if there is a vermin problem or insufficient food storage space.

Under the Housing Acts, the local authority can take action where a property is unfit for human habitation, where it is in serious disrepair, where there are conditions which might interfere with a tenant's personal comfort and where property is in multiple occupation. Local authorities often take action on the first ground mentioned above. In deciding whether a property is unfit for human habitation the authority must ask whether it is so defective in relation to various matters (e g repairs, stability, freedom from damp, ventilation, sanitary arrangements etc) that it is not reasonably suitable for occupation. If it is possible that the property could be made fit for human habitation, the local authority will serve a 'repairs notice' on the landlord requiring him to carry out the necessary work. Otherwise a 'closing order' may be made, requiring that the property should no longer be used for human habitation. In this case, however, the tenant will be rehoused by the local authority and given compensation for being required to move.

In the case of houses in multiple occupation, the local authority has powers enabling it to prevent serious overcrowding of houses and to ensure that the property is reasonably suitable for the number of people occupying it (e g in terms of fire escapes, lighting, ventilation, water etc). These powers are extensive, and tenants concerned about overcrowding and poor facilities would be well advised to discuss the issue with their local authority.

(d) Third parties. Where a landlord is in breach of his repairing covenant, it will normally be the tenant who wishes to take action to make him comply with his obligations. It is sometimes the case, however, that a third party (e g a relative of the tenant or people visiting his property) may wish to bring a claim against the landlord. For example the landlord may fail to repair the bannisters on a staircase and a visitor to the property may slip and fall and suffer injury as a result. It was at one time the law that third parties had no claim against a landlord for injury resulting from a breach of his repairing obligations. This was changed however by the Defective Premises Act 1972. It provides that, where a landlord *either* is under an obligation to a tenant (whether imposed by statute or not) for the maintenance or repair of the property *or* is or can become entitled to enter the premises to maintain or repair them, then he owes a duty to *all persons* who might reasonably be expected to be affected by defects in the premises to take reasonable care to see that they and their property are reasonably safe from injury or damage. The landlord can only be liable under this section where he knows or ought to have known of the defect in the property which required repair. It is impossible for the landlord to contract out of this liability.

3. HOUSING ASSOCIATION TENANCIES

Housing associations play an important part in the provision of rented accommodation. They come in a variety of forms and are in a slightly strange position in that they do not belong entirely either to the private or the public sector; instead they rather tend to straddle the two. Some housing associations are of ancient origin,

having traditionally provided accommodation for people unsuccessfully seeking council housing. Often such associations have helped the sorts of people who come low down on a local authority's 'points' system. But there are also many modern associations, established with the purpose, for example, of converting existing properties or building new ones, which then grant leases to tenants on a non-profit making basis. The Housing Corporation is an important body with a central role in the development of the housing association movement. It has many powers – e g to borrow and lend money and to acquire land for development – and has acquired considerable expertise in this field of housing. Housing associations which register with it become eligible for privileges, including, most importantly of all, substantial loans.

There are two particular issues which need to be considered as far as housing associations are concerned: the first is whether tenants of housing associations enjoy security of tenure and the second is whether the rents charged by housing associations can be regulated. For these purposes a housing association is defined in section 189 of the Housing Act 1957 (now re-enacted as section 1 of the Housing Association Act 1985) as a society, body of trustees or company established for the purpose of, or amongst whose objects or powers are included those of, constructing, improving or managing or facilitating or encouraging the construction or improvement of, houses and which does not trade for profit.

(i) Security of Tenure

Until 1980, tenants of housing associations did not enjoy security of tenure at all. This was because the Rent Act 1977, which granted security of tenure to many tenants in the private sector (see page 72), excluded lettings created by housing associations registered with the Housing Corporation, designated by the Secretary of State, or registered under the Industrial and Provident Societies Act 1965. Lettings by the Housing Corporation itself were also outside the Rent Act system. However, in 1980 Parliament extended the security of tenure system from the private to the public sector and at the same time afforded protection to tenants of housing associations and the Housing Corporation. The relevant provisions are now contained in the Housing Act 1985 and are different in some respects from those originally introduced in 1980. They will be explained in more detail in the section on council housing (see page 97), but essentially the nature of the tenant's protection is as follows. The tenant of a housing association has what is termed a 'secure' tenancy. It can *only* be terminated by a Court order. A landlord seeking such an order must serve a notice on the tenant in the prescribed form. The notice must state the ground or grounds for possession on which the landlord is relying as well as the reasons why the landlord is relying on them. The Court can only make an order if it is satisfied that one or more of these grounds for possession exist, and even then there are further limitations. In the case of grounds 1–8 the Court must also be satisfied that it would be reasonable to make an order; in the case of grounds 9–11 it must be satisfied that there is reasonable alternative accommodation available (this term is defined in Part IV of Schedule 2 of the 1985 Act); and in the case of grounds 12–16 it must be satisfied on both these points. Briefly the grounds are as follows:

Ground 1: the tenant has failed to pay his rent or is in breach of covenant;

Ground 2: the tenant has been guilty of nuisance, annoyance etc;

Ground 3: the condition of the property has deteriorated because of the tenant's neglect;

Ground 4: the furniture has deteriorated;

Ground 5: the tenant obtained the tenancy by deceit;

Ground 6: the tenant was party to an exchange of council houses and money changed hands when this happened;

Ground 7: the property was let to the tenant in conjunction with his employment and his subsequent conduct in some way makes it reasonable for the landlord to remove him;

Ground 8: the property was let to the tenant while repairs were carried out to his real home;

Ground 9: the property is overcrowded;

Ground 10: the landlord intends to demolish or reconstruct the property;

Ground 11: the tenant's presence in the property conflicts with the objects of the landlord, it being a housing charity;

Grounds 12–15: the property is particularly suitable for the needs of an incoming tenant and the landlord requires it for that person;

Ground 16: the property is larger than is needed for the successor of a secure tenant.

Obviously these provisions are of great importance to tenants of housing associations; they apply to tenancies created both *before* and after the Housing Act 1980. It is also important to note that, in general, a secure tenancy can be transmitted on death to a successor. Only one such succession is provided for. To qualify as a successor, the person in question must have occupied the dwelling-house as his only or principal house at the time of the secure tenant's death and be either the tenant's spouse or another member of the tenant's family residing with the tenant throughout the twelve months ending with the tenant's death.

(ii) Rent Regulation

Tenants of housing associations do benefit from rent regulation. The relevant provisions are much the same as those that obtain in the case of private sector regulated tenancies (page 81). The relevant legislation is now contained in Part VI of the Rent Act 1977. There is a special part of the rent register kept by local authorities in which fair rents may be registered in respect of housing association tenancies. Tenants and/or the housing association may apply to the Rent Officer for the registration of a fair rent, and he will be guided by the criteria already discussed in the context of private sector tenancies (page 82). If the rent payable under the tenancy exceeds the rent fixed by the Rent Officer, the excess is irrecoverable from the tenant. If the rent fixed exceeds the contractual rent, the former is recoverable, except that there are rules which require that the increase be brought into effect gradually (this is known as 'phasing'). Even if there is no fair rent registered, section 88 of the Rent Act 1977 strictly controls the extent to which the rent may be increased by the housing association: the effect of section 88 is to encourage the use of the fair rent procedure. If any problems occur as to the relevant rent limits in respect of housing association tenancies, the County Court has a general jurisdiction under section 96 of the Rent Act 1977 to resolve disputes.

4. COUNCIL HOUSING

Very many tenants live in properties owned by local authorities. Until relatively recently there was very little statutory law controlling the relationship of landlords and tenants in the public sector. The basic position was that the respective rights and duties of the parties were those laid down in the tenancy agreement itself which would deal with such issues as rent, rent increases, the duration of the lease and repairs.

Obviously local authorities were in a much stronger bargaining position than their tenants, and although many authorities were 'good' landlords, there was much dissatisfaction about the extent of their powers over their tenants. It was even possible for a local authority to evict one of its tenants who had not misbehaved in any way and without giving any reasons for the dismissal. The Housing Act 1961, which imposed certain repairing obligations on landlords, did apply both to public and private sector tenancies. Apart from that, it was not until the Housing Act 1980 that Parliament took action to confer substantial rights on council house tenants. This Act (and subsequent legislation) have radically altered their position. We shall look at four particular issues, security of tenure, rent regulation, the rights and obligations of the parties and the council tenant's right to buy his house.

(i) Security of Tenure

The Housing Act 1980 conferred security of tenure upon council tenants analogous to that already enjoyed by many tenants in the private sector. The relevant legislation is now the Housing Act 1985. Protection is given to 'secure tenants.' A secure tenant is a tenant of a local authority (and various other similar institutions such as the Commission for the New Towns and development corporations) who has a tenancy of a property as a separate dwelling and who occupies that dwelling as his only or principal residence. There is an important provision in section 79(3) of the 1985 Act which states that the protection extends not only to tenants in the technical sense but also to licensees; this avoids the lease-licence problem which arises in the case of private sector tenancies (page 71). Tenancies which came into existence *before* the Housing Act are just as protected as those created after it.

There are a number of exceptions to the definition of secure tenancies given in the Act. They are as follows: (a) long tenancies (i e for more than 21 years); (b) service tenancies; (c) tenancies of dwellings on land acquired for development; (d) tenancies or accommodation used for homeless persons; (e) tenancies or accommodation provided on a temporary basis for people seeking employment; (f) certain short-term tenancies; (g) tenancies of temporary accommodation while repair works are being carried out; (h) tenancies of agricultural holdings; (i) tenancies of public houses; (j) student lettings; (k) business tenancies; (l) tenancies of almshouses.

It is impossible for a secure tenancy to be brought to an end except by Court order. The Housing Act 1980 established a special regime whereby the local authority wishing to remove a tenant must serve a notice on him in the form prescribed by the Secretary of State, informing him of the ground or grounds on which possession is sought and explaining why the landlord is relying on those grounds. The relevant Act is now the Housing Act 1985. It sets out 16 grounds on which possession may be claimed; however, even if the Court is satisfied that one or more of the grounds is established, there are further limitations upon its power to make a possession order. In the case of grounds 1–8 it may only make an order if it is also satisfied in all the circumstances that it would be reasonable to do so. In the case of grounds 9–11 it may only make an order if it is satisfied that there is reasonable alternative accommodation available for the tenant. In the case of grounds 12–16 the Court must be satisfied upon both of these issues. To qualify as suitable alternative accommodation, two tests have to be satisfied. First, it must be let as a separate dwelling under a secure or protected tenancy (i e the tenant must continue to enjoy security of tenure). Secondly, the accommodation must be suitable to the personal needs of the tenant and his family. For these purposes, various issues must be considered by the Court e g the proximity of the alternative property to the tenant's place of work or to other members of his family if their proximity is essential to his well-being. The 16 grounds for possession are as follows:

Ground 1: the rent lawfully due under the tenancy has not been paid or the tenant is in breach of other obligations under the tenancy agreement;

Ground 2: the tenant or someone else living in the property is guilty of conduct which is a nuisance or annoyance to neighbours or has been convicted of using it for illegal or immoral purposes;

Ground 3: the condition of the property has deteriorated as a result of acts of waste by, or the neglect or default of, the tenant or anyone else living in the property. If a lodger or sub-tenant commits the acts of waste, this ground is only available if the council tenant has failed to take action to remove that person;

Ground 4: the condition of furniture included in the tenancy has deteriorated because of ill-treatment by the tenant or someone else living in the property. In the latter situation the same proviso exists as in ground 3;

Ground 5: the tenancy was granted to a tenant who induced the local authority to do so by making a false statement knowingly or recklessly;

Ground 6: the tenant was party to an exchange of council houses and money changed hands when this happened;

Ground 7: the property was let to the tenant in conjunction with his employment and his subsequent conduct makes it reasonable for the landlord to remove him;

Ground 8: the property was made available to the tenant while improvements were being carried out on his previous house;

Ground 9: the property is overcrowded (overcrowding for these purposes is defined in Part X of the Housing Act 1985);

Ground 10: the landlord intends within a reasonable time of obtaining possession to demolish or reconstruct the building and cannot do so without obtaining possession of it;

Ground 11: (this ground relates to tenancies by housing charities and is inapplicable in the case of council tenants);

Grounds 12–15: the property is particularly suitable for the needs of defined categories of tenants (e g employees, the disabled or other people with special needs) and the landlord requires the property for such people;

Ground 16: the accommodation in the dwelling is more extensive than is reasonably required by the tenant, and the current tenant is a tenant by succession (see below).

Succession. Apart from the fact that a local authority can only terminate a secure tenancy by taking Court proceedings and where one of the grounds just described exists, the Housing Act also provides a statutory right of succession to members of a deceased secure tenant's family. Only one statutory right of succession exists, however (although there is nothing to prevent a local authority granting a *fresh* tenancy to later successors). In order to succeed to a secure tenancy, the person in question must have occupied the property in question as his or her only or principal house and must be either the secure tenant's husband or wife or another member of the secure tenant's family who has lived with the secure tenant throughout the twelve months immediately preceding the secure tenant's death. Various people may qualify as members of the secure tenant's family including so called 'common-law' husbands and wives, parents, grandparents, children, grandchildren, brothers, sisters, uncles, aunts, nephews and nieces.

(ii) Rent Regulation

Whereas most private sector tenants and the tenants of housing associations enjoy the benefit of rent regulation under the Rent Acts, there is no statutory control over the rents chargeable by local authorities. Section 24 of the Housing Act 1985 provides that local authorities may make 'such reasonable charges for the tenancy or occupation as they may determine.' They also have a duty from time to time to review rents and to make such changes of rents generally or of particular rents as circumstances may require. Various tenants have brought actions in the Courts complaining that their rents are unfair, but none of these actions has ever been successful and, given the breadth of the discretion conferred upon such authorities, it is highly unlikely that any such action will succeed. In recent years the tendency has been for central government to bring pressure to bear on local authorities to *increase* their council house rents, and in this respect it has been to a large extent successful.

(iii) Rights and Obligations of the Parties

Generally speaking the rights and obligations of the local authority and the tenant are contained in their tenancy agreement. Until recently the only important statute regulating their relationship was the Housing Act 1961 which imposed a duty on the landlord to keep in repair (a) the structure and exterior of the property (including drains, gutters and external pipes) and (b) the installations in the dwelling-house (i) for the supply of water, gas and electricity and for sanitation (including basins, sinks, baths and sanitary conveniences but not fixtures, fittings and appliances for making use of water, gas or electricity) and (ii) for space heating or heating water. This provision, which is now contained in the Landlord and Tenant Act 1985, applies equally to public and private sector housing. The authority will only be liable for breach of this covenant if it has notice of the disrepair in question. The Act permits the authority to enter the property at reasonable times of the day to view the condition of the premises and their state of repair, but it must give at least 24 hours notice of its intention of doing so.

Apart from this statute and the covenants normally implied in a lease by the landlord not to interfere with the tenant's quiet enjoyment of the property and not to derogate from his grant, the council tenant had no rights against his landlord other than those set out in the tenancy agreement. This caused much dissatisfaction, and there was a widespread feeling that a greater measure of protection ought to be given to such people. The Housing Act 1980 introduced important changes in the law. Apart from conferring security of tenure upon council tenants (see page 98), it also introduced what has become known as 'The Tenants' Charter' setting out a series of rights which they now enjoy. The relevant provisions are now contained in Part IV of the Housing Act 1985. It is impossible for the local authority to contract out of these provisions. The tenant's rights under the charter are as follows:

(a) Every secure tenant may allow anyone to reside in his property as a lodger.

(b) Every secure tenant has the right to sub-let part of his property to a sub-tenant. However, this can only be done with the written consent of the local authority; the authority is not allowed to withhold its consent unreasonably: if it does so, consent will be deemed to have been given. Where the authority does withhold consent, the onus is on it to prove that it acted reasonably.

(c) Secure tenants must not make any improvements to the property without the consent of the local authority; however, the local authority must not withhold its consent unreasonably, and, if it does so, consent will be deemed to have been given. Two important further provisions should be noted. First, where the authority gives its consent to the improvement and it materially adds to the value of the property, it has *power* (but not a duty i e the matter is discretionary) to reimburse the tenant at or after the end of the tenancy such sum of money in respect of the improvement as it considers appropriate. Secondly, the Housing Act provides that the local authority is not permitted to increase the rent on the property because of improvements made to it at the tenant's own cost. However, the tenant would be liable for any increase in *rates* attributable to the improvement.

(d) Secure tenants are to be given the right to carry out repairs for which their local authority is liable (either expressly under the lease or by virtue of the Landlord and Tenant Act 1985) and to recoup this cost from the authority. This provision was added to the Housing Act 1980 by the Housing and Building Control Act 1984 and is now contained in section 96 of the Housing Act 1985. This new system will not come into effect until the Secretary of State for the Environment has issued regulations as to how it should be operated. Once in effect, it will overcome the dissatisfaction often felt by tenants who consider that local authorities either delay unduly in carrying out repairs or execute repairs of poor quality.

(e) All secure tenants have a right to exchange their homes with other secure tenants. The consent of the local authority (or both authorities if the tenants are from different parts of the country) is needed, but consent can only be refused on certain specified grounds e g that the authority has already begun possession proceedings against one of the tenants on one of the grounds in the Housing Act (see page 98) or that the exchange would mean that one of the tenants would end up with substantially more accommodation than he needs for himself and his family. It is not permissible to take a lump sum payment when exchanging council houses: the local authority would be allowed to take possession proceedings against a tenant receiving such a sum.

(f) Secure tenants now have important rights to obtain information from their local authority. Each authority has a duty to publish information about its tenancies and in particular about:
    (i) the express terms of its secure tenancies
    (ii) the relevant provisions of the Housing Act 1985 dealing with tenants' rights to buy and with tenants' repairs and improvements and
    (iii) the authority's responsibilities under the Housing Act 1985. This information must be kept up to date so far as is reasonably practicable, and a copy of it must be supplied to each secure tenant. Authorities must also publish details of their procedures for allocating council houses and permitting transfers.

(g) Secure tenants also now have a right to be consulted by their local authority on housing management issues, and to have their views taken into account before the authority makes important decisions that would affect them.

(h) If a local authority intends to vary the terms of a secure tenancy (e g by increasing rents) there is a special statutory procedure which must be followed before the variation can be brought into effect. The procedure is designed to ensure that the tenant has adequate notice of the proposed variation together with an opportunity to make representations to the authority before the variation is actually brought into effect.

(iv) The Right to Buy

The Housing Act 1980 also introduced the right of a council tenant to buy his home together with a right to assistance with the financial side of the acquisition. The relevant law is now contained in Part V of the Housing Act 1985. A tenant of a local authority has a right to buy his home provided that:

(a) he is not an undischarged bankrupt;
(b) he has not had a possession order made against him;
(c) he is not in arrears with his rent;
(d) he has been a tenant of a public sector landlord for at least two years. The period was three years until the Housing Building and Control Act 1984. It is not necessary that this period of two years should have been spent in the same property or as a tenant of the same landlord. Time spent in the property by a tenant's spouse, ex-spouse or deceased spouse can count towards the two year period. When a secure tenancy is vested in two people jointly, the right to buy belongs to them jointly. If the tenant has a council house, he is entitled to buy the freehold of it (provided that the authority is itself the freehold owner: if not the tenant is entitled to a long lease). Where the tenant occupies a council flat, he can call for a long lease of the property.

(A) Procedure. A tenant wishing to purchase his home must serve a notice on the authority to which the authority must reply within four weeks either admitting the tenant's right or denying it, with reasons. Once the question of the tenant's right to buy has been sorted out, the authority must, as soon as practicable thereafter, serve a notice on the tenant dealing with the purchase price, the terms that must be inserted in the conveyance of the freehold or grant of the leasehold and the entitlement to financial assistance.

(B) Purchase price. The Housing Act 1985 contains important provisions whereby the price the council tenant must pay for his property must be calculated. Basically the price payable is the value of the property at the time the tenant decides to exercise his right to buy less any discount to which he is entitled. The value of the property for these purposes means its open market value calculated as though it could be sold with vacant possession. In the event of a dispute between the parties, it has to be resolved by the District Valuer. The discount to which the tenant is entitled is calculated by reference to the period for which he or his spouse (or deceased spouse) has been a secure tenant, and has occupied the property as his or her principal home. If the period to be taken into account for these purposes is less than four years, the minimum discount available is 32% of the purchase price. If the relevant period is more than four years, the available discount increases by 1% for each complete year by which the period exceeds two years. The maximum discount available is 60%. (Note that the minimum and maximum discount figures in the Housing Act 1980 were altered by section 7 of the Housing and Building Control Act 1984; the relevant provision is now section 129 of the Housing Act 1985.) There are two further limitations upon the amount of discount to which the tenant is entitled. The Secretary of State has laid down that no discount may exceed £25,000: Housing (Right to Buy) (Maximum Discount) Order 1980; and section 131 of the Housing Act 1985 provides that the discount may not be so large that the tenant ends up paying less than it cost the local authority to build or improve the property, provided that it incurred this expenditure since 31 March 1974.

In certain circumstances the right to a discount may be reduced or even lost altogether. If the secure tenant has already had the benefit of a discount in the past, his entitlement to a further discount is reduced as a result (section 130 of the Housing Act 1985). Furthermore, a tenant who buys with the benefit of a discount but then resells within five years is liable to repay some or all of the discount received. The sum repayable is

101

the amount of the discount less 20% for each complete year after the original sale that the tenant remained in the property.

Some disposals (e g from a husband to wife on divorce) fall outside the provisions for repaying discounts.

(C) The right to a mortgage. A person who has the right to buy his council house also has the right to obtain a mortgage to finance the purchase from the local authority (although there is nothing to prevent him arranging a loan privately should he prefer to do so). Notice must be served on the local authority within a prescribed time limit (which may be extended in some cases) should the tenant wish to receive a loan. The authority must then send the tenant a notice stating how much it is prepared to lend, how it arrived at that figure and what terms any mortgage deed will have to contain. The maximum amount of the loan will be the aggregate of (a) the purchase price of the house (b) the costs (up to £50) incurred by the tenant in taking out the mortgage and (c) expenses such as legal and surveyor's costs paid for by the authority. However, notwithstanding this, the amount available to the tenant will be limited according to his income. Special rules have been laid down in the Housing (Right to Buy) (Mortgage Limit) Regulations 1980. The Housing Act also lays down rules whereby the interest rate for local authority mortgages must be calculated.

(D) Completion. Once a secure tenant has indicated his desire to purchase his home, the law requires the authority to proceed with a minimum of delay. There does not have to be a formal exchange of contracts as in the normal case of buying and selling a house. Once completion has taken place, title to the property must be registered at HM Land Registry. The local authority has to provide the secure tenant with a certificate which should make it a simple matter for him to register his title. In some situations the tenant on completion will receive the freehold to the property and in others a long lease (see page 101). Whether he receives the freehold or a leasehold interest, the legal document which the local authority executes must contain certain terms e g a covenant by the tenant to repay some or all of his discount should he resell, rights of way necessary for the tenant to enjoy the property fully and a promise to indemnify the local authority should it be sued for breach of a restrictive covenant

taken for the benefit of other property in the area of the secure tenant's home.

(E) Housing Defects Act 1984. This Act was passed to deal with the problem of secure tenants purchasing their homes and subsequently discovering that their value is substantially less than was originally thought owing to some defect in the construction or design of the property in question. The relevant law is now contained in Part XVI of the Housing Act 1985. In such cases, the Act confers two possible remedies on the tenant: either the right to receive a reinstatement grant from the authority, i e a grant towards reinstating the property and remedying the defect or the right to have the local authority repurchase the property in question. In order for the Act to apply, the Secretary of State or local authority must firstly have designated the particular type of property as one which should qualify for assistance. The first designation under the Act was made in November 1984 and related to 22 types of prefabricated houses. Copies of the designations made can be obtained from HM Stationery Office. Any designation made must also state the period within which any claim under the Act must be made. The November 1984 designation requires claims to be made within ten years. Section 527 of the 1985 Act defines the people eligible to benefit from its provisions: essentially the answer to this is secure tenants who purchased their house from the local authority (as opposed to *subsequent* purchasers from the original council tenant). Anyone wishing to make a claim under the Act must make a written application to the local authority (there is no particular form in which this must be done) within the period laid down in the designation. The authority must then reply, indicating whether or not it accepts the claim and whether or not the case is one for a reinstatement grant or for repurchase. The Act prescribes rules for determining which of these two remedies should be available.

(F) Reinstatement grants. The local authority will pay a reinstatement grant if four conditions are satisfied:

(1) the defective dwelling is a house (not a flat);
(2) if the proposed work of reinstatement were carried out, the property in question would be likely to provide satisfactory housing accommodation for at least 30 years and a prospective purchaser of the property would

be likely to be able to raise a mortgage on it;
(3) giving a reinstatement grant is justified taking into account on the one hand the amount of the grant that would be available and on the other the likely value of the property after the work has been carried out;
(4) the amount of the grant payable should not exceed the price that the authority would have to pay to repurchase the property under the Act plus the costs incurred by the tenant e g in obtaining a surveyor's report or in instructing a solicitor.

Where a grant is payable under the Act, the authority will notify the applicant. Its notice must contain certain information e g as to the work which must be done to reinstate the property, the amount of the expenditure which it would be reasonable to incur and the period which it should take to carry out the work. The Act also lays down rules for calculating the amount of the grant available. In the normal case 90% of the expenditure stated in the local authority's notice will be made available, although in cases of hardship this may be increased to 100%. There is also a maximum limit for any reinstatement grant which is fixed at the moment at £14,000 by the Housing Defects (Expenditure Limit) Order. In some circumstances it is possible for the local authority to claim repayment of the grant e g because the work has not been carried out within the stipulated period (although power does exist to extend this period in appropriate cases).

(G) Repurchase. In other cases the local authority may decide to repurchase the property. In this case a notice must be served on the owner to that effect and the authority and the owner have to negotiate a reasonable repurchase price. Any disputes on this issue are taken to the District Valuer. In general, if the local authority repurchases the property, it has to grant a secure tenancy to the vendor who then will benefit from the various provisions contained in the Housing Act (e g the 'Tenants' Charter' and security of tenure).

(H) Shared ownership leases. In some cases a council tenant may wish to purchase his own house but discover that financially he is unable to proceed. It may be, however, that he is entitled in such circumstances to claim a 'shared ownership lease.' This system was introduced by the Housing and Building Control Act 1984. The relevant legislation is now contained in Part V of the Housing Act 1985. What happens is that the tenant can buy a fixed percentage interest in the property (the minimum being a 50% interest). He can then, over a period of years, acquire further 12½% interests until eventually he becomes the absolute owner. Until he becomes absolute owner, he continues to have to pay a rent to the local authority, but the rent payable is reduced according to the extent of the interest he has already acquired. In order to qualify for a shared ownership lease, various conditions must be complied with:

(a) the tenant must establish a right to buy;
(b) he must have applied for a public sector mortgage;
(c) he must be ineligible for a 100% mortgage (e g because his earnings are inadequate to cover the loan);
(d) he must pay a deposit of £100 to the local authority. The legislation contains various provisions as to the notices and counternotices that have to be served by the respective parties. The purchaser is entitled to mortgage help with his acquisition of the property, including with the successive 12½% shares that he purchases. The Act also contains rules on discount entitlement, the price to be paid for subsequent shares, the rent payable etc.

5. LONG LEASES

Residential tenancies vary considerably from case to case. Some tenants are granted a mere weekly tenancy while others may be given a long lease – for 99 years or even 999 years – at a rent which is so low as to be nominal only. Long leases are sometimes granted for technical conveyancing reasons (to enable the landlord to enforce positive obligations by his tenants, e g to repair the property); also many long leases were granted, in particular in the nineteenth century, to developers of land who intended to build on it. The freeholder would grant a 99 year lease to the developer; the developer would develop the site and sell individual houses on it at a profit; at the end of the 99 year period the freeholder would claim the property back with the benefit of the houses on it. Long leases at low rents normally do not fall within the protection of the Rent Act 1977, because that Act does not apply when the annual rent payable is only nominal (see page 76). However, Parliament has legislated to grant important rights to long leaseholders. This protection falls into two categories: first, security of tenure under the Landlord and Tenant Act 1954 and, secondly, the right in certain circumstances to buy the freehold or a long leasehold of the property in question under the Leasehold Reform Act 1967.

(i) Landlord and Tenant Act 1954

A tenant qualifies for the protection of this Act if he has a long tenancy (i e for more than 21 years) and if he would qualify for Rent Act protection but for the lowness of the rent he pays. This means therefore that he must satisfy all the other requirements of the Rent Act 1977 (e g the property must be let to him as a separate dwelling and the rateable value must be within the specified limits: see page 76). Assuming that the 1954 Act applies, when the long lease expires by effluxion of time at common law, the Act maintains it in existence until it is brought to an end in accordance with its provisions. The tenant may end it by giving one month's notice, but the landlord can only do so by giving not less than six and not more than twelve months' notice. Such notice may be in one of two forms. First he may serve a 'landlord's notice to resume possession,' stating that, unless the tenant is willing to give up his tenancy, he intends to apply to the Court for possession. The tenant may either oppose this notice, in which case the landlord has to apply to the Court for possession within two months. Basically the Court can only make an order in the landlord's favour on the same grounds that obtain in a case under the Rent Act 1977 (see page 78). If the tenant does *not* oppose the landlord's notice, the tenancy comes to an end on the date contained in that notice, and the tenant must leave. The other type of notice that the landlord may serve is a 'landlord's notice proposing a statutory tenancy.' In this case, the parties are left to negotiate the terms of the statutory tenancy themselves, except that the Court will do so if they cannot. The rent payable under the new statutory tenancy will be the full market value (as opposed to the original nominal amount). Being a statutory tenancy, the rent regulation provisions of the Rent Act 1977 will now apply to the tenancy, and the Rent Officer can be asked to fix a fair rent.

Repairs. The Landlord and Tenant Act 1954 contains special provisions designed to deal with the situation where a property is in disrepair at the end of a long lease. Basically these entitle the landlord to carry out repairs to put the property back into a reasonable condition and for him to recover the cost of so doing from the tenant, either in a lump sum or in instalments.

(ii) Leasehold Reform Act 1967

Under this Act, tenants with long leases may in certain circumstances call for the freehold to the property (this is known as 'leasehold enfranchisement') or insist upon a 50 year extension of their tenancy. For this Act to apply, five conditions must be complied with:

(a) The tenancy must be a long one i e lasting for 21 years or more. It is not necessary for the applicant under the Act to be the *original* tenant – he may only have acquired the tenancy by assignment. Nor does the original tenancy necessarily have to have been for 21 years or more; if a yearly periodic tenancy has in fact lasted for longer than 21 years, it would qualify.

(b) The tenancy must have been granted at a 'low rent' i e less than ⅔rds the relevant rateable value.

(c) The rateable value must be less than specified limits. This is a rather complex matter depending on various factors and in particular the date on which the property first appeared on the valuation list. In respect of properties first rated since 31 March 1973, the relevant figures are £750 if the property is outside London and £1,500 if within it.

(d) The property in question must be a house and not a flat or maisonette.

(e) The person claiming the benefit of the Act must have occupied all or part of the property under the long tenancy as his only or main residence for at least the last three years or three of the last ten years. Successors of a deceased tenant may also make a claim.

A person wishing to make a claim under the Act must serve a notice on the freeholder. The legislation lays down a strict system of notice and counter-notice which must be complied with. When there is a disagreement as to the price to be paid for the freehold or the rent to be paid if the lease is extended, the matter must be taken to the Leasehold Valuation Tribunal (which is in practice the same as the Rent Assessment Committee) with an appeal to the Lands Tribunal. Other disputes between the parties are resolved by the County Court. There are some situations in which the landlord is exempt from having to enfranchise the leaseholder or extend his tenancy. In particular the landlord may apply to the County Court for possession of the property when the lease expires if he requires the property for himself or an adult member of his family as his only or main residence and if he can show the Court that it would cause greater hardship to him or his family not to make the order than there would be if the tenant gave up possession at the end of the tenancy. The landlord cannot rely on this provision if he became the owner of the property after 18 February 1966. If the landlord is successful, the tenant will be able to claim compensation. The landlord can also resist a claim under the Act from a tenant who has himself given notice to terminate the tenancy or if he delays for more than two months in replying to a landlord's notice to end the tenancy under the Landlord and Tenant Act 1954. There are also provisions enabling the landlord to recover possession of the property where he intends to demolish or reconstruct the whole or part of the premises in question for redevelopment purposes. A tenant in this case will be entitled to compensation. The Crown is not bound by the Act, so that tenants of the Crown cannot call for the freehold or an extended tenancy (though in practice the Crown often does observe the terms of the legislation). It is impossible to contract out of the Act.

(A) Extension of the tenancy. Where the tenant only seeks to extend the original tenancy (for example, because he cannot afford to buy out the freehold) he will be entitled to a 50 year tenancy to begin after the existing one expires. Basically the new tenancy will be on the same terms as the original one, although the terms can be varied by agreement and any ones which are no longer reasonable, given the changes that have taken place since the original tenancy was granted, may be modified or even excluded. The Act contains provisions for calculating the rent that should be paid under the extended tenancy. Basically this should only be a ground rent i e the letting value of the site itself *excluding* anything for

the value of the building on the site. If the site is ripe for redevelopment, this is taken into account in fixing the new rent. The new lease when granted must give the landlord the right of resuming possession for the purposes of redevelopment: if the landlord exercises this right he must pay compensation to the tenant. If the tenant exercises his right to an extended tenancy, the right to call for the freehold under the enfranchisement provisions will be lost once the new term begins to run. Furthermore, at the end of the new 50 year term, he will not be entitled to any further protection under the Act.

(B) Leasehold enfranchisement. Where the tenant makes a claim to have the freehold conveyed to him, two particular issues call for comment; the purchase price and the terms on which the land is to be conveyed to the claimant. As far as price is concerned, the basic policy of the Act is to enable the tenant to purchase the property as if the landlord owned only the site itself, as opposed to the site with a house already built on it. This means that the tenant can acquire the freehold at a very reasonable price indeed. The price is actually calculated in one of two different ways, depending on the property's rateable value. If the rateable value is less than £1,000 (in London) or £500 (elsewhere), the price that the tenant has to pay will be more favourable than if the rateable values are between £1,001 and £1,500 (in London) or £501 and £750 (elsewhere). As to the terms on which the freehold is conveyed, many of the covenants in the original lease will no longer be appropriate after the leasehold has been enfranchised. However, the land will be conveyed subject to any restrictive covenants which benefit other property retained by the landlord (e g not to use the land for business or commercial purposes) and the landlord may also draw up a 'scheme of arrangement' (which has to be approved by the High Court) where this is necessary to maintain the appearance and condition of a housing estate originally within his sole control. The purchaser will be bound to comply with such a scheme, which may oblige him for example to make contributions towards the maintenance and repair of the property and to abide by restrictions imposed by the original landlord for the benefit of the estate generally.

1. INTRODUCTION

The ownership of land carries with it many rights and duties. The owner of the freehold of a piece of land is, of course, entitled to occupy it or to grant a lease of it to a tenant in return for a rent. But quite apart from this basic right, there are many other legal rules which affect the way in which the land may be used. For example, neighbours may have rights of way across it or the right to prevent its use except for certain purposes, while the local authority has power to decide how the land can be used or what types of building can be erected on it. It may even be entitled compulsorily to purchase the property in exercise of its planning powers. In this section these issues will be explored in some detail; first we shall look at the legal relationship between neighbouring owners of land, then the law on planning permission and lastly the compulsory purchase powers of local authorities.

2. NEIGHBOURS

Everyone has neighbours and, unfortunately, not all neighbours succeed in getting on amicably. There are numerous ways in which legal disputes can break out between adjacent occupiers and the law reports are full of such cases. The client who approaches his solicitor with a complaint about his neighbour is frequently told that it would be much more sensible to sort the problem out over a gin and tonic/pint of beer/cup of tea rather than to spend hundreds of pounds on legal fees. This is often very good advice: swallowing one's pride and reaching a compromise is usually better than years of litigation. Nevertheless it is as well to have some idea of one's legal rights and duties as against the neighbours, while sometimes starting legal proceedings may be unavoidable.

(i) Land Is Three-Dimensional
The first point that should be made about the ownership of land is that, in general, the owner of land owns not just the surface of the land itself, but also everything above and below it. This means therefore that the owner of land can prevent a neighbour trespassing in his air-space e g by allowing the jib of a crane to protrude into it

and also that he owns the subsoil and the mineral deposits beneath it. However, there are some exceptions to this basic principle. First, the rule that a landowner owns all the airspace above it is subject to a common sense limitation that he only owns so much of it as he could reasonably make use of. Thus he cannot bring a claim for trespass against the pilot of an aircraft who crosses the land several hundred feet above it. Furthermore, the Civil Aviation Act 1949 specifically states that an action cannot be brought in trespass or nuisance by reason only of an aircraft flying over a property at a height which is reasonable, having regard to the wind, weather and all the circumstances of the case. Secondly, there are exceptions to the rule that the landowner owns everything beneath his land. It may be that a previous owner of the land reserved the rights to minerals beneath it, in which case the current occupier of the land would have to respect this fact. Also some important natural resources such as gas, oil and coal belong to the Crown as a result of Acts of Parliament (e g the Coal Nationalization Act 1946). Also there are some ancient doctrines which provide, for example, that the Crown is the owner of all gold and silver which is available to be mined and also that the Crown is entitled to 'treasure trove.' This term has a specific legal meaning: to qualify as treasure trove, the objects in question must consist of gold or silver, they must have been *deliberately* hidden, and their true owner must be unknown. Therefore, if a pot of gold coins is found and it appears that the pot was not simply lost but instead was hidden, it is the Crown which can claim the coins and not the owner of the land where they were found. However there is a system whereby the landowner can be paid compensation for the find out of Government funds.

In *Attorney General v Overton* (1981) a Mr Kilshaw searched some farmland in Lincolnshire with a metal detector for Roman coins. He found a pot containing 7,811 antoniniani. He was convicted of theft, as he should have handed them to the owner of the land. The question then arose whether Mr Overton could keep them or whether the Attorney General could successfully claim them for the Crown. In the Court of Appeal it was held that the coins belonged to Overton since they contained only 18% silver at most (the Roman coinage of the time having been debased). Had they have been 'substantially' silver (say 50% or more) the Attorney General would have won.

(ii) Lost Property

A difficult legal problem which quite often arises concerns lost property. Suppose that someone drops a gold ring while in a shop and cannot now be traced; at a later date another customer enters the shop and picks up the ring. As between the owner of the shop and the customer, who is entitled to keep the ring? According to the principle that a landowner owns everything above and below the land, one might imagine that the shopkeeper would win. The legal position is actually a little more complex than this, however. If the lost property actually becomes physically attached to the land itself (e g where a ring is dropped in a garden and becomes embedded in the soil itself) then indeed the owner of the land would prevail. Where the item in question is simply lying loose in or around the property, the position is less straightforward. If the finder was a trespasser, a Court would certainly find in favour of the landowner; otherwise the important question is whether the landowner intended to exercise control over all items of property found on his land. If so, the lost property is his; if not, the finder can keep it. This test obviously means that the law is somewhat vague, but it would mean, on the one hand, that an item found in someone's house would inevitably belong to that person, who clearly intends to control everything within it; on the other hand, a local authority which owns a 30 acre park would find it very difficult to claim that a wallet or a bracelet found in the park belongs to it rather than the finder. In between these examples one will of course come across some difficult cases where the issue is far from clearcut.

In *Parker v British Airways Authority* (1981) the plaintiff found a bracelet in the executive lounge of British Airways at Heathrow Airport. He handed it in to an employee of the airline. The true owner never claimed it. British Airways sold it for £850. The plaintiff claimed that, since the true owner had not come forward, the bracelet belonged to him and so sued for the £850 plus interest. The Court of Appeal found in his favour, since British Airways had not manifested an intention to control all the property in its executive lounge.

(iii) Rights of Way

It is very common for the owner of one piece of land to have a right of way across his neighbour's, for example, to give him access to a shed or garage or to a side road. At the same time, the neighbours may have similar rights over his own land. Such rights are known as 'easements.' To qualify as an easement, the right of way across one piece of land must be of direct benefit to another piece of land in the area: in the legal jargon, there has to be a 'dominant tenement' (the land with the benefit of the right of way) and a 'servient tenement' (the land over which the right is exercisable). Assuming that an easement does exist, the benefit of it will automatically pass to a purchaser of the dominant tenement and the burden will usually bind a purchaser of the servient one. Easements such as this may be created in various ways. Normally they are established when a piece of land is being developed by builders and sold off in plots to individual purchasers. It will often be necessary for all the individuals concerned to have various rights of way across one another's land, and it is a fairly straightforward matter for the conveyancers dealing with the matter to ensure that the necessary legal formalities are complied with. In this sort of situation, the conveyance to each purchaser will state what rights of way come with the land and what rights it will be subject to. In some situations the conveyance may omit to create easements which are clearly necessary to enable the land to be enjoyed properly, and in that situation the law will often imply the creation of an easement, notwithstanding the failure to create one expressly. It may also happen that one neighbour decides that he would like to acquire a right of way over a neighbour's land. In this case there is nothing to prevent him approaching the neighbour to see if he would be prepared to grant him an easement: if so a formal 'deed of grant' should be drawn up. However, the prospective servient owner is under no obligation to grant the right of way and is free to negotiate whatever price he can as a condition of doing so. It is not unusual for the owner of the dominant tenement to pay several thousand pounds for the grant of an easement. There is one other way in which an easement may be created, known as prescription. The idea of this is that, if X has exercised a right of way over Y's land uninterruptedly as of right for a sufficiently long period, a time comes when Y can no longer prevent him from exercising that right. The subject is a very complex one, but normally X (or his predecessors) in this situation would have to have exercised the right for at least 20 years, and must not have done so in a secretive way or with the tacit approval of Y.

A right of way may be general or limited. A general right of way gives the owner of the dominant tenement an unlimited right to cross and recross the servient land for all purposes and at all times. However, it is possible for the right of way to be limited e g by providing that it can only be exercised during daylight hours or that it can only be used by the dominant owner himself but not his cattle or vehicles. If the easement was created expressly in a legal document, the terms of the document will indicate whether it is a general or limited one. Where the easement is one implied by law, the extent of the right of way will depend upon what is necessary to enable the owner of the dominant tenement to make reasonable use of his property. If the easement was acquired by prescription, its extent will depend upon the type of use which has been made of the right of way over the prescription period. Someone who has merely crossed land by foot for the past twenty years could not now claim to have a right to drive his car over it.

It is an important point to note that where X has a right of way over Y's land, it is for X and not Y to construct and maintain any necessary pathway or drive (unless the parties expressly enter into some other agreement). In the normal case, Y's only obligation is not to block X's right of way e g by building a fence or wall. X does, however, have a right to come onto Y's land to keep the way in reasonable repair. Should Y block X's right of way, X has two remedies available. Provided that he does not use any more force than is reasonably necessary, X may 'abate' the interference by removing any obstruction. For example he would be entitled to force open a lock upon a gate or to remove an unreasonable barrier. He is allowed to do this without notifying the servient owner. However, the law does not favour self-help remedies such as these (which may well lead to unpleasant disturbances and even violence). X's other remedy would be to apply to the Court for an injunction ordering Y to remove the obstruction; he could also claim damages if he can show he has suffered some pecuniary loss. Going to Court may, of course, be costly and time-consuming, but it may well be that a plaintiff will be granted an interim injunction against the defendant requiring him to remove the obstruction pending the final hearing of the dispute, if the matter is one of urgency and if the balance of convenience lies on the plaintiff's side. In this case, however, should the plaintiff ultimately lose the case (e g because the defendant succeeds in proving that he never had a right of way in the first place) the plaintiff may be ordered to pay compensation to the defendant.

(iv) Rights of Light

Another important right which one neighbour may have against another (and which causes many disputes in practice) is the right of light. Arguments frequently erupt when one neighbour wishes to build, say, a loft extension, which will deprive the neighbour of light through his kitchen or living-room window. There is no natural right to light: X can only assert such a right against Y if he has acquired an easement to that effect (although it may be that X can prevent Y building on his land by virtue of the law of restrictive covenants: see page 110). X may well find that his best remedy is to get in touch with the local planning authority, which may have power to prevent Y going ahead with the proposed development or to impose conditions and obligations on Y which will protect X's position. However, X may have an easement of light in which case he himself can bring an action against Y without having to rely on the involvement of the local authority. Rights of light can be obtained in just the same way as the rights of way considered above, that is to say expressly, impliedly or by prescription. In practice, however, express and implied rights of light are unusual, and it is much more likely that X will claim to have acquired a right of light by prescription. Indeed, many conveyances of property expressly state that a purchaser of land shall *not* be capable of acquiring a right of light over neighbouring land: a developer who builds on a site and then sells off 1000 individual houses may well insist that each conveyance should contain a clause to this effect. It follows that if and when a dispute about the right to light breaks out, one should consult the title deeds to the property to see whether they deal with the problem. As far as prescription is concerned, there are two Acts of Parliament which contain specific provisions dealing with rights of light: it is actually easier (for technical reasons) to acquire a right of light by prescription than other rights such as rights of way or a right to have a building supported by a neighbouring house. The Prescription Act 1832 provides that the actual enjoyment of the access of light to a dwelling-house, workshop or other building for twenty years without interruption shall make the right absolute and indefeasible unless enjoyed by written consent or agreement. One problem caused by the fact that a neighbour can acquire a right of light by prescription is that it is not easy to know how one can object to the acquisition of such a right. At common law, the most effective way of doing so was to erect a hoarding or screen within the prescription period of twenty years so that, at the end of that time, the neighbour could not claim to have enjoyed an uninterrupted access to light for the relevant period. Such action is obviously highly cumbrous, however, and the Rights of Light Act 1959 therefore introduced a new system whereby the acquisition of a prescriptive right to light can be prevented. A notice can be registered with the local authority as a 'local land charge' with the prior approval of the Lands Tribunal. Such a notice acts as though the access to light had been physically obstructed. Should the would-be dominant owner wish to do so, he then has a year within which to claim that he had already obtained a right to light.

Assuming that a right to light does exist, the owner of the dominant tenement is entitled to the amount of light which will enable him to enjoy comfortable use of his property. The amount of light needed may vary according to the type of property in question. For example, in *Allen v Greenwood* (1979) the plaintiff owned a greenhouse. The defendants built a fence and parked a caravan near to the greenhouse which excluded sunlight from half the greenhouse and seriously reduced the chances of growing tomatoes, melons etc. The Court of Appeal held that the plaintiff was not just entitled to light, but to sufficient light to enable him properly to use the greenhouse. Thus the plaintiff was awarded an injunction ordering the defendant to stop interfering with the *sun*light to the greenhouse. However it is important to appreciate that having a right to light does not necessarily mean that a neighbour may do nothing that would restrict the amount of light available. Provided that the owner of the dominant tenement will still have enough light to make *comfortable use* of his property, the servient owner is allowed to carry out development of his site even if this will substantially limit the available light. Furthermore, in considering whether the dominant owner's right to light is infringed, the Court will consider alternative sources of light available to him e g through a skylight in his own property. Where someone considers that his right of light is being infringed, he would theoretically be entitled to abate the infringement himself by removing the obstruction, but much the wiser course of action would be to seek an injunction from the Court.

(v) Rights of Support
Every land-owner has a natural right to have his *land* supported. For example, X can prevent a neighbour Y from removing soil or minerals from his own land if this will result in subsidence to X's land. However this right only extends to the land itself and not to buildings upon it. Neighbours can only acquire the right to have a *building* supported through the law of easements, i e the right to support is the same kind of legal creature as the right to light and a right of way. Easements of support may be created expressly or by legal implication but they are commonly acquired through prescription. For example, where a pair of semi-detached houses were built more than twenty years ago, it is highly likely that each owner will have the right to have his house supported by the other. It will be an infringement of this right for one owner to demolish his property if this removes the support from the other. For example, in *Dalton v Angus* (1881) the plaintiffs owned a coach factory which adjoined a house owned by the defendants. This state of affairs had lasted for a long time – much longer than twenty years. The defendants then employed a contractor to pull the house down; the effect of this was that the coach factory almost entirely fell down. The House of Lords held that a right of support had arisen by prescription and that the plaintiffs could claim damages for the harm suffered. Where an easement of support exists, this entitles the dominant owner to enter the servient property and carry out any repairs that may be necessary to ensure that the support is sound, but it does not put the servient owner under a duty to keep the supporting building in repair.

(vi) Other Easements
The law recognises many other types of easement of which the three types just discussed are perhaps the most common. The unifying characteristic of easements is that the right which exists over the servient piece of land in some sense benefits or accommodates the dominant piece of land. Without this relationship of dominant and servient land, there cannot be an easement. Other types of easement would be, for example,

the right to run drains or pipes under a neighbour's land, a right to store coal in another person's coalshed, a right to hang washing on or over someone's land and a right to permit rainwater to drop from a roof on to someone's land (the original meaning of 'eavesdropping'). There are many other types of easement. However it is important to know that it is *not* possible to enjoy a right to a view as an easement (although it may be that a neighbour can be prevented from building if there is a restrictive covenant (see below) or by the local planning authority); nor is there a right to have one's building protected from severe weather by a neighbour's. In *Phipps v Pears* (1964) the defendant owned 14 Market Street, Warwick. In 1962 he pulled it down, leaving the flank wall of No 16 exposed to the weather. This wall had not been rendered or plastered; rain got in and then froze and considerable damage was caused. The plaintiff claimed that he had a right to have his property protected from the weather, but the Court of Appeal unanimously agreed that no such easement existed in law.

(vii) Restrictive Covenants

Another very important legal interest which affects the relationship between neighbours is the restrictive covenant. A restrictive covenant can enable the owner of one piece of land to prevent his neighbour using his land in a particular way. Common restrictive covenants in practice are the right to prevent a neighbour building on his land, using it for business or commercial purposes, keeping animals on it or using it in an illegal or immoral way. To qualify as a restrictive covenant, the restriction upon one piece of land must be of benefit to the neighbouring piece of land (just as with easements there has to be a dominant and a servient tenement). Once a restrictive covenant has been created, and assuming that various legal formalities are properly complied with, both the benefit and the burden of the covenant are said to 'run with the land,' that is to say anyone happening to own the 'dominant' land at any time can enforce it, and the owner of the 'servient' land will always be bound by it. It is important to appreciate that, to qualify as a *restrictive* covenant, the covenant must be purely negative in nature. For example, a covenant not to build on a piece of land imposes on the servient owner a purely passive obligation; however, a covenant 'not to let property fall into disrepair,' though worded in a negative form,

actually imposes a *positive* obligation to maintain the property. It is not therefore a restrictive covenant. The question to be asked is, does the covenant in any sense require the servient owner to incur expenditure or to take any positive action; if so, one is outside the law of restrictive covenants. Restrictive covenants can only be created by express agreement (easements such as rights of way can also be created by prescription: see above). Restrictive covenants are very common in practice, and have been since the middle of the nineteenth century. Many home owners will find, if they read their title deeds, that they are subject to numerous obligations of this kind, although, by the same token, they will normally have reciprocal rights against their neighbours. When companies develop a housing estate, they will impose restrictive covenants upon all their purchasers as this is a useful way of ensuring that the environment of the estate generally is maintained (and also, therefore, the value of the properties). Restrictive covenants are a very important part of preserving the character and atmosphere of an area. If a neighbour threatens to act in breach of a restrictive covenant, the obvious remedy for the plaintiff is to seek an injunction from the Court ordering the defendant not to do so.

Many restrictive covenants were created a considerable time ago, perhaps as long ago as the mid-nineteenth century. It may well be the case that the original reason why the covenant was imposed has long since gone: large Victorian houses built as private dwellings may now be more suitable for business purposes and yet a restrictive covenant may make this impossible. In such a situation it is possible for the servient owner to make an application to the Lands Tribunal under section 84 of the Law of Property Act 1925. It has power to modify or discharge restrictive covenants on various grounds, for example that they have become obsolete. If the Tribunal decides to do so, it may order the servient owner to pay compensation to the dominant owner (or owners), although it is not bound to do so.

(viii) Positive Covenants

Having seen that one neighbour may have a right to restrict the way in which another can use his land, the next question must be whether it is possible for neighbours to enforce *positive* duties against one another. For example, can X insist that Y maintains and repairs his half of a semi-detached property? In general, the answer to this question is no. It would always be possible for X and Y to enter into a private agreement between themselves to maintain and repair, but the problem is that these covenants do not 'run with freehold land' i e a successor of X could not enforce the covenant against a successor of Y. Easements do not involve the servient owner in doing anything – they simply prevent him infringing the dominant owner's rights (the one exception to this being the rather unusual easement of fencing). Restrictive covenants are purely passive in character. However, the law has never been prepared to allow positive covenants to be enforced against freehold land, even though in policy terms it is highly desirable that they should be. When a housing estate is developed, it is in everyone's interests that the whole area should be kept in reasonable condition e g through periodic repainting and maintenance work. Also where a number of people buy flats in a large old house, it is necessary to ensure that the common parts are lit and kept clean and periodically decorated and that all the owners should contribute to this work. To overcome the problem that positive covenants cannot be enforced against freeholders, many people are granted long leases, often for 999 years. The point is that positive duties *can* be enforced against a tenant by the landlord. Similarly, where land is purchased subject to a rentcharge, positive covenants are enforceable against the owner of the land at any particular time (even, in this case, if he has the freehold). In other words, there are conveyancing devices whereby the defect in the law on positive covenants can be circumvented, although the position is still far from satisfactory. Many people must have wondered what the point of their having a 999 year lease rather than a freehold is: the answer is almost always that this is a way of compelling them to comply with various positive obligations. The Law Commission has recently looked into the whole problem of positive covenants in great detail, and has concluded that various types of positive obligation should be enforceable between neighbours in much the same way as restrictive covenants are. The law will almost certainly be altered in due course, although probably only with prospective and not retrospective effect.

(ix) Noise

One of the most common complaints about neighbours is that they make too much noise. It may be possible to take legal action against them, but it is highly desirable in practice for the parties to try to resolve disputes of this nature amicably. In particular, the need to compromise is important, for what is an acceptable noise level to one person may be unacceptable to another and it is difficult for a Court to set down specific rules on an issue such as this. Where someone finds that a neighbour absolutely refuses to reduce the amount of noise he makes, there are two options available to him in law: one is to bring an action in 'nuisance', a civil wrongdoing known as a tort; the other is to get in touch with the Noise Abatement Officer of his local authority, who has various powers available to him under the Control of Pollution Act 1974.

(A) Nuisance. The tort of nuisance is committed when one person unreasonably interferes with the use or enjoyment of another piece of land. Obviously the making of excessive noise may amount to an actionable nuisance, in which case the plaintiff may seek an injunction to bring it to an end and damages for any annoyance suffered as a result. The law recognises where there is an actionable nuisance from noise that a plaintiff would rather have the noise stopped rather than be paid more compensation. In *Kennaway v Thompson* (1980) the plaintiff owned a house near a lake in the Cotswolds. A club started to use the lake for motor boat races. Over a number of years the number of races increased, and by 1977 it had become a venue for national and international events, and was used far more frequently than in the past. The plaintiff brought an action in nuisance. The High Court agreed there was a nuisance, but awarded Mrs Kennaway £16,000 damages rather than an injunction. She appealed to the Court of Appeal, which granted her the injunction she wanted. The club was only allowed to hold a very limited number of meetings in future and was told to keep such noise as was made below certain specified levels. The difficulty with the tort of nuisance is to decide at what point the level of noise becomes an unreasonable interference with the use of neighbouring land. The law has the very difficult problem of trying to strike a balance between the right of one occupier to make use of his own land as he wishes and the right of his neighbour not to be interfered with. A Court will expect some give and take between neighbours and will look very closely at the circumstances of any given case before deciding whether the noise level is unacceptably high. It will wish to hear evidence as to the level of any noise, its frequency and the times at which it occurred. It will also consider the nature of the locality in which the noise is created; the same level of noise may be acceptable in a busy main road in a city centre and unreasonable in a quiet village. Similarly, noise caused by a factory established in a predominantly residential area is more likely to be condemned than the same noise on a trading estate. The law on this subject is necessarily somewhat vague, and this is why it is really much better to try to settle any disputes without becoming involved in litigation.

(B) Control of Pollution Act 1974. If it is necessary to take action against a neighbour, it is normally more sensible to proceed under this Act rather than by bringing a private action in nuisance. It may be possible to get the local authority to bring the action; local authorities employ a Noise Abatement Officer to deal with such cases. Even if the authority won't act, the aggrieved individual may be able to take proceedings in the Magistrates' Court (which will certainly be cheaper than bringing a tort action in a County Court or the High Court). The Act applies whenever there is a 'noise nuisance'. Nuisance for these purposes has the same meaning as in the tort of nuisance i e an unreasonable interference with the use of land. When the local authority is satisfied that a noise nuisance exists, it *must* serve a notice on the person creating it, requiring its abatement. That person then has 21 days to appeal against the notice to a Magistrates' Court.

The Control of Noise (Appeals) Regulations 1975 establish the grounds on which an appeal may be made e g that there is no noise nuisance or that there is some defect in the authority's notice. Assuming that there is no appeal, or that any appeal is lost, it is an offence to fail to comply with the authority's notice and a fine of £200 can be imposed for a first offence. The fines get steeper for subsequent offences. Also the authority can seek an injunction in the High Court if they are of the opinion that fines in the Magistrates' Court would be inadequate. Refusal to obey an injunction to abate a noise nuisance would be a contempt of court, and a guilty party could even be imprisoned by way of penalty. It is also possible for an aggrieved individual to bring proceedings in the Magistrates' Court under the Control of Pollution Act 1974 even if the local authority will not act. The Court can make an order requiring the nuisance to be abated, and the same penalties as mentioned above can be imposed on a person failing to obey the order. Where an individual wishes to seek an injunction, however, this can only be done by bringing an action in the civil Courts, based on the private tort of nuisance.

(x) Trees

Another common cause of complaint between neighbours is the tree with overhanging branches or encroaching roots. Branches that protrude into one's property may be unsightly, dangerous and annoying while roots may adversely affect one's gardening aspirations and, more seriously, cause damage to the foundations of a house. These problems are normally dealt with under the law of nuisance.

(A) Overhanging branches. There must inevitably be a certain amount of 'give and take' between neighbours, and it is almost impossible to prevent any intrusion by a tree or shrub into one's airspace. Action should only be contemplated against a neighbour where it is really justified e g because a branch has become dangerous or is having a serious effect on the design of a garden. Where a landowner has a legitimate grievance, his claim will be based on the tort of nuisance i e that a neighbour is unreasonably interfering with the comfortable use of his property. The main question that arises in such cases relates to remedies: is it necessary for the aggrieved party to go to Court, or can he take action himself by cutting off the offending branches? The answer to this is that it is permissible to 'abate' a nuisance by taking action oneself. However, if it is necessary to go on to the neighbour's land to chop the branches off, notice must first be given to the owner. On the other hand, it was established by the House of Lords in *Lemmon v Webb* (1895) that it is not necessary to give notice if the necessary action can be taken entirely from one's own property. All the same, it would be worthwhile discussing the matter with the neighbour first: unilateral action by one person is often liable to provoke an equal (or greater) reaction from the other and neighbour disputes in particular have an unfortunate tendency to escalate.

(B) Encroaching roots. The situation here is a little more complex, because, since the encroachment is not visible, the neighbours probably will not realise that there is a problem until, for example, physical damage is caused to a building. There is no doubt that someone whose land is invaded by roots from a neighbour's tree or shrubs can bring an action for nuisance against him, but the neighbour will only be liable to the extent that he knew or ought to have known of the danger caused by the tree. In *Solloway v Hampshire County Council* (1980), the plaintiff owned a house near the highway. A chestnut tree on the pavement had grown to about 18 metres and its roots had encroached onto the plaintiff's property. The two hot summers of 1975 and 1976 caused the roots to draw moisture from around the foundations of the house and serious subsidence occurred which cost about £6,000 to rectify. The High Court awarded the plaintiff damages against the highway authority, but the Court of Appeal reversed the decision as the authority could only be liable if it knew, or ought to have known, of the danger of damage occurring. In this case the possibility of such damage was altogether too vague for the plaintiff to succeed. However, if that test is satisfied, a plaintiff may recover. In *Bridges and Others v Harrow London Borough* (1981) the plaintiffs' house was seriously damaged by the roots from some oak trees. They sued the borough council, and the legal argument was about who owned the trees. The judge held on the facts that the council did, and awarded the Bridges £8,000 and their neighbours, who also suffered damage, £6,000. Where a landowner discovers roots encroaching onto his land, he is entitled to sever the offending roots, although it is not clear in law whether he must first give notice to the neighbour who owns the tree. Because of this uncertainty, the sensible advice must be to give prior notice.

(xi) Animals

Animals give rise to many heated disputes between neighbours. There are various ways in which the law may be invoked to control neighbours' animals.

(A) Nuisance. Where a neighbour's animals cause an unreasonable interference with the comfortable enjoyment of someone's own property, an action in nuisance may be brought. As has already been said, the law expects a certain amount of give and take between neighbours, and a Court will not be particularly sympathetic to a plaintiff objecting to the fact that a neighbour's dog barks sometimes. However, if the barking is *unreasonable* (e g because there is a large number of dogs, all of which bark conti-

nually – perhaps from early in the morning until late at night) then an action in nuisance will succeed and the dogowner can be ordered to bring the nuisance to an end: obviously this may mean that he will have to get rid of them. Actions have been successfully brought before the Courts by plaintiffs complaining about cockerels crowing loudly at 4.00 a m, although it must be remembered that, in considering what is unreasonable, the Court will consider the nature of the locality in which nuisance is alleged: a cockerel crowing in rural Devon is much less likely to be a nuisance in law than the same behaviour in suburbia. An action in nuisance could also be brought where the neighbour's animals cause a noxious stench.

(B) Trespass. Where the neighbour's animals physically go onto someone else's land, this does not, as might be imagined, necessarily amount to a trespass. To qualify as a trespass it is necessary to show that the neighbour intended the animals to go on to the plaintiff's land or that he was negligent in allowing them to do so i e he failed to take reasonable steps to prevent it happening. In *League Against Cruel Sports v Scott* (1985) the League owned land on Exmoor and the defendants were responsible for the Devon and Somerset Staghounds. On several occasions the Hunt's hounds went onto the League's property. The League sued for trespass, and the judge held that the defendants were liable in respect of some of the incursions into the League's property because they had failed to take reasonable care to prevent that happening.

(C) Assault and battery. Where a neighbour deliberately lets his animals loose with the intention of their harming or scaring an adjoining occupier, he may be guilty of a criminal offence under the Offences Against the Person Act 1861.

(D) Negligence. An owner of an animal has a duty to exercise reasonable control over it and to ensure that it does not behave in a way which could be harmful to other people. If he fails in this responsibility and the animal in fact causes harm which is of a reasonably foreseeable nature, the victim may bring an action for damages. It follows that a neighbour who fails to keep a dog under reasonable control could be sued if the dog escapes and attacks an adjoining owner.

(E) Dangerous animals. The Animals Act 1971 establishes special rules relating to 'dangerous species' of animals i e species which are not commonly domesticated in the British Isles and whose fully grown animals normally have such characteristics that they are likely, unless restrained, to cause severe damage or that any damage they may cause is likely to be severe. The owners of such animals are strictly liable for any harm caused by them i e the victim does not need to show that the lion's owner was negligent in allowing it to maul him, simply that it did so. This may be reassuring to the neighbour of a zoo or safari park.

(F) Tame animals. In some circumstances the Animals Act also imposes strict liability upon the owner of a tame animal which causes damage. To be liable three conditions have to be satisfied: the damage must be of a kind which the animal, unless restrained, was likely to cause and which was likely to be severe; this likelihood must have been attributable to characteristics of the animal not normally found in animals of that species (e g it must be a particularly temperamental or difficult animal); and the owner must have known these characteristics.

(G) Straying livestock. The Animals Act also deals with the problem of straying livestock. 'Livestock' is defined in the Act and includes many beasts from cattle to quails. The Act imposes strict liability on the owner of livestock for any damage done by them to someone else's land; he must also pay for any expenses incurred in keeping the straying livestock under control. There is a defence to an action where the plaintiff was at fault in allowing the livestock to stray on to his land, but for these purposes the mere fact that he could have kept the livestock out by fencing his land does not mean he is at fault. However, he would be at fault if he was under a *duty* to fence his land (e g because he had entered into an agreement to do so). It is also a defence if the livestock in question strayed onto the plaintiff's land from the highway, and their presence on the highway was itself lawful.

(H) Dogs upsetting livestock. The Animals Act also provides that the owner of a dog which causes damage by killing or injuring livestock is strictly liable for the damage. There are three defences: that the damage was the fault of the person suffering it, that the person suffering it voluntarily accepted the risk and that the damage was done to livestock which had strayed onto the dogowner's land. The important question that arises in cases such as this is whether the owner of the livestock is entitled to kill the offending dog. The Act does permit him to do this provided that he acted for the protection of his livestock, that within 48 hours he gives notice of what he has done to an officer in charge of a police station, and that he was entitled (within the terms of the Act) to take such action. This is so where the dog is worrying or about to worry the livestock and there are no other reasonable means of ending or preventing the worrying, or the dog has been worrying livestock, is still in the vicinity and is not under the control of anyone and there is no way of finding out to whom it belongs.

(I) General straying. It is also important to point out that the owner of one piece of land can sometimes be liable for harm done to someone else's animals when they come onto the former's property. In *Tutton v A D Walter* (1984) the plaintiff kept bees and the defendant grew rape. He sprayed the rape when in full flower. The plaintiff had warned that this could cause harm to the bees. In fact the bees were all killed by the poisonous spray, and the High Court held that the defendant was liable in negligence and had therefore to compensate the plaintiff. The defendant had failed to take reasonable care not to harm the plaintiff's bees.

(xii) Other Nuisances

Apart from the irritation that can be caused by a neighbour's noise, trees and animals, there are many other activities to which objection might be taken. For example, the neighbours may tend to behave in an unhygienic way, leaving rubbish lying around or failing to dispose properly of waste matter. It may be that noxious fumes emanate from a neighbouring property, or that machinery is used there which causes alarming vibrations capable of doing damage to buildings. They may fail to keep their drains clear, with the result that from time to time there is a discharge of drainage matter onto neighbouring property. Where this type of problem is encountered, the aggrieved party may bring an action based on the tort of nuisance. As has been seen above, this tort is committed when a neighbour interferes unreasonably with the comfortable use of someone else's property, and there is no doubt that the sort of behaviour just described could amount to a nuisance. In deciding what is reasonable or unreasonable, the Court must look at all the circumstances including e g the nature of the locality, the general utility of the behaviour complained of and the need for 'give and take' between neighbours. This might of course mean that the emission of noxious fumes as a result of industrial activity is reasonable in one area and unreasonable in another. On the other hand, some types of anti-social conduct (e g overflowing drainage) would almost certainly amount to a nuisance if conducted in a residential area. In order to succeed in an action for nuisance, the plaintiff will have to show a course of conduct which has interfered with the use of his property: a single, isolated act would not be sufficient. Anyone considering taking action against a neighbour would be well advised to keep a record of each and every occasion e g that the drains overflowed or that noxious fumes invaded their property.

The plaintiff in a nuisance action will want above all to have the offensive activity discontinued: a monetary award in such circumstances is normally considered to be a poor second best. In general, a successful plaintiff will indeed be granted an injunction in such cases, ordering the defendant to stop the nuisance in question, although the Court does have power to award damages in lieu of an injunction. Normally it will only award damages in lieu where the nuisance is of a trivial nature. Where there is a substantial interference with the plaintiff's use of his property, the Court will grant an injunction: otherwise it would almost mean that a defendant could compulsorily purchase (by the payment of damages) the right to cause a nuisance. Thus in *Kennaway v Thompson* (see page 111), the Court granted an injunction ordering the defendants to have fewer motor boat races. However, in *Miller v Jackson* (1977) the Court of Appeal proceeded differently. The plaintiffs lived near a cricket ground in a village and frequently found their Sunday afternoons were disturbed by batsmen hitting sixes into their garden, sometimes damaging property and even the plaintiffs themselves. In fact the cricket club was established before the plaintiffs' house was built, and it was arguable that their house had been built too close to the ground. However, the Court agreed that the defendants, the cricket club, were liable both in negligence and nuisance but refused to grant an injunction, saying that the public interest (of playing and watching village cricket) should prevail over the plaintiffs' desire to have the game stopped. Therefore the plaintiff had to be content with damages 'in lieu'. No doubt many people would sympathise with the Court's decision, but

legally it is somewhat questionable and it is more likely in future that *Kennaway v Thompson* would be followed rather than *Miller v Jackson*.

It is important to point out that it may also be possible to persuade the local authority to take action against a neighbour in various circumstances. The advantage of this is that it avoids the expense of having to bring a legal action oneself, and that it is often the case that the involvement of a disinterested third party can help to bring about a sensible resolution of a dispute in a way that the neighbouring owners are unable to do themselves. The local authority's powers to take action against unreasonably noisy neighbours have already been described (page 112). But there are other problems in respect of which the authority can take action. Under Part III of the Public Health Act 1936 it can.act where premises are in a state which is prejudicial to health etc; under the Control of Pollution Act 1974 it can take action in respect of matters such as the disposal of waste etc; and the Clean Air Acts 1956 and 1968 enable it to control conduct which could produce atmospheric pollution. It is obviously sensible therefore to discuss these types of problem with the relevant department of one's local authority.

(xiii) Boundaries and Fences

Disagreements with neighbours over boundaries and fences are regrettably common. Three particular problems tend to crop up: where precisely is the boundary, who owns the fence or wall dividing two properties from one another, and who (if anyone) has the duty of erecting and maintaining fences?

(A) Boundaries. It can be very difficult to tell precisely where the boundary between two properties runs, especially where they are old and ramshackle or in a rural area. Of course the most obvious way of finding out about the boundaries is to look at the title deeds of the property, but all too often they fail to deal with the issue or turn out, on close inspection, to be ambiguous. Even if the title to land becomes registered in HM Land Registry, the Registry does not guarantee the boundaries of the property. If there is some dispute with a neighbour and the title deeds fail to provide a clear answer, there is everything to be said for trying to reach a sensible and amicable compromise with him which can then be formally recorded: a proper plan can also be drawn up. If it is impossible to do this, then the matter can be taken to Court. One owner can start an action for trespass against the other, and the Court will have to hear evidence and look at all the circumstances of the case before it can give judgment. However, it is questionable whether it is worth spending hundreds or even thousands of pounds on legal costs where there is only a suggestion of a minor encroachment onto one's land. It is important to appreciate also that, even if the title deeds show that the boundary between two properties suggest that a neighbour has 'stolen' one's land, he may have acquired a right to that land by what is known as 'adverse possession.' If he has occupied someone else's land uninterruptedly and without any complaint for a minimum of twelve years, then the Limitation Act 1980 provides that he gets a good title to it and the neighbouring owner loses his. In practice this frequently happens.

(B) The ownership of fences and walls. A fence or wall built entirely on one person's land will naturally belong to that person. The more difficult situation, however, is where the fence or, more probably, the wall straddles the land of each neighbour. In this situation, the wall will normally be a 'party wall', and section 38 of the Law of Property Act 1925 provides that party walls shall be treated as being severed vertically but that each owner shall have a right to have his part of the wall supported by the other. What this means is that each neighbour owns the half of the wall on his side of the boundary, but that neither can remove his part of the wall if this would mean that the other part collapses. In the absence of agreement, there is no positive duty on either party to keep his part of the wall in repair: simply a duty not to remove any necessary support to the other part. When a purchaser buys land, a standard preliminary enquiry is sent to the vendor (or his solicitor) asking who owns and maintains the various boundaries, walls and fences: it is highly desirable that a newcomer to a property should be clear upon this issue, as this may avoid misunderstanding and arguments at a later date.

(C) Erecting and maintaining fences. The basic position is that no one has a duty to erect fences on his land or to repair and maintain such fences as there are. However, there are some exceptions to this. As far as erecting a fence is concerned, there are some situations in which statute requires someone to do so. For example, the Highways Act 1959 imposes a duty to erect a fence when carrying out excavations on land adjacent or near to a public highway. Also the

Occupiers' Liability Act 1957 requires an occupier of premises to make them reasonably safe for visitors, and it may be necessary to put up a fence to discharge this duty. It is also possible that one owner of land has an enforceable right against his neighbour that he should fence his property in: such a right is a type of easement (just like the right of way and right of light described earlier) and it may be created expressly or arise from prescription. This is an unusual easement, since it requires the servient owner to expend money on maintaining the fencing: no other easement requires positive action by the servient owner. In *Crow v Wood* (1970) the plaintiff owned a farm in Yorkshire and the defendant had a right to let his sheep stray on some nearby common land. They actually strayed onto the plaintiff's land and caused considerable damage. The plaintiff sued and the County Court awarded her £205 damages. However, the Court of Appeal allowed the defendant's appeal, since the plaintiff was under a duty, through the easement of fencing, to fence her property in. It followed that it was the plaintiff's own fault that the damage occurred and that the defendant escaped liability. It is also possible for neighbours to enter into an agreement with one another that a fence or wall be built and maintained at shared expense. The problem with an agreement (or 'covenant') such as this is that, although it is enforceable as between the original contracting parties, and although the benefit of the covenant (i e the right to enforce it) passes to subsequent purchasers, it is not normally possible to enforce the burden of the covenant against later owners. This is because the burden of positive covenants does not 'run with the land' (see page 110), although the law may soon be changed in this respect. There are some conveyancing techniques whereby such covenants can be made to bind later purchasers: e g if the land is subject to a rentcharge, or if the occupier of it owns a leasehold interest rather than the freehold, positive covenants do run with the land.

In the absence of an enforceable right against a neighbour to compel him to maintain a wall or fence, there are some other possibilities. If it is in a dangerous condition, it may be possible to bring an action in tort to have the danger removed and the Court could grant an injunction compelling the person responsible to take the necessary action. Also it would be possible to complain to the local authority, which has powers under the Public Health Act 1961 to order someone to make good a dangerous structure or to carry out the necessary repairs at his expense. Two final points should be made on this subject. First, it is possible to subject property to a restrictive covenant *preventing* owners from fencing in their land; such covenants being negative rather than positive do run with the land and bind subsequent purchasers. Houses in modern 'open plan' developments frequently have such covenants imposed upon them, which makes it very difficult to keep marauding dogs from one's front lawn. Secondly, inhabitants of London should be advised that there are special rules laid down in the London Building Acts (Amendment) Act 1939 dealing with rights and obligations in respect of party walls.

3. PLANNING AND COMPULSORY PURCHASE

(i) Introduction

Quite apart from the various rights that neighbours may have over one's property, it is important to appreciate that there are also many restrictions that can be imposed on the use and development of land under the planning laws and also that, in some circumstances, it is possible for a local authority compulsorily to acquire land in the public interest. It is very important for the purchaser of land to find out how the planning laws affect the property in question: it is obviously pointless to buy premises from which to run a business if the local authority is going to refuse to allow it to be used except for residential purposes. This is one of the issues which a local search of the records of the local authority prior to exchanging contracts should sort out (see page 43).

(ii) Planning Laws

The modern system of planning laws began with the Town and Country Planning Act 1947. The most important legislation is now the Town and Country Planning Act 1971 which consolidated earlier legislation; various amending Acts have added to the Act since 1971. Under this legislation, every county planning authority has a duty to prepare a 'structure plan' for the area of its responsibility. The structure plan consists of a written statement of the general proposals of planning policy for the area in question, and has to be submitted to the Secretary of State for the Environment for his approval. The county authority is also required to draw up 'local plans' which contain a more detailed review of planning policy for each part of the county. Local plans do not have to be submitted to the Secretary of State. Between them the structure plan and the local plans of a county constitute the 'development plan' for that county. It is possible for the local authority, when granting planning permission, to deviate from the terms of the development plan. However, the development plan is obviously very important as it gives a pretty clear indication of how the local authority is likely to respond to an application for planning permission: it is unlikely to allow a factory to be built in an area designated as primarily residential, while it will have indicated in the plans where it considers more houses or light industry ought in the future to be located. Any member of the public is entitled to inspect the authority's structure and local plans.

The area of planning law most likely to affect the individual is that dealing with 'development'. Generally speaking, anyone wishing to 'develop' land can only do so with planning permission which has to be obtained from the local authority. However, there are some exceptions from this general rule, and there are some situations in which planning permission is deemed to have been given.

(A) 'Development'. The application of the planning laws hinges upon this key term. Section 22 of the Town and Country Planning Act 1971 defines development as: '(i) the carrying out of building, engineering, mining or other operations in, on, over or under land *or* (ii) the making of any material change in the use of any building or other land.' It is very important to recognise that material change of use requires planning permission; most people know that they cannot build a house without permission, but fail to recognise that conversion of a house into, say, a shop also has to be sanctioned by the local authority. Precisely what constitutes a 'material change of use' can be a difficult question, and sometimes it is necessary to take the matter before a Court for the judge to adjudicate upon the problem. The Act does make clear, however, that the conversion of one dwelling-house into two or more separate units *does* constitute a change of use requiring planning permission. Anyone thinking of dividing his rambling old Victorian house into two or three parts must therefore apply to his local authority for permission to do so. The Act does provide, however, that some operations which might be thought to amount to 'development' as defined do not in fact require planning permission. In particular, works for the maintenance, improvement or alteration of a building which do not materially affect its external appearance, the use of buildings or other land within the curtilage of a house for any purpose incidental to the enjoyment of the house as such, the use of land for agricultural purposes and the change of use from one use to another within the same 'use class' do not require planning permission. The Town and Country Planning (Use Classes) Order sets out 18 classes of use e g use as an office, use as a light industrial building and use as a shop: thus planning permission is not necessary if someone wishes to use a former toy shop as a shoe shop. This area of law is complex, and proper legal advice should be sought before relying on these provisions.

Where someone proposes to develop his land in the sense just described, he must generally apply for planning permission. However, there are some exceptions to this; one is of particular importance to the homeowner wanting to improve his property. The Town and Country Planning General Development Order 1977 grants the necessary planning permission for any development falling within the 23 classes set out in the order i e it is unnecessary in such cases to apply *individually* to the authority for planning permission. Of particular significance, the Order authorises limited enlargements and alterations to houses, including the building of a garage. The Order permits such an enlargement provided that (a) the cubic content of the original dwelling-house is not exceeded by more than 50 cubic metres or one-tenth, whichever is the greater, subject to a maximum of 115 cubic metres; (b) the height of the building as so enlarged does not exceed the height of the highest part of the roof of the original dwelling-house and (c) no part of the building when enlarged projects beyond the forward-most part of any wall of the original dwelling-house which fronts on a highway. Thus it may well be possible to go ahead and build a conservatory or a granny annexe without having to ask permission. However, one word of warning: quite apart from needing planning permission, many building operations also require building regulation consent. Such consent also has to come from the local authority, though from a different department from the one dealing with planning laws. Building regulation consent is designed to ensure that the building will be safe and hygienic and will be of a suitable standard. It is often tempting to turn a blind eye to the need for building regulation consent in the hope and expectation that no one from the local authority will even find out about the work in question, let alone take any action in respect of it. However, it is worth pointing out that when the property is put on the market, the purchaser or his solicitor may well ask to see a building regulation consent in respect of any recent building operations, and if none is available a sale may be lost as a result.

(B) Applications for planning permisson. Application must be made in the prescribed form, and a fee is payable. The local authority keeps a register of planning applications, and neighbours ought to have an opportunity to make their views known before permission is actually given. When granting permission, the authority may do so unconditionally or it may grant it subject to such conditions as seem to be appropriate. The conditions must be related in some way to the proposed development and must not be unreasonable. When permission is given, it will remain valid for five years or for such other time as the authority specifies. If the development is not commenced within that time, the permission lapses and a new application must be made. Where an applicant objects to the authority's refusal to grant him permission or to the conditions attached to a grant of planning permission, he may appeal to the Secretary of State. Normally the matter is then determined by an inspector from the Department of the Environment, though sometimes the Secretary of State himself deals with the case. On appeal, the matter proceeds as though it were a fresh application, and the Secretary of State (or inspector) can come to whatever decision seems appropriate: he could even overturn a conditional grant of planning permission and refuse permission altogether. If dissatisfied with the outcome of the appeal, the applicant may within six weeks apply to the High Court on the ground that the decision reached was 'ultra vires' i e one which could not be legally justified under the Town and Country Planning Act. A *neighbour* who objects to the grant of planning permission to the person in the house next door can also challenge the decision, normally by applying to the Divisional Court (a branch of the High Court) for 'judicial review' (i e a review of the legality or reasonableness of the local authority's decision).

(C) Enforcement. Where development takes place without proper planning permission in breach of a condition, the local planning authority has power to issue an enforcement notice. As a general rule, the notice must be issued within four years of the alleged breach. It has to describe the breach and state what steps should be taken to remedy it, and also it must state within what period the necessary remedial action should be taken. The recipient of an enforcement notice may appeal to the Secretary of State and a public local inquiry is then held, unless the parties are prepared to deal with the matter on the basis of written representations alone. The Secretary of State on appeal has wide powers to discharge, modify or confirm the enforcement notice. There is a further right to appeal to the High Court from his decision on points of law. If someone fails to comply with a valid enforcement notice, he can be prosecuted and fined on conviction and he can also be penalised for continuing to disobey it after conviction. The local authority also has power to enter on the land and remove structures erected without planning permission. Where the use of a property has been changed without permission, the authority can seek an injunction from the Court ordering the cessation of that use. Disobedience of the injunction can be punished by fines and even imprisonment. If a local authority has served an enforcement notice on someone but it has not yet become effective (e g because an appeal is pending), it can serve a 'stop notice'. This is an interim order requiring the development to cease until the matter is finally sorted out. Disobedience of a stop notice is a punishable offence. However, an aggrieved party served with a stop notice who subsequently wins an appeal against an enforcement notice, may claim compensation from the local authority.

(D) Miscellaneous provisions. Apart from the general law relating to planning permission, there are various other important powers which may affect the way in which a homeowner uses or develops his property. Under the Town and Country Planning Act 1971, it is possible for the Secretary of State to list certain buildings as being of special architectural or historic interest. Once a building has been listed, it is an offence to demolish, alter or extend it without obtaining 'listed building consent'; it is also an offence to damage such a building. Under the same Act, the local authority may make a tree preservation

order, in which case it is an offence to cut down the trees in question without consent. Also it is possible to designate an area as a 'conservation area', in which case it is unlawful to demolish a building or to fell any trees without consent. The purchaser of a house will find out whether these provisions apply to the property from his local search (see page 43).

(iii) Compulsory Purchase

There are various circumstances in which statutory powers are conferred on specific institutions (e g local authorities or statutory undertakings such as Electricity Boards or British Gas) to acquire land compulsorily. Another obvious example is a highway authority needing to widen an existing road or to build a new one. Where such a power is exercised, it can only be used for the purposes described in the empowering statute, and any attempt to use the power for some other reason can be prevented by challenging the institution in question in court. One of the most common uses of the compulsory purchase system arises where a planning authority needs to acquire land in order to develop, redevelop or improve an area within its control. Also in some circumstances a homeowner whose property has been 'blighted' by adverse planning proposals or decisions can insist that a local authority should compulsorily purchase his house. For example, it may be known that in the future a dual-carriageway road will be built on the site of one's home: in that case, it will be impossible to sell it on the open market but the local authority can be forced to purchase it.

Whenever the compulsory purchase system is invoked, it is necessary for the authority in question to follow the procedure laid down in the Acquisition of Land Act 1981. This Act establishes that proper notice must be sent out and that representations and objections must be heard and gives limited rights of appeal against any compulsory purchase order made. Assuming that the order stands, the acquiring authority must act on it within three years. It will write to the people affected asking them to make their claims for compensation. Assuming that a figure can be agreed, a conveyance is drawn up and executed much as would happen in the case of a private sale and purchase, except that there is no need to draw up a written contract.

Compensation. The most likely dispute between the parties will relate to the amount of compensation payable. The Land Compensation

Act 1961 deals with this problem. Disputes are resolved by the Lands Tribunal, a specialized body which consists both of lawyers and valuers. Under the Act, the basis of compensation is the market value of the property ie the amount which the land, if sold in the open market by a willing seller, might be expected to realise. However, if the property acquired is unfit for habitation, it is only the value of the *site* which can be taken into account. Working out the market value is a complex and specialised matter on which advice should always be taken; in particular, it is permissible in some situations to look not only at the existing use value of the land, but its value were it to be developed with the benefit of planning permission. The land's 'prospective development value' may considerably exceed its 'existing use value'. An authority compulsorily purchasing land may also be required to pay compensation for the depreciation in value of any land retained, and for the disturbance caused to someone forced to leave his property.

SECTION 3
THE LAW AND YOUR JOB

Every employee has a contract of employment with his employer. Often the agreement is not written down, although contracts of apprenticeship must be in writing. The contract is made in the same way as any other contract, on the basis of the terms offered and agreed at the job interview or in a follow-up letter containing an offer of employment.

Once the job applicant has accepted the offer, either orally, in writing or by turning up on the stated day and starting work, the contract automatically comes into existence, even though there may be nothing at all in writing. It follows from this that it is impossible for employees to have no contract of employment. At the most, they might have no written contract. In such cases, the question of what are the contractual rights and duties of employers and employees might have to be determined by the courts if there are serious disputes which cannot be resolved by negotiation.

There are some duties which are implied into all contracts of employment – unless there is a written contract which makes express provision otherwise – and the most important of these are set out below.

1. EMPLOYEE'S DUTIES

The employee's basic duty is to serve his employer faithfully, and in principle anything he does which is detrimental to the employer's interests is a breach of that duty. An obvious example is 'moonlighting' by competing with the employer. So, in the case of *Hivac v Park Royal Scientific Instruments Ltd* (1946), some of Hivac's employees worked for the defendants, a rival company, in their spare time. This was held to be a breach of the contract of employment, and the Court in fact granted an injunction restraining the defendants from continuing to employ them. The duty is very wide in its scope: the employee must not engage in any conduct which is detrimental to the employer's interests. In the old case of *Pearce v Foster* (1886), for example, Pearce was employed in the City of London as a confidential clerk advising his employers on stock exchange transactions. His employers discovered that he was speculating privately in stocks and shares,

and dismissed him. The court held that they were entitled to do so since his activities suggested that he could no longer give objective and disinterested advice to his employers.

However, this will only apply when the employee's second job might damage the employer. In the case of unskilled or semi-skilled employees it has been held by the courts that there is no breach of their duty of fidelity if they take on a second job – say, in the evenings.

Another aspect of the duty is that if an employee makes any discovery during the course of his work, using his employer's time and materials, the benefit of the discovery belongs to the employer and not to the employee personally. So, in *British Syphon Co Ltd v Homewood* (1956), Mr Homewood, who was the employer's chief technician, invented a soda water dispenser. He patented it in his own name and then started work for a rival company. The Court ruled that the patent must be held for the benefit of his former employers.

The Patents Act 1977, however, provides that employees may apply to the Comptroller of Patents for an award of compensation in certain circumstances. The necessary forms for making such claims can be obtained from the Stationery Department, Patent Office, 25 Southampton Buildings, London WC2.

Some of the employee's duties continue to bind him after he has left the employment. In particular, he is under a duty not to disclose any confidential information acquired during the course of his employment to an unauthorised third person. However, this is a developing area of the law, and recent cases suggest that information acquired by the employee in the course of his service – and not subject to a special contract term – falls into three groups:

(a) Information which, because of its trivial character or easy accessibility from public sources, is not confidential at all. The employee is at liberty to impart it during his employment or afterwards to anyone he pleases, including competitors. This class of information will not readily be extended by the Courts.

(b) Information which the employee must treat

Inventions at work

During the course of his work, an employee may invent something, and contracts of employment sometimes contain a clause which sets out to deal with the situation. The position is in fact governed by the Patents Act 1977. This states (section 39):

(a) An invention made by an employee belongs to the employer provided either it was made during his normal duties, or, the duties were specifically assigned to him.

(b) In either case the circumstances must be such that an invention might reasonably be expected to result from those duties.

(c) An invention will also belong to the employer where, because of the employee's special responsibilities, he has a special obligation to further the employer's interests.

Only inventions covered by these fairly restrictive provisions belong to the employer and even in that case the employee may be entitled to an award of compensation, i e, a fair share in the benefits. To get compensation, the employee must apply to the Comptroller General of Patents (or the Patents Court) and all the circumstances will be taken into account in assessing the compensation award. These include, for example, the input of other employees, and any assistance from the employer. All other inventions belong to the employee – whatever the contract of employment says – and if he transfers the right to the employer, and the financial reward is inadequate, it is possible to apply for compensation. This only applies to inventions which can be patented. The position with copyright (i e, rights in literary works) is different. The Copyright Act 1956 covers the matter. If the work was written in the course of employment – a sales brochure or technical manual, for example – the copyright belongs to the employer. But this does not extend to work written outside the course of employment – for example, an engineer who gives lectures at a technical college in his spare time has the copyright in his lecture material.

as confidential, either because he is expressly told that it is confidential, or because from its character it is obviously so. Once learned, this information necessarily remains in the employee's head and becomes part of his own skill and knowledge. The legal position then is quite clear:

> 'So long as the employment continues, he cannot otherwise use or disclose such information without infidelity and therefore breach of contract. But when he is no longer in the same service the law allows him to use his full skill and knowledge for his own benefit in competition with his former master'.

This statement was made in *Faccenda Chicken Co Ltd v Fowler* (1985), where the Court found against an employer who claimed damages against ex-employees for alleged abuse of confidential information. Faccenda marketed fresh chickens. Mr Fowler was their sales manager and, at his suggestion, Faccenda adopted a method of selling from refrigerated vans travelling particular routes. Each van salesman acquired sales information about customers, prices and so on. Fowler left the plaintiff's employment and set up his own business, conducting it in the same area as Faccenda, using the same routes and serving the same type of customers. Five of Faccenda's van salesmen joined the rival firm. The High Court held that they were entitled to do so and dismissed Faccenda's claim for damages.

(c) Specific trade secrets so confidential that, even though they have been learned by heart and even though the employee may have left his employer's service, they cannot lawfully be used for the benefit of anyone but the employer. This is a narrow class of trade secret – special formulae, unique processes and the like – and the category is fairly restricted.

Employees also have a duty to obey all reasonable orders given by their employer. What is 'reasonable' will clearly depend on the nature of the job they have been employed to do and the particular circumstances prevailing at the time. For example, if an office has just flooded it may well be reasonable for employers to ask clerks to set to work mopping up, whereas it would not be reasonable to ask them to wash floors in normal times.

2. EMPLOYER'S DUTIES

The contract of employment is not a one-sided agreement. Corresponding duties are imposed on

123

the employer. Thus the employer is bound to pay the agreed wage or remuneration and if, unusually, nothing were said about this vital subject, the employee would be entitled to 'reasonable remuneration' as decided by the Court. In general, however, the employer is not obliged to provide his staff with any work. This is subject to two exceptions:

(a) If the work is essential to enable the employee to earn his remuneration, e g, a commercial traveller employed on a commission only basis.

(b) If doing the work is essential to enhance the reputation of the employee. This unusual situation is illustrated by the decision of the House of Lords in *Herbert Clayton & Jack Waller Ltd v Oliver* (1930) where a young actor, Barrie Oliver, was engaged to play one of the three leading comedy parts in a new musical. The producers later cast Barrie Oliver for a subsidiary part, which he refused to accept. He was held entitled to do so and was awarded damages for the loss of publicity he had suffered.

These two cases apart, there is no duty on employers to provide the work. As was said in the 1940 case *Collier v Sunday Referee Publishing Co Ltd*: 'Provided I pay my cook her wages regularly, she cannot complain if I choose to take any or all of my meals out'.

An important basic obligation imposed on all employers is to provide a safe system of work for all their employees; this is a personal duty and the employer cannot absolve himself from liability by delegating the responsibility to someone else. The duty is a three-fold one. It is to (a) supply and maintain safe plant and appliances, proper for the work for which they are required or to be used; (b) ensure a safe system of working; and (c) engage reasonably competent fellow employees. If the employer is in breach of this duty, and an employee is injured as a result, the employee can sue the employer for negligence. This is so even where the injury is caused by the wrongful act of a fellow employee, since an employer is liable for the actions of his employees provided the wrongful act was done 'in the course of the employee's employment'.

This simple and sensible rule has thrown up a large body of case law, and its application in practice is shown by *Harrison v Michelin Tyre Co Ltd* (1985). Mr Harrison, a tool-grinder employed by Michelin, was injured at work while standing on a duck-board by his machine talking to another employee. Mr Smith, one of his co-workers, was pushing a truck along a passageway in front of Mr Harrison, and decided to indulge in horseplay by turning the truck suddenly and pushing it under the duck-board. The duck-board tipped up and Mr Harrison fell off and was injured. He successfully sued Michelin for damages, and the Court laid down a simple test for deciding whether or not the wrongful act was in the course of employment. This is in the form of two questions:

1. Was the incident part and parcel of the employment in the sense of being incidental to it, even if the incident was prohibited or unauthorised? If the answer is 'yes' the employer is liable.

2. Was the incident so divergent from the employment as to be plainly alien to and wholly distinguishable from it? If it is, then the employer is not liable.

Finally, there is a duty on employers to act reasonably – in other words, not to do anything which might gratuitously undermine the employment relationship. There may thus be a breach of the employment contract if the employer behaves in such a way (and without good cause) as to make it impossible for the employment relationship to continue. However, any actions on the employer's part which are expressly allowed for in the contract cannot give rise to a claim for breach of contract.

These are the basic terms which the law will imply into a contract of employment which is unwritten or incomplete. They are so obvious that they go without saying. The usual practice in the company or industry may also help fill in any gaps and today, very importantly, there are collective agreements which apply to many industries. Collective agreements – negotiated between trade unions and employers' organisations – now embrace not only wage rates and hours but the wider aspects of conditions of employment. If the terms of the collective agreement are specifically referred to in the contract of employment, there is no doubt that they form part of the contract of employment, even if the particular individual is not a union member. So, in *National Coal Board v Galley* (1958), a colliery deputy's contract of service was held to be regulated by an agreement between the union and the employer. By working to the terms of the agreement he had accepted it. Mr Galley was held liable for damages for breach of contract for refusing to work on Saturdays, although the collective agreement provided that deputies should 'work such days or part days as may reasonably be required'.

The position is not clear where there is no mention of the collective agreement in the contract of employment, either written or oral, but most lawyers think that employees will be bound by the terms of such agreements, and the Courts are likely to find that the agreement is incorporated as part of the terms of employment, even if the employee is not a member of the union.

3. WRITTEN PARTICULARS OF EMPLOYMENT

Where there is no comprehensive written contract of employment, the Employment Protection (Consolidation) Act 1978, as amended, requires an employer to give each employee a written statement of the main terms of the contract of employment, with a note on disciplinary and grievance procedures. These provisions are set out in sections 1 to 7 and 11 of the Act. The 'written particulars' are not a contract of employment; they merely summarise the contract's most important requirements and are evidence of the terms of an unwritten contract.

The written particulars must be provided within thirteen weeks of an employee starting work, the only exception being where an employer re-engages on the same terms an employee whose period of employment ended within the previous six months. He or she need not be given another written summary of terms. The following groups of employee are *not* entitled to a written statement: (a) those who have written contracts of employment which already cover the matters in question, though they must be notified about disciplinary and grievance procedures; (b) part-time employees who normally work less than sixteen hours a week – part-timers are covered when they have been continuously employed by the employer for at least eight hours a week for at least five years; (c) Crown servants; (d) registered dock workers and certain merchant seamen and fishermen; and (e) employees who ordinarily work outside Great Britain.

The written statement must contain certain basic details and a note on disciplinary and grievance procedures, although the employer can simply refer in the written particulars to other documents, such as works manuals, staff handbooks and so on, which contain the information, provided they are readily accessible to the employee. The statement must give the following details: (a) The names of employer and employee. (b) The date when the employment began. (c) Whether any employment with a previous employer counts as part of the employee's continuous period of employment and, if it does, the date on which the period of continuous employment began. The period of continuous employment is important in respect of the employee's various statutory rights, since the longer he has worked for his employer, the more rights he is entitled to. This requirement is especially important where, for example, a company is taken over, and employees are asked to work for a new company. (d) Particulars of basic terms of employment correct to a specified date which must not be more than a week before the statement is given to the employee:

(i) Scale or rate of remuneration or the method of calculating it, e g details of piece-rates, overtime payments, etc.

(ii) The intervals when the remuneration is payable, e g, weekly or monthly.

(iii) The hours of work, to include the normal working hours.

(iv) Details of holiday entitlement and holiday pay in sufficient detail to enable the employee's entitlement to any accrued holiday pay to be precisely calculated should the employment be terminated.

(v) Sickness arrangements and sickness pay.

(vi) Details of any pension or pension scheme. This does not apply where a special statutory pension scheme applies under the terms of which the employer is already obliged to provide pensions information.

(vii) Details of notice entitlement. This must cover the length of notice which the employee is obliged to give and is entitled to receive. If the contract is for a fixed term, the date when the contract expires must be stated.

(viii) The title of the job which the employee is employed to do.

If there are no agreed terms under any of these headings – for example, there is no company pension scheme – the written statement must set this fact out.

The law also requires that the written statement must contain a note about the applicable

```
FROM: Hopes Bakery,
      Wine Lane,
      Stoke Bishop,
      Avon.

TO:   Miss L. Small
      6 Goldney Lane,
      Bristol,
      Avon.
```

This statement sets out certain particulars, as at the date of the statement of the terms and conditions of your employment which are required to be given to you under s.1 Employment Protection Act 1978.

1. Your employment commenced on 1.1.86. Employment with your previous employer, Deans Bakery forms part of a continous period of employment which began on 26.5.78.

2. The title of your job is Shop Assistant and your place of work is Hope Bakery, Wine Lane, Stoke Bishop, Avon.

3. Your remuneration is £85 per week, payable at weekly intervals on Thursdays.

4. Your normal hours of work are from 8.30a.m. to 4.30p.m. Monday to Friday inclusive. You will not be asked to work overtime, but any overtime worked by you at our request will be paid at one and a half time the normal rate per hour.

5. You are entitled to 28 days' holiday in each calender year to be taken at times convenient to us, in addition to public holidays. During holidays you will be entitled to your normal basic remuneration. On termination of your employment your entitlement to accrued holiday pay will be in direct proportion to the length of your service during the calender year in which termination takes place. No holidays may be taken during a period of notice.

6. You will be paid your normal remuneration during absence through sickness or injury up to a maximum of three weeks in any period of twelve months, provided that you supply a medical certificate in the event of any such absence for seven or more consecutive days. Such remuneration will discharge our liability to pay you Statutory Sick Pay and you will be required to give credit for any other national insurance sickness benefits payable to you as a result of such absence.

7. There is no pension scheme applicable to you.

1

8.1.The diciplinary rules which apply to you are set out in the schedule hereto.

8.2.If you are dissatisfied with any diciplinary decision relating to you, you may apply to the Bakery Manager. Similarly if you have any greviance relating to your employment you may seek redress by applying to the Shop Supervisor.

9.1.The length of notice which you are obliged to give us to terminate your employment is one week.

9.2.The length of notice you are entitled to recieve from us to terminate your employment is:

One week's notice if your period of continuous employment is less than two years,

One week's notice for each year of continuous employment, if your period of continuous employment is two years or more, subject to a maximum of twelve weeks' notice after twelve years continuous employment.

Please acknowledge receipt of this statement by signing the acknowledgement at the end of the copy attached and by returning it to us at the above address.

Dated the....*18th*....day of.*October*.

....
[Signature of employer or agent]

2

127

disciplinary and grievance rules and procedures, and this must cover four areas: (a) Any disciplinary rules which apply to the employee must be specified or else must refer to a document, which is reasonably accessible to the employee, where the rules are specified. This does not extend to disciplinary rules relating to health and safety offences. (b) The person to whom the employee can apply should he be dissatisfied with any disciplinary action taken against him, or for the purpose of seeking redress of any employment grievance which he has, must be specified by name or description, e g, 'the Personnel Manager'. (c) Any further steps which the employee may take in such cases must be set out, e g, rights of appeal. (d) If a 'contracting-out' certificate is in force under the Social Security Pensions Act 1975 for the employment, this must be stated.

In practice, disciplinary and grievance matters are best set out in separate documents, and this is certainly the case with the larger employers. The employer can quite properly refer to other documents – including collective agreements – and it is quite permissible for these to be displayed on a notice board. The main point is that the written particulars must tell the employee where the relevant information can be seen.

The employer must keep the written particulars up to date. For example, if there is a change in the terms, or a new rule, the employer must inform the employee of the change within one month of its introduction. The administrative burden on the employer is considerable, and the easiest method for him is to meet this obligation by keeping reference documents up to date. He can do this provided he gives a written undertaking – which he can do in the written particulars – to do so. He does not then have to notify each employee of any changes, but he must up-date the document within a month of any change. However, it must be stressed that terms of the contract can only be changed by agreement between employer and employee: it is **not** open to employers to change terms merely by following this procedure.

A typical form of written particulars is set out on pages 126–127.

4. CHANGE OF EMPLOYER

Sometimes the employer's legal identity will change. For example, a business may be sold as a going concern because its owner is retiring; or a limited company, or part of its business, may be bought by another. Employment rights are protected in these circumstances, and in general the new employer must issue a new and full written statement to employees within thirteen weeks of the change.

Essentially, there are four main ways in which a business is likely to change hands:

Share transfer: when a business is sold by means of its shares being acquired by new shareholders, the position of employees does not change. They are still employed by the same legal entity. There should thus be no need for their written statements to be amended unless the name of the company changes in which case they must be notified of the change.

Transfer of a business: when commercial undertakings are sold other than by share transfer, the position of employees is protected by law and they may only be dismissed fairly for a technical, organisational or economic reason connected with the transfer.

Other transfer: when businesses which do not qualify as commercial undertakings are transferred to a new owner, the employees transfer automatically also. Their contractual terms and continuous service are preserved.

Sale of assets: if only the assets of a business are sold – i e it is not sold as a going concern – the employees have no rights against the new owner. In such cases, they will not often be able to claim a redundancy payment (see page 158) from the old employer.

5. TERMS AND CONDITIONS OF EMPLOYMENT

Before taking a job, it is essential to agree with the employer on all important aspects of the job, and not leave too much unsaid. An employee cannot expect to change the terms and conditions after he has started work. All important matters such as pay, pay increases, 'fringe benefits', sickness arrangements and so on should be sorted out at the job interview. It is the agreement reached before work is started that is the contract of employment. It is best to get a letter of appointment setting out all the points agreed and in most cases, the employer will ask the successful job applicant to sign a copy of the appointment letter. This should only be done if the letter contains all the details which the applicant believes are important. Once signed, the letter is legally binding. A typical letter of appointment is set out opposite.

LETTER OF APPOINTMENT

Barchester University,
Barchester Towers,
Barchester.

24th October 1986

Mr Colin Piper,
8,Ashcroft Close,
High Wycombe,
Bucks.

Dear Mr Piper,

    I am writing formally to offer you appointment as Research Assistant within the Faculty of Law of the University for two years from 1st November 1986, or such earlier date as may be agreed with Professor Curry, with the possibility of extension for a third year. The salary will be £6,600 on range 1B of the Research and Analagous Staff salary scale (under review). You will be eligible for an increment on 1st November 1987.

    You will be required to participate in the University's Superannuation Scheme, contributing annually 6.35% of your salary, and as a consequence you will be contracted out of the earnings related part of the State Pension Scheme.

    As this contract of employment is for a fixed term of one year or more, it is a condition of appointment that you agree, in writing, to exclude any claim in respect of your rights under Section 54 of the Employment Protection (Consolidation) Act 1978 (as subsequently amended or re-enacted) arising out of a dismissal consisting only of expiry of that term without it being renewed.

    I should be grateful if you would let me know whether you accept this offer of appointment and if so will you please complete and return to me the enclosed staff record form.

Yours sincerely,

Registrar and Secretary

Copy to Professor Curry.

6. VARYING THE TERMS

In principle, once the contract of employment has been made, any change in its terms must be mutually agreed between employer and employee. The employer is not allowed to change the terms unilaterally. However, changes in the employment contract are often made in practice, as when an employee gets a pay rise, and changes of this sort simply take effect by the implied mutual agreement of employer and employee. Technically, the employer is bound to give written notice of the change within one month of its taking effect.

Where there is a written contract of employment, or a formal letter of appointment, this will often cover possible changes of a more fundamental nature. The contract may provide, for example:

'These terms and conditions may be subject to variation from time to time, but changes will not be implemented without reasonable prior notification. When such changes occur, the contract of employment will be deemed to be varied accordingly'.

However, even such terms are likely to be held by the courts to be restricted to 'reasonable' variations.

If changes in terms and conditions are not provided for, expressly or by implication, a change which goes to the root of the contract will put the employer in breach of the contract. In such cases, the employee can resign and claim compensation before an industrial tribunal and, possibly, damages in Court as well. The sort of changes which would be fundamental would be a reduction in pay or a demotion.

The only way an employer may make such changes in the absence of agreement from employees is by giving proper notice to terminate the employment contracts and offering re-engagement on the new terms. However, such a course of action would constitute a dismissal and so the employees concerned (providing they had sufficient qualifying service) would be able to make unfair dismissal claims to an industrial tribunal.

7. WAGES AND OTHER BENEFITS

Wages or salary are usually fixed by negotiation between employer and employee. They can also be fixed by the terms of a collective agreement made between the employer (or, more usually, an employer's association representative of several employers or a whole industry) and a trade union. The rates laid down in collective agreements will become part of the individual's contract of employment either by express reference in a letter of appointment or in the written particulars or by implication.

So important are wages that under the employment protection legislation, employers must provide employees with a detailed written pay statement at or before the time of payment. Its purpose is to enable an employee to see how his pay is made up and this is a statutory right: section 8 of the Employment Protection (Consolidation) Act 1978. This *itemized pay statement* must set out: (a) the gross amount of the wages or salary; (b) the net amount payable; (c) details of fixed and variable deductions and the purposes for which they are made. This covers trade union subscriptions and any other deductions.

There are two types of pay statement. The first is a pay statement which specifies the amount and purpose of every deduction as a separate item and is often adopted by small employers. Larger employers choose the second option, which is a standing statement of fixed deductions. This must set out the amount of the deductions, the intervals at which they are made and the purposes of the deduction. Standing statements must be reissued at least once every year and are valid for up to twelve months. The employee is then entitled to written notification of any changes made in the interim. If an employer fails to comply with these requirements, the employee's remedy is to apply to an industrial tribunal. Application must be made during the period of employment or within three months of the date when it ceased. If unnotified deductions have been made, the tribunal can award a discretionary amount of compensation of the total of unnotified deductions made during the thirteen weeks before the date of the application to the tribunal. The tribunal can also say what the statement should have contained.

(i) Statutory Protection of Wages

The agreed method of payment of wages or salary is usually written into the contract of employment, and the employer's failure to pay wages as agreed is a breach of contract on his part. Payment may be made in cash, by cheque or directly into a bank account. The Truck Acts 1831–1940 used to govern the method of payment

```
        ITEMISED PAY STATEMENT          BRIGGS & CO.

   ┌──────────────────┬─────────┬────────────────┬───────────┬──────────┐
   │ SURNAME          │ INTLS.  │ N.I.NUMBER     │ WORKS NO. │ DEPT.    │
   │ Brown            │ J.      │                │ 357       │ Despatch │
   ├──────────────────┴─────────┴────────────────┴───────────┴──────────┤
   │ PAY PERIOD ...April.1986.....                                       │
   ├──────────────────┬──────────────────────────┬──────────────────────┤
   │ PAY/ALLOWANCES   │ DEDUCTIONS               │ CUMULATIVE DEDS.     │
   │                  │                          │                      │
   │ Basic  £650.00   │ Income Tax   £144.24     │ Income Tax   £144.24 │
   │ O/time £ 50.00   │ N.I.Conts.   £ 58.50     │ N.I.Conts.   £ 58.50 │
   │                  │ Pens.Fund    £ 50.00     │ Pens.Fund    £50.00  │
   │                  │                          │                      │
   │ Total  £700.00   │ Total        £252.74     │ Total        £252.74 │
   ├──────────────────┴──────────────────────────┴──────────────────────┤
   │ NET PAY: ..£447.26.....                                             │
   └─────────────────────────────────────────────────────────────────────┘
```

of wages to manual workers and the deductions which could be made from their pay. However, these Acts have been repealed by the Wages Act 1986. Until 1 January 1987 manual workers had to be paid in cash unless they had given their written consent to be paid by cheque or by bank giro. Although this provision has been repealed, manual workers may still have a contractual right to be paid in cash and it may therefore constitute a breach of contract if their employer insists, unilaterally, in paying them in some other form.

(ii) Deductions from Pay

The Wages Act also governs deductions from pay for all employees. Specifically, it provides that deductions from pay for poor workmanship or other reasons, and provides that they may only be made if:

(a) the deduction is required or authorised by statute (e g PAYE or N.I. contributions); or

(b) the deduction is in accordance with a term of the contract and this contract term has been notified to the employee in writing or the employee has agreed to the deduction being made.

However, these provisions do not apply to deductions in respect of overpayments of wages or deductions in respect of court orders. There are also other – very limited – exceptions.

There are separate rules in the Wages Act covering deductions from the pay of workers in the retail trade, made in respect of stock losses or cash deficiencies. The Act states that such deductions will be lawful **only** if the employer:

(a) has written to the employee stating the total liability for the loss; and

(b) has issued a written demand for payment; and

(c) where the deduction is greater than 10% of the employee's gross wages due on any pay day, staggers payment so that no more than 10% is deducted in any one pay period; and

(d) has made the deduction no later than twelve months from the date when the shortage was first established.

However, if a retail worker leaves employment while deductions are still owing, the 10% rule does not apply to any monies due on termination.

(iii) Guaranteed Payments

Whether or not an employer is entitled to put an employee on short-time or temporary lay-off which is unpaid or paid at lower than average levels of pay depends on the individual's contract of employment. Many national agreements make provision for lay-off or short time, e g, the working rules governing the building and civil engineering industries. Unless there is a provision in the contract of employment dealing with lay-off or short time, the employee is entitled to be paid in full whether or not any work is provided. Thus, if a factory has to close down for a week, the employees must still be paid in full for that week unless there is a contractual provision to the contrary or they have agreed to waive their right to be paid.

Even when the employer is entitled to lay them off without full pay, section 12 of the Employment Protection (Consolidation) Act 1978 gives employees who have at least one month's continuous service a right to a guaranteed payment if they are laid off and have lost a full day's work. The daily amount of the guaranteed payment varies, but is at present £10.70. To qualify for the payment four conditions must be satisfied: (a) Employees must not be laid off or on short time owing to a strike or other industrial action involving employees of the employer or an associated employer such as a subsidiary company. (b) A complete working day must be lost. No guarantee payment is due in respect of a day in which some work is provided, even if it is provided outside normal working hours. (c) Employees must comply with the employer's reasonable requirements to ensure that their services are available. For example, the employer might require employees to report for duty at a specific time. (d) Employees must not unreasonably refuse an offer from the employer of suitable alternative work. This need not be work they are employed to perform.

This guaranteed payment is payable for a maximum of five days in any three month period.

If there is a contractual right to a guaranteed payment, e g under a collective agreement, the contractual amount will be off-set against the statutory amount and, indeed, the Act makes provision for exemption from the guaranteed pay provisions for certain employers and employees who have their own collective agreement.

Employees who do not receive guaranteed pay to which they consider they are entitled can complain to an industrial tribunal. There is a general time limit of three months from the day for which the payment has not been made, although tribunals have a discretion to accept complaints made outside this period if it was not reasonably practicable to have made the complaint earlier.

(iv) Sickness Pay

There is a statutory right to sickness pay, and the written particulars of employment (see page 125) must set out the arrangements which the employer makes for employees who are sick. The general rule is that where an employee has a period of incapacity for work in relation to his employment contract, his employer is liable to pay him Statutory Sick Pay (SSP) and the employer recovers amounts so paid from the Department of Health and Social Security provided he goes through the correct procedures. Very complex and detailed regulations deal with the matter, and entitlement to SSP depends on the employee being absent from work through incapacity for a period of four or more calendar days – including days when he would not have been expected or indeed allowed to work. An employee's right to SSP ends when he reaches his maximum statutory entitlement. The employer's maximum liability is to pay 28 weeks' SSP in any one period of incapacity for work. There are a number of exceptions to the right to SSP and those groups of people who are excluded from SSP are set out below:

(a) people over State pension age;
(b) people employed on fixed-term contracts of three months or less;
(c) people earning less than the lower earnings limit for N.I. purposes;
(d) people who have received State sickness benefit in the preceding 57 days;
(e) people who are pregnant during the period 11 weeks before and seven weeks after the expected date of confinement;
(f) people abroad in a non-EEC country or in prison;
(g) people involved in strike action.

Exclusion of an individual from SSP entitlement does not affect any contractual entitlement which an employee may have to receive sickness payments from his employer. The right to SSP is a minimum right, and many occupational pay schemes will provide employees with a better deal although there is no legal duty on them to do so. Operation of SSP depends on the employee notifying the employer of his absence, often backed up by a doctor's note. Many employers have introduced quite elaborate self-certification schemes so that the employee certifies his own illness in a special form. The rates of SSP vary and full information on current rates can be obtained from the local Social Security office.

8. HOURS OF WORK

Hours of work and overtime are fixed by the contract of employment. In general, an employee cannot be required to work overtime unless it is a term of his contract that he should do so, but various cases establish that a term about overtime may be readily implied in certain industries. Moreover, if an employee agrees to work overtime on a regular basis, he may find that his contract has been varied by implication so that he is then bound to work overtime. This is illustrated by *Tovey v F F Robinson Ltd* (1975) where lorry drivers entered into a new agreement with their employer. This said nothing about overtime payments. Previously, drivers had often worked unpaid overtime for short periods. Mr Tovey was asked to do unpaid overtime and, when he refused, he was dismissed. It was held that his dismissal was fair; he had accepted the new agreement and, on the basis of past practice, was bound to work short periods of unpaid overtime.

9. HOLIDAYS

Holidays with pay will depend on express or implied agreement between the parties and will be one of the matters covered by the contract of employment or written particulars. If nothing were said about holidays, the law would probably imply into the agreement a term that the employee was entitled to a reasonable period of paid holiday. Its length would depend on the custom and practice of the industry concerned as well as the employee's status, but of course Sundays would always be excluded. Employees are entitled to public holidays – New Year's Day, Good Friday, Easter Monday, spring holiday, late summer holiday, Christmas Day and Boxing Day – unless their contract of employment requires them to work on those days. Shop assistants are, by law, entitled to a half day's holiday a week on early closing day.

10. TIME OFF WORK FOR PUBLIC DUTIES

Sections 29, 30 and 32 of the Employment Protection (Consolidation) Act 1978, as amended, required employers, in certain circumstances, to permit employees holding specified public positions reasonable time off of perform the duties associated with them. In broad terms, the provisions apply to employees who are:
(a) Justices of the Peace; (b) local authority councillors; (c) members of regional or district Health Authorities; (d) members of statutory tribunals; (e) governors or managers of local authority educational establishments; (f) members of a water authority. *Note:* there is no mention of Jury Service in this part of the Act, but employees *must* attend for Jury Service if summoned. Employers are not obliged to pay them for this time off.

There is no right to time off with pay; it is a right to take 'reasonable' time off without pay, and what is reasonable will depend on all the circumstances of the case. Relevant factors include: (a) the circumstances of the employer's business and the effect of the employee's absence on it; (b) the amount of time off generally required to perform the public duty and the amount required on a particular occasion; (c) the amount of time off already allowed, whether for public duties or for trade union duties: see page 145. A qualified employee who is refused time off has the remedy of complaining to an industrial tribunal. There is a time limit of three months. If the tribunal finds that the complaint is justified it may, in its discretion, order the employer to pay compensation to the employee. Cash awards tend to be small.

11. MATERNITY RIGHTS

Expectant mothers are given four valuable rights by employment legislation. They are a right to:
(i) Paid time off for ante-natal care.
(ii) Maternity pay.
(iii) Return to work after a period of absence on account of pregnancy or confinement.
(iv) Complain of unfair dismissal if sacked because of pregnancy.
These are minimum rights and a woman's employment contract may make a better provision. The statutory rights are available to women employees whether they are married or unmarried, but they are subject to various limitations. Members of the police service or armed forces are excluded from the provisions and the

rights to maternity pay and leave are subject to two years' qualifying service.

(i) Time Off for Ante-natal Care

A pregnant employee is entitled to time off work with pay for the purpose of receiving ante-natal care provided she has made an appointment for the purpose and has requested time off. Except for the first appointment, the employer can ask to see the appointment card or letter and a medical certificate stating that she is pregnant. Pay is at the appropriate hourly rate for the period of absence from work and the rate is averaged out where the employee's hours vary.

If the employer refuses either to allow time off or to make the appropriate payment, a complaint can be made to an industrial tribunal. If the tribunal finds that the employer has unreasonably refused time off, it will order the employer to pay the employee an amount equal to the sum she would have received had she received time off. Where the tribunal finds that the employer has failed to make the appropriate payment, it will order the employer to pay an equivalent sum. The complaint must be made within three months of the day of the appointment.

(ii) Maternity Pay

Contrary to popular opinion, the legislation has not required the employer to pay the employee her salary or provide other employment benefits if she is away from work because of pregnancy or confinement. The law merely gives a woman who is absent because of pregnancy or confinement a right to receive *maternity pay* for a limited period during the early stages of her absence from work and a *right to return to work* up to a certain time after her confinement. These rights are hedged around with restrictions and limitations.

To qualify for maternity pay – which is 90% of the employee's normal week's pay as defined in the Act, less the amount of the flat-rate national insurance maternity allowance – the employee must:

(a) Continue to be employed by her employer until immediately before the beginning of the eleventh week before the expected date of confinement, as certified by a doctor or a midwife. She does not actually need to be at work – she might be absent because of sickness – but she must continue in employment. She will lose her right to maternity pay if she resigns her job before the eleventh week.

(b) Tell the employer at least 21 days before she stops work that she intends to stop work because of her condition. She must give this three weeks' notice unless it is not 'reasonably practicable' to do so, in which case she must notify her employer as soon as it is reasonably practicable. The employer can ask for notice in writing and may also require a medical certificate stating the expected week of confinement. Failure to comply with these provisions means the loss of the right to maternity pay.

(c) Have been continuously employed with the employer for at least two years immediately before the beginning of the eleventh week before the baby is due if she is a full-time employee. In the case of part-time employees – those normally working between eight and sixteen hours a week – the qualifying period is five years.

If the employee is contractually entitled to maternity pay – an unusual situation! – this is offset against the statutory payment. Maternity pay is payable for a period of six weeks only and is taxable under Schedule E and so income tax is deductible where appropriate along with any national insurance contributions due. The Act does not say how maternity pay should be paid. It can be paid as a lump sum when the employee leaves, or on a weekly or monthly basis. Since the intention of the statutory provision is to maintain a woman's earnings during the first six weeks of absence, it is contrary to the spirit of the Act to pay it in a lump sum at the end of the six week period.

The employer recoups the payment he makes from the Maternity Pay Fund. If an employer fails to pay maternity pay when due, or has not paid the full amount, the employee can ask the Department of Employment to pay her direct provided she has first tried to get her employer to pay which means, in most cases, that she has made a complaint against the employer to an industrial tribunal, which is her basic remedy. However, where the employer is insolvent, she can apply to the Department immediately.

(iii) The Right to Return to Work

Subject to a number of conditions, an employee has a right to get her job back after her confinement at any time before the end of a period of 29 weeks beginning with the week in which the baby was born. The basic conditions are that the employee must have been employed for at least two years and have continued in employment until at least the eleventh week before the expected date of confinement. Other requirements to be met are:

(a) She must give the following information to her employer *in writing* at least three weeks before she stops work:
   - She intends to be absent from work to have a baby.
   - She intends to return to work after her absence.
   - The expected week of confinement or, if it has occurred, the date of confinement.

(b) If requested to do so by the employer, she must produce a supporting medical certificate.

(c) After maternity absence has begun, the employer can ask for written confirmation of the intention to return to work. He can do this no earlier than 49 days from the date he was notified as the expected date of confinement, and the employer's request must warn her that she must give the required written confirmation within fourteen days after receiving the request.

(d) She must write to her employer informing him of the date she proposes to return to work at least 21 days in advance.

Although the date of the return to work is a matter for the employee to decide, she must in general return to work before the end of 29 weeks beginning with the week in which the child was born. If she is ill, and produces a medical certificate, she can defer her return for a further month from the notified date of return or, if she has not notified a date, for up to a month from the end of the 29 weeks' period. The date of return to work may also be put off, for example, because of industrial action or something similar causing an interruption of work, and it must be noted that the employer can put off the date of return for a maximum period of up to four weeks from the notified date of return, provided he gives reasons and tells the employee of the date when she can return.

These rights are not as generous as might appear at first sight since, unless the employment contract provides otherwise, then for the purpose of assessing seniority, pension rights, pay increments and so on, the period of absence is not required to be counted. Where the employee exercises her right to return to work, the period of maternity absence does count for the purposes of the various statutory benefits, such as redundancy, unfair dismissal protection and so on.

There are also restrictions in the right to return to work:

(a) The former job may no longer be available because of redundancy (see page 158). In that case, the employer must offer the employee 'suitable alternative work', and if he cannot do so, she may be entitled to redundancy pay.

(b) If it is not 'reasonably practicable' for a reason other than redundancy to offer the employee her original job back, he can offer her 'suitable alternative work'. This means work which is both suitable and appropriate for the employee, and of which the 'terms, conditions and location' are not substantially less favourable than those of her employment before her maternity absence. In other words, she has no right to her actual job back, unless the contract of employment is very specific in its job description.

(c) In the case of small employers – those employing five people or less – and it is not reasonably practicable for the woman to return to her job or to offer her suitable alternative work.

If a qualified employee, satisfying all these conditions, is not allowed to return to her job, she can complain of unfair dismissal to an industrial tribunal which, if it finds the complaint justified, may order the employer to re-instate her in her old job, or to re-engage her in another. If it is not practicable to do this, or the employee does not want it, the tribunal can make a cash compensation award: see unfair dismissal compensation, page 175. The time limit for complaints is three months from the day the employee intended to return to work.

It should be noted that if a woman is not allowed to return to work because, for instance, her temporary replacement turned out to be more efficient the dismisal is very likely to be adjudged unfair. The woman will have had no chance to improve or otherwise to convince her employer that she should not be dismissed.

(iv) Unfair Dismissal Because of Pregnancy

An employee has a right to complain of unfair dismissal if she is dismissed by her employer because of, or for a reason connected with, her pregnancy. Except in limited circumstances, such a dismissal will automatically be unfair. A dismissal by reason of pregnancy will not necessarily be unfair where the employee's condition makes it impossible for her to do her job adequately or if it would be against the law for her to do that particular job while pregnant. However, the employer sheltering behind these exceptions must be able to show that he has offered the employee a suitable alternative vacancy, if one is available, before or on the date on which her employment was due to be terminated, and if dismissed for one of these two reasons, in general the employee does not lose her maternity entitlements. See page 153 as to unfair dismissal.

If a woman who does not qualify for maternity or unfair dismissal rights (because she has been employed for less than two years) is sacked because she is pregnant, she may well be able to make a successful claim to an industrial tribunal that she has been unlawfully discriminated against on the grounds of her sex.

12. DISCIPLINARY RULES

One of the implied duties of every employee is to obey his employer's 'lawful and reasonable orders'. Whether or not the orders are lawful and reasonable is a question of fact, but the employee's disobedience to a reasonable order will be a breach of contract because it is the legal duty of every employee to obey such orders. An employee can, of course, lawfully refuse to do work for which he has not been employed and must, of course, refuse to obey an order which would involve a breach of the law. In other cases, however, failure to obey the employer's orders may result in dismissal. In an exceptional case, refusal to obey an order may be grounds for 'summary dismissal', that is dismissal without notice. So, in *Pepper v Webb* (1969), Mr Pepper was employed by Major Webb as a gardener on his Surrey estate. One Saturday morning, Mrs Webb told Mr Pepper to put some plants in at once or they would die. He replied 'I am leaving at twelve o'clock; you can do what you like about them. If you don't like it you can give me notice'. When it was nearly twelve noon, Major Webb went out into the garden, said the job would only take half an hour, and asked Mr Pepper why he was making so much trouble and fuss about it. Mr Pepper's reply was unprintable, but amounted to a very rude refusal to do what was required. Major Webb then dismissed him forthwith, without notice or wages in lieu. Mr Pepper claimed damages for wrongful dismissal. The Court of Appeal found against him. He had broken his contract by refusing to obey orders.

Summary dismissal may still be justified in extreme cases, though the test to apply is that of men and not angels, and normally dismissal must be by notice or payment of wages in lieu (see page 137). Moreover, even if the dismissal is justified at common law, the employee may still have a statutory claim for unfair dismissal, as explained on page 123. Dismissal is the last resort, and most employers will wish to exercise other disciplinary measures. Whether or not they can do so will largely depend on the terms of the contract of employment.

(i) Warnings

An employer can always give a recalcitrant employee a warning or reprimand. The contract need not expressly provide for this, though disciplinary procedures will usually do so.

(ii) Suspension

Since in general the employer is not bound to provide work for the employee, he is equally entitled to suspend an employee on full pay. Suspension on full pay is not an effective disciplinary measure and is the remedy normally adopted when alleged serious misconduct is being investigated. The employer can only suspend an employee without pay, or on reduced pay, if there is an express or implied term of the contract entitling him to do so. An employee who is wrongly suspended without pay can recover his lost wages by way of an action for damages, and could also regard himself as being constructively dismissed and bring a claim for unfair dismissal. Disciplinary procedures often provide for suspension without pay as a disciplinary measure.

(iii) Demotion

Demotion is only permitted as a disciplinary measure if there is a term to this effect in the employment contract. Demotion will otherwise be a breach of contract by the employer, and the employee can treat himself as dismissed and bring a claim for unfair dismissal.

Further information on disciplinary procedures is given in section 3.4(5) on page 156.

13. ENDING THE CONTRACT OF EMPLOYMENT

An employer can end an employee's contract at any time, either with or without notice. The contract itself may lay down the period of notice which is required. Monthly-paid employees, for example, are often both required to give and are entitled to receive at least one month's notice of termination of employment. The law lays down minimum periods of notice for most groups of employees, and the period of notice entitlement increases with length of service:

Length of Service	Minimum Notice
At least one month but less than two years	One week
At least two years but less than twelve years	One week for each complete year
Twelve years or more	Twelve weeks

Whatever the contract says – or the law provides – an employer may still end the contract of employment either with or without notice but in that case he may have to pay compensation, though to obtain redress it may be necessary to take proceedings either in court or in an industrial tribunal.

Contractual provisions for notice cut both ways. The contract may itself provide for the employee to give a specific period of notice and this he is then bound to do, unless the employer waives the right to notice. Either an employer or an employee can waive the right to notice and this is commonly done by employers in practice. The employer must then make a payment in lieu of notice.

Once he has been employed for four weeks or more, every employee is bound to give at least one week's notice of intention to leave his job, this minimum being laid down by section 49(1) of the Employment Protection (Consolidation) Act 1978. This period does not increase with length of service, although the contract may require him to give a longer period of notice. An employee who fails to give proper notice is in breach of contract and, in legal theory at any rate, the employer can sue him for damages. This is unlikely to happen in practice, although the employer might well retaliate by refusing to provide a reference. Refusal of a reference may well provide an effective sanction because prospective employers are put on guard. Indeed, the employer might well provide a reference which is to the detriment of the former employee!

The employer is not bound to give a reference or to answer any enquiries from prospective employers. If he does so, then he must tell the truth to the best of his knowledge and belief. In rare cases, an ex-employee who was the subject of a bad reference might be able to sue for libel and, by the same token, if an employer stated that an ex-employee was trustworthy when, in fact, he had been dismissed for dishonesty, the new employer could sue the old for any loss which he suffered as a result of relying on the reference.

(i) Dismissal by the Employer with Notice

The more usual case is where the employer ends the contract by notice. He, too, must give any length of notice which is laid down or to be implied in the contract of employment, and in the case of most staff statutory minimum periods of notice are required once the employee has been employed for four weeks or more. Notice need not be in writing – unless the contract requires this.

Unless the contract states otherwise, notice can be given at any time and on any day. In general, the notice period runs from the start of the following day, but many employment contracts provide that notice can only be given so as to expire at the end of a pay week or month. The minimum notice periods laid down by Parliament do not apply in every case. The following groups of employees do not qualify.

(A) Part-time employees. Part-time employees are those who normally work less than sixteen hours a week, unless they have been continuously employed by the employer for at least eight hours a week for at least five years.

(B) Registered dockworkers.

(C) Overseas workers. Employees who ordinarily work outside Great Britain under their contracts of employment. This is a limited group, and most offshore oil workers and so on are in fact covered by the provisions. It should be noted though, that workers in other countries may well be covered by the legislation of those countries.

(D) Some mariners. Masters and crew members engaged in share fishing who are paid solely by a share in the profits or gross earnings of a fishing vessel. Certain merchant seaman are also not covered.

(E) Most employees who have fixed-term contracts. In general, it is not necessary to give notice of the expiry of a fixed-term contract, but if the contract is brought to an end before the date it is due to expire, at the very least the minimum notice provisions will apply. In most cases, though, the employees will be able to sue for damages in lieu of the wages they should have earned between the date the contract terminated and its proper end-date.

(ii) Dismissal Without Notice

If an employee is dismissed without notice – and is not in one of the groups listed above – the employer will, in most cases, have acted in breach of contract. The employee could therefore make a claim for damages in the County Court equal to the amount of wages or salary that would have been payable during the notice period. However, there would be no breach of contract if the dismissal was for gross misconduct, e g theft, fighting, etc.

(iii) Written Statement of Reasons for Dismissal

Most employees whose contract is terminated, with or without notice, have a statutory right to receive from their employers a written statement of the reasons for dismissal. Employees working under fixed-term contracts which expire without being renewed have a similar right. In both cases the right is conditional on a request from the employee and on the employee having six months' continuous service with the employer. The request need not necessarily be in writing; an oral request is sufficient, but it is best to make a written request.

The employer must comply with the employee's request for a written statement within fourteen days of it being made. The written statement is important because it can be used in evidence in any industrial tribunal proceedings.

If the employer refuses to provide a written statement of reasons for dismissal, or provides one which gives untrue or inadequate reasons, the employee can make a complaint to an industrial tribunal. The application to the tribunal must normally be made within three months of dismissal, although the tribunal has a discretion to extend this time period if it considers that it was not reasonably practicable for the time limit to be met. If it upholds the employee's complaint, it may make a declaration as to what the reasons for dismissal were and will award the employee compensation equivalent to two weeks' pay.

(iv) Minimum Pay During Notice Period

Most employment contracts specify normal working hours – for example, 9.30 a m to 5 p m. Where the contract does so, any employee who works throughout those hours during the notice period is entitled to receive his or her normal pay. Indeed, with one or two exceptions, the 1978 Act guarantees all qualified employees a minimum average hourly rate of pay during the statutory minimum period of notice for any period during normal working hours that the employee is: (a) ready and willing to work – but no work is provided; or (b) incapable of work because of sickness or injury; or (c) on holiday in accordance with the terms of the contract. The right to minimum pay applies whichever party has given notice. However, if the employee has given notice, the employer need not make the statutory minimum payment unless and until the employee leaves his employment in accordance with the notice given.

There are three cases in which the guarantee of minimum pay during the notice period does not apply:

(a) Where the contract of employment specifies a notice period which is at least one week longer than the statutory minimum period. In such cases, payment during the notice period will depend on the contractual terms.

(b) Where an employee has given notice to his employer and then takes part in a strike of employees of the employer.

(c) Where, during the period of notice, the employee takes time off at his or her own request.

1. INTRODUCTION

The employee's safety at work is the responsibility not only of the employer, but also of the employee himself and his colleagues. The Health and Safety at Work etc Act 1974 imposed new statutory duties as to health, safety and welfare on specified people – employers, employees, the self-employed and those in control of premises, amongst others – but the 1974 Act (and regulations made under it) are only one aspect of safety legislation. Detailed regulations governing the health, safety and welfare of workpeople are laid down in the Factories Act 1961, the Offices, Shops and Railway Premises Act 1963, and many Acts and sets of regulations covering particular industries.

In addition to this industrial legislation, the employer is under a duty to provide for the safety of his employees under the common law, and if he breaches this duty – and death or injury is caused – the injured person (or his dependents) may bring an action for damages, i e financial compensation. Even under the legislation the employer, quite rightly, has the major share of responsibility for health, safety and welfare at work, because he controls the premises, plant and equipment.

2. COMMON LAW DUTIES

Although there is no liability on the employer in respect of the ordinary risks of the job, at common law he is under a threefold obligation – to provide 'a competent staff, adequate material, and a proper system and effective supervision'. These duties are personal to the employer, and he cannot escape liability by delegating them to someone else. The duty is not an absolute one. It is a duty to take *reasonable care* and this means that if the employer can establish that he has acted in a reasonably careful and prudent manner he will not be liable. This is in contrast to duties imposed by some Acts of Parliament under some of which the employer is made absolutely liable.

Case law establishes, however, that if to the employer's knowledge, an employee is suffering from a disability which increases the risk should an accident befall him, that special risk of injury is relevant in deciding what precautions the reasonable employer would have taken. So, in *Paris v Stepney Borough Council* (1951), Mr Paris was employed as a fitter in the Council's garage. To the Council's knowledge he had the use of only one eye. Whilst repairing a van, he was totally blinded when a chip of metal flew off and entered his good eye. The Council did not provide safety-goggles for fitters, and there was no evidence that it was the ordinary practice of employers to do so. The Council was held liable. In the special circumstances known to them, the Council should have provided Mr Paris with eye-protection and he recovered £5,250 damages and costs.

(i) A Safe Workplace and Safe Working Conditions

Statute apart, the duty of the employer is to see that the place of employment is safe, and this liability continues so long as the employee is doing something ordinarily and reasonably incidental to his employment, e g, washing himself before going home. This provision applies even when the employee is not working in the employer's premises – e g is working at another site or is travelling from company to company. However, as was stated above, the duty is to take *reasonable* care and so the employer is not expected to obviate every conceivable risk.

(ii) Safe Plant and Appliances

The employer cannot shift the blame for unsafe plant and appliances in normal circumstances. The plant, tools, equipment, etc provided must be safe and suitable for the work being done in the conditions which are prevalent at the time. The situation is well-illustrated by the case of *Bradford v Robinson Rentals Ltd* (1967), where Oliver Bradford claimed damages against his employers in respect of permanent injury which he suffered caused by frostbite from prolonged exposure to cold during a journey in his employer's van. In January 1963 he was sent on a journey to change an old van; the round journey was almost 500 miles. Both the old and new van were unheated, and the radiator of the old van was defective. Before going on the job, Mr Robinson told his employers that the journey was hazardous and he ought not to undertake it. But he was instructed to go. Oliver Bradford's claim for damages was successful; the employers were liable for negligence in exposing him to a foreseeable risk.

Most tools and equipment are, of course, purchased by the employer from third parties; but the employer cannot absolve himself from liability in this way. As a result of the Employers Liability (Defective Equipment) Act 1969, if an employee suffers personal injury in consequence of a defect in equipment supplied by the employer, the injury is treated as being the employer's responsibility even if the defect is attributable to a third party's fault and even though the employer has taken reasonable care.

(iii) Safe System of Work

'The common law demands that employers should take reasonable care to lay down a reasonably safe system of work'. This statement was made in the case of *General Cleaning Contractors Ltd v Christmas* (1952), where a window cleaner was cleaning the windows of a club. While he was standing on the sill of one of the windows to clean the outside of a window, and was holding one sash for support, the other sash came down on his fingers, causing him to let go and fall to the ground. He was following the usual practice adopted by the company's employees in working in this way. The employers had made safety belts available, but Mr Christmas, an experienced window cleaner, had not used one because there were no hooks to which the belt could be attached. Mr Christmas's claim for damages was successful. The employers were in breach of their duty to provide a safe system of work, e g, by providing wedges to prevent sashes closing. Their duty was to see that the system adopted was as reasonably safe as it could be made and they ought to have instructed all employees as to the steps to be taken to avoid accidents. Indeed, one of the Law Lords said that where a practice of ignoring an obvious danger has grown up, it is not reasonable to expect individual employees to take the initiative in devising and using precautions. It is the employer's duty to consider the situation, devise a suitable system, instruct his employees what they must do, and provide them with any implements that may be required.

In the end, every case must depend to some extent on its own facts. No two cases are identical. Various factors are taken into account: the work and its layout, provision of warnings, instruction, training and so on are all relevant factors. The employer is liable if he permits an unsafe method of working to continue.

The emphasis at common law is on reasonableness; whether the employer has fulfilled his duty is a question of fact in each case. Thus, if sued for negligence, the employer will not be liable at common law if he did all that a reasonable employer could have been expected to do in the circumstances. In *Latimer v AEC Ltd* (1953), owing to exceptionally heavy rain, a factory was flooded with surface water which became mixed with an oily liquid which was normally collected in channels on the factory floor. After the storm, the factory floor was covered with an oily film which made the floor slippery. The employers spread sawdust on the floor, but there was insufficient to treat the whole floor area. Mr Latimer slipped and was injured. His claim for damages failed. On the facts, the employers had taken every step which an ordinarily prudent employer would have taken in the circumstances and so they were not liable.

3. HEALTH AND SAFETY AT WORK ETC ACT 1974

The 1974 Act is a great advance in the law and practice relating to health, safety and welfare of people at work. Basic obligations are imposed on employers, the self-employed, employees, those in charge of non-domestic premises, people providing plant, etc for industrial use, and on manufacturers, designers and installers of work materials and equipment. It covers all employed people – except those in domestic employment in a private household. When it came into force, in 1975, about five million workpeople were brought under statutory protection for the first time. It applies to people at work wherever they may be; it also gives protection to people affected by work-activities. It is concerned with people and not premises in contrast to other legislation, e g, the Factories Act 1961, which concentrates on places.

Breach of the Act's provisions does not, of itself, give rise to any right to compensation. The Act works through the criminal law, and so if someone is in breach of any of its provisions, the sanction is a fine or – in an extreme case – imprisonment. The Act is enforced by Inspectors of the Health and Safety Executive, who have very extensive powers including a power to enter premises at any reasonable time or, if there is a dangerous situation, at any time.

A major feature of the Act lies in enforcing the law by new techniques, a criminal prosecution being the last resort. Co-operation and not compulsion is the keynote, and the most effective way of enforcing the law is found in the issue of improvement and prohibition notices.

(i) An improvement notice may be served by an inspector on any person who is contravening any relevant health and safety provision in circumstances which make it likely that the contravention will be repeated or will continue. The notice is in standard form, and states what the fault is and the time within which it must be put right. The time given for improvement must not be less than 21 days from the date of issue and may, in practice, be considerably longer. In effect, by issuing an improvement notice the inspector is condoning a breach of the law and is giving the offender a chance to put matters right. Disregard of an improvement notice is a criminal offence.

(ii) A prohibition notice, in contrast, is a drastic sanction. A prohibition notice can be served on any person who is in control of 'any activities which are being or are about to be carried on' and which are covered by relevant provisions. The notice can only be served where there is a risk of serious personal injury. It directs that the activity shall cease or not be carried on until the risk of contravention is remedied. It calls a total halt and, unlike an improvement notice, even if it is appealed against (see below) it remains effective until the outcome of the appeal is known. A prohibition notice can be issued where no breach of a specific statutory provision has occurred, but where it is clear that if the activity is started or continued, statutory provisions will apply.

The notice must specify three things: (a) the work, plant or substance creating the risk; (b) the relevant statutory provisions and the reasons for the inspector's opinion; (c) the activities which must be stopped.

Where the risk of serious personal injury is or will be *imminent* – which means that it will happen soon unless prevented – the notice can take immediate effect. In other cases, the notice will be deferred, and will not take effect until after the expiry of the specified period. Both types of notice can include directions for remedying the fault.

More than 16,000 improvement and prohibition notices are issued each year – in contrast to 2,000 or so criminal prosecutions. In practice there are few successful appeals against either type of notice. Appeals can be made on various

grounds and are decided by an industrial tribunal which can cancel, modify or affirm the notice.

Reporting a dangerous work practice to the Health and Safety Executive is a very effective means of dealing with health, safety and welfare problems at work!

The Statutory Duties

(A) Employer's duties. The employer's basic obligations towards his employees are laid down in sections 2 and 3 of the 1974 Act. They are general obligations which must be observed 'so far as is reasonably practicable' in the light of current knowledge.

Section 2 starts off by making it the duty of every employer to ensure, so far as is reasonably practicable, the health, safety and welfare at work of all his employees. That general duty is then particularised, since the employer must:

(a) Provide and maintain plant and systems of work which are safe and without risks to health.

(b) Make arrangements for ensuring safety and absence of risk to health in connection with the use, handling, etc of articles and substances for use at work.

(c) Provide information, instruction, training and supervision.

(d) Ensure that places of work under his control are safe and without risks to health – this extends to access to work places.

(e) Provide and maintain a safe and healthful working environment with adequate facilities and arrangements for employees' welfare at work.

Broadly speaking, these duties equate with the employer's common law duties. The employer must act reasonably.

But there is an additional obligation which is imposed on employers by (iii) opposite which is not based on any common law duty. All employers – except those employing less than five employees – must prepare and issue a *written safety policy* and revise it as necessary and have arrangements for carrying out that policy. The safety policy must be brought to the notice of all employees and the intention is that every employer should think out the problems with which he must deal. Effective policy, organisation and arrangements can only result from the individual company's efforts. The policy document is the statement of the company's intent, and the Health and Safety Commission has emphasised that every employer, large or small, must have a safety organisation. This need not be a formal structure – there is no general requirement to appoint a safety officer, for example – but the duties and the extent of responsibilities at specified line management levels for health and safety must be defined. An individual at the highest level must have overall responsibility, e g, one of the directors. The written policy may need supplementing by more detailed rules.

Safety representatives and safety committees need to be appointed where the employer recognises a trade union for purposes of collective bargaining and the trade union so requests, and there are special regulations (Safety Representatives and Safety Committee Regulations 1977) which lay down the detailed procedures. Safety representatives, appointed by the trade union, are entitled to reasonable time off with pay for carrying out their duties and attending any necessary training courses.

Employers and the self-employed also owe statutory duties to third parties. The basic duty is spelled out in section 3: the undertaking must be carried on so as to ensure – so far as reasonably practicable – that third parties, e g, members of the public, are not exposed to risks to their health or safety. People who control non-domestic premises are under a duty to take such measures as are reasonable in the circumstances to ensure that the premises, including access to them, and plant or substances in them, are as safe as may be. The key factor here is that the non-domestic premises must be made available to people who are not the controller's employees – students in a College for example – either as a place of work or as a place where they may use plant or substances provided for their use. It is under this provision, therefore, that an employer owes a duty to an outside contractor working on his premises and, less obviously, by a University to a student in one of its laboratories. Although the student is obviously not using the laboratory as a 'place of work' in the legal sense, he is using it as a place where he may use the equipment provided.

Duties are also imposed on any person who, in the course of business, designs, manufactures, imports or supplies any article or substance for use at work.

(B) Employee's duties. Health and safety at work depend on the co-operation of everyone involved, and section 7 of the Act imposes a basic duty on all employees while at work. The duty is to act in the course of their employment with reasonable care for the safety and health of themselves, other workers and the general public, and to co-operate with the employer and others to see that statutory provisions are observed. The employee's duty of co-operation is qualified by the phrase 'so far as is necessary'.

In an industrial situation, the application of section 7 is obvious, but white-collar workers often assume, wrongly, that they are unlikely to face health and safety problems in their working environment. A moment's thought will show that this is incorrect. The modern office, for example, is jumbled with electrical and other equipment.

The Health and Safety Commission – which is the national body responsible for implementing the Act – has issued a number of Codes of Practice and guidance notes on various aspects of health and safety at work. Codes of Practice are intended to provide practical guidance for those affected by the statutory provisions or any regulations made under them. They are guides to good practice, and if someone fails to follow a Code's recommendations he may be guilty of an offence unless he can show that he has met the legal requirement in some other way.

Heavy penalties are laid down for breach of the Act's provisions and, interestingly, if an offence committed by a corporate body – such as a local authority or a limited company – is shown to have been committed with the consent or connivance of or through the neglect of one of its senior officers – directors and so on – section 37 provides that the individual concerned can also be prosecuted, and there have been a number of successful prosecutions under this provision. In one Scottish case, for example, a top local authority official was prosecuted for failing to prepare, issue and put into effect a safety policy. Currently, the maximum fine is £2,000 by magistrates but, in more serious cases, the prosecution would be brought before the Crown Court in which case the amount of the fine could be unlimited. Indeed, in five specific cases – one of which is failing to observe a prohibition notice (above) – there is the possibility of up to two years' imprisonment.

4. OTHER LEGISLATION

Eventually – and it is a long-term aim – all the other industrial legislation governing places of work will be repealed and replaced by new provisions, but until that is done there are many Acts of Parliament and sets of regulations which govern particular situations.

The Factories Act 1961, and various detailed regulations made under it, is of wide application, as most industrial situations are covered. It is enforced by Health and Safety Executive Inspectors. In all premises covered by the Act a summary of the rules must be prominently displayed. Employers who fail to comply with the regulations can be prosecuted and fined; employees can also be prosecuted and fined if the offence could have caused death or serious injury.

Restricted hours of work for women and young people

In factories the hours of work of women and young people are restricted by law:

(a) Total hours must not exceed 9 hours a day or 48 a week.

(b) No more than 11 hours a day may be worked including overtime.

(c) Earliest permitted starting time is 7 a m and latest finishing time is 8 p m.

(d) Maximum of 6 hours overtime a week; 100 hours a year.

(e) Half-hour break after 4.5 hours of work.

There are some exceptions e g, factory cleaners, and exemption is possible. There are also restrictions on the sort of factory work which women and young people can be employed to do and other restrictions in particular industries. A woman cannot work underground in a mine.

(i) Accident Reporting

Employers are legally obliged to report serious accidents at work to the Health and Safety Executive Inspectorate. They must do this as quickly as possible after the accident happens, e g, by telephone, and must also report it in writing within seven days, using a special form, F2508. Records must be kept of all accidents for at least three years, and form F2509 may be used for this purpose. Not every accident has to be notified; only serious accidents are reportable. Serious accidents are those which cause death or a major injury. Major incidents, such as explosions, collapse of a scaffold, and so on, must also be reported.

(ii) Claiming Compensation

Nearly 800,000 people are injured at work in the United Kingdom every year. The interests of employees who are injured at work are well-protected by law, and an injured employee can claim compensation in many cases. To make a successful claim, the employee must be able to establish that: (a) the employer was negligent, i e, failed to take reasonable care; or, (b) the employer was in breach of a statutory duty, i e, has failed to carry out statutory safety requirements. The cases discussed on pages 139 to 140 show the sort of circumstances in which employers have been held liable, and anyone who is seriously injured at work should always take legal advice.

In some cases, the injured employee himself is partly to blame for the accident; he is then said to be 'contributorily negligent'. This does not mean that the employer can escape liability; all that it means is that the employee's damages are reduced proportionately. This is the effect of the Law Reform (Contributory Negligence) Act 1945, which provides that if someone is injured, partly as a result of his own fault, and partly because of someone else's fault, the damages may be reduced to the extent which the court thinks just. In practice this is done on a percentage basis.

In addition to claiming damages, an injured employee may be entitled to claim statutory sickness pay from the employer while absent from work (see page 132) or State sickness benefit from the Department of Health and Social Security.

Anyone who is injured at work – even if the injury is trivial – must take immediate steps to safeguard the position:

(a) Report the accident immediately, either to the employer or someone in authority such as a foreman.

(b) Make sure the details are recorded in the firm's accident book. If there is no accident book, it is best to write formally to the employer setting out the details.

(c) The employee should see his own doctor and, if necessary, get a medical certificate.

(d) Collect evidence about the accident, e g, obtain signed statements from witnesses.

(e) Consult a trade union representative, if appropriate, and see a solicitor if necessary.

143

5. SUSPENSION ON MEDICAL GROUNDS

Any employee who has been continuously employed for more than one month will be entitled to be paid if he is suspended from work as a result of certain statutory provisions. These mainly cover certain hazardous processes such as those involving lead or radioactive substances. Not every suspension on medical grounds qualifies; employees qualify only if they have been suspended under the following provisions:

Regulation 12 of the Indiarubber Regulations 1922

Regulation 30 of the Chemical Works Regulations 1922

Regulation 16 of the Control of Lead at Work Regulations 1980

Regulation 16 of the Ionising Radiations Regulations 1985

An employee who is so suspended must receive from his employer a normal week's pay for every week of the suspension, up to a maximum of 26 weeks. If the contract of employment already provides for payment during suspension, that is sufficient. But the employer must always make up the difference to a normal week's pay.

An employee who is entitled to medical suspension pay and does not receive it can complain to an industrial tribunal. The complaint must be made not later than three months after the first day for which payment is claimed. Tribunals can also deal with claims for underpayment and with claims from employees who have been dismissed because of their medical suspension.

It should be noted that these rules apply **only** to employees who are fit to work but whose health may be endangered if they continue: they do not cover people who are away from work because of sickness.

Every employee has certain rights in relation to trade union membership. These rights are guaranteed by law. They are as follows.

1. THE LEGAL RIGHT TO JOIN AN INDEPENDENT TRADE UNION AND TO TAKE PART IN ITS ACTIVITIES

An independent trade union, in law, is one which is recognised by and registered with an official called 'the Certification Officer'. The essence of 'independence' is that the Union must not be under the domination or control of the employer. Independent trade unions include not only the traditional trade unions such as the Transport and General Workers Union, the Association of Scientific, Technical and Managerial Staff and so on, but also various 'staff associations'. Recognition by the TUC is not essential for a union to be regarded as 'independent' in law; what is vital is registration with the Certification Officer. He is an independent Government official who, amongst other things, issues a 'certificate of independence' as proof that a trade union is independent. If the trade union does not have that certificate, any proceedings to decide whether or not an individual's union membership rights have been infringed will have to be delayed until the Certification Officer makes a decision. The right to belong to a trade union of one's choice – or the right not to belong subject to certain conditions (see below) – is one of the basic freedoms of the individual which is guaranteed by law.

Coupled with the right to belong to a trade union is the right to take part in its activities 'at an appropriate time'. This is defined as a time which is either: (a) outside working hours, or, (b) within working hours at which the employer has agreed that the employee may take part in trade union activities: section 23(2) of the 1978 Act. 'Outside working hours' can cover activities which take place when the employee is on the employer's premises but not actually required to be working, such as lunch breaks, but there may be cases in which a person can be victimised but is not protected. If the employer does not recognise the trade union for purposes of collective bargaining (see below), and has not given per-

mission for members to take part in its activities during working hours, the trade unionist who does so cannot claim compensation if he is victimised.

So, in *Robb v Leon Motor Services Ltd* (1978), Leonard Robb joined Leon's staff. He was a keen member of the Transport and General Workers Union, which the employers did not recognise. Mr Robb tried to recruit new members for the union during his normal hours of work, and the employers transferred him to another job which isolated him from his colleagues. He claimed that he had been victimised because of his trade union activities. His claim for financial compensation failed. Although he had been victimised, he was not entitled to redress because his activities took place during working hours without the employer's permission.

Such permission may be implied from the employer's behaviour as, for example, in the case of keyboard operators who are allowed to talk while working. If such an operator were to be dismissed for talking to colleagues about the benefits of union membership, it is likely that the dismissal would be on grounds of union activities and so would be unfair.

'Trade union activities' are not defined in law. They include recruiting members, collecting subscriptions, distributing literature and attending meetings off the employer's premises or on them during meal-breaks. The activities must not cause 'substantial inconvenience' to the employer's business and industrial action, such as a strike, does not form a 'union activity' for this purpose.

Officials of independent, recognised trade unions have the right to take reasonable time off work, with pay, to carry out their duties connected with industrial relations matters affecting the employer of the members they represent. The protection against victimisation only extends to employees; it does not extend to prospective employees. So, in *Birmingham District Council v Beyer* (1978), Beyer, a skilled bricklayer, was a militant trade union activist, keen to see all building workers in his union. His methods over the years had earned criticism and hostility from building employers, and he was convinced that no large employer would give him a job if it knew

Picketing

Peaceful picketing during an industrial dispute is lawful provided the rules laid down in section 15 of the Trade Union and Labour Relations Act 1974, as amended in 1980. This says that it is lawful for 'a person in contemplation or furtherance of a trade dispute' to attend: (a) at or near his own place of work; or (b) if he is a trade union official, at or near the place of work of a member of the union whom he is accompanying and whom he represents; (c) for the purpose only of peacefully obtaining or communicating information, or peacefully persuading any person to work or to abstain from working. The provision covers employees, trade union officials, and ex-employees sacked because of the trade dispute.

The right to picket peacefully is very limited. It only covers the specific acts mentioned and not other actions. In particular, pickets have no right to stop vehicles, as illustrated by *Broome v Director of Public Prosecutions* (1974) where, during a strike of building workers, John Broome – a union official – held a poster on the highway in front of a lorry and asked the driver to draw to the side of the road, which he did. Mr Broome urged the driver not to make a delivery to a nearby building site. His persuasion failed and the driver began to move. Broome stood in front of the lorry to prevent the lorry going on. He refused the driver's request to move and also refused a police request to get out of the way. There were no angry words or violence during the incident, which lasted about ten minutes. John Broome was arrested and charged with obstructing the highway. The House of Lords ruled that he was guilty of the offence.

'Flying pickets' and mass picketing are unlawful. In *Thomas v National Union of Mineworkers* (1985), mass picketing was held to be a nuisance at common law and an injunction was granted to restrain it. Unless an act is lawful within section 15, the picketing is unlawful and can attract civil liabilities as well as criminal penalties. There is a Code of Practice on Picketing which lays down the ground rules to be observed.

his true identity. He deceived the council by giving a false name and a bogus reference and was taken on. Within a few hours his true identity was discovered and he was sacked. Beyer claimed that he had been unfairly dismissed on account of 'trade union activities', namely that he had to resort to deceit and that this deceit was a trade union activity! His claim failed. The Employment Appeal Tribunal ruled that the situation envisaged by the Act is some trade union activity after employment has commenced. It did not refer to activities outside and before the employment began. Mr Beyer had been dismissed for deceit and not for trade union activities.

Union members are entitled to *reasonable time off* for trade union duties and activities if the employer has recognised the union, but not otherwise. Legislation does not specify what is meant by 'reasonable time off', but ACAS has published a Code of Practice No 3 giving guidance, the kernel of which is paragraph 10:

'To take account of [the] wide variety of circumstances and problems, employers and unions should reach agreement on arrangements for handling time off in ways appropriate to their own situations. Subsequent advice in the Code should be read in light of this primary point of guidance which ACAS considers fundamental to the proper operation of time off facilities. The absence of a formal agreement dealing specifically with time off for trade union duties and activities should not of itself preclude the granting of release'.

2. THE LEGAL RIGHT NOT TO BELONG TO A TRADE UNION

Employees also have the right not to belong to a trade union, but the extent of this right is varied where there is a 'closed shop'. Where there is no closed shop, an employee has the right not to join a trade union. He has the right not to be dismissed for not belonging to a trade union, or for refusing to join one, and is also protected against other action taken by the employer to compel him to be or become a member of the union. There is also a right not to be chosen for redundancy because he is not a trade union member.

The basic position where there is no closed shop is shown by *Dunbar v Ford Motor Company Ltd* (1975). Dunbar was disenchanted with his union and fell into arrears with his subscriptions. He returned to work after a short illness, and his colleagues refused to work with him because he was not a union member. The company encouraged union membership, but there was no closed shop agreement. Mr Dunbar persisted in his refusal to pay the arrears and also refused suggested alternative employment. After some days,

Fords dismissed him. The dismissal was held to be unfair.

The situation is different where there is a closed shop, which is called technically 'a union membership agreement'. In brief, it is an agreement or arrangement between an employer and one or more trade unions which requires certain employees to be members of a union or one of a number of unions. The law gives closed shop agreements a special status, and it is important to note that the requirement of union membership may depend on custom and practice and need not necessarily be set out in a formal written agreement. In a closed shop situation, the employee's right not to belong to a trade union depends primarily on whether the closed shop has been *approved in a secret ballot*. The law sets out very complicated rules about how the ballot must be conducted and who is entitled to vote in it.

If the closed shop has not been approved in a ballot, employees have the same rights not to belong to a union as if the closed shop agreement did not exist. But where a closed shop agreement has been approved by ballot, the employer can insist that employees join a union, and can dismiss them if they refuse to join, unless one of the following exceptions applies:

(a) The employee 'genuinely objects on grounds of conscience or other deeply held personal conviction to be a member of any trade union whatsoever, or of a particular trade union'. This exception is not confined to religious belief, but it is for the employee to establish that he has a genuine and sincere objection either to trade unionism in general or the particular union.

(b) The employee was an existing employee at the time the closed shop agreement came into effect and was not a member of the union at that time or at any time since then. Existing employees cannot be compelled to become union members.

(c) The employee is bound by his or her qualifications to observe a written code of conduct and has left or been expelled from the union, or refused to join it, because of a conflict between the professional code of conduct and a union directive to take industrial action.

(d) Where the closed shop agreement has not received the required level of support in the ballot. The required level of support depends upon the date the agreement took or takes effect. This is 80% or more of those entitled to vote or, if the agreement has previously been approved on this basis, either 80% or more of those entitled to vote or 85% or more of those actually voting. The agreement is subject to a fresh ballot at least once every five years.

(e) Where, at the time of the dismissal, the employee has been found by an industrial tribunal to have been unreasonably excluded or expelled from membership of the required trade union or has lodged a complaint to that effect with the tribunal.

In addition to the right not to be dismissed for not belonging to a trade union, employees have additional rights: (a) the right not to be dismissed for refusing to make a payment in lieu of union membership, e g, to a charity; and (b) the right not to have any other action taken against them by the employer to compel them to make such a payment.

3. EXCLUSION OR EXPULSION BY THE UNION

Closed shop agreements are very common in many areas of business and industry and even in some professions, such as acting. Where a closed shop agreement requires individuals to be members of a particular union, they have the right not to be unreasonably excluded or expelled from the union. Unfortunately, the law does not define the circumstances where an expulsion or exclusion is unreasonable. This has to be decided on the merits of each case, but guidance is given in the ACAS Code of Practice: Closed Shop Agreements and Arrangements. Any individual who works in, or is seeking, a job which requires membership of a trade union can complain to an industrial tribunal that they have been unreasonably excluded or expelled from the trade union in question. This applies to job-seekers as well as employees. Complaints must normally be made within six months of the action complained of. The remedies available are: (a) a declaration that the individual has been unreasonably excluded or expelled. This is often a sufficient remedy. (b) Compensation to be paid by the union concerned.

The complainant may also make a further application for compensation not sooner than four weeks and not later than six months after the tribunal's decision. If the applicant has been admitted or readmitted to the union, the application is to the industrial tribunal; if not, then it goes to the Employment Appeal Tribunal. The compensation awarded will be the sum the tribunal considers just and reasonable to compensate for the loss involved but subject to a statutory maximum: £12,560 by an industrial tribunal; £20,710 by the Employment Appeal Tribunal.

Apart from this special statutory procedure, other remedies are available. An employee who loses his job because he has been expelled from a trade union or because the union has refused to accept him as a member, can appeal to the Independent Review Committee of the Trades Union Congress if the union concerned is affiliated to the TUC, and its rulings are normally obeyed by affiliated unions, though not legally enforceable.

The individual concerned may also have the right to bring an action in the ordinary courts if the union takes action against him which is contrary to the union's own rules, or is contrary to the principles of natural justice, which covers the right not to have action taken against one without a full and fair hearing. A court has no power to order admission to membership, but a rule which arbitrarily restricts membership may be invalid as being contrary to public policy.

4. MAKING A COMPLAINT

These rights do not depend on age, length of service or hours of work. They are basic rights, and if allegedly infringed a complaint can be made to an industrial tribunal. If dismissed, the employee can bring a claim for *unfair dismissal*. If not, the complaint is one for *action short of dismissal*. Where the employee thinks that he or she has been unreasonably excluded or expelled from a trade union in a closed shop situation, the complaint is one of *unreasonable exclusion or expulsion*. In all cases, the complaint is made on application form IT1, which must be completed and sent to the Central Office of Industrial Tribunals.

The procedure will vary according to the nature of the complaint, but is substantially the same in all cases. An important power is that of the Tribunal to grant *interim relief* where an employee complains that his rights in connection with a trade union have been infringed. The applicant can ask the tribunal to make an order requiring the employer to continue the employee's contract of employment or to re-

employ him until the tribunal has given a decision on the complaint of unfair dismissal. There is a strict time limit to be observed. The application for interim relief must be made no later than seven days after the effective date of termination of the employment. Interim relief is appropriate only where there is a dismissal and, if the employee alleges that he has been dismissed because of trade union membership or activities, he must also get a signed certificate from a trade union official in support of his complaint. This certificate must state: (a) at the date of dismissal the employee either was or proposed to become a member of the union and (b) there are reasonable grounds for believing that his trade union membership or proposed membership was the reason for the dismissal. See section 3.4 on page 151 for unfair dismissal.

5. ACTION SHORT OF DISMISSAL

This covers discrimination in promotion, transfer or training opportunities as well as threats of dismissal or redundancy. It is very difficult to prove, and there is no statutory definition of what is embraced by the term. It is up to the industrial tribunal to decide on the merits of the case. The important point is that the actions must have been taken against the employee personally or against a number of employees as individuals and with the intention of pressurising those concerned in respect of union membership or activities or non-membership.

6. UNION RECOGNITION

Employers can no longer be compelled to recognise a trade union for purposes of collective bargaining, even if the majority of the employees are union members. Recent legislation has tended to cut back on the privileges which trade unions earlier enjoyed, and the Employment Act 1982 has in fact prohibited companies, local authorities and so on from imposing on contractors 'union labour only requirements' or 'recognition requirements', i e, requirements which make it a condition of getting on a tender list or obtaining a contract that the contractor employs only trade union members or recognises a trade union.

Recognition is a voluntary act by the employer. If a trade union is recognised, the employer is obliged to supply the union's authorised representatives with bargaining

Going on strike

A strike is a breach of contract by the employee which entitles the employer to dismiss him. As long as the employer dismisses *all* the strikers, or offers to re-engage all of them within three months, then the industrial tribunal is precluded from considering whether the dismissal is fair or unfair. But the employer cannot be selective; he cannot pick and choose who to keep on, and he may lose the protection from an unfair dismissal claim if he tries to dismiss someone before the strike has started or after it is over. Similar protection is given to the employer if he dismisses for 'other industrial action', which includes a 'work to rule' or 'going slow' or a 'sit-in'. In *Power Packing Casemakers Ltd v Faust* (1981), during a dispute about wages, employees refused to do overtime, which they were not contractually bound to do. All of them were dismissed. The ruling was that their refusal amounted to 'other industrial action' and so they could not make a claim in a tribunal.

Even if the employer elects not to dismiss striking employees, they forfeit their right to pay during the continuance of the strike, though the striker's family may be able to claim supplementary benefit from the Department of Health and Social Security.

Broadly speaking, strikers are given immunity from civil liability – claims for damages – as a result of strike action in a genuine 'trade dispute', but in certain circumstances the Trade Union Act 1984, sections 10 and 11, requires secret ballots before industrial action is taken, and failure to do so means that the civil immunity of trade unions from actions for damages is removed unless a ballot is taken and its result is affirmative. Until recently the law conferred blanket legal immunities on trade unions, thus giving them protection from civil liability. These protections have been cut down in the last few years. If a trade union is successfully sued, there are limits to the amount of damages which may be awarded, dependent on the size of the membership of the union.

There is no immunity in respect of criminal acts during a strike, and there are special criminal provisions set out in the Conspiracy and Protection of Property Act 1875. For example, section 7 of the Act makes it a criminal offence to do any of the following things with a view to compelling someone to abstain from doing an act which he has a right to do, e g, the right to go to work: (a) Use violence to or intimidate that other person or his wife or child or injure his property; (b) Persistently follow that person from place to place; (c) Hide or interfere with any of that person's property; (d) Watch or beset his home or business premises; (e) Follow that person with two or more other people in a disorderly manner. Section 7 is wide in its scope. For example, in *Galt v Philp* (1984), workers engaged in a 'sit in' and barricaded laboratories so as to prevent other employees from entering. They were found guilty of the offence of 'besetting'.

information to enable them to do their job properly, and to consult the union if redundancies are envisaged or if it is proposed to sell the business. Union officials have a right to take reasonable time off work for purposes of trade union duties and activities. The union also has the right to appoint safety representatives: see page 141.

Just as importantly, section 2 of the Employment Act 1980 obliges such employers to agree in certain circumstances to the use of their premises for the purpose of giving employees a reasonable opportunity of voting in a secret ballot for trade union purposes. The conditions to be met are: (a) there must be at least twenty employees of the employer and any associated employer; (b) the recognised trade union must propose that a ballot be held; (c) application must be made by an authorised representative of the trade union. If these conditions are met, an employer who recognises a trade union must permit his premises to be used for purposes of the ballot. Whether or not to recognise a trade union is a matter of industrial relations practice and not of law. Recognition is very much to the advantage of the union.

7. MEMBERSHIP OF A TRADE UNION

In general, a trade union can lay down in its rules who is eligible for membership, but, as indicated above (page 147), in some cases a person who is refused membership of a trade union is given a remedy by law.

The trade union rules constitute a contract between the union and its members and must be strictly observed, both by the member and by the union and its officials. Once someone has become a member of a union, he has a legal right to take part in its activities, and the law will protect him against any misuse of powers by union officials.

On the whole, the courts have tended to be suspicious of trade unions and if the rules are ambiguous, the ambiguity will be resolved in favour of the individual rather than of the union. An individual trade unionist's rights are in essence threefold: (a) he has a right to attend meetings and take part in union activities and receive benefits in accordance with the rules; (b) he has a right to take part in union elections and to stand for office, if qualified; (c) he has a right not to be expelled from the union, except in accordance with its rules – and any disciplinary proceedings must comply with the requirements of 'natural justice'. So, in *Taylor v National Union of Seamen* (1967), Taylor worked for the NUM and had a policy argument with the union's general secretary and as a result he was dismissed and lost some of his membership rights. He appealed against his dismissal, and was given a hearing, but the general secretary who had dismissed Taylor chaired the meeting and, in Taylor's absence, spoke to the appeal committee about Taylor's conduct. The appeal committee confirmed the dismissal. The court held that the dismissal was unlawful, because the rules of natural justice had not been observed.

Unions cannot discriminate against applicants or members on grounds of race or sex. It is also unlawful to discriminate against a member who refuses to contribute to the union's political fund, and if this is done a complaint can be made to the Certification Officer who registered the union. Most unions in fact have set up a 'political fund', but any member who wishes to do so has an absolute right to 'contract out' of the political fund, if he wishes. A union member is free, at any time, to give notice that he objects to making contributions to the political fund. This notice will be effective from the beginning of the following year unless it is given on joining the union, when it is effective immediately.

3.4 DISMISSAL

1. INTRODUCTION

Until the early 1970s, an employer was entitled to dismiss an employee for any reason or, indeed, for no reason at all. The only contractual obligation was for the employer to give the employee the appropriate period of contractual notice or to make payment in lieu of notice. In some cases, the employee's conduct might well warrant instant dismissal (summary dismissal) without notice.

All that was changed by the Industrial Relations Act 1971 which created a right for those employees qualified to invoke the 'unfair dismissal' procedure; this is a purely statutory right, and the relevant rules are now contained in sections 54 to 65 of the Employment Protection (Consolidation) Act 1978, as amended by the Employment Acts 1980 and 1982.

The statutory right not to be 'unfairly dismissed' builds on to the old law relating to summary, lawful and wrongful dismissal, and in some cases a dismissed employee has an option. He can bring an action at common law in the ordinary courts or else pursue a claim for compensation for unfair dismissal before an industrial tribunal. He can opt for whichever remedy produces the most advantageous result to him. For example, there is a statutory maximum on the amount of compensation which an industrial tribunal may award: see below. A very highly-paid employee may be better off suing for damages at common law if he can establish that he has been wrongfully dismissed, i e, dismissed in breach of contract. Similarly, there are strict time limits in which to bring a claim for unfair dismissal before an industrial tribunal – generally three months from the effective date of termination – but the time limit for bringing an action in court for breach of contract is six years from the date of the breach. The rules relating to unfair dismissal build on to the common law rules and, while a dismissal under the terms of the contract of employment may be deemed 'unfair dismissal' by an industrial tribunal, it may not be a 'wrongful dismissal' at common law.

Under the general law there are a number of cases where an employer may dismiss an employee summarily and without notice. These include gross misconduct, gross neglect, dishonesty and so on. So, for example, in *Stewart v Western SMT Co* (1978) the dismissal of an employee who falsified his own time records was held to be fair. The Employment Appeal Tribunal stated that: 'False clocking, or false claims in respect of hours done are serious offences of dishonesty which can justify instant dismissal'.

Although the basic rules laid down by the 1978 Act represent the basis of the law, industrial tribunals place much importance on a non-statutory document, called The Code of Practice on Disciplinary Practice and Procedures, published by the Advisory Conciliation and Arbitration Service. The principles enshrined in the Code, while not mandatory, are always taken into account by an industrial tribunal, although failure to observe it will not necessarily make a dismissal 'unfair'. In fact, the Code's recommendations merely represent good employment practice. It should be noted that the Code was under revision at the time this book went to press, but the principles set out in section 3.4(5) will remain unchanged.

2. WHAT IS DISMISSAL?

Dismissal is a technical concept, and there are three ways in which it can take place.

(i) Where the Employer Terminates the Contract, Either With or Without Notice

This is the most straightforward case: the employer tells the employee that his or her services are no longer required and the employee leaves. However, there may be grey areas; for example, in *Sheffield v Oxford Controls Co Ltd* (1979) an employee first threatened to leave and then said he would go if he was paid £10,000. He was then threatened that if he did not resign he would be dismissed. After negotiations on severance terms, he signed an agreement and left. While in most cases a threat to an employee to resign or be dismissed will constitute a dismissal, it was held in this case that it was not the threat of dismissal which had caused him to resign. He had left because of a mutual agreement and so there was no dismissal.

(ii) Where the Employee Himself Terminates the Contract, Either With or Without Notice, Because of his Employer's Conduct

Oddly, the law recognises a concept called 'constructive dismissal'. This means that, although the employee has terminated his contract – either with or without notice – the circumstances are such that he is entitled to do so. The limitation is that the employer's conduct must effectively amount to a breach of the employment contract itself. It is not necessarily sufficient that the employer is unpleasant or unreasonable. It is not every sort of unreasonable conduct by the employer that will entitle the employee to resign and claim 'constructive dismissal'. The employer's conduct must constitute a major breach of the contract – for example, trying to change the contract terms unilaterally by lowering the employee's earnings.

The law was finally settled by the Court of Appeal in the case of *Western Excavating Co Ltd v Sharp* (1978), where the employer dismissed Mr Sharp for taking unauthorised time off work. Mr Sharp appealed under the company's disciplinary procedure, and the appeal committee substituted a penalty of five days' suspension without pay. As he was short of cash, Mr Sharp subsequently asked if he could have a 'sub' – an advance of accrued holiday pay due to him. This was refused, and so he resigned in order to get his holiday pay. Subsequently, he brought a claim for unfair dismissal alleging that he was forced to resign because of the employer's conduct. He said that the employer's conduct was so unreasonable that he could not fairly have been expected to put up with it. Surprisingly, an industrial tribunal upheld his claim, but this decision was eventually overruled by the Court of Appeal. There had been no breach of contract by Mr Sharp's employers. They were under no contractual obligation to make him a 'sub' (an advance) and therefore there was no dismissal, actual or constructive.

Case law subsequent to this decision is still confused, but the basic principle is that the employee claiming 'constructive dismissal' must prove that the employer has broken a major term of the contract. The term in question need not necessarily be contained in writing: it might be one of the terms which are implied into all employment contracts, for example, regarding the employee's health and safety or the duty on the employer not to undermine the employment relationship (see section 3.1(2)). Whether an employer's conduct amounts to a constructive dismissal is a question of fact to be determined by the tribunal.

When the employer goes bankrupt

(a) All employees* have special rights when they lose their job and the employer owes money which he cannot pay because of insolvency. There is no qualifying period.

(b) The debts covered are:

(i) Arrears of pay up to £155 a week for a maximum of eight weeks. Pay includes salaries, wages, overtime, etc and certain statutory payments.

(ii) Holiday pay up to a maximum of six weeks at £155 a week maximum. This covers accrued holiday pay as well as pay for holidays actually taken.

(iii) Special payment for employer's failure to give notice. This is broadly equivalent to the amount of the employee's notice entitlement, less any earnings or state benefits in the interim and any tax liability.

(iv) Any unpaid basic award made by an industrial tribunal for unfair dismissal.

(v) Apprentice premiums or articled clerk's fees.

(c) The first step is to apply to the liquidator, trustee, or receiver and fill in the appropriate forms (IP1 and IP2) and return them to him. The liquidator, etc, can pay any debts owed to you above the £155 limit, if there are funds available.

(d) You will then be asked to sign a statement of the amount owed and transferring your rights to the Secretary of State for Employment. The Department of Employment will then fund the liquidator or, exceptionally, may pay you direct. The Department of Employment cannot pay anything above the limit of £155 a week and so only if there are surplus funds will higher-paid employees receive any more.

(e) These rights survive the employee's death and pass to personal representatives (executors or administrators) for the benefit of the estate.

* Registered dock workers, share fishermen, merchant seamen and those ordinarily working outside EEC territories are excluded from the scheme.

There can be a deemed dismissal where a woman is entitled to return to work after confinement and has purported to exercise her right to return, but is not allowed to do so: see maternity rights, page 133.

(iii) Expiry of a Fixed-term Contract

Where an employee is employed by a company for a fixed term, there is a dismissal if the contract period expires without the contract being renewed. This basic principle is subject to the following exceptions:

(a) A fixed term contract of more than two years made before February 1972 where the dismissal alleged consists solely of failure to renew on expiry.

(b) A fixed term contract of one year or more where the dismissal alleged consists of failure to renew, if the employee has agreed in writing to exclude any claim in respect of his dismissal. All well-drafted fixed-term contracts in this category will contain such an exclusion, but the only statutory requirement is that the employee must agree to the exclusion in writing before the fixed-term expires. There cannot be an exclusion clause if the fixed term is for less than one year. A contract is for a fixed term even if it contains a provision providing for either side to terminate it by notice before the specified term expires. However, if it is terminated early, the exclusion clause will not apply.

3. FAIR AND UNFAIR DISMISSAL

It might be thought, with some justification, that employers are in a somewhat difficult situation when it comes to dismissing an employee who falls under the protection of the 1978 Act.

Section 57 in fact lays down five grounds on which a dismissal is capable of being fair. These are as follows: (a) The capability or qualifications of the employee for performing the work of the kind which he or she was employed to do. 'Capability' is broadly defined. It includes any assessment by reference to skill, aptitude, health, etc. 'Qualifications' means a degree, diploma, academic, technical or professional qualification relevant to the employee's position. (b) The conduct of the employee. This is the most common ground for dismissal and covers a very wide field. (c) Redundancy. This is a technical concept: see below page 158. (d) Statutory disqualification. This is a limited ground. (e) 'Some other sub-stantial reason' which is such as to justify the employee's dismissal from holding the position which he or she held.

A dismissal based on one or more of these five reasons will not necessarily be a fair dismissal. Whether it is so will depend on whether in all the circumstances of the case the employer acted reasonably or unreasonably in treating it as a sufficient ground for dismissing the employee, and this matter has to be determined 'in accordance with equity and the substantial merits of the case': section 57(3) of the 1978 Act, as amended. The circumstances taken into account include the size and administrative resources of the employer's business.

Although the employee claiming unfair dismissal must establish that he has in fact been dismissed – and surprisingly there are many disputes about this – it is the employer who must show the reason for the dismissal; and the reason shown must be one of the five reasons listed above. If the employer fails to do this, the dismissal is automatically unfair. This is illustrated by *Raynor v Remploy Ltd* (1973) where Remploy dismissed a manager with five years' service for alleged general inefficiency and lack of sound business judgment. There was no evidence that the manager was incapable. The dismissal was held to be unfair.

From the employer's point of view, there are two important practical factors: (i) it must be established that the employer went through the proper procedures in reaching the decision, i e, following the recommendations of the Code of Practice; (ii) the employer must consider all the circumstances of the case. These include any mitigating factors. At the end of the day, the question which the industrial tribunal will ask itself is 'Would a reasonable employer have dismissed this employee?'.

4. GROUNDS FOR DISMISSAL

The five reasons for dismissal recognised by the Act cover a wide field, and must be considered in more detail.

(i) Capability or Qualifications

Incompetence in one's job is clearly a ground on which a reasonable employer may decide to dismiss. The lack of capability may be due to a natural lack of ability, or it may take the form of neglectful incompetence. Minor lapses should be tolerated, but the employee should be warned of the likely result of a failure to improve.

Incapability can take the form of ill-health; if someone is sick he is clearly incapable of doing his job, and long-term sickness resulting in absence from work is a valid ground for dismissal. Contrary to popular mythology, someone may be fairly dismissed when he is absent through sickness. The employer is entitled to consider the needs of his business as well as those of the employee. Dismissal for sickness should never be automatic; various cases have established that the employer should make inquiries from the employee and from his doctor. A warning is not appropriate in the case of long-term sickness; you cannot warn someone that his or her health must improve!

Short-term sickness on a persistent basis is different. A warning may be appropriate and a succession of absences through minor ailments, resulting in absences from work, can undoubtedly entitle the employer fairly to dismiss the employee, even if the absences are covered by medical certificates. This was the situation in *International Sports Ltd v Thompson* (1980), where Ms Thompson was frequently away from work with a variety of minor complaints. The employer reviewed her attendance record and gave her a series of warnings. There was no improvement and, after seeking the advice of their own doctor, they dismissed Ms Thompson. The dismissal was fair.

There are numerous reported cases on the problems of ill-health and dismissal and, at the end of the day, each case turns on its own particular facts. The key-note is that the employer must act reasonably in dismissing on grounds of ill-health and he must treat the employee with sympathetic consideration. The correct approach is illustrated by *East Lindsey District Council v Daubrey* (1977). The tribunal held that the dismissal of a sick employee was unfair on two main grounds:

(a) A full report on his health had not been obtained by his employer;

(b) He had not been given the opportunity to discuss the matter with his employers before he was dismissed.

On appeal, the tribunal's decision was upheld. The Appeal Tribunal said that employers should take sensible steps to consult the employee, discuss the matter with him and inform themselves of the true medical position.

Lack of qualifications is a different matter. The 'qualifications' must be relevant to the job and there must be a contractual obligation to have the qualification. This may be express or implied. For example, in *Tayside Regional Council v McIntosh* (1982), Mr McIntosh was employed as a vehicle mechanic. A driving licence was essential to his job, since he had to test-drive vehicles, though his contract made no mention of a driving licence. He was disqualified from driving and lost his licence. His dismissal was upheld as being fair.

(ii) Conduct

Misconduct is of various degrees. It can range from the trivial to the gross, e g dishonesty. Lateness and absenteeism without permission are examples of minor misconduct which, if persisted in after warning, may well result in dismissal. A problem area is that of theft. In principle, theft is gross misconduct, and the employer does not have to apply the same investigative methods as the police. What the employer must do is follow a fair procedure, and it is irrelevent whether or not criminal charges are involved; indeed, a subsequent acquittal on criminal charges is irrelevant to the fairness of the dismissal. The reason for this is that the standard of proof in unfair dismissal cases is quite different from that in criminal cases. The employer has only to show that he had a genuine belief that the employee had committed the act and this belief was reasonable.

The position regarding thefts from employers is shown by *Trust House Forte Hotels Ltd v Murphy* (1977). Murphy was a night porter who had charge of a small bar for hotel guests. Stocktaking revealed a deficiency of £10. He admitted taking this for his own use. The Employment Appeal Tribunal ruled that his dismissal was fair.

Theft or indeed other misconduct outside the employment may also lead to dismissal and that dismissal may be held to be fair. No general rule can be laid down, except to say that the misconduct must have some bearing on the job or the employer's confidence in the employee or, in the case of a public employee, the confidence of the public. For example, in *Nottinghamshire County Council v Bowly* (1978) the dismissal of a school teacher, because he had been convicted for gross indecency with a man in a public lavatory, was held to be fair. The Appeal Tribunal upheld that decision.

(iii) Redundancy

Redundancy is a valid reason for dismissal, and an employee may be entitled to a redundancy payment: see page 158. But dismissal for redun-

Rehabilitated Persons

Sometimes a person's criminal record can be kept secret. Convictions for criminal offences are treated as if they had never been committed, and ex-offenders need not mention their past when applying for a job. The protection also extends to other types of application – mortgages, insurances, club memberships and so on.

This is the result of the Rehabilitation of Offenders Act 1974, under which convictions become 'spent' at the end of a fixed period – called the rehabilitation period – which runs from the date of the conviction, the only proviso being that the ex-offender must not have committed a further serious offence during that period. The 'rehabilitation period' varies according to the severity of the original sentence (see Table) and a sentence of more than 30 months imprisonment will never become 'spent'.

Questions cannot be asked of a rehabilitated person about his past and, if asked, the person can deny his previous conviction.

Section 4(3)(b) of the Act says that, in general, a 'spent' conviction or failure to disclose it is not a ground for dismissing or excluding the person concerned from any occupation or employment or from prejudicing him in any way in that employment. So, in *Property Guards Ltd v Taylor and Kershaw* (1982), Taylor and Kershaw were employed as security guards. At the beginning of their employment both of them signed a statement that they had never been found guilty of a criminal offence. Both had convictions for minor offences. Their subsequent dismissal by the employer, on discovery of the truth, was unfair.

But there are exceptions to the Act. It does not apply to:
(a) Questions asked of a person when applying for admission to certain professions – medical, legal, accountancy, dentistry and so on.
(b) Questions asked of someone when applying for certain jobs, which range from legal appointments, police, and traffic wardens to social work, teaching and jobs looking after children.

'Spent convictions' can be revealed to the Courts by the prosecution in subsequent criminal proceedings, and also in custody, care, adoption, wardship or guardianship proceedings.

Main rehabilitation periods

Sentence	Period*
Imprisonment more than 6 months up to 30 months	10 years
6 months imprisonment or less	7 years
Youth custody	7 years
Fine or Community Service Order	5 years
Probation, Conditional Discharge, Binding Over, Care or Supervision Order	1 year or the length of the order, whichever is longer
Absolute discharge	6 months
Disqualification	When it ends

* Reduced by half for those under 17 at time of conviction

dancy is not automatically fair. The reasonable employer will consider alternatives and will try and find the employee another niche if possible. The Industrial Relations Code of Practice, which can be taken into account by tribunals in claims of unfair redundancy dismissals, states that employers should give as much warning as possible to employees of impending redundancies, should consider introducing a scheme of voluntary redundancy and retirement, and transfers to other parts of the company, and should offer the employees help in finding new work.

There are two cases where selection for redundancy is automatically unfair. If the applicant can show that other employees holding similar positions to him were not made redundant and the reason he was chosen was either (a) because he was or was not a trade union member or (b) his selection was in breach of an agreed or customary procedure, and there were no special reasons for not following it, the dismissal is unfair: section 59 of the 1978 Act.

(iv) Statutory Restriction

There are some legal restrictions on the employment of people in some circumstances. For example, a man cannot be employed as a driver unless he has a valid driving licence, and in some industries certain employees must hold certificates of competence. A driver who is disqualified from driving or someone whose competence certificate is revoked may render himself liable to dismissal for this reason. Equally, dismissal of an employee who required a work permit would be

155

British Aircraft Corporation v Austin (1978)
Ms Austin needed to wear eye protection at work. Her employers had provided goggles but she complained that, as she wore glasses, she could not wear the goggles and she stopped using them.

She spoke to the safety officer, saying she wanted goggles fitted with her own prescription lens. He said he would check to see whether the employers were prepared to pay.

Ms Austin heard no more from the employers and so she left and claimed she had been constructively dismissed. The industrial tribunal and the Employment Appeal Tribunal agreed. Employers are under a general contractual duty to take care for their employees' safety. In failing to investigate Ms Austin's complaint, her employers were in fundamental breach of that duty and had thus constructively dismissed her.

for this reason if the permit were revoked or if it expired and could not be renewed.

(v) Other Substantial Reason

This is a sweeping-up ground and various different things have been held to fall under it. For example, in *Wilson v Underhill House School* (1977), Ms Wilson, a school teacher at a private school which was in financial difficulties, refused to accept anything less than a full pay award, although all her colleagues did so. It was held that she was fairly dismissed. Similarly, refusal of new contractual terms necessitated because of the firm's commercial needs has been held to be 'some other substantial reason'. The employer must, of course, as in all cases, act reasonably in treating it as sufficient reason for dismissal.

5. DISCIPLINARY RULES AND PROCEDURES

Employers must have adequate disciplinary rules and procedures. The ACAS Code of Practice on Disciplinary Practice and Procedures in Employment makes the point (paragraph 2):

'Disciplinary rules and procedures are necessary for promoting fairness and order in the treatment of individuals and in the conduct of industrial relations. They also assist an organisation to operate effectively. Rules set standards of conduct at work; procedure helps to ensure that the standards are adhered to and also provides a fair method of dealing with alleged failures to observe them'.

Indeed, as we have seen (page 125), the law requires employers to provide written information to their employees about disciplinary rules and procedures which are applicable to them and, except in a very small business, the absence of a disciplinary procedure makes it difficult, if not impossible, for the employer to argue that he has not acted unfairly in a dismissal situation. The Code of Practice recommendations are important; failure to follow those recommendations – which have no legal effect – does not necessarily render any action taken unfair, but an employer ignores those recommendations at his peril.

It is the employer's responsibility to draw up a disciplinary procedure. Where there is trade union representation, the trade union representatives should be involved, but the important point is that the procedure, once established, must be followed.

The Code of Practice lays down eleven essential features of any disciplinary procedure. These are:

(a) The procedure should be in writing.
(b) It must specify to whom the procedures apply.
(c) It must provide for speedy settlement of disciplinary matters.
(d) It must indicate what disciplinary actions may be taken – warnings, suspension, dismissal and so on.
(e) It must specify the management's levels with authority to take the various forms of action. A basic principle is that immediate superiors should not normally have the power to dismiss without reference to senior management.
(f) It must provide for the employee to be told what is alleged and give him or her an opportunity to put his or her side of the case before decisions are reached.
(g) It must allow individuals a right to be accompanied by a trade union representative or a work colleague of their own choice.
(h) It should ensure that no employee is dismissed for a 'first offence' except in exceptional cases.
(i) It must ensure that no disciplinary action is taken until after a full investigation of the case.

(j) It must ensure that employees are given an explanation of the disciplinary action taken.

(k) It must provide a right of appeal and detail any procedure to be followed.

These are general counsels or principles; obviously the small employer cannot be expected to have a full procedure and everything depends on the size of the firm and the circumstances of each case. The procedure must be flexible and so, in a large organisation, it may be possible to by-pass early stages in the procedure in a serious case. The keynote is fairness; and disciplinary procedures are not to be judged by the same standards as would be applied by a court of law.

If the employer's action is challenged before an industrial tribunal it will be for the employer to establish that: (i) he has a genuine belief that the employee is guilty of what was alleged; (ii) he carried out a reasonable investigation into the matter and treated the employee fairly; (iii) he has reasonable grounds on which to establish his belief in the employee's guilt. In addition to a disciplinary procedure, there must also be disciplinary rules which the employee is expected to observe. These rules must be brought to the attention of the employees, and merely putting them up on the notice board is not necessarily sufficient. It should be quite clear that the rules are 'disciplinary rules' and not merely counsels of perfections or exhortations. For example, in *Rigden-Murphy v Securicor Ltd* (1976) a disciplinary rule was set out in a handbook containing 'Ten golden rules', some of which were merely exhortations such as 'Beware of complacency'. Although there was a statement at the end of the 'Ten golden rules' saying that non-compliance might result in dismissal, Mr Rigden-Murphy's dismissal for one of the substantive legal rules was held unfair.

Disciplinary rules may be couched in general terms – some types of misconduct are anathema to any employer. But the employer may specify the sort of misconduct which he will not tolerate, although other employers might. In the financial world, for example, in the City of London, where the highest standards of probity are expected, it is quite common (and sensible) for disciplinary rules to make it a disciplinary offence to 'fail to disclose any personal financial difficulties' to the employer. Similarly, in *Turner v Pleasurama Casinos Ltd* (1976), Mr Turner was employed by a casino to oversee the honesty of croupiers at the gaming tables. He was sacked for 'neglect of duty' after a client had been caught blatantly cheating in his presence. His dismissal was upheld as fair.

There is no rule of law which says that an employer cannot dismiss an employee until he has given him one or more 'warnings', but the Code of Practice does lay down some ground rules: (a) Informal oral warnings should be given by immediate supervisors for minor infractions. The purpose of an informal warning is so that the miscreant can improve his or her conduct. (b) Except where summary dismissal is warranted, if disciplinary action is needed, a three-stage procedure should be observed. (i) In the case of minor offences, a formal oral warning or, in a more serious case, a formal written warning should be given. This must set out the nature of the offence and the likely consequences of repetition. In both cases, the individual must be told that this constitutes the first formal stage of the procedure. (ii) A final written warning should be issued in the case of any further misdemeanour. This should specify the likely penalty for a further infraction, e g, suspension or dismissal. (iii) The final stage of the procedure. This, according to the Code of Practice, 'might be a disciplinary transfer' if allowed by the employment contract but, in practice, could be dismissal; whether dismissal is justified depends on the nature of the offence.

There will of course be cases where it is fair to dismiss employees on conduct grounds without having first given warnings. Such cases will arise when the employee has committed an act which constitutes gross misconduct (e g theft, fighting, etc). They may also occur in respect of acts which, potentially, are likely to result in such serious risk to life or property that no reasonable employer could tolerate the continued employment of the employee.

There should be a speedy and effective method of dealing with appeals, although in a small organisation it may be impracticable to have a formal appeals procedure. But in a large organisation this is possible and should, where there is trade union involvement, be agreed with the trade union.

3.5 REDUNDANCY

1. INTRODUCTION

When an employee loses his job because the work for which he was employed has ended or diminished he is regarded in law as redundant. Redundant employees are entitled to a redundancy payment which is paid as a lump sum, free of tax. It is payable even if the employee finds another job straight away. The object of a redundancy payment is to compensate an employee for his past services; in effect, he is treated as having a right in his job, acquired on the basis of his past services, and the payment is to compensate him for the loss he has suffered. Redundancy payments do not affect the employee's right to unemployment pay.

2. WHO QUALIFIES FOR REDUNDANCY PAY?

The general qualification is that the employee must have two years' continuous employment with the employer. This is the minimum qualifying period and any service before the employee's eighteenth birthday does not count towards the total. The employee must be at least twenty years old in order to qualify.

Some categories of employee are excluded from the right to a redundancy payment. These are as follows. (a) A person who is employed under a fixed-term contract for two years or more and who, before the expiry of the fixed-term, has agreed in writing to exclude his right to a redundancy payment. (b) People who ordinarily work outside Great Britain. (c) Part-time employees who normally work less than sixteen hours a week. (Part-timers who work for more than eight hours a week and have done so for at least five years do qualify.) (d) Civil servants, registered dock workers and share fishermen.

Only *employees* qualify for a redundancy payment. The self-employed have no right to a redundancy payment. For example, in *Challinor v Taylor* (1972), Mr Challinor drove a taxi cab at night for its owner, Mr Taylor, who paid all the running expenses of the cab and retained 65 per cent of the gross takings. He also made a contribution towards Mr Challinor's national insurance stamp, although Mr Taylor was treated as a self-employed person for tax purposes and paid tax under Schedule D rather than on a PAYE basis. When Mr Taylor sold the cab, Mr Challinor was 'redundant': his job had gone. He was held not entitled to a redundancy payment; he was not an employee.

Members of a partnership do not qualify for redundancy pay because they are self-employed. Executive directors – that is, working directors – of limited companies do qualify if they work under a contract of employment, but the position is less clear in the case of directors of 'one man' companies where, effectively, the director is working for himself.

3. WHAT IS DISMISSAL FOR REDUNDANCY?

A qualified employee is only entitled to redundancy pay if he is *dismissed* by reason of redundancy. As we have seen, 'dismissal' is a technical concept (see page 137) and if the employee resigns of his own initiative, he is not entitled to claim. Of course, the situation is different where the employee can establish a constructive dismissal, i e, where the employer has behaved in such a way that the employee was entitled to terminate the contract.

In many cases, an employer will call for 'volunteers' for redundancy. The volunteers will qualify for the payment provided they do not act hastily and there is an actual dismissal. For

---

No entitlement to redundancy pay
Some groups of employees have no right to a redundancy payment. The main excluded groups are: (a) Men and women who have reached retirement age: 65 for men and 60 for women. (b) Apprentices whose service ends at the end of the apprenticeship contract. (c) Employees on fixed-term contracts of two years or more where the contract contains a waiver clause. (d) Domestic servants working in private households who are close relatives of the employer. (e) Civil servants. (f) Merchant seamen, share fishermen, and registered dock workers. (g) Employees normally working abroad. (Northern Ireland is not abroad for this purpose).

example, in *Morton Sundour Fabrics Ltd v Shaw* (1966), Mr Shaw's employers warned the workforce of impending redundancies. Mr Shaw took the initiative, left the company and found another job. He was held not entitled to redundancy pay as he had not been dismissed.

The dismissal must also be by reason of redundancy. There are three types of redundancy situation. (a) Where the employer has ceased, or intends to cease, to carry on his business for the purposes for which the employee was employed. This is the straightforward situation and causes few problems in practice. It covers not only complete cessation of business but also where part of it – such as a department or site – is closed down. (b) Where the employer moves or intends to move his place of business. This is again an easily recognised situation but problems can and do arise. For example, an employee who, by his contract, can be required to work anywhere in the country will not be redundant just because his employer moves to another business. Equally an employee whose employer moves to new premises in the same locality will not normally be redundant on the grounds of the move. (c) Where fewer employees of a particular kind are (or are expected to be) needed. This type of redundancy situation can arise because of reorganisation, technological advances, and so on, all of which result in fewer employees being required for existing work. An employer is entitled to reorganise his business to improve its efficiency and to dispense with the services of his employees if they do not agree to the changed conditions of employment. This does not of itself create a redundancy situation. It might also arise if the employer decides to sub-contract out the work, as happens when local authorities privatise some of their services. Again, fewer *employees* are required as the work is being carried on by independent contractors.

The leading case is *Lesney Products & Co Ltd v Nolan* (1977) where, due to a falling off in sales, the company wished to reduce its output and staff at its Hackney factory. There was a redundancy situation. The night shift was taken off altogether. The machine setters who worked on the day shift were reorganised. The shift system was changed. All the machine setters were asked to stay on but, instead of working one long day shift plus overtime, they were required to work two day shifts. Those who refused were dismissed and brought claims for redundancy. The Court of Appeal ruled against them. The amount of work

coming into the factory remained the same as before reorganisation and the machine setters did the same work as before. They simply did not do the same amount of overtime; the saving was for reasons of efficiency and not redundancy.

Even if the employer can establish a redundancy situation – and it is for him to do so – he must also show that he acted reasonably. He is not necessarily justified in dealing with it by dismissal and, as we have seen, there can be an 'unfair dismissal by reason of redundancy'.

One of the major reasons for a redundancy dismissal to be unfair is if the employer has failed to give consideration to the possibility of offering alternative work to an employee whose job disappears.

4. OFFER OF A NEW JOB

A redundant employee will not be entitled to redundancy payment if he is offered a new job with the same employer and unreasonably refuses the offer: section 82 of the 1978 Act. In broad terms, this is the effect of a new job offer, but the following points must be noted: (a) The new job must be offered before the old contract of employment expires and must start within four weeks of the old job coming to an end. (b) The offer need not be in writing – though it commonly is. (c) It need not be the offer of exactly the same job. The terms and conditions may differ; but it must be 'an offer of suitable alternative employment'. Whether or not this is so is a matter of fact in each case. All the circumstances must be taken into account: the nature of the job, hours, pay, conditions, and the employee's qualifications and experience.

The approach taken to this issue is demonstrated in *Hindes v Supersine Ltd* (1979). It was held that the test of suitable employment is an objective test: is the work of a kind that is suitable when compared with the previous work done by the employee. If it is, it must then be considered whether it is 'reasonably' suitable for the employee, thus requiring account to be taken of factors personal to the employee, in terms of travelling times, the working environment, etc.

Whether or not the alternative work is suitable is to be judged objectively, although the employee's personal problems can be taken into account. For example, domestic difficulties and lack of suitable schools for children have been amongst the factors taken into account and held to be reasonable grounds on which to reject the

Redundancy Pay Calculation Table

(a) Read off the employee's age and number of complete years of service.

(b) Multiply the number of weeks shown by the current weekly pay factor (now £155). This will show the amount due.

Note that for a woman over 59 and a man over 64, the total amount due must be reduced by 1/12 for every complete month over those ages.

Service (years)

Age (years)	2	3	4	5	6	7	8	9	10	11	12	13	14	15	16	17	18	19	20
20	1	1	1	1	—														
21	1	1½	1½	1½	1½	—													
22	1	1½	2	2	2	2	—												
23	1½	2	2½	3	3	3	3	—											
24	2	2½	3	3½	4	4	4	4	—										
25	2	3	3½	4	4½	5	5	5	5	—									
26	2	3	4	4½	5	5½	6	6	6	6	—								
27	2	3	4	5	5½	6	6½	7	7	7	7	—							
28	2	3	4	5	6	6½	7	7½	8	8	8	8	—						
29	2	3	4	5	6	7	7½	8	8½	9	9	9	9	—					
30	2	3	4	5	6	7	8	8½	9	9½	10	10	10	10	—				
31	2	3	4	5	6	7	8	9	9½	10	10½	11	11	11	11	—			
32	2	3	4	5	6	7	8	9	10	10½	11	11½	12	12	12	12	—		
33	2	3	4	5	6	7	8	9	10	11	11½	12	12½	13	13	13	13	—	
34	2	3	4	5	6	7	8	9	10	11	12	12½	13	13½	14	14	14	14	—
35	2	3	4	5	6	7	8	9	10	11	12	13	13½	14	14½	15	15	15	15
36	2	3	4	5	6	7	8	9	10	11	12	13	14	14½	15	15½	16	16	16
37	2	3	4	5	6	7	8	9	10	11	12	13	14	15	15½	16	16½	17	17
38	2	3	4	5	6	7	8	9	10	11	12	13	14	15	16	16½	17	17½	18
39	2	3	4	5	6	7	8	9	10	11	12	13	14	15	16	17	17½	18	18½
40	2	3	4	5	6	7	8	9	10	11	12	13	14	15	16	17	18	18½	19
41	2	3	4	5	6	7	8	9	10	11	12	13	14	15	16	17	18	19	19½
42	2½	3½	4½	5½	6½	7½	8½	9½	10½	11½	12½	13½	14½	15½	16½	17½	18½	19½	20½
43	3	4	5	6	7	8	9	10	11	12	13	14	15	16	17	18	19	20	21
44	3	4½	5½	6½	7½	8½	9½	10½	11½	12½	13½	14½	15½	16½	17½	18½	19½	20½	21½
45	3	4½	6	7	8	9	10	11	12	13	14	15	16	17	18	19	20	21	22
46	3	4½	6	7½	8½	9½	10½	11½	12½	13½	14½	15½	16½	17½	18½	19½	20½	21½	22½
47	3	4½	6	7½	9	10	11	12	13	14	15	16	17	18	19	20	21	22	23
48	3	4½	6	7½	9	10½	11½	12½	13½	14½	15½	16½	17½	18½	19½	20½	21½	22½	23½
49	3	4½	6	7½	9	10½	12	13	14	15	16	17	18	19	20	21	22	23	24
50	3	4½	6	7½	9	10½	12	13½	14½	15½	16½	17½	18½	19½	20½	21½	22½	23½	24½
51	3	4½	6	7½	9	10½	12	13½	15	16	17	18	19	20	21	22	23	24	25
52	3	4½	6	7½	9	10½	12	13½	15	16½	17½	18½	19½	20½	21½	22½	23½	24½	25½
53	3	4½	6	7½	9	10½	12	13½	15	16½	18	19	20	21	22	23	24	25	26
54	3	4½	6	7½	9	10½	12	13½	15	16½	18	19½	20½	21½	22½	23½	24½	25½	26½
55	3	4½	6	7½	9	10½	12	13½	15	16½	18	19½	21	22	23	24	25	26	27
56	3	4½	6	7½	9	10½	12	13½	15	16½	18	19½	21	22½	23½	24½	25½	26½	27½
57	3	4½	6	7½	9	10½	12	13½	15	16½	18	19½	21	22½	24	25	26	27	28
58	3	4½	6	7½	9	10½	12	13½	15	16½	18	19½	21	22½	24	25½	26½	27½	28½
59	3	4½	6	7½	9	10½	12	13½	15	16½	18	19½	21	22½	24	25½	27	28	29
60	3	4½	6	7½	9	10½	12	13½	15	16½	18	19½	21	22½	24	25½	27	28½	29½
61	3	4½	6	7½	9	10½	12	13½	15	16½	18	19½	21	22½	24	25½	27	28½	30
62	3	4½	6	7½	9	10½	12	13½	15	16½	18	19½	21	22½	24	25½	27	28½	30
63	3	4½	6	7½	9	10½	12	13½	15	16½	18	19½	21	22½	24	25½	27	28½	30
64	3	4½	6	7½	9	10½	12	13½	15	16½	18	19½	21	22½	24	25½	27	28½	30

men only { (ages 60–64)

160

alternative job. But this must not be taken too far. In *Fuller v Stephanie Bowman Ltd* (1977), Miss Fuller worked as a secretary in Mayfair. The employers decided to move the office to Soho and Miss Bowman rejected the alternative job because the new office was above a sex shop and she said that she would find being in close proximity to a sex shop distasteful. The London industrial tribunal rejected her claim for a redundancy payment; her refusal to move to the new premises was unreasonable.

The employee is entitled to a trial period where he is offered a new job. The trial period is four weeks although this may be extended beyond four weeks by written agreement between employer and employee if retraining is necessary. If the employee rejects the new job before the trial period ends, because it turns out to be unsuitable or for some other good reason, he is regarded as redundant from the date the original employment ended.

5. CALCULATING REDUNDANCY PAY

The amount of the lump-sum payment depends on how long the employee has been continuously employed by the employer, on the weekly pay, and the employee's age. The diagram opposite shows a straightforward method of calculating the lump sum payment according to the employee's age and length of service, but the rules are very complicated. The maximum number of years of service for redundancy pay is twenty years. The exact figure is calculated by multiplying a week's pay (or one half or one week and a half a week's pay, depending on age) by the number of complete years of service: for each complete year of employment when the employee was 18–21 = half a week's pay; for each such year when the employee was 22–40 = one week's pay; for each complete year in which the employee was 41 to 65 (for men) or 60 (for women) – one and a half week's pay. The week's pay (subject to a statutory maximum) is calculated on the normal rate of pay; overtime earnings are excluded. For people paid on piece-rates, it is averaged out over the preceding twelve weeks. The present (1986) limit on the amount of a week's pay that may be reckoned is £155.

The amount of the payment is reduced for employees who are within one year of state retirement age by $\frac{1}{12}$ for each month over 64 (men) or 59 (women).

The payment is, or should be, made automatically by the employer when the employee leaves. There is no need for the employee to make a claim unless the employer fails to pay or disputes the entitlement, e g, because he disputes that there is a redundancy situation. In that case, the employee must either make a written request to the employer or make a claim to an industrial tribunal, or both, within six months from the date the employment ended. Failure to do this will normally mean that the right to redundancy pay is lost.

Legitimate claims which are not satisfied will be met by the Department of Employment out of the Redundancy Fund. If the employer is insolvent, or is unwilling or unable to pay, the employee can apply to the Department for direct payment. This is subject to two conditions: (a) the employee must have written to the employer for payment within six months of the date the employment ended; (b) the employee must have taken reasonable steps to obtain payment.

Employers who employ fewer than 10 people are entitled to claim a rebate of 35% of redundancy payments from the Redundancy Fund.

6. LAY-OFF AND SHORT-TIME WORKING

When an employer is in temporary economic difficulties – he has a low order book, for example

---

Redundancy – time off for job hunting

(a) An employee who has been employed for more than two years and is under notice because of redundancy has a right to reasonable time off with pay during working hours to look for another job or make arrangements for training for other employment.

(b) The time off must be allowed before the notice period expires.

(c) The employee does not have to produce a list of appointments for interviews: he is entitled to 'reasonable' time off with pay to look for work.

(d) What is 'reasonable' time off is a question of fact and common sense.

(e) Employees who are unreasonably refused time off or who are not paid can complain to an industrial tribunal within three months.

(f) The sanction is an award of up to two days' pay, less any sum paid by the employer towards the sum due.

– he sometimes lays-off employees temporarily or puts them on short time as an alternative to dismissing them. Lay-off and short-time are endemic in some industries, and contracts of employment often provide for it. If lay-off or short-time lasts for more than four consecutive weeks (or more than six in any thirteen weeks), the employee can give the employer a written notice that he intends to claim a redundancy payment. He must do this within four weeks of the finish of the lay-off or short-time period. If the employer believes that he will be able to offer the employee at least thirteen weeks' full-time working, he must serve a counter-notice on the employee stating this. If he does not do so, the employee may resign and claim the redundancy payment. The counter-notice must be served within seven days of the employee's notice. Disputes are then settled by the industrial tribunal if the counter-notice is not withdrawn.

It should be noted that if an employee is laid-off or put onto short-time working and this is *not* provided for in the employment contract, the employee may make a claim for damages in the county court or may resign and claim constructive dismissal (see section 3.4(2)).

3.6 DISCRIMINATION IN EMPLOYMENT

1. INTRODUCTION

In recent years, legislation has had a considerable effect on employment policies and practice. This has been particularly noticeable in the area of sex and racial discrimination and, more recently, in the field of equal pay.

The Sex Discrimination Act 1975 is designed to prevent unlawful discrimination against people on grounds of sex or marital status. It is not aimed merely at discrimination against women but, intentionally or otherwise, it is not unlawful to discriminate against single people! It is, however, not permissible to discriminate in favour of a single person. Discrimination can take one of two forms: direct or indirect discrimination.

(i) Direct Discrimination

Direct discrimination is where a person of one sex is treated less favourably than someone of the opposite sex because of the sex of the person involved. The most obvious example is to refuse to employ a woman on the grounds that it is a 'man's job', and the employer's motive for discriminating is irrelevant. Discrimination can, however, take more subtle forms.

(ii) Indirect Discrimination

Indirect discrimination is where the employer imposes a requirement or condition of such a sort that the proportion of people from one sex who can comply with it is considerably smaller than the other sex, unless the employer can show that the condition is justified irrespective of sex. Examples of indirect sex discrimination include minimum height requirements – which would exclude more women than men – or a requirement that employees weigh less than a certain amount since this would preclude more men than women.

2. DISCRIMINATION PROHIBITED

Part II of the Sex Discrimination Act 1975 prohibits unlawful discrimination in employment. It is not confined to the employer/employee relationship, and can apply to the self-employed. For example, in *Quinnen v Howells* (1984), a male self-employed demonstrator in a department store successfully complained that two female demonstrators were receiving a higher rate of pay than he was!

The Act applies to arrangements for taking on employees, their terms and conditions of employment, access to training, promotion and benefits and to dismissal.

The arrangements made for the purpose of deciding who shall be employed cover job advertisements, questions at interviews and on application forms, and so on. Job descriptions with sexual connotations in advertisements are assumed to be discriminatory unless the advertisement contains an indication to the contrary, such as 'Persons of either sex may apply'. The test is the ordinary and natural meaning of the words used and so such terms as 'waiter' or 'stewardess' are assumed to be discriminatory, but not, it is thought, terms which have no sexist connotation such as 'steeplejack' or 'engineer' or 'architect'. However, since the Equal Opportunities Commission is very active, wise employers will make sure that job advertisements make it plain that people of either sex are welcome to apply.

Even if the advertisement passes the test, this is not enough. Subsequent events are just as important. An employer who offers a job to a woman on terms less favourable than those offered to a male applicant discriminates unlawfully, but this is subject to an important exception. Unless the Equal Pay Act 1970 (see page 164) imposes an equality clause, money payments are excluded; and it is also lawful to discriminate on terms relating to death or retirement, since these are excluded from the Act.

A refusal or deliberate ommission to offer employment because of a person's sex is unlawful. For example, in *Munro v Allied Suppliers* (1977), a man was refused a job as a cook because, said the employers, women would not work with him. This was unlawful discrimination. But there must be evidence of discrimination – not every rejection will amount to discrimination.

Equally, it is unlawful to deny a woman admission to a training course on the assumption that she will be leaving soon because, for instance, it is known that her husband is moving out of the

163

area. Unless there is evidence that she will also be moving, it would be unlawful discrimination to treat her unfavourably on the basis of a generalised assumption about married women.

Sexual harassment is discrimination

In *Porcelli v Strathclyde Regional Council* (1984), Mrs Porcelli was employed as a school laboratory technician. She alleged that male colleagues were sexually harassing her by brushing against her and making suggestive remarks. She applied for a transfer to another school. She complained of unlawful discrimination; she had been subjected to a 'detriment' in having to seek the transfer. The Employment Appeal Tribunal upheld her claim. The employers agreed they were responsible for the acts of their employees.

There are a number of exceptions to the Act:

(a) It is allowable in some circumstances if the employment is in a private household.
(b) Special provisions may be given to women in connection with pregnancy or childbirth.
(c) Provisions about death or retirement are excluded.
(d) It is not unlawful to discriminate on grounds of sex in order to comply with legislative requirements passed before the 1975 Act.
(e) Genuine occupational qualifications of sex for a job are excluded, e g where the job needs to be held by a man or a woman to preserve decency or privacy and related matters. The sex of the person to do the job must be relevant if it is to be regarded as a genuine occupational qualification.

3. EQUAL PAY

The Equal Pay Act 1970, as amended, deals with equal terms and conditions of employment, and because of Britain's membership of the Common Market, account must be taken of the provisions of Article 119 of the Treaty of Rome. That requires equal pay for equal work, and it overrides national legislation. 'Equal pay' covers any benefits, in cash or kind, which are received directly or indirectly in respect of employment. For example, in *Worringham and Humphreys v Lloyds Bank Ltd* (1982), the bank's pension scheme was held, by the European Court of Justice, to be a violation of Article 119. It required male employees under the age of 25 to contribute 5% of their salary to the pension scheme while female employees of the same age were not required to make any contribution. The male employees got 5% extra salary to compensate them and, if they left the bank's employ before reaching the age of 25 they received a refund of their contributions.

Whenever a woman is employed on 'like work' or work 'rated as equivalent' or 'work of equal value' with that of a man in the same job, the woman's contract of employment is deemed (i e, treated as if it actually includes the clause) to include an equality clause. Effectively this may modify the terms and conditions of employment.

'Like work' is work which is the same or broadly similar, any differences not being of practical importance. Different responsibilities may be taken into account in deciding whether or not the work is 'like work'. So, in *Eaton Ltd v Nuttall* (1977), a man and a woman were employed as production schedulers by a company which manufactured fork lift trucks. They worked in the same department. Mrs Nuttall was responsible for ordering items up to the value of £2.50, while the male employee's job involved responsibility for items ranging in value from £5 to £1,000. The Employment Appeal Tribunal upheld the employer's contention that the work Mrs Nuttall did involved a different and lesser degree of responsibility than that done by the man because an error on his part would have more serious consequences than an error on hers. Account must therefore be taken not only the work done but also the circumstances in which it is done and the degree of responsibility involved. Different hours and different duties are also relevant considerations.

Work being rated as equivalent comes into its own where there has been a job evaluation scheme; and few problems arise here. The position is different with regard to work of 'equal value' and, under the Equal Pay (Amendment) Regulations 1983 a woman can claim equal pay on the ground that her work is of equal value to that of a man. Where there is no job evaluation scheme, the industrial tribunal can commission an independent expert who will make an assessment of the value of the woman's job and that of the man in order to determine whether or not they are of equal value. Under the regulations the industrial tribunal can make a back-dated award, the cut-off point being 1 January 1984.

In *Hayward v Cammell Laird Shipbuilders Ltd* (1985), the first successful case under the new rules, Ms Hayward, a catering worker, was successful in her claim that she was doing work of equal value to other skilled workers – painters, insulation engineers and joiners.

The Act provides a loophole where the employer can show that the variation in pay 'is genuinely due to a material factor which is not the difference of sex': section 1(3) of the 1975 Act. This enables account to be taken of such things as additional qualifications, long service increments, responsibility allowances for extra duties and so forth, as well as experience and training.

4. REMEDIES

Claims in respect of employment discrimination are dealt with by industrial tribunals. The complaint must be made within three months of the date of the act complained of although, in limited cases, the tribunal can extend this period. The conciliation officer will try and bring about an agreed settlement but, if this fails, the tribunal determines the complaint. If it is upheld the tribunal can:

(a) Make an order declaring the rights of the complainant.
(b) Order compensation up to £8,000. This may include something for injured feelings.
(c) Recommend what action the employer should take to deal with the matter. Failure to comply with such a recommendation (if made) will result in an increase in compensation.

The Equal Opportunities Commission can bring proceedings in the County Court in the case of some contraventions of the Act, e g, those relating to discriminatory advertisements, and also gives advice and help to people who feel that they have been discriminated against. Where cases involve what the Commission considers to be an important matter of principle, they often finance the case.

The Equal Opportunities Commission has extensive powers including a power to carry out formal investigations into an employer's policies and practices. It can, if the investigation establishes discrimination or contravention of the equal pay provisions, issue a non-discrimination notice.

Complaints about equal pay are also dealt with by industrial tribunals. If the tribunal upholds the complaint it can order payment of arrears or compensation.

5. RACIAL DISCRIMINATION

It is unlawful to discriminate against someone on racial grounds and, as in the case of sex discrimination, direct and indirect discrimination are covered. The motive for the discrimination is irrelevant and there is a large and unfortunately growing body of case law on the Race Relations Act 1976.

To be caught by the Act, the discrimination must be on racial grounds. These are defined (section 3 of the 1976 Act) as meaning colour, race, nationality or ethnic or national origins. Religion is not caught by the Act as such, but of course in many cases religion will fall under one of the other headings, e g, 'Jewish' can mean membership of a race as well as membership of a religion. But in England and Wales at any rate it is not unlawful to discriminate by stating 'No Roman Catholic applicants considered', though the position is different in Northern Ireland where such discriminatory conduct is specifically declared unlawful. Racial discrimination in general is prohibited and unlawful, but there are special provisions for employment discrimination.

Section 4 of the 1976 Act deals with racial discrimination in employment. It is unlawful to discriminate against someone on racial grounds:
(a) in the arrangements for determining those to

Safety rules justify discrimination
Mr Kuldip Singh worked for British Rail repairing railway carriages. In 1983 British Rail decided that bump caps – a form of protective headgear – had to be worn. Mr Singh was a Sikh who always wore a turban in accordance with his religious beliefs. He refused to wear the protective headgear and was obliged to take a different job with less pay. He claimed that he was unlawfully discriminated against contrary to section 1(1)(b) of the Race Relations Act 1976.

Mr Singh lost his case. The requirement was justifiable in the interests of safety. The test was objective. The reasons for the requirement were adequate; it was not essential for the employers to prove that the headgear was absolutely necessary. (*Singh v British Rail Engineering Ltd* [1985])

165

whom employment will be offered; (b) in the terms on which employment is offered; (c) by refusing or deliberately omitting to offer a person employment.

Once a person is employed, it is unlawful to discriminate against him or her on racial grounds as regards: (a) the terms of employment; (b) access to job opportunities or other benefits, facilities or services; (c) by dismissal or some other detriment.

There are three exceptions. (a) Employment in a private household is not covered. (b) Civil Service posts may be the subject of discrimination on grounds of birth, nationality, descent or residence. (c) Where being a member of a particular racial group is a genuine occupational qualification. This covers such things as entertainment or modelling work as well as working in a restaurant where race is required for authenticity, e g, an Indian restaurant, or where the job involves providing people of a particular group with personal services promoting their welfare.

Discriminatory practices, advertisements, etc are all unlawful, and the Commission for Racial Equality can take proceedings for breaches of the provisions. The Commission has very wide powers similar to those of the Equal Opportunities Commission.

An individual alleging discrimination can take industrial tribunal proceedings (section 54). The general time limit for the application is three months from the alleged violation. The complainant must prove that an act of discrimination took place – which is not always easy to do in practice. If the complaint is upheld the tribunal can: (a) make a declaration of the claimant's rights; (b) order payment of compensation up to £8,000 – including something for injured feelings; (c) recommend the action to be taken by the employer. Failure to comply can result in the compensation award being increased.

6. VICTIMISATION

As well as the provisions against discrimination on grounds of sex or race, victimisation is unlawful. It is illegal to victimise or treat a person less favourably because he or she has brought proceedings under the legislation, or given evidence or information, or made allegations of contravention.

7. SEGREGATION

It is also unlawful discrimination to segregate employees on the grounds of their sex or race – e g to keep all women on one shift or to employ Asians only in a particular department.

1. INDUSTRIAL TRIBUNALS

Industrial Tribunals approximate to the 'labour courts' of other countries. They have a wide and growing jurisdiction, but they still cannot deal with all aspects of employment law. They have no power to deal with claims for breaches of contract, and so if an employee wishes to bring a claim for *wrongful dismissal*, i e, dismissal in breach of contract, he must bring a claim in the ordinary Courts – usually in the local County Court. Higher-paid employees who can prove wrongful dismissal may well be better off bringing an action at common law in the ordinary Courts. Suppose, for example, a company director has a fixed-term five year contract at £20,000 a year, and the employer dismisses him during the fixed term in breach of the contract provisions, the director would be better off bringing a common law action for breach of contract. The industrial tribunal only has jurisdiction to deal with claims for *unfair dismissal* and can only award a limited amount of compensation.

The Courts cannot adjudicate on unfair dismissal, which is a creation of statute, and the industrial tribunals cannot adjudicate on dismissal in breach of contract, but of course they can take the breach of contract into account in considering whether or not the dismissal is unfair.

In *Treganowan v Robert Knee & Co Ltd* (1975), Miss Treganowan worked with other girls in an office. The atmosphere in the office became tense and unbearable and this was seriously affecting the company's business. The trouble was a personality clash between Miss Treganowan and her work colleagues for which Miss Treganowan was to blame. The hostility arose 'from a difference of opinion as to the merits of the permissive society . . . she already had an illegitimate child and was boasting of her association with a boy half her age'. She was summarily dismissed. The dismissal was held to be fair – it was for 'some other substantial reason' – but the High Court ruled that a tribunal could not award an employee who had been wrongfully dismissed without notice wages for the period during which notice should have run unless the dismissal was also 'unfair'. The mere fact that the dismissal was

in breach of contract, being summary instead of by notice, did not make the dismissal unfair.

Although there is now a statutory power to give the industrial tribunals jurisdiction to deal with common law claims, it has not yet been activated, with the result that complaints about unpaid wages, unpaid holiday pay, and other breaches of contract, have to go to the County Court.

An industrial tribunal consists of three members. There is a legally-qualified chairman, who must be either a barrister or solicitor, and two lay members. The chairman may be full or part-time but the lay members are all part-timers. They are selected from a panel which is drawn up after consultation with employers' organisations and trade unions. There must always be a representative from each side of industry at an actual hearing; the chairman can sit with one lay member only if the parties agree.

The decision can be reached by a majority vote, but this is unusual. More than 96% of tribunal decisions are unanimous. Tribunals sit at major centres throughout the country. There is a Central Office of Industrial Tribunals in London and Glasgow, together with sixteen Regional Offices in England and Wales and three in Scotland.

The addresses of the Central Offices are:

93 Ebury Bridge Road,
London SW1W 8RE
Tel: 01-730 9161

Saint Andrew House
141 West Nile Street,
Glasgow G1 2RU
Tel: 041-331 1601

There are strict time limits for making complaints, and if an application is received out of time, the tribunal will only consider the complaint if they believe it was not reasonably practicable for the employee to have made the complaint within the specified period.

(i) Applying to the Tribunal
Legal aid is not available for legal representation before an industrial tribunal, but (see section 1) 'legal advice' is available under the Legal Aid Act

to people whose income and capital are within certain prescribed limits. Such people can obtain up to £25 worth of legal advice from a solicitor for little or no cost. This means that the solicitor can give advice, help draw up documents and so on. Someone wishing to obtain advice under the scheme should consult a solicitor direct or through the local Citizens' Advice Bureau. In some parts of the country there are Neighbourhood Law Centres or Rights Centres, and trade unionists can always get help from their trade union officials. Many applicants are represented at tribunal hearings by a trade union official. The Equal Opportunities Commission has power to assist applicants under the equal pay and anti-discrimination legislation and will often do so where the complaint raises a question of principle.

Complaints to an industrial tribunal should be made on form IT1 which can be obtained from job centres or unemployment benefit offices. It is fairly easy to complete and quidance on tribunal procedure is contained in a special leaflet (ITL1) which accompanies form IT1 (see opposite).

When completed, form IT1 must be sent to the appropriate Central Office of the Industrial Tribunals at the address given on the form. It is essential to keep a copy of the form. When received by the Central Office, copies will be sent to the employer and to the conciliation officer from the Advisory, Conciliation and Arbitration Service (ACAS). The employer has a short time in which to reply (again on a special form) and copies of the employer's reply will be sent to the employee.

Over 60% of claims to industrial tribunals are, in fact, settled without the need for a formal hearing. In the process of claims settlement the conciliation officer plays an important role.

(ii) Conciliation

The Advisory, Conciliation and Arbitration Service (ACAS) is a statutory body charged with the general duty of promoting the improvement of industrial relations. It is completely independent from Government control. ACAS has its own staff, and these include conciliation officers whose job it is to attempt to settle by conciliation matters which are the subject of industrial tribunal proceedings. That is why the conciliation officer gets a copy of the complaint and the employer's reply and he always contacts both parties to see whether there is any chance of settling the claim without a tribunal hearing.

Indeed, either party can request a conciliation officer to intervene before the complaint is presented and, from the employer's point of view, there is an advantage in an early settlement of this sort. An agreement which is reached under his auspices is binding once he has recorded it on the appropriate form and it has been signed by the parties and registered with the Central Office of Industrial Tribunals.

In the majority of cases the conciliation officer intervenes after the complaint has been presented. He will contact the parties and see whether or not they wish to reach a voluntary settlement. If this seems likely, and a hearing date has been set, application can be made for it to be postponed. Many claims are disposed of on the basis of the employer making some financial payment to the applicant, but this involves 'give and take' on both sides. The conciliation officer cannot force the parties to settle; he is not involved with the merits of the case, and must not get involved on one side or the other.

(iii) Pre-hearing Assessments

If conciliation fails – or neither party wants to settle – in due course the Central Office of Tribunals will set a date for the hearing of the case. However, in some cases there will be a pre-hearing assessment. The object of pre-hearing assessments is to try and eliminate frivolous or hopeless cases. Either party can apply for a pre-hearing assessment or the tribunal may order one in any case. The tribunal will only do this if it considers that the claim or defence is hopeless or frivolous, and such orders are rarely made in practice on the tribunal's own initiative.

But employers may well apply for a pre-hearing assessment. This is an informal hearing at which the parties will outline the position. The purpose is so that the tribunal can consider whether there is any substance in the case and whether it should proceed to a full hearing. A case will not be dismissed or decided at this stage and no evidence is taken, but, if the tribunal comes to the conclusion that either claim or defence has no merit, it will warn the party concerned that he may be liable to costs if he proceeds with the claim or defence.

If, despite the warning, the party persists in a case which is subsequently found to be without merit, costs may be awarded against him at the conclusion of the full hearing – thus providing an exception to the normal rule that no order for costs is normally made. This filter system does

Originating Application to an Industrial Tribunal

NOTES FOR GUIDANCE

Before completing the application form please read —

THESE NOTES for guidance

LEAFLET ITL I which you were given along with this form

THE APPROPRIATE BOOKLET referred to under the relevant Act of Parliament — see paragraph 2 below.

1   QUALIFYING PERIODS AND TIME LIMITS

IN ORDER TO MAKE A VALID APPLICATION YOU MUST SATISFY ANY APPROPRIATE QUALIFYING PERIOD OF CONTINUOUS EMPLOYMENT AND YOUR APPLICATION MUST BE RECEIVED WITHIN THE APPROPRIATE TIME LIMIT. Information on both of these requirements is given in the booklets mentioned in paragraph 2 below. For example, to be able to complain of unfair dismissal you must normally have been employed by the same employer for the appropriate minimum period and the time limit for the receipt of such an application is normally 3 months from and including the effective date of dismissal. There is no qualifying period of employment for certain jurisdictions eg Equal Pay, Sex Discrimination or Race Relations complaints or where dismissal is for trade union activities, but time limits for making an application apply.

2   RELEVANT ACTS OF PARLIAMENT

You can ask the Tribunal to decide various questions as provided for in relevant Acts of Parliament. Details of these questions, the relevant Acts of Parliament and the titles of booklets explaining in simple terms the provision of these Acts and what the Tribunal can decide are given in ITL I which should be issued to you with this form. These booklets are obtainable FREE from any employment office, jobcentre or unemployment benefit office. This form may be used for any of the matters referred to in leaflet ITL I.

3   PREPARATION OF APPLICATION FORM

When completing the application form you should fill in items 1, 2, 4 and 12 and any other items which are relevant to your case. You should keep a copy of entries on the form. If in doubt about the respondent to name in item 4 you may seek advice from any employment office, jobcentre or unemployment benefit centre. A Citizens' Advice Bureau or Trade Union may be able to help you complete the form or advise you as to whether you have a complaint which an Industrial Tribunal could consider.

4   PREPARATION OF YOUR CASE AND REPRESENTATION AT THE HEARING

At the hearing you may state your own case or be represented by anyone who has agreed to act for you. If you intend to have a representative it is advisable that he or she should be consulted at the earliest possible stage — preferably before the application form is completed (but see note above regarding time limits). In cases under the Equal Pay and Sex Discrimination Acts the Equal Opportunities Commission, and in cases under the Race Relations Act the Commission for Racial Equality, may provide assistance or representation — see appropriate booklet. IF YOU NAME A REPRESENTATIVE ALL FURTHER COMMUNICATIONS WILL BE SENT TO HIM OR HER AND NOT TO YOU; YOU SHOULD ARRANGE WITH YOUR REPRESENTATIVE TO BE KEPT INFORMED OF THE PROGRESS OF YOUR CASE AND OF THE HEARING DATE.

Do not forget to sign the form.

PLEASE DETACH THESE NOTES before sending the application form to the Central Office of the Industrial Tribunals. KEEP THE NOTES FOR FUTURE REFERENCE.

CENTRAL OFFICE OF THE INDUSTRIAL TRIBUNALS

IT I (Revised September 1981)

Printed in the U.K. for H.M.S.O.   Dd 8886594 40M 8/85 G615

ORIGINATING APPLICATION TO AN INDUSTRIAL TRIBUNAL

IMPORTANT: DO NOT FILL IN THIS FORM UNTIL YOU
HAVE READ THE NOTES FOR GUIDANCE.
THEN COMPLETE ITEMS 1, 2, 4 AND 12
AND ALL OTHER ITEMS RELEVANT TO YOUR CASE,
AND SEND THE FORM TO THE FOLLOWING ADDRESS

For Official Use Only	
Case Number	

To: THE SECRETARY OF THE TRIBUNALS
CENTRAL OFFICE OF THE INDUSTRIAL TRIBUNALS (ENGLAND AND WALES)
93 EBURY BRIDGE ROAD, LONDON SW1W 8RE

Telephone: 01 730 9161

1   I hereby apply for a decision of a Tribunal on the following question. **(STATE HERE THE QUESTION TO BE DECIDED BY A TRIBUNAL. EXPLAIN THE GROUNDS OVERLEAF.**

WHETHER I WAS UNFAIRLY DISMISSED

2   My name is (Mr/Mrs/Miss Surname in block capitals first):—

MR BROWN, J

My address is   45, HIGH STREET, BRADFORD

Telephone No.

My date of birth is   27.12.46

3   If a representative has agreed to act for you in this case please give his or her name and address below and note that further communications will be sent to your representative and not to you *(See Note 4)*

Name of Representative:—   NOT APPLICABLE

Address:—

Telephone No.

4   (a)   Name of respondent(s) (in block capitals) ie the employer, person or body against whom a decision is sought *(See Note 3)*

BRIGGS AND CO. LTD

Address(es)   39, MAIN STREET, BRADFORD

Telephone No.

5   Place of employment to which this application relates, or place where act complained about took place.

AS ABOVE

6   My occupation or position held/applied for, or other relationship to the respondent named above (eg user of a service supplied in relation to employment).

GENERAL LABOURER

7   My employment began on   23.6.83   and *(if appropriate)* ended on

8   (a)   Basic wages/salary   £120 PER WEEK.

     (b)   Average take home pay   £95 PER WEEK

9   Other remuneration or benefits   SUBSIDISED CANTEEN

10   Normal basic weekly hours of work   40

11   (In an application under the Sex Discrimination Act or the Race Relations Act)
Date on which action complained of took place or first came to my knowledge

Please continue overleaf

IT I (Revised September 1981)

12   You are required to set out the grounds for your application below, giving full particulars of them.

I HAVE A GOOD RECORD AT WORK, NEVER HAVING BEEN GIVEN ANY
WARNINGS ABOUT MY CONDUCT OR GENERAL WORK PERFORMANCE.
I HAVE BEEN AWAY FROM WORK ILL WITH A BAD BACK SINCE JUST
BEFORE CHRISTMAS. MY EMPLOYERS WROTE TO ME AT THE END
OF JANUARY ASKING WHEN I WOULD BE FIT TO RETURN TO WORK.
I TOLD THEM I WAS NOT DUE TO SEE MY DOCTOR UNTIL THE END
OF FEBRUARY, AND THEY DISMISSED ME BECAUSE THEY SAID
THEY COULD NOT KEEP THE JOB OPEN ANY LONGER.

I HAVE NOW BEEN TO SEE MY DOCTOR, WHO THINKS I SHALL BE
FIT TO GO BACK TO WORK WITHIN TWO TO THREE WEEKS.

13   If you wish to state what in your opinion was the reason for your dismissal, please do so here.

14   If the Tribunal decides that you were unfairly dismissed, what remedy would you prefer? (Before answering this question
please consult the leaflet "Unfairly dismissed?" for the remedies available and then write one of the following in answer
to this question: reinstatement, re-engagement or compensation)

....

Signature .... J. Brown .... Date FEBRUARY 28TH, 1987.

FOR OFFICIAL USE
ONLY

Received at COIT	Code	ROIT	Inits

NOTICE OF APPLICATION TO AN INDUSTRIAL TRIBUNAL

INDUSTRIAL TRIBUNALS (RULES OF PROCEDURE) REGULATIONS 1985

NOTICE OF ORIGINATING APPLICATION

REGIONAL OFFICE OF THE
INDUSTRIAL TRIBUNALS,
2ND FLOOR, PRINCE HOUSE,
43 - 51, PRINCE STREET,
BRISTOL, BS1 4PE.
Tel: BRISTOL 298261.

Case No.

1.   I enclose a copy of an originating application for a decision of a tribunal in which you are named as respondent. Under the rules of procedure you are required to enter an appearance within 14 days of receiving the copy of the originating application. You can do this either by completing and sending to me the enclosed form of notice of appearance or by sending a letter giving the information called for on the form. This form and any other communications addressed to me may be sent by post or delivered to me at the above address.

2.   The proceedings on this application will be regulated by the rules of procedure contained in the above Regulations and these are explained in the enclosed leaflet. The case number of the application is indicated above and should be quoted in any communications with regard to these proceedings.

3.   If you name a representative at item 3 of the form, further communications regarding the case will be sent to him and not to you, and you should arrange to be kept informed by him of the progress of the case and of the hearing date. When the application is heard by the tribunal the parties (other than a respondent who has not entered an appearance) may appear and be heard in person or be represented by anyone they choose.

4.   If you do not send me the completed form (or other notice of appearance) you will not be entitled to take any part in the proceedings (except to apply for an extension of time to enter an appearance). If you do not take part in the proceedings a decision which may be enforceable in the county court may be given against you in your absence. Whether or not you enter an appearance you will be notified of the date of hearing and sent a copy of the tribunal's decision.

5.   In all cases where the Act under which the application is made provides for conciliation the services of a conciliation officer are available to the parties. In such cases a copy of the application is sent to the Advisory Conciliation and Arbitration Service accordingly, (see leaflet ITL1 page 6).

Signed .... Dated ....
for Secretary of the Tribunals

To the Respondent(s)

IT2

172

tend to eliminate hopeless cases, although surprisingly few applications for pre-hearing assessments are made. The tribunal does not go into the merits of the case at this stage.

(iv) Witnesses and Evidence

If the case proceeds to a hearing, the tribunal must decide the case on the evidence put to it. Both sides are entitled to call witnesses, who will normally be required to give evidence on oath or affirmation at the hearing.

The person calling the witness has the task of telling him of the date and place of the hearing when it is set, but it may be that a witness is reluctant to attend. In that case, the person calling him can apply to the tribunal to make a witness order, requiring the reluctant witness to attend. If a witness order is applied for, granted, and served, and the witness fails to appear, he will be liable to a fine of up to £100 for non-compliance.

The tribunal also has power, at the request of either party or of its own initiative, to order further and better particulars of the case, and also to require the production of documents. For example, an employee claiming unfair dismissal may wish to see his personnel file or get a copy of the works rules. These orders are not granted automatically; the applicant must show that he will be prejudiced unless he has the information requested. These applications must be made in writing to the Regional Office of Industrial Tribunals dealing with the case and will be considered by the Chairman on their merits.

Confidentiality is no reason for not producing documents. If one party claims that a document is confidential – another employee's assessment, for example – the chairman will consider the matter and decide whether disclosure is necessary in the interests of justice, which are paramount.

(v) The Hearing

Once all the preliminary matters have been settled, the Regional Office of Industrial Tribunals will send the parties a notice of the hearing on an official form IT4. Usually, the hearing will be scheduled for 10 a m; if a later time is given, the hearing may have to be postponed if the earlier case overruns. If the date and time is not convenient, e g, because of holidays or prospective witnesses or representatives will not be available, it is possible to apply for a postponement by writing to the regional office explaining the circumstances. The hearing will usually be postponed if a good reason is shown, but requests for postponement should be avoided if at all possible. The tribunal itself has power to postpone the hearing of its own volition, but this is rarely done. Indeed, the Employment Appeal Tribunal has emphasised that:

> 'A claimant before an industrial tribunal is entitled to have his claim quickly disposed of, in what is intended to be a simple, readily available form of proceedings; and it is not desirable, except in unusual cases, to have to delay or postpone the hearing . . .'

Settlements are, in fact, often made 'at the door of the court', e g, the employer may offer to pay the employee a sum of money. If a settlement offer is made and accepted, rather than withdraw the application to the tribunal it is best for the applicant – usually the employee – to ask the tribunal to record it and make a decision to that effect. There is a standard form for this purpose. The advantage of adopting this procedure is that the tribunal's decision can be enforced simply in the County Court.

The procedure before the tribunal is relatively informal, but there is a certain degree of formality. The clerk to the tribunal will usually explain the procedure in outline if asked. There are separate waiting rooms for applicants and respondents, and just before the time set for the hearing the parties (and their representatives and witnesses) will be asked to go to the hearing room, which is usually set out very much like a Court of law, although there is no witness stand. Evidence is usually given on oath or affirmation. The hearing is in public – in rare cases it can be held in private – and this means that public and press are admitted although, in the nature of things, there are very seldom any spectators!

The decision of the tribunal is taken by the chairman – a lawyer – and the two lay members together; if necessary it can be by a majority, and it is possible for the lay members to out-vote the chairman.

If a party fails to appear or be represented at the hearing, the tribunal is entitled to dispose of the application, but must take into account any written submissions the absent party has made. It is, indeed, possible for either party to rely on written submissions, by sending them to the tribunal and the other party in advance, but this is not a wise course of action because the written submissions cannot be tested by cross-examination. An applicant can conduct a case himself – the tribunal is always very helpful to unrepresented applicants but cannot, of course, conduct the case for them – or else he can get a friend, trade union official or a lawyer to represent him if he wishes.

The usual order of the hearing is that the party who has to prove the relevant matter begins. In an unfair dismissal case, for example, the onus is on the employer to prove that the dismissal was for a fair reason and so he will put his evidence first. If the employer claims that the employee was not dismissed, or if the employee resigns and is claiming 'constructive dismissal', the employee begins, and whoever begins has the right to have the last word in addressing the tribunal.

Each party presents his case, and questions his witnesses. The other party can then cross-examine them. Cross-examination takes the form of questions about the evidence which the witness has already given, and it is not possible to cross-examine one's own witness to get him to change his story! Members of the tribunal have the right to ask questions as well.

When all the witnesses have been called, each party will then summarise his case, and the tribunal will reach a decision. Often the tribunal will adjourn for a short time. The tribunal's decision is normally announced, with reasons, immediately after the close of the hearing, although in a complex case the ruling may be postponed.

In due course, both parties (or their representatives) will receive a decision in writing, and the reasons given are usually very full. If the tribunal orders payment of compensation, the person against whom the award is made must pay it direct to the other party within 42 days. If he does not do so, the successful party can recover the sum due by proceedings in the County Court.

2. REVIEWS AND APPEALS

(i) Reviews

A review is not the same as an appeal. There is no general power to review a tribunal's decision, and the tribunal will only agree to a request for a review – which must be made within fourteen days of the decision – on five limited grounds:

(a) The decision was wrongly made as a result of an error on the part of the tribunal staff.

(b) A party did not receive notice of the proceedings.

(c) The decision was made in the absence of a party entitled to be heard. For example, where last minute illness has prevented the applicant from attending, or where the employer did not attend in the erroneous belief that having made a settlement offer to the conciliation officer he would be contacted further if his attendance was required.

(d) New evidence has become available since the date of the decision. It must be shown that the new evidence could not have been presented at the original hearing and that it has substance.

(e) A review is required 'in the interests of justice'. For example, in *Help-the-Aged Housing Association (Scotland) Ltd v Vidler* [1977], Vidler was awarded £4,700 compensation on the basis that he was 60 years old and that it would be a considerable time before a man of his age found another job. In fact, he got a new job within two weeks of the tribunal's decision, thus making the original assessment of compensation (see opposite) wrong. The 'interest of justice' required a review. If the tribunal grants a review, the procedure will follow that of the original hearing, and the tribunal is free to review the whole of its decision and re-open the matter.

(ii) Appeals

The Employment Appeal Tribunal (EAT) can only hear appeals 'on points of law'. The appeal must be made within 42 days from the date when the document setting out the tribunal's decision was sent, but in exceptional cases the EAT can extend this time. Legal aid is available in the EAT. An appeal has no chance of getting off the ground unless there is a point of law and the appeal notice must state the point involved precisely. Generalisations are not sufficient. Competent legal advice is essential. A further appeal lies from decisions of the EAT to the Court of Appeal and thence to the House of Lords.

3. REMEDIES

There are three possible remedies for unfair dismissal. Two of them involve re-employment of the applicant by the employer. The three remedies are: (a) reinstatement; (b) re-engagement; (c) compensation.

(i) Reinstatement and Re-engagement Orders

Form IT1 – the application form used in tribunal proceedings – asks the applicant what remedy he is seeking. Does he want his job back or only compensation? Section 69 of the 1978 Act says that if a tribunal finds that an employee has been unfairly dismissed, it should explain to him that it has power to make an order that he be reinstated or re-engaged, but it has a discretion as to whether to make either order.

Under a reinstatement order, the employee is treated in all respects as though he had not been dismissed, while a re-engagement order directs that he is to be re-employed, but not necessarily in the same job or on the same terms and conditions. If the tribunal is minded to make such an order, it must take the applicant's wishes into account, and will first consider a reinstatement order. The main consideration taken into account in either case is whether it is practicable for the employer to comply with the order. Such orders are not therefore likely to be made in a redundancy situation or where the parties mistrust each other. In the case of a small firm, an order will only be made in the most exceptional cases. If an order is made and it is not complied with, then compensation will be ordered.

(ii) Compensation Awards

In practice, an award of money compensation is the typical remedy in an unfair dismissal situation. There are overall financial limits on the amount which can be awarded, but quite large sums can be involved. Usually, the award consists of two parts: (a) The **basic award** – based on the employee's age, length of service and weekly pay. A maximum of twenty years' employment is to be counted, and the week's pay limit is at present £155. (b) The **compensatory award** – this is the amount which the tribunal considers just and equitable for the loss suffered by the employee as a result of the dismissal.

(A) Calculating the basic award. Once the tribunal has found that a dismissal is unfair, and does not make an order for reinstatement or re-engagement, it must make a basic award, except where the dismissal was by reason of redundancy and the employee has been paid redundancy pay. It is calculated in exactly the same way as a redundancy payment (see page 160). The calculation is straightforward:

* One and a half week's pay for each complete year of employment between the ages of 41 and 65 (for men) or 41 and 60 (for women).
* One week's pay for each complete year of employment between the ages of 22 to 40.
* One half a week's pay for each year below the age of 22.

Since the maximum multiplier is 30 (based on 20 years' service) and the current statutory maximum week's pay which can be counted is £155, the maximum basic award is currently £4,650. A week's pay in this context is the normal week's pay, excluding overtime, but no earnings in excess of £155 a week can be counted. (The statutory maximum is reviewed each year in April.)

Note: Where the dismissal is held to be unfair on grounds of trade union membership or non-membership, the minimum basic award is £2,200: section 73 (4A) of the 1978 Act. But the basic award can be reduced in some circumstances. If the employee is aged over 64 (or 59 if a woman) it will be reduced by one-twelfth for each month after that age. The basic award must also be reduced where the employee has been awarded or has received a redundancy payment.

More importantly, the basic award can be reduced where the employee has been wholly or partly the author of his own misfortune, when it will be reduced by such amount as the tribunal considers just and equitable. So, if the employee caused or contributed to his own dismissal, or has unreasonably refused an offer of reinstatement, or has been guilty of improper conduct before the dismissal, the basic award may be reduced. However, contributory conduct will not affect the amount of the basic award if the reason for the dismissal was redundancy.

(B) Compensatory award. A dismissed employee may also get a compensatory award, based on the loss which he has suffered as a result of the dismissal, insofar as the employer is responsible for that loss. The compensatory award is akin to an award of damages at common law. There is a maximum amount which can be awarded of £8,000. This is the maximum after taking into account any payments already made and any reductions made in the amount awarded because of the employee's contributory conduct. It is over and above the basic award.

The usual headings which the tribunal consider are as follows:

(1) The immediate loss of wages.

(2) Loss of future earnings. This often ends up as a 'guestimate' unless the employee has already obtained other employment. The state of the job market is taken into account, as well as the claimant's personal characteristics. For example, in *Fougere v Phoenix Motor Co Ltd* (1976), because of his poor state of health, Mr Fougere was likely to face an extended period of unemployment, and the EAT ruled that this was a factor to be taken into account.

(3) Loss of perks, such as pension rights, subsidised mortgages, cars and so on.

(4) Expenses in connection with the finding or taking up of the new employment.

Something is also awarded for loss of acquired rights to unfair dismissal and redundancy protection, and the more senior the dismissed employee was, in practice, the more he gets. However, the compensatory award can be reduced under several heads. First, where the employer has made an *ex gratia* payment by way of compensation, this will be offset, as will any earnings from other employment between the dismissal and the tribunal hearing. Again, the dismissed employee must take reasonable steps to minimise his loss by seeking other employment. He cannot simply sit back and do nothing. If he does, then in legal language he has not 'mitigated his loss'. The most important factor which will go to reducing a compensatory award is, however, if the dismissed employee has contributed to the dismissal by his conduct, and in one or two cases this has been as much as 100%. The House of Lords has ruled that it is permissable for the tribunal to make a nil award if in the circumstances it would be just and equitable to do so, e g, where the employee has suffered no injustice because of the dismissal.

(iii) Additional and Special Awards

As well as the basic and compensatory awards, in certain cases additional or special awards can be made.

(A) Additional award. Where an employer ignores or refuses to comply with an order for reinstatement or re-engagement, the tribunal can make an additional award, and will do so unless the employer is able to satisfy it that it was not practicable to comply. In *George v Beecham Group Ltd* (1977), Mrs George was unfairly dismissed because of a reason connected with her pregnancy. She had a bad record of absenteeism through sickness, and the employers refused to comply with an order for her reinstatement because of this. She received 20 week's pay as an additional award. The additional award is normally between 13 and 26 weeks' pay, but where the dismissal was unfair because it was through racial or sex discrimination, it will be between 26 and 52 weeks' pay – subject to the statutory maximum of £155 a week.

(B) Special award. The only case in which a special award can be made is where the dismissal is found to be unfair because of trade union membership or non-membership. It is made when the employee has asked the tribunal for a reinstatement or re-engagement order, and either the tribunal has decided against this or it makes the order and the employer fails to comply with its terms.

(1) Where the tribunal makes no order for reinstatement or re-engagement, the special award amounts to 104 weeks' pay or £11,000, whichever is the greater, subject to an overall maximum of £22,000. In this case, the week's pay is not subject to the statutory limit and higher paid employees gain accordingly.

(2) Where the tribunal makes the order asked for, and the employer fails to comply, then unless he satisfies the tribunal that it was impracticable to comply, the special award will amount to 156 weeks' pay or £16,500, whichever is the greater.

A tribunal can reduce a special award on a number of grounds, including the employee's conduct, and the special award is extinguished entirely at retirement age. Moreover, despite the potentially large sums which can be awarded, the majority of special awards have been fairly moderate.

SECTION 4
THE LAW AND YOUR MONEY

1. INTRODUCTION

Buying and selling involves making a contract, which is an agreement which the law will enforce. Writing is not in general a requirement for a contract in English law, though there are some exceptions to this rule. Verbal agreements are quite valid and enforceable, and all that is required is an offer and an acceptance and 'consideration'. Each party must confer a benefit on the other because gratuitous promises are not binding unless made under seal. In the practical context of buying and selling, consideration is always present since the seller agrees to deliver goods and the buyer agrees to pay the price.

An offer is one party's indication of the terms on which he is willing to contract, but the contract only comes into existence when the offer has been accepted. There is usually no problem about this when the parties are negotiating face to face, as in a shop. For example, I go into a newsagents to buy the morning paper. I make the offer by telling the assistant the paper I want. He accepts the offer by handing the newspaper over. But there are cases where what might appear to be an offer is not in fact so in law. So, in the well-known case of *British Pharmaceutical Society v Boots Cash Chemists Ltd* (1952), it was held that the display of goods on the shelves of a self-service store was not an offer, but rather what the law calls 'an invitation to treat'. The customer makes the offer at the cash desk, and the assistant is quite free to accept or reject the offer. Similarly, the display of goods in a shop window is not an offer in the legal sense (*Fisher v Bell* (1961)) nor is a catalogue or price list. This was established in *Grainger & Son v Gough* (1896) where a wine-merchant canvassed orders by sending out a price list. It was argued that the circular amounted to an offer in law. The Court ruled that it was not; it was an attempt to induce offers. The Court said:

> 'The transmission of such a price list does not amount to an offer to supply an unlimited quantity of the wine described at the price named, so that as soon as an order is given there is a binding contract to supply that quantity. If it were so, the merchant might find himself involved in any number of contractual obligations to supply wine of a particular

description which he would be quite unable to carry out, his stock of wine of that description being necessarily limited'.

The practical consequence of this rule is that a shop is not bound to sell goods at the marked price or at all. This protects the shopkeeper, for example, if the price tag is wrong or in fact the goods are already sold.

Today's consumer is well protected by the law, and there is a large and growing body of consumer legislation, which is discussed in this section. So far as buying and selling goods is concerned, the main protection is contained in the Sale of Goods Act 1979 which sets out certain terms which apply in every case and gives the consumer valuable protection should the goods prove to be defective. The law relating to liability for defective goods is very complex, and there are three heads of liability: (1) liability in contract, i e, under the contract between the parties and on the basis of the Sale of Goods Act 1979; (2) liability in negligence if the goods are manufactured negligently and cause injury; (3) criminal liability, where statutory protection will apply, e g, under the Trade Descriptions Act 1968.

2. CONTRACTUAL LIABILITY

In large-scale commercial transactions, the parties often expressly agree on the contract terms, and go into considerable detail. The terms so agreed are called *express terms*. Terms can also be *implied* and this is the case under the Sale of Goods Act 1979. Not everything said between the parties during negotiations necessarily becomes a term of the subsequent contract. Untrue factual statements made with a view to inducing one party to contract may amount to misrepresentations, which will in themselves give rise to liability (see page 180), but such statements must be distinguished from the seller's age-old over-commendation of his wares, which the law regards as 'mere puffs' which nobody is expected to believe.

The modern judicial tendency is to impose liability if it is possible to do so, as is well illustrated by *Andrews v Hopkinson* (1956), where a second-hand car dealer's sales manager assured a commercial traveller, George Andrews, who knew little about cars, that a 1934 Standard saloon car was 'a good little bus' and added 'I would stake my life on it. You will have no trouble with it'. Mr Andrews agreed to take the car on hire purchase terms from a finance company and acknowledged in a delivery note that he was satisfied as to the car's condition. The steering mechanism was grossly defective, and the defect could have been discovered by a competent mechanic. It was held that quite apart from the contract with the finance company there was a contract between Mr Andrews and the dealer, under which the latter guaranteed the car.

Sections 13 to 15 of the Sale of Goods Act 1979 lay down certain terms which will be implied in every contract of sale and these cannot be excluded in consumer sales. These implied terms are as follows.

(i) Description

If the consumer orders goods by description, they must correspond to the description. Most sales of goods are sales by description since the sale may fall into that category even though the buyer has himself selected the goods from stock without anything being said, as in the case of self-service stores where the customer selects the goods from the shelves.

(ii) Merchantability and Fitness for Purpose

Section 14 of the Sale of Goods Act 1979 sets out two implied conditions which are in fact interrelated and which apply 'where the seller sells goods in the course of a business'. This in fact excludes few cases other than that of the private seller, since the Act does not say 'in the course of the business of selling goods'. The two conditions are that the goods must be of 'merchantable quality' and also that they must be reasonably fit for the purpose for which they are bought.

What is meant by 'merchantable quality'? Section 14(6) gives a rather generalised answer. It says that goods are of merchantable quality 'if they are as fit for the purpose or purposes for which goods of that kind are commonly bought as it is reasonable to expect having regard to any description applied to them, the price (if relevant) and all the other relevant circumstances'. Merchantability relates to the actual condition of the goods, and the condition is applied to both new and second-hand goods. In the case of a second-hand sale, the description and the price

are very important factors in deciding whether the goods fulfil their function. A car that does not start is clearly not of merchantable quality, but what of a second-hand car whose engine seizes up after 2,300 miles?

This was the very point in *Crowther v Shannon Motor Co* (1974), where dealers sold Andrew Crowther a second-hand Jaguar car for £390. The car was eight years old and had 82,165 miles on the clock. The dealers said that 'it would be difficult to find a 1964 Jaguar of this quality inside and out' and added that it 'was hardly run in'. Mr Crowther bought the car but, three weeks later, after he had driven it 2,300 miles, the engine seized up completely. On examination the engine was found to be in extremely bad condition and had to be replaced. The Court of Appeal held that the car was not of merchantable quality.

There are two exceptions to the duty to provide goods of merchantable quality: (a) it does not apply where the goods are unmerchantable because of defects which have been specifically drawn to the buyer's attention before the contract is made; (b) it does not apply where the buyer has actually examined the goods before purchase in respect of defects which the examination ought to have revealed. Even a cursory examination brings this exception into operation, and so the buyer may be better off not to examine the goods at all.

The implied condition of fitness for purpose is covered by section 14(3) which says that in certain circumstances goods must be reasonably fit for the purpose for which they are bought. In order to bring section 14(3) into operation the following conditions must be met:

(a) The buyer must make known to the seller the purpose for which the goods are required so as to make it plain that he is relying on the other's skill and judgment. In practice this requirement is easily met. Where an article has only one natural purpose, merely asking for it is sufficient to make known by implication the particular purpose for which it is required. In *Jackson v Watson* (1909), for example, the request was for 'tinned salmon', and this was held to be sufficient to establish that the customer required the goods for eating;

(b) The sale must be in the course of business;

(c) The obligation does not apply 'where the circumstances show that the buyer does not rely, or that it is unreasonable for him to rely, on the skill or judgment of the seller. The seller is under an absolute obligation to see that the goods sold are reasonably fit for their purpose. He does not have to be at fault. So in *Jackson v Watson* (above) it was irrelevant whether, as would usually be the case, the grocer had no means of knowing that the tinned salmon was unfit for eating.

(iii) Sales by Sample
Where there is a sale by sample – usually, but not necessarily in the case of bulk commodities – the following terms are implied by section 15 of the Sale of Goods Act 1979: (a) that the bulk will correspond with the sample in quality; (b) that the buyer will have a reasonable opportunity of comparing bulk with sample; (c) that the goods will be free from defects, rendering them unmerchantable, which would not be apparent on reasonable examination of the sample.

(iv) Exclusion of Liability
An important question is whether the seller can, by express contractual terms, cancel the customer's rights to protection. In the case of consumer sales, the seller's obligations under sections 13 to 15 of the Sale of Goods Act 1979 cannot be excluded. Any exclusion clause is made totally ineffective by section 6(2) of the Unfair Contract Terms Act 1977. A consumer sale in this context is one if: (a) the customer does not make the contract in the course of business nor hold himself out as doing so; (b) the other party does make the contract in the course of business; and (c) the goods concerned are of a type ordinarily supplied for private use and consumption.

Because of the provisions of section 6(2) – which outlaws exclusion clauses in consumer sales – if a customer wants to retain the extensive protection given by the Sale of Goods Act 1979, he must make sure that he does not unwittingly take himself outside the Act's protection. Obviously, a private sale between two private individuals is not a consumer sale, but there are borderline cases which are not always obvious. To save money, an individual may obtain a 'trade card' to enable him to buy from a wholesale warehouse at trade rates. This is probably not a consumer transaction because in fact the customer is holding himself out as a retailer.

The rights conferred by the Sale of Goods Act 1979 are against the seller. They are rights which arise in contract and so the customer's remedy (if anything goes wrong) is against the seller. Some shopkeepers will try and fob off dissatisfied customers by suggesting that his recourse is against the manufacturer. The legal position is that if the goods do not work properly, it is the shopkeeper who is primarily liable, for they are responsible for the fitness and quality of the goods which they sell.

(v) Untrue Pre-sales Statements
Untrue statements made by a seller in the course of negotiations leading up to a contract may be treated as terms of the contract, but then if not they may amount to *misrepresentations* and themselves give rise to liability. The customer can sue the seller if he made false statements of fact about the goods which induced the customer to buy them.

Statements of opinion do not amount to misrepresentations. If, for example, the customer is buying a television set and the salesman says 'I think the colour on this TV is the better of the two' the customer has no redress, in contrast to the situation where a car salesman says: 'This model has twin carbs'.

A purchaser who has bought goods relying on a misrepresentation is entitled to damages unless the person who made the misrepresentation can prove that he had reasonable grounds to believe that the misrepresentation was true.

(vi) Manufacturer's Guarantees
Most major manufacturers of consumer durables give a 'guarantee' of the goods. The following wording is typical:

> 'The above-mentioned equipment is guaranteed against material or workmanship defects for twelve months after the date of purchase. In case of need, free in-warranty service shall be rendered by any one of the authorised service operators listed in this guarantee card, in accordance with the warranty policy and procedure explained in the operating manual, provided that the equipment has not been abused, altered, operated contrary to instructions, or repaired by unauthorised repair shops.'

These 'guarantees' are usually honoured by the manufacturer in practice, but in the normal case the customer wishing to rely on them must comply with any conditions laid down. Often these conditions include liability to heavy packaging-charges and, in some cases, to paying for any labour involved. In many instances it will be better for the customer to rely on his Sale of Goods Act rights against the seller of the equipment. If, for example, you buy a camera from a chain-store and a few days later it becomes defective, the best course will be to seek redress against the chain store and either get your money back or obtain a replacement.

Unless the goods which are the subject of the 'guarantee' have been bought directly from the manufacturer – by post, for example – (when there will be a contract of sale and the Sale of Goods Act will apply) the guarantee may be legally worthless and ineffective. If the goods are bought from a retailer, the contract is between retailer and customer; there will be no contractual relationship with the manufacturer.

The legal position is not, however, entirely clear, and in those cases where (as is often the case) the customer is required to return the guarantee card to the manufacturer, including a good deal of information about the customer's age group, occupation and so on, it may be that the terms of the guarantee are directly enforceable as between customer and manufacturer, though it would take litigation to establish the position!

The position is different where a payment is made in respect of the 'guarantee', as is often the case with consumer durables such as washing machines, television sets, and so forth, when the customer is paying for the item to be either serviced on a regular basis or repaired on call.

3. LIABILITY IN NEGLIGENCE – DIRECT CLAIMS AGAINST MANUFACTURERS

The consumer's usual remedy in respect of defective goods is against the person who sold the goods to him. But, quite independently of this liability – which is based upon contract – someone who is injured by defective goods may have a claim against the manufacturer or, indeed, against the wholesaler or other intermediaries, any of whom may have to answer if the goods are defective and cause damage. This liability does not depend upon a contractual relationship; it is an independent liability imposed by the law of tort, and in particular by that specific tort or legal wrong called negligence. The basic principle was stated by the House of Lords more than 50 years ago in these words:

'A manufacturer of products, which he sells in such a form as to show that he intends them to reach the ultimate consumer in the form in which they left him with no reasonable possibility of intermediate examination, and with the knowledge that the absence of reasonable care in the preparation or putting up of the products will result in an injury to the consumer's life or property, owes a duty to the consumer to take reasonable care'.

[Lord Atkin in *Donoghue v Stevenson* (1932)]

Subsequent case law has extended the meaning of the word 'manufacturers'; it covers wholesalers, retailers, and a wide variety of other people. And the principle is not limited to sales of goods, but extends to those who supply goods by way of hire purchase, hire, and so on, as well as to those who repair goods. So, in *Stennett v Hancock* (1939), a lorry-repairer negligently replaced a wheel which flew off and struck a passer-by. The repairer was held liable for the pedestrian's injuries.

Donoghue v Stevenson (1932) is still the leading case, and its facts are unforgettable. Mrs Donoghue and a friend went to a café, and the friend purchased a bottle of ginger-beer, manufactured by Stevenson. The ginger beer was in an opaque bottle and, in fact, contained the decom-

Your rights at sales
The Sale of Goods Act 1979 applies to purchases at sale time just as it does to other consumer purchases. This means that the goods must (a) be of merchantable quality; (b) correspond with description; (c) be reasonably fit for their purpose. Many sale goods are sold as 'seconds' or 'slightly defective'. You must accept minor defects. If things go wrong with the goods, notify the shop immediately. Notices saying 'No refunds on sale goods' or 'No refunds without a receipt' are not binding on you. They are illegal and your rights cannot be taken away by them. You are not bound to accept a credit note or an exchange. If the goods are seriously defective, you have a right to your money back. You are not entitled to your money back if you simply changed your mind. Failing satisfaction with the shop, complain to the local authority Consumer Advice Department. If all else fails, you can go to Court. There is a special 'small claims' procedure in the County Court. (See Section 1.)

posed remains of a snail. Mrs Donoghue became very ill as a result of imbibing the contaminated ginger beer. She could not sue the retailer (the proprietor of the café) because it was the friend and not she who had bought the ginger beer, but instead sued the manufacturer. Her claim was successful, and her case became the foundation of the modern law.

In a negligence claim, it is for the consumer to show that the manufacturer etc was careless, but, a court may easily infer that snails do not find their way into carefully bottled ginger beer. The need to prove negligence can be very important in relation to newly discovered products, such as pharmaceuticals. So a major problem for the victims of thalidomide was to show that the manufacturers and distributors ought to have known that it was dangerous to foetuses. It is virtually certain that legislation will be introduced shortly to remove the need to prove negligence where defective products lead to personal injury. At the moment it seems that the manufacturer cannot be sued simply because the product is defective: it is necessary to show that the defective product has caused personal injury or damage to property.

4. STATUTORY PROTECTION

Despite the availability of legal aid and advice, going to law is both costly and uncertain, although there are many organisations which will help the consumer in particular situations: see below. Another line of approach where goods are defective is through the medium of the criminal law; this will not result in any financial recompense as such to the consumer, but merely in the person in default being subjected to criminal penalties, such as a fine. There is now a broad spectrum of legislation protecting the consumer, the advantage being that its enforcement lies in the hands of central and local government officials.

(i) The Trade Descriptions Act 1968
This is the most important single consumer protection legislation, and about 30,000 prosecutions are brought under its provisions every year. Its enforcement lies in the hands of the Trading Standards Department of the local authority, to whom complaints may be made.

Section 1(1) of the 1968 Act says:

'Any person who, in the course of a trade or business: (a) applies a false trade description

Consumers' Association
14 Buckingham Street
London WC2N 6DS   Tel. 01-839 1222

Consumers in the European Community Group (CECG)
24 Tufton Street
London SW1 3RB   Tel. 01-222 2662

Consumer Credit Trade Association
3 Berners Street
London W1P 3AG   Tel. 01-636 7564

Consumer Credit Association of the United Kingdom (CCAUK)
Queens House
Queens Road
Chester CH1 3BQ   Tel. (0244) 312044

Institute of Consumer Advisers (ICA)
20 Eagle Close
Enfield EN3 4RS

National Federation of Consumer Groups (NFCG)
12 Mosley Street
Newcastle upon Tyne NE1 1DE
Tel. (0632) 618259

Research Institute for Consumer Affairs (RICA)
14 Buckingham Street
London WC2N 6DS   Tel. 01-930 3360

to any goods; or (b) supplies or offers to supply any goods to which a false trade description is applied; shall, subject to the provisions of this Act, be guilty of an offence'.

The case law establishes that this provision is very wide in its scope. Many statements which would not give rise to civil liability in the law of contract have been held to be 'false trade descriptions' for the purposes of the Act, and in general liability under the Act does not depend on proof that the person applying the trade description knew it to be false. In some cases, however, the seller can disclaim liability for a false trade description, provided the disclaimer is 'as bold, precise and compelling as the trade description itself and [is] effectively brought to the notice of any person to whom the goods may be supplied' (*Norman v Bennett* (1974)) as, for example, by pasting a notice over the mileometer of a second-hand car stating that 'The accuracy of the recorded mileage is not guaranteed'. False or misleading indictions as to the price of goods are prohibited by section 11 of the 1968 Act, which creates three separate offences:

(a) False comparisons with a recommended price. It is unlawful for someone to offer to supply goods giving a false indication that their price is equal to or less than the price recommended by the manufacturer, though there is a loophole where the manufacturer recommends a price so high that all retailers sell the goods well below that price;

(b) False comparisons with the retailer's own price. This is especially important in respect of goods bought in retailer's sales. It is an offence for a retailer to make false price comparisons with his own previous price unless in fact he has offered the goods at a higher price for a period not less than 28 days in the preceding six months. The protection is not so wide as appears because (a) in the case of multiple stores all that is required is to show that the goods were in fact offered at a higher price elsewhere and (b) the retailer can state that he has offered the goods at the higher price only for a short period. This is illustrated by *Westminster City Council v Ray Alan (Manshops) Ltd* (1982), where the accused put casual sweaters on sale at its Oxford Street, London W1, shop, for 75p, with a tag saying 'Fantastic Reductions!'. It was held that the accused was entitled to establish as a defence that the 'fantastically reduced' sweaters had in fact been offered for sale at higher prices in its shops in Rotherham and Leeds!;

(c) Indicating that the price is less than that actually being charged. It is an offence to suggest that the customer is in fact being charged less than he actually is. So, for example, in *Sweeting v Northern Upholstery Ltd* (1982), Northern Upholstery advertised: 'Envoy suites in dralon at £699'. Only suites covered in beige dralon were in fact available at this price; if the customer wanted other colours he had to pay more. The advertisement was held to constitute an offence.

Not all price comparisons are caught by the provisions of section 11 of the Trade Descriptions Act 1968 nor is all misleading advertising caught by the Act. However, under the Price Marketing (Bargain Offers) Order 1969 the following comparisons are prohibited: (a) 'Worth £50, yours for £25'; (b) 'Save up to half price'; (c) 'At least £100 elsewhere, only £75'.

The 1968 Act does not only apply to trade descriptions about goods; section 14 also covers services, though in this case the defendant must have known that the statement which he was making was true or else have made it recklessly. The situation is illustrated by the case of *Wings*

Ltd v Ellis (1984), where Wings' holiday brochure for 1981–82 winter season mistakenly indicated that certain hotel accommodation in Sri Lanka was air-conditioned, when it was not. In May 1981 Wings discovered the mistake and immediately took steps to correct the error by circularising travel agents. In January 1982 a customer booked a holiday with Wings through a travel agent relying on an uncorrected brochure, and neither Wings nor the travel agent informed him that the hotel was not air-conditioned. On his return home he complained both to Wings and to his local trading standards officer. The House of Lords held that Wings were properly convicted under section 14. A great many of the cases under section 14 have, in fact, involved holiday operators or airlines, and those who have been subjected to the common airline practice of overbooking can take comfort from the ruling in *British Airways Board v Taylor* (1976), where the airline issued a ticket to a passenger confirming his reservation for a named flight. The court very properly held that the statement that the seat was confirmed was a false statement even though, at the time the statement that the seat was confirmed was made, the flight was not then overbooked.

There are defences available to someone charged with an offence under the Trade Descriptions Act 1968. Section 24(1) provides that it is generally a defence to show: (a) that the commission of the offence was due to a mistake or reliance on information supplied to him by a third person, or to that person's act or default, or to an accident or some other cause beyond his control; and, (b) that he took all reasonable precautions and exercised all due care to avoid the commission of the offence by himself or his employees, etc.

(ii) The Consumer Safety Act 1978

The Consumer Protection Act 1961 empowered the Secretary of State to make regulations imposing requirements in respect of classes of goods so as to prevent or reduce the risk of death or personal injury. The regulations issued covered a variety of goods ranging from babies' dummies, stands for carry-cots, perambulators and pushchairs to oil heaters and oil lamps. The 1961 Act is concerned primarily with criminal liability, but under section 3(1) anyone who is injured as a result of breach of regulations made under the Act is given a right of action for damages.

The 1961 Act is gradually being replaced by

the Consumer Safety Act 1978 which is designed to be much more comprehensive. The detail is gradually being filled out by regulations, which again cover a wide variety of products which are potentially dangerous. In addition to making regulations, the Secretary of State is authorised to issue: (a) Prohibition orders, the effect of which is to prohibit people from supplying goods, etc., which are set out in the order, because he does not consider them to be safe. (b) Prohibition notices addressed to a particular person forbidding that person to supply unsafe goods, etc. (c) Warning notices ('notice to warn') about specified goods. The Secretary of State is also given extensive powers to obtain information.

Other consumer protection measures include the Fair Trading Act 1973 which set up the office of Director General of Fair Trading, who also has important responsibilities under the Consumer Credit Act 1974: see page 194. Various important regulations have been made under the 1973 Act covering such things as business advertisements and mail order transactions.

5. SALES BETWEEN PRIVATE INDIVIDUALS

So far as legal protection goes, you are generally better off buying from a commercial source, such as a retailer, since it is only in such cases that the full legal protections discussed in this section apply. Many sales, however, are made by private individuals, resulting from advertisements or from word of mouth. In private sales, only one of the basic Sale of Goods Act obligations will apply, namely that imposed by section 13, that 'the goods will correspond with description', but the private seller is under the same obligation as anyone else not to make false statements of fact ('misrepresentations')' Otherwise, the maxim of the law is expressed in the Latin tag *caveat emptor* – let the buyer beware.

6. AUCTION SALES

An auction sale is one where goods are sold to the highest bidder, and the very nature of an auction presupposes a conflict between the bidders and the vendors. The bidder wishes to purchase the goods as cheaply as possible, and the vendor wishes to obtain the highest price he can. Auction sales are, however, governed by the same basic principles of law as apply to other contracts of sale, although they are also subject to special rules. At an auction, it is the bidder who makes

the offer by making his bid. The auctioneer's request for bids is merely an attempt to set the ball rolling. The auctioneer accepts the bid when the hammer falls and then the sale is complete. Neither party can then back out of the transaction, and the bidder is bound in law to pay for the goods.

Most auctions are governed by conditions of sale which are drawn up by the auctioneer – they will usually be printed in the catalogue and displayed in the auction room. At the outset of the sale the auctioneer will make it clear that all sales are subject to those conditions. Bidders are then bound by the conditions. Since these conditions are drawn up in the seller's interests, almost inevitably they will exclude liability for any defects in the goods bought. It is, therefore, essential to examine the goods carefully. It is quite usual for the conditions to exclude the Sale of Goods Act obligations of fitness for purpose, merchantable quality, and description as well as liability for 'misrepresentation' or false sales talk.

Section 6(3) of the Unfair Contract Terms Act 1977, allows this subject to what it calls the test of 'reasonableness'. If there is a dispute as to whether or not the exclusion clause is reasonable, this is a matter for the court to decide 'having regard to the circumstances which were, or ought reasonably to have been, known to or in the contemplation of the parties at the time the contract was made' (section 11 of the 1977 Act) subject to guidelines set out in the Act.

The conditions of sale can also reserve for the seller or someone acting on his behalf the right to bid, thus pushing up the price. Well-drafted conditions of sale will also state whether or not the sale is 'subject to reserve', i e, a price below which the goods will not be sold. The auctioneer is not bound to disclose what the reserve price is, but if it is not reached, the goods will be withdrawn from the sale.

What happens where the sale is advertised as being 'without reserve'? Does this constitute a definite offer to sell to the highest bidder? The answer is probably yes.

What is clear is that an advertisement of an auction sale is not an offer in the legal sense. If, therefore, the sale is cancelled, disappointed would-be purchasers have no claim against the auctioneer. This was established in *Harris v Nickerson* (1873), where Nickerson advertised that some furniture would be sold by auction on a certain day. Harris attended the sale, but the lots in which he was interested were withdrawn. He sued Nickerson to recover for his loss of time and expenses involved in attending the abortive sale. His claim failed, the judge saying that it was 'an attempt to make a mere declaration of intention into a binding contract'.

The purchaser is not, however, entirely without protection. If, for example, he is induced to pay an inflated price at an auction by bids which, though apparently independent, were actually made on behalf of the vendor, he would not be bound by the sale unless, of course, the right to so bid had been reserved.

The auctioneer is the seller's agent. He works on a commission basis. The actual contract of sale is made between the buyer and the seller: the auctioneer is merely the intermediary. People selling goods at auction are also protected by the law. The auctioneer is liable for negligence in conducting the sale but, more importantly, auction 'rings' are illegal. An auction ring is an agreement between intending bidders – usually dealers – whereby one or more of them do not bid, so as to damp down the price at which the lot is purchased or an arrangement under which the lots are to be divided amongst members of the ring either in agreed proportions or by a subsequent auction between them. Auction rings are prohibited by the Auctions (Bidding Agreements) Acts 1927–1969, but prosecutions are very rare because of the difficulties in establishing that a dealers' ring is in operation. The 1969 Act was introduced after a well-publicised affair in the late 1960s, in which a painting, which was bought for £2,700 at a country auction, was sold shortly afterwards to the National Gallery for £150,000. Suspicions that a dealers' ring was in operation were never proved, but the publicity led Parliament to strengthen the law.

Mock Auctions

A mock auction is one at which people are tricked into buying shoddy goods at grossly inflated prices. At one time this confidence trick was very common in London, at seaside resorts and fairgrounds. A variety of techniques were used, but usually the intended victims were lured by the promise of an auction at give-away prices. Attractive looking goods were displayed, and these would then be auctioned. In each case, most of the money paid would then be refunded, so that the actual price paid was that stated at the outset. Once trapped, bidders believed they were going to get bargains, and a number of expensive-looking items, which had not been on show, would be put up and sold to bidders for many times their real value: the lots were often specially-manufactured shoddy merchandise.

To remedy this situation the Mock Auctions Act 1961 was passed. This makes it a criminal offence – punishable by a fine of up to £1,000 and/or two years' imprisonment to promote or conduct, or to assist in the conduct of, a mock auction of lots including any of the following: plate, plated articles, linen, china, glass, books, pictures, prints, furniture, jewellery, household, personal or ornamental articles, musical instruments, scientific apparatus. A sale is a mock auction for this purpose if: (a) any lot is sold to a person at a lower price than his highest bid, or if part of the price is repaid or credited to him, unless this is to reimburse him for a defect discovered after he made his bid; or (b) the right to bid for any lot is restricted, or said to be restricted, to those who have bought or agreed to buy one or more articles; or (c) any articles are offered or given away as gifts. Prosecutions under the Act are comparatively rare, and mock auctions still take place.

7. BUYING THROUGH MAIL ORDER

Buying goods by post is governed by the same principles of the law of contract as apply to any other sale. There are also some special rules. Advertisements or catalogues must include the supplier's name and business address.

The customer has the same legal protection as if he had bought the goods over the shop counter. The seller must supply goods which are fit for their intended use, of reasonable quality, and be as described. In fact, in buying goods by post the customer has to rely almost entirely on the description in the catalogue or advertisement; if they are unsatisfactory and are not as described, he is entitled to have his money back or to claim compensation, as appropriate. If the goods are damaged in the post or in transit, this is the seller's responsibility, but the customer should take care to sign for any goods received from a carrier as 'unexamined' and then write to the seller immediately explaining the position.

Most reputable mail order concerns offer a 'money back guarantee' in any case, and many of the larger companies offer goods 'on approval'; the customer may return them if he is not satisfied, or even if he merely changes his mind. If goods are not sent 'on approval', then the customer can only claim the money back if there is something wrong with them.

Mail order customers are also protected by voluntary codes of practice which are in effect more stringent than legal controls. The Advertising Standards Authority (ASA), the Association of Mail Order Publishers (AMOP), and the Mail Order Traders Association all have codes of practice which protect the customer; most of the major newspapers and magazines take part in a scheme which guarantees the customer his money back if the advertiser's business becomes insolvent and the orders are not met. This scheme, however, only applies to 'display advertisements' and not to small advertisements in the classified columns. The main points to note are: (a) Both the ASA and AMOP codes of practice provide that 'cash with order' advertisements must state a waiting period of delivery – it is usually 28 days – and failure to meet this requirement should produce an automatic

---

Mail order advertising protection

Advertisements in many magazines are governed by the British Code of Advertising Practice. Magazines participating in the scheme usually print a notice about it: see Illustration. Mail order advertisements which require payment in advance are covered by the Code. The advertiser must fulfil orders within 28 days unless he has stated a longer delivery period. The customer who returns the goods undamaged within seven days of receipt is entitled to his money back. If you return goods, make sure that you get proof of posting from the Post Office as you may need this receipt.

The Mail Order Protection Scheme usually applies. Where it does, and you pay for mail order goods in advance in response to an advertisement in the magazine, you may be able to get your money back from the publisher if the buyer becomes insolvent. You must write to the publisher not earlier than 28 days from the day you sent your order and not later than two months from that day if you have not received the goods or a refund. Claims made under the scheme will be honoured by the publisher if and when the advertiser is formally declared bankrupt or insolvent. The scheme does not cover: (a) classified advertisements; (b) sales from catalogues, etc (only direct response sales are covered) (c) defective goods.

---

refund. (b) The Newspaper Proprietors' Association Scheme has established a system for vetting prospective advertisers and, subject to the conditions of the scheme, will refund the money to the customer if the order is not fulfilled. It is wise to keep a copy of any advertisement or catalogue, and a copy of any correspondence.

8. UNSOLICITED GOODS

Inertia selling is a well-known though dubious sales-technique. Goods are sent which are not ordered in the hope that the recipient will pay for them. The same technique is applied to entries in trade directories: a business is sent a proposed entry in a 'trade directory' and then receives an invoice for payment. The Unsolicited Goods and Services Acts 1971 and 1975 deal with this racket, and make provision for the protection of those who receive unsolicited goods or services.

A customer is not obliged to pay for goods or services which he did not order and, as far as unsolicited goods are concerned, he has two options:

(a) He can keep the goods safe for a period of six months. They then belong to him and he can sell or dispose of them if he thinks fit. He can safely ignore any 'invoice' or request for payment, and need not return them at his own expense. But the sender is entitled to collect them during this six-month period. If they are not so collected the goods are treated as an unconditional gift;

(b) He can write to the sender stating that he did not order the goods and requiring them to be collected either from his address or another stated address. If the goods are not then collected within 30 days, they become his property.

During the six month or 30 day periods the recipient cannot use the goods; he must store them safely, and not cause deliberate damage to them. The recipient is not, however, liable for accidental damage to the goods.

By going through the prescribed procedure the receipient can make the goods his property – but he must not unreasonably refuse to allow the sender or his representatives to collect them. It is a criminal offence – punishable with a fine of up to £200 – to send an invoice or demand for payment for any unsolicited goods, and if the sender threatens to take legal action, or tries to collect the 'debt' he faces a much heavier fine. In fact, the 'invoice' or demand seeking payment for unsolicited goods must state boldly in red: 'THIS IS NOT A DEMAND FOR PAYMENT – THERE IS NO OBLIGATION TO PAY'. This statement must appear at the top left-hand corner of the demand, which must also have boldly printed diagonally across the page 'THIS IS NOT A BILL'. There are similar controls over directory entries. The same legislation also makes it an offence to send any book, magazine, leaflet or advertising material for such items which describe or illustrates human sexual techniques if it is known or ought reasonably to be known that it is unsolicited.

Despite the legislation, this high-pressure sales technique is still common. Anyone who receives a threatening letter in respect of unsolicited goods or services should inform the police and/or the local Trading Standards Department.

9. BUYING ON THE DOORSTEP

Many reputable firms employ doorstep salesmen, and the door-to-door salesman has the same legal obligations as any other seller of goods. The trouble with buying on the doorstep is that, if something goes wrong, it may be difficult to trace the salesman or his company. Doorstep purchasers should, therefore, ensure that they have proof of the salesman's identity, his address and the company's address. It may well be difficult to complain about faulty or unsatisfactory goods unless the firm is a reputable one.

Credit purchases made on the doorstep are subject to special rules, as explained in section 4.4. Briefly, when goods are bought on the doorstep on credit, such as hire-purchase, the salesman is usually obliged to give a copy of the contract to the customer who has a right to back out of the transaction within three days. This is called the 'cooling-off period' and the customer has a right of cancellation.

Under section 49(1) of the Consumer Protection Act 1974 to canvass certain types of credit on the doorstep – these include most credit sales – is illegal but the prohibition does not apply if the salesman comes in response to the prospective customer's request which might, for example, be made through a newspaper advertisement. Broadly speaking, offering credit on the doorstep is illegal.

Contracts for repairs and services are basically governed by the Supply of Goods and Services Act 1982 and by the Unfair Contract Terms Act 1977, and these provisions give consumers valuable rights. Until the 1977 Act, many suppliers of goods and services traded on standard terms and conditions which limited the trader's liability or in some cases attempted to exempt him entirely if things went wrong.

Now, provided the contract is a 'consumer transaction', contract terms controlled by the 1977 Act are subject to the test of 'reasonableness'.

1. THE CONTRACTOR'S OBLIGATIONS

Where a consumer employs a firm to carry out a repair or service, there is a contract between them. It is a contract for work and materials, i e, a contract under which the contractor supplies both services and materials. The 1982 Act writes implied terms into contracts of this kind. The most important of them are as follows.

(a) Where the contractor or supplier is acting in the course of a business, there is an implied term that he will carry out the work with reasonable care and skill. The customer has the right to have the job done properly and to a reasonable standard. This is a very difficult test to apply in practice. The test is the average standard of the reasonably skilled member of the profession or trade in question. So, for example, in *Worlock v Saws* (1982), David Hicks was a carpenter by trade, but he had decided to branch out into general building work. Mrs Worlock wanted a small bungalow built and Mr Hicks agreed to build it. This was the first time he had undertaken responsibility for a new dwelling, though he had carried out some conversion work. He did the work badly in that he put in insufficient foundations. When sued by Mrs Worlock, the question arose as to the standard of care he ought to have shown. The court, while sympathetic to Mr Hicks, found him to be liable. His lack of experience did not help him. The judge said:

> 'The law is quite clear. He held himself out as a building contractor. He must therefore be

judged as such because it was as a building contractor that he was engaged . . . and . . . he was required to exercise generally over the work upon which he was engaged that standard of care which would be expected from a reasonably competent contractor'.

This ruling is of general application and all repair and service work must be done to a reasonable standard. If it is not, the contractor is in breach of this implied term.

(b) Any materials used by the contractor will be fit for their purpose and of proper quality. If a replacement part is fitted, it must be 'fit for its purpose', so if the customer takes a television set in for repair, he is entitled to expect that good quality replacement parts will be used.

(c) Where no time is fixed for performance of the contract, there is an implied term that the supplier will carry out the job 'within a reasonable time'. This is a question of fact. A complicated job will take much longer than a simple one, and what is a reasonable time in one case will not be so in another. It is always best to agree with the repairer how long the job should take.

(d) The contractor has a duty to take reasonable care of the goods entrusted to him and to protect them from damage, fire and theft. The contractor is liable if he is negligent but the law does permit the contractor to exempt himself from liability to a limited extent by means of an exemption clause printed in notices on the premises, receipts, tickets and the like. A typical garage exemption clause might read:

> 'We will not accept responsibility for any loss or damage sustained by the vehicle, its accessories or contents, however caused'.

An exemption clause of this type will in fact be valid to the extent that it is 'reasonable' under the Unfair Contract Terms Act 1977. Various factors are taken into account in deciding whether the clause is fair and reasonable and these include the customer's knowledge of the clause.

There is an important further control. Even if the clause would otherwise be valid, if its effect has been misrepresented to the customer by or on behalf of the contractor, it will not be enforceable.

For example, in *Curtis v Chemical Cleaning and Dyeing Co Ltd* (1951), Mrs Curtis took a white satin wedding dress to the defendants for cleaning. The assistant asked her to sign a 'receipt' which contained a clause that the dress 'is accepted on condition that the company is not liable for any damage howsoever arising'. Before she signed, Mrs Curtis, asked why her signature was necessary. The assistant told her that the effect of the document was merely to exclude damage to beads or sequins. Mrs Curtis then signed the 'receipt' without reading it. The dress was badly stained. Mrs Curtis's claim for the cost of a new dress succeeded. The cleaners could not rely on the condition because, however innocently, they had misrepresented its effect.

2. PRICE OF REPAIRS

It is always best to get an estimate or quotation before handing over goods for repair or servicing. Many firms have minimum charges, which can be quite exorbitant. In fact, where no price is agreed for the service, there is an implied term that the customer will pay a reasonable charge. This again is a question of fact, and the best guide is what other traders are charging, though the customer must expect to pay more for quick service. In most cases, a repairer can refuse to hand over the goods until he has been paid. In law, he has what is called 'a lien' over the goods.

3. UNCOLLECTED GOODS

Sometimes customers fail to collect goods which they have left for repair or servicing. In such cases the repairman has a statutory right to sell them, after going through the correct procedure. If he knows how to contact the customer, the repairer must give the customer a written notice of intention to sell, which must be sent by registered letter or the recorded delivery service. The period between the notice and the proposed date of sale must give the customer 'a reasonable opportunity of taking delivery of the goods' and, when any payment is due, such as a repair charge, it must not be less than three months. If the repairer cannot notify the customer, because, for example, he does not have an address, he may be at risk in selling on the basis of not having taken 'reasonable steps' to trace him and so in such cases the repairer must be very careful.

In the straightforward case, if the customer fails to respond to the notice and collect the goods and pay the charge, the repairer can sell them,

Excluding liability for negligence

For a contract term or notice to exclude effectively or limit contractual liability for negligence, three conditions must be satisfied: (a) The clause must be a term of the contract. This will be the case if the customer signs a document containing the clause, even if he does not read it. A notice displayed in the shop may be equally effective. (b) The wording of the clause must be explicit. It must explicitly exclude or limit liability for negligence. Generalised wording is not sufficient. Any ambiguity will be resolved in the customer's favour. (c) The person relying on the clause must satisfy the Court that the clause is fair and reasonable, having regard to the circumstances which were, or ought to have been known, or were in the parties' contemplation, at the time the contract was made.

Court decisions suggest that many factors are relevant in deciding on whether the term is 'fair and reasonable'. The most important factors are:

(a) A clause which tries to limit liability to a stated financial amount will be more favourably regarded than a clause giving a total exemption from liability. The following clause from a computer-maintenance contract is typical:

'AB shall at its own expense make good any damage to the equipment caused by the error or negligence of its personnel. AB will indemnify the customer for personal injury (including death), direct physical damage to property (not including any loss of data) provided that such injury or damage is caused by the negligence of the AB engineer or other AB employee while on the site. AB's total liability to any one customer in respect of damage to property is limited to £500,000 for any one occurrence or series of related occurrences'.

Note. Liability for negligence resulting in death or personal injury can never be excluded, however widely the contract term is drawn.

(b) If the customer is a consumer, a negotiated clause is more likely to be held reasonable than one imposed on him.

(c) The availability of insurance is a very relevant factor.

deduct the amount owing and the sale costs, and pay the balance over to the customer. The repairer must adopt the best method of sale in the circumstances. This may mean selling expensive goods by auction and, indeed, if the goods are valuable, the wise repairer will apply to the Court for an order for sale, as this will then protect him.

These rules are set out in the Torts (Inter-ference with Goods) Act 1977, which permits arrangements more favourable to the repairer to be made. Many repairers in fact write a term into their conditions or put a written notice up on the premises, to this effect. Under a specially agreed term, for example, the repairer may reserve the right to sell the goods after a shorter period and keep the profit.

Consumer hire contracts are often called 'rental agreements'. They are subject to control under the Consumer Credit Act 1974 which lays down very strict rules that must be complied with. They are growing in importance, and today almost anything can be hired: fancy dress, a morning suit for a society wedding or a car for a holiday, either on short or long term. Television sets and video recorders are often rented on a long term basis, while such things as floor sanders, rotavators and so on are hired in the short term.

There is no legal significance in the terminology used by the owner: renting, leasing and hiring are synonymous in law. Unlike contracts for the sale of goods, under a hire contract ownership does not pass from one party to the other; the goods remain the owner's property, but the hirer has the use of them. Hire differs from hire-purchase (see page 194) in that the hirer never becomes the owner of the goods, however long the agreement may last. Under a hire-purchase contract the hirer has the opportunity of acquiring ownership of the goods and, indeed, that is the purpose of the transaction. Under a rental agreement there is simply a transfer of possession, subject to the owner's terms and conditions.

Section 15 of the 1974 Act contains its own definition of a 'consumer hire agreement'. It is an agreement: (a) other than a hire purchase agreement; (b) made with an individual hirer; (c) capable of lasting for more than three months; (d) where the hirer is not required to make payments exceeding £15,000.

The Act also covers 'small agreements' under which the hirer is not required to make payments in excess of £50 and, effectively, all consumer hire agreements are covered. (The hire of telephone and metering equipment from British Telecom is, however, exempt.) There are strict rules about the way in which the hire agreement must be set out and what it must contain, and the main point for the consumer to watch is whether there is any minimum or fixed period of hiring. Hire concerns usually stipulate for a minimum period of hiring – which generally cannot be longer than eighteen months – and if the hirer wishes to terminate the agreement before that minimum period, he will have to pay an agreed sum for earlier determination. Most hire contracts in fact contain a minimum payment clause.

The situation is illustrated by *Robophone Facilities Ltd v Blank* (1966) where an accountant hired a telephone answering machine for a period of seven years, at a rental of just over £17 a quarter, the value of the machine being £350. Clause 11 of the agreement was a minimum payment provision, under which Mr Blank undertook to pay a sum equal to 50% of the total rental which would thereafter become payable. Immediately after signing the agreement Mr Blank changed his mind and purported to cancel the agreement. The Court ruled that he must pay £245 11s as compensation.

Subject to a few exceptions, section 101 of the 1974 Act entitles the hirer to give written notice of termination after eighteen months from the date of the agreement. The period of notice must equal the intervals of payment, e g, a week's notice if the rental is payable weekly, or three months, whichever is the less. Terminating the arrangement does not affect the hirer's liability to pay any overdue rent, and the section 101 provision does not cover agreements under which the annual payments exceed £900 (£17.31 a week or £75 a month).

A few hire contracts are for a fixed length of time; others run from week to week or month to month. In periodic agreements, the notice required to terminate will usually be laid down. If nothing is said, a notice equivalent to the period of hire is sufficient to bring the agreement to an end. Owners usually stipulate that the goods must be kept at a particular place, and can at any time require the hirer to give information about where the goods are. If the hirer fails to pay the rental due, the owner has the right to repossess the goods without a Court order, although he must give a default notice. The hirer does not have the same statutory protection against repossession as does the buyer under a hire-purchase agreement. However, where the owner has repossessed the goods, section 132 of the 1974 Act enables a Court, on the hirer's application, to order repayment to him of all or any part of his payments and cancel any sums owed by him. This power is rarely exercised and so far as cancellation of payments is concerned, probably refers to future payments and not existing liabilities.

1. OWNER'S OBLIGATIONS

The Supply of Goods and Services Act 1982 imposes certain liabilities on the owner of the goods under a contract of hire, which is defined so as to include all normal hire transactions. The owner's statutory obligations are:

(i) There is an implied condition that the owner has the right to hire out the goods for the period of the hire and that he will not interfere with the hirer's 'quiet enjoyment' throughout the hire period. It follows that the hirer can sue the owner if his possession of the goods is interfered with by a third person because, for example, the owner's legal title is defective. This is of importance where the hirer is dealing with an 'owner' who does not in fact own the goods because, e g, they are subject to a hire-purchase agreement.

(ii) There is an implied condition that the goods will correspond to description.

(iii) Where the owner is supplying the goods in the course of a business, there are implied conditions that the goods will be of merchantable quality and reasonably fit for the particular purpose for which they are supplied: see section 4.1(2). If the owner is in breach of these terms, the hirer can return the goods and treat the contract as at an end unless the owner can replace them or remedy the defect immediately.

In the case of consumer transactions, these terms cannot be excluded by a clause in the hire contract. In a non-consumer situation, they can be excluded to the extent that it is 'reasonable' to do so.

2. HIRER'S OBLIGATIONS

There are corresponding liabilities on the hirer. His obligations are:

(i) He must pay the agreed charge or rental at the times and in the manner specified in the agreement. Failure to pay will entitle the owner to serve a default notice, terminate the agreement and repossess the goods. The hirer is still bound to discharge any arrears and the owner may be entitled to claim damages. This can be important in the case of a fixed-term contract because then, in principle, the owner is entitled to recover the whole of the rental which would have been payable for the fixed period.

(ii) He must take reasonable care of the goods and observe any restrictions placed upon their use by the terms of the agreement. He is responsible if he carelessly damages the property. The hirer is not, however, an insurer and is not, therefore, liable if the goods are damaged by an accidental fire or if they are stolen. However, some hire contracts impose on him an obligation to insure the equipment for its full value. There is usually an express term dealing with the hirer's responsibility for safekeeping, e g,

'THE HIRER is responsible for the safekeeping of the goods and for their use in a proper manner, and is strictly liable for any loss of or damage to the goods, from whatsoever cause arising, fair wear and tear excepted.'

A clause in this form makes the hirer strictly responsible and under it the hirer would be responsible even if he was not negligent, thus altering the general rule.

The hirer is not under any obligation to repair the goods and, indeed most hire agreements provide that he 'shall not repair or attempt to repair the goods'. If he fails to observe the terms of a non-repair clause he is liable for any resulting damage.

(iii) He must return the goods at the end of the contract. Quite apart from his contractual liabilities, the hirer is liable under the law of tort. If he sells or disposes of the goods, he breaks the contract, and brings the hire arrangement to an end. Selling hired goods is also a criminal offence, quite apart from the fact that the owner can sue the hirer for the tort of conversion and claim damages. It also amounts to conversion if the hirer refuses to hand over the goods should the owner make a lawful demand for their return. The third party will not become the owner of the hired goods. The position is illustrated by *Hillesden Securities Ltd v Ryjack Ltd* (1983), where a car was leased for a period of three years and the hirer sold the car during this period. Hearing of the wrongful disposal, the owner demanded the car back. When its demand was not complied with, the owner sued for conversion. The car was in fact handed back after a few months, just before the Court case. The judge ordered the hirer to pay damages at the rate of £115 a week – the rental of the car – from the time of the 'sale' until the date when it was returned.

The Office of Fair Trading has produced a guidance note called 'Hire Agreements' which explains the rules about the form and content of hire agreements. Copies can be obtained from the local Trading Standards Officers or from the Consumer Credit Licensing Branch, Room 407/11, Government Building, Bromyard Avenue, Acton, London W3 7BB or from the Office of Fair Trading, Chancery Lane, London WC1.

Apart from bank overdrafts and bank loans, there are three common forms of credit under which the customer purchases the goods by instalments: hire purchase, conditional sales and credit sales. These credit transactions are all governed by the Consumer Credit Act 1974, which is one of the most complex measures on the Statute Book. It was not until 19 May 1985 that the last of its major provisions came into effect, and even now some of its provisions are not in force. The Act largely regulates what are called 'consumer credit agreements' which are defined as a contract for credit: (a) not exceeding £15,000; (b) made to an individual or group of individuals, such as a partnership. The protection given by the 1974 Act does not extend to limited companies. Most consumer credit transactions are caught by the Act, few individual consumers buy anything worth more than £15,000 on credit terms. The 1974 Act introduces its own classification of credit-type purchases, and the statutory definition of credit is so elastic as to catch transactions that have not yet been invented.

In law, hire purchase, credit sales and conditional sales are three distinct forms of transaction:

(i) Hire purchase, strictly speaking is not a sale. What the hire purchaser is doing is agreeing to hire the goods for a period and pay the hire rent; at the end of the period he has an option to buy the goods on payment of a small additional sum. In *Helby v Matthews* (1895) the House of Lords ruled that under a hire purchase contract, because the hirer is not legally bound to exercise the option to purchase, the contract is not one of sale. The result of this ruling is that during the currency of the transaction the hirer does not own the goods and he cannot transfer ownership to someone else. It is only on the exercise of the option to purchase that the ownership passes to the customer.

(ii) A credit sale, in contrast, in its simplest form is a straightforward contract for the sale of goods. The buyer is allowed to defer payment of the price or part of it. Usually there will be a schedule of payments. The buyer will become the owner usually on delivery.

(iii) A conditional sale is different again. It is an agreement to sell. The buyer gets the goods on payment of a deposit, and pays the unpaid balance of the price in fixed instalments. Ownership does not pass to the buyer until he pays all the instalments. During the currency of the agreement, the buyer cannot transfer ownership.

In all cases, the liability for the condition and quality of the goods lies on the creditor – who may be the dealer or the finance company, depending on the technicalities of the transaction. The legal refinements do not generally concern the actual consumer because all these transactions are made on standard sets of documents which specify the type of transaction concerned.

Despite the protection afforded to consumers by the 1974 Act, it is still necessary to be very careful. Oral agreements for credit are allowed under the general law, which does not lay down special requirements unless the agreement is *regulated* by the 1974 Act, and if for some reason the agreement is not caught by the Act's provisions, the customer may be in a very difficult position. Whatever the legal position may be, it is always dangerous to sign a form of agreement in blank and allow the dealer to fill in the details.

The dangers of doing so are graphically illustrated by *United Dominions Trust Ltd v Western* (1975), where Eric Western wished to buy a second hand Ford Corsair on display at the premises of Romanay Car Sales. As a result of discussions between Mr Western and Mr Romanay, Mr Western agreed to buy the car for £550, and paid a small deposit as he wished to buy on hire-purchase terms. He then signed what he took to be a standard hire purchase agreement, leaving the dealer to fill in the blanks. In fact, it was UDT's standard form of loan agreement, and the figures filled in were not those which had been agreed between Western and Romanay. The price of the car was put in as £730, and a larger deposit was mentioned. UDT accepted the transaction in good faith and sent Mr Western a copy of the agreement. He did nothing about it, but became dissatisfied with the car, which was later stolen. He failed to pay any instalments due under the agreement. The Court of Appeal held that he was bound by the terms of the document, and upheld the trial judge's order that Mr Western should pay £750, plus costs.

Buying stolen goods

The basic rule of the common law, affirmed by the Sale of Goods Act 1979, is that the sale of goods by someone who is not the true owner, or acting with his authority, cannot make the buyer the owner. He gets no legal title to the goods, even if he acted innocently and in good faith, and will be obliged to give the goods up to the true owner.

Buying stolen goods knowingly is a criminal offence – punishable with imprisonment – and the circumstances in which the goods were bought is always a factor which the police take into account in deciding whether or not to prosecute. It is not an offence to buy stolen goods unless the buyer knows or believes them to be stolen, and in practice stolen goods are often purchased innocently. Obviously, if a consumer buys goods from a reputable source, and it turns out subsequently that the goods are stolen, and have to be returned to their true owner, the buyer will have a claim against the innocent seller, who is liable for breach of the implied term that he has the right to sell the goods. The innocent seller, in turn, would have a claim against the person from whom he bought, but eventually the chain comes to an end. This straightforward and simple rule is subject to a number of exceptions, but only two of them are of much practical importance:

(a) Where goods are bought in 'market overt' the buyer acquires a good title to them subject to certain conditions. A sale in 'market overt' is essentially a sale in a long-established market, on a market day, or any open sale in a shop in the City of London, for such things as are usually sold in the shop. The sale must be by and not to the shopkeeper, and must be of an item which is of a type usually sold in the shop. For example, a sale of jewellery in a grocery shop would not be a sale in market overt. The sale must also take place openly, that is in a saleroom to which the general public is admitted. Outside the City of London, the sale must be in a legally-constituted market, on a market day, and in accordance with the custom of the market. In both cases, the buyer will become the owner of the goods provided he buys them in good faith and does not know that the seller cannot transfer ownership.

(b) Of more practical importance, there are special statutory provisions relating to private purchases of motor vehicles which are in fact on hire-purchase or conditional sale terms. This exception is set out in Part III of the Hire Purchase Act 1964. If a private purchaser buys a motor vehicle which is subject to a hire purchase or credit sale agreement, he acquires a good legal title to it if he bought in good faith and without knowledge of the hire purchase or credit sale agreement. The exception does not apply to dealers but, curiously, if a private purchaser buys such a motor vehicle from a dealer, he will become the owner of the car, even though the original sale was not effective to transfer the ownership to the dealer.

There is little justification for the market overt rule, which is a hangover from mediaeval days. Citizens' Advice Bureaux and the motoring organisations, such as the AA and RAC, can make searches of the records of Hire-Purchase Information Ltd (HPI). HPI was set up by the finance companies to prevent hire-purchase fraud, and member companies notify HPI of any motor-vehicle hire-purchase agreement which they enter into. HPI records the information and answers queries from member finance companies and motor dealers, and so on, but not from private individuals.

Since most hire purchase and allied agreements are today caught by the 1974 Act, a similar case is not likely to arise, but the court's ruling emphasises how dangerous it is for anyone to sign a blank or partially-completed agreement.

Note. All consumer credit agreements within the 1974 Act are 'regulated agreements' unless exempted. There are no exemptions for hire purchase and conditional sale agreements.

1. HIRE PURCHASE

A hire purchase agreement is defined (section 189(1) of the 1974 Act) as an agreement under which the purchaser takes the goods on hire initially, with an option to become the owner at a later stage if he so desires. The form and content of hire purchase agreements is laid down by regulations, and it is important to realise that the financial limit of £15,000 (which brings the agreement within the statutory provisions) is not the price of the goods. It is the amount of the credit (see page 197 for an example of a hire purchase contract). The document must contain the following information and the first page must be headed prominently 'HIRE PURCHASE AGREEMENT REGULATED BY THE CONSUMER CREDIT ACT 1974':

(a) The names and postal addresses of each party;

195

(b) A description of the goods;

(c) Their cash price;

(d) The amount of the deposit, which is to include any part-exchange allowance;

(e) The amount of the credit i e the difference between the cash price and the deposit;

(f) The total charge for credit, i e the sum of the last three items;

(g) The amount of each instalment;

(h) The Annual Percentage Rate (APR), i e, the actual rate of interest;

(i) Description of any security, e g, a guarantee by a third party;

(j) Details of any charges payable if the customer defaults.

The agreement must also set out, in a red box, a very clear warning: 'This Document contains the terms of a hire purchase agreement. Sign it only if you want to be legally bound by them.' The signature of the hirer is appended.

The goods will not become your property until you have made all the payments. You must not sell them before then.

Other information must be given in the document, and notably details of the hirer's rights on termination and the legal position about repossession. These statements must be printed boldly.

The customer will therefore always know if he is signing a hire-purchase agreement. Before he signs it he must be told the cash price of the goods, the rate of interest, and the total credit price; usually this is done by a label on smaller goods. It is not enough merely for it to be set out in the agreement.

Under a hire-purchase agreement, just as under an ordinary sale of goods, certain obligations are written in by statute. These are conditions that: (a) the owner or seller has the right to sell the goods; (b) the goods must be of 'merchantable quality' that is free from serious defects; (c) they must be reasonably fit for the purpose for which they are required. Dealers or finance companies cannot exclude these implied obligations in a consumer contract of hire-purchase. The law protects the hire purchase customer in many other ways, and in the majority of cases the customer can back out of the agreement within a short space of time. He is not necessarily legally committed because he has signed the agreement – he is moving towards a legal commitment. There are two cases to consider.

(i) Cancelling Before the Agreement Is Completed

At any time before the completion of the agreement, either party may withdraw from the transaction. This is the rule under the general law of contract but has special application in the field of hire purchase. Sections 62 and 63 of the 1974 Act stipulate that the customer must be given at least one copy, and often two copies, of the agreement. In the usual case, the customer will receive two copies. Suppose, for example, a customer has decided to buy a car on hire purchase terms. In the nature of things, the finance company will want to make inquiries about the customer's credit worthiness. So the dealer will fill out the form and the customer will sign and must be given a copy of the agreement. At that point it is not legally binding; it will not be binding until it is signed as accepted by the finance company, and this will often be several days later. So at any time before it is accepted by the finance company the customer can back out. If he decides to do so, he would be wise to send his cancellation by recorded post to both the finance company and the dealer, quoting the details of the transaction from the unexecuted agreement. Once the agreement has been accepted by the finance company, it is too late to back out – unless the agreement was made 'off trade premises': see below.

The customer is entitled to a second copy of the agreement, this time of the agreement as accepted by the finance company. This copy must be given to him within seven days following the making of the agreement, i e, when it was accepted by the finance company. The seven day period starts to run on the day following the making of the contract. This requirement is satisfied if the copy agreement is posted, even though it arrives after the expiry of the seven day period.

(ii) Cancellable Agreements

For many years legislation has protected customers against the unfair pressure sometimes exerted by door-to-door salesmen and has given the customer the right to cancel the contract for a limited period – called 'the cooling off period'. This applies wherever the customer signs the agreement away from the business premises of the dealer, the finance company, or the salesman. There is also a requirement that the salesman or negotiator should have made oral representations to the customer, but this requirement is invariably satisfied.

The agreement must then contain,

HPC **Hire Purchase Agreement** *regulated by the Consumer Credit Act 1974*   Original
With right of cancellation

Agreement No. _____

This agreement sets out below and overleaf the terms on which we (the owners) agree to supply the goods described below on hire purchase to you (the customer)

The Owners
Name and address

The Customer
Full names please

Address

Particulars of Goods		Cash Price Incl. VAT	
Qty.	Description	£	p
	Identification Nos:		
	Total Cash Price (incl. VAT) (a)		

Financial Details and Payments		£	p
Total Cash Price	(a)		
Less Deposit: Cash £ Pt Ex £			
= Credit Extended			
Add: Charges	(b)		
= Balance Payable			
Total Amount Payable	(a) + (b)		
A.P.R.			%
Number of monthly payments			
Day of month on which payable			
First Payment due (month and year)		19	
Amount of each payment			
Amount of final payment (if different)			

TERMINATION: YOUR RIGHTS

You have a right to end this agreement. If you wish to do so, you should write to the person authorised to receive your payments. We will then be entitled to the return of the goods and to half of the total amount payable under this agreement, that is £ _____ .[1] If you have already paid at least this amount plus any overdue instalments, you will not have to pay any more, provided you have taken reasonable care of the goods.

[1] Insert one half of the total amount payable.

REPOSSESSION: YOUR RIGHTS

If you fail to keep to your side of this agreement but you have paid at least one third of the total amount payable under this agreement, that is £ _____ ,[2] we may not take back the goods against your wishes unless we get a court order. (In Scotland, we may need to get a court order at any time.) If we do take them without your consent or a court order, you have the right to get back all the money you have paid under the agreement.

[2] Insert one third of the total amount payable.

DECLARATION BY CUSTOMER

By signing this agreement you are declaring that:

★ Your particulars given above are correct

★ All the information you have given us is correct

★ You realise that we rely on that information when deciding whether to enter into this agreement.

Witness: Signature

Name
Block letters please

Address

Witness: Signature
Second witness required in Scotland only

Name
Block letters please

Address

Signature of (or on behalf of) Owners

Date of Owners' Signature (Date of Agreement)

This is a Hire-Purchase Agreement regulated by the Consumer Credit Act 1974. Sign it only if you want to be legally bound by its terms.

Signature(s)
of Customer(s)

Date(s) of Signature(s)
The goods will not become your property until you have made all the payments. You must not sell them before then.

YOUR RIGHT TO CANCEL
Once you have signed this agreement, you will have for a short time a right to cancel it. Exact details of how and when you can do this will be sent to you by post by us.

✂ -

CANCELLATION FORM
(Complete and return this form ONLY IF YOU WISH TO CANCEL THE AGREEMENT).
To: [1]
I/We* hereby give notice that I/we* wish to cancel

agreement _____ [2]

Signed

Date

Name

Address

Notes for cancellation form:
[1] Owners to insert name and address.
[2] Owners to insert reference number, code or other identification details.
* Delete inapplicable pronoun.

HPC
Original

TERMS OF THE AGREEMENT

1 Payment

Before signing this agreement you must have paid the deposit shown overleaf. By signing this agreement you agree to pay the Balance Payable by making the payments set out overleaf, by their specified dates, to us at the address stated overleaf or to any person or address notified by us in writing. Punctual payment is essential. If you pay by post you do so at your own risk.

2 Failure to pay on time

We have the right to charge interest at the annual percentage rate shown overleaf on all overdue amounts. This interest will be calculated on a daily basis from the date the amount falls due until it is received and will run both before and after any judgment.

3 Ownership of the goods

You will become the owner of the goods only after we have received payment of all amounts payable under this agreement, including under Clauses 2 and 11. Until then the goods remain our property.

4 Selling or disposing of the goods

You must keep the goods safely at your address and you may not sell or dispose of them or transfer your rights under this agreement. You may only part with the goods to have them repaired. You may not use the goods as security for any of your obligations.

5 Repair of the goods

You must keep the goods in good condition and repair at your own expense. You are responsible for all loss of or damage to them (except fair wear and tear) even if caused by acts or events outside your control. You must not allow a repairer or any other person to obtain a lien on or a right to retain the goods.

6 Change of address

You must immediately notify us in writing of any change of your address.

7 Inspection

You must allow us or our representative to inspect and test the goods at all reasonable times.

8 Insurance

You must keep the goods insured under a fully comprehensive policy of insurance at your own expense. You must notify us of loss of or damage to the goods and hold any monies payable under the policy in trust for us. You irrevocably authorise us to collect the monies from the insurers. If a claim is made against the insurers we may at our absolute discretion conduct any negotiations and effect any settlement with the insurers and you agree to abide by such settlement.

9 Your right to end the agreement

You have the right to end this agreement as set out in the notice 'Termination: Your Rights' overleaf. You must then at your own expense return to us the goods, together with in the case of a motor vehicle, the registration document, road fund licence and test certificate.

10 Our right to end the agreement

We may end this agreement, after giving you written notice, if:

(a) you fail to keep to any of the terms of this agreement;

(b) you commit an act of bankruptcy (such as failing to pay a debt ordered by a court) or have a receiving order made against you;

(c) you make a formal composition with or call a meeting of your creditors;

(d) execution is levied or attempted against any of your assets or income or, in Scotland, your possessions are poinded or your wages arrested;

(e) the landlord of the premises where the goods are kept threatens or takes any step to distrain on the goods or, in Scotland exercises his right of hypothec over them;

(f) where you are a partnership, the partnership is dissolved;

(g) you have given false information in connection with your entry into this agreement;

(h) the goods are destroyed or the insurers treat a claim under the above policy on a total loss basis.

If we end this agreement then, subject to your rights as set out in the notice 'Repossession: Your Rights' overleaf, we may retake the goods. You will also then have to pay to us all overdue payments, and such further amount as is required to make up one half of the Total Amount Payable under this agreement. If you have failed to take reasonable care of the goods you may have to compensate us for this.

11 Expenses

You must repay on demand our expenses and legal costs for:

(a) finding your address if you change address without first informing us or finding the goods if they are not at the address given by you;

(b) taking steps, including court action, to recover the goods or to obtain payment for them.

12 General provisions

(a) The word 'goods' includes replacements, renewals and additions which we or you may make to them.

(b) No relaxation or indulgence which we may extend to you shall affect our strict rights under this agreement.

(c) Where two or more persons are named as the customer, you jointly and severally accept the obligations under this agreement. This means that each of you can be held fully responsible under this agreement.

(d) We may transfer our rights under this agreement.

13 When this agreement takes effect

This agreement will only take effect if and when it is signed by us or our authorised representative.

IMPORTANT — YOU SHOULD READ THIS CAREFULLY
YOUR RIGHTS

The Consumer Credit Act 1974 covers this agreement and lays down certain requirements for your protection which must be satisfied when the agreement is made. If they are not, we cannot enforce the agreement against you without a court order.

The Act also gives you a number of rights. You have a right to settle this agreement at any time by giving notice in writing and paying off all amounts payable under the agreement which may be reduced by a rebate.

If you would like to know more about the protection and remedies provided under the Act, you should contact either your local Trading Standards Department or your nearest Citizens' Advice Bureau.

To: UNITED DOMINIONS TRUST LTD.
51 Eastcheap, London EC3P 3BU

Specific Guarantee:
ACT CONDITIONAL SALE

In consideration of your entering into a Conditional Sale Agreement with the person named in the Schedule hereto ("the Principal") for the goods briefly described in the Schedule hereto having a balance of total purchase price as specified in the Schedule I the Guarantor mentioned in the Schedule ("the Guarantor") hereby guarantee the due performance and observance by the Principal of all the terms of the said Conditional Sale Agreement including in particular the punctual payment by the Principal of all instalments of the balance of total purchase price payable thereunder as and when they become due and agree that in the event of the Principal failing promptly to pay any such sum to pay the same when called upon by you to do so.

I further agree that this guarantee shall be not affected by any time or other indulgence which you may grant to the Principal and that the expression "the Guarantor" wherever used herein includes as many persons or bodies corporate as may be named as Guarantor in the Schedule hereto and if more than one person or body corporate is so named then all obligations on the Guarantor shall be several as well as joint.

SCHEDULE

(To be completed in Block Letters)

THE PRINCIPAL (Name and address)	THE GOODS
	Serial/Registration No.
	Balance of Total Purchase Price £

THE GUARANTOR

Where the Guarantor is a body corporate:

Name .... Registered No. ....

Registered Office ....

Where the Guarantor is an individual:

Age ....

Name .... Tel. No. ....

Address ....

| Relationship to Principal (if any) | Married/Single/ Widowed/Divorced .... | No. of dependants (including spouse) .... |

| How long at present address .... House/Flat/Rooms .... | Tenant/Owner/ Living with parents .... |

Previous address (if at above address less than 3 years) ....

Present employer's name .... Occupation ....

and address .... How long with present employer ....

Previous employer (if less than 3 yrs. with present employer) ....

Bankers name .... How long have you had an account there ....

and address ....

Largest current credit commitment: Company .... Purpose ....

Ref. No. .... Amount outstanding £ .... Date to be paid in full ....

Where there are additional Guarantors please show the name and address and registered number (if applicable) below and provide overleaf particulars of individuals similar to those requested above.

Witness(es) to Guarantor's Signature

Signature ....

Name ....

Address ....

*Signature ....

Name ....

Address ....

Date of Guarantee .... 19 ....
*Second witness required in Scotland

NOTICE TO GUARANTOR

If you do not understand your obligations you should seek advice BEFORE signing.

Signature ....

If this your guarantee is acceptable to United Dominions Trust you will be sent a photo-copy of the agreement and this guarantee which will become binding on you once the agreement is made.

Additional Guarantors and Witnesses to sign overleaf as necessary   D230 (11/80) immediately adjacent to the box for signature, a special and boldly printed notice: 'YOUR RIGHT TO CANCEL'. Once you have signed this agreement you will have for a short time a right to cancel it. Exact details of how and when you can do this will be sent to you by post by the creditor. However, the customer need not wait to hear from the finance company or other creditor, but he must exercise his right to cancel within the cooling-off period. The normal period runs from the time the customer signed the agreement to the end of the fifth day following the day on which he receives the second copy of the agreement through the post. In effect, once he receives the document he has six days in which to cancel.

Cancellation must be by written notice posted or given by the customer. Finance companies often provide special forms, but no special wording is required. All the customer has to do is to write indicating his intention to withdraw from the agreement. Although the Act says that where a notice is posted it takes effect on posting, whether or not it is actually received, it is best to use recorded delivery post to avoid arguments. Cancellation destroys the agreement; it is treated as though it never existed, and the customer is entitled to receive back all the money he has paid, less a small fee.

(iii) Practical Problems

(A) Early settlement. Sometimes the customer will decide that it is in his interests to settle the agreement before the agreed date by offering to pay off the outstanding balance. Section 94 of the 1974 Act gives the customer a right to settle agreements early by giving written notice to the finance company and paying off the outstanding balance, less a rebate for early settlement. There is a very complicated formula for calculating the rebate, and what the customer must do is to write to the finance company asking for a settlement figure. If the customer does then settle early, the agreement is at an end and the goods become the customer's property.

(B) Repossession of goods. Failure to make payments to the finance company as they fall due is a breach of the terms of the agreement. Since the goods are not the customer's property, the finance company is entitled to repossess them or claim them back. Many customers in fact fall into arrears through no fault of their own, and if this happens most of the finance companies will be reasonably sympathetic and will accept reduced

payments or come to some compromise agreement. There are restrictions on the finance company's right to repossess the goods in any case.

Once the customer has paid one third of the total credit price, the goods become 'protected goods' under section 90 of the 1974 Act. This means that the finance company cannot recover the goods without a Court order. The company must, in any event, serve a *default notice* in a special form and no action can be taken by the finance company until at least seven days after the notice has been served.

There is, however, a loophole, even in the case of 'protected goods' because, having served a default notice, the finance company can recover possession if the customer consents. In some cases it will be to the customer's benefit to do this – but in others it is best to rely on the statutory protection because the finance company must then take Court proceedings. The judge will not necessarily allow the goods to be reclaimed. Indeed, if there is a reasonable prospect of the indebtedness being discharged by smaller instalments over a reasonable period of time, it is likely that the court will make an order for the debt to be paid off by instalments.

Where the goods are not protected – because, for example, less than a third of the credit price has been paid, no Court order is required. A default notice must still be served and in any case the finance company's representatives cannot come on to the customer's property to recover the goods without the customer's consent. Whatever the agreement may say, section 92 of the 1974 Act forbids the finance company from entering premises without a Court order. Indeed, any attempt to do so which is calculated to cause distress, alarm or humiliation to the customer or his family may well constitute a criminal offence.

2. CREDIT SALE AGREEMENTS

A credit sale agreement differs from hire purchase in that under it the customer becomes the owner of the goods immediately. He can, therefore, sell the goods while the agreement is running, though most credit sale agreements contain a clause requiring the immediate repayment of any balance due if the goods are sold. Credit sale payments are made on the basis of five or more instalments and interest rates are similar to those under hire purchase agreements.

Where the goods turn out to be unsatisfactory, the customer's legal rights are exactly the same as in an ordinary sale of goods: see page 178. The consumer cannot lose his legal protection by a contrary term in the credit sale agreement.

The main difference between a credit sale agreement and a hire purchase agreement is that the seller cannot repossess the goods after the agreement has been made, even if the customer defaults on the instalment payments. The seller's only right is to sue for what is owed. Credit sale agreements are still subject to the requirements of the Consumer Credit Act 1974. The customer is entitled to be informed of the cash price of the goods, the total credit price and the rate of interest, and the customer's signature will have to be in a special box on the form of agreement, which must also contain the following warning, printed in a red box: 'This is a Credit Agreement regulated by the Consumer Credit Act 1974. Sign it only if you want to be legally bound by its terms.' The signature of debtor and the date of signature is appended.

Basically, the customer's rights of cancellation and so on are the same as under a hire purchase agreement.

Guaranteeing a Credit Agreement

This branch of the law is very technical, but being a surety is a risky business, even though sureties are protected to a limited degree.

Someone who obtains goods on credit may be asked to provide a guarantor – that is, a third person who agrees to make good any obligations incurred under the terms of the credit agreement. Guarantees are frequently called for where the customer is not considered a good risk by the finance company. Sureties of this sort fall into two groups in law – 'guarantees' and 'indemnities'. The difference between a guarantee and an indemnity is straightforward: under a guarantee the guarantor is only liable if the debtor defaults, but an indemnity is a promise to pay in any event, so that the finance company can take direct action against a person who has signed an indemnity without involving the original debtor. An indemnity is a promise that the creditor will suffer no loss from granting the credit, and so an indemnity is fully enforceable even if the customer is under the age of eighteen. This was the ruling of the Court of Appeal in *Yeoman Credit Ltd v Latter* (1961), where Clifford Owen signed a document headed 'Hire-Purchase Indemnity and Undertaking' so as to enable Terry Latter to buy a motor-car on hire-purchase terms. Mr Latter never paid any of the instalments and the

car was repossessed, and Clifford Owen was held liable. He would not have been liable if the document had been a guarantee in the legal sense.

The Consumer Credit Act 1974 now governs guarantees and indemnities and works very much in favour of the guarantor. Section 113(1) effectively reduces nearly all indemnities to the level of guarantees: (a) The guarantee or indemnity cannot allow the finance company to recover more from the surety than he would from the customer. (b) If the hire purchase or credit sale agreement is itself unenforceable, e g, because the formalities have not been complied with, the guarantee is similarly restricted. (c) Guarantees taken in relation to prospective agreements are not enforceable until the main agreement comes into effect. This means that in most cases the surety can withdraw the guarantee until that time.

Finance companies will always insist on an indemnity if the customer is under age – a young man buying a motor-cycle, for example – and recognising the special position in such cases the Act does allow indemnities to be enforced. Regulations lay down the form and content of guarantees and indemnities. There must be a signature box warning the surety that he may have to pay instead of the customer and illegible print is outlawed. The surety gets a copy of the agreement when it is handed or sent to him for signature.

3. OTHER FORMS OF RETAIL CREDIT

Although hire purchase and credit sales are the most common form of retail credit, a variety of other schemes are available, most of them for obtaining credit on a short-term basis. Bank loans and overdrafts are considered on page 208. Here we deal with other types of credit transaction, all of which are subject to the Consumer Credit Act 1974.

(i) Budget Accounts

Many department stores operate a form of revolving credit for their customers. These schemes are called by a variety of names, but broadly speaking they all operate in the same way. The customer makes regular payments into the account of a set amount each month and is given a 'credit limit', which is usually 12 or 24 times the monthly payment. So if a customer agrees to pay £20 each month he will be given a 'credit limit' of £240 or £480 and is then allowed to charge his purchases to the account, up to the credit limit. How much credit is available at any time depends on how much the customer has charged to the account and how much he has paid in.

This is an expensive form of credit. A charge is almost invariably made for the facility, either by way of interest on the amount outstanding or on the basis of the value of purchases made during the previous three months.

Some large groups of retail stores operate these schemes themselves, in which case the credit contract is a standing offer to supply goods on the instalment terms set out in the terms and conditions, and each sale is a credit sale. In other cases, the credit will be supplied by a separate company. The 1974 Act describes this sort of transaction as 'running-account credit'. The customer's legal rights in respect of goods bought on a budget account are exactly the same as those in a straightforward sale of goods transaction: see page 178.

(ii) Budget Option Accounts

This is a variant of the budget account, and such schemes are usually operated by a specialist company, which is either independent or set up by the retailer for this purpose. Once again, a credit limit is given. This is not based on the amount of repayment but on the company's assessment of the credit risk. The usual credit limit varies from £350 to £1,500. The customer has the option of paying the account in full (without interest) or of taking extended credit and paying a specified minimum monthly sum and becoming liable to interest on the balance. The minimum amount payable will be set out on the statement and this is once again a very expensive form of credit. The customer's rights in respect of goods purchased are again identical to his rights under an ordinary sale of goods transaction which, indeed, the purchase is: see page 178.

(iii) Credit Cards

Credit cards are commonly known as 'plastic money' and enable the customer to make purchases without having to carry cash. They may be issued by a bank, e g, a Barclaycard, or by a credit-card company, and in both cases the customer has legal protection under the Consumer Credit Act 1974 and has rights against the credit-card company if the goods or services purchased with the card are unsatisfactory. This operates very much in the customer's favour. Two different types of facility are offered.

(A) Travel and entertainment cards. American Express and Diner's Club cards are typical travel and entertainment cards. They allow credit on a short-term basis since the entire current debt must be cleared once a month. The customer has no pre-fixed credit limit, although retailers and so on who participate in the scheme may have a 'floor limit' set by the credit card company which means that if the customer wishes to purchase above that limit, the retailer will telephone the credit card company for authorisation. Cards of this type are a useful alternative to cash and can be used world-wide. The credit card company makes very searching inquiries about an applicant's credit-worthiness before issuing the card, for which it makes an annual charge. The credit-card company is not liable for the quality of goods or services which are bought with the card and the customer's redress is against the supplier of the goods or services.

By signing the card the card holder becomes responsible for it and is bound by the Conditions of Use. If the card is stolen or misused, so long as the customer has acted properly, his liability is limited to £30 under sections 83 and 84 of the Consumer Credit Act 1974. The Conditions of Use form the basis of the contract between the card holder and the credit card company and should be read and understood. Typically, the conditions provide as follows:

(a) Only the card holder is authorised to use the card;

(b) The card can only be used during its period of validity – usually two years from date of issue;

(c) Statements must be settled in full on receipt. A period of grace for payment is usually allowed – 40 days after statement date is common – and if payment is not made in full by that date a default or service charge is added;

(d) If the card is lost or stolen, the card holder must inform the credit card company immediately. There is usually a charge of £5 for a replacement card;

(e) The card company has the right to stop the customer's use of the card by telling suppliers not to accept it;

(f) The card remains the credit company's property and must be returned on demand;

Credit card application form

As explained in the text, the application form is the basis of the contract between you and the credit card company.

The form must be fully completed in every respect:

★ The company may require further information from you.

★ The company will certainly make credit checks and take up references.

★ Some companies seek details of your outgoings as well.

★ County Court judgments registered against you or even non-payment of a debt may disqualify you as you are then a bad credit risk.

★ Although the company is not bound to give you any reason for refusing to issue the card, it must, if asked by you, give you details of any credit reference agency used.

★ The credit card company is seeking to establish that you are a stable credit risk; hence the questions about length of occupancy of your home and the number of years you have been with your employer.

(g) 'Diners Club is not responsible for the standard, quality or suitability of any goods, tickets or services purchased with the card; all statements must be paid in full and without set-off or counterclaim. This does not, however, affect any statutory rights which you may have as a consumer or your rights against the [supplier] with whom all claims should be settled direct. Diners Club is not responsible if any [supplier] refuses to accept the card';

(h) The rules may be changed by the credit card company notifying the card holder to that effect.

(B) Ordinary credit cards. In contrast to travel and entertainment type cards are credit cards such as Barclaycard, Visa and Access. Technically, they are 'credit token agreements' and are covered by section 14 of the Consumer Credit Act 1974. Their main function is to allow the customer to obtain goods or services from suppliers which have arrangements with the credit card company, and the important point about cards of these types is that anything the customer buys with the card becomes a 'linked transaction', which means that the customer has equal rights against both the supplier and the

credit card company. The card company is jointly liable with the supplier for a consumer purchase made with the card of a cash value between £30 and £15,000: section 75 of the 1974 Act. This is a valuable protection and, in recent years, has proved beneficial to card holders who purchased holidays or air tickets with a credit card when the holiday company or airline subsequently became insolvent.

A feature of this type of card is that the customer is given a pre-set credit limit – usually in the range of £250 to £1,500 – and may make purchases within this limit. They offer extended credit. The card holder has the option of settling the account in full on a monthly basis (in which case no credit charge is incurred) or alternatively of making a minimum payment, in which case he is charged interest on the amount due, usually at something like 22%, though this varies in accordance with the bank base rates.

The card holder is bound by the conditions of use and in all other respects the situation is the same as with travel and entertainment type cards. The customer must not overshoot his credit limit although in practice the card companies have a generous and rather optimistic outlook on this. Some of the companies will respond to over-spending by raising the credit limit! Nevertheless, deliberately to exceed the limit may be a criminal offence (see page 448).

What to do if you are refused a credit card

Nobody has a right to a credit card and the credit-card companies make inquiries about credit-worthiness. Fill in the application form fully and correctly and answer all the questions truthfully. Sometimes a covering letter may explain doubtful points. The credit-card company need give no reason for declining an application and refusing to issue a card. If you are refused a card, ask the company whether they consulted a credit reference agency and, if so, its name and address. They are bound to give you this information. Check the position with the credit-reference agency. They sometimes make mistakes. Your bank manager may be able to advise you of other possible reasons for rejection: he is always asked to give a reference. Unless you have a bad credit record, it may be that the company thinks your income is fully committed. You can always apply again if things improve.

CREDIT CARD APPLICATION FORM

Card company will seek reference

Owning your own home, even if mortgaged, adds to your credit rating

CREDIT CARD APPLICATION FORM

PERSONAL DETAILS PLEASE USE BLOCK CAPITALS IN BALLPOINT PEN OR FELT TIPPED PEN

Title	Surname
MR	JORROCKS

Forename
JOHN

Address
21, SURTEES ROAD

FOXTOWN

WESSEX

Post Code	Telephone No.
WX1 2PA	0000-1234.

Own Home	Tenant	Years of Residence	Date of Birth
✓		10	1/4/30

Marital Status: Single ___ Married ✓ Divorced ___   Number of Dependent Children 2

Professional/Academic Qualifications
MASTER OF FOXHOUNDS

Primary Use of Card: Business ✓ Personal ___   Is a Member of Your Family a Barchester Express Cardmember Yes ___ No ✓

Please send statement to: Home Address ___ Office Address ✓

Have you previously held a Barchester Express Card: Yes ___ No ✓

Other Cards held: Access ✓ Diners ✓ Visa ✓

| J | O | H | N | | J | O | R | R | O | C | K | S | | | | | | | |

Please spell out your name as you wish it to appear on the Card using no more than 20 letters or spaces

Short residence will elicit further enquiries

Checks will be made with credit card companies whose cards you hold

Employer's Name
SELF-EMPLOYED

Address
1297, MINCING STREET

LONDON

Post Code	Telephone No.
EC9 4DA	01-007-5678

Nature of Business
WHOLESALE GROCER

Position Held
SOLE PROPRIETOR

Years with Employer	My Annual Income is £
25	£52,000

If self-employed, name of your accountant whom we may contact regarding your income

Name
S. SPONGE

Address
14, DUMBLETON STREET

LONDON

Post Code	Telephone No.
EC9 1BA	01-007-3456

Annual income and length of service with employer both taken into account in assessing credit worthiness

If self-employed, your accountant will be asked to confirm your income

LONDON & SOUTHERN COUNTIES BANK LTD

18, BROAD AVENUE, LONDON

EC9 5PQ	01-007 9112

00707707

Type of Bank Account: Current ✓ Deposit ✓ Mortgage ___   Years with present Bank 25

Do you have a Building Society Account Yes ✓ No ___

Savings ___ Mortgage ___ Both ✓   Time with Society 10 YRS

FOR OFFICE USE ONLY
T 06 005 BB 85

I warrant and represent that this information is true and I authorise Barchester Express Europe and its representatives to contact my employer, my bank or any other source to obtain any information it may require. I understand that Barchester Express may decline the application without giving a reason and without entering into correspondence. Conditions of use will accompany the Barchester Express Card(s) when issued.
This application is for a Card billed in sterling. Send no money. The annual subscription of £22.50 and the enrolment fee of £15.00 will be included in your first statement.
The Barchester Express Card can also be issued to members of your immediate family, for only £12.50 each. This £12.50 annual subscription will be charged to your account, as will all subsequent transactions charged by your family to the Card.

Signature	Date
X *John Jorrocks*	1/4/86

Barchester Express Cards for your family

Title	Surname

Forename(s)

Relationship	Date of Birth

Signature of family member requiring Card
X

Basic Cardmember's signature
X

• False statements are a criminal offence
• Credit card company need give no reasons for refusal
• You authorise the company to seek information from any source

An enrolment fee and annual subscription are payable for the use of this card

Using a credit card sensibly
Try to pay off your monthly outstanding balance in full, thus avoiding interest, which is currently about 22% with Access and Barclaycard. The interest rate is usually higher on store cards. Time your purchases correctly. The standard period of free credit is 25 days from the date of the statement. Purchases made just before or on the statement date are not normally included in the next month's statement, so giving in effect an interest-free period of 50 days or slightly more. Use your credit card for purchases of more than £100 as then the credit card company is equally liable with the supplier for defects in the goods, etc. The purchase must be between £100 and £10,000.

(iv) Check and Voucher Trading

There are a number of check-trading organisations and this form of credit is quite popular in the north of England. The customer buys checks or vouchers, and uses them to buy goods from stores taking part in the scheme. Each check has a face value which the customer pays to the check-trader by weekly instalments, which include a hefty premium for interest. The store accepting the check supplies the customer with goods up to its face value, and receives payment – less a substantial discount – from the check trader. The credit is for a fixed amount. There is no rebate for repaying earlier and the true rate of interest is usually about 25%. The repayment period is often 21 weeks.

Vouchers are similar, but a voucher usually has a greater face value than the check, and the amounts of credit involved are larger. Vouchers are often repayable on a monthly basis and invariably over a longer period – 100 weeks is not uncommon. No rebate is granted for early payment. In both cases, if the customer agrees to buy checks or vouchers, he must be given a copy of the written agreement, signed on the check trader's behalf, when he receives them.

If the goods are faulty or unsatisfactory the customer has the usual Sale of Goods Act rights against the supplier.

4. REGULATION OF CREDIT BUSINESS

The Consumer Credit Act 1974 regulates all those who deal in credit. Credit dealers must all have a licence from the Office of Fair Trading and the Act covers not only those who provide credit, e g, under hire purchase agreements, and credit brokers who introduce individuals to sources of credit, but also debt-adjusters, debt-counsellors and most debt-collectors. A licence is required to carry on business falling into these categories unless the credit never exceeds £30. Unlicensed trading is an offence and, in the case of a creditor (lender) or credit broker, makes any subsequent agreement unenforceable unless the Director General of Fair Trading makes an order to the contrary. Canvassing for credit away from trade premises is strictly controlled; canvassing for debtor-creditor agreements, which are loans which are not made under an arrangement with a supplier, and credit-brokerage, debt-adjusting and debt-counselling may not be canvassed at all. Other forms of credit can be canvassed only if there is a licence. It is an offence to send circulars offering credit or about credit facilities to a minor – a person under eighteen years of age. It is also an offence to give a person a credit token (which includes a credit card) if he has not asked for it, unless of course it is a renewal under an existing agreement. A 'credit token' is not limited to a credit card. There are also restrictions on advertisements for retail credit and the 1974 Act, in an endeavour to protect people from themselves and from the 'hard-sell', has hedged the granting of credit about with numerous restrictions.

5. CREDIT RATING AND REFUSAL OF CREDIT

Anyone over the age of eighteen can obtain credit, provided they are considered a good risk. The supplier (or finance house) may wish to take up references from other suppliers or the customer's bank. Most finance houses also check with a credit reference agency – such as Dun and Bradstreet – to check the customer's credit rating. The agency keeps records – usually on computer – about bad payers and those who have had court judgments registered against them for debt. Anyone who has ever bought anything on credit is likely to have a file kept on him by one or other of the agencies. The information which they keep is both favourable and unfavourable.

The customer is always entitled to know what information is on file about him, whether or not credit is refused. The 1974 Act and regulations made under it require the creditor or dealer to disclose the identity of any credit reference agency consulted. This information must be

205

supplied within seven days of a written request, which can be made within 28 days of the date when the parties last had dealings. The consumer can then write, sending a fee of £1, for a copy of his file. This must be in plain English, and must be supplied within seven days of the customer's request, along with a notice in a special form telling him of his right to have any inaccurate information corrected. If the agency has no file on the customer it must tell him so. If the customer thinks that the information is incorrect, he can give written notice requiring its removal or correction. The agency has 28 days to reply and supply him with a copy of any amended entry. If the entry has not been removed from the file, the customer has a further 28 days in which to insist that there be added to the file a note of correction which he has drafted. This cannot be more than 200 words in length. In turn, the agency has 28 days in which to tell the consumer either that it intends to comply or that it will refer the matter to the Office of Fair Trading, e g, because the correction is defamatory. The OFT will often try to act as conciliator. Inaccuracies can and do creep into credit reference agency files, and unfortunately some of these files are based on addresses rather than on individuals, and this has led in some cases to credit being refused.

Most credit application forms require the customer to give a great deal of detail about himself—his name and address, occupation, details of his employment, and whether he owns or rents property. It is a criminal offence to give false information on an application and the applicant's answers must be truthful. They are always checked out. The pitfalls of falsehood are shown by *The Crown v Webb* (1961), where Webb applied for a mortgage. He stated on the application form that he was earning £1,250 a year, whereas his real income was only £780. He also stated that he was the manager of a motor repair firm, whereas he was in fact a partner. The building society wrote to the firm for confirmation of these statements. Webb intercepted the letter and typed a fraudulent reply on the firm's notepaper and forged his partner's signature. The building society advanced money to him. Subsequently Webb was made bankrupt by another creditor. Although the building society realised the mortgage security without making a loss, Webb's fraudulent activities came to light and he was prosecuted and convicted. Webb was jailed for six months. When seen by the police, he was alleged to have said 'I'm sure I'm not the only

one who has had to boost his income to get a mortgage'. The position about false information is exactly the same under any form of credit application.

It is unlawful to discriminate against women in connection with the grant of credit just as it is to do so on the grounds of race. Discrimination means either (a) less favourable treatment or (b) imposing conditions which are harder for such applicants to meet and which cannot be shown to be justifiable.

The position is neatly illustrated by *Quinn v Williams Furniture Ltd* (1981) where Mrs Quinn applied for hire purchase. She was told that her husband must act as guarantor. She asked twice whether she would have had to guarantee her husband's repayments and was told 'no'. Mrs Quinn had a good job, had paid over half the cash price by way of deposit and had substantial sums in a deposit account. The Court of Appeal held that this amounted to discrimination. Lord Denning said:

> 'By requiring, or even suggesting or advising, that she should get her husband to sign the guarantee form in order to facilitate the agreement being entered into, it seems to me that there was unlawful discrimination against Mrs Quinn'.

The remedy for unlawful discrimination is an injunction, the effect of which may be to force the granting of credit in such cases. The discrimination is not a criminal offence.

6. EXTORTIONATE CREDIT BARGAINS

Since 1977, the courts have had power to reopen 'extortionate credit bargains' and, effectively, to vary the rate of interest where credit has been granted to an individual. This applies to all credit bargains and not merely to credit agreements regulated by the Act. The customer is given the right to challenge the agreement on the ground that it is an 'extortionate credit bargain' by applying to the Court. The power is also exercisable if, for example, the creditor is seeking to enforce the agreement. It applies to agreements 'whenever made' and the power could scarcely be wider.

No doubt many borrowers think that they are being charged an exorbitant rate of interest, but this is not the same as an extortionate bargain. A bargain is only extortionate if: (a) it requires payments which are *grossly* exorbitant; or (b) it otherwise *grossly* contravenes the ordinary principles of fair dealing. The Consumer Credit Act 1974 lays down several criteria for determining whether the agreement is extortionate and in practice very few attempts to vary interest rates are successful. The criteria are very restrictive. They are:

(i)   The rates of interest prevailing at the time the agreement was made. All the factors must be taken into account. There is no rule of thumb for assessing whether interest rates are too high. A high rate of interest may be justified, for example, if the lender was the borrower's last-resort because he was unable to get credit elsewhere or because he is a bad risk. The giving of security – for example a second mortgage – is also relevant. There is a tariff for most forms of credit – and a true interest rate of 48% is not uncommon in some situations – and the tariff is likely to be upheld in most cases;

(ii) The age, experience, business capacity and state of health of the customer;

(iii) The financial pressure on the customer;

(iv) The degree of risk involved and the security available. The position is well illustrated by the case of *A. Ketley Ltd v Scott* (1980), where Mr Scott had the chance to buy his home as a sitting tenant. He failed to obtain finance before signing the contract of purchase, when he paid a deposit of £2,500 on the price of £22,500. As a last resort, since he was in danger of losing his deposit, he approached Ketleys who agreed to lend him £20,500 for a short period at an annual interest rate of 48%. The Court ruled that this was not an 'extortionate bargain' in the circumstances. The lenders were taking a big risk – the shortness of time had prevented them making proper inquiries and the loan represented a high percentage of the value of the property;

(v)   The relationship of the creditor with the customer;

(vi) Other relevant factors.

Even if the credit bargain is found to be extortionate, the Court will not necessarily re-open it. For example, if the customer has not disclosed information about himself which shows that he is a bad risk the Court would refuse to intervene. But if the customer's challenge is successful, the creditor cannot proceed to judgment against him, and the Court has power to alter the terms of the agreement.

7. RATES OF INTEREST – CALCULATING THE ANNUAL PERCENTAGE RATE

Interest rates are misleading. Most customers are concerned with how much they have to repay a month and in the past lenders did not have to provide customers with the rate of interest. Now they must do so. The customer must be given:

(A) An accurate percentage rate. Flat rates are inaccurate. A flat rate is the monthly or annual rate of interest but this is not the same as the true rate of interest. If a man borrows £100 repayable over a year at a flat rate of 10% in monthly instalments, each instalment reduces the debt. A true rate of interest is almost 20% because, in the example, the debt averaged out over twelve months is about £55. A rough and ready calculation for finding the true rate is to multiply the flat rate by a factor of 1.8, but more accurate figures can be obtained by more sophisticated calculations.

(B) A common comparison or yardstick, which is what the debtor who pays annually would pay. The end result is called the Annual Percentage Rate – the APR – and this is what must be stated. There are very complicated rules for working out the APR.

4.5 BANK ACCOUNTS

Today's consumer is faced with a bewildering choice of banking facilities. These range from the traditional 'current account' or cheque account operated by the 'clearing banks' to what are effectively deposit accounts (on which interest is paid) which include a facility to draw cheques. Banking facilities are offered not only by the traditional banks but also by building societies, finance houses, and National Giro, which is a special bank run by the Post Office. Competition is fierce, and the services provided are similar. All of these institutions hold their customers' money, make regular payments on customers' behalf by 'standing order', and enable payments to be made by the customer to third parties. Some of the institutions offer other facilities as well: they provide foreign currency or travellers' cheques for use abroad, and offer advice on investments, stocks and shares and insurance. In many cases they offer loans or overdrafts as a means of raising finance.

1. TYPES OF ACCOUNT

(i) Current Account

A current account gives the customer a cheque book which enables him to withdraw money from his account at any time, either by making out a cheque to 'cash' or by making it payable to someone else. A cheque is the customer's written instruction to the bank requiring payment to be made. The bank will also arrange periodical payments to third parties by standing order and direct debit, both based on the customer's written instructions. Current account customers may also be able to arrange to borrow money by way of an overdraft or a bank loan: see page 212.

Until recently, most current accounts were operated by the 'clearing banks' of which Barclays, Lloyds, National Westminster, and Midland are the best known – who collect payments for cheques paid in through the London Bankers' Clearing House. Nowadays they face stiff competition from other financial institutions and it pays to shop around. The main advantage of an account with one of the major clearing banks is that they have branches in most towns and cities throughout the country, whereas some of the competing institutions have very few branches. All the major clearing banks also offer a 'cash card' facility through which the customer can withdraw money from automatic machines when the bank is closed, including evenings and weekends. The clearing banks' short opening hours – 9.30 a m to 3.30 p m on five days a week – have been a prime reason for the growing competion from other deposit takers, although some of the big clearing banks are now reversing their policy against Saturday opening (when most people want to use the bank) by opening major branches for short periods on Saturday mornings.

Current accounts may also be opened with other financial institutions, and sometimes these accounts offer significant advantages. A recent innovation is a package offered by a number of banks which combines:

(a) A current account with no charges and no minimum balance requirement;

(b) A borrowing option, often called the credit limit option, under which the bank offers a pre-arranged credit facility up to a given amount. Some of these accounts also cater for customers who occasionally overdraw without realising it, e g, because a payment into the account has been delayed, and allow the customer to overdraw a small sum for a few days without special prior arrangement;

(c) A savings option, providing for automatic transfers to deposit account where the money will earn interest;

(d) In some cases, the package includes payment of interest on balances in the current account as well as no charges, though to qualify there is sometimes a minimum balance requirement or a differential rate of interest, depending on the amount involved. The various schemes on offer should be carefully compared, as to conditions and restrictions and certainly the non-clearing bankers usually require more information about a prospective customer and his financial commitments than do the 'high street banks'. For example, on one application form currently in use, the applicant has to make a special declaration (see illustration opposite).

Current Accounts & Savings Application Form

To Barchester Trust & Savings
I/We wish to apply for an account and agree to make regular monthly payments into the account of not less than £150.

Please transfer to savings section each month £ _____ (*optional*)

Do you want a cheque guarantee card? ☐ YES ☐ NO (*Please tick*)

Are you an existing or previous Barchester Trust & Savings customer ☐ YES ☐ NO
If, yes, please give details _____

To help us with your request for an account, please complete this form carefully. All the information you provide will be treated confidentially unless otherwise authorised by you.

1

Full Name:
Mr ☐ Mrs ☐ Miss ☐

_____

_____

Date of Birth _____

Married ☐ Single ☐ Widowed ☐

Separated ☐ Divorced ☐

No. of Children _____

Their ages _____

2

Permanent Address:

_____

_____

_____

_____ Postcode _____

At this address since _____

Telephone Number _____

Owner ☐   Tenant Unfurnished ☐

Tenant Furnished ☐   Lodger ☐

With Parents ☐

3

If at present address less than 3 years
Previous Address: _____

_____

_____

_____

4

Occupation: _____

Employer's Name and Address

_____

_____

Employer's Telephone No.

_____

With this employer since _____
If necessary may we seek confirmation
YES ☐   NO ☐
We may not need to contact your employer if you enclose a recent cumulative pay-slip.

5

Joint Applicant's name

Date of Birth _____

Occupation _____

Employer's Name & Address

_____

_____

_____

_____

With this employer since _____

If necessary may we seek confirmation YES ☐ NO ☐

6

Banker's name and address (*if any*)

_____

Account No. _____

Type of account
Current ☐ Deposit ☐ Loan ☐

Cheque guarantee card No. (*if any*)

7

Access Card Number (*if any*)

Barclaycard Number (*if any*)

Other credit card (*if any*)
Please give name and number

I/We enclose our cheque for £ _____

as an opening deposit (*minimum deposit £5*) and accept the terms and conditions prevailing at the date of application and understand that where I/we have more than one account with you, you reserve the right to restrict the use of any individual account in the event of the incorrect performance of any other account.
If this account is to be held in joint names, we hereby authorise you to honour payment instructions signed by either one of us. Should any such instruction overdraw the account we acknowledge that our liability for this overdraft and any charges shall be joint and several.
We understand that in the event of either of us dying while the account continues, any credit balance shall be placed in the sole name of the survivor.

Signed _____
(*First applicant*)

Signed _____
(*Joint applicant*)

Date _____

> **Banks – the customer's duties**
> Unless there is express agreement to the contrary, the customer's duty to his bank in the operation of his current account is limited to writing out his cheques in such a way as to make fraud or forgery difficult. The customer must also inform the bank of any unauthorised cheques drawn on the account as soon as he becomes aware of them. The customer is not under a duty to take reasonable precautions in the management of his business with the bank to prevent forged cheques being presented for payment. Neither is the customer under a duty to check his bank statements periodically as they come in.
>
> The business of banking is the business of the bank and not of the customer. The bank offers a service, which is to honour the customer's cheques when drawn on an account in credit or within an agreed overdraft limit. If the bank pays out forged cheques, they are acting outside their mandate, and they must bear the loss. These basic principles were re-stated in 1985 in a case where a bank argued, unsuccessfully, to the contrary.

(ii) Cheque Guarantee Cards

An important facility offered with most current accounts is a *cheque card* which gives a guarantee by the bank that any cheque supported by the card will be met by the bank, even if the customer has insufficient funds in his current account. Cheque cards are not credit cards. They are a promise by the bank to pay the supplier who accepts a cheque backed by the card that it will be duly honoured provided it does not exceed a certain amount. The current limit imposed by most banks is £50, although one or two banks issue cheque cards for greater amounts. Barclaycards – although primarily credit cards – also function as cheque cards.

Before a customer can be given a cheque card by his bank he must enter into an agreement with the bank authorising it to meet cheques backed by the card. A payment by cheque with a cheque card cannot be countermanded except in case of fraud, and the customer's undertakings to the bank are extensive: see the box above. The cheque card also has conditions printed on its back, and the bank will only meet the cheque if those conditions are observed. The standard conditions are: (a) The cheque msut be signed in the presence of the payee and the signature must correspond to that on the cheque card; (b) The cheque is drawn on a bank cheque bearing the code number of the card; (c) The cheque must be dated before the expiry date of the card; (d) The payee must write the card number on the back of the cheque. It is not sufficient if the customer writes the number; the person in whose favour the cheque is drawn (or someone authorised on his behalf) must write the number on the back of the cheque.

(iii) Payment by Cheque

Apart from small items, most consumer purchases are paid by cheque. Cheques are either 'crossed' or 'uncrossed', and the practical difference is that a crossed cheque can only be paid into another bank account whereas an 'uncrossed cheque' can be exchanged for cash. Crossing a cheque is a protection against fraud.

The relationship between a bank and its customer is based on contract. The main terms of the contract are that the bank will honour its customer's cheques – which are an instruction to the bank to pay – provided there is sufficient money in the account or an overdraft facility has been agreed, and that the bank will maintain its customer's confidences. It must not disclose details of his financial position or dealings to anyone else without the customer's authority which can, of course, be given where the customer gives the bank's name as a reference.

Sometimes a cheque will be dishonoured or, to use a popular expression, 'bounced'. The bank is only entitled to dishonour a customer's cheque on very limited grounds.

(A) If there are insufficient cleared funds in the account and there is no agreed overdraft limit. All banks reserve the right to withhold payment of cheques drawn against what are called 'uncleared effects', which are payments in by cheque which have not been cleared through the clearing house system. So, if the customer pays a cheque into his account on Monday, he should not draw cheques against its value for several days – it takes at least three working days to 'clear' a cheque through the system. Although the account may be credited with the amount of the in-payment, the bank still has the right to refuse to pay against the sum credited until it is cleared. Similarly, if there are insufficient cleared funds in the account to meet the value of a cheque drawn, the bank can bounce the cheque, just as it can where to pay it would exceed any overdraft limit previously agreed.

(B) Where there is a mistake on the cheque – for

example, if the customer has forgotten to sign or date it or some other discrepancy. A common mistake is for the words and figures to differ.

Banks use different terms when dishonouring cheques – they are returned to the collecting banker and the matter is then between the customer and the payee. A cheque can be 'stopped' by the customer in certain circumstances (see below). A cheque can, therefore, be dishonoured for a number of reasons, and to have a cheque 'bounced' can cause serious embarrassment and difficulty to the customer. Banks frequently make mistakes, but the private customer is in a difficult position. Although by wrongfully bouncing a cheque the bank is in breach of contract, the customer's only entitlement would be to a pound or two by way of nominal damages.

This is shown in the case of *Gibbons v Westminster Bank Ltd* (1939), where the bank wrongfully dishonoured a cheque drawn by Mrs Gibbons in payment of her rent. The mistake was entirely the bank's since Mrs Gibbons had paid in more than sufficient to meet the cheque; the payment had been credited to the wrong account. As a result, the landlords insisted that all future payments of rent be made by cash and not by cheque. Although the bank was liable, Mrs Gibbons was held entitled to recover only nominal damages of £2. The position would have been different if Mrs Gibbons could have proved that she suffered some specific financial loss.

The position is different in the case of a business account. A trader whose cheque is wrongfully dishonoured is entitled to recover substantial damages – often many hundreds of pounds – and in an extreme case a tradesman might be able to recover damages from the bank for defamation of character (libel).

The rights of the payee of a dishonoured cheque are well protected by law. If the cheque is dishonoured for technical reasons, or because it is marked 'Refer to drawer: please represent' or 'Effects not cleared' most people simply represent the cheque for payment and, indeed, it is banking practice to do this. However, as the Court of Appeal has pointed out, a cheque is for all practical purposes 'to be treated as cash; it is to be honoured unless there is some good reason to the contrary' (Lord Denning in *Fielding & Platt v Najjar* (1969)) and one result is that the payee has an independent right to sue on the cheque as opposed to the transaction to which it relates.

In some cases the customer has the right to 'stop' a cheque – that is, to instruct the bank not to pay it. A cheque backed by a cheque card cannot be 'stopped'. Where a cheque is stopped, the bank will mark it 'orders not to pay'. A stop can be put on a cheque by telephone, but the bank will insist on having written confirmation giving the number of the cheque, its date and details of the payee and the amount.

A buyer should not stop the cheque because he has decided that after all he does not like the goods. Although the instruction to the bank not to pay will be effective to stop the cheque, it will be a breach of both the contract of sale and of the seller's rights under the cheque. Even if, as between buyer and seller, the customer is entitled to stop the cheque, he may find that he is under some liability to a third party who took the cheque in good faith. Furthermore, if a cheque is wrongfully stopped, and it can be proved that the customer had no intention of paying for the goods, he may be subject to a criminal prosecution. Where the customer knows that he is expected to pay on the spot for goods supplied to him or services rendered to him it is an offence for him dishonestly to go away without having paid and never intending to pay.

It is a criminal offence, punishable by imprisonment, to write out a cheque knowing that the bank is unlikely to meet it and, indeed, anyone who 'bounces' a cheque may find himself subject to prosecution for obtaining a financial advantage by deception. Misuse of a cheque card is similarly an offence.

A cheque is 'negotiable' – that is, it can be transferred to third parties by being endorsed over by the payee – and the third party who takes the cheque in good faith and for value has direct rights against the drawer. So, if the payee has endorsed the cheque to an innocent third party, the endorsee will be entitled to sue on the cheque.

Payment by cheque is not complete until the cheque is actually delivered, and until then the risk of misappropriation is on the customer as between himself and a seller of goods. Cheques may be lost or stolen and then misused. Sometimes the customer loses his cheque book or it may be stolen, and a wrongdoer manages to obtain money by using it. Provided the customer has not been negligent, it is the bank which bears the loss. Cheque books are valuable documents and should be kept carefully – the customer must take reasonable care. It is not taking reasonable care to sign a blank cheque or to write it in such a way that the figures can be easily altered. All cheque books have a series of warnings printed on their inside front cover. These warnings include instructions to prevent fraud. The amount of the cheque, in words and figures, should begin as far as possible over to the left of the space provided so that no other words and figures can be inserted. Any alterations should be confirmed with the customer's full signature. Cheque books and cheque cards should not be kept together – this facilitates fraud.

(iv) Budget Accounts

A budget account is a variant of the current account which enables the customer to spread his expenses over the year by regular payments. It is a current account with a built-in overdraft facility. The customer agrees with the bank the total of his likely regular expenses for the year – mortgage payments, rates, heating and lighting, telephone and so on – and signs a standing order transferring a fixed sum of money from his current account to his budget account each month – the total of the agreed expenses plus a charge, divided by twelve. The bank then gives him a special cheque book and the customer can overdraw on the account when several bills arrive at the same time. The budget account is a means of spreading payments over the whole year, and is otherwise subject to the same rules as an ordinary current account.

(v) Loan Accounts

Banks are in the business of lending money and will make loans to finance a customer's purchase from a dealer or for other purposes. Such loans – repayable by instalments over a fixed period, which may be up to five years – are 'consumer credit agreements' if they do not exceed £15,000 and are then subject to the provisions of the Consumer Credit Act 1974, including all its formalities, including warning boxes, supply of copies of the agreement, and so on. Perhaps unintentionally, the 1974 Act has made borrowing from a bank more complicated – though overdraft arrangements are not caught by the 1974 Act.

(vi) Deposit Accounts

A deposit account is one form of savings account. The customer puts money on deposit with the bank, and receives interest in return. The rate of interest varies according to bank rate. Usually, seven days' notice to withdraw money is required – though the exact details vary from bank to bank – and a higher rate of interest may be obtained by keeping large sums in the account. SAVINGS ACCOUNTS are a variant of the ordinary deposit account – the customer agrees to pay in a regular sum each month – and the accumulated balance earns interest.

2. BANK GIRO

The banks run a credit-transfer system – called bank giro – which is an alternative to paying bills by cheque. The customer fills out a special form for each firm he wants to pay – many major concerns print standard forms on their accounts – and hands them to the bank with the total amount in cash or by cheque. Several bills can be paid at the same time using one cheque. A similar service is operated through the National Giro-bank (the Post Office bank) and is called Transcash.

More and more people are getting into debt, often because they take on commitments which they cannot really afford. In other cases disaster strikes because someone loses his job, and finds that on a depleted income he cannot pay bills which he has run up. If this happens, all is not lost because creditors only take legal action as a last resort.

When someone runs into difficulties, the first step is to inform the creditor as soon as possible. This applies whether it is an unpaid bill, a hire-purchase agreement, or any form of credit. In practice, most creditors will adopt a sympathetic approach, and accept payment by instalments or over a longer period. The essential point is that the debtor should be frank and explain his difficulties and make realistic proposals and keep to them.

Unless the debtor acts sensibly in this way, the creditor is going to take a strong line and, unless the amount involved is very small, will attempt to recover the money. Very small debts may, in practice, be written off, but it would be rash to assume that this will happen. Both tradesmen and lending institutions have their own procedures for recovering debts due to them.

1. DEBT COLLECTING AGENCIES

Debt collecting agencies need a licence from the Director-General of Fair Trading. Operating as a debt-collector without a licence is a criminal offence. The agencies usually operate on a commission basis, and the larger agencies have local agents throughout the country. Sometimes they send someone to call on the debtor, but more usually they start off by writing to him on the creditor's behalf.

Debt collectors have no special legal status, and both they (and the creditor) can only attempt to collect the debt by legal means. It is a criminal offence to harass a debtor by making frequent or threatening demands for payment, and there are various controls:

(i) Neither the creditor nor the collector must ask for payment in such a way as to indicate that they are acting in an official capacity, e g, as a Court official, and amongst other things they are not allowed to send demands which look as though they are official Court forms.

(ii) They must not harass or bully the debtor so as to subject him or his family to alarm, humiliation or distress. This means, for example, that shops cannot display 'shame lists' of debtors – though there is nothing to prevent trade organisations from exchanging lists of debtors amongst themselves or advising their members of bad debtors and this happens frequently in practice. Any debtor who thinks he is being harassed should report the matter to the police. A typical case of harassment would be by parking a van marked 'Debt Collector' outside the debtor's front door. The majority of debt-collecting agencies are reputable and responsible, and it may be possible to make arrangements even at this stage to pay off what is owed by instalments.

2. COUNTY COURT PROCEEDINGS

The creditor may decide to use the Courts to recover his money. Most debt recovery proceedings are taken in the County Court which has jurisdiction where the amount claimed does not exceed £5,000 although some larger creditors – banks and hire-purchase companies, for example – may opt to start proceedings in the High Court. But the vast majority of creditors' claims for debt are disposed of in the County Courts.

The first step in the process will usually be a letter from the creditor's solicitor demanding repayment of the money. The letter will usually state that failure to pay the debt in full within a short period of time – seven or 14 days – or the making of satisfactory proposals for repayment, will result in legal proceedings. Even at this stage, creditors will often accept instalment payments, provided the debtor's proposal is realistic. If the debtor owes £1,000, for example, it is not realistic to offer to pay the debt off by weekly instalments of £1.

It is best to arrange to pay if this can be agreed because, if Court proceedings are started, the debtor will be liable for legal costs as well and these soon mount up. A letter offering to pay off the debt due by instalments should always

PLAINT NOTE (DEFAULT SUMMONS)

In the BRISTOL County Court

BETWEEN .... WILLIAM SMITH .... PLAINTIFF

AND

CASE No.	DEFENDANT	ISSUE FEE	DATE OF POSTAL SERVICE	JUDGMENT
	JOHN EVANS	£24.80	3 JUNE '86	

Full name of plaintiff

Full name of defendant

In this case the summons has been served by post

The court fee is on a sliding scale. Its amount depends on the sum claimed

To the Plaintiff

The above action(s) was/were issued today and you will be entitled to judgment 14 days after the date of service of the summons, unless within that time the defendant pays into court the total amount of the claim and costs or delivers at the court office a defence, an admission with an offer of payment or a counterclaim. If payment is made you will be notified. If a defence, or counterclaim is delivered you will be sent a copy. If the defendant does not reply to the summons or if he delivers an admission without an offer of payment you must apply for judgment to be entered.(1) If you do not, the action will be struck out twelve months after the date of service.

The summons must be served within twelve months from today. You may apply for this period to be extended provided your application is made before the summons expires.(2)

Always bring this plaint note with you when you come to the court office for any purpose connected with these proceedings.

If judgment is entered then, unless otherwise directed the defendant will be ordered to make payments into the court. The court will send the money to you. If you receive any money from the defendant you must notify the court.

(1) Order 9 Rule 10
(2) Order 7 Rule 20

DATED   3/6/86

Address all communications to the Chief Clerk AND QUOTE THE ABOVE CASE NUMBER(S)

THE COURT OFFICE AT

GREYFRIARS, LEWINS MEAD, BRISTOL, BS1 2NR,

is open from 10 a.m. to 4 p.m. Monday to Friday.

N.205—Plaint note (default summons). Order 3 Rule 3(2)(d)(I).

MCR 345285/1/F24840 20m 8/85 TL

WARRANT No.	AGAINST DEFENDANT	ISSUE FEE	WARRANT No.	AGAINST DEFENDANT	ISSUE FEE

No. OF OTHER PROCESS	AGAINST DEFENDANT	ISSUE FEE	DATE, TIME AND PLACE OF HEARING

include a payment on account as a token of good faith. If the debtor fails to respond to the solicitor's letter, and the creditor decides to take Court proceedings, the solicitor will go along to the Court office and issue a 'default summons', which will be sent by the Court to the debtor by post unless the solicitor arranges (for an extra fee) to have the summons served personally by a County Court bailiff. The default summons (see opposite) requires the debtor to admit or deny the claim within fourteen days. It will be accompanied by a form which the debtor must fill in and return to the Court within the fourteen day period. This form enables the debtor to make an offer to pay by instalments if he wishes, and he must then provide details of his income and outgoings.

The creditor is not bound to accept payment by instalments but once again, in practice, may well agree to do so. If he does not – for example, because he thinks the proposal is unrealistic – the case will proceed to be heard. Smaller claims are dealt with by the County Court Registrar, who may well make an order that the debt be paid by instalments which are geared to the debtor's income and commitments, but he is not bound to do so. If an instalment order is made, it is essential that the instalments are made promptly to the County Court office as specified in the order. Payments have to be made in cash or by cheque (backed by a cheque guarantee card) at the Court office, or they may be made by post, using postal orders or cash (sent by registered post). The Court will not accept cheque payments by post.

Where a debt is disputed, the Court proceedings will be held in public and there will be a trial. But if the debt is admitted, and the creditor is merely disputing the question of repayment, there will be a private hearing 'in chambers'. The Court will fix a date for this hearing – called 'the disposal date' – and the debtor must turn up then, taking with him evidence of his means. The registrar will hear what the parties have to say, there will be questions asked, and then will decide the method of payment and make the order.

3. ENFORCING A JUDGMENT

When the debtor refuses to pay, or ignores the Court order, the consequences are drastic. There are several ways open to the creditor to enforce

his judgment and recover his money from the debtor. Only in a very few cases will it not be worth the creditor's while to enforce the judgment, for example, if the debtor has moved on and left no forwarding address. Even in these cases, however, if a substantial sum is involved, a larger creditor will undoubtedly make strenuous efforts to trace the defaulter.

The consequences of failure to pay a judgment debt are unpleasant, the last resort being that the debtor can be made bankrupt.

(i) Seizing the Debtor's Goods

The most common form of enforcing a judgment is by 'levying execution' against the debtor's goods, which means putting the bailiffs in. The debtor's goods are seized by the bailiffs and then sold to pay off what is due. This method is available both for the whole amount and where there are instalments outstanding. The creditor applies to the Court to issue a 'warrant of execution' – a fee is payable, depending on the amount involved. The debtor is informed when the warrant is issued and then has a further seven days in which to pay up. He can also pay the bailiff when he calls.

Alternatively, the debtor can apply to the Court to suspend the warrant, and even at this stage the Court may do so (after a hearing) and make an order for payment by instalments. But the Court is unlikely to suspend a warrant on more than one occasion.

Often the mere issue of the warrant is enough to make the debtor pay up, but if he does not do so – or take one of the other actions outlined – the bailiffs will enter his house and seize goods to the value of the warrant. The trouble with this method of enforcement – from the creditor's point of view – is that when the goods are sold by auction they usually fetch very little.

The bailiff cannot take the debtor's own clothes, bedding or the tools of his trade up to a value of £250, but can take anything else which belongs to the debtor. He cannot seize goods which belong to the debtor's family, or which are on hire-purchase or rental. The seized property is then valued and auctioned and, after the (heavy) expenses involved have been deducted, the creditor gets the balance.

In some cases the bailiff will take what is called 'walking possession'. He lists the property seized and asks the debtor to sign a form agreeing not to dispose of the listed goods and leaves the goods behind.

215

(ii) Deductions from Earnings

The debtor can apply to the Court for an attachment of earnings order which requires the employer to make regular deductions from his wages or salary to satisfy the judgment. The employer pays the money to the Court which in turn pays it to the creditor. This method can only be used if the debtor has a regular job and not if he is self-employed. If the creditor applies to the Court for an attachment of earnings order, the debtor is informed and must give the Court full details of his income, outgoings and other relevant facts. The Registrar then decides how much the debtor can afford to pay. If the debtor changes his job, he must inform the Court within seven days, because the attachment order lapses and a fresh one must be made.

When an order is made a 'protected earnings figure' is specified, and the employer does not make a deduction if the debtor's earnings fall below this figure.

(iii) Garnishee Order

Another method of enforcing a judgment is a 'garnishee order' which is useful where the debtor is in business and is owed money by others or has money in his bank account. To get this information, it is usual for the creditor to apply to the Court for an inquiry into the debtor's means. A hearing is held at which the debtor must answer questions put to him about his assets and liabilities. If it emerges that he is owed money, the creditor asks the Court for a garnishee order requiring the third party who owes money to the debtor in the ordinary course of business to pay the amount direct to the creditor.

(iv) Judgment Summons

If a judgment debt is unpaid – or the debtor falls behind with an instalment order – the creditor can, if he wishes, issue a judgment summons requiring the debtor to appear before the Court to give an explanation of why he has not paid. In many instances, the likely result will be a variation of the original order.

4. ADMINISTRATION ORDER

The debtor may himself apply to the Court for an administration order to be made, the effect of which is to help him organise his financial affairs.

This is a useful technique where the debtor has got into financial problems and has several judgment debts against him, and his total debts do not exceed £5000. Only the debtor can apply for an administration order. If it is made, the Court will decide the amounts to be paid to each creditor by instalments.

5. BANKRUPTCY

Bankruptcy is the ultimate method of enforcing a judgment but is definitely the last resort, though it is widely used by the Inland Revenue against people who owe arrears of income tax, as well as by the Customs and Excise in respect of unpaid value added tax. It has a number of disadvantages from the creditor's point of view – notably the fact that if, as is usual, several people are owed money, there is usually very little left to share out amongst the general body of creditors because certain creditors – such as the Inland Revenue – get preferential treatment and are paid before others, and the costs of the procedure are enormous.

The bankruptcy laws were first shaped in the 19th century. The law is now contained in the Insolvency Act 1986. The practical effect of being made bankrupt is that the bankrupt loses his property and assets which are sold and the proceeds are distributed amongst the creditors.

The purpose of bankruptcy is two-fold: (a) To ensure equal distribution of assets amongst the creditors – but this is subject to an 'order of preference' and in most cases the ordinary creditors only get a few pence of each pound they are owed; and (b) To protect the debtor from the pressing demands of his creditors and to allow him to wipe the slate clean. This is the theory; the practice is very different, and attitudes in the United Kingdom are still coloured to a large extent by the residual feeling towards bankrupts which was common in the world of Mr Micawber and 19th century debtor's prisons. Bankruptcy laws are quasi-criminal in their operation and the undischarged bankrupt is subject to a number of serious disabilities. In fact, the situation in recent years has become so serious that there is now an Association of Bankrupts (4 Johnson Close, Abraham Heights, Lancaster LA1 5EU) which exists to advise people in this position and to press for reforms in the law.

SECTION 5
THE LAW AND YOUR BUSINESS

The law allows those who wish to run a business to do so in a variety of different ways. A business may be operated by a sole trader, or two or more individuals may combine together as a partnership, or a company may be formed to run the business. Some businesses are co-operatives, but these are less common and will not be dealt with here.

1. SOLE TRADERS

Operating as a sole trader, either entirely alone or with employees, is the simplest way of starting a business. Anyone can set himself up as a sole trader without going through any formalities. (But see Business Names below.) The sole trader has total control over his business, but he will be personally liable for all its debts, and hence he can be made bankrupt if the business fails. This means that not only the assets used in the business, for example business premises and stock, but also all the trader's personal assets, including his house, may be sold to satisfy the business's debts.

2. PARTNERSHIPS

A partnership is defined in the Partnership Act 1890 as 'the relation which subsists between persons carrying on a business in common with a view to profit'. It follows from this definition that if two or more people are in business together, the law will treat them as a partnership regardless of whether they have formally entered into a partnership agreement, or indeed, whether or not they even realise that they are in partnership. The legal consequences which flow from being in partnership will now be considered, and then we will go on to look at the ingredients of a typical partnership agreement.

(i) The Responsibility of Partners to Those with Whom the Firm Deals

(A) Partnership contracts. All the partners in a firm will normally be liable on contracts entered into by any one of them if the contract is related to the firm's business. The fact that the partners have agreed between themselves that the authority of an individual partner to bind the firm should be limited, will not normally affect an outsider. There are exceptions if the outsider is aware of the restriction on the partner's authority, or he does not realise that he is dealing with a partner. It will not make any difference that the rest of the partners object to a contract that a particular partner has entered into, so long as it would appear to the other contracting party that the contract in question is one which is related to the business of the firm. If, for example, the firm runs a newsagency and the partners agree that they will no longer sell cigarettes, the partners will nevertheless be bound to pay for cigarettes that one of their number orders, since it would appear to the supplier that this is a legitimate part of the firm's business.

(B) Employees. The firm's employees are similarly able to bind the partners in contracts with third parties. This will be so where either the employee is authorised by the partners to enter into contracts of the type in question, or where it would appear to third parties that the employee is so authorised, even if he is not. It is very important, therefore, that the partners should not give the impression to outsiders that the scope of an employee's authority is greater than they intend it to be.

(C) Torts. If a partner commits a tort (civil wrong) his partners will also be liable, even though they are not personally implicated, so long as the tort was committed in the course of the partnership business. Thus, if a partner drives negligently whilst he is attending to the firm's business and injures another road user, his fellow partners will also be liable, despite the fact that they will obviously not have authorised him to drive negligently. The question is not whether the manner in which a partner has behaved was authorised, but whether he was engaged in the business of the partnership when the tort was committed. The same principle applies with respect to fraudulent acts. If a partner receives a customer's money or other property for the firm to look after, all the partners will be liable if the partner who received the property misappropriates it. The principles referred to in this paragraph also apply with respect to employees: the partners will be liable for their torts too.

(D) New and retiring partners. If a new partner joins the firm, he will not be responsible for any of the liabilities which were incurred by the firm before he became a partner. A partner retiring from the firm, on the other hand, will remain liable for obligations which arose while he was a partner, unless it is agreed with the firm's creditors that his liability should be extinguished. A retired partner may, in certain circumstances, become liable for debts incurred by the firm even after he has retired. To avoid this possibility, it is essential that the firm should send a circular to established customers and others with whom the firm has dealt and may deal with again, notifying them of the retirement. With respect to other potential creditors, the position of a retired partner will be sufficiently protected if the firm gives notice of the retirement in the official government newspaper, the *Gazette*. It makes no difference whether or not the creditor sees the notice.

(E) Personal liability for partnership debts. We have seen above that a partner may frequently be made legally responsible for the actions of his fellow partners. It is important to realise that a creditor of the firm may sue any partner for the entire amount that is owed to him – the wealthiest partner being the obvious target. Having been sued, a partner can require a contribution from his fellows in whatever proportions the partnership agreement may have provided for. Such internal arrangements, however, have no effect on the rights of third parties to proceed against the partner of their choice for the entire debt. As distinct from the position of a shareholder in a limited liability company, the entire personal wealth of a partner is available to meet the firm's obligations. His exposure is not limited to his investment in the business.

(F) Limited partners. A special form of partnership, called a limited partnership, should briefly be mentioned in this context. A partnership of this kind must be registered under the Limited Partnership Act 1907, and must be made up of at least one partner, called a general partner, who will have unlimited liability for the debts of the firm. One or more of the other partners can be limited partners whose liability will be confined to their investment in the business. The limited partners must not take any part in the running of the business – if they do, they will lose their limited liability status. For this reason limited partnerships are not a popular medium through which to run a business. If limited liability is required a company structure is much more flexible, and so no more will be said about limited partnerships.

(ii) Forming a Partnership and the Partnership Agreement

No formalities, such as registration, are necessary for the formation of a partnership (but see Business Names below). A firm may not have more than twenty partners, though there is an exception to this in the case of some professions, such as solicitors and accountants, where there is no limit on the size of the firm. Partnership should not be entered into lightly: we have already seen that a partner can expose his fellow partners to potentially unlimited liability to others. Many partnerships fail owing to disagreements among the partners. This is often a result of the partners not thinking through all the details in advance. Many difficulties will be avoided if a formal partnership agreement is entered into before business is commenced, setting out the respective rights and obligations of the partners. A formal agreement is not a legal necessity, however, and where no express agreement is made these matters will be governed by the terms of the Partnership Act 1890 (see below). The Act will also supplement a partnership agreement which is silent on certain matters which are covered by it. Partners owe a duty to act with the utmost good faith in their dealings with one another. One consequence of this is that intending partners must make a full disclosure of all relevant circumstances before entering into partnership. Failure to do this will give the other partners the right to set the partnership agreement aside. All facts relevant to the business must also be disclosed during the course of the partnership. In addition, a partner must not make an undisclosed personal profit out of his position as a partner, even though he does this quite innocently. A partner is not, for example, entitled to keep a commission which he is paid as a result of the partnership entering into a contract with a supplier, nor may he acquire materials in which the partnership deals and then sell them to the partnership at a profit.

(A) The partnership agreement. Not all the rules set out in the Partnership Act may be thought to be appropriate to the firm's requirements. We will now, therefore, look at some of the matters which are typically provided for in a 'tailor-made' partnership agreement. The agreement should ideally be drawn up by a solicitor or

Partnership Act 1890, section 24
The rules, set out in section 24 of the Partnership Act 1890, which will apply to the firm unless it is agreed otherwise, are as follows:
'(1) All the partners are entitled to share equally in the capital and profits of the business, and must contribute equally towards the losses whether of capital or otherwise sustained by the firm.
(2) The firm must indemnify every partner in respect of payments made and personal liabilities incurred by him: (a) In the ordinary and proper conduct of the business of the firm; or (b) In or about anything necessarily done for the preservation of the business or property of the firm.
(3) A partner making, for the purpose of the partnership, any actual payment or advance beyond the amount of capital which he has agreed to subscribe is entitled to interest at the rate of five per cent per annum from the date of payment or advance.
(4) A partner is not entitled, before the ascertainment of profits, to interest on the capital subscribed by him.
(5) Every partner may take part in the management of the partnership business.
(6) No partner shall be entitled to remuneration for acting in the partnership business.
(7) No person may be introduced as a partner without the consent of all existing partners.
(8) Any difference arising as to ordinary matters connected with the partnership business may be decided by a majority of the partners, but no change may be made in the nature of the partnership business without the consent of all existing partners.
(9) The partnership books are to be kept at the place of business of the partnership (or the principal place, if there is more than one), and every partner may, when he thinks fit, have access to and inspect and copy any of them.'

accountant, but the intending partners will need to address their minds to the issues which are discussed below before the agreement can be drafted. Where a firm is prospering, it is likely that the partnership agreement will rarely be looked at, but it may be of vital importance if things go wrong.

(B) Partners' names. The names of the partners should be set out in the agreement. It may be convenient to name them in a schedule to the agreement if there is a large number of partners or the composition of the firm is likely to change frequently.

(C) Partnership name. The name the partners intend to trade under should be stated in the agreement (see Business Names, page 262).

(D) Nature of business. It is important to define carefully the type of business in which the firm is to engage because this will be relevant in determining whether a partner has actual authority to bind his fellows with regard to a particular transaction. It must be remembered, however, that where it would appear to an outsider that a partner is authorised, the firm will be bound even though the partner has no actual authority.

(E) Duration of the partnership. If the time for which the partnership is intended to last is not stated in the partnership agreement, it will be susceptible to dissolution by any of the partners at any point. The appropriate duration for a partnership will obviously depend on the particular circumstances of the partners and the nature of the business. Usually the partners will not wish to agree a closing date, but if, instead, they state that the partnership may not be dissolved without the agreement of all the partners, this will protect the firm from an unexpected and damaging dissolution. If a date for dissolution is fixed but the firm nevertheless carries on business beyond that date, the partnership will continue on the terms set out in the agreement, but may be brought to an end by a single partner at any time.

(F) Provisions concerning capital. Partners may contribute cash or property, such as business premises, at the start of the partnership. Where property is contributed, it is useful to state its value in the partnership agreement because this makes it easy to see what the proportionate capital contribution of each partner is. Where the partners do not make equal contributions, it may be intended that they should not share equally in the firm's capital (for example, where the partnership is dissolved and the assets are divided amongst the partners) or in profits. If this is the intention it is necessary to spell it out in the partnership agreement, since otherwise the Partnership Act will prevail and all the partners' shares in capital and profits will be the same. If a partner advances money to the partnership over and above the amount that has been agreed as his contribution to capital he will be entitled to interest on this sum. If a more commercial rate than the 5% specified in the Act is thought appropriate, this should be stated in the partnership agreement. It should also be made clear in the agreement whether assets which are to be used in the business are to become partnership property or are to remain the property of an individual partner. Failure to do this may give rise to a dispute if a partner leaves the firm or it is dissolved.

(G) Profits and losses. The partnership agreement may state that profits are to be shared in whatever proportions the partners wish. Since it will not normally be known what level of profit a firm has made until the end of its accounting year, it is often provided that the partners may make drawings from the partnership bank account during the year, subject to an obligation to repay any excess drawings once the firm's profit for the year has been calculated. Alternatively, it may be provided that partners are to receive fixed salaries during the year, and then should divide what remains of the profits between them in the agreed proportions at the end of the year. The partners may choose to share income profits – the result of successful trading – in different proportions from capital profits – the result of the firm's assets increasing in value. The partners may also share the business's losses in whatever proportions they choose. If the partnership agreement is silent on this question, losses will be shared in the same proportion as profits. It should be remembered that the sharing of losses is a purely internal affair – it does not affect the right of a creditor to sue an individual partner for the entire amount owed to him.

(H) Accounts and banking. It is common to have a clause in a partnership agreement stating the date to which the firm's profit and loss account and balance sheet should be drawn up, and requiring the keeping of proper books of account. The bank and branch at which the firm's account is to be kept is normally specified, together with the requirements for signing cheques. It will obviously be most convenient if the signature of only one partner is necessary, but it must be borne in mind that this will authorise the bank to pay out on the cheque, so long as it is within the usual scope of the firm's business, whether the payment is in the partnership's interest or not. A sensible compromise is to state in the agreement that above a certain figure the signature of two partners is necessary. The bank will need to be informed of the firm's cheque signing procedures.

(I) Other business interests of partners. It is frequently stated in a partnership agreement that the partners will devote the whole of their time to the affairs of the firm. If it is intended that any of the partners should be allowed to be actively engaged in other businesses, in order to avoid disputes this should be provided for in the agreement. This is particularly important where a partner has an involvement in a business which operates in the same field as the partnership business, with the result that the two businesses are in competition. The partnership agreement should expressly provide that the partner in question is permitted to be involved in the competing business, since otherwise any remuneration or profits he derives from the competing business can be claimed by the partnership. Many partnership agreements impose restrictions on partners starting up rival businesses if they leave the firm. Such restrictions will be enforceable only if they are reasonable. In deciding this issue, the Court will have regard to such factors as the size of the geographical area within which the former partner may not compete, the length of time for which the restriction will operate, and the range of activities which are prohibited. If any of the restrictions go beyond what is necessary to protect the legitimate interests of the partnership, the entire clause imposing the restrictions will be ineffective. The Court will also declare the clause void if it is against the public interest, for example, because it restricts competition. A valid clause may be enforced by injunction, that is, the Court will order the party in breach of the restriction to comply with it. A remedy in damages will also be available.

(J) Management of the partnership. All the partners have an equal right to take part in management decisions unless the partnership agreement states otherwise. It is not uncommon to provide in the agreement for certain matters to be decided upon only by more senior partners. It is also possible to give the partners different voting rights. The Partnership Act provides that 'ordinary matters' are to be decided on by a majority, but that the decision to change the nature of the business of the firm and the decision to admit a new partner must be reached unanimously. If intending partners consider that any particular matters are of such fundamental importance to them that they would not wish to be bound by majority decision, these matters should be set out in the partnership agreement as being ones requiring unanimous consent.

(K) Retirement from the partnership. If the partnership agreement does not provide for a date on which the partnership will end, nor state that it may only be dissolved by unanimous agreement, a partner will be able to retire from the firm at any time. This will have the effect of bringing the entire partnership to an end, unless the agreement provides otherwise. Where, on the other hand, the partnership has been created for a fixed period or it is only dissoluble by unanimous consent, in the absence of a contrary indication in the partnership agreement, a partner may not retire without the consent of all the other partners. Even if the partners do agree, this will bring about a dissolution of the partnership, again subject to contrary provision in the partnership agreement. Since dissolution will generally be undesirable, it is common to provide in the agreement that the continuing partners will remain in partnership and that the interest of the withdrawing partner shall vest in them.

(L) Expulsion of a partner. Unless otherwise provided in the partnership agreement, it is not possible to expel a partner. It may be thought desirable, therefore, to include either a general power to expel by majority decision, or a power to expel on certain specified grounds, such as mental or physical incapacity, repeated breaches of the partnership agreement, or refusal to take part in the running of the business. Powers of expulsion must, however, be exercised in good faith. This means that the partners must be motivated by a desire to protect the interests of the partnership and not, for instance, by personal animosity towards the partner expelled.

(M) Dissolution of partnership. A number of events have been referred to above which will bring about an automatic dissolution of the partnership unless contrary provision is made in the partnership agreement. The death or bankruptcy of a partner will also have this effect and hence it will normally be desirable to state that if any of these events occur the partnership will continue and the share of the out-going partner will automatically vest in the continuing partners. As an alternative, the remaining partners could be given the option to acquire the deceased or bankrupt partner's interest in the firm on dissolution.

(N) Valuation of departing partner's interest. Where a partner retires or is expelled or otherwise leaves the firm, many of the difficulties of buying him out will be lessened if some formula is provided in the partnership agreement for the valuation of partners' interests. One way of doing this is by reference to the value of the firm's assets as written in the latest accounts. An alternative method is to value the partner's interest in accordance with a multiple of profits earned over the latest year for which accounts are available, or perhaps the average annual profits made over a number of years. Yet another way would be to state in the partnership agreement that a valuer should be appointed to decide on a fair price.

(O) Tax continuation clause. Where a partner withdraws from the firm, the trade may be treated as having ceased for tax purposes, which could have expensive consequences. A special provision is often included in the partnership agreement to help avoid this problem (see Tax and Your Business on page 273).

(P) Insurance. The death or incapacity of a partner may have a serious effect on the running of the firm. It is often sensible to provide in the partnership agreement that each partner should insure his life for the benefit of the other partners, or that the partners should insure one another's lives. If this is done, the insurance money can be used to buy out the deceased or incapacitated partner's interest in the business.

(Q) Arbitration. A provision in the partnership agreement that disputes between the partners should be referred to an arbitrator will help avoid costly recourse to the courts. It is common to provide that the president of an appropriate professional body or trade association should appoint the arbitrator if the parties cannot agree on a name. Failing that, the agreement might stipulate that the President of the Chartered Institute of Arbitrators should make the appointment.

3. LIMITED COMPANIES

In this section we will examine the law relating to the formation and running of companies. It is worth listing at the outset the main advantages of operating a business through the medium of a limited company.

(1) The most obvious advantage is that the owners of a company – its shareholders – are

Partnership agreement checklist

The following is a checklist of points which should be considered prior to having a partnership agreement drawn up. Some of the points have been discussed in greater detail above.

1. Name of firm
2. Commencement date of partnership
3. Duration of partnership
4. Place(s) of business
5. Proportions in which capital is to be contributed and proportions in which capital is to be owned
6. Proportions in which profits are to be shared. Extent to which partners are to be allowed to make drawings. Partners' remuneration, if any
7. Proportions in which losses are to be shared
8. Rate of interest, if any, to be paid on capital contributions made by partners in excess of amounts stipulated in partnership agreement, and on loans made by partners
9. Provisions concerning salaried partners (i e non-profit sharing partners), if any
10. Matters requiring unanimous agreement and matters requiring majority decision
11. Voting rights of partners
12. Provisions concerning appointment and role of senior partner, if any
13. Date to which accounts are to be drawn up
14. Whether accounts to be prepared by independent accountants
15. Name of bank. Who may sign cheques and financial limit on cheques which may be signed by a single partner
16. Insurance against death, sickness, professional negligence or other matters
17. Whether partners required to devote entire time and attention to affairs of firm
18. Whether partners permitted to have other business interests
19. Partners' holidays
20. Provisions permitting retirement or requiring compulsory retirement on reaching a stated age
21. Semi-retirement and consultancy
22. Provisions allowing expulsion, generally or subject to conditions
23. Death of partner – deceased partner's interest to vest automatically in other partners or partnership to be dissolved and other partners to have option to purchase deceased partner's interest
24. Method by which value of deceased or withdrawing partner's interest to be ascertained
25. Tax position on withdrawal of a partner
26. Arbitration clause

largely insulated from liability for its debts should it become insolvent.

(2) The corporate form offers a flexible administrative structure. Once a business has grown beyond a certain size the partnership form will be unwieldy.

(3) A range of advantages flow from the fact that a company is a separate legal person. The business – its premises and all its other assets – are owned by the company. The members hold shares and have no direct stake in the assets. The interest of a member in the business can, therefore, be transferred without disrupting the running of the company, which makes it easier for new members to join a company, and for members to leave, than is the case with a partnership. There are also fewer problems when a participant dies or is declared bankrupt.

(4) There may be tax advantages in adopting a corporate structure (see Tax and Your Business on page 273).

(5) Perhaps surprisingly, given that the liability of shareholders for a company's debts is limited, it is often easier for companies to raise loan finance. This results in part from the reluctance of financial institutions to lend to private individuals, but also from the ability of companies – not shared by sole traders or partnerships – to give a special form of security for borrowings. This is known as a floating charge (see page 246). In what follows, references to the Companies Act are to the Companies Act 1985.

(i) Types of Company

Companies may be registered with limited or unlimited liability. In the latter form of company the shareholders (the terms 'shareholder' and 'member' are largely interchangeable) will be liable for the company's debts if it goes into liquidation. Since limited liability is generally the main reason for adopting the company form, it is not surprising that unlimited trading companies are extremely rare. Their main use is by professional firms whose regulatory bodies will not permit limited liability practice.

A company may be limited either by shares or by guarantee. In the case of a company limited by shares, the members' responsibility for the debts of the company is confined to the nominal value (which means the same thing as 'face' or 'par' value) of their shares. If the full nominal value of his shares has been paid to the company, therefore, a member will not be liable to make any further contribution if the company goes into liquidation. If the full amount of the nominal value has not been paid (that is, the shares are 'partly paid') the member will be required to contribute towards the discharge of the company's debts on liquidation to the extent of the amount that is unpaid. Thus, if a member has 100 shares with a nominal value of £1 each, and 50 pence has been paid on each share, that member will be required to pay a further £50 if the company goes into insolvent liquidation. Shares are nowadays usually issued fully paid, but they might be issued partly paid if it is anticipated that a further injection of capital will be needed at some time in the future.

Where a company is limited by guarantee, the members do not make an initial capital contribution by subscribing for shares, but instead undertake to be liable for a stated amount if the company goes into liquidation. The guarantor can be required to undertake responsibility for any amount – frequently the figure chosen is £1, which will be the limit of his liability. Most companies limited by guarantee are not trading companies but are, for example, charities, which are attracted to this form of incorporation because they may be allowed, subject to fulfilling certain conditions, to drop the word 'limited' from the company's name.

Public and private. The other main distinction is between public and private companies. A public company must be registered as such and must have issued shares of a nominal value in excess of £50,000. There are no minimum capital requirements in the case of a private company. Most of the rules of company law apply to public and private companies in the same way. The principal difference is that a public company may offer its shares to the public, but a private company cannot. A public company must also have at least two directors, whereas a private company is only required to have one. Both types of company need only have two shareholders. A variety of other regulatory requirements are stricter with regard to public companies, for example, the rules governing when a dividend can be paid, and restrictions affecting the making of loans by a company to its directors. The name of a public company must end with the words 'Public Limited Company' or 'PLC' or for a Welsh company 'Cwmni Cyfyngedig Cyhoeddus' or 'CCC'. Private company names end in 'Limited', 'Ltd',

'Cyfyngedig' or 'Cyf'. Companies are very rarely formed as public companies. A business is normally incorporated as a private company and then if it prospers and grows its directors may decide to have it re-registered as a public company. By far the most popular and most suitable corporate vehicle for a new business is the private company limited by shares, and so the following discussion will be confined to that form of company unless otherwise stated.

(ii) The Formation of a Company

If it is decided to operate a business as a company, either a new company can be formed specifically to take the business over, or an existing company can be acquired for this purpose. Where the latter course is followed, a 'clean' company should be obtained from one of the commercial company registration agents. A company bought from a friend or colleague may be in default with respect to the filing of accounts and other statutory requirements and may have incurred tax liabilities which have not been discharged. Companies bought from registration agents are often referred to as 'ready-made' or 'off-the-shelf' companies. Before we look at the procedures for forming or acquiring a company, we will examine the legal requirements concerning a company's constitution.

(A) The corporate constitution. All companies must have a written constitution. This is made up of two documents, the first called the memorandum of association and the second called the articles of association. The memorandum states the purposes for which the company exists and governs its relations with the outside world. The articles are largely concerned with internal affairs.

(B) The memorandum of association. The memorandum of a private company will contain five principal clauses. These are concerned with: (a) the company's name; (b) the registered office; (c) the company's objects; (d) the liability of the members; (e) the company's authorised share capital.
We will now examine each of these clauses in some detail.

(a) The company's name (sections 25–34 of the Companies Act). Every company must have a name, which will appear on its certificate of incorporation. A company may trade under a name which is different from its registered name;

this is called its business name. A company whose registered name is 'John Smith Limited', for instance, might have adopted the business name of 'Smith's Leisure Goods'. Business names will be considered separately below (see page 262).

It is important to check before forming a company or changing the name of an existing company that the proposed name is available. This may be done by inspecting the index of names which are already in use, and therefore unavailable, which is kept at Companies House in London and Cardiff. Alternatively, a firm of company registration agents will perform this service for a fee. When registering a name, it may be advisable to offer an alternative in case the first choice is already in use or otherwise inappropriate.

The Registrar of Companies will not register a name which: (a) includes the words 'limited', 'unlimited', or 'public limited company', or their Welsh equivalents, or abbreviations of these words, otherwise than at the end of the name; (b) is the same as an existing registered name; (c) the use of which by the company would, in the opinion of the Secretary of State for Trade and Industry, constitute a criminal offence; (d) which in the opinion of the Secretary of State is offensive.

The Secretary of State has the power to order a company to change its name within twelve months of registration if he considers it to be 'too like' an existing name. The Secretary of State may act after receiving a complaint from a company that another company has been registered with a name so similar to its own that confusion is likely to result. The Secretary of State may also order a change of name where misleading information was provided for the purpose of registration, or where a company's name is so misleading that it is likely to cause loss to the public.

With respect to names which include certain specified words, the approval of the Secretary of State, or of some other body designated by him, must be obtained before registration. This will be the case, for example, if words such as 'Parliament' or 'Department' appear in the name, thereby giving the impression that the company is connected with HM Government or a local authority. Words which suggest national or international pre-eminence, such as 'European' or 'British', or words suggestive of some representative role, for example, 'Association' or 'Federation' must also be approved in advance. There is a long list of words, such as 'Patent', 'Building Society' and 'Contact Lens', which may create the impression that the company is involved in providing certain specific services, for which advance permission must also be obtained.

The Department of Trade and Industry publishes information giving full details of names which require advance permission and from whom the permission must be sought. This information may be obtained by writing to: The Registrar, Companies Registration Office, Crown Way, Maindy, Cardiff CF4 3UZ.

(b) Registered office. A company's memorandum must state where its registered office is to be. This does not mean the address of the company, but simply whether the company's registered office is to be in England (which includes Wales for this purpose), or Wales (to the exclusion of England) or Scotland. This determines the jurisdiction in which the company is resident, and is for practical purposes unalterable.

(c) The objects clause. It is crucial that all the types of business in which the company might wish to engage are set out in its objects clause. If the company enters into a transaction of a kind which is not provided for in the objects clause, or which is not reasonably incidental to the company's stated objects, the transaction will be beyond the powers of the company, or *ultra vires* as it is technically known. An *ultra vires* transaction is void, (unenforceable) and if the company suffers a loss as a result of entering into such a transaction, the directors may be required to compensate the company. The theory is that if a company is only allowed to be involved in the activities which are set out in its memorandum, investors and creditors will be able to assess the risks inherent in the business, in the knowledge that the company will not be able to change its business and move into totally unexpected fields. In reality, many investors and creditors do not read objects clauses and in any event most companies' objects clauses permit them to undertake almost every conceivable activity, thus preventing the *ultra vires* doctrine from operating. The doctrine can, however, still occasionally trap the unwary by causing a transaction to be unenforceable. Parliament has to some extent come to the aid of those dealing with companies by providing that so long as a transaction is decided on by the directors and the person (which includes another company) dealing with the company does not realise that it is *ultra vires*, the transaction will be

enforceable against the company (section 35 of the Companies Act). It is not entirely clear when a transaction can be said to have been decided on 'by the directors' for this purpose, though the expression probably extends to a transaction decided by a company's managing director on his own.

Whilst a company can change its objects (see page 236), it will obviously be more convenient if it is equipped from the outset with an objects clause which will allow it to expand, without formality, into any new area which appears profitable. The usual practice is for the company's principal intended activities to be set out first, and this is then followed by a list of every type of business that it is conceivable the company might wish to enter into in the future. In order to defeat any argument that some of the stated objects are merely ancillary to the main objects of the company, and thus can only be pursued if the company is still carrying on its 'main' business, or can only be pursued in a way which assists the carrying on of the 'main' business, it is customary to include a provision stating that all the activities mentioned in the objects clause are to be treated as independent objects. This is sometimes referred to as a *Cotman v Brougham* clause, after the case in which it was decided that this device is effective.

It is also sensible to include a *'Bell Houses'* clause (named after the case of *Bell Houses Ltd v City Wall Properties Ltd* 1966). This clause is used as a safety net, in case the company wishes to become involved in a type of business which is not otherwise covered in its objects. It will state that the company may carry on any kind of trade or business whatsoever that, in the opinion of the directors, may be advantageously carried on in connection with, or ancillary to, any of the company's other businesses.

(d) The liability clause. In a company limited by shares this will simply say that the liability of the members for the company's debts is limited. If the company is limited by guarantee, the amount which each member undertakes to contribute in the event of the company being wound up must also be stated.

(e) The capital clause. This clause will state what the company's authorised share capital is to be, and the number and nominal value of its shares. The authorised share capital is the figure – often £100 in the case of a newly-formed company – up to which the company can issue shares. The members can subsequently resolve to increase the original share capital (see page 236). The capital can be divided into shares of any denomination. The capital clause of a company with an authorised share capital of £100 might, for instance, state that the company may issue 100 shares with a nominal value of £1 each, or 50 shares with a nominal value of £2 each. It should be noted that the market value of a share – what it can be sold for – need bear no relation to its nominal value. A company with an issued share

---

Shares and capital – some technical terms explained

A number of technical terms have been used with respect to shares and capital. It may be helpful to summarise their meanings.

Authorised (or nominal) share capital means the maximum amount up to which the company can issue shares.

Issued share capital means the aggregate nominal value of the shares which have actually been issued. It may be the same or less than the company's authorised share capital.

Nominal value means the same as 'par' or 'face' value, that is, the monetary amount that is actually stated on the share itself.

Fully-paid share. This is a share the full nominal value of which has been paid to the company.

Partly-paid share. This is a share with respect to which the full nominal value has not been paid to the company. The unpaid amount will be susceptible to being called up by the company, and will be required to be paid in order to help discharge the company's debts if it goes into insolvent liquidation.

Paid-up capital means the amount which has been received from members; if the company has partly-paid shares the paid-up capital will be less than the issued capital.

Premium. A company can issue shares for a price greater than their nominal value. The amount paid over and above the nominal value of the share is called a premium. If shares have been issued at a premium, but the whole of the premium has not been paid at the time the company goes into liquidation, the holder of the shares in question will be required to pay the premium to the company.

capital of £100 might have assets of a value considerably in excess of £100, and hence its shares will be worth correspondingly more than that figure. It is possible to issue shares with different rights attached to them (for example, with different numbers of votes or a preferential right to dividend). These rights are usually set out in the company's articles of association, rather than in the memorandum.

When shares are disposed of, the previous holder is normally discharged from any liability for amounts unpaid on them. There is an exception to this, however, where a member disposes of shares and the company goes into liquidation within twelve months of the disposal. In these circumstances, he remains liable for unpaid amounts to the extent that the current members are unable to satisfy their contributions.

(f) Declaration of association. As well as the five clauses just discussed, a company's memorandum must also declare that the subscribers (initial members) are desirous of being formed into a company in pursuance of the memorandum and that they agree to take the number of shares set out against each of their names. This clause is signed by the subscribers and must be witnessed.

The inclusion in the memorandum of the clauses considered above is compulsory. A company may also put into its memorandum any provision which would more normally be found in the articles of association.

(C) Articles of association. As mentioned above, a company's articles are concerned with the regulation of its internal affairs. There need to be provisions governing at least the following matters: (1) share capital, (2) transfer of shares, (3) meetings of members, (4) appointment and removal of directors, (5) powers of directors, (6) dividends and reserves.

If a company does not adopt its own tailor-made articles, the provisions of the model articles known as 'Table A', which used to be contained in a Schedule to the Companies Act, but which are now published as separate regulations, will automatically apply. It is usually thought desirable to make a number of amendments to Table A. These will be considered below. It should be noted that a company whose articles are based on Table A will be governed by the provisions of the Table A which was current at the time the articles were adopted. A company's articles will not change automatically when changes are made to the model articles.

A company may adopt 'long form' or 'short form' articles. Articles are in long form where all the provisions are set out, even though many of them may duplicate Table A. Short form articles simply list amendments to, and exclusions from, the provisions of Table A. Unless a particular provision of Table A is expressly or impliedly excluded, it will be incorporated. The Companies Act requires articles to be printed; this means that they must be in a form which is relatively permanent and difficult to alter. Hence, a photocopy of typed articles is acceptable but the original typed version is not.

Alterations to Table A. Some of the alterations which are commonly made to Table A articles will now be considered. It should be emphasised that it will normally be unwise to form a company without the advice of a solicitor or accountant, or a company registration agent. The following discussion is intended as an explanation of some of the issues and policies on which a professional adviser or company registration agent will require a decision.

(a) Directors' discretion to refuse to register a transfer of shares. Table A permits the directors to refuse to register a share transfer where, amongst other things, the shares in question are not fully paid. It is often thought desirable to extend this power to give the directors an absolute discretion to refuse to register transfers. In a small company it is important that the participants should know and trust one another; if a member could freely transfer his shares to an outsider this trust might be undermined. Restrictions on transfer can also be used to prevent changes in the control of the company, for instance, with a view to keeping control within the family, or to avoid upsetting the existing balance of power. A wide discretion of this kind is obviously capable of abuse, and so the law requires that it be exercised in good faith. Thus, the directors would not be permitted to refuse to register a share transfer if their motive in so doing was to obtain the shares themselves at an unfairly low price. Nonetheless, a wide discretion with regard to share transfers will give the directors considerable freedom to influence the relative shareholdings within the company and hence it is often thought desirable to incorporate more sophisticated restrictions into the articles. Thus, the articles might provide that a member has an unrestricted right to transfer his shares either to members of his family or to existing members of

227

the company. Alternatively, where a member proposes to transfer some of his shares, he could be required first to offer them to existing members, and only if any of the shares remain unsold would he be permitted to transfer them to outsiders. Where an article of this kind is adopted, it should also be stated that the shares cannot be offered to an outsider for a price lower than the one at which they were offered to members, or alternatively a method for valuing the shares should be set out. Otherwise, the object of the restriction could be evaded by offering the shares to members at an excessively high price. Another possible restriction is to state that shares may only be transferred if all the existing shareholders consent.

(b) Allotment of shares. The directors of a company are not authorised to issue shares unless they have authority from the members to do so (section 80 of the Companies Act). This is designed to give the members some control over the size of the company's issued share capital. The necessary authority may be given by ordinary resolution, either in respect of a particular issue of shares, or for the issuing of shares in general. In the latter case, the authority cannot last for more than five years and the authority must state the maximum number of shares that can be issued. As an alternative to this, authority to issue shares could be given in the articles; again, the authority cannot last for more than five years (from incorporation), and the maximum number of shares which can be issued must be stated. In all cases, the authority is renewable and cancellable by ordinary resolution.

Unless contrary provision is made, if a company wishes to issue shares it must first offer them to existing members, in proportion to their existing holdings (sections 89–96 of the Companies Act). The purpose of these rights of pre-emption is to prevent the value of members' shares being diluted if new shares are issued at less than their market value, and also to prevent the directors from manipulating voting control by issuing shares to their supporters. These provisions only apply if the shares are issued for cash. If a member does not wish to subscribe for his allocation of the shares being issued, they can, after his refusal, be issued to someone else. It is possible, in the case of a private company, to exclude pre-emption rights by a suitable provision in the articles. If the company has authority provided by its articles to issue shares, as discussed in the preceding paragraph, and that authority is inconsistent with pre-emption rights, the rights will, to the necessary extent, also be excluded. Thus, if a company wishes to devise its own pre-emption rights, this will have the effect of excluding the statutory rights. If pre-emption rights are not excluded or modified by the articles, a special resolution of the shareholders will be necessary to exclude or vary them.

(c) Removal of directors. No matter what a company's articles may say, a director may be removed from office by an ordinary resolution of the shareholders (section 303 of the Companies Act). The articles cannot impose a more rigorous requirement than this – for example, that a removal resolution must be passed by at least 75% of the votes cast. This being so, directors are vulnerable to removal by the shareholders, with all the implications that this has for loss of control of the running of the company's affairs and loss of remuneration. In order to safeguard the position of directors, therefore, a provision is often inserted in the articles enhancing a director's voting rights (in his capacity as a shareholder) if a resolution is put at a shareholders' meeting for his removal. This is sometimes referred to as a '*Bushell v Faith* device', after the case in which it was decided that such provisions are effective. Thus, if a company has three shareholders, each with an equal number of shares, in the absence of a *Bushell v Faith* device it will be open to any two of them to 'gang up' on the third and remove him from his office as director. If, however, the articles state that on a resolution for the removal of a director the shares of the director in question will carry, in the example above, three times their normal votes, the resolution to remove him will be defeated by his using his enhanced voting rights. As an additional precaution, it might be provided that on a resolution to change this particular article, a director under threat of removal will have increased voting rights as well.

Table A provides for automatic retirement (though there can be immediate re-appointment) of directors by rotation. In a small company with few directors it will be preferable to remove these provisions.

(d) Chairman's casting vote. Table A provides that both at meetings of shareholders and of directors, the chairman of the meeting shall have a casting vote (that is, a vote in addition to his ordinary vote) if there is a tie. This may be thought to give excessive power to the chairman, particularly in a two-shareholder or two-director company, where such an article will give the chairman

effective control. The relevant articles are, therefore, often removed.

(e) Directors' interests. If a director (or certain persons who are connected with him) has an interest in a contract or other matter which might conflict with the company's interests, he is not, under Table A, entitled to vote at the board meeting at which the matter is considered and he cannot be counted in determining whether there is a quorum. (The quorum is the minimum number of directors who must be present for the meeting validly to take place.) If, for example, a director is proposing to sell property to the company, he will not be allowed to vote on the contract. If a company only has two directors, and it has a quorum of two, this would make it impossible for the contract to be agreed on because the meeting would necessarily be inquorate. Table A allows the shareholders by ordinary resolution to relax or suspend the above prohibitions, thus avoiding this difficulty, but as an alternative it might be preferred to amend Table A to allow a director with an interest to be counted in the quorum, and, if so desired, to vote. (For other provisions concerning directors' interests in company contracts, see page 238, Company Officers and Decision Making).

(f) Board resolutions. Table A provides that a written resolution signed by all the directors will be effective even if a board meeting has not been held. This is designed to avoid difficulties in making decisions where directors are unable to attend meetings. It may not be much easier, however, to arrange for all the directors to sign the resolution, and so it is sometimes provided in the articles that a decision will be validly made simply where all the directors agree on it, or a sufficient number of them to constitute a quorum, agree. Properly drafted, such an article will allow the directors to make decisions by telephone. It is desirable that such decisions should subsequently be confirmed in writing by the directors concerned, and they must, of course, be minuted.

The legal effect of the articles. The articles constitute a contract between the company and each of its members. The company is, therefore, contractually bound to respect the rights of the members set out in the articles. A member will be entitled, for instance, to bring an action if he is deprived of the right to vote. Whilst the articles are a contract between the company and its members, however, a member only has contractual rights in his capacity as a member. Thus, if the articles state that a specified member is to be the company's permanent solicitor, for example, the member will not be able to enforce that right merely on the basis of the articles, because it is not a right which he has by reason simply of being a member. It may be possible, however, to argue that the articles constitute evidence of the terms of a separate contract entered into between the company and the member in his capacity as solicitor, particularly if he has begun to perform services.

(iii) The Formalities of Registering a Company

Having examined the contents of the memorandum and articles of association, it is now necessary to look at the procedure for registering a company. The term 'promoter' will occasionally be used below. A promoter is a person who takes a leading role in the formation of a company. Someone who decides to form a company and transfer his business to it, for example, is a promoter, as is someone who is engaged in the formation procedures and later becomes a director or shareholder in the company. A professional adviser, on the other hand, so long as his role is limited to the provision of professional services, will not be a promoter.

For a company to be registered, the following documents must be delivered to the Registrar of Companies: (1) memorandum of association, (2) articles of association, (3) Form 10, setting out the particulars of the first directors and secretary and the intended situation of the registered office, (4) Form PUC 1, dealing with the company's authorised share capital, (5) Form 12, which is a statutory declaration of compliance with the requirements of the Companies Act, (6) registration fee (currently £50).

The forms mentioned above are official companies forms and can be obtained from law stationers or company registration agents.

Form 10 (see page 230) contains details of the company's first directors and secretary, and the intended situation of the company's registered office. The company may have one or more directors, but if it only has one, that person cannot also be the company secretary. If there are two or more directors, one of them can be the secretary. In view of the technical nature of the secretary's duties, it is common in small companies to appoint a professional adviser, such as a solicitor or accountant, to that office. In the context of

G

COMPANIES FORM No. 10

Statement of first directors and secretary and intended situation of registered office

10

Pursuant to section 10 of the Companies Act 1985

Please do not
write in
this margin

To the Registrar of Companies

Please complete
legibly, preferably
in black type, or
bold block lettering

For official use

Name of company

* insert full name
of company

> . C. POOTER & COMPANY LIMITED

The intended situation of the registered office of the company on incorporation is as stated below

> THE LAURELS, BRICKFIELD TERRACE
> HOLLOWAY, LONDON
> Postcode   N7 1SB

The address of the Company's registered office

If the memorandum is delivered by an agent for the subscribers of the memorandum please mark 'X'in the box opposite and insert the agent's name and address below

Postcode

This may be left blank if the form is completed by the subscribers to the memorandum

Number of continuation sheets attached (see note 1)

Presentor's name address and
reference (if any):

C. POOTER
THE LAURELS
BRICKFIELD TERRACE
HOLLOWAY
LONDON

For official Use
General Section

Post room

Page 1

230

A private company must have at least one director

The name(s) and particulars of the person who is, or the persons who are, to be the first director or directors of the company (note 2) are as follows:

Please do not write in this margin

Name (note 3) CHARLES POOTER	Business occupation CLERK
Previous name(s) (note 3) —	Nationality BRITISH
Address (note 4) THE LAURELS BRICKFIELD TERRACE, HOLLOWAY LONDON Postcode N7 1SB	Date of birth (where applicable) (note 6)
Other directorships † NONE	

I consent to act as director of the company named on page 1
Signature *Charles Pooter*   Date 14.6.86

† enter particulars of other directorships held or previously held (see note 5) if this space is insufficient use a continuation sheet.

It will not usually be necessary to insert the date of birth

If the director is the director of another company, its name must be given here

Date on which form is completed

A director must give his written consent to act

Name (note 3) LEO CUMMINGS	Business occupation CLERK
Previous name(s) (note 3) —	Nationality BRITISH
Address (note 4) LONGSHANKS BRICKFIELD TERRACE, HOLLOWAY LONDON Postcode N7 4SJ	Date of birth (where applicable) (note 6)
Other directorships † NONE	

I consent to act as director of the company named on page 1
Signature *L Cummings*   Date 14.6.86

Name (note 3)	Business occupation
Previous name(s) (note 3)	Nationality
Address (note 4) Postcode	Date of birth (where applicable) (note 6)
Other directorships †	

I consent to act as director of the company named on page 1
Signature   Date

The company only has two directors, so this box is left blank

Page 2

Please do not write in this margin

Please complete legibly, preferably in black type, or bold block lettering

The name(s) and particulars of the person who is, or the persons who are, to be the first secretary, or joint secretaries, of the company are as follows:

Name (notes 3 & 7)   CARRIE POOTER

Previous name(s) (note 3)   —

Address (notes 4 & 7)   THE LAURELS, BRICKFIELD TERRACE, HOLLOWAY, LONDON

Postcode   N7 1SB

I consent to act as secretary of the company named on page 1

Signature   C Pooter   Date   14.6.86

All companies must have a secretary

Name (notes 3 & 7)

Previous name(s) (note 3)

Address (notes 4 & 7)

Postcode

I consent to act as secretary of the company named on page 1

Signature   Date

Usually there will only be one secretary, so this box is left blank

delete if the form is signed by the subcribers

Signature of agent on behalf of subsribers   Date

The subscribers to the memorandum may appoint an agent to execute the form on their behalf

delete if the form is signed by an agent on behalf of the subscribers.

All the subscribers must sign either personally or by a person or persons authorised to sign for them.

Signed C Boter	Date 14.6.86
Signed L Cumnings	Date 14.6.86
Signed	Date
Signed	Date
Signed	Date
Signed	Date

The subscribers are the persons to whom shares are allotted on the formation of the company. There must be at least two of them

Page 3

Notes

1 If the spaces on Page 2 are insufficient the names and particulars must be entered on the prescribed continuation sheet(s).

2 'Director' includes any person who occupies the position of a director, by whatever name called.

3. For an individual, his present christian name(s) and surname must be given, together with any previous christian name(s) or surname(s).

"Christian name" includes a forename. In the case of a peer or person usually known by a title different from his surname, "surname" means that title. In the case of a corporation, its corporate name must be given.

A previous christian name or surname need not be given if:—

(a) in the case of a married woman, it was a name by which she was known before her marriage; or

(b) it was changed or ceased to be used at least 20 years ago, or before the person who previously used it reached the age of 18; or

(c) in the case of a peer or a person usually known by a British title different from his surname, it was a name by which he was known before he adopted the title or succeeded to it

4 Usual residential address must be given or, in the case of a corporation, the registered or principal office.

5 The names must be given of all bodies corporate incorporated in Great Britain of which the director is also a director, or has been a director at any time during the preceeding five years.

However, a present or past directorship need not be disclosed if it is, or has been, held in a body corporate which, throughout that directorship, has been:—

(a) a dormant company (which is a company which has had no transactions required to be entered in the company's accounting records, except any which may have arisen from the taking of shares in the company by a subscriber to the memorandum as such).

(b) a body corporate of which the company making the return was a wholly-owned subsidiary;

(c) a wholly-owned subsidiary of the company making the return; or

(d) a wholly-owned subsidiary of a body corporate of which the company making the return was also a wholly owned subsidiary.

6. Dates of birth need only be given if the company making the return is:—

(a) a public company;
(b) the subsidiary of a public company; or
(c) the subsidiary of a public company registered in Northern Ireland

7 Where all the partners in a firm are joint secretaries, only the name and principal office of the firm need be stated.

Where the secretary or one of the joint secretaries is a Scottish firm the details required are the firm name and its principal office.

Form 10, the 'situation' of the registered office means its address; this can be changed at any time so long as it remains within the country which is specified in the registered office clause of the memorandum. If the company does change the address of its registered office, the Registrar of Companies must be informed within fourteen days on the prescribed form, Form 287.

Form PUC 1 (Statement of capital on formation). This form states the company's authorised share capital. A tax, called capital duty, must be paid when a company raises capital. The rate is £1 per £100 or part of £100, and is charged on the greater of (a) the nominal value of the shares alloted or (b) the actual amount paid or value of assets transferred to the company as consideration for the shares. If nothing is paid on the company's shares on incorporation, no duty will be payable until a later date. (See page 236.) The number of shares to be taken on incorporation will, nevertheless, be shown on the form.

Form 12 (Statutory declaration of compliance with requirements on application for the registration of a company – opposite). An application for registration must be accompanied by a statutory declaration, in the prescribed form, to the effect that the requirements for registration have been complied with. This must be completed either by the solicitor engaged in the formation of the company, or by a director or secretary of the company named in Form 10.

Certificate of Incorporation. On receipt of the above documents the Registrar will examine them, and provided that they are in order and the name chosen is still available, he will issue a certificate of incorporation. This will state the company's name and its registered number. From the date stated on the certificate the company is a separate legal entity, distinct from its members.

(iv) Ready-Made or Shelf Companies

We have seen above the steps which must be taken to form a company. There is an obvious advantage in forming a company specifically for the business venture that the promoters have in mind, in that the company's memorandum and articles will be tailor-made to their needs. However, this process can take several weeks and it may be more convenient to buy a company which has already been formed, from a company

registration agent. It should be borne in mind, however, that in addition to the cost of purchasing a ready-made company (£100 upwards), there will be further expense if, as is likely, it is necessary to change its name, or to amend the memorandum and articles. On the other hand, the registration agent may offer support services, such as the supply of statutory books and draft minutes of shareholders' and directors' meetings, which will make the early stages of running the company easier.

(A) Procedure to transfer ownership of a ready-made company. Practice varies, but the following procedure is typical of the way control of the company will be transferred.

(1) Before parting with control of the company, the registration agent will normally require the purchaser to complete a Form 287 and a Form 288. The first of these is a notice of change in the situation of the company's registered office (i e its address) and the second is a notice of change of directors and secretary and consent to act as such. This will be accompanied by the registration agent's fee.

(2) The first directors and secretary of the company (usually employees of the registration agent) will resign and the persons mentioned in Form 288 will be appointed in their places.

(3) The Forms 287 and 288 will be filed at the Companies Registry by the registration agent.

(4) The registration agent will forward the certificate of incorporation, resolutions appointing the new directors and secretary, and the resignations of the first directors and secretary. These will be accompanied by a certificate to the effect that the company has not traded (thus confirming that it has no liabilities).

(5) As well as the above documents, the purchasers of the company will receive two stock transfer forms (or forms of renunciation) in respect of the two subscriber shares. The transfer of these shares into the names of the new members will result in the transfer of the ownership of the company. The new directors should resolve to register the transfers at their first board meeting. It may be, of course, that the directors and members are the same people. Company law insists that all companies must have at least two members. If it is intended that only one person should effectively own the company, the second member can hold his share as a nominee for the other. This may be done by the nominee executing a declaration of trust in

This form may be completed either by a solicitor engaged in the formation of the company, or a director or secretary

G

COMPANIES FORM No. 12

Statutory Declaration of compliance with requirements on application for registration of a company

12

Please do not write in this margin

Pursuant to section 12(3) of the Companies Act 1985

Please complete legibly, preferably in black type, or bold block lettering

To the Registrar of Companies

For official use

For official use

* insert full name of Company

Name of company

· C. POOTER & COMPANY LIMITED

I, DAISY MUTLAR

of 15, STATION ROAD, LONDON N1

† delete as appropriate

do solemnly and sincerely declare that I am a [Solicitor engaged in the formation of the company]†
[person named as director or secretary of the company in the statement delivered to the registrar under section 10(2)]† and that all the requirements of the above Act in respect of the registration of the above company and of matters precedent and incidental to it have been complied with,
And I make this solemn declaration conscientiously believing the same to be true and by virtue of the provisions of the Statutory Declarations Act 1835

Declared at HOLLOWAY

Declarant to sign below ◄

Signature of person making declaration

the 14th day of JUNE
One thousand nine hundred and EIGHTY SIX
before me R PADGE

Daisy Mutlar

A Commissioner for Oaths or Notary Public or Justice of the Peace or Solicitor having the powers conferred on a Commissioner for Oaths.

This declaration most be made before a suitably qualified person not involved in the formation of the company

Presentor's name address and reference (if any):

C. POOTER
THE LAURELS
BRICKFIELD TERRACE
HOLLOWAY
LONDON

For official Use
New Companies Section

Post room

235

favour of the other member and his signing a blank share transfer, which should be kept by the real owner of the share.

(B) First board meeting after change in control. At the first board meeting, as well as approving the registration of the transfers of the subscriber shares into the names of two new members, it may also be resolved to issue and allot further shares, either to those members or to additional members. At this stage it will become necessary to pay capital duty on the subscriber shares and on any further shares which are issued. As explained above, capital duty is charged on either the nominal value of the shares issued, or the value of the assets handed over to the company in return for the shares, if this is greater than their nominal value. Thus, where an existing business is sold to the company, capital duty will be charged on the value of the business; transferring the business in return for a small number of shares of low nominal value will not reduce the amount of duty payable. The Registrar must be informed of the amount paid for shares on the appropriate PUC form. It will also be necessary at the first board meeting to appoint auditors and to select an accounting reference date. These two matters will be dealt with below (see page 238).

(C) Changes to a ready-made company's memorandum and articles. Having acquired a ready-made company, the new controllers may find that some of the provisions of its memorandum and articles are inappropriate. The memorandum and articles cannot be changed by the directors – this must be done by the members, though where all the members are also directors, there is in practice no need for separately convened meetings. Separate minutes, however, should be kept. Where some of the members are not also directors, it will be necessary to convene a shareholders' meeting. Proper notice of the meeting must be given unless there is consent to short notice. The following changes to the company's constitution may be necessary: (1) name, (2) objects, (3) authorised share capital, (4) articles.

(a) Change of name. The ready-made company may have a name which is inappropriate or unattractive. One way of surmounting this problem is to trade under a business name (see Business Names on page 262). Alternatively, it may be decided to change the company's registered name. Before doing this, the availability of the proposed new name should be checked with the Registrar, in the same way that it would be if a new company were being formed. If the new name is available, it is then necessary to convene a meeting of shareholders and a special resolution to change the name must be passed. The appropriate fee (currently £40), together with a copy of the resolution should then be sent to the Registrar. A company registration agent will perform these services, if so requested. The new name should not be used until the change of name certificate has been issued.

(b) Changing the objects. It is unlikely that the objects of the company will need to be changed, because the registration agent will keep a stock of companies with a range of different objects to suit most businesses. If, however, the company's objects are for some reason not satisfactory, they can be changed by special resolution. A copy of the resolution must be sent to the Registrar within fifteen days. A copy of the amended memorandum must also be sent to the Registrar between 22 and 36 days of the passing of the resolution. (This strange time limit results from the fact that the members have the right to object to changes in the objects clause within 21 days of the resolution to change it being passed.)

(c) Increase in authorised share capital. Most ready-made companies have an authorised share capital of £100 divided into £1 shares. If it is desired to increase the company's authorised capital (for instance, because one hundred £1 shares does not allow sufficient flexibility in holdings), it can be increased by ordinary resolution. The increase must be registered on Form 123 within fifteen days. There is no registration fee.

(d) Change in articles. A ready-made company may have Table A articles or the registration agent's own standard form articles. The agent may be able to offer companies with a range of different articles, or may provide options for changes in the articles of the company acquired. Some of the changes which might be thought appropriate have been discussed above. A special resolution is required to alter the articles; a copy of the resolution, together with a new set of articles, must be forwarded to the Registrar within fifteen days.

(v) Matters Arising Before Commencement of Business

Entering into contracts before the company is registered. It may be necessary to enter into contracts, for example, with suppliers or professional advisers, before the company is formed. Before a company is registered, however, it has no legal existence and thus no capacity to enter into contracts. If a promoter enters into a contract, either in the name of the company or as agent for it, he will be personally liable to the other contracting party unless they agree in advance that this will not be so. If the company is for some reason never registered, or is unwilling or unable to perform its obligations under the contract, the promoter will, therefore, have to meet the liability himself. This is obviously something to avoid. One way of overcoming the problem is for the contract to be signed by the other party only, and for the company's objects clause to state that on registration, the company will enter into the contract in question. This will only be appropriate with respect to major contracts, for example for the transfer of a business to the company. Even where a contract has been entered into by the 'agent' of a company which has not yet been formed, however, it may still be possible for the 'agent' to avoid personal liability. This will be so if, after registration, the company has shown that it considers itself to be bound by the contract, for example, by performing its terms. It will then be possible to argue that the company's conduct amounts to entering into a new contract with the other party, which will have the effect of releasing the promoter from his obligations under the original contract.

(vi) Transfer of Assets or of a Business

(A) Promoters. If a promoter sells an asset to the company he has been involved in promoting, he must make a full disclosure of his interest in the matter and of the size of the profit that he is making. This disclosure must be made either to an independent board of directors or to existing and intending shareholders. If disclosure is not made, the company will be entitled to rescind the contract of purchase (i e cancel it and demand repayment of the price) and/or claim any secret profit that the promoter has made. Where a promoter incorporates his business, therefore, unless he is to be the sole effective owner of the company, he will be required to make known to his fellow incorporators any facts which are relevant to the value of the business being transferred.

(B) Directors. A promoter will often become a director of the company which he promotes, in which case additional requirements may have to be satisfied on the transfer of assets or a business. A company's articles of association will normally allow a director to be interested in a contract made with the company so long as he does not vote, is not counted in the quorum, and discloses the nature of his interest to the board. Failure to disclose an interest can result in a fine (section 317 of the Companies Act). Further to this, however, if the sale of the business to the company constitutes a 'substantial property transaction', the approval of the shareholders, in the form of an ordinary resolution, will also have to be obtained (sections 320–322 of the Companies Act). The purchase of assets by the company will be a substantial property transaction if the value of the assets transferred is either £50,000 or more, or equal to ten per cent of the value of the company's net assets, if the latter amount comes to less than £50,000. Contracts for less than £1,000 are, however, excluded. If the shareholders' approval is not obtained, the contract can be set aside by the company and the director required to account to the company for any profit he makes. It is, however, possible for the shareholders to approve the purchase retrospectively.

Other matters to be considered on the transfer of a business to a company

1. Transfer of business premises; consent of landlord to assignment of lease to company.
2. Consent of lender to transfer of long term loans, hire purchase contracts etc.
3. Notification to customers, suppliers, public utilities etc that business has been transferred. The former owner of the business can bring his personal liability on existing contracts to an end by a 'novation'. This involves the company entering into a new agreement with the company's creditors, on the terms of the old agreement, acknowledging that the company is stepping into the former owner's shoes.
4. Transfer employment contracts (with directors and employees) and make pension and insurance arrangements.

The tax implications of running a business as a company, and of transferring an existing business to a company, will be considered below.

The provisions mentioned in the previous paragraph make it necessary to convene a meeting of shareholders if a business, or any other assets of the requisite value, are sold to the company. There will be no need to call a meeting, however, if all (not just a majority) of the shareholders consent to the acquisition. It is a principle of company law that a unanimous informal agreement on the part of the shareholders is as effective as a resolution which satisfies the company's formal procedures.

(vii) Company Officers and Decision-Making

(A) Directors.

(a) Appointment of directors. The persons notified to the Registrar of Companies as being willing to serve will become a company's first directors automatically on registration. The qualifications and method of appointment of subsequent directors will be set out in the company's articles. Unless required by the articles, there will be no need for a director also to be a shareholder. The normal method of appointment of a director is by ordinary resolution of the shareholders. Table A also permits the directors to make an appointment to fill a casual vacancy or to increase the size of the board. A director appointed in this way will automatically cease to hold office at the next annual general meeting, unless the members re-elect him. Where Table A applies, there is no limit to the number of directors the company is allowed to have, though a limit can be imposed by ordinary resolution.

(b) Removal of directors: retirement by rotation. Table A provides for the retirement of directors by rotation. Thus, at the company's first annual general meeting (see below) all directors retire from office and at subsequent annual general meetings one third of the directors retire each year. The retiring directors are eligible for re-election, however, and will, in fact, be automatically re-elected unless someone else is appointed, the meeting resolves not to appoint them, or it is resolved not to fill the vacancy. As discussed above, it may be thought convenient to exclude these provisions from the company's articles.

(c) Removal by the members. As well as having the opportunity not to re-appoint directors on their retirement (if the relevant article has not been excluded) the shareholders can, at any time, remove a director by ordinary resolution. The

articles cannot take away this right, nor can they require a greater majority of those voting than fifty per cent. We have seen above, however, that the incorporation of a *Bushell v Faith* device into a company's articles can make a director practically unremovable. It is also possible to protect a director's position by the use of a shareholders' agreement (see below), and a dismissed director may, in certain circumstances, be able to have the company wound up, or have some less drastic remedy, such as re-instatement, ordered by the Court (see below, Minority Shareholder Remedies). In addition, if a director has a service contract and this is prematurely terminated by the company removing him from office, he will be able to obtain damages for breach of contract.

Certain notice requirements must be satisfied if a director is to be removed from office by the members. A member wishing to put such a resolution must give *special notice* of it. This means that the member must give notice of the resolution to the company at least 28 days before the meeting at which the resolution is to be moved is held. Any attempt on the part of the directors to frustrate the intentions of the person moving the resolution by calling a meeting, after they have received the required notice, for a date which is less than 28 days away, will fail, because in these circumstances sufficient notice of the resolution will be deemed to have been given. Having received the notice, the company must notify the members of it at least 21 days before the meeting. Notice must also be given by the company to the director whom it is proposed to remove, and the latter also has the right that the company circulate, with the notice calling the meeting, a written statement made by him in his defence. He also has the right to address the meeting.

(d) Automatic removal. Table A provides that a director will lose his office if: (a) he becomes bankrupt; (b) becomes of unsound mind; or (c) is absent from board meetings without permission for six consecutive months and the directors resolve that he should be removed. If the articles require a director to hold qualification shares, a director will automatically vacate office if the shares are not obtained within two months of appointment.

(e) Disqualification. The companies legislation contains a number of provisions for the disqualification of directors. A Court can disqualify a person from acting as a director: (a) if he is convicted of an indictable offence in connection with

the management of a company; (b) if he is guilty of persistent default in the filing of returns to the Registrar of Companies; (c) where it appears in the winding up of a company that the director has been guilty of fraud or some other breach of duty; (d) under the Company Directors Disqualification Act 1986, where the director is a director of a company which has become insolvent and his conduct makes him unfit to be a director.

(f) Managing director. If the articles permit, a company may appoint a managing director. The appointment will normally be made by the board. The functions of a managing director will vary from company to company; normally he will have a service contract and this will set out his duties. Table A provides that the board of directors may delegate any or all of their powers to a managing director, to the exclusion of its own powers, if so desired. The board can, however, take back the powers it has delegated at any time, though this may put the company in breach of the managing director's service contract. The advantage of appointing a managing director is that decisions can be made and implemented without summoning a board meeting.

(g) Chairman. The chairman of the board is not an officer in the sense that a director or secretary is. Unlike a managing director, he has no special power to make decisions or to bind the company. His role is simply to preside at directors' meetings – that is, to supervise the orderly administration of business. Table A envisages the election by the directors of a chairman who shall chair all board meetings, unless unable to do so, but articles could provide for the election of a chairman at each meeting. The person appointed chairman of the board is often also appointed chairman of general meetings of shareholders.

(h) Committees of directors. It may be convenient to appoint a committee of directors to deal with particular matters. The committee can be given such power as the board chooses under Table A articles and can consist of only one director. This is a useful way of allowing decisions to be made and implemented without involving the whole board.

(i) Alternate directors. Table A now provides for the appointment of alternate directors. An alternate director is a person who is appointed to act as a director in the temporary absence of the director who has appointed him. An alternate director may either be an existing director or some other person who has been approved by the board. When acting in the place of his appointer, the alternate will have all the appointer's rights (such as the right to receive notice of directors' meetings) and obligations. An alternate should be someone in whom the appointer has total confidence, since the alternate is not merely an agent – he is empowered to act in accordance with his own judgment.

(B) The company secretary. Every company must have a company secretary. In the case of a company with only one director, that director cannot also be the secretary; otherwise, the secretary can be one of the directors. The secretary will be responsible for the keeping of the various books and registers that a company is required to maintain. The secretary will commonly also be responsible for the issuing of share certificates, the taking of minutes at board and general meetings, and the payment of dividends. In addition to his statutory duties (for breach of which a secretary can be liable to criminal penalties), many company secretaries are appointed to look after a company's administration generally. This may, for instance, involve them acting as office manager. In the case of a small company where the directors lack the time or expertise to deal with the complex matters which fall within the secretary's responsibilities, it will be sensible to appoint an outside professional adviser, such as a solicitor or accountant (but not the company's auditor) to act as secretary. Some company registration agents also provide a secretarial service.

(C) Proceedings of directors. Depending on the form of articles which the company has adopted, there are usually few formalities governing directors' meetings. Notice must be given to all the directors (though not, under Table A, if a director is abroad), but it can be very short (so long as it is possible for all the directors to act on it), and need not be in writing. Table A states that the directors may determine what the quorum shall be, but if they do not, that it shall be two. Thus, a valid board meeting may be held even though all the directors are not present, so long as there is a quorum and all the directors have been given notice of the meeting. It is usually provided in the articles that decisions shall be made by majority vote. Under Table A articles the chairman of the board (if there is one) has a casting vote in the event of a tie. It has been suggested above that in some companies it may be desirable to omit this provision. If a director is wrongfully excluded from a board meeting he can be granted an injunction restraining the company from excluding him in future. A director who is directly or indirectly interested in a contract made with the company must declare his interest at a board meeting (he can be fined for failing to do so, section 317 of the Companies Act), and under Table A articles he will not be allowed to vote or be counted in the quorum. There is a statutory obligation to keep minutes of all board meetings.

(D) The division of power between the board and the members. The division of power between the board and the shareholders is largely a matter for the articles, though there are certain powers of which the shareholders cannot be deprived, such as the right to remove a director by ordinary resolution or to change the company's articles by special resolution. Table A provides that the company shall be managed by the directors who may exercise all the powers of the company. The only way in which the shareholders can interfere in the making of actual decisions is by passing a special resolution (i e one requiring a majority of 75% of the votes cast). However, since the shareholders can by ordinary resolution (50% of the votes cast) remove the directors, it is possible for a majority to exercise effective control over the board. This is only likely to be practicable where a majority of the votes are held in a small number of hands.

Despite the existence of an article which gives total management power to the board, there are some circumstances in which the shareholders will have a residual power of management. Thus, if the board has for some reason ceased to exist, for example because its members have all died, or the board is deadlocked, the shareholders in general meeting can act to relieve the situation until there is a functioning board again. In one case (*Barron v Potter*, decided in 1914) a company had two directors, one of whom would not speak to the other. This made running the company impossible because no board decisions could be made. In those circumstances the court held that the shareholders in general meeting had the power to deal with the situation.

(E) Directors' duties to the company.
(a) Duty to act in the company's interest. The power directors have over the running of the company's affairs brings with it certain responsibilities.

Directors are required to act in good faith for the benefit of the company in carrying out their duties. This means that they may not use the company's property for their own purposes, and they may not obtain any illicit financial advantage from their position as directors. Thus, in one case (*Cook v Deeks*, decided in 1916), two directors of a company set up a second company and diverted a contract to it which, without their intervention, would certainly have gone to the first company: they were required to pay the profit that had been made on the contract to the first company. Not only must directors act in the best interests of the company, they must also be seen to be acting in its best interests. They are not, therefore, allowed to retain any profit they might make in a situation in which their personal interests could conflict with their duty to the company. A commission paid by a supplier to a director personally, for instance, must be handed over to the company. Where, however, the company's interests have not been damaged, a director can keep a profit if a majority of the shareholders consent.

(b) Voting control. Another aspect of a director's duty forbids him to exercise his powers for the purpose of manipulating the voting control of the company. The directors may not, for example, issue shares to their supporters, not in order to raise money, but so the supporters can use their votes to keep the directors in office. This acts as a supplement to the rule that new shares must first be offered to all the existing members, which, as we have seen, can be modified by the company's articles or by special resolution.

(c) Negligence. A director owes duties of care and skill to his company, though they are generally not very onerous. A director must exercise such skill in the performance of his duties as is to be expected of a person of his knowledge and experience. This means that a higher standard is expected of someone with particular qualifications or expertise. A qualified accountant, for example, might be liable for mismanaging a company's finances where a person with no accounting experience would not. Unless he has a full-time service contract, a director is not required to spend all his time on the company's business and he will not necessarily be liable for failing to attend board meetings at which he might have discovered that something was wrong (see Wrongful Trading on page 262).

(d) Relief from liability. Where a director has committed a breach of duty he can be relieved of liability by the Court if he has acted 'honestly and reasonably' and the Court considers that in all the circumstances he ought fairly to be excused. This discretion is unlikely to be used except where the breach of duty is a mere technicality.

(F) Arrangements to protect the interests of directors and minority shareholders. We have seen that a company's directors usually have exclusive powers of management. However, since shareholders who control more than 50% of the votes will be able to sustain in office directors of their own choosing, majority shareholders can, in effect, determine company policy. This means that minority shareholders are potentially at the mercy of the majority. If, for example, a company has three shareholders with an equal number of votes, two shareholders acting together will have the power to make all the decisions. Thus, depending on the articles, they might remove the third shareholder from his office as a director, causing him to lose his salary. He would as a result also be deprived of any say in how the company is run – the directors might, for instance, decide to sell the company's business, or diversify into new areas. They might also adopt a policy of not paying dividends, thereby depriving the out-of-favour shareholder of any return on his shares, and when he decides that he has had enough, they might then refuse to register a transfer of his shares, making his interest unsaleable. Company law provides some remedies for oppressed minority shareholders (see page 242), but it will be preferable to prevent these problems from arising in the first place. Some of the ways in which this may be done will now be discussed. We have already seen that it will generally be impossible to remove a director without his consent where a *Bushell v Faith* device is included in the articles.

(a) Director's service contracts. A person can be appointed to the office of director without having a service contract. Where this is so, a dismissed director will not be entitled to a redundancy payment under the employment legislation, nor will he be entitled to claim unfair dismissal. If a director does have a service contract, as well as these possible benefits, he will be able to claim damages from the company if the contract is prematurely terminated. This is despite the fact that the Companies Act gives to a majority of the shareholders the right to remove a director. A service contract is, therefore, a valuable protection for a director who cannot rely on majority support. It is common for a company to enter into a service contract where a director is appointed to a specific job, such as managing director, or finance director.

We have seen above that, depending on the articles, a director who is interested in a contract made with the company cannot be counted in the quorum and cannot vote on the contract. This applies to directors' service contracts too. An additional restriction is that a service contract which the company is unable to terminate in less than five years cannot be entered into without the approval of a majority of the shareholders (section 319 of the Companies Act). A long service contract can mean that a company will be faced with a large damages claim if it tries to get rid of a director. Payments to departing directors, in excess of their contractual entitlements, must be approved by the shareholders (section 312 of the Companies Act).

Copies of directors' service contracts must be available for inspection by members during business hours for at least two hours each day (section 318 of the Companies Act). If a director's contract is not in writing, a written memorandum of its terms must similarly be made available for inspection. Copies must be kept at the company's registered office, the place where its register of members is kept, or its principal place of business. If the copies are not kept at the registered office, the Registrar of Companies must be informed.

(b) Shareholders' agreements. A shareholders' agreement is an agreement, distinct from the company's articles, entered into between all or some of the members of a company, governing how the company is to be run. The shareholders agree that they will exercise their voting rights in such a way as to ensure that the terms of the agreement are complied with, and that they will procure that the directors act in accordance with it. This is, therefore, a method by which the interests of minority shareholders can be safeguarded. An agreement can, for example, put minority and majority shareholders on equal terms in respect of the matters to which it relates, by stating that decisions about them must be made unanimously. It should not be expected, however, that a shareholders' agreement will give complete protection against a majority shareholder who is determined to ignore the minority's interests.

241

Examples of matters which often require the consent of all the members

The following are some of the matters which it is often stated in a shareholders' agreement shall require the consent of all the members:

1. changes to the memorandum or articles;
2. changing the nature of the company's business, or disposing of the company's business or assets, other than in the ordinary course of business;
3. declaring dividends or making other forms of distribution of profits;
4. issuing new shares or altering the rights attached to shares; transferring shares;
5. borrowing in excess of a stated amount;
6. charging the company's assets to secure debts;
7. guaranteeing the obligations of any other person, company or firm;
8. lending, other than the granting of ordinary trade credit.

A wide range of other matters could be covered by the agreement. It might, for example, be provided that each of the shareholders shall be entitled to have a director appointed (which could be himself), or it could be stated that a certain shareholder shall have the right to a fixed proportion of the company's profits.

Many of the issues which are dealt with in a shareholders' agreement could alternatively be provided for in the company's articles. The advantage of a shareholders' agreement is that it cannot be varied without the assent of all the signatories, whereas the articles can be altered by a 75% majority.

(G) Minority shareholder remedies. Where a minority shareholder has not protected himself by the methods suggested above, or where he is treated unfairly in a way that has not been anticipated, the position may still not be hopeless. An aggrieved shareholder can apply to the Court for redress in a number of different situations, which we will now briefly consider.

(a) Winding up (section 557(1)(g) of the Companies Act). The Court has a discretion to wind a company up where it would be 'just and equitable' so to do. Thus, the Court may put an end to the business and have its assets divided amongst the members where the relationship of trust between the participants has broken down. This will particularly be so if there was some prior understanding as to how the business was to be run, or as to who its directors were to be, and this understanding has been breached. It will be easier to establish that an understanding of this kind exists where a formal shareholders' agreement is entered into. The case (at right), decided in 1972, is an example in which a company may be wound up on this ground.

(b) Unfairly prejudicial conduct (section 459 of the Companies Act). Winding up is obviously an extreme solution to the problems of the oppressed minority shareholder. The assets of the business will have to be divided, goodwill may be

Ebrahimi v Westbourne Galleries Limited

Nazar and Ebrahimi originally ran a carpet business in partnership. They formed a company to take over the business and both were directors and equal shareholders in it. Some time later Nazar's son was made a director and shares were issued to him, which meant that Ebrahimi was now in a minority position. Ebrahimi eventually fell out with the Nazars and they voted him out of office as director. As a result he had no say in the running of the business, and despite the fact that the company was profitable, he received no dividends, as all the profits were paid out in the form of directors' remuneration. The Court held that it would be just and equitable to wind the company up, because there had been an understanding between the parties that Ebrahimi was to have an equal share in the running of the business, and this understanding had been disregarded.

damaged, and it may be difficult for the ex-members of the company to start up in business on their own. There is, therefore, a more flexible remedy available where it can be shown that the affairs of the company have been conducted in a manner which is unfairly prejudicial to the interests of some of the members. Such a situation might exist, for instance, where the directors refuse to register the transfer of a member's shares without good cause, or where the company's profits are paid out as salaries to directors and not as dividends, thus depriving a minority shareholder who is not also a director of return on his investment. Where unfair prejudice can be made out, the Court has the discretion to award any remedy that it considers appropriate to rectify the situation. In the examples suggested above, it could order the directors to register a transfer, or to pay dividends and make recompense for failure to pay dividends in the past. In extreme cases, the Court could order the majority to buy the minority's shares, or force the majority to sell its shares to the minority.

(c) Duty of majority shareholders to act for the benefit of the company. It is sometimes said that shareholders must exercise their votes in good faith for the benefit of the company. The decided cases suggest that this principle is not very extensive, but it does mean that an attempt to change the articles to give the majority the right to confiscate the minority's shares, for example, would be invalid, and it will prevent the majority from surrendering the company's rights to take proceedings against directors who have acted fraudulently or have otherwise deliberately harmed the company.

(d) Action in company's name. Because the directors owe their duties to the company (as a separate legal entity) and not to the members, minority shareholders cannot sue the directors for breach of duty. In certain circumstances, however, minority shareholders may be allowed to bring legal proceedings against the directors on behalf of the company (and compel the company to pay the legal costs). The rules about this are very complicated, but an action will be possible where the directors enter into a transaction which is beyond the capacity of the company, and also where the directors have defrauded the company, at least if the directors have a majority of the votes. Any damages awarded against the directors will be payable to the company and not to the minority shareholders. With respect to other breaches of duty, the decision to sue a director must either be made by the board, or by a majority of the shareholders. As the law stands, there is probably little that a minority shareholder can do to complain about negligence on the part of the directors.

(e) Enforcement of articles of association. As the articles constitute a contract between the company and its members, a member can, at least with respect to certain provisions in the articles, bring a breach of contract action against the company if the articles are not complied with. It has been held, for example, that a shareholder can complain if he is denied the right to vote, or if a dividend which has been declared is not paid.

(H) Meetings of members.

(a) Types of meeting. Meetings of shareholders are called general meetings, to distinguish them from board meetings. There are two types of general meeting, the annual general meetings ('AGM's'), and all other general meetings, which are called extraordinary general meetings ('EGM's').

(b) Annual general meetings. Every company must hold an AGM in each calendar year (i e one in 1986, another in 1987 etc), and meetings may not be more than fifteen months apart. So long as a newly-formed company holds its first AGM within the first eighteen months of incorporation, it need not have a meeting during both the first and second calendar years of its existence.

The business to be conducted at an AGM is dependent on the company's articles. The latest edition of Table A does not prescribe any particular business for the AGM, but the following matters are normally dealt with: (1) presentation and consideration of accounts and directors' report; (2) declaration of a dividend; (3) election of directors; (4) appointment of auditors. So long as proper notice has been given, business of any other kind may be done at the meeting, including, for example, changing the articles.

(c) Extraordinary general meetings. Where business arises which must be conducted before the next AGM, it will be necessary to convene an EGM. The meeting may be called by the directors, and also by members who together hold at least one tenth of the company's paid up share capital. They must send a signed requisition to the directors, stating the reason for the meeting. Under Table A, the directors are then required to call the meeting for a date not more than eight weeks after the receipt of the requisition.

(d) Notice of meetings. Notice of general meetings must be sent to all members, the directors and the auditors. The accidental omission to give notice will not invalidate the meeting. The period of notice is 21 days in the case of an AGM and also of an EGM if a special resolution is to be proposed at it. Otherwise the required notice is fourteen days. Table A provides that a notice sent by post is deemed to be served 48 hours after posting, regardless of the class of post and the destination. Thus, a notice posted on 1 March is deemed to be served on 3 March, and the period

of notice will run from 3 March. If 21 days' notice is required, the earliest date the meeting could be held, therefore, is 25 March. A meeting may be held on shorter notice than this: in the case of an AGM, if all the members agree, and in the case of an EGM, if members holding at leat 95% in nominal value of the share capital agree.

The notice must state the time and place at which the meeting is to be held, and must state that a member who is entitled to attend and vote is entitled to appoint a proxy to attend and vote instead of him (see below). The notice must set out the general nature of the business to be conducted at the meeting; the test of adequacy of notice is whether it is sufficient to enable a member to decide whether it is worthwhile attending. Business may not be conducted if no notice has been given of it. If a special or extraordinary resolution is to be proposed, the resolution must be set out verbatim in the notice, and no amendments of substance may be made to it at the meeting. This is not so with respect to an ordinary resolution, and so amendments can be validly moved so long as they are within the scope of the business of which notice has been given.

(e) Resolutions. An *ordinary resolution* may be passed by a simple majority. It should be noted that the majority required is a majority of those who actually vote, not a majority of the members present and still less a majority of all the members. Any matter may be decided by ordinary resolution that is not required by the Companies Act or the articles to be determined by special or extraordinary resolution.

A *special resolution* must be passed by 75% of those voting and 21 days' notice of it must be given. The articles may require a wide variety of matters to be dealt with by special resolution (though not, for example, a resolution to remove a director), and the Companies Act provides that certain matters of major importance, such as changing the articles, must be decided in this way. A special resolution must be registered within fifteen days' of its passing.

An *extraordinary resolution* needs a majority of 75%, but unlike a special resolution, only fourteen days' notice is required. An extraordinary resolution must be registered. The Companies Act provides that certain matters connected with winding up must be determined by extraordinary resolution.

(f) Members' resolutions. Members holding not less than one twentieth of the total voting rights attached to the company's shares may have a resolution of their choosing put onto the agenda of a meeting. They must deposit a copy of the resolution at the company's registered office at least six weeks before the meeting. They may also have a statement not exceeding one thousand words sent out on their behalf by the company. In both cases, the requisitionists may be required to pay the company's expenses.

(g) Proxies. A proxy is a person appointed by a member to attend and vote at a meeting on his behalf. A proxy need not be a member himself. He has the right to speak at a meeting, and under Table A articles he must be counted for quorum purposes. A proxy may vote in a poll, but not on a show of hands; he is, however, entitled to demand a poll (under Table A).

(h) Conduct of meetings. It is important that meetings be conducted in accordance with the general law and the company's articles; otherwise, the proceedings may be invalid.

1. *Quorum.* The quorum requirements are dependent on the articles. Under Table A, two members must be present, either personally or by proxy, throughout the meeting. If there is no quorum, the meeting is automatically adjourned for seven days.
2. *Chairman.* Table A provides that the chairman of the board, or some other director chosen in advance, shall be the chairman of a general meeting. If neither of these turns up, another director, elected by his fellows, shall be chairman.
3. *Resolutions.* All resolutions should be put to the meeting by the chairman. Amendments should only be allowed if they fall within the scope of the notice of the meeting.
4. *Voting.* Voting may either be by show of hands or a poll (usually conducted by the members signing a sheet for or against the motion). On a show of hands, each member only has one vote, regardless of the number of shares held. Under Table A, any two members, or any member or members with 10% of the votes or with shares which constitute 10% of the company's paid up capital, may demand a poll. The number of votes attached to a share will depend on the articles or terms of issue.
5. *Adjournment.* The chairman may move an adjournment with the consent of the meeting. An adjourned meeting is a continuation of the

original meeting; hence, no business may be conducted at it which could not have been conducted at the original meeting. Under Table A, if the adjourned meeting is held fourteen days or more after the original, at least seven days notice of it must be given.

6. *Minutes.* Minutes must be kept of all general meetings and the members have the right to inspect the minute book.

(j) Written resolutions and waiver of irregularities. It is not essential to hold a meeting in order to pass a resolution. A resolution, be it ordinary, special or extraordinary, can be passed if all the members who are entitled to attend and vote at a general meeting consent to it in writing. Irregularities in the calling or conduct of a meeting, for example, insufficient notice or the acceptance of an improper amendment, will also be cured if all the members consent.

(viii) Financing the Company
(A) Share capital. The advantage of financing the company from share capital is that a return need only be paid (in fact, *can* only be paid) on the shares if the company has made a profit. The return on shares is called a dividend and will be considered below (page 260). If the company borrows, on the other hand, it will be contractually bound to pay interest and this will be a drain on the business. In addition, a loan will eventually have to be repaid; this is generally not the case with shares. The main disadvantage of raising money by issuing shares is that there may be a limited number of people – perhaps only relatives and friends – who are prepared to take them. We will see, however, that there is a growing number of institutions offering what has become known as 'venture capital' (see Financing Your Business, below). Shares normally have voting rights attached to them, but it is possible to issue non-voting shares. This is sometimes done where there is a wish to raise capital without losing voting control.

Transfer of shares. A member may transfer his shares by gift or sale. A transferee will not become a member of the company until the transfer is registered by the directors (for the directors' discretion to refuse to register transfers, see page 227). Share transfers are subject to stamp duty (2%), and must be made on a 'proper instrument of transfer' if the shares are fully paid (section 183 of the Companies Act and section 1 of the Stock Transfer Act 1963). A stock transfer form should be used for this purpose. If the shares are not fully paid, the requirements set out in the company's articles must be complied with. The normal procedure on transfer is for the transferor to execute a stock transfer form in favour of the intended transferee, which, together with the share certificate, is then handed to the latter, in exchange for payment. The transferee then lodges these documents with the company, which will issue a new certificate to him on registering his holding. The transferee pays the stamp duty. Where only part of a holding is transferred, the member sends his share certificate, and the transfer, to the company. The company secretary marks the transfer 'certificate lodged', and returns it to the member. The member then gives the transfer to the transferee, who sends it to the company for registration. If a member dies, his shares will vest in his personal representative automatically; the personal representative must apply to be registered if he plans to retain the shares, but if he wishes to dispose of them he can transfer them without becoming a member first.

(B) Borrowing. (For borrowing in general, see Financing Your Business on page 264.)
(a) Power to borrow. All trading companies have the power to borrow, whether or not this is mentioned in their objects clause. The directors should, however, have regard to any limits on borrowing which might be contained in the objects clause or in the articles.

(b) Borrowing from the members. As well as subscribing for shares in the company, the shareholders can provide finance by making loans to it. This has the advantage from the shareholder's point of view that he will have a contractual right to interest, and if the company goes into liquidation he has a better chance of recouping his investment. Shareholders receive nothing in respect of their shares on a winding up ('liquidation' and 'winding up' refer to the same process) until all the company's debts have been paid off. A loan by a shareholder, however, is a debt like any other, and hence the shareholder will rank with the other creditors for payment. If it is proposed to secure the loan on the company's assets, however, it should be borne in mind that outside lenders, such as banks, will insist on their loans having priority.

(c) Secured loans. A company gives security for a loan by 'charging' (i e mortgaging) an asset or assets. This means that if the loan is not repaid,

245

the debt is satisfied from the proceeds of selling the asset which has been charged. Companies give two main kinds of security – fixed charges and floating charges.

(d) A fixed charge is a mortgage over a specific asset, such as a building or a machine. If property is subject to a fixed charge, it cannot be sold without the consent of the lender (the 'chargee').

(e) A floating charge is a charge over the company's assets generally (or sometimes a more limited range of assets). The company is free to dispose of these assets without the consent of the lender unless the charge has 'crystallised'. When a floating charge crystallises it attaches to all the assets which are subject to it and becomes, in effect, a fixed charge over each of those assets. Crystallisation can be triggered off by the commencement of winding up, the appointment of a receiver, or on the occurrence of any other event mentioned in the charge. A receiver is a person appointed by the lender; his function is to dispose of the assets charged, in order to release funds to pay off the debt owed to his appointer. Only companies can create floating charges, which means that companies are in a position to borrow more than sole traders or partnerships because they can give more security. A company, by creating a floating charge, can use its stock as security; this is practically impossible for a sole trader or partnership, because a fixed charge would have to be used. This would mean that every time an item of stock was sold it would first have to be released from the charge by the lender. Loans secured by a floating charge are sometimes called 'debentures', though the term can be used to refer to a loan which is not secured.

(f) Registration. All company charges must be registered with the Registrar of Companies within 21 days of creation (section 395 of the Companies Act) (see opposite). It is the duty of the company to do this and officers of the company who are in default will be liable to a fine. The lender may also register the charge, and it is very much in his interests to see that it is registered since a charge which is not registered in time will be void, unless an extension of time is granted. When registered, the following information will be put on the company's file, which is open to public inspection: (a) the date the charge was created; (b) the amount secured by the charge; (c) brief details of the property charged; (d) the person entitled to the charge. The company must also keep a register containing this information, and must keep copies of all charges.

(g) Priority of charges. If a company is wound up because it is insolvent, there will not, by definition, be enough assets to pay off all the creditors. The order in which the company's debts will be met by the liquidator is, therefore, of great importance. The basic principle is that the holder of a fixed charge will be paid in full, ahead of the other creditors, assuming that the amount of the debt does not exceed the value of the asset charged. The holder of a floating charge will be paid before the unsecured creditors. Where the company has created more than one fixed or floating charge over the same asset(s), the charges will rank in the order in which they were created, unless special steps have been taken to vary this order. A category of 'preferential creditors', which includes the Inland Revenue, rank after the holders of fixed charges, but before the holders of floating charges.

(ix) Running the Business
(A) Publicising the company's name and business stationery.
Once the company's name has been accepted by the issue of its certificate of incorporation, appropriate name-plates and stationery can be ordered. Company law imposes a number of requirements with respect to publicising a company's name (sections 348–351 of the Companies Act).

(a) The registered name of the company must appear in a conspicuous position on the outside of each of the company's offices and other places of business.
(b) The company's name must be engraved on its seal. A seal is necessary to enable a company to enter into formal deeds.
(c) The company's name must be clearly stated on all the company's letters, notices, cheques, orders, receipts, invoices etc – in effect, on all its stationery.

If the company's name is not stated outside each place where it carries on business, the company and each officer of the company who is in default will be liable to a fine. Where the company's name is missing from a cheque or order, as well as possibly being fined, the officer responsible will be personally liable if the company does not pay. This is, therefore, one occasion when the Court will ignore the separate legal status of the company and impose personal liability on its officers for its debts. (The expression 'officer' means

M

COMPANIES FORM No. 395

Particulars of a mortgage or charge

395

Pursuant to section 395 of the Companies Act 1985

Please do not write in this margin

Please complete legibly, preferably in black type, or bold block lettering

* insert full name of company

To the Registrar of Companies

For official use

Company number

Name of company

* **C. POOTER & COMPANY LIMITED**

Date of creation of the charge

21 JUNE 1986

The date appearing on the charge

Description of the instrument (if any) creating or evidencing the charge (note 2)

MORTGAGE

The type of security given should be entered here

Amount secured by the mortgage or charge

£10,000

(TEN THOUSAND POUNDS)

The amount of the debt that is secured by the mortgage or charge

Names and addresses of the mortgagees or persons entitled to the charge

**PERKUPP (MERCHANT BANKERS) PLC
2, MAMMON STREET, LONDON**
Postcode **EC1 2UY**

The details of the lender or creditor who has the benefit of the security should be entered here

Presentor's name address and reference (if any):

**C. POOTER
THE LAURELS
BRICKFIELD TERRACE
HOLLOWAY
LONDON**

For official Use
Mortgage Section

Post room

Page 1

Time critical reference

247

Short particulars of all the property mortgaged or charged

BUSINESS PREMISES AT
THE LAURELS, BRICKFIELD TERRACE,
HOLLOWAY,
LONDON

Details of the property over which the security is created

Particulars as to commission allowance or discount (note 3)

NONE

Signed *Charles Pooter*   Date **23 June 1986**

On behalf of [company][mortgagee/chargee]†

† delete as appropriate

This form may be completed either by an officer of the company that has given the security, or by the person who has the benefit of it

Notes

1   The original instrument (if any) creating or evidencing the charge, together with these prescribed particulars correctly completed must be delivered to the Registrar of Companies within 21 days after the date of creation of the charge (section 395). If the property is situated and the charge was created outside the United Kingdom delivery to the Registrar must be effected within 21 days after the date on which the instrument could in due course of post, and if dispatched with due diligence, have been received in the United Kingdom (section 398). A copy of the instrument creating the charge will be accepted where the property charged is situated and the charge was created outside the United Kingdom (section 398) and in such cases the copy must be verified to be a correct copy either by the company or by the person who has delivered or sent the copy to the registrar. The verification must be signed by or on behalf of the person giving the verification and where this is given by a body corporate it must be signed by an officer of that body. A verified copy will also be accepted where section 398(4) applies (property situate in Scotland or Northern Ireland) and Form No. 398 is submitted.

2   A description of the instrument, eg "Trust Deed", "Debenture", "Mortgage" or "Legal charge", etc, as the case may be, should be given.

3   In this section there should be inserted the amount or rate per cent. of the commission, allowance or discount (if any) paid or made either directly or indirectly by the company to any person in consideration of his;
   (a) subscribing or agreeing to subscribe, whether absolutely or conditionally, or
   (b) procuring or agreeing to procure subscriptions, whether absolute or conditional,
for any of the debentures included in this return. The rate of interest payable under the terms of the debentures should not be entered.

4   If any of the spaces in this form provide insufficient space the particulars must be entered on the prescribed continuation sheet.

Page 2

a director, the company secretary or a manager.) The Courts have been very strict in the way they have applied this requirement. In one case, a director was made personally liable on a cheque drawn by the company merely because an ampersand was missing from the company's name. In another, a director was personally required to pay £34,000 on a company cheque because the word 'limited' was omitted. It is, therefore, of the utmost importance that the company's name be stated fully and accurately on all the documentation it uses, especially if there is any risk that the company may become insolvent.

Other information required on stationery. The company must state on all letters and order forms (a) its place of registration and its number (which will appear on its certificate of incorporation) and (b) the address of its registered office. If the company has been granted permission to drop the word 'limited' from its name, it must state in its correspondence that it is a limited company. If a company puts the name of any of its directors on its letters, trade circulars, trade catalogues or showcards, it must state the names of all of them (surnames, and forenames or initials). Where a company makes any reference to its share capital on its stationery, the reference must be to paid-up share capital. If the company is registered for VAT is must state its VAT registration number on its invoices and credit notes.

(B) Statutory books and records. Companies are legally required to maintain the books and records mentioned below. The company can prepare its own books but it will often be more convenient to buy them from law stationers.

(a) Register of directors and secretaries (See page 250 section 288 of the Companies Act). Every company must keep a register of its directors and secretaries at its registered office; failure to do so is a criminal offence. The register must set out the full names, any previous names (though not the maiden name of a married woman), and the residential addresses of all the directors and the secretary. The nationality, business occupations (if any) and other directorships currently held or held within the previous five years must also be disclosed with respect to directors. Other directorships need not be disclosed if they are of companies which are inactive, or, in certain circumstances, of companies in the same group. If a director or secretary is in another company, its registered name and registered office must be disclosed.

(b) Register of directors' interests (section 325 of the Companies Act). There is a series of complex rules providing for the disclosure of the interests of directors and their spouses and infant children in the shares and debentures of a company. This is designed to enable shareholders, and others who may be interested, to discover the scale of the direct and indirect holdings in the company of a director. The company must keep a register containing this information, and the directors are under a duty to inform the company of relevant changes. On receiving notification from a director, the company must enter the appropriate details next to his name and the date the information is entered. The register must be kept at the company's registered office if the register of members (see below) is kept there; if the register of members is kept elsewhere, the register of directors' interests may either be kept at the same place or at the registered office. The register must be available for inspection at the company's annual general meeting.

(c) Register of members (section 352–369 of the Companies Act). Every company must keep a register of members. The information which must be disclosed in it is as follows:

1. The names and addresses of all members.
2. The number and class (if there are different classes) of shares held by each member. If the shares are numbered, the numbers should be given. If the company's shares have been converted into stock the amount and class of stock held should be indicated.
3. The amount paid up on each share held.
4. The date the member was registered as such.
5. The date the member ceased to be a member.

If the company has more than fifty members, the register must either be arranged alphabetically, or be indexed. Apart from this, the register is not required to be in any particular form. It could, for instance, be kept on computer, so long as it is possible to produce a print-out of the information stored on it. The register of members can either be kept at the company's registered office or the place at which it is made up. If it is kept at the latter place, notice of this must be sent to the Registrar of Companies.

(d) Register of Charges (section 407 of the Companies Act). A company must keep a register of

G

COMPANIES FORM No. 288

Notice of change of directors or secretaries or in their particulars

288

Pursuant to section 288 of the Companies Act 1985

Please do not write in this margin

To the Registrar of Companies

For official use

Company number 987431

Enter the company's number

Please complete legibly, preferably in black type, or bold block lettering

Name of company

* insert full name of company

. C. POOTER & COMPANY LIMITED

ø specify the change and date thereof and if this consists of the appointment of a new director or secretary complete the box below. If this space is insufficient use a continuation sheet.

notifies you of the following change(s):

ø LEO CUMMINGS HAS RETIRED AS A DIRECTOR OF THE COMPANY

Indicate the nature of the change

Particulars of new director or secretary (see note 1)

Name (note 2 and 3) LUPIN POOTER	Business occupation§ CLERK
Previous name(s) (note 2) WILLIAM POOTER	Nationality§ BRITISH
Address (notes 3 and 4) THE LAURELS BRICKFIELD TERRACE, HOLLOWAY LONDON Postcode N7 1SB	Date of birth (where applicable) (note 5)§

§ Applicable to directors only.

Other directorships (note 6)§

HOLLOWAY COMEDIANS LIMITED

Previous name

Any other directorships must be entered here

† delete as appropriate

I consent to act as [director][secretary]† of the company named above

Signature L Pooter   Date 19. 9. 86

Continued overleaf

Presentor's name address and reference (if any):

C. POOTER
THE LAURELS
BRICKFIELD TERRACE
HOLLOWAY
LONDON

For official Use

General Section

Post room

Particulars of new director or secretary (see note 1) continued

Name (note 2 and 3)	Business occupation§	§ applicable to directors only.
Previous name(s) (note 2)	Nationality§	
Address (notes 3 and 4)		
Postcode	Date of birth (where applicable) (note 5)§	
Other directorships (note 6)§		

I consent to act as [director] [secretary]† of the company named on page 1   † delete as appropriate

Signature   Date

number of continuation sheets attached (see note 7)

Signature   *Charles Pooter*   [Director][~~Secretary~~]† Date   **20. 9. 86**

Signature of the person who has completed the form

Notes

1 'Director' includes any person who occupies the position of a director, by whatever name called, and any person in accordance with whose directions or instructions the directors of the company are accustomed to act.

2. For an individual, his present christian name(s) and surname must be given, together with any previous christian name(s) or surname(s).

"Christian name" includes a forename. In the case of a peer or person usually known by a title different from his surname, "surname" means that title. In the case of a corporation, its corporate name must be given.

A previous christian name or surname need not be given if:—

(a) in the case of a married woman, it was a name by which she was known before her marriage; or

(b) it was changed or ceased to be used at least 20 years ago, or before the person who previously used it reached the age of 18; or

(c) in the case of a peer or a person usually known by a British title different from his surname, it was a name by which he was known before he adopted the title or succeeded to it

3 Where all the partners in a firm are joint secretaries, only the firm name and its principal office need be given.

Where the secretary or one of the joint secretaries is a Scottish firm, give only the firm name and its principal office.

4 Usual residential address must be given. In the case of a corporation, give the registered or principal office.

5 Date of birth need only be given if the company making the return is:—

(a) a public company;
(b) the subsidiary of a public company; or
(c) the subsidiary of a public company registered in Northern Ireland

6 The names must be given of all bodies corporate incorporated in Great Britain of which the director is also a director, or has been a director at any time during the preceeding five years.

However a present or past directorship need not be disclosed if it is, or has been, held in a body corporate which, throughout that directorship, has been:—

(a) a dormant company (which is a company which has had no transactions required to be entered in the company's accounting records, except any which may have arisen from the taking of shares in the company by a subscriber to the memorandum as such).

(b) a body corporate of which the company making the return was a wholly-owned subsidiary;

(c) a wholly-owned subsidiary of the company making the return; or

(d) a wholly-owned subsidiary of a body corporate of which the company making the return was also a wholly owned subsidiary.

7 If the space overleaf is insufficient, the names and particulars must be entered on the prescribed continuation sheet(s).

charges. The register must detail the terms of the charge and identify the property which is subject to it. Copies of the documents creating charges must also be kept.

(e) Memorandum and articles of association. Copies of these must be kept at the registered office.

The members of a company are entitled to inspect the above registers and documents, free of charge. They must be available for inspection during business hours, for at least two hours per day. Members of the public are also entitled to inspect them, and they may be charged no more than the designated fee (currently five pence) to exercise this right. Copies of entries in registers may be made. Directors' service contracts (if any) and the minutes of general meetings must also be made available to members on request.

Every company must also keep accounting records which satisfy the requirements of the Companies Act (see page 255) and minutes of directors' meetings. These are not required to be made available for inspection by members.

(C) Entering into contracts.

(a) The form of company contracts. A company, not being a natural person, can only act through its agents, that is, its officers and employees. The extent of an agent's authority to bind the company will be considered below. In this paragraph we are concerned with the form of company contracts. There are, in fact, no special rules as to the form which company contracts must take. Thus, those contracts which can be made orally by an individual can also be entered into orally by a company, acting through its agents. Most contracts can be made orally, the main exceptions being contracts for the transfer of an interest in land and contracts of guarantee, which must be evidenced in writing. Where a contract must be in writing, no special formula is required for the company to be bound; it is simply necessary to state that the company's agents are signing on its behalf. Similarly, a company need only enter into a transaction under seal where the law would also require an individual to do so. The principal example is a conveyance of land (as opposed to a contract to convey, which must be in writing but does not require a seal). In practice, companies apply the corporate seal to a wider range of documents than is legally necessary, for example, share certificates and mortgages. Where the seal is applied, the form of words which goes with it

(the testatum) is: 'The common seal was affixed hereto in the presence of:', followed usually (depending on what the company's articles say) by the signatures of a director and the secretary. The signatures do not need to be witnessed by any today.

(b) Authority to bind the company. Many of the contracts which a company enters into will not be decided on by the whole board. The power to enter into a wide range of contracts will be delegated to the company's agents, that is, individual directors or employees. In order to determine whether an agent has the authority to bind his company, two questions must be considered. The first is whether the transaction is within the capacity of the *company*. The second is whether the particular agent is authorised to enter into it. We will look first at the question of the company's capacity.

(c) The objects clause. The importance of setting out the company's objects in its memorandum has been discussed (see page 225). If a transaction is entered into which falls outside the company's stated objects, or it is not reasonably incidental to those objects, it will be *ultra vires* and hence, subject to what will be said below, void. An example of a transaction which will be reasonably incidental to the company's objects is the borrowing of money, where the money borrowed is to be used to further the company's objects. If the company does not have the capacity to enter into a transaction, it is impossible for an agent to have the authority to do so.

In the case of ordinary business transactions the company's capacity will not normally be a problem, because the likelihood is that the company will have an objects clause which is drawn so widely as to permit it to enter into every conceivable kind of business. Even where the company does enter into a transaction which is beyond its capacity, it will still be bound if the other party can satisfy certain conditions. These are that the other party dealt with the company in good faith and that the transaction in question was decided on by the directors (section 35 of the Companies Act). A party will not be in good faith if he knows that the transaction is beyond the company's capacity. A transaction will be treated as decided on by the directors if it has been considered by the board or, probably by a director, such as a managing director, to whom authority to enter into contracts has been delegated.

Where an agent has purported to enter into a contract which is beyond the capacity of the company, if the other contracting party suffers a loss as a result of not being able to enforce it, he may be able to recover that loss from the agent in question, on the ground that the agent has misstated his ability to bind the company. It is important, therefore, that those representing a company first check that the company is able to enter into the relevant transaction. It may also be noted that, in certain circumstances, it will be possible for a party who has paid money or delivered goods to a company in pursuance of a contract which was beyond the company's capacity, to recover them.

(d) The authority of agents. An agent will be able to bind his company if he has actual or apparent (sometimes called ostensible) authority. Actual authority exists where the agent has been validly appointed to his office and the transaction entered into falls within the scope of the authority given to him. Apparent authority will exist, even though the two requirements just mentioned are not satisfied, where it would appear to an outsider that the agent is authorised. Actual authority will be examined first.

(e) Actual authority. A company's articles will often give authority to the board to exercise all the company's powers. This is the effect of article 70 of the latest edition of Table A. It is, however, important to check the company's articles because power can be divided between the board and the general meeting of shareholders, and limits can be imposed on the directors' authority, to any extent that is desired.

A single director (unless the company only has one director) will not, as such, have any actual authority to bind the company. For him to have actual authority, power must be delegated to him by the board, assuming that the articles permit this. The articles might provide, for example, for the appointment of a managing director, to whom all or any of the board's powers can be delegated. If the company appoints a managing director, therefore, he will have such actual authority to bind the company as has been validly delegated to him. Alternatively, the board might delegate authority to a single director for the purpose of entering into a specific transaction or series of transactions. The company secretary, by reason of his appointment, will have authority to make contracts in connection with the administration of the company, for instance, for office

equipment. He will not, however, be authorised to enter into contracts in connection with the company's business generally, for example, for the borrowing of money. Depending on the size of the company and the practicalities of day-to-day management, it is common for companies to delegate considerable power to employees.

Where a company's articles impose restrictions on the authority of the board (there might, for example, be a limit on the amount of money that can be borrowed) and these restrictions are breached, the shareholders in general meeting can, by ordinary resolution, ratify the board's act and thereby make it binding on the company. The board can similarly ratify the acts of a director or employee who exceeds the scope of his authority. Acts which are beyond the capacity of the company cannot be ratified, even by a unanimous resolution of the shareholders.

Where a transaction has been 'decided on by the directors' (see above), a party dealing with the company in good faith will be able to enforce it even if there are restrictions on the directors' powers in the articles (section 35 of the Companies Act). The Companies Act also provides that the acts of a director or manager are valid notwithstanding any defect that may afterwards be discovered in his appointment or qualifications (section 285 of the Companies Act). This means that a transaction will be binding even though the agent who has acted on the company's behalf has not been properly appointed. The provision will not apply, however, if the agent has not been appointed at all to the office which he purports to occupy.

(f) Apparent authority. Even though a person acting on behalf of a company does not have actual authority, he may still be able to bind it. This will be so if he has apparent authority. Authority of this kind will exist where the agent is represented by the shareholders, or, more usually, by the board, as having authority. This representation having been made, the company is not entitled to deny its truth. An agent may lack actual authority either because he has not been appointed at all, or because he has exceeded the authority which has been granted to him. The agent may have apparent authority in either of these cases. The representation which is needed to create apparent authority need not be an express one. Where a company knows that one of its officers or employees is acting as though he were authorised, and the company takes no steps

253

to prevent this or to deny his authority, its inaction will be sufficient to constitute a representation that he is authorised. It will be helpful to illustrate these principles with the example of *Freeman & Lockyer v Buckhurst Park Properties (Mangal) Ltd*, decided in 1964.

Freeman & Lockyer v Buckhurst Park Properties (Mangal) Ltd

In this case the director of a company, which was involved in property development, entered into a contract with a firm of architects in connection with the development of a site. The director in question had never been appointed to the office of managing director, though he acted as such. When the development failed, the company refused to pay the architects' fees, claiming that the director had no authority to enter into the contract with them. The Court held that he had no actual authority, as a single director, and as he had not been appointed to the office of managing director he could not have actual authority on that basis. However, since the board had been aware of his conduct and had acquiesced in it, this was held to amount to a representation that he was managing director, and thus the company was bound on the basis of apparent authority.

Where an agent lacks actual authority, the other party to the transaction will not be able to rely on apparent authority if he knows that actual authority is lacking. In such a case the transaction will be unenforceable unless it is ratified by the company.

Another principle of company law, called the indoor management rule, will protect outsiders from the effects of irregularities in the company's internal procedures. If, for example, a company's articles state that a certain kind of contract can only be entered into if sanctioned by an ordinary resolution of the shareholders, failure to pass the resolution will not affect the other party's rights so long as he had no reason to suspect that the proper procedures had not been satisfied. Similarly, an outsider will not be affected if the board meeting at which a contract is decided on is not properly convened, or if there is no quorum.

Where a director has ceased to be a director of the company, the company will not be allowed to rely on this fact as against a third party, if the third party is unaware of it, unless the change has been 'officially notified'. This means that the company must inform the Registrar of Companies on the appropriate form that there has been a change of directors (see above) and the Registrar must then advertise this fact in the official *Gazette*. If this has not been done, the ex-director will still be able to bind the company.

(D) Personal liability in respect of company contracts. The following are the circumstances in which a director or employee may be personally liable as a result of entering into a contract which he intends to make on the company's behalf.

1. As discussed above, if the complete name of the company, including the word 'limited' or 'public limited company', as appropriate, is not stated on company cheques, other bills of exchange or promissory notes, the person signing or who authorises signature will be personally liable.

2. A person entering a contract on a company's behalf should make it clear that that is exactly what he is doing, and that he is not entering it on his own account. All signatures on business documents should, therefore, be accompanied by the words 'on behalf of' and then the full name of the company. Where this is not done there is a risk that the contract will be interpreted as one made by the agent personally. It may be possible to resist this conclusion where the contract is made, for instance, on company notepaper, but it is prudent not to take the risk. In the case of a negotiable instrument (e g a cheque), it is not enough merely to state that the agent is acting in a representative capacity; it must also be stated who his principal is, that is, the name of the company. If an employee signs *per pro* an officer or more senior employee, it must clearly be established what the relationship between the officer or senior employee and the company is. It is not sufficient merely to name them.

3. If a person purports to enter into a contract on behalf of the company but has no authority to do so, he will be liable to the other party to the transaction if he has represented that he does have authority. The representation need not be an express one – it could be inferred from the circumstances. It is of obvious importance, therefore, that directors and employees of companies should ensure that they have authority before attempting to contract on the company's behalf. Where power is delegated by the board to a director or manager, there should be a minute to this effect, unless there has already been a general

delegation of power to the individual in question. Where a more junior employee is authorised to enter into a transaction by a manager he should, in his own interests, seek written confirmation of his authority, and ideally, confirmation of the manager's authority to delegate.

4. We saw above that even though an agent may not have actual authority, his company will still be bound to a third party if he has apparent authority. In some circumstances it may be possible for the company to insist on the agent reimbursing the company for any losses it may have suffered as a result of being bound by the unauthorised transaction.

(x) Keeping the Members and Creditors Informed.

(a) Accounts. All limited companies must publish annual accounts, in the required form and containing the specified information, and they must be audited. The accounts must be made available to the members and filed with the Registrar of Companies. Sole traders, partnerships and unlimited companies are not required to publish accounts, though less formal accounts will be required for income tax and Value Added Tax (VAT) purposes.

(i) Accounting records (section 221 of the Companies Act). The annual accounts will be prepared from accounting records, which every company is required to keep. If proper records have not been kept, the auditors are required to say so in their report on the accounts. Failure to keep proper records is a criminal offence. Amongst other things, all monies paid and received by the company, and the underlying transactions, must be recorded, and there must be a statement as to the company's stock (where the company deals in goods) at the end of the financial year. The records must reveal, with reasonable accuracy, the company's financial position at any time. As well as being a legal requirement, the keeping of proper accounts is essential to the proper running of a business. Where a company has not maintained adequate accounting records, it will be more difficult to resist charges of wrongful trading if the company goes into liquidation (see page 262). All directors are entitled to inspect the accounting records at any time, but the members have no right to see them. A private company must keep its accounting records for at least three years and they must be accessible.

(ii) Accounting reference date (See Form 224 on page 256) (section 224 of the Companies Act). A company may within six months of registration inform the Registrar of Companies when its financial year (known as its 'accounting reference period') will end; if it fails to do so, its year end (the accounting reference date) will be 31 March each year, though this can be changed. It will be convenient to have the end of a month as the accounting reference date, and there may be tax advantages in choosing one date rather than another. A company's annual accounts must cover the period starting on the day after its accounting reference date and ending on its accounting reference date in the next year, and a copy of the accounts must be sent to the Registrar within ten months of the latter date. If the accounts are filed late, the directors responsible can be fined; they can also be disqualified from acting as directors if they are persistently in default of filing requirements. The accounts must also be laid before the members in general meeting during this ten month period. This is usually done at the annual general meeting; copies of the accounts should be sent to all members with the notice of meeting.

(iii) Form and content of accounts (section 228 of the Companies Act). The accounts must contain a profit and loss account for the accounting reference period and a balance sheet made up to the accounting reference date. The Companies Act prescribes in detailed terms the form that these accounts must take and their contents. This is a job for an accountant; in small companies the auditor frequently draws up the accounts as well as auditing them. The overriding requirement is that the accounts must give a 'true and fair view' of the company's affairs. This reflects the fact that there may be more than one way of expressing the company's results and the value of its assets, but whichever way is chosen the accounts must be accurate, present the reader with all relevant information and not mislead.

As well as detailing the company's trading results and assets, the accounts must contain the following information.

1. Directors' emoluments. The accounts must reveal the total amount of directors' emoluments, directors' and previous directors' pensions, and any compensation paid to directors for loss of office. If the total figure for emoluments exceeds £60,000, the actual remuneration of the chairman must be given, together with the numbers of directors whose remuneration falls within successive

G

COMPANIES FORM No. 224

Notice of accounting reference date
(to be delivered within **6 months** of incorporation)

224

Pursuant to section 224 of the Companies Act 1985

Please do not write in this margin

Please complete legibly, preferably in black type, or bold block lettering

* insert full name of company

To the Registrar of Companies

For official use

Company number

987431

The number given to the company by the Registrar on formation

Name of company

* C. POOTER & COMPANY LIMITED

gives notice that the date on which the company's accounting reference period is to be treated as coming to an end in each successive year is as shown below:

Important
The accounting reference date to be entered alongside should be completed as in the following examples:

5 April
Day   Month

0 5 0 4

30 June
Day   Month

3 0 0 6

31 December
Day   Month

3 1 1 2

Day   Month

0 5 0 4

Insert the company's accounting reference date in the manner indicated

The form may be completed by a director or secretary of the company

† Delete as appropriate

Signed *Charles Pooter*   [Director][Secretary]† Date 21.6.86

Presentor's name address and reference (if any):

C. POOTER
THE LAURELS
BRICKFIELD TERRACE
HOLLOWAY
LONDON

For official Use
General Section

Post room

256

bands of £5,000 (e g how many directors earn between £1 and £5,000, £5,001 and £10,000, 10,001 and 15,000 etc).

2. *Details of staff.* The accounts must state the average number of employees employed during the year and their total remuneration, as well as total social security and pension contributions. The number of employees earning amounts in successive bands of £5,000 must be revealed in the case of employees earning £30,000 or more.

3. *Loans, quasi-loans and credit transactions.* As will be discussed below (see p 000 below), there are restrictions on the permissibility of a company making loans to its directors. All these transactions must be disclosed in the accounts, whether they are lawful or not, subject to certain exceptions when the amounts in question are small.

4. *Other transactions involving directors.* Details of every transaction in which a director has a material interest must be revealed in the accounts, except where the total value of such transactions falls below the stated limits. It is open to the directors, other than the director with the interest, to decide that the interest is not material, in which case it need not be disclosed.

(iv) Modified accounts (sections 247–249 of the Companies Act). All limited companies, regardless of size, must prepare full accounts, setting out the information required by the Companies Act. Copies of these full accounts must be presented to the shareholders. Since 1981, however, it has been possible for smaller companies to file with the Registrar modified accounts, that is, accounts containing less detailed information. Companies which are subject to these less onerous filing obligations are referred to as 'small companies' and 'medium-sized companies'.

(b) The directors' report (section 235 of the Companies Act). As well as accounts, every company must prepare a directors' report. The report is attached to the accounts and every member is entitled to receive a copy. The report must contain a fair review of the development of the business of the company during the financial year and the company's position at the end of it. The directors must also state the amount which they recommend be paid as dividends, and the amount, if any, which they propose to carry to reserves. More particular information must also be given, which includes:

(a) *Details about the company's business*, such as its principal activities and significant changes in its fixed assets;

(b) *Information about directors*, that is, the names of the persons who were directors during the year, and details of their holdings in the company's shares and debentures, unless this information is given in the profit and loss account or balance sheet;

(c) *Charitable and political donations* must be disclosed if the company makes payments totalling more than £200. The amount given must be shown, and in the case of a political donation, the recipient.

Information must also be given if the company acquires its own shares, and in companies employing more than 250 people, details of steps taken to encourage employee participation and the company's policy on employing the disabled must be supplied.

(c) Audit. The accounts of all limited companies must be audited (sections 236 and 237 of the Companies Act). This means that they must be examined by an independent accountant, who is

---

Limited filing requirements

Small company. A small company's accounts need not include a profit and loss account, the balance sheet can be in a summarised form and there is no obligation to file a directors' report (see below). A small company is defined as one where for the accounting reference period, and the preceding one, any two of the following conditions are satisfied: (a) turnover was £1,400,000 or less; (b) assets were £700,000 or less; (c) the average weekly number of employees was 50 or less.

Medium-sized company. A medium-sized company may file a modified profit and loss account in which some items are aggregated, but it must submit a full balance sheet. A medium-sized company is defined as one where for the accounting reference period, and the preceding one, any two of the following conditions are satisfied: (a) turnover was £5,750,000 or less; (b) assets were £2,800,000 or less; (c) the weekly average number of employees was 250 or less.

required by law to report on the accounts to the members. The person appointed as auditor must be a member either of the Institute of Chartered Accountants or the Association of Certified Accountants.

The auditor's report must deal with the profit and loss account and the balance sheet; he is not required to comment on the directors' report unless it is inconsistent with the accounts. He must state whether the accounts have been prepared in accordance with the provisions of the Companies Act, and whether the balance sheet and profit and loss account give a true and fair view of the company's affairs. If he considers that the accounts are misleading or inaccurate, or there are material omissions, he must say so, in which case the report is said to be a 'qualified report'. He must also comment if he considers that adequate accounting records have not been kept. Where information on directors' remuneration and directors' interests in contracts with the company is missing from the accounts, he is specifically required to provide it in his report, in so far as he is able.

Unless a shareholder is also a director, he will not be entitled to detailed information about the day-to-day running of the company's affairs. The auditor fulfils the vital role of keeping a watchful eye on the directors to ensure that they do not use the company's assets improperly or otherwise abuse their positions. His report on the accounts, if unqualified, acts as an assurance to the members and creditors that they can rely on the information that the accounts contain. In order to carry out his duties properly, the auditor has the right to inspect all the books, accounts and records of the company at any time. Auditors may make 'spot checks' at unexpected times, and they are entitled to such information and explanations from the directors and others as they may require. To encourage full and frank disclosure by directors, any officer of the company who knowingly or recklessly makes a misleading, false or deceptive statement to an auditor will be liable to criminal prosecution (section 393 of the Companies Act).

The auditor's report must be annexed to the accounts which must be sent to all members and laid before them in general meeting. The auditor has the right to attend general meetings and to speak on any matter that concerns him as auditor, for example, if he thinks that the directors are misrepresenting his report or the accounts in general.

Appointment, removal and resignation of auditors (sections 384–391 of the Companies Act). A company's first auditor can be appointed by the directors. Otherwise, the auditor will be appointed by the shareholders in general meeting, and his appointment will be effective until the next meeting at which accounts are considered. He must then be reappointed or a new auditor appointed. This will normally mean that an appointment will run from one annual general meeting to another. An auditor can be removed from office by ordinary resolution in mid-term, though the company will be required to pay damages if this involves a breach of contract. The auditor is entitled to have a written statement by him circulated to the members and he may speak at the meeting at which it is proposed he be removed. If an auditor resigns during his period of office he must either state that there are no circumstances connected with his resignation which ought to be brought to the attention of members or creditors, or if there are such circumstances, what they are. The details must be notified to the members and debenture holders by the company. The auditor is also entitled to have his own written statement circulated and he can insist that a general meeting be called. The purpose of these provisions is to ensure that an auditor who has discovered irregularities and resigns, perhaps out of a sense of loyalty to the directors, cannot avoid disclosing them.

(d) Annual return. Every company which has a share capital must file an annual return with the Registrar of Companies (section 363 of the Companies Act). It is not necessary to submit a return in the first year of incorporation, nor in the following year if the company was incorporated after 1 July. The following is a summary of the information which must be set out in the return.

1. The address of the company's registered office.
2. Details of the company's share capital, including the amounts paid up in cash and otherwise.
3. The total amount of the indebtedness of the company in respect of all mortgages and charges which are required to be registered.
4. Names and addresses of all members and the number of shares each holds. A full list need only be given every three years, provided that details of changes are given in the return in intervening years.
5. Particulars of directors and secretary.

The annual return must be filed within 42 days after the annual general meeting for the year, and must be accompanied by the filing fee of £20. The information in it must be made up to the fourteenth day after the AGM. The return must be signed by a director and the company secretary. If an AGM is not held (which is an offence), an annual return must still be filed. It should in this case be made up to 31 December.

(xi) Maintenance of Capital and Distribution of Profits

(A) The concept of capital. Because the members of a company have limited liability, whether or not all the company's creditors are paid will ultimately depend on the company having sufficient assets to discharge its debts. The value of a company's assets will, to some extent, depend on the amount that has been raised from the members in return for the shares issued to them. Since persons lending money to a company will often be influenced by the size of the company's issued share capital in deciding whether to risk their money, it would be unfair if capital contributed by the members could subsequently be returned to them, since this would reduce the amount available to meet the company's liabilities. A company's capital is, therefore, often said to constitute a guarantee fund for the benefit of creditors. It is not, however, anything like a complete guarantee, because if the company trades unsucessfully and makes losses, its capital will be eroded and there may be very little left for creditors if the company is forced into liquidation. To say that a company's capital constitutes a guarantee fund does not, therefore, mean that the company must lay its capital to one side and preserve it intact. It simply means that the capital raised from the members cannot be returned to them. This principle is referred to as the 'maintenance of capital'.

The rules of company law are, to a limited extent, designed to see that a company gets full value for the shares that it issues, and to a greater extent, that its assets are not returned to the members. As regards getting full value for its shares, a company may not issue shares at a discount, that is, for less than their nominal value. As explained above, shares can be issued partly-paid, but in that case the holder remains liable to pay the difference between the issue price and the nominal value of the share at a later date. Where shares are isued in exchange for something other than cash, however, there is no requirement, as far as private companies are concerned, that the company should obtain full value; only if there is fraud, or the inadequacy of the assets contributed is manifest, can the validity of the issue be called into question.

One important consequence of the rule that a company cannot return its capital to the members is that dividends can only be paid out of profits. Thus, a dividend can only be paid where the company has 'profits available for the purpose', which means that its accumulated realised profits must exceed its accumulated realised losses (section 263 of the Companies Act). The effect of the word 'accumulated' is that if the company has made a loss in a previous year, that loss must be made up before a dividend can be paid. The word 'realised' is concerned with capital profits and losses. When a fixed asset is sold at a profit the profit is a realised profit; if the asset is simply revalued in the company's books, the profit is unrealised and does not count for dividend purposes. Whether the company has profits available for distribution is calculated in accordance with its audited accounts. If a company which does not have available profits nevertheless pays a dividend, the recipient will be required to return it if he knew, or ought to have realised, that it was paid improperly. The directors will be liable to reimburse the company if the invalid dividends are not recovered from the members.

(B) Other rules relating to maintenance of capital. As discussed above, if a company issues shares for an amount in excess of their nominal value, the shares are said to be issued at a premium. Share premiums are notionally put into a 'share premium account'. This is treated virtually as though it were part of the company's capital, and hence the amount standing in the account may not be returned to the members. The share premium account may, however, be used to pay up bonus shares. These are shares which are issued to existing members, in proportion to their existing holdings, free of charge. The sum required to pay up the shares is transferred from the share premium account and becomes fully a part of the company's capital. Since no money has been returned to the members, the position of the company's creditors is not affected by this procedure. It should be realised that the amount standing in the share premium account, like the rest of the company's capital, is not kept

259

to one side; it can be used in the business and hence will be susceptible to being lost. The significance of the share premium account is simply that the amount it represents cannot be returned to the members.

Subject to satisfying a number of procedural safeguards, companies may reduce their capital with the consent of the Court (sections 135–141 of the Companies Act). Since a reduction of capital may mean that the assets available to meet the company's debts will be reduced, the Court will need to be satisfied that creditors will not be prejudiced by the reduction. Companies rarely go through this procedure and hence it will not be discussed further.

The law has recently been changed to allow companies to purchase their own shares, and they may also issue redeemable shares (sections 159–181 of the Companies Act). A share is redeemable if it can be repaid at the option of the company or its holder. A company may decide to buy back or redeem some its shares where, for example, a member dies and the person who has inherited the shares wishes to dispose of them, but none of the existing members want to buy. The purchase or redemption of shares will cause the company's capital to be reduced, and hence there are certain safeguards for creditors. The money that is repaid may only come out of capital if there are insufficient distributable profits to finance the repayment and the proceeds of a fresh issue of shares would also be insufficient. Where shares are repaid out of profits, there is still a reduction in capital because the repaid shares are cancelled. The company must, therefore, establish a 'capital redemption reserve' equal to the reduction in capital. This reserve is treated in a similar way to ordinary capital and the share premium account. If the repayment is made out of capital, the directors must make a declaration to the effect that the company is solvent and that it will be able to continue in business as a going concern for at least another year.

Companies may not, subject to a number of complex exceptions, provide financial assistance to a third party (be it an existing member or otherwise) for the purchase of the company's shares (sections 151–158 of the Companies Act). This prohibition is justified in part on capital maintenance grounds. It is also designed to prevent men of straw using the company's assets to acquire its shares and thereby take control.

(C) Dividends. A dividend is a payment to a shareholder which constitutes the income from his investment. It is distinguishable from interest in that a lender will have a contractual right to receive interest (usually at a fixed rate) regardless of whether the company makes a profit. Interest is an expense of the business which is deducted from the company's income before it can be determined whether a profit has been made. A dividend, on the other hand, as we have seen above, can only be paid to the extent that there are profits available for the purpose.

A member will have no entitlement to a dividend unless one is declared. The procedure for declaring dividends will be set out in the company's articles. Under Table A the directors recommend a particular dividend to the shareholders (normally at the AGM, but it can be done at an EGM); the shareholders can accept the amount suggested, reject it, or reduce it, but they cannot increase it. The directors are under no legal compulsion to declare a dividend, even where the company has made large profits. They may, if they wish, retain profits for use in the business, or simply put them in the bank.

The dividend payable to a shareholder will depend on the nominal value of the shares held by him. Premiums are irrelevant for this purpose. Some companies issue preference shares. A preference share is a share which gives its holder a preferential right to dividend, which will usually be expressed as a percentage of the share's nominal value. This means that if a company pays any dividends at all, it must satisfy the preference shareholders' rights first. A holder of 10% preference shares each with a nominal value of £1, for example, will be entitled to a dividend of 10 pence per share before anything is paid to ordinary shareholders. If preference shares are 'non-participating' their holders will be entitled to nothing more than the preferential dividend; the remainder of the profits, no matter how large, will go to the ordinary shareholders. In the case of 'cumulative' preference shares, if the full preferential dividend was not paid in a previous year, outstanding amounts are carried forward and must be paid before ordinary shareholders benefit. Preference shares will be non-participating and cumulative unless the company's articles or the terms of issue state otherwise.

(D) Interest. Where a shareholder has made a loan to the company, his entitlement to interest will not depend on there being distributable profits. The amount of interest payable to him is an expense of the business in just the same way as is interest payable to the bank.

(E) Directors' remuneration. Directors' remuneration can take two forms, namely directors' fees or a salary paid under a service contract. Fees are awarded by the shareholders in general meeting (there is usually a power in the articles to this effect) and the amount paid is at their discretion. If a director has a service contract it will state what his salary is to be. So long as the amounts paid to directors genuinely constitute payment for services rendered, they will constitute an expense of the business and hence need not be met from distributable profits. If, however, they significantly exceed the value of the directors' services and the company subsequently goes into liquidation, the Court may order the directors to reimburse the company to enable it to discharge its debts. Even where there are available profits, minority shareholders might be able to object to excessively generous remuneration, and hence the amount of remuneration paid should always be linked to the value of the directors' services unless all the members agree otherwise. The tax implications of distributing profits as remuneration rather than as dividends, will be shown on page 278.

(xii) Restrictions on Other Methods of Extracting Assets from a Company

A company is a separate legal person. Its assets are not the property of its members or directors and hence they are not freely transferable. There is a temptation for the directors of small companies to ignore this fact, especially if they own all the shares. They might, for example, transfer cash balances to themselves or make gifts of the company's property to friends or relatives. As with the payment of excessive remuneration, this will not matter so long as the company remains solvent and there are no minority shareholders whose interests might be prejudiced by such transactions. If the company does go into liquidation, however, or a minority objects, the directors may be required to compensate the company for any losses they have caused it.

(A) Transactions with the company. We have already seen (page 237) that there are procedural safeguards where a director buys from or sells to his company. He must declare his interest at a board meeting and, depending on the articles, he will not be allowed to vote on the contract. The consent of the shareholders must be obtained in the case of a 'substantial property transaction'. Subject to these requirements being satisfied, a director may enter into a transaction with his company so long as he does not exploit his position to make an excessive profit.

(B) Pensions. A company can grant a pension to a retired director or director's dependent so long as this could be said to be 'reasonably incidental' to the company's business. This will be so if the pension is part of the director's overall remuneration, ie it constitutes payment for services. There are, however, cases where the Court has held that a pension has been paid without regard to the interests of the company, in fact, simply as a gift to the director or his widow. In

---

Re Halt Garage

This case, reported in 1982, is an example of the Court requiring remuneration to be repaid on the ground that it was excessive.

The company, which operated a petrol filling station, had two directors, a husband and wife, who were also its only shareholders. The company's articles authorised payment of remuneration for the mere holding of office as director. From the year 1968/69 onwards, the company was insolvent. The husband received £50 per week from the company from April 1969 and the wife £30. From May 1970 the husband received £70 per week and the wife received £10, until the company finally went into liquidation in March 1971. Owing to ill-health, the wife had played no active part in the business from December 1967. The liquidator sought to recover on the company's behalf all the remuneration paid to the wife during the period in which she had been inactive, and such amounts from the husband as were in excess of the market value of his services. The judge held that £10 per week constituted a reasonable payment for the mere holding of office by the wife, but that anything she had received beyond that during the period in which she was inactive must be repaid; the latter amounts could not be described as remuneration but were really a gift. The amounts paid to the husband genuinely represented payment for the services he had performed and hence were valid.

some of these cases the Court has required the pension to be repaid.

(C) Loans to directors. There are specific statutory prohibitions on companies making loans to their directors. They may not guarantee loans made by third parties, or give security for such loans, either. There is an exception where the total amount lent to a director does not exceed £2,500, or where the loan is made to enable him to carry out his functions as a director.

(xiii) Circumstances in Which Directors or Members Can Be Made Liable for a Company's Debts

(A) Trading with fewer than two members (section 24 of the Companies Act). A company must have at least two members. If it trades with only one member for more than six months, that member will be liable, with the company, for all the debts incurred after those six months if he is aware that he is the only member.

(B) Failing to use the company's name (section 349 of the Companies Act). If a director or other person signs or authorises the signature of a cheque, promissory note, order for goods etc, which does not have set out on it the full name of the company, he will be personally liable unless the company pays. (See pages 246 and 249.)

(C) Fraudulent trading (section 630 of the Companies Act). If, while a company is being wound up, it is discovered that the business of the company has been carried on with intent to defraud creditors, the persons responsible can be declared by the Court to be personally liable for such debts of the company as the Court thinks fit, which can mean all its debts. The kind of situation in which liability will be imposed is where the directors realise that the company is insolvent, but nevertheless continue to obtain goods on credit, knowing that the company will never be able to pay for them. Liability may be imposed on a person who is not a director if he has been a party to the carrying on of the business; this would cover a controlling shareholder who gives instructions to the directors.

(D) Wrongful trading (section 214 of the Insolvency Act 1986). It is difficult to impose liability under the above provision because of the need to show knowledge that the company will not be able to repay debts incurred. As a result, a new provision has been introduced which will allow the Court to impose personal liability on a director, or other person in accordance with whose instructions the directors act, in the following circumstances:

(a) the company has gone into insolvent liquidation;

(b) at some time before the commencement of winding up, the person in question knew, or ought to have realised, that there was no reasonable prospect of the company avoiding going into insolvent liquidation;

(c) that person failed to take every step which he might reasonably be expected to take to minimise loss to creditors.

The effect of this provision is to give the Court power to impose personal liability where the directors cause the company to continue to incur debts where they *should* have realised that the company will not be able to repay them. Directors who do not make themselves properly aware of the company's financial position may, therefore, be at risk. Liability might also be imposed where the effect of continuing to trade is to make the company's deficit worse. If there is no reasonable prospect of an upturn, the safest course may be to stop trading and put the company into liquidation. It should be noted that the Court has the discretion to impose liability on the directors for the whole of the company's debts if it so wishes, not just debts incurred after it should have realised that the company could not avoid going into liquidation.

4. BUSINESS NAMES

Business names are regulated by the Business Names Act 1985. A sole trader or partnership trades under a business name if a name other than the surnames and forenames or initials of the proprietors are used. A company has a business name if it trades under a name which is different from its registered name.

Prohibitions. The use of some names is prohibited, and others require the consent of the Secretary of State for Trade and Industry or some other designated body. The types of names which fall within these provisions, and the procedures for obtaining consent, are similar to those discussed in connection with companies' registered names (see above). Use of a prohibited name, or the unauthorised use of a name that requires consent, is a criminal offence.

Disclosure of the owners' names. The name of the proprietor, the names of all the partners, and in the case of a company, its registered name, must be disclosed if a business name is used. This disclosure must be made on all letters, written orders for goods, invoices and receipts, and written demands for payment of debts made in the course of the business. The address at which service of any document relating to the business will be effective must also be disclosed. In addition, the names and address mentioned above must be displayed in a prominent position at all the business's premises to which customers and suppliers have access. If anyone with whom the firm does business, or with whom anything related to the business is discussed, requests this information, it must be supplied to him immediately. A firm with more than twenty partners need not set out the names of all the partners on its business documents, so long as none of the partners' names is mentioned and the firm maintains at its principal place of business a list of partners' names, and this fact is disclosed on its letters etc.

Consequences of failure to make proper disclosure. If the information mentioned above is not properly disclosed, the persons responsible will be liable to a fine. Further, the business will not be allowed to enforce a contract made at a time when it was in breach of the disclosure requirements if the other contracting party has been unable to pursue its rights arising out of the contract against the business, by reason of the breach, or has otherwise suffered a financial loss as a result of the breach. This is subject to the Court's discretion to allow enforcement if it considers it just and equitable so to do.

Passing off. It is possible to bring a civil action for damages or an injunction against a trader who commits the tort of passing off. Using a name which is the same as or very similar to another trader's name can amount to the tort if the impression is likely to be given to customers that goods being sold are those of the plaintiff or that the two businesses are in some way linked. Merely using one's own name, however, will not in normal circumstances amount to passing off even if there is another trader with the same name in a similar line of business. (See page 287 for Copyrights, Patents, Designs and Trade Marks.)

1. DIFFERENT WAYS OF RAISING CAPITAL

(i) Shares

Issuing shares is a source of finance which is only available to companies. Many of the legal rules relating to shares have been looked at in the preceding section. In this section we will look at share capital in the wider context of a company's overall financial position.

(A) Risk capital. A company's ordinary share capital is often referred to as its 'equity' or 'risk capital': it is what the shareholders will lose if the business fails. It is also the foundation on which the company's finances are built and hence it must be large enough, for example, to support the company's borrowing. Share capital does not have to be repaid (unless the company has issued redeemable shares) and dividends can only be declared if profits are made (see page 259). Share capital is, therefore, a permanent source of finance – it cannot be withdrawn if the fortunes of the business decline – and unlike a loan, it need not be serviced by regular payments of interest, and so is not a drain on the company's resources.

(B) Gearing. Suppliers of loan finance, such as banks, will generally not be prepared to lend amounts greater than the company's share capital, in the case of a new company. This is because they do not wish to have a greater risk than the proprietors of the business, and also because the ability of a company to service its debt commitments will, to an extent, depend on the size of its capital base. Once a company has an established track record, a lender may be prepared to be more generous. The ratio of a company's borrowing to its share capital is referred to as 'gearing'. A company which, for example, has borrowed £1 for every £1 of its share capital, has a gearing of 1:1. The owners of a company which is profitable will benefit from high gearing; the company will have to pay interest on the amount it has borrowed, but if its rate of profit exceeds the interest rate the surplus will go to the holders of the comparatively small number of shares. The percentage return on the shares of a company with low gearing, on the other hand, will be lower, because more share capital will have to have been invested to make the same profit. Excessively high gearing, however, is dangerous. If profits are not forthcoming, or interest rates rise, the company may find itself unable to service its debt commitments and it might be forced into liquidation.

(C) Sources of equity finance. As well as the founders of the business, it may be that friends, relatives and business contacts will be prepared to buy shares. Under the terms of the Business Expansion Scheme (see page 267), tax relief is available to the purchasers of shares in new businesses. This has increased the flow of investment in the equity of small companies. There are also now a large number of Business Expansion Funds; these are approved organisations in which individuals put their money, and which then invest the money in a number of different companies, thus spreading the risk. Funds are unlikely to be interested in investing less than £30,000, but they might be able to put the company in touch with an individual who would consider such an investment. A company's solicitor, accountant or bank manager might similarly know of someone who is prepared to invest in the business.

In addition to individuals and Business Expansion Funds, there is a growing number of financial institutions of different kinds who are prepared to make investments in the equity of new businesses. These bodies, which are often subsidiaries of banks, insurance companies or pension funds, provide what is referred to as 'venture capital' or 'development capital'. A provider of venture capital will generally intend its investment to be a long-term one, whereas an institution offering development capital will want to recoup its investment, usually, in three to five years, by selling its shares in the business. Many institutions are prepared to offer a financial package, made up of an investment in the company's share capital together with loan finance. Amounts available will range from £5,000 upwards.

(D) Size of holding. The size of the stake in the company taken by the outside investor will have to be negotiated. The presence of a shareholder with interests independent of the company's controllers will mean that the latter will lose a certain amount of freedom of action, and the company's affairs will probably have to be conducted with greater formality. In addition, the more shares the outside investor holds, the smaller will be the proportion of profits that the company's controllers will be able to retain. The outside investor may also insist on having an option to acquire more shares, or to convert preference shares or loan capital into ordinary shares. The terms of options should be carefully scrutinised, since if they are exercised the interests of the controllers will be diluted.

(E) Dividends. An investor who plans to retain his stake indefinitely will want regular dividends. The company cannot pay dividends if it has not made a profit, but the investor may make it a condition of his investment that a certain proportion of such profits as are made are distributed, rather than retained in the business. This may conflict with the interests of the other shareholders. The investor might also insist on preferential dividend rights, which will diminish the amount available for the other shareholders unless the company makes large profits. An investor who is interested in capital appreciation, on the other hand, may not be concerned about dividends, but will want to dispose of his shares, usually after five years at the latest. The effect of this and how it is to be done should be carefully considered at the outset.

(F) Board representation and restrictions on management. An investor taking a significant stake in a company (perhaps 15% or above) may want a representative on the board to oversee its investment. This can be useful to the company because the representative will usually have financial and management expertise which the other directors may lack. The investor may wish to impose restrictions on management with respect to directors' remuneration, the company's borrowing powers, alterations in share capital, transfers of shares and outside interests of directors, amongst other things.

(ii) Borrowing

Borrowing is a source of finance available to all types of business, regardless of their legal form. Repayment terms and interest rates will vary depending on the type of loan. 'Short term' loans are repayable within three years; 'medium' and 'long term' loans last for three years or more. It should be borne in mind that all forms of financing have tax implications; appropriate advice should be obtained before entering into any commitments.

(A) Overdrafts. Bank overdrafts are the commonest source of short term finance. They can be arranged without formality and they have the advantage that sums can be drawn from the bank and repaid within the limits agreed, thus matching the needs of the borrower. Whilst the interest rate might be higher than that on a loan for a fixed period, interest will only be paid on the amount outstanding from day to day at any given time, and so an overdraft can work out cheaper overall. The interest rate will not be fixed, however, and so the cost of servicing an overdraft might suddenly increase dramatically. Usually the interest rate will be a given percentage over the bank's base rate. Overdrafts are subject to another serious disadvantage: they are repayable on demand. This means that the bank can, without warning, insist on immediate repayment. It is unlikely that the bank will do this, though it may become alarmed if the account is managed erratically. If the business is experiencing difficulties, it is better to explain these to the bank.

(B) Term loans. Rather than, or as well as, an overdraft, the business might borrow for a fixed period. The loan may be repayable in full on a stated date, or by instalments. With a term loan the borrower has the security of knowing that the money lent cannot suddenly be withdrawn at the whim of the lender, and he will be able to organise the affairs of the business so that it will be in a position to repay the loan at the appropriate time. The loan agreement may, however, specify 'events of default', the occurence of which will entitle the lender to demand immediate repayment. Such events might include failure to pay an instalment of interest or capital within a certain time after the due date, a default under any other financing arrangement, or, in the case of a borrower which is a company, a change in the control of the company. Such terms should be carefully scrutinised by the borrower to ensure that the lender does not have too wide a discretion to 'pull the rug' from under the business.

(C) Interest. The interest rate on a term loan may be fixed or variable. The choice of a fixed interest rate will prove to have been a good one if interest rates in general rise, since the borrower will not be affected, but if they fall he will find that he is paying more than the market rate. The risk with a variable interest rate is that it might rise to a level which cannot be satisfied from the profits of the business. A fixed rate also makes forward planning easier.

(D) Security. For all but the smallest loans the lender will require security. Fixed and floating charges have been considered above (see (Financing the Company)). A loan to a company will be secured on the company's assets, but it is very likely that a lender will also seek a personal guarantee from directors and/or shareholders, and this guarantee might well be secured on their private assets. The effect of giving such a guarantee is that as far as the loan guaranteed is concerned, limited liability is lost. It should also be borne in mind that unless express provision is made, the person giving the guarantee will not be able to call on the other shareholders (unless they are co-guarantors) to make a contribution to any sums he might have to pay under it. It may be appropriate, therefore, for the shareholders to enter into an agreement whereby they promise to indemnify the guarantor in respect of any sums he has to pay under the guarantee, in proportionate shares. This could be included in the shareholders' agreement, if the company has one (see Company officers and decision making above).

(iii) Other Forms of Finance

(A) Leasing. Instead of buying assets outright (either from its own resources or with the help of a loan), a business might decide to lease them. This avoids tieing up what might be large amounts of money which could be used more profitably in some other way. Almost any equipment that might be used in a business can be leased, ranging from industrial machinery to computers and office furniture. Ownership of the asset leased remains with the leasing company throughout. The lessee pays rent and may use the asset in the business in the ordinary way, but unlike in the case of a hire purchase arrangement, the asset never becomes the property of the lessee. Most leases run from three to five years. Leasing is sometimes referred to as 'off-balance sheet borrowing'; this is because paying rent is in some ways similar to paying interest on a loan to buy the leased equipment. As a matter of legal analysis, however, there is no borrowing because there is no capital sum which must be repaid, only an obligation to pay rent. The financing of the asset does not show up as a liability on the business's balance sheet and, therefore, will not affect its gearing. Government grants for the purchase of equipment will be available to the lessor and not the lessee, but the lessee will take some of the benefit of these in the form of a reduced rent. Leasing may also be advantageous to the lessee where he has insufficient profits to absorb the capital allowances available on the purchase of equipment (see below); the availability of these to the lessor will be reflected in the rent.

Types of leasing
(i) Finance leasing. With a finance lease, the lessee selects the item he wants from a supplier, the lessor buys it and then leases it to the lessee. The lessor will wish to recover the cost of the item and make a profit, which fact will be reflected in the rent charged. At the end of the initial rental period the lessor will usually be prepared to renew the lease at a much reduced rent, because it will by then have already recouped its investment. It should be borne in mind that under this kind of arrangement the lessor will give no warranty as to the condition or suitability of the item leased, and the obligation to maintain and repair it will be placed by the lease on the lessee. The lessee will also be responsible for insurance.
(ii) Operating leasing. With an operating lease the lessor will not intend to recover all his costs and profit over the life of the lease, because the item leased will have a second-hand value. This form of leasing is useful for equipment which may become obsolete as a result of technical advances, such as computers, or for vehicles, where the lessee may not wish to use old and deteriorating cars and vans. Whether the lessee is responsible for repairs, maintenance and insurance will depend on the terms of the lease.
(iii) Sales-aid leasing. In this form of leasing there is a connection between the lessor and the manufacturer or vendor; it is used to promote the products of the latter.
(iv) Contract-hire. Under this type of arrangement, commonly used for vehicles, the lessor agrees to make available from a pool equipment of a specified type, but the particular equipment supplied at any given time may vary. The lessor will normally be responsible for repair and maintenance, but this is not universal, so the terms of the agreement should be carefully checked.

So long as the lessee pays the rent, the lessor will not be able to withdraw the equipment. This is a considerable advantage over an overdraft as a method of financing. The way in which the rent payable is calculated should be carefully examined; the rent might be variable, for example, with changes in corporation tax, or there might be provisions for accelerated payment. It may suit the lessee for the rent to vary seasonally, where his cash-flow is subject to seasonal variations, for example in farming or the tourist trade. Leasing companies will often be prepared to accommodate such special requirements.

(B) Factoring. Factoring is a means of obtaining cash on trade debts before the debts are actually paid, and is thus of assistance in improving cash-flow. The business sells its debts to the factoring company, up to an agreed limit, and then receives up to 80% of the value of the debts from the factor. The factor collects the debts from the customers, and when they have all been paid, the factor pays the balance to the business, less its charges for the factoring service. This will usually work out at a little more than the rate for a bank overdraft, but as well as receiving cash on its debts immediately, the business will be spared the time and trouble of debt collection and will have the benefit of the factor's expertise in this area. If a non-recourse factoring agreement is entered into, the factor will not be able to demand reimbursement from the business in respect of a bad debt, thus providing the business with a 100% guarantee of payment. The factor will, however, carefully scrutinise debts before accepting them. Factoring should be distinguished from *invoice discounting*. Here selected debts are sold to the factor who advances a percentage of their value to the business, but (unlike ordinary factoring) the business itself collects them and forwards the money to the factor. The factor then pays the balance of the value of the debts to the business, less its charges. Under this system the business's customers will not know that their invoices have been discounted.

(C) Government grants and tax concessions
(a) Grants and other schemes. There are well over one hundred schemes operated by central and local government, the EEC and some private bodies offering grants and loans on favourable terms to new and developing businesses. Grants are available from central government, for example, in the Assisted Areas, under the Regional Development Grant and Regional Selective Assistance schemes. Much of Scotland, the North East, the North West, Wales, the Midlands and the South West have Assisted Area

status. Grants are also available under other schemes in coal, steel, textile and shipbuilding closure areas. There are schemes offering grants for high technology projects throughout the UK, and for capital projects which will provide or improve tourist amenities. A range of schemes are also available to encourage employment. There is, for example, the Enterprise Allowance Scheme, which provides an income of £40 per week for up to a year to someone who was previously unemployed who starts up a new business. Other schemes include the Young Workers Scheme, which offers a subsidy for employing young people, and the Job Splitting Grant, which enable an employer to obtain a grant for splitting a full-time job into two part-time jobs. There are also incentives to employ young people under the Youth Training Scheme and the Community Programme. As well as these national schemes, there is a wide range of programmes offering financial assistance which are operated by local authorities and other local bodies.

(b) The Small Firms Service. The Small Firms Service is run by the Department of Trade and Industry and is designed to provide advice on all aspects of setting up and managing a business. As well as advising on technical matters, training, marketing, exporting etc, the Service has up-to-date knowledge of the full range of financial assistance which is available to small businesses. There are thirteen Small Firms Centres and over 100 Area Counselling Offices around the country. The address of the nearest Centre can be discovered by dialling 100 and asking the operator for Freephone Enterprise.

(c) The Business Expansion Scheme. This scheme is designed to encourage individuals to invest in the equity shares of small companies by offering tax concessions. An investor can claim tax relief, at his highest income tax rate, on an investment of up to £40,000 for each year of the scheme. The current scheme has been in force since April 1983 and will continue indefinitely. As an example, someone investing the maximum of £40,000 and who pays income tax at 60% on at least £40,000 of his income, will obtain relief worth £24,000. £40,000 can be invested for each of the years that the scheme operates. The investment can be in one company, or spread between a number of companies. But there is a minimum qualifying amount of £500 which must be invested in any one company, unless the investment is made through an approved investment fund.

To qualify for relief, the following requirements must be satisfied.

(a) The investment must be in new ordinary shares, which have no special rights attached to them (such as preferential rights to dividend). The company's shares can have different voting rights, but all its shares must be fully paid up.

(b) The shares must be retained for at least five years.

(c) The company must not be listed on the Stock Exchange or on the Unlisted Securities Market.

(d) Most kinds of company which trade wholly or mainly in the UK are included, but the Scheme does not apply to companies involved in the provision of financial services, property development, farming and a number of other areas.

(e) Relief is not available to persons who are closely connected with the company. Someone will be 'closely connected' if he owns more than 30% of the company's ordinary shares, either alone or with close relatives or business partners, is a paid director of the company, or is a partner or employee of the company.

To claim relief, a certificate showing that the company satisfies the conditions of the Scheme should be sent by the investor to his Inspector of Taxes together with his claim. The certificate may be issued by the company after obtaining authorisation from its Inspector of Taxes.

(D) Investment funds. The Inland Revenue has approved a number of investment funds. A fund will invest an individual investor's money in a number of different qualifying companies, allowing the investor to have the benefit of tax relief on his investment, but with less risk. The normal minimum investment of £500 per company does not apply in this case.

2. PROBLEMS OF GETTING PAID

(i) Suing a Customer

If customers fail to pay for goods or services which you have provided, it may ultimately be necessary to take legal action against them, in other words, to sue them. It will often be found that a letter from your solicitor, warning the customer that unless the amount outstanding is paid within a certain number of days legal action will be taken, is all that is needed to persuade the customer to pay.

If this proves unsuccessful, the commencement of proceedings will have to be considered. It should be borne in mind that there will be little point in suing if the defendant lacks the means to pay, though, as we will see below, the court can order payment by instalments. Where the customer is a company, information about its assets can be obtained by inspecting the company's file at Companies House in London or Cardiff (or by employing agents to do this). Often, however, this information will be out-of-date. The reason why the customer has failed to pay should also be considered. If, for instance, it is because the goods supplied were defective, an action for payment may produce a counterclaim for compensation by the customer.

Proceedings for payment of a debt can be commenced in the County Court for sums up to £5,000; for amounts above that figure, the case will be heard in the High Court. Claims in the County Court for less than £500 will automatically be referred to the Small Claims Court, which is part of the County Court, for arbitration. For claims below this amount, the cost of employing a solicitor cannot be recovered by the winning party from the loser. Where the amount in dispute is more than £500 the matter can still be decided by arbitration if both parties agree; solicitor's costs are recoverable in these circumstances unless the parties agree otherwise.

Small Claims Court. The rule that the cost of employing a solicitor cannot be recovered in a Small Claims Court action for less than £500 is meant to ensure that proceedings in the Small Claims Court are cheap, and to discourage excessive formality. Where the amount in dispute is not very great, therefore, it is likely that only a 'do-it-yourself' action will be financially viable. Proceedings may be commenced simply by visiting the nearest County Court office and filling in a form known as a 'request'. The nature of the claim being made must be briefly set out, for example that the defendant bought certain goods from the plaintiff on a specified date and has failed to pay for them. If interest on the debt is being claimed, the amount must also be stated. The court officials will be happy to give advice on how to make a claim and will supply a useful free booklet, entitled 'Small claims in the County Court', on request. A fee, of around 10% of the amount claimed, will be payable on the commencement of proceedings. If the defendant resides in a different County Court area, the position is a little more complicated because an action must be commenced either in the Court for the area in which defendant is based, or for the area in which the contract giving rise to the debt was made. The officials at your local County Court will be able to advise on this. If an action must be conducted in a Court which is some distance away, the extra time and expense to which this will give rise should be borne in mind.

After the plaintiff has made the request and paid the fee, the court will serve a summons on the defendant, but it is the responsibility of the plaintiff to ensure that he has given the Court the correct address. Where the defendant is a company, the summons must be served at its registered office. The address of this ought to appear on the company's notepaper, but, if it does not, it can be discovered by inspecting the company's file at Companies House. If the debtor is a sole trader or partnership, the summons can be served at any place the firm carries on business, or at the private address of a partner. In the case of a partnership, it will be sensible to sue the firm in the partnership name, rather than naming a particular partner or partners. This is because if a partner is sued and judgment is given against him, but he is unable to pay, it will not be possible to sue the other partners thereafter. If the name of the partnership does not consist of the full names of the partners, the firm must display the partners' name at its business premises and on its business documents. Partners are under an obligation to disclose their full names and the address of the firm if so requested.

Once the summons has been served on the defendant, he has fourteen days in which either to pay or make proposals about payment (for example, by instalments), or to deny the claim. If he does nothing the plaintiff has the right to have judgment made in his favour. An application should be made to the Court for judgment in default. If the defendant makes an offer of payment by instalments or delayed payment, this must be accepted or rejected through the Court office within fourteen days. Where the defendant files a defence, the Court will fix a date for a 'pre-trial review', at which either the dispute will be resolved or arrangements will be made for a hearing. In the latter case, the issues which are in dispute will be clarified at the pre-trial review and the nature of the evidence which will be required will be discussed. The proceedings at the hearing will be held in private and will be informal. The rules of procedure and evidence are more relaxed than at a formal hearing, and

evidence will normally be given from behind a desk rather than from the witness box. The parties are allowed to have a friend or adviser to help them, but they will be required to give evidence personally. It is also possible to call witnesses. Having heard the evidence and the argument, the judge or registrar in charge of the case will normally give judgment immediately.

(ii) Enforcement of Judgments

Even though judgment has been obtained against a defendant (the debtor), he may still be reluctant to pay. Obtaining a favourable judgment is only the first stage in securing payment of a debt. Whilst in making its judgment the Court will have ordered the defendant to pay, the responsibility for seeing that this order is complied with is borne by the plaintiff (the creditor). A creditor can, however, apply to the Court for a number of different enforcement procedures. As with the initial decision to take legal action, the creditor should be satisfied that the debtor will be able to pay before he incurs further expense in having the judgment enforced. One way of determining what the debtor's financial position is is to apply to the Court for an examination as to his means. This is a procedure whereby the debtor is summoned to Court and is obliged to answer questions put to him by the creditor as to his financial affairs, for example how much he earns, what his savings are and so on. We will now consider a number of methods by which judgments may be enforced. If one method fails, another may be used, but this may turn out to be expensive.

(A) Warrant of execution against goods.
Under this procedure, which is the commonest method of enforcing judgments, the creditor applies to the Court for a warrant empowering a bailiff to sell the debtor's goods and hand over the proceeds to the creditor in satisfaction of his debt. If the bailiff considers that the debtor does not own goods of sufficient value to meet the debt, plus the cost of removal and sale, the bailiff will report this to the Court, which will notify the creditor. Where the Court has ordered the debtor to pay by instalments, however, each instalment is regarded as a separate debt for this purpose, and so a warrant of execution can be issued if an instalment goes unpaid, even though the debtor has insufficient assets to meet the whole debt. The threat of seizure is normally sufficient to persuade a debtor to pay up. The bailiff will give the

debtor time to raise the necessary money before removing goods provided the debtor signs a 'walking possession agreement'. If the debtor then fails to pay, the bailiff can break into his home and seize his goods. Without a walking possession agreement a bailiff cannot forcibly enter a private residence, but he can so enter business premises.

(B) Attachment of earnings. A Court can order that a debt be paid off in instalments taken from the debtor's earnings. For this to be possible, the debtor must be an employee; attachment of earnings is not available against a sole trader or partner, though it will be against a company director who is paid a salary. A state old age pension, disability pension and social security benefits cannot be attached. After an application has been made to the Court by the creditor for an attachment of earnings order, the Court will request details from the debtor of his earnings and expenses. The Court may also obtain a statement of the debtor's earnings from his employer. On receipt of this information, the court will set a 'protected earnings rate'; if the debtor's income falls below this no deductions will be made from it. The Court will also fix a 'normal deduction rate', which is the amount which will be deducted weekly or monthly (depending on how often he is paid) from the debtor's earnings, so long as they are above the protected earnings rate. The amount fixed is deducted by the employer and sent to the Court, which will then pay it to the creditor. The Court may hold a hearing before deciding what the appropriate rates are to be.

(C) Garnishee proceedings. A garnishee order is an order by the Court to someone who owes money to the debtor to pay that money to the creditor, instead. Its main use is to enable a creditor to get at money in the debtor's bank account, which is a debt owed to the debtor by the bank. After an application by the creditor to the Court, the Court will order the debtor's bank to hand over to the Court such amount standing in the debtor's account as is necessary to meet the debt. If there are insufficient funds in the account, the creditor can accept whatever amount is offered without prejudice to his right to receive the balance from the debtor. The summons will only affect the money which is in the account at the time the summons is served on the bank – it will not apply to subsequent deposits. It is important, therefore, to have the summons served at a time when it is likely that the debtor's account will be substantially in credit, in the case of an employee, for example, shortly after he has been paid.

(D) Charging orders. A Court can impose a charging order on land (for example, the debtor's house) or on securities (shares in a company or government stock). This is equivalent to imposing a mortgage in favour of the creditor on the property charged. The debtor will not be able to sell it free of the creditor's interest. If the debtor does not pay, the Court, at its discretion, can order the charged property to be sold and for the debt to be satisfied from the proceeds of sale. This procedure should not be attempted without the assistance of a solicitor.

(E) Appointment of a receiver. A receiver is a person who is appointed by the Court to collect amounts which are due periodically to the debtor, for the benefit of the creditor. If, for example, the debtor owns a house which he lets to tenants, a receiver can be appointed to collect the rent on behalf of the creditor. Receivership is a complex matter which requires the involvement of a solicitor.

All the enforcement procedures referred to above are available in the County Court. Where the debt is for more than £5,000 the original action (as distinct from enforcement proceedings) will have to be fought in the High Court. High Court judgments (for whatever amount) can, however, be enforced in the County Court. The High Court also has its own enforcement procedures, which require the assistance of a solicitor and will not be discussed here.

(iii) Legal Position in the Event of the Insolvency of Customers

An individual who cannot pay his debts may be declared bankrupt. The equivalent process for a company is called liquidation or winding up. Once bankruptcy proceedings or winding up have commenced, the debtor will no longer be free to pay off his debts or otherwise dispose of his property as he chooses. The policy behind the insolvency legislation (now contained in the Insolvency Act 1985 with regard to individuals, and in the same Act and the Companies Act 1985 with regard to companies) is to secure the fair and orderly payment of the insolvent person's debts, given that the assets available will be insufficient to meet all the debts in full. Thus, once insolvency proceedings have commenced, a creditor who does not have full security for his debt will not receive payment for the whole of the amount he is owed. In addition, in certain circumstances a creditor may be forced to repay sums which were paid to him by the debtor in satisfaction of a debt, even though they were paid before the commencement of bankruptcy proceedings or winding up (proceedings commence, in most cases, within six months). This will be so if the debtor was insolvent at the time the payment was made, and the debtor's intention was to 'prefer' the creditor, that is, put him in a stronger position than he would have been in if bankruptcy proceedings or winding up had commenced. Certain other payments or dispositions of property (for example, gifts and transactions at an undervalue) may also be set aside once insolvency proceedings begin.

(A) Commencement of insolvency proceedings. If the other methods of obtaining payment of a debt appear likely to fail, or it is feared that the debtor's assets are about to be diminished to the prejudice of the creditor, a creditor may decide to apply to the court to have the debtor declared bankrupt or wound up. Proceedings are commenced in the County Court or the High Court, depending on financial limits and geographical considerations.

(B) In the case of an individual debtor a creditor may petition for a bankruptcy order if:

(1) the debtor owes the petitioning creditor or creditors at least £750;

(2) the debt, or each of the debts, is (generally) unsecured, is of a determinable amount, and is payable immediately or at a time in the future which is certain; and

(3) the debtor is unable to pay the debt or debts and there is no reasonable prospect of payment. A debtor will not normally be treated as being unable to pay a debt unless a demand for payment has been made and at least three weeks have elapsed since the demand was served, without a satisfactory response being made by the debtor. Nor will it be accepted that there is no reasonable prospect of payment unless a similar notice has been served. As an alternative to the service of a notice, it will be accepted that the debtor cannot pay his debts if a method of execution has wholly or partly failed.

(C) When a debtor is a company a creditor can petition for winding up if:

(1) alone, or with other creditors, he is owed at least £750; and

(2) the company is unable to pay its debts. It will be accepted that this is the case if a demand for payment has been made at least three weeks previously without a satisfactory outcome, or execution in favour of a creditor has been unsuccessful in whole or in part. In addition, even though a company may be able to pay its debts for the time being, it will be deemed to be unable to pay its debts if its assets are less than its liabilities, taking into account its prospective and contingent liabilities.

The above are the requirements for a 'compulsory' winding up. A company may also be wound up, without these requirements being satisfied, if the members so resolve. The winding up will, in this case, be a 'voluntary' winding up.

Once insolvency proceedings have been commenced, the assets of both individual and corporate debtors will be frozen – they will not be able to dispose of them except in accordance with proper procedures, and creditors will not be allowed to levy execution on the debtor's property. The debtor's property will be collected in and sold by the trustee in bankruptcy in the case of an individual debtor, and by the liquidator in the case of a company. The amount realised will then be used to pay off the insolvent's debts in the following order: (1) debts secured by fixed charges, to the value of the property charged; (2) the costs of the insolvency proceedings; (3) preferential claims – these include certain debts owed to the Inland Revenue, remuneration owing to employees and so on; (4) (only where the debtor is a company) amounts secured by floating charges; (5) unsecured debts; (6) (in the case of an individual only) debts owed to a person who was the debtor's spouse at the commencement of the winding up. The members of each category are paid in full before anyone else is paid. It should be borne in mind that there may be little or nothing left for the unsecured creditors by the time those appearing higher in the list have been paid.

A person who is declared bankrupt will eventually be discharged from bankruptcy, either automatically or by order of the court. When the process of winding up has been completed, the insolvent company will be struck off the register and will cease to exist.

(D) Voluntary arrangements. Instead of proceedings being taken for a bankruptcy order or a winding up, it is possible for a debtor to enter into an arrangement with creditors, whereby it is agreed, for example, that the creditors will accept payment of part of the amounts owed to them in full settlement, or deferred payment. Where the required majority of creditors agree, a scheme which is drawn up will be binding on all the creditors (but the rights of secured and preferential creditors cannot be affected without their consent). The purpose of this procedure is to give a breathing space to a debtor whose financial difficulties are capable of being overcome.

5.3 TAX AND YOUR BUSINESS

1. INCOME TAX

Income tax is payable on the income profits of sole traders and partners. Income must be distinguished from capital receipts: sums received from selling stock or supplying services are income, whereas amounts obtained on the sale of fixed assets, for example, business premises or machinery, are capital. Only income profits are chargeable to income tax. A profit made on the sale of a capital asset may, however, be subject to capital gains tax (see page 279). Generally, income tax is paid on receipts which are of a recurrent nature, though in certain circumstances it can be charged on 'one-off' receipts.

(A) The tax schedules. Different rules apply to different types of income to determine the way in which expenses are to be deducted and the period over which income is to be assessed. These rules are largely contained in the Income and Corporation Taxes Act 1970 (generally referred to as the 'Taxes Act'), with separate Schedules dealing with each type of income. Thus, income from an employment is assessed under Schedule E, whilst profits from a trade, profession or vocation are assessed under Schedule D. We will now examine the Schedule D rules.

(B) Deduction of expenses under Schedule D. Income tax is charged on the profits of a business over the relevant period. In order to determine what profits have been made, expenses incurred during the period are deducted from income, but not all expenses may be deducted for tax purposes, and so taxable profit may be different from that shown in the profit and loss account. In order to be deductible, expenditure must (a) be of a revenue, rather than of a capital nature and (b) be 'wholly and exclusively' for the purposes of the business. The distinction between revenue and capital expenditure is similar to that between income and capital receipts, mentioned above. Thus, sums spent on buying business premises, machinery, office equipment and so on are of a capital nature and so are not deductible in arriving at a profit figure (but see capital allowances, below), whereas sums spent on employees' wages, rent of business premises and repairs (but not improvements)

can be deducted. The 'wholly and exclusively' requirement means that expendiure which is incurred for mixed business and private purposes will not be deducted if it can be shown that an identifiable part of it was incurred wholly for the purposes of the business. Thus, no deduction can be made for a combined business trip and holiday, but a mileage allowance can be claimed for exclusively business journeys in a car which is also used for private purposes. Where part of a private house is used exclusively for business purposes, an allowance may be claimed for heat, light and repairs to the part concerned (though doing so could increase the likelihood of a capital gains tax liability arising when the house is sold). The Revenue will also normally agree to a small deduction being made where a trader's home is used for business purposes, even though the rooms so used are not used exclusively for business.

(C) Capital allowances. As explained in the preceding paragraph, capital expenditure cannot simply be deducted from income in calculating taxable profits. Relief is, however, given on certain capital expenditure by means of capital allowances (as provided in the Capital Allowances Act 1968, as amended), which can be set-off against profits. The rules vary as between different types of capital expenditure; the main category, which we will examine here, is for expenditure on plant and machinery. (Other categories include new industrial buildings and agricultural buildings.) In deciding whether an asset constitutes 'plant and machinery', regard will be had as to whether the asset performs a function in the carrying on of the business, as opposed to its merely being part of the setting in which business is carried on. Interior decoration, for example, will not constitute plant, unless it is designed to create an atmosphere which will encourage customers to buy. Allowances will be given on plant which is used partly for business and partly for private purposes, in such proportion as is reasonable, having regard to the private element.

The rules governing the way in which capital allowances are calculated where changed in the Finance Act 1984. With regard to expenditure incurred after 31 March 1986, allowances take the form of annual writing-down allowances of 25%, calculated by the reducing balance method. This means that 25% of the cost of an asset may be deducted from the profits earned in the accounting period in which it was purchased, and in successive accounting periods, 25% of the 'written-down' value of the asset is deductible. Thus, if an asset costs £2,000, the allowance in the first year will be £500, in the second year it will be £375 (25/100 × 1,500), and so on. The idea is that the cost of obtaining an asset will eventually be fully allowed against the profits which the asset contributes towards creating. The total allowances given over the lifetime of the asset, however, will not be permitted to exceed the cost of the asset after allowing for any sale proceeds. So if an asset is sold and the sale price exceeds its written-down value, the difference will be subject to tax, by means of a 'balancing charge'. If there is a short-fall when the asset is disposed of, the taxpayer will be credited with a 'balancing allowance'. Where allowances are claimed on more than one item, the expenditure incurred will usually be pooled; the proceeds of an item which is sold will be deducted from the pool before writing-down allowances are calculated, and a balancing charge will only be made if the proceeds exceed the amount in the pool. Individuals (as opposed to companies) must make a specific claim for capital allowances. A taxpayer whose income is insufficient to use up all his personal reliefs should not waste them by claiming capital allowances: the latter can be saved for future years, whereas personal allowances cannot.

(D) Cars and tax. Writing-down allowances of 25% are available on cars used in the business. There may be a greater tax-saving if cars are leased rather than bought, since it will usually be possible to deduct the whole of the leasing charge from profits. Full relief, whether the car is bought or leased, will not be available if the car is also used for private purposes. Running expenses and repairs ascribable to business use can also be deducted from profits, but it should be noted that the expense of travelling between home and the business's premises is not allowable.

(E) Year of assessment. The year of assessment (or 'tax year') runs from 6 April in one year to 5 April in the next year. A trader's accounting year need not coincide with the tax year: the dates of an accounting period are at the discretion of the

business. It will, however, prove inconvenient to have an accounting period which lasts more than 12 months. An accounting period which ends early in the tax year (for example, the end of April) will often be advantageous, since, as we will see below, this will maximise the time-lag between a profit being made and tax on it being due for payment. Where the tax year and the business's accounting period do not coincide, it will be necessary to allocate profits made over the accounting period to the relevant tax year. Normally, profits will be assessed on the 'preceding year basis'; this means that the profits which are assessable for a given tax year will be those made during the accounting period which ended in the previous tax year. Thus, if a business's accounts are made up to 31 December, the profits assessable for the tax year 1985/6 will be those earned during the accounting period which ended in the tax year 1984/85, namely 1 January 1984 to 31 December 1984. Income is allocated to the year of assessment in which it is earned, even though payment may not be received until later. Tax due is payable in two equal instalments, on 1 January of the tax year and on 1 July. Under Schedule D, therefore (unlike Schedule E), there will be a considerable period between the receipt of income and the date on which tax must be paid. This will assist the cash-flow of the business, but the prudent trader will ensure that he has funds available to meet his tax liability when the date for payment arrives.

(F) Opening and closing years. Special rules apply to the opening and closing years of trade – in the opening year because there is no preceding year on which to assess tax, and in the closing years in order to prevent the business being terminated after a profitable year, with a view to avoiding tax being paid by reference to that year's profits. In the first year of trade, the assessment is based on the profit made from the date of commencement to the following 5 April (with apportionment on a time basis if necessary). The second year's assessment is based on the profits of the first twelve months. The trader can choose in the second and third years (only, and the choice must be made for both or neither) to be taxed on the actual profits of those years; this will be worth while only if profits are falling, since tax is charged on the later, lower profits. In the last year of business, the assessment is based on the profits from 6 April to the date the business ceases. For the two preceding tax years, the

Revenue has the discretion not to apply the preceding year basis, but instead to assess tax on the basis of profits actually made in those years, which they will do if profits were rising when the business was closed down.

(G) Rate of income tax and reliefs. Income tax is progressive, which means that tax is charged at higher rates as more is earned. The rates for 1986/87 are: the first £17,200 29%; the next £3,000 40%; the next £5,200 45%; the next £7,900 50%; the next £7,900 55%; the remainder over £41,200 60%.

Various reliefs and allowances are deducted from income; the above rates apply to the amount of income that is left after these deductions. Reliefs include the personal allowance (single person's allowance, or the higher married man's allowance), dependent relative relief, and so on. As we have seen, the purchase of capital equipment or shares in a company are capital transactions and so the amounts spent cannot be off-set against income, but relief can often be claimed on interest on loans taken out for these purposes. 'Allowable interest' includes interest on a loan to buy plant and machinery, to acquire a stake in a partnership, or for putting capital into a partnership or lending to it. A director or employee may set-off interest on a loan to buy shares in a trading company, so long as it is a close company (one owned by five or fewer shareholders or controlled by its directors), and the lender either owns more than 5% of the company's ordinary shares, or works full-time for the company. (Schedule 1, Finance Act 1984.)

(H) Tax treatment of losses. If the business makes a loss, there will, of course, be no taxable profit. As well as no tax being payable, relief can be claimed on losses, by setting them off against future or earlier income, or against income from other sources.

1. A loss can be carried forward against later profits of the same trade (section 171 of the Taxes Act). Relief is obtained by deducting losses from the income of the next tax year in which there are profits, and if the loss is not fully absorbed, in future years, until the loss is used up. The disadvantages of this method of relief are that there will be a time-lag before a loss can be used to reduce the tax bill, and if the nature of the trade changes, or the business comes to an end, no relief can be claimed. Further, the whole of the loss will be off-set against the profits of the next year (if sufficient) and this may lead to personal allowances being wasted. (Personal allowances cannot be carried forward.)

2. The loss can be set against income from any source in the year of assessment on which the loss is made and in the following year, so long as the taxpayer is still carrying on the trade with a view to profit (section 168(1) of the Taxes Act.) A claim has to be made within two years of the end of the year of assessment in question. Any unrelieved losses can also be set-off against a spouse's income.

3. Losses made during the first two years of a trade, or of a partner's being a member of a partnership, can be carried back against income, from any source, in the previous three tax years (section 30 of the Finance Act 1978). This provision enables the founders of a new business which makes losses in the early years to obtain a repayment of tax paid on his earnings in a previous employment. A 'repayment supplement' (which is equivalent to interest) will also be paid. It will be preferable not to carry losses back where this has the effect of extinguishing so much income that personal allowances are wasted. In such circumstances losses should be off-set against current or future income. A claim under this section must be made within two years after the end of the year of assessment in which the loss is incurred.

4. Where a loss occurs in the last year of a trade, it can be carried back against the income, from any source, of the previous three years of assessment (section 174 of the Taxes Act). If losses were made in those years as well, there will, of course, be nothing to off-set the losses of the final year against unless the taxpayer has an alternative source of income.

Capital allowances for periods in which losses are made, or in which profits are insufficient to absorb them, may be carried forward to future years. Alternatively, they can be used to convert a profit into a loss, or to increase the size of a loss.

(I) Partnerships. The income tax treatment of partners is essentially the same as that of sole traders – tax is normally assessed on the preceding year basis, for example. The partnership accounts will probably treat partners' salaries and interest or capital supplied by partners as charges against profits, but for tax purposes these amounts will be treated as constituting part of the profits earned by the business and hence they will not be deductible. A single assessment will be issued by the Revenue, showing the tax liability of each partner, taking into account personal allowances and other deductions, and calculated in accordance with the rate appropriate to the particular partner's income. The assessment will, however, be made in the partnership name, and any partner will be liable for the whole of the tax due if it is not paid.

It should be noted that an assessment is allocated between the partners in accordance with the profit-sharing proportions applicable to the year of assessment, and not to the period covered by the accounts which form the basis of the calculation of the amount of that assessment. This will be of significance if profit-sharing ratios change, or where there is a change in the partners and it is elected that the trade be treated as continuous (see next paragraph). In the latter case, profits actually received by an out-going partner may be assessed on an incoming partner.

(J) Continuation election. For tax purposes, there is a cessation of the trade of a partnership every time a partner leaves or a new partner joins. This means that the closing year rules will apply to the period before the change, which, as mentioned above, will be disadvantageous where profits are rising. This result can be avoided, provided at least one partner remains a partner throughout, if all the partners (including out-going and in-coming ones) elect in writing within two years of the date of the change that the change should be ignored for tax purposes. The Revenue must be informed of the election. It is sensible to provide in the partnership agreement that an out-going partner may be required to sign such an election, since otherwise he will be able, if he so wishes, to affect adversely the tax position of the continuing partners and thereby hold them to ransom. Since an election may increase the tax liability of an out-going partner, however, it should also be provided that an indemnity will be payable for any loss suffered. Balancing the interests of continuing and out-going partners can be a highly complex matter; it is, therefore, sometimes provided in the partnership agreement that any disputes which arise should be resolved by an independent arbitrator.

(K) Spouse's earnings. If the proprietor's wife is employed in the business, and she is paid a salary below the levels of the wife's earned income allowance and the national insurance earnings limit (in 1986/87, £44.90 and £35.50 per week, respectively), the wife will have no tax or national insurance liability, and the wages paid can be deducted from profits as an expense of the business. If the wife is paid more than £35.50, it might be more advantageous for her to be a partner rather than an employee. This is because national insurance contributions might be lower, and whilst a partner's salary is not a deductible expense of the business, husband and wife partners can divide income from the business between them in any proportion they choose, so long as they are both, to some extent, involved in the business. This may have the effect of lowering the total amount of tax they pay, if they elect for separate tax treatment (see below). It should be borne in mind that a spouse (or anyone else, for that matter) who is *employed* in the business should be paid no more than a commercial rate. Otherwise, the Revenue is likely to treat the excess as not being wholly and necessarily for the purposes of the business, and therefore not a deductible expense.

A husband and wife's earnings are normally combined for tax purposes, but they can be separated by use of the 'wife's earnings election'. This must be made by both spouses at least six months before, and no more than twelve months after, the end of the tax year for which it is to apply. The effect is that the husband and wife will be taxed as if they were single; the husband will lose the married man's personal allowance (which is higher than the single man's), but since the two incomes are no longer aggregated, they may, depending on the level of their incomes and other personal circumstances, benefit from lower tax rates.

(L) Informing the Revenue and books and records. When a new business commences, the local inspector of taxes should be informed of the name of the business, the date of commencement, the nature of the business, the names of the proprietors and whether there are any employees. (This information should be supplied on Form 41G, obtainable from the local inspector of taxes.) Once in business, it is important that full records of all financial transactions are kept, so that an accurate tax assessment can be prepared and all allowances claimed can be supported. Thus, all sales and purchases should be recorded, there should be a record of amounts owed to and by the business, and all expenses and capital expenditure should be noted. Where possible, cheque stubs, invoices, receipts and so on should be retained in order to substantiate entries in the accounts. Stock and work in progress will need to be valued at the end of an accounting period, since their value must be known in order to determine the amount of profit that has been made. Stock and work in progress are normally valued at the lower of cost and market value; items that are used up in the course of running the business should be valued at cost. Any sums which are drawn from the business for the personal use of the proprietors, and goods taken from the business for personal use, should be recorded. These will be treated by the Revenue as part of profits.

The inspector of taxes should be informed if the business is converted into a company. As discussed above (pages 255–257), companies are required to keep accounts which comply with the requirements of the Companies Act 1985.

(M) Appeals. The rules concerning appeals against income tax assessments are also much the same for corporation tax and capital gains tax. An appeal must usually be made within 30 days of the disputed assessment, though this limit is sometimes extended. The appeal will be heard by General Commissioners or Special Commissioners (in the case of more specialised appeals). Further appeals lie on points of law to the High Court and the appellate Courts. The tax claimed is payable on the due date notwithstanding the appeal, but an application, separate from the appeal, can be made for postponement.

2. CORPORATION TAX

Corporation tax is paid by companies on their profits. A company's taxable income is computed in much the same way as the taxable income of an individual is calculated for income tax purposes. The rules as to what expenditure can be deducted, for instance, are largely the same, though one difference is that directors' remuneration is an allowable expense of the business, unlike the payment of salaries in an unincorporated firm. Directors' remuneration is, however, chargeable to income tax in the hands of the directors (under Schedule E, as employees). Capital allowances are available to companies. They are deducted from income as trading expenses, balancing charges being treated as trading receipts. Capital gains are chargeable to corporation tax, and not capital gains tax, as is the case with an unincorporated business.

(A) Basis of assessment. A company's profits are calculated for a chargeable accounting period, which usually means the period for which the company's accounts are made up. This will normally be twelve months, ending with the company's accounting date. Unlike profits chargeable to income tax, therefore, the assessment is not made on the previous year basis. Corporation tax is payable nine months after the end of the accounting period. The effect of these rules is that tax will be payable significantly earlier than it would be if the business were not a company.

(B) Rates of tax. Corporation tax rates are fixed for financial years, which run from 1 April to 31 March in the following year. Financial years are referred to by the calendar year in which they begin; the financial year 1986 is, therefore, the year to 31 March 1987. Where a company's accounting period does not end on 31 March, and so straddles two financial years, profits are apportioned between the two years if rates change. Tax rates were fixed in the Finance Act 1984, as amended up to 31 March 1987. Rates vary according to the size of profits. The small company rate is 29%. The term 'small company' does not refer to the size of the company, but to the size of its profits. A company is 'small' for this purpose where the sum of the three following items does not exceed £100,000: (1) income chargeable to corporation tax; (2) the chargeable fraction of capital gains; and (3) franked investment income (dividends received from another company). A company which has profits in excess of £500,000 pays corporation tax at 35% (for the financial year 1986). Marginal relief is available where profits lie between £100,000 and £500,000.

(C) Corporation tax and dividends. When a company pays a dividend (or makes a distribution in kind, which will also be subject to tax), it becomes liable to pay corporation tax within fourteen days of the quarter ending 31 March, 30 June, 30 September or 31 December in which the dividend is paid. Corporation tax payable in this way is called 'advance corporation tax' or 'ACT', because the obligation to pay tax has been brought forward by the payment of the dividend. The advance payment is at the rate of $^{29}/_{71}$ of the dividend (which is equivalent to basic rate income tax on the gross amount of the dividend, plus the ACT payable on it). If a small company (paying tax at the rate of 29 per cent) distributed all its profits, its tax liability would be extinguished by the payment of ACT. If the whole profits are not distributed, or the company pays tax at a rate higher than 29%, the amount that is left after ACT has been deducted ('mainstream corporation tax') will be payable in the usual way. ACT can only be set off against mainstream tax to the extent of the company's income profits for the current year, though there are rules which allow the eventual recouping of any surplus tax paid. As a result of this system, the dividend that a shareholder receives will already have had tax deducted from it at the rate of 29 per cent; in order to avoid double taxation he will be given a tax credit of 29%, thereby discharging his liability to income tax on the dividend if he pays tax at the basic rate. If the shareholder pays higher rate tax, the credit will be off-set against his liability, and if he does not pay tax at all (because his personal allowances have not been exhausted, for example), the value of the credit will be paid to him by the Revenue.

(D) Close companies. A close company is one under the control of its directors or (broadly) five or fewer shareholders. The rules which required close companies to distribute all their profits, or otherwise face serious tax consequences, have largely been repealed with regard to trading companies. There are, however, still a few differences between the tax treatment of close companies and other companies. Benefits in kind paid to participators (unless already chargeable to income tax in the hands of the recipient) and loans made to participators, are liable to tax as if they were distributions. 'Participators' are, broadly speaking, shareholders. It should be noted that loans to directors in excess of £2,500, subject to certain limited exceptions, are prohibited (see page 262).

(E) Treatment of losses. Tax relief on losses suffered by companies is similar to that available to individuals. There are a number of ways of obtaining relief.

1. A loss may be set-off against current profits (section 177(2) of the Taxes Act). For this purpose, profits includes not only income, but also the chargeable part of capital gains.

2. A loss can be carried back against capital or trading profits for a period of time equal to the accounting period in which the loss was incurred, so long as the trade was carried on during that period (section 177(3)(3A) of the Taxes Act).

3. A loss which is not relieved against current or earlier profits can be carried forward and set off against future trading (not capital) profits of the same trade (section 177(1) of the Taxes Act).

4. A company may carry back a loss incurred during the last twelve months of trading (a 'terminal loss') for up to three years, subject to claiming relief under 1 and 2 above, first (section 178 of the Taxes Act). A terminal loss can only be set off against trading profits.

5. Capital losses may be set off against capital gains of the same accounting period. Unrelieved losses may be carried forward and set off against future capital gains. Capital losses cannot be set off against income profits.

Since a company is a separate person, the directors or shareholders cannot set off any losses which the company suffers against their own tax liability. An individual who owns an unincorporated business and also a company, can, however, off-set losses incurred by the unincorporated firm against his income from the company.

(F) Remuneration or dividends. The different tax consequences of distributing a company's profits as remuneration rather than as dividends are not as significant as they were, because of the abolition of the higher rate of tax payable on investment income and the reduction in corporation tax rates (the small company rate and the basic rate of income tax both now being 29%). Some differences still remain, however. One is that national insurance contributions are payable on remuneration, but not on dividends. Another is that remuneration is subject to PAYE, which will result in tax being payable earlier than it would be on a dividend. The payment of a dividend will result in a repayment of tax if it is paid in a year in which no taxable profit is made (but there must be profits available for distribution, see page 259). It is not possible to set off the ACT payable on the dividend against the current year's corporation tax liability, but this can be carried back to earlier years, resulting in its repayment, which will mean that the dividend will have been paid tax-free. This advantage would be lost if the amount in question were paid as remuneration. On the other hand, there will usually be a benefit in paying remuneration to a director's or shareholder's wife, who is employed in the business, since this will be earned income and so use can be made of the wife's earned income relief, or, in appropriate circumstances, the separate taxation election (see above). In addition, tax exemption on pension scheme contributions will only be available where there is a source of earned income, and future entitlements under a scheme may be adversely affected by limiting the amount of remuneration that is paid.

(G) Issue of shares to directors and employees on advantageous terms. If shares are issued to directors or employees at less than their true value, or the value of the shares is artificially reduced by subjecting them to restrictions, the difference between the price and the value of the shares may be subject to income tax. In certain circumstances, the increase in the value of the shares, even though they are not sold, may also be subject to tax. The issue of shares at an undervalue is not, therefore, an effective means of avoiding tax on rewards to directors and employees. More favourable tax treatment may be obtained if the complex requirements of an approved profit-sharing scheme are satisfied.

(H) Retention of profits. If profits are retained in the company, as opposed to being paid out as remuneration or dividends, the effect will be to increase the value of the company's assets, and therefore, of its shares. Retained profits are subject to corporation tax to the same extent as distributed profits, and the increase in the value of the company's shares means that there will be a higher capital gains tax liability on their disposal. Whether retention of profits results in an overall increase in tax liability, however, will depend on the personal circumstances of the directors and shareholders, for example, the rate at which they would pay income tax on remuneration or dividends. It should also be borne in mind that the payment of remuneration (but not dividends) may, in appropriate circumstances, mean that the company's profits fall into a lower corporation tax rate band, or might convert a profit into a loss, which will be subject to loss relief. On the other hand, the elimination of profits by the payment of remuneration will mean that there is nothing against which to carry back later losses.

Whilst benefits in kind supplied to directors and employees earning more than £8,500 per annum are taxable, there may be an advantage in the company's buying an asset for a director or employee's use, rather than paying him the money with which to buy it. This is because benefits are not subject to national insurance contributions, and there will be an overall tax saving where the director or employee pays income tax at a higher rate than the company pays corporation tax.

3. CAPITAL GAINS TAX

Capital gains tax is paid by individuals; capital gains made by companies are calculated on capital gains tax principles, but are actually charged to corporation tax. A capital gain is the profit made on the disposal of a capital asset, taking into account its cost, money spent on improving it and the cost of disposal. An amount is deducted from the profit to reflect inflation (referred to as the 'indexation allowance'). If income tax is payable on the disposal of an item (because the sale of such items is part of the business) there will not be a charge to capital gains tax too. Tax is payable on gifts as well as sales; in the case of a gift, the 'profit' is calculated on the basis of the market value of the asset. Capital gains tax is not payable on transfers on death (but inheritance tax is, see page 280). The rate of tax is 30% of the realised gain. This is also the effective rate at which capital gains made by companies are charged to corporation tax. The first £6,300 (for 1986/87) of an individual's gains each year is exempt from tax; this annual exemption does not apply to companies. A number of types of property are specifically excluded from tax. These include an individual's main residence, and business chattels where the sale proceeds do not exceed £3,000. The gains and losses made on the disposal of assets over the course of the year are aggregated to give the net chargeable gains or allowable losses for the year. Where losses exceed gains, the former can be carried forward to be set off against the next gains made. Tax due must usually be paid on 1 December after the end of the tax year. An application to pay by instalments may be made.

Reliefs

1. Roll-over relief. If the proceeds of sale of a business asset are used to acquire another business asset, liability to pay tax can usually be deferred (if so desired) until the replacement asset is disposed of, or indefinitely, if the sale proceeds are always reinvested (sections 111A and 115–119 of the Capital Gains Tax Act 1979). The new asset must be purchased twelve months before or three years after the disposal of the original asset.

2. Retirement relief. Relief is available to an individual over 60 (or someone below that age retiring because of ill-health) on the disposal of all or part of a business, interest in a partnership or share in a family trading company, up to a limit of gains of £100,000 (section 124 of the Capital Gains Tax Act 1979; sections 65, 66, and Schedule 17, Finance Act 1985). There is a proportionate reduction in the relief available where the business has not been owned for the previous ten years, or, in the case of a family company, where the taxpayer has not been a full-time working director during that period.

3. Transfer of a business to a company. The relief available in this situation is discussed below.

4. INHERITANCE TAX
(formerly Capital Transfer Tax)

Inheritance tax is charged on gifts made by individuals on death or during the seven years before death. The lifetime charge on gifts between individuals has been abolished. Liability to pay the tax is primarily on the recipient of a gift. Inheritance tax has implications for the way in which a business is owned, but it is not payable by businesses as such and so will only be discussed in brief outline. As with all tax matters, professional advice should be sought in appropriate cases.

No tax is payable unless the donor's estate exceeds £71,000 (for 1986/87). Gifts made between three and seven years from death are not charged to tax at the full rate; a gift made three years from death, for example, is charged at 80% of the death rate, and a gift made seven years from death at 20%. The full rate of tax ranges from 30% of the value of the estate, to 60% where the estate is worth more than £317,000. Transfers made more than seven years from death are not counted in calculating whether the level at which tax is payable has been reached, nor in determining what the rate of tax is. The first £3,000 of transfers in each tax year is exempt, and gifts of a value of up to £250 ('small gifts') may be made to any one person in a tax year. No tax is payable on transfers between spouses.

(A) Relief. Business property relief is available on the transfer of certain business property, to the extent that it is still owned by the first transferee on the death of the donor. The rate of relief is 50% of the value of a business, or of an interest in a partnership or of a controlling shareholding in a company. If the shares of a husband and wife added together give them control, each is treated as having control for this purpose. Relief is only available at the rate of 30% on the transfer of a minority shareholding, and on the transfer of plant and machinery used by a company in which the owner of the plant and machinery has a controlling shareholding, or used by a partnership in which he was a partner.

(B) Tax planning. There is obviously an advantage in disposing of a business, or of an interest in a business, more than seven years before the death of the owner. If the business is incorporated, it will be easier to transfer the owner's interest progressively, enabling him to make use of the annual exemption on transfers not exceeding £3,000, and of the 'small gifts' exemption. It should be borne in mind, however, that once control of the company is lost, the rate of business property relief on subsequent transfers will be reduced.

5. TRANSFER OF A BUSINESS TO A COMPANY

(A) Income tax assessment on transferor. If a sole trader or partnership decides to form a company and transfer the business to it, the trade of the sole trader or partnership will cease for income tax purposes, which means that the closing year rules will apply (see above). The effect of this will be an increased income tax liability where profits are rising, though this can generally be reduced by making the transfer after the end of the tax year, rather than before, since this will maximise the profits that escape assessment. Provision should, nevertheless, be made for the payment of what might be a considerable amount of additional income tax before the business is transferred.

(B) Loss relief. If there are any unrelieved trading losses, these cannot be carried forward and off-set against the company's profits. They can, however, be used to give relief against the ex-sole trader or partner's income from the company, either in the form of directors' remuneration or dividends (in that order), provided that the business was sold to the company mainly in exchange for shares and the shares are still held when the loss is set off (section 172 of the Taxes Act).

(C) Capital allowances. The transfer of a business to a company constitutes a disposal of the business's assets. Plant and machinery will be deemed to be disposed of at market value, and so if the capital allowances claimed on those assets exceed the amount by which they have fallen in value, a balancing charge will be payable. This can usually be avoided if the sole trader or partner, and the company, elect that the business should not be treated as discontinued for capital allowance purposes (Schedule 8(13) to the Finance Act 1971).

(D) Capital gains tax. Subject to what will be said below, the transfer of a business to a company will constitute a disposal for capital gains tax purposes. Plant and machinery are unlikely to be valued at more than cost, so there will be no chargeable gain, but freehold and leasehold property, and goodwill, will be treated as being transferred at their market value, and hence there might be a considerable tax liability. There are three ways, however, in which this liability might be mitigated.

1. Roll-over relief on transfer (section 123 of the Capital Gains Tax Act 1979). Relief is available where a business (which means all the assets, though cash need not be handed over) is transferred to a company in exchange for shares in the company issued to the former owner(s) of the business. Where the payment is entirely in shares, the whole tax liability is deferred until the shares are eventually disposed of (and other reliefs, such as retirement relief, might be available at this time). Proportionate relief is given where payment is only partly in shares (the rest, for example, being in cash).

2. Retention of assets. If the original proprietor retains ownership of business assets, for example, the premises, but allows the business to use them either free or for rent, there will be no charge to tax because there will have been no disposal. This may mean that roll-over relief is lost on the assets which are transferred (because it is a condition of relief that all assets be transferred), but this might be considered acceptable in order to avoid 'double taxation'. This arises where an asset is transferred to a company and later disposed of at a profit; the profit is a chargeable gain, and it will also cause the value of the company's shares to increase, the increase being chargeable to tax as well, when the shares are eventually disposed of. It may be possible to obtain roll-over relief, and at the same time retain some assets, if those assets are taken out of the business before the business is transferred. The Revenue may challenge this, however, as being an artificial device to avoid tax. Unless precautions are taken, retaining business assets on a transfer to a company may also endanger roll-over relief on the replacement of the retained asset, retirement relief, and business property relief against inheritance tax.

3. Gifts of business assets (section 126 of the Capital Gains Tax Act 1979). If an asset is given to a company or sold to it at less than its market value by the previous owner of the business, the capital gains tax liability can be held over until the asset is disposed of by the company. The tax will then be payable by the company, not the transferor. The company's acquisition cost will be treated as being the cost at which the previous owner acquired the asset in the case of a gift; the sale price to the company will be the company's acquisition cost where the company buys the asset at an undervalue. This will, however, have the effect of reducing the allowance for inflation when the company comes to sell the asset.

(E) Stamp duty. Stamp duty is payable on written instruments by which property is transferred. If property can be transferred without the use of a document, no duty will be payable. Duty can, therefore, be avoided on the transfer of stock, plant and machinery, but it will be difficult to escape duty on freehold and leasehold property (assuming that these are transferred) and goodwill. Duty is payable, in most cases, at the rate of 1% of the sale price, and the liability to pay it is on the transferee.

(F) Capital duty. Capital duty will be payable by the company on the shares it issues in return for the assets transferred to it. The rate is 1% of the value of those assets.

(G) Value added tax. If the business is registered for VAT, an application should be made for its VAT registration number to be transferred to the company. No VAT liability will usually arise on the incorporation of a business, and the company will take over the previous business's VAT position.

6. SOLE TRADER/PARTNERSHIP VERSUS COMPANY

Non-tax considerations, in particular, the increased administrative burden, should be borne in mind in considering whether to operate the business as a company. The following is a brief summary of the main tax advantages/disadvantages of the corporate form.

(A) Rates of tax. Sole traders/partners are charged to income tax on profits, whether or not they are taken out of the business. Where profits are such that higher rate income tax would be payable, there is an advantage in operating as a company, since profits retained in the business will only be taxed at 29% (where the small pany rate is applicable). Retention of profits may, however, have the effect of increasing capital gains tax payable on a disposal of shares in the company. Where both spouses are involved in the business and incomes are high enough to warrant making the wife's earnings election, the lowering of tax that can be achieved by each being a partner is also a factor to bear in mind (see above).

(B) Time of payment. The income of sole traders and partners is taxed on a preceding year basis (an advantage where profits are rising) and, depending on the accounting date, there will be a gap of between 9 and 21 months between earning profits and having to pay tax on them. Companies pay tax much sooner, and director's remuneration is subject to almost immediate taxation through the PAYE scheme.

(C) Losses. The rules applicable to the tax treatment of losses are different for companies from those applicable to individuals. Broadly, the company rules are less favourable, especially in the early years, since losses cannot be carried back to the period before the company was formed, whereas an individual can off-set them against income which was earned before the business was commenced.

(D) Capital gains. A disadvantage of incorporation is that gains are effectively taxed twiced if profits are retained in the company, since corporation tax is charged on the profits when they are earned, and then the increased value of the company' shares will be subject to capital gains tax when they are disposed of.

(E) Inheritance Tax. The company form permits more flexible tax planning, since an interest in a company can be disposed of more gradually than one in an unincorporated business.

(F) Pensions. The rules concerning contributions to pension schemes are more favourable with respect to companies. Self-employed persons are entitled to relief on their earned income on pension premiums of between 17.5% and 32.5% of profits, depending on age. A company which has its own pension scheme, on the other hand, can claim relief on premiums of any amount. Contributions (if any) of employees (which includes directors) are also deductible from their earned income.

7. VALUE ADDED TAX

Value added tax is a tax on expenditure by consumers. It is charged on the supply of goods and services in the United Kingdom, if the supply is a 'taxable supply', made to a 'taxable person'. The tax is generally borne by consumers, not by businesses, but businesses are responsible for administering it. A business pays tax on taxable supplies made to it (known as 'input tax'), and charges tax on taxable supplies made by it (known as 'output tax'). At the end of a tax period the business calculates the difference between the input and the output tax. If there is a surplus of output tax, the surplus is paid to Customs and Excise; if input tax exceeds output tax, this is recovered from Customs and Excise. The eventual consumer purchaser of goods, however, cannot reclaim tax paid on them.

(A) Taxable persons – registration. If the taxable turnover of a business exceeds £20,500 in total over four consecutive quarters (this is the figure for the year beginning 19 March 1986), the business must be registered for VAT. The local VAT office should be notified within ten days of the end of the quarter in which the turnover limit is reached (on Form VAT 1). Registration must also be obtained if turnover in a particular quarter exceeds £7,000, unless Customs and Excise can be persuaded that turnover in that and the next three quarters will not exceed £20,500. On registration, a certificate of registration will be issued, showing the business's VAT number. If a business which is required to register fails to give notice to this effect, it will still eventually have to pay tax from the date on which registration should have taken place. By this time, of course, it may no longer be possible to recover tax from customers. There are also penalties for failure to register. Input tax on goods and services obtained before registration for the purposes of the business can be deducted from output tax after registration. An application for registration to be cancelled can be made where it is possible to show that turnover in the next twelve months will be £19,500 or less. This can also be done where the business has been registered for at least two years, turnover in each year has been less than £20,500, and there are no reasonable grounds for believing that it will reach that amount within the next tax year. Customs and Excise must be notified within 10 days if the form of the business changes (for example, from sole trader to partnership, or on incorporation).

These changes will necessitate a new registration, or the transfer of an existing registration. Other changes, such as to the name of the business or its address, or the composition of a partnership, must be notified within 21 days.

(B) Taxable supplies. Apart from items which are specifically exempt, all supplies of goods and services are taxable supplies. Exempt supplies broadly consist of the supply of land, insurance, finance, and health and educational services. A business which only makes exempt supplies may not be registered. Goods which are taken out of the business for use by the proprietors are chargeable to tax on the cost of the goods. No distinction is made between the supply of revenue and capital items: the sale of capital equipment, for instance, is equally a taxable supply. Generally, secondhand goods are taxable on the full selling price, but there are special schemes for certain items, such as cars and antiques, whereby VAT is charged only on the difference in value between cost and the selling price.

(C) Business. It should be noted that whilst VAT is only charged on supplies made by a business, 'business' is widely defined for this purpose. A club which provides facilities for its members, for example, will be treated as a business as far as VAT is concerned.

(D) Rates of tax. There are currently two rates of tax – the standard rate of 15%, and the zero rate (section 16 and Schedule 5 of the Value Added Tax Act 1983). The main zero-rated items are:
(1) food (but not food supplied in catering, which includes hot take-away food, and 'non-essential' food, such as ice cream and crisps); (2) books; (3) construction work (but not repairs, maintenance, alterations etc); (4) children's clothing and footwear; (5) fuel and power (but not petrol); (6) transport (but not taxis or hire cars); (7) drugs on prescription; (8) exports.

As with exempt supplies, no tax is paid on zero-rated supplies, but there are two important differences. First, a zero-rated supply is counted in determining whether a business's turnover has reached the limit at which the business becomes taxable and the person must register. Secondly, the making of exempt supplies may affect the ability of the business to recover input tax. A business which only makes exempt supplies cannot recover any of the input tax which it has paid on supplies made to it. Where exempt supplies only constitute a small proportion of turnover, the business may reclaim all input tax (Statutory Instrument 1985/886 Part V); if exempt supplies are more than a 'small proportion' of turnover, only a percentage of input tax will be recoverable.

(E) Voluntary registration. Even though a business's turnover is below the limit at which registration is compulsory, it may prove beneficial to register, since this will enable input tax to be recovered from Customs and Excise. It must be borne in mind, however, that once registered, the business will also be required to charge VAT. This means that voluntary registration will not usually be advisable where the business mainly sells to the public, since prices will be higher as a result of the VAT which the business must now charge, and retail customers will not be able to recover it. The burden that administering VAT will impose on the business should also be considered before applying for voluntary registration. It should be stressed that the acceptance of the voluntary registration is at the discretion of Customs and Excise; registration will not be allowed unless the trade is on a significant scale and the business would otherwise be at a serious disadvantage as a result of its inability to recover input tax.

(F) Tax invoices (Statutory Instrument 1985/886). Where a standard rated supply is made to another taxable person, a tax invoice must be issued within 30 days and a copy kept. The invoice must contain the following information: (1) identifying number; (2) date of supply ('tax point'); (3) supplier's name, address, and VAT registration number; (4) customer's name and address; (5) type of supply (sale, hire purchase, etc); (6) description of goods or services supplied; (7) total amount payable, excluding VAT, and rate of tax on each type of goods; (8) rate of any cash discount given; (9) total tax payable. If the supplier is a retailer, a tax invoice need only be provided if the customer asks for it, and if the price, including tax, is £50 or less, not so much information need be given (only items (2), (3), (6) and (7), above).

(G) Tax point (sections 4 and 5 of the Value Added Tax Act 1983). The usual tax point is the date when the goods are delivered or otherwise made available to the customer, or when the services are performed, unless an invoice is issued earlier or payment is made in advance, in which case the tax point will be the earlier date. If goods or services are invoiced within fourteen days of supply, the date of the invoice will be the tax point. It is important to know what the tax point is because this will determine into which quarterly period the supply will fall.

(H) Books and records (Schedule 7 of the Value Added Tax Act 1983). Taxable persons must keep full records of all transactions affecting the business's VAT position. These include supplies of goods and services to the business on which VAT is charged, supplies by the business (including zero-rated and exempt supplies), and taxable supplies for private use. There are special schemes for retailers which avoid the need for every separate transaction to be recorded. Tax invoices on supplies to the business must be kept – these are evidence of input tax paid by the business – and copies of invoices issued by the business must also be retained. The business must keep a VAT account, showing the results of each tax period. Customs and Excise officers are likely to make periodic visits (at intervals of between one and three years) to check the adequacy of records and that VAT is being properly calculated. Penalties can be imposed where records are inadequate. All records must be kept for at least six years.

(I) Tax returns. A tax period is normally three months. A business which makes a significant proportion of zero-rated supplies may apply for a one month period in order to gain the benefit of monthly repayments, but the burden of completing additional tax returns should be borne in mind. A VAT return must be made within one month of the end of each tax period, on form VAT 100. It is possible to have the quarterly return dates altered to coincide with the business's accounting period. Tax is payable at the same time that the return is due. Late payment may result in a 'default surcharge' where there has been another late submission within the previous twelve months. The Finance Act 1985 has imposed additional penalties for the sending of late or inaccurate returns.

(J) Appeals. Where a taxpayer disputes the amount of tax payable, or objects to the way he has been treated by Customs and Excise with respect to a variety of other matters (for example, cancellation of registration), he may appeal to an independent VAT tribunal within 30 days of the decision in question. There is a right of appeal from a tribunal's decision to the Courts.

8. NATIONAL INSURANCE CONTRIBUTIONS

A variety of State benefits are paid to individuals in return for compulsory contributions by them and, where they are employees, also by their employer. Self-employed persons pay two types of national insurance contribution (unless they are exempt), namely Class 2 and Class 4 contributions.

(A) Class 2 contributions (section 7 of the Social Security Act 1975). These are payable weekly at a flat rate. Contributors are entitled to most forms of contributory benefit, except unemployment benefit, the earnings-related supplement to retirement pension, invalidity pension and widow's benefit. Payment is either by buying a special stamp from a post office (which is then stuck on a contribution card) or by direct debit. The rate for 1986/87 is £3.50 per week.

(B) Class 2 exemptions. There are a number of exemptions from the obligation to pay Class 2 contributions. The most important are as follows.
1. Men over 65 and women over 60 are exempt.
2. Contributions need not be paid in respect of a week for the whole of which the contributor was incapable of work or was receiving sickness or similar benefits or maternity allowance.
3. A person with 'small earnings' who has obtained a certificate of exemption is exempt. 'Small earnings' for 1986/87 are net earnings of £1,925 or less. Application should be made on form CF10, obtainable from the Department of Health and Social Security.
4. A person who is not ordinarily self-employed is exempt. Someone earning less than £800 in a tax year from part-time self-employment will be treated as not ordinarily self-employed and hence need not apply for a certificate of exemption.

(C) Class 4 contributions (section 9 of the Social Security Act 1975). Payment of Class 4 contributions does not give rise to any additional entitlement to benefits; they are simply a way of making the self-employed pay their share of the cost of the social security system. They are payable at a percentage rate of profits which are chargeable to income tax under Schedule D. For 1986/87, income of between £4,150 and £13,780 is charged at a rate of 6.3%. Below the lower limit there is no liability to Class 4 contributions and there is no additional liability above the upper limit. Half the amount paid as Class 4 contributions is deductible from total income in calculating income tax liability. The contributions are collected by the Inland Revenue at the same time as income tax for the relevent year.

(D) Class 4 exemptions. The main exemptions are for men over 65 and women over 60, and for persons who are not ordinarily self-employed (see above). Someone who is both an employee and self-employed may, in certain circumstances, be able to defer Class 2 and Class 4 contributions.

(E) Company directors. Directors are not self-employed, and so they do not pay Class 2 or Class 4 contributions. They are classified as employees, and so, as with other employees, Class 1 contributions are payable both by the director and the employing company. Directors' remuneration is also subject to PAYE.

9. TAKING ON EMPLOYEES

A business which has employees must pay employer's national insurance contributions with respect to each employee (unless the employee is exempt), and operate the Pay as You Earn (PAYE) and statutory sick pay schemes.

(A) Employer's national insurance contributions (sections 2 and 4 of the Social Security Act 1975). Class 1 contributions are payable both by the employee and the employer, unless the employee is exempt. The main ground for exemption is that weekly earnings are £35.50 or less (for 1986/87). The rates with respect to the employer's contribution are on a graduated scale, starting at 5% of gross pay and rising to 10.45%. Employees' rates go from 5 to 9%, with a maximum weekly contribution of £23.85. Reduced rates are payable by employers and employees where the employee has contracted out of the earnings-related element of the State retirement scheme.

(B) PAYE. Income tax must be deducted from the wages and salaries of all employees each time they are paid. The Inland Revenue supplies the employer with a tax code for each employee, together with a set of tax tables, which will enable the employer to calculate the amount to be deducted. National insurance contributions are also deducted in the same way. The amounts collected must be sent to the Inland Revenue within fourteen days of the end of each tax month (by the 19th of each month). At the end of every tax year, all employees must be given a form P60, detailing pay and tax deducted for the year. A form P35, which summarises tax and national insurance contributions in respect of all employees, must be sent to the Revenue.

(C) Statutory sick pay. Employers must pay statutory sick pay to employees where the absence does not exceed eight weeks in a given tax year. There are three flat rates of sick pay, depending on the employee's average weekly earnings. Sick pay is subject to deductions for income tax and national insurance contributions. Employers can recover amounts paid as statutory sick pay, and national insurance contributions paid in respect of it, by deducting the gross sum from the monthly national insurance contributions that they pay as part of the PAYE scheme. Records of periods of sickness absence and amounts of sick pay awarded must be kept by the employer.

(D) Further information. The above discussion of employer's national insurance contributions, PAYE and statutory sick pay constitutes only a brief outline. Detailed information is available in booklets published by the Inland Revenue in respect of PAYE, and the Department of Health and Social Security with regard to national insurance and sick pay.

1. INSURANCE

A number of the risks incidental to running a business can be guarded against through insurance. An efficient broker will be able to advise on the types of cover that are available, and to arrange insurance in appropriate markets at a competitive rate. He will also be of assistance in processing claims under the policy. The relationship between a person taking out insurance and the insurer is said to be one of 'utmost good faith'. This means that full and accurate disclosure must be made to the insurer of all matters relevant to the risk that is being insured, both when the policy is initially taken out and when it is renewed. Innocent non-disclosure of a material fact, even if it appears trivial, can result in the policy being invalid. A clause in the policy may, in addition, impose a duty on the insured to disclose, during the currency of the policy, any matters which might cause the risk which is being insured against to increase. With respect to a fire policy, for example, the business may be required to notify the insurer that it has started to deal in inflammable materials. An insurer may also be able to deny liability if the terms of the policy are not strictly adhered to. For example, if it is agreed that a vehicle will be kept in a garage overnight but this is not done, there may be no cover if the vehicle is stolen, even though failure to keep it in a garage did not contribute to the theft. A contract of insurance will not be effective until the insured person's offer (usually contained in a proposal form) has been accepted by the insurer. Temporary cover, however, can be given on the basis of a 'cover note', which will normally incorporate the terms set out in one of the insurer's standard policies.

(i) Types of Cover
(A) Business premises. Premises can be insured against fire, and the policy may usually be extended, on the payment of an additional premium, to cover such events as explosions, overflowing water tanks, and malicious damage. It will often be necessary to insure leasehold, as well as freehold, premises. The lease may impose an express obligation on the tenant to insure, or to repair the premises, in the event of damage. In each of these cases the insurance will need to cover the whole value of the buildings. Where the tenant is not under an obligation to insure or repair, the lease may nevertheless oblige him to continue paying rent even though the premises are damaged or destroyed. In this case, insurance should be taken out in respect of the rent payable for the remainder of the term of the lease. Where equipment and stock of significant value are kept on the premises these should also be insured against damage. Cover can be obtained for theft of property where the premises have been forcibly entered, but it is unlikely that it will be possible to insure against shoplifting. The insurance company will probably insist that certain precautions against theft, for instance the installation of a burglar alarm, be taken.

(B) Goods and money. It is possible to insure goods owned by the business, even though they have not yet been delivered, for example, where they are still in the seller's warehouse. Damage or decay resulting from adverse conditions can be covered, but normal wear and tear and inherent vice (for instance, the death of animals from natural causes) will be excluded. Loss of money can be insured, for example, against it being stolen from an employee whilst in transit.

(C) Fidelity cover. Cover can be obtained in respect of losses caused to the business arising out of dishonesty on the part of an employee or partner. Negligence will only be covered if specifically mentioned.

(D) Personnel. It is possible to take out insurance against death or incapacity of the proprietors of the business or key personnel. Payment under such a policy would, for example, enable a firm to buy out of the interest of a deceased partner or employ someone to manage the business.

(E) Motor vehicles. It is a criminal offence to drive a motor vehicle on the public highway without proper insurance. The minimum insurance which is legally necessary is cover for causing death or personal injury to others. It is usual, however, to have insurance which goes beyond this and extends at least to liability for causing damage to the property of others (third party cover). Other policies will give cover against fire and theft and a comprehensive policy will cover all the above events and also accidental damage to the vehicle.

(F) Liability insurance. There is a wide variety of circumstances in which the operators of a business may become liable to the public or employees. These include liability arising out of the occupation of business premises, for example, injury to customers or their property which results from negligence on the part of the business, loss caused to third parties as a result of the dishonesty of employees, and damage caused to members of the public owing to defects in the business's products. Public liability insurance normally covers most forms of liability to third parties, but does not extend to employees. The Employers' Liability (Compulsory Insurance) Act 1969 imposes an obligation on all employers (subject to certain limited exceptions, e g where only members of the family are employed) to take out suitable insurance with respect to liability for injury to employees. The certificate of insurance must be displayed at the business premises.

(ii) Policy Terms

The terms on which policies are based vary considerably; it is important to read through the wording before entering into the insurance contract to make sure that cover is adequate. A policy insuring premises or goods, for example, may not extend to consequential loss, that is, additional loss which results from physical damage. It is important to check whether loss of profits, or rental income, where appropriate, would be compensated for if the premises burnt down, for instance. As well as liability for wear and tear and inherent vice being excluded, as mentioned above, it is likely that there will be no cover for damage caused by riot or civil commotion, unless specific cover is agreed. Many policies provide for what is referred to as an 'excess'. This is an amount, usually with regard to each claim made, for which the insurer will not be liable. With respect to a policy covering theft, for example, it might be provided that the insured person must meet the first £10 of the claim himself, or the figure may be expressed as a percentage of the claim. Acceptance of a large excess will probably bring about a reduction in premiums, but will obviously diminish the usefulness of the policy. The basis on which the claim will be settled should also be noted. If

the policy only provides for the payment of the value of an item at the time of its loss or destruction, the insured may receive considerably less than what it will cost to buy a replacement. A 'new for old' policy, on the other hand, will enable the insured to claim the full replacement cost. In some cases property will be valued at the time the insurance contract is made, and the agreed value stated in the policy. This will then be the amount which can be claimed in the event of loss, even though it no longer represents the value of the item concerned.

2. COPYRIGHTS, PATENTS, DESIGNS AND TRADE MARKS

If a business sells a product which it has invented, it will obviously be in its interests to prevent others from marketing a similar product. A distinctive design, or the goodwill attached to a trade name, are similarly assets of the business which are worthy of protection. The law provides a number of different ways of safeguarding these interests; some apply automatically, whereas others are dependent on registration.

(i) Copyright

Copyright is capable of subsisting in literary and artistic works, including sound recordings, films and television programmes (Copyright Act 1956). The general principle is that it is possible to have copyright in works which are of 'artistic craftsmanship'. A wide range of products could come within this category, for example, furniture, crockery or toys. It must be intended that the item be of some artistic merit, and this aim, at least to an extent, must be realised. Preliminary designs and drawings, on the other hand, will be protected even though they have no artistic merit.

Copyright will subsist in a work without formality – there is no need to go through any registration procedures, or to state on the work that it is copyright material. The latter is often done, however, by marking the work with the symbol © and stating the name of the copyright owner and the year of creation. This is necessary to give protection in some overseas countries. The period of protection is the lifetime of the creator, plus 50 years. The effect of copyright is to give the copyright owner the exclusive right to reproduce the work. Copyright is infringed if an unauthorised copy is made which is substantially the same as the original. Unlike the protection afforded by a patent, however, there will be no infringement if someone independently arrives at the same idea and expresses it in a very similar form. There is a range of remedies for breach of copyright, both civil and criminal. Thus, the copyright owner can bring an action for damages, which may be calculated on the basis of the profits that the copyright owner has lost as a result of the infringement. The copyright owner might, for example, have lost sales, or his reputation may have been damaged through the availability of inferior copies. Alternatively, the infringer may be required to hand over the profits he has made as a result of infringement. An additional civil remedy is that of an injunction – an application can be made for the Court to order infringement to stop, or to require the infringer to hand over infringing copies or let the copyright owner search his premises for them. Criminal penalties can he imposed where infringement is by way of trade.

(ii) Patents

A patent is a document which recognises that a person has exclusive rights to an invention. In order to take out a patent it is necessary to make a formal application to the Patent Office in London. This can be a highly technical matter and advice should be obtained from a professional patent agent. The Patent Act 1977 lays down four requirements that an invention must satisfy in order to be patentable.

(1) The invention must be new. This means not only that the invention must not have been patented before, but also that it must never have been publicly disclosed. Someone wishing to take out a patent should, therefore, keep his invention secret until an application is filed.

(2) The invention must involve an inventive step. An inventive step will not be involved if the invention is merely a development of an existing product or process which would be obvious to someone with a good knowledge of the relevant subject.

(3) The invention must be capable of industrial application. This means that it must be something which can be made by, or used in, some form of productive process.

(4) The invention must not be an 'excluded' invention. A literary or artistic work, a scientific theory, or a business method, are excluded inventions. Purely intellectual conceptions, therefore, as opposed to the practical embodiment of an idea, are not patentable.

(A) Protection given by a patent. It is not necessary to obtain a patent in order to exploit an invention; its purpose is to prevent others from making use of an idea without the consent of the inventor. If a business does not patent an invention, however, there is always a risk that someone might, and this will then prevent the business from trading in it. The person who has taken out the patent (the 'patentee') has, in effect, a monopoly right to the invention during the period of the patent, which will be up to twenty years from the date of making the patent application. Annual fees will have to be paid to keep the patent alive from after the end of the fourth year of registration. A British patent will only be effective in the UK. It is possible to obtain a European patent which will be effective in selected European countries. In addition, an international application can be made under the Patent Cooperation Treaty. This will be of assistance in obtaining individual registrations in the large number of countries which are signatories to the treaty.

It is open to a patentee to sell his invention or to give permission to someone else to exploit it for a period of time, by way of a licence, in return for royalties. A person who makes a patented item without the consent of the patentee will commit an infringement, as will someone who sells, uses or merely keeps the item. This will be so whether or not the infringer knows of the patent, and even though the infringer has invented the item in question quite independently, without copying. A patentee can obtain an injunction to prevent further infringement, and can claim for damages. Damages may be calculated on the basis of a notional royalty for each infringing item, or in accordance with what the patentee would have charged the infringer for a licence to exploit the invention, as well as on the more conventional basis of loss of profits. An infringer can also be required to hand over the profits he has made from infringement.

(B) How to obtain a patent. Obtaining a patent is a lengthy and complex process. The first stage is to make an application on the appropriate forms, which can be obtained from the Patent Office in London. (The Patent Office, the address of which is 25 Southampton Buildings, London WC2 1AY, also issue a number of useful booklets concerning patent applications.) The application must be accompanied by a full description of the invention, together with the filing fee (currently £10). If the forms are properly filled in, the application will be given a filing date, which will give the application priority over any subsequent applications with respect to the same invention. Within the next twelve months further forms must be filed; these include 'claims' and an abstract of the invention. The 'claims' are a description of the invention which define precisely what will be protected if the application is granted. The Patent Office will also make a search of existing patent specifications (for which a fee, currently £75, will be charged), since these may show that the invention is not new, or is obvious. The next stage is for the invention to be published, which means that anyone who wishes to examine the application will be able to do so. The final stage is that of examination by the Patent Office (there is another form and another fee, currently £90). Amendments to the application may need to be made as a result of this. If the requirements of the Patent Act 1977 are then satisfied, a patent will be granted.

(iii) Registered Designs

Industrial designs can be protected under the Registered Designs Acts 1949-1961. The term 'industrial' means that the article in question must be one which is manufactured in quantity. A 'design' is the outward appearance of an article, for example its shape and any ornamentation or pattern applied to it. The function of an article, the way it is made or the materials from which it is constructed are not part of the design, and so cannot be protected as such. In order to be registerable, a design must be new. It must not, therefore, have been revealed to anyone before the application for registration, except in confidence. Unless a design makes a materially different appeal to the eye from other articles of a similar type it will not be considered to be new. There is some overlap between the protection given by registration and the automatic protection given by copyright. When a design is registered, however, a similar design cannot be used by anyone else even though it was created without reference to the registered design; copyright can only be infringed by a direct copy. It may also be wise to register a design when there is some doubt as to whether the article is of a type in which copyright is capable of subsisting. It may not, for example, be of sufficient merit to constitute a work of 'artistic craftsmanship' (see above). Once registered, a design will normally be protected for five years, and on application, registration can be renewed for two further periods of five years each. The usual civil remedies are available for infringement.

How to obtain a registration. Registration is obtained by making an application on the appropriate form, accompanied by a representation or specimen of the design, and an explanation of why the design is novel. A fee must also be paid (in most cases, £40). If all the formalities have been complied with, and a search of the Designs Registry and other sources of information does not reveal that the design is not sufficiently novel, a certificate of registration will, in due course, be issued. The Designs Registry is a branch of the Patent Office. In order to gain international protection it is necessary to register a design in each country in which protection is sought.

(iv) Trade Marks

The law relating to trade marks is contained in the Trade Marks Act 1938. A 'trade mark' is a 'device, brand, heading, label, ticket, name, signature, word, letter, numeral, or any combination thereof' which is used to indicate a connection between goods and the person who has the right to the mark. To be protected under the Act (but see Passing off, below), a mark must be registered in the Register of Trade Marks, which is administered by the Patent Office. The Register is divided into two parts, Part A and Part B. Registration in either part gives the registered proprietor the exclusive right to mark, but the proprietor of a Part B mark will not be able to obtain relief if the defendant can show that the use of the mark is not likely to decieve, or be taken as indicating that there is a connection between the goods and the proprietor of the mark. To be registerable under Part A a mark must be distinctive of the proprietor's goods, and contain or consist of at least one of the following:

1. the name of a company, individual or firm, represented in a particular manner;
2. the signature of the applicant for registration or a predecessor in business;
3. an invented word or words;
4. a word or words having no direct reference to the character or quality of the goods, and not being a geographical name or surname;
5. any other distinctive mark; a name, signature, or word other than such as fall within 1 to 4 above is not registerable, except on evidence of its distinctiveness.

A Part B mark is one which is capable of distinguishing goods as being of the proprietor, but which does not yet have this effect. In other words, a Part B mark is one which is not associated in the public mind with the proprietor's goods, but it is hoped that it will become so in the course of use, at which point application can be made for registration in Part A. Registration lasts for seven years initially, but this can be renewed for successive periods of 14 years. Application for registration must be made on the prescribed form. The usual civil remedies are available for infringement.

(v) Passing Off

A civil action will lie where a trader markets his goods in such a way as to create the impression that they are the goods of another trader, thereby 'cashing in' on the latter's goodwill. There are a number of ways in which a false impression of this kind can be created. One is by a straightforward statement to the effect that the goods are manufactured by the plaintiff. Passing off may also be committed by trading under the same name as the plaintiff, if the business is of a similar kind, such that confusion is likely to result. Carrying on business in one's own name, however, is usually unobjectionable, even if this does give rise to some confusion. Use of a distinctive description or trade name which is strongly associated with the plaintiff's products (for example, 'Yorkshire Relish') can constitute passing off, but no complaint can be made about words which merely describe the function or characteristics of a product (for example, 'vacuum cleaner' or 'shredded wheat'). A passing off action is a useful supplement to the other forms of protection discussed above. It might be used, for example, where a new company is formed with a name confusingly similar to that of the plaintiff. Use of someone else's trade mark can also amount to passing off, even though the mark is not registered or is otherwise invalid. Similarly, imitating the appearance of the plaintiff's goods might be actionable on this basis, even though no action for breach of copyright or infringement of a registered design would be available. Similarity of appearance which merely results from similarity of function does not amount to passing off, but the incorporation of decorative or other non-functional characteristics which make the product look like the plaintiff's can give rise to an action. Where passing off is proved to have occurred, an injunction and damages are available.

Where a trader applies a false description to his goods he may commit an offence under the Trade Descriptions Act 1968. If a business discovers that its interests are being damaged by the use of misleading descriptions by another trader, it can report the matter to the Trading Standards Department of the local Weights and Measures Authority, who are responsible for conducting prosecutions.

A seller must not misdescribe in his advertising the goods or services which he is offering, nor should an advertisement contain material which is obscene, racially or sexually discriminatory, or defamatory. With regard to the last of these, it is possible to slander goods, as well as a person. Thus, if a trader compares his goods in an advertisement with the goods of another supplier, the latter's products must not be disparaged in a way which is untrue, since otherwise a civil action for 'slander of goods' will lie. It is permissible to make adverse comparisons, but only if this is done accurately.

(i) Offer or Invitation to Treat?

A legally binding contract comes into existence when one party has made an offer which has been accepted by the other. Once this has happened, a party can only get out of the contract if the other party consents, and failure to comply with the contract can result in an action for breach. The general rule is that an advertisement does not constitute an offer, but instead is an 'invitation to treat', in other words, an encouragement to a potential customer to make an offer. If it were otherwise, a contract would come into existence as soon as a customer expressed an intention to buy the advertised goods, which could create difficulties for the seller, for example where the goods in question are sold out.

(ii) Misrepresentation

A misrepresentation is a statement of fact which is untrue. If a customer relies on an advertisement which contains a misrepresentation, and buys the advertiser's goods, he will usually be able to claim his money back or damages. A misrepresentation should be distinguished from what lawyers call a 'mere puff', which is not actionable. This is a statement extolling the virtues of the seller's goods, but which does not refer to verifiable facts which are intended to be taken seriously. The assertion that the advertiser's washing powder washes 'whiter than white', for instance, is of this character. Misrepresentations involve a more definite statement of fact, for example that a car is new, or that a washing machine is in perfect working order. A

misrepresentation will be actionable even though it was not the main reason why the purchaser entered into the contract, so long as it was one of the reasons. A purchaser to whom a misrepresentation has been made is entitled to return the goods and demand his money back (to 'rescind' the contract). He may lose this right if he cannot return the goods in substantially the condition in which he received them, or if he delays in returning the goods, or otherwise acts in such a way that it appears that he intends to retain them. The purchaser will also have a right to damages if the seller did not believe the misrepresentation to be true, or made it without taking reasonable care. Damages will be useful if the purchaser wishes to retain the goods, despite the misrepresentation, enabling him to obtain compensation for the fact that the goods are not as valuable as he was led to believe. It is possible that in some circumstances a statement in an advertisement will be treated as a term of the contract. If the term is held to have been breached, for example because the goods do not comply with the promised specification, the purchaser will be entitled to damages even though the statement was made honestly and with reasonable care. It may also be possible to return the goods and claim a refund in some situations.

(iii) Trade Descriptions Act

As well as civil liability, the inclusion of misleading information in an advertisement can give rise to criminal prosecution, under the Trade Descriptions Act 1968. The Act prohibits false trade descriptions, false statements about services, accommodation or facilities and misleading information about prices.

(iv) False Trade Descriptions

A trade description with respect to goods is an indication, direct or indirect, and by whatever means, of any of the following matters:
1. quantity, size or gauge;
2. method of manufacture, production, processing or reconditioning (e g home-made);
3. composition (e g sterling silver);
4. fitness for purpose, strength, performance, behaviour or accuracy (e g showerproof);

5. any physical characteristics not included in the preceding paragraph;
6. testing by any person and the results thereof (e g MOT tested);
7. approval by any person or conformity with the type approved by any person;
8. place or date of manufacture, production, processing or reconditioning:
9. person by whom manufactured, produced, processed or reconditioned;
10. other history, including previous ownership or use (e g government surplus).

Only a person buying and selling goods who makes a false trade description in the course of a business can be prosecuted. The offence is committed both by applying a false description to goods, and also selling goods to which a false description has already been applied, for example, by the manufacturer. A false description is 'applied' to goods if it is used in a way likely to be taken as referring to the goods. Thus, information contained in advertisements, circulars, catalogues and price lists is caught by the Act, as is information which is attached to goods or their wrapping or containers. The description must be 'false to a material degree', which means that the error must be sufficiently serious that is could be regarded as inducing a purchase, though it is not necessary to show that any particular purchase has been induced by it. A statement will also be treated as false, even though it is literally true, if it is materially misleading. For example, it may be true that a car has run at the stated miles per gallon, but if this could not be achieved under ordinary motoring conditions, the statement can result in prosecution.

(v) Statements as to Services, Accommodation or Facilities
Misdescribing services etc will, in appropriate circumstances, constitute an offence. False statements must not be made as to any of the following:
(1) the provision in the course of any trade or business of any services, accommodation or facilities;
(2) the nature of any services, accommodation or facilities provided in the case of any trade or business;
(3) the time at which, manner in which or persons by whom any services, accommodation or facilties are so provided;
(4) the examination, approval or evaluation by

any person of any services, accommodation or facilities so provides;
(5) the location or amenities of any accommodation so provided.

A picture can constitute a false statement for this purpose; for example, if a hotel is depicted as being in the wrong location, or as having a swimming pool which does not exist, an offence may be committed. The Act will also be infringed if inaccurate statements are made about the results to be expected from repairs or processes, for example that a course of treatment will eradicate damp, if this is untrue. Nor must the possession of professional qualifications be falsely asserted.

(vi) Pricing Offences
Giving false or misleading information about the price of goods can be an offence. It is an offence to suggest that goods are offered at a price below the recommended price, or at a price which is lower than the price at which the goods were previously offered by the seller, if this is untrue. A 'recommended price' is the price recommended by the manufacturer or supplier for retail sale in the relevant area; where goods are offered at a price which is said to be less than the previous higher price, the goods must have been offered at that higher price for a continuous period of at least 28 days within the previous 6 months, unless the contrary is stated. It is also an offence to suggest that goods are being offered at a price which is less than the true price, for example, by omitting to state the VAT.

(vii) Defences
In order to be liable for making a false statement with respect to services etc, it is necessary to show that the defendant either knew that the statement was false, or made the statement recklessly, that is, without regard to whether it was true or false. Blameworthiness of this kind is not necessary in order to establish the offence or making a false statement with regard to goods, or with respect to misleading pricing, however, but the Act does provide a number of defences. Thus, a prosecution will fail if the defendant can show that the false statement was due to 'a mistake or to reliance on information supplied to the [defendant] or to the act or default of another person, an accident or some other cause beyond his control' *and* '[the defendant] took all reasonable precautions and exercised all due diligence to avoid the commission of such an offence by himself or any person under his control' (section 24(1) of the

Trade Descriptions Act). There is a separate defence where the defendant can prove that he did not know, and could not with reasonable diligence have ascertained, that the goods did not conform to the description or that the description had been applied to the goods. A retailer may be protected on this basis from liability in respect of a false statement contained in packaging or sales material produced by the manufacturer, on the accuracy of which he has reasonably relied.

(viii) Penalties

On conviction, a fine and/or imprisonment can be imposed. Prosecutions must be commenced not later than three years from the commission of the offence. Where the offence is committed by a company, a penalty can also be imposed on the officers responsible. It is open to the court to require a person convicted under the Act to pay compensation to a person who has suffered a loss as a result of the offence. It should be noted that proceedings cannot be commenced by individuals, but are the responsibility of the local weights and measures authority (sometimes called consumer protection or trading standards authorities).

(ix) The Business Advertisements (Disclosure) Order 1977

Under this provision it is an offence to publish an advertisement with respect to goods which are for sale in the course of a business if it is not reasonably clear that the seller is a business, rather than a private individual. This may be apparent from the context in which the advertisement appears, or its format or content.

(x) Code of Practice

The Advertising Standards Authority have produced a code of practice (The British Code of Advertising Practice) which lays down principles to which all advertisers should adhere. Compliance with the Code is voluntary (though breach of its provisions may be independently unlawful). Its essence is that advertisements should be 'legal, decent, honest and truthful'. A copy of the Code, and other useful information, may be obtained from the Advertising Standards Authority, Brook House, 2/16 Torrington Place, London WC1E 7HN.

SECTION 6
THE LAW AND YOUR FAMILY

1. INTRODUCTION

Despite all the social changes of the last twenty or thirty years, marriage remains very popular and the decision to marry is for many people one of the most important decisions they make in their lives. Even among those marriages which end in divorce, many of the partners enter upon a second marriage. It seems probable that there has been an increase in the number of couples who decide to live together without getting married, even though each of them is free to marry the other but this is still very much a minority practice.

As we shall see marriage has certain automatic effects on the rights of the parties, for example, a widow has succession rights against her husband's estate if he dies intestate (that is without having made a valid will). Some of these effects, for example, the widow's right to certain social security benefits, cannot be produced without a marriage. It will often be important therefore to tell whether the parties are validly married even though the day to day life of a cohabiting couple may look very like that of a married couple.

Since it is not possible to get married on the spur of the moment, marriage is necessarily preceded by a period when the parties have agreed to get married. In practice, of course, this period of *engagement* is usually of some weeks or months or even years and the process of getting engaged is regarded as an important preliminary to marriage. Until 1970 English Law regarded mutual promises to marry as creating a contract so that, if either party refused to marry, the other could bring an action for 'breach of promise'. In practice the vast majority of such actions were brought by women who sometimes recovered large sums of damages to compensate them for their injured feelings. The Law Reform (Miscellaneous Provisions) Act 1970 abolished such actions but introduced new rules for gifts exchanged upon engagement (see left).

Gifts between engaged couples

Before 1970 gifts made by one engaged party to the other in contemplation of marriage were treated as a pledge that the marriage would take place. This meant that the party who broke off the engagement could not recover his or her gifts and that the other party could. The 1970 Act makes a distinction between engagement rings and other gifts. In the case of engagement rings there is now a presumption that the ring is intended as an out and out gift so that the lady can normally keep the ring even though it is she who has broken off the engagement. This presumption could be rebutted in special circumstances, for instance, where the ring was an heirloom of the man's family or where the man is so unromantic as to say at the time of the engagement that the ring is to be returned if the marriage does not take place.

In the case of other gifts it no longer matters whose fault it is that the engagement has come to an end (indeed, it was the desire to avoid such unedifying enquiries which prompted the Act). In principle therefore the gifts are returned when the engagement comes to an end. However, the person who has received the gift could in some circumstances argue that the gift, although made while the parties were engaged, was not made 'in contemplation of marriage' because it was an ordinary birthday or Christmas present.

Poor Mrs Shaw

In *Shaw v Shaw* (1954) 'Mrs' Shaw discovered on the death of her 'husband' that she was not married at all as he had forgotten to tell her that he already had a wife. This had potentially serious consequences as he had not left a will so that his property would go to his widow and not to her. The Court of Appeal held that she could bring an action for breach of promise of marriage against his estate and recover as damages the money she would have got if he had carried out his promise to marry her. This possibiity is no longer open since the 1970 Act abolished an action for breach of promise but the Act allows a person who has in good faith entered into a void marriage with someone who is now dead to apply for reasonable provision out of his estate exactly as if she were his widow.

The Act also dealt with the special problem of the fiancé who goes through the 'marriage' and forgets to mention that he already has a wife.

When is a marriage valid? This involves two questions. Has the marriage been completed according to the correct formalities? If so, did the parties have capacity to marry (each other)?

2. FORMALITIES

In England there was no legislation about the way in which marriages should be celebrated until 1753. Before that date English law simply followed the Canon Law. If the marriage was valid in the eyes of the Church, it was valid in the eyes of the State. The early Church had extremely informal rules. Although a religious ceremony was desirable, it was not essential.

Marriage could be created by the parties living together as man and wife or by exchanging promises forthwith to be married. This informality came to be regarded as clearly undesirable and in 1753 Lord Hardwicke's Act required a public Church ceremony after the calling of banns on three successive Sundays. There were special provisions for Quakers and Jews but both Roman Catholics and Non-conformists had to marry in Church of England churches if their marriages were to be valid. This pattern was changed in 1836 to provide two systems: (i) marriage in the Church of England; and (ii) marriage under the Marriage Act 1836 which provided for a purely civil ceremony in a Register Office or, in certain circumstances, in non-Anglican places of worship. This dual system still operates today. In certain circumstances 'parental' consent is required (see the box below). The law imposes

---

Parental consent

If either party to the marriage is under eighteen the consent of that party's parents is required unless the infant is a widow or widower. The rules as to who shall give consent are complex and depend on whether the child is legitimate and whether the parents are alive and living together.

(A) **Child is legitimate**	**Who must consent**
(1) *Both Parents alive*	
(a) Parents living together	Both parents
(b) Parents divorced or separated by consent or Court order	Whichever parent has custody
(c) One parent deserted by the other	The deserted parent
(d) Both parents have been deprived of custody by Court order	The person to whom custody has been granted
(2) *Only one Parent alive*	
(a) No other guardians	The surviving parent
(b) If a guardian has been appointed by the deceased parent or the Court	The surviving parent and the guardian unless one of them is the sole guardian in which case the sole guardian
(3) *Both Parents dead*	The guardian or guardians appointed by the parents or the Court
(B) **Child is illegitimate**	
(1) *Mother is alive*	The mother unless she has been deprived of custody by Court order – in which case the person who has custody
(2) *Mother is dead*	Guardian appointed by mother

If the person whose consent is necessary refuses to give it application may be to the High Court, the County Court or the magistrates. In practice nearly all applications are made to the magistrates. Where the consent refused cannot be obtained because of absence or inaccessibility application may again be made to the Court or the Superintendent Registrar may dispense with the consent.

If the parties succeed in getting married without a required consent, the marriage is valid.

requirements both as to the necessary preliminaries and as to the ceremony itself.

(i) Marriages in Church of England Churches

(A) Preliminaries. There are three different procedures:

(a) Banns. This is the usual procedure. If the parties live in the same parish the banns must be published there; if they live in different parishes, then in each of them. The banns must be entered in an official register and published audibly in the prescribed words on three Sundays before the ceremony. Parties may marry immediately after the third publication. The marriage must take place in one of the churches where the banns have been published, so that if the parties intend to marry in a church in a parish where they are not resident, the banns should be published there too.

(b) Common licence. In order to obtain such a licence one of the parties has to swear an affidavit that there is no lawful impediment, that residential qualification has been complied with and that any necessary parental consents have been obtained. The licence can only permit a marriage either in the parish where one of the parties has had his usual place of residence for fifteen days immediately before the grant of the licence or in the church which is the usual place of worship of either or both parties. Once the licence is issued the marriage can take place immediately.

(c) Special licence. The Archbishop of Canterbury has power to licence marriages at any hour of day or night in any convenient place whether consecrated or not. Such licences are usually used to permit marriages in churches other than a parish church (for instance the chapel of an Oxford College). There is a fee of £25.

(B) The ceremony. The marriage must be celebrated by a clergyman in the presence of two or more witnesses according to the rite laid down by the Book of Common Prayer or any alternative form of Service currently authorised.

(ii) Civil Marriages

(A) Preliminaries. The Act of 1836 established the office of Superintendent Registrar of births, deaths and marriages. All marriages other than those solemnised in the Church of England, have to be preceded by preliminaries for which the Registrar of the relevant district is responsible.

Again there are three different procedures.

(a) Superintendent Registrar's certificate. Notice has to be given to the Registrar of the Registration District(s) where the parties have resided for seven days beforehand (so if one party does not live in this country this procedure cannot be used). The notices must be accompanied by a solemn declaration that there are no impediments to the marriage, that the residential requirement has been satisfied, and that any necessary consents have been obtained. All notices are recorded in a marriage notice book which is open for public inspection and the notice is displayed in the Registrar's Office. The Registrar must issue a certificate twenty-one days after the giving of the notice. The marriage may then take place within three months from the day when notice was entered in the marriage notice book. There is a fee of £6.

(b) Superintendent Registrar's certificate and licence. This procedure is often (wrongly) called a 'special licence'. It is similar to the previous procedure with the following changes. Notice need only be given of the district in which one of the parties has been resident for the last fifteen days; notice must be entered in the notice book but it is not displayed in the Registrar's Office and there is a fee of £27. If this procedure is followed marriage may take place at any time after one whole day has expired from the giving of notice.

(c) Registrar General's licence. This is a procedure introduced in 1970 similar to the Archbishop of Canterbury's special licence. It is specifically provided that it will not be used as a preliminary to an Anglican wedding. It was intended to provide for situations where one of the parties was seriously ill and not expected to recover but the Marriage Act of 1983 entitles the Registrar to issue a certificate in such cases.

(B) The ceremony. The parties may state in their notice that they wish to be married in a Register Office. The ceremony takes place in the Office with open doors in the presence of the Superintendent Registrar. The ceremony must be secular and basically must consist of the exchange of vows.

(iii) Marriage According to a Non-Anglican Religious Ceremony

Such a marriage has to follow the civil preliminaries but there is in practice wide freedom as to the

Dp 157663

*The statutory fee for this certificate is 3s. 9d.
Where a search is necessary to find the entry,
a search fee is payable in addition.*

CERTIFIED COPY of an
ENTRY OF MARRIAGE

Pursuant to the
Marriage Act, 1949

[Printed by authority of the Registrar General].

M. Cert.
Church

Registration District *London Borough of Lewisham*

1965 Marriage solemnized at *the Church of St. John Baptist, Bexborough*

of *St. John Baptist, Bexborough* in the *London borough of Lewisham* in the Parish

No.	When married	Name and surname	Age	Condition	Rank or profession	Residence at the time of marriage	Father's name and surname	Rank or profession of father
213	27th Nov. 1965	John Vernon Howard	23	Bachelor	Architect	28, Wrightsbridge S. Norwood S.E.25	Ivan Temple Howard	Clerk
		Iris Dey	24	Spinster	Tailoress	57, Ballamoulough Downham Kent	George Thomas Dey	Porter

Married in the *Church of St. John* according to the rites and ceremonies of the *Church of England* or after *banns* by me,

This marriage was solemnized between us,	John Vernon Howard Iris Dey	in the presence of us,	J.T. Dey W.F. Howard	Antony Toller Curate.

I, *Antony Toller, Curate* of *St. John Baptist, Downham* in the *Parish of St. John Baptist, Downham* do hereby certify that this is a true copy of the Entry No. 213, in the Register Book of Marriages in the said Church.

WITNESS MY HAND this 27th day of November, 1965,

Antony Toller
Curate.

State "Rector", "Vicar", or "Curate"

CAUTION.—Any person who (1) falsifies any of the particulars on this certificate, or (2) uses a falsified certificate as true, knowing it to be false, is liable to prosecution.

Insert in this margin any notes which appear in the original entry.

form of the ceremony. The certificate must state where the marriage is to be held and this must be a registered building. The Registrar General is the person who has to decide whether the building should be registered. Such a building must be one where activities of worship connected with a religion take place. Marriages in registered buildings must be attended either by the Registrar or by an 'authorised person' who is in practice always a minister of the relevant religion.

(iv) Quaker and Jewish Marriages

Quaker and Jewish marriages have been treated differently than those of other non-Anglican religions since 1753. Today it is necessary to follow one of the prescribed forms of civil preliminaries but the marriage need not be celebrated in a registered building, by an authorised person or in public.

3. CAPACITY TO MARRY

Not only must the parties go through a valid ceremony but they must have capacity to marry each other. Some kinds of incapacity are absolute, for instance, no person under sixteen can contract a valid marriage; others are relevant to the other party, for instance, an uncle and niece may not marry each other.

For historical reasons English law has come to put such grounds of invalidity into two groups – those which make the marriage *void* and those which make it *voidable*. If the marriage is void, the law treats it as if it never existed; it is not necessary to get a decree declaring it void and a decree pronouncing it void may be sought at any time (even after the death of the parties) by any one who has an interest to do so (for example, a relative who stands to acquire property rights by showing that the marriage is void). On the other hand if the defect makes the marriage voidable, then the marriage is valid unless annulled and only the parties to the marriage can take proceedings to have it annulled.

The modern law is laid down by the Nullity of Marriage Act 1971.

(i) Void Marriages

The marriage is void in the following circumstances.

(A) Prohibited decrees. Most, if not all, societies prohibit marriages between some classes of

relative though there are wide variations in detail as to which classes are prohibited. There are in fact two different kinds of objection. The first concerns close blood relationship. Many systems prohibit marriages between first cousins, which are permitted by English law. Here the arguments are largely genetic, that is, there is a greater chance of transmitting faulty genes to children in such cases. (There is extensive experience of this in the breeding of show dogs, where breeding between close relatives is widely practiced in order to increase the chances of developing desired breed characteristics.) The other objection concerns relationships themselves arising from marriage. For instance English law until 1907 prohibited a man from marrying his deceased wife's sister. One of the arguments in favour of this law was that a man's relationship with his sister-in-law should be asexual, which it could not be if they could look on each other as potential spouses. In practice, however, the most common cases where such marriages were desired seem to have arisen where the husband had been widowed and his wife's sister had been the most natural person to turn to for help in raising his children.

The present table of prohibited decrees is set out in the box below.

(B) Age. The marriage is void if either party is under sixteen.

Prohibited marriages

A man may not marry his
   Mother, daughter, grandmother, granddaughter, sister, aunt, or niece

   Father's wife, grandfather's wife, wife's daughter or wife's granddaughter (unless both are over 21 and the younger party was not at any time before the age of 18 a child of the family in relation to the other party – that is they lived in the same household and the younger was treated by the older as a child of his family)
   Wife's mother (unless both are over 21 and both wife and wife's father are dead)
   Son's wife (unless both are over 21 and both son and mother of son are dead)

Similarly a woman may not marry her
   Father
   Son and so on

(C) Bigamy. The marriage is void if one party at the time of the ceremony is lawfully married to someone else. This is so even where the married partner honestly thinks that his or her former spouse is dead (in which case the crime of bigamy would not have been committed).

(D) Invalid formalities. This has already been discussed.

(E) Both parties are of the same sex. At first sight this might seem a blinding statement of the obvious! It does, however, have some practical significance. It means that so called 'homosexual marriages' cannot be marriages under English law. More difficult questions have arisen in relation to marriages where one of the parties is a 'transexual', that is born with the physical characteristics of one sex but psychologically a member of the opposite sex and has had a so called 'sex change' operation.

'Marriages' between members of the same sex

In *Corbett v Corbett* (1971) the respondent April Ashley had undergone a sex change operation and indeed had worked successfully as a female model. She had been treated as a woman for national insurance and passport purposes. It was held however that for marriage purposes 'she' was a man since all the relevant biological tests pointed that way. Implicitly this decides that sex is fixed at birth.

(ii) Voidable Marriages

(A) Incapacity to consummate. Canon law regarded ability to consummate as essential to the validity of the marriage. Although the incapacity will be manifested after the ceremony, it is treated as a defect existing at the time of the ceremony and historically it is this theory which justified treating this as a ground of nullity and not of divorce. This was of great importance in a society which did not permit divorce at all and it is still important for those whose religion forbids divorce.

It is important to note that it is the ability to have sexual relations and not the ability to have children which is important. So a wife who discovered after the wedding that her husband had had a vasectomy which he had not revealed, would not get a decree of nullity. It is now well known that incapacity is often psychological rather than physical and may indeed arise out of the relationship with the other partner. A decree can certainly be granted on these grounds so that it is no defence to show that the respondent to the petition had had sexual relations with another partner or even with the petitioner before marriage. The incapacity must, however, be permanent and incurable (except where the relevant partner refuses to undergo a curative operation).

Before 1971 it was possible in some instances to petition on the grounds of one's own incapacity. It is thought that this now turns on the rules as to approbation, discussed in the box below.

(B) Wilful refusal to consummate. This ground was introduced in 1937. In practice it overlaps with the previous ground and petitioners usually allege both grounds. The petitioner must show a settled and definite decision not to have intercourse for which there is no lawful excuse. So a single refusal will not do and the Court will examine the whole history of the marriage to see if the refusal is 'wilful'.

(C) Lack of consent. The parties will be invited to say during the ceremony whether they agree to the marriage. Clearly if one of them indicates absence of consent the ceremony will not be com-

---

Failure to consummate

In *Potter v Potter* (1975) the wife had a physical defect which prevented consummation. In due course she had an operation which cured the defect. The husband then made one further attempt to consummate which was unsuccessful because the wife was suffering from post-operative stress. In due course the wife petitioned but failed as it was held that the failure to consummate resulted from the husband's 'loss of ardour' which was not wilful.

In *Kaur v Singh* (1972) a civil ceremony took place between two Sikhs. Under Sikh religious law a religious ceremony (which it was the husband's duty to arrange) was necessary for the marriage to be complete. The husband refused to make the arrangements for the religious ceremony and it was held that this amounted to a wilful refusal to consummate.

In *Baxter v Baxter* (1948) it was held that a refusal to have intercourse unless a contraceptive sheath was used did not amount to wilful refusal.

---

pleted. However, one of the parties may appear to consent only to argue later that this consent was not real because it was only given under duress or as the result of a mistake. In the case of duress the petitioner must show that his will was overcome by fear so that his apparent consent was not real. In the case of mistake it is necessary for the petitioner to show that he was mistaken as to the identity of the person he married or as to the nature of the ceremony (see the box below) and it is not enough to show that the petitioner was mistaken about the personal qualities of the respondent. Obviously many marriages take place when one of the parties mistakenly thinks the other is wealthy, good natured or chaste and such a mistake certainly does not invalidate the marriage.

Hall v Hall

In *Hall v Hall* (1908) the petitioner went through a marriage ceremony in Kensington Register Office. She thought that marriages could only take place in church and believed that she was registering her name. A decree was granted.

(D) Other grounds. Three other grounds were originally introduced in 1937. They are that at the time of the marriage the respondent was pregnant by some person other than the petitioner; that at the time of the marriage the respondent was suffering from venereal disease in a communicable form; or that at the time of the marriage either party was suffering from mental disorder of such a kind or extent as to be unfitted for marriage.

(iii) Bars to Decree

Even though there are grounds for granting a decree that the marriage is voidable, the granting of a decree is barred in certain circumstances. (There are no similar bars to a decree that the marriage is void.)

(A) Time limits. Proceedings in respect of lack of consent, venereal disease, and pregnancy by another must be brought within three years of the marriage.

(B) Knowledge. Petitions founded on venereal disease or pregnancy by another will fail unless the petitioner can show that at the time of the

marriage he was ignorant of the relevant facts. In the case of pregnancy by another he need not show that he did not know his wife was pregnant, so long as he can show that he did not know that he was not the father.

(C) Approbation. It has always been the case that the petition might be rejected on the basis that although the petitioner had shown grounds, he had also behaved in such a way as to recognise the validity of the marriage. The precise limits of this idea were unclear but the question has been cleared up by the 1971 Act which provides that the respondent must show three things: first, conduct by the petitioner which reasonably led the respondent to think that the petitioner would not seek to have the marriage set aside; secondly, it must be shown that at the time of the consent, the petitioner knew that he was entitled to have the marriage annulled; and thirdly it has to be shown that it would be unjust to the respondent to grant a decree.

4. EFFECTS OF A NULLITY DECREE

Traditionally English law attached draconian consequences to the discovery that the marriage was void: the children of the marriage were illegitimate and the usual consequences of marriage, such as the right to inherit the spouse's property when he or she had died without making a will, did not take place. Exactly the same happened when a marriage was declared voidable, even though the marriage had been valid until avoided.

In effect this was to treat voidable marriages in exactly the same way as cases where a man and women had lived together without getting married at all. To modern eyes this seems an unduly doctrinaire view and the present trend is in the opposite direction. So by 1949 it had been enacted that the child of a voidable marriage must be treated as legitimate and in 1959 it was provided that the children of a void marriage were to be treated as legitimate if at the time of the intercourse resulting in the birth or at the time of the celebration of the marriage if it were later, either or both of the parents reasonably believed that the marriage was valid.

Historically if the marriage was void the 'wife' would not be entitled to maintenance, as she was not a wife. Today, however, when a Court grants a decree of nullity it has exactly the same power to order financial provision by one party for the other as it would have if it were granting a decree of divorce. Similarly a 'spouse' who has obtained a decree can apply to the Court for reasonable provision out of the other's estate after death.

Since 1971 a decree that the marriage is voidable has ceased to have retrospective effect. The voidable marriage is now treated as having been valid between the date of the ceremony and the date of the decree.

5. MARRIAGES ABROAD

It may be necessary to decide in England whether a marriage celebrated abroad is valid, for instance, because the parties are now living in England and the 'wife' says that the 'husband' should support her. In deciding whether such a marriage is valid, English law distinguishes between the formal validity of the ceremony and the parties' capacity to marry each other.

As far as formalities are concerned the marriage will be valid if it is valid by the law of the country where the ceremony took place and usually invalid if it is not valid by the law of that country.

However, under the Foreign Marriages Act 1947 marriages between parties, at least one of whom is a member of Her Majesty's Forces serving in a foreign territory, may be solemnised by a Forces Chaplain or by anyone authorised by the Commanding Officer of such forces. Under the Foreign Marriages Act 1892 a marriage abroad between parties at least one of whom is a British citizen may be celebrated by a 'marriage officer'. 'Marriage officers' are British consuls and ambassadors and members of their diplomatic staff provided that they hold a marriage warrant from the Secretary of State.

The capacity of the parties to marry each other is governed by the law of their domicile, that is the law of the country that is their principal home.

Void marriage

In *Brook v Brook* (1861) a man wished to marry his deceased wife's sister. Both of them were domiciled in England and English law at that date prohibited such marriages. The parties paid a visit to Denmark, the law of which permitted such marriages and went through a ceremony there. They lived together and had five children. The 'husband', 'wife' and one of their children died during a cholera epidemic. It was held that the marriage was void and the children illegitimate and therefore that the surviving children had no succession rights to the property of the deceased child (the father on his death bed having made a will dividing his estate between his five children by name).

Valid and invalid marriages

In *Bethiaume v Dastous* (1930) two Roman Catholics who were domiciled in Quebec in Canada were married in a Roman Catholic church in France. The priest who married them took no steps to arrange a civil ceremony as required by French law. The marriage was held invalid.

In *Starkowski v Attorney General* (1954) two Roman Catholics who were domiciled in Poland were married in a Roman Catholic Church in Austria without a civil ceremony in May 1945. At that date Austrian law required a civil ceremony but a few weeks later a law was passed in Austria retrospectively validating such marriages if they were registered. The marriage was not in fact registered until 1949 by which time the parties had become domiciled in England and had separated. In 1950 the wife 'married' another man. It was held that the Austrian marriage was valid and the wife's second marriage therefore void.

6. POLYGAMOUS MARRIAGES

In Victorian England it was confidently stated in a leading case that marriage was 'the voluntary union for life of one man and one woman to the exclusion of all others' and so a Mormon marriage in Salt Lake City was invalid, even though the husband had never taken a second wife, because polygamy was part of the Mormon doctrine and commonly practised in Utah. Now that there are many people living in England who belong to religions which permit polygamy it has become clear that this is too simple a view. In certain circumstances it has been seen to be proper to recognise the validity of some polygamous ceremonies.

It is clear that a ceremony which takes place in England cannot create a valid polygamous marriage. If parties go through, say, a Muslim religious ceremony, this would not comply with the laws about formalities of marriage set out above. If the parties have previously gone through a civil ceremony that would create a monogamous marriage, whose character would not be changed by the later religous ceremony.

However, if the marriage takes place in a country which permits polygamy, the position may be different. The first question will be to decide whether the marriage is a monogamous or polygamous one since those countries which permit polygamy usually also permit monogamy. The decision will depend on the law of the place where the ceremony is conducted and the critical question will be whether that law permits that husband to take a second wife or further wives. So a first marriage will be polygamous if second wives are permitted even though the husband never takes a second wife and never intends to.

If the marriage is in a form which the local law recognises as creating a valid polygamous marriage, then the next question will be whether the parties have capacity to enter into polygamous marriages, which will depend again on the law of their domicile. English law clearly does not permit English domiciliaries to contract polygamous marriages. So if a Pakistani man comes to England and lives here long enough to acquire an English domicile and then returns to Pakistan to marry, he would not in the eyes of English law have capacity to contract a valid polygamous marriage. However, a marriage in Pakistan between a man and a woman, both domiciled in Pakistan, and which according to Pakistan law creates a valid polygamous marriage would be treated as a valid marriage for most purposes in England.

So it is clear, for instance, that the children of such a marriage are legitimate and have the usual succession rights of legitimate children. Similarly the surviving wives of a polygamous marriage can succeed to their husband's property if he dies intestate. Under the Social Security Act 1975 the wife of a polygamous marriage is entitled to the Social Security benefits that go to wives so long as she is in fact the only wife.

7. UNMARRIED UNIONS

This section on marriage so far has been considering cases where parties have gone through a ceremony of marriage even though in some cases the result has not been to create a valid marriage. The parties may, however, choose to live together without going through any ceremony at all. It is widely believed that this practice is increasingly common although there do not appear to be any reliable statistics to back up this view. What does seem clear is that the social status of such arrangements has changed so that many parties do not find it necessary to pretend that they are married. When divorce was more difficult such unions often arose when one or both parties had left their respective spouses but were unable to get a divorce. This is now less likely to be the case in the long run although there seem to be few inhibitions about living together while awaiting divorce. It seems likely too that there has been an increase in the practice of living together as a preliminary to marriage but perhaps the greatest change is the increase in the number of couples who deliberately reject marriage and explicitly agree to live together in an unmarried state.

This changing scene is reflected in the confused and unsatisfactory terminology used to describe these kinds of relationships. The woman is often referred to as a 'common law wife' but this is legally inaccurate. The term 'mistress' has an old-fashioned ring and in any case also covers relationships when the parties are not living together at all. Lawyers often describe such parties as co-habiting. The law is in a similar state of flux. Even 50 years ago it could have been confidently stated that the parties to such a union had none of the rights and duties of husband and wife. This is still largely true, particularly in relation to benefits conferred by general legal rules or by the State though there are odd anomalies, so that for instance a man and woman each of whom is earning a substantial income may well be better off for income tax purposes than if they were married. An unmarried couple may regulate their relationship by contract. At one time it would have been thought that such a contract was sexually immoral and invalid but it seems clear that this is no longer the case. As we shall see these developments are very important in relation to property disputes which arise if the relationship breaks up.

1. PARENTAL RIGHTS AND OBLIGATIONS

In the nineteenth century English law treated it as clear that a father had extensive rights over his children. The position today is very different for a number of reasons. First, the father now has to share any rights with the mother on a completely equal basis. Secondly, as between father and mother on the one side and the child on the other there has been a marked shift in the balance of power. The law has shifted from a basic support for parental authority to a decisive concern for the child's welfare. In any of the many ways in which questions about the position of the child may come before the Courts, it has been said that the Court 'will concern itself solely with the question what course of action will best promote the welfare of the child'.

Nevertheless, although many cases involving children do come before the Courts, the majority of disputes involving children do not. In practice the parents' day-to-day decisions will usually be decisive since they will be effective unless someone takes steps to challenge them. This is a natural corollary of the parental responsibility for the child. In practice it will be very seldom that parent and child will resort to the Courts to resolve disputes between themselves; such proceedings are much more likely to result from disagreements between the parents or intervention by outsiders.

Historically the rights which parents have enjoyed included the following:

(i) Right to Physical Possession

Parents have in the past been able to compel the return of children by issuing a writ of *habeas corpus*. Today a Court would be unlikely to compel a child to return home where the child was unwilling to do so and wanted to live with others. This assumes that the child is old enough to have views of his own. In the case of younger children the parents will normally be entitled to have the child back and this can be the cause of much distress where young children have been placed with foster parents although as we shall see there are various ways in which the parents' decision to reclaim the child can be challenged.

(ii) Power to Control Education

In practice today the statutory rules for the control of education, which are considered below, are much more important.

(iii) Discipline

The parent has the right to inflict moderate and reasonable corporal punishment. No doubt, however, today's ideas of what is moderate are not those of a century ago.

(iv) Choice of Religion

This is perhaps unlikely to be a critical question except where the parents are of different religions. The old rule that the father had all the parental rights meant that he was entitled to determine the child's religion contrary to the wishes of the mother. Now that the views of father and mother are equal this cannot happen. If the parents could not agree and called on a Court to adjudicate, the Court would in principle decide what was best for the child though this might offer an uncertain test in this area.

(v) Administration of Property

A parent has certain rights of administration over the child's property.

(vi) Litigation

A child can only bring proceedings by his 'next friend' and a child who is sued must be represented by a guardian *ad litem*. A parent would *prima facie* be the person entitled to act unless he had personal interests contrary to those of the child.

(vii) Consent to Medical Treatment

In English law a doctor is not entitled to give medical treatment to a patient simply because the treatment is good for the patient – the patient must consent. Certainly as far as young children are concerned, the parent is the appropriate person to give consent. The position is more complicated in the case of older children. The Family Law Reform Act 1969 provides that children over sixteen may effectively consent to surgical, medical or dental treatment and that it is not necessary to obtain parental consent. What about children under sixteen?

305

There are a number of different possibilities. If the parents consent to an operation and the child does not, a prudent doctor would choose not to proceed. If the parents consented and the child did not appear to object the doctor would probably be safe to rely on the parents' consent (see the box below).

The converse case is perhaps even more difficult. Suppose a fifteen-year-old girl wishes to have an abortion because she has been raped and her parents object on religious grounds, the position is unclear (see the bottom box below).

If time permits the child can be made a ward of Court and the Court's consent substituted for that of the parents.

Wardship sterilisation

In *Re D (A Minor) (Wardship Sterilisation)* (1976) the mother of an eleven-year-old girl, who was handicapped, was worried that the child might be seduced and give birth to a handicapped child. She took the advice of a consultant paediatrician and a consultant gynaeocologist and it was decided to sterilise the child. In fact a social worker who knew of the proposal made the child a ward of Court and the Court refused its consent to the operation but it was clearly assumed that the doctor could lawfully have carried out the operation otherwise, relying on the parent's consent.

Contraceptive advice to girls under sixteen

In *Gillick v West Norfolk and Wisbech Area Health Authority* (1985) Mrs Gillick, mother of five daughters under the age of sixteen, sought a declaration that advice given by the DHSS to doctors that in certain circumstances they could properly give contraceptive advice to girls under sixteen without their parents' consent was unlawful. The House of Lords held by a majority of three to two that the declaration should not be granted. The view of the majority was that though the doctor should normally try to persuade the girl to discuss the matter with her parents and that usually if she refused he should refuse to prescribe contraceptives, yet there was no absolute rule that in all circumstances it was wrong to give contraceptive advice without parental consent. Ultimately the matter was one for the doctor's clinical judgment.

2. WHO IS ENTITLED TO EXERCISE PARENTAL RIGHTS?

(i) The Parents

As we have seen, all parental rights used to be vested in the father. Under the Guardianship Act 1973, however, the mother now has the same rights as the law had previously given to the father. The Act provides that the rights of the father and mother are equal and that each may act without the other. This means, for instance, that a doctor who seeks parental consent may safely rely on the consent of either parent. It would probably be imprudent for a third party to rely on one parent's authority when the other parent was actually known to disagree. If the parents disagree on any question affecting a minor's welfare either may apply to the Court for directions and the Court may make such order as it thinks proper. It is obviously not very likely that in a satisfactory marriage the parents would often think that this was the best way to resolve disputes.

If the child is adopted the adoptive parents have full parental rights. On the death of one parent, parental authority will pass to the survivor together with any guardian appointed by the deceased parent. If a child is illegitimate parental rights belong exclusively to the mother.

(ii) Guardians Appointed by Deed or Will

Either parent may appoint by deed or will any person to be a guardian of the child after his death. Such a guardian would normally act jointly with the surviving parent. If the surviving parent objects or if the guardian considers the surviving parent unsuitable, there can be an application to the Court. The Court may either leave the surviving parent sole guardian, order the surviving parent and guardian to act jointly or order that the guardian shall act as sole guardian.

(iii) Guardians Appointed by the Court

Under the Guardianship of Minors Acts 1971 and 1973, either the High Court, the County Court or a Magistrates' Court may appoint a guardian in the following circumstances: (a) if a child has no parent, guardian or other person having parental rights; (b) if either parent dies without appointing a guardian; (c) if either parent dies and the guardian that he has appointed dies or refuses to act; or (d) if the Court removes a guardian, it may appoint another to act in his place.

It will be seen that this scheme means that parental rights will only pass to non-parents by a formal process. This is of increasing importance today when the large number of divorces means that a large number of children are being brought up in families where the two adult members of the family are not the natural parents of all the children. The step-parent will have no 'parental rights' even though he or she is in fact performing the role of the parent. Similarly where the father and mother are living together but not married, the father will have no parental rights.

(iv) The Courts

There is a very large collection of procedures under which different Courts may make orders which affect the exercise of parental rights and duties. These are as follows:

(a) The *wardship* jurisdiction of the High Court.

(b) The jurisdiction to make legal custody orders under the Guardianship of Minors Acts 1971-73.

(c) The jurisdiction to make legal custody orders under the Domestic Proceedings and Magistrates' Court Act 1978.

(d) The divorce jurisdiction under the Matrimonial Causes Act 1973.

(e) The power to make custodianship orders under Part II of the Children Act 1975.

(f) The power of the Juvenile Court to make care orders under the Children and Young Persons Act 1969.

(g) The power to make adoption orders.

We need to consider each of these powers in turn.

(A) Wardship. The wardship jurisdiction of the High Court is very old and is usually said to be based on the Crown's position as *parens patriae*. This phase may be roughly translated by saying that the King is the father of his people. This may be no more than an example of the habit of English lawyers to obscure dubious reasons by translating them into Latin but since the seventeenth century this power has in fact been exercised by the judges and since 1971 by the judges of the Family Division (though wardship proceedings may be transferred by the High Court to the County Court or heard by a County Court Judge sitting as a Deputy High Court Judge).

Until the end of the nineteenth century the typical ward of Court was a wealthy orphan but the jurisdiction has become much wider in the twentieth century. One of the great advantages of the system is that it can be called into operation at great speed since all that is necessary is to issue a summons. The child then automatically becomes a ward until the Court rules otherwise. The applicant need not be a parent or even a relative. Indeed applications have successfully been made by social workers (see box opposite) and local authorities. If the Court considers that the applicant has no legitimate interest in making an application it will dismiss the application.

Once the child has been made a ward, no important step in the child's life can be taken without the Court's consent. So the child cannot leave the country or get married without the Court's consent. This is often important since wardship applications may be used to prevent another parent from taking a child out of the country or to stop a sixteen or seventeen year old girl from contracting an unwise marriage. Wardship applications can be made at very short notice and there is a duty judge, who can if necessary, be contacted on the telephone or at his home.

Any minor may be made a ward. This can be useful because many of the other powers only apply to particular classes of minors. On the other hand the Courts are nowadays rather unwilling to use the wardship jurisdiction where the real purpose of the application is to attack a decision made by a local authority under the statutory scheme for children in care.

The Court will decide what it considers to be in the best interest of the child. This may involve rejecting all the views put before it and choosing a

---

Supervised access to child

In *Re E* (1984) the lower courts thought that they had to choose between returning the child at once to his father or allowing him immediately to be placed for adoption. The House of Lords held that this was wrong. Although those were the only alternatives put to the Court, the Court should decide independently on the best course, which the House of Lords thought was to allow the father a period of supervised access to see whether father and son could establish a satisfactory relationship.

course of action which no party has suggested (see box on page 307). In performing this task the Court is often helped by the Official Solicitor who will be appointed to act as the ward's guardian *ad litem* where the Court feels the child should be separately represented. In such cases the Official Solicitor will make his own investigations and report to the Court.

(B) Guardianship of Minors Acts 1971 and 1973. Under these Acts the father or mother of a minor may apply for legal custody, access or maintenance. Under these Acts other interested persons such as grandparents, step-parents, and foster parents cannot apply. The Acts are principally useful where the marriage has broken down and the applicant does not wish to seek other matrimonial relief, for instance, because there are not yet any grounds for divorce. The Court will make an order if it believes it to be in the child's interest to do so. Applications can be made to the High Court, the County Court or the Magistrates' Court.

In the usual case the Court will give custody to one parent and access to the other. Custody will be given to the parent who is to have physical custody of the child but the Court may well think that the other parent ought to have a continuing voice in the child's upbringing. In such a case the Court may provide that the parent who does not have custody shall have such of the parental rights and duties as the Court may specify and shall have them jointly with the other parent.

Although only the father or mother may apply under this Act, the Court may award custody to a third party or in exceptional circumstances commit the care of the child to a local authority.

A parent may apply for access without applying for custody. This is particularly useful for the father of an illegitimate child who has no parental rights in the absence of a Court order.

Where the Court makes an order giving actual custody to one parent it may make an order against the other parent requiring that parent to make either a lump sum payment or periodic payments either to the child or to the other parent for the child's benefit.

(C) Matrimonial proceedings in the Magistrates' Court. These are now governed by the Domestic Proceedings and Magistrates' Court Act 1978. Under this Act applications have to be based on certain grounds (set out elsewhere) but once an application is made the Magistrates' Court is required to consider whether to make an

order for legal custody, maintenance and access whether or not it finds the grounds proved. So the Courts' power to decide questions of custody depends on the application being made and not on it being successful. In the same way the Courts' powers are independent of either party having invited the Court to make an order as to custody.

Under this Act only a party to a marriage can apply. So the Act is not available to parties who are living together but are not married. On the other hand the power to make custody orders applies to any 'child of the family' and this expression is very widely defined.

'Child of the family'

The expression 'child of the family' includes not only all children of both parties of the marriage whether legitimate, legitimated, adopted or illegitimate but also any other child who has been treated by both parties of the marriage as a child of their family. So in the now common case where both partners have children from a previous marriage, such children will be children of the family provided that they have been treated as one of the family as, of course, they usually will. Further children who are not biologically related at all may be included. The only groups of children who are explicitly excluded by the statute from this possibility are those who have been boarded out by local authorities or voluntary organisations. This would exclude most foster children but not those privately fostered.

The Court can make an order as to the legal custody of any child of the family under the age of eighteen and as to access to such a child by either of the parties to the marriage or of any parent of the child. As in the guardianship legislation above the Court can give the parent who does not get custody specific parental rights and duties and can in exceptional circumstances commit the child to the care of the local authority. The Court may also make orders for periodical payments or for a lump sum (not exceeding £500). The Court may make such an order against a spouse who is not the child's parent but in doing so it must consider whether that person (for example, a stepfather) has assumed any responsibility for maintaining the child and whether in assuming that responsibility he was aware that the child was not his own.

(D) Divorce proceedings. Under modern divorce law (discussed on page 373 Ending a Marriage) it is very unusual for there to be a real dispute as to whether the parties are to be divorced. Real disputes are about children or about the division of the matrimonial assets (see page 327: Family Assets).

The procedures set up under the Matrimonial Causes Act (1973) are designed to separate the consideration of the arrangements for the children from other disputes. Again the jurisdiction extends to any child of the family (see box opposite). Under the 1973 Act the Court is required not to make a decree absolute of divorce unless it is satisfied either that there are no children of the family or that arrangements have been made for the welfare of every child of the family which are satisfactory or which are the best which can be made in the circumstances. This means that even if the parties agree as to custody, the judge will still consider the question and there will be a special 'children's appointment' for this purpose. The petitioner has to set out in detail the proposed arrangements and the respondent can suggest alternative arrangements. If the Court is doubtful about the arrangements it can refer the matter to a Court welfare officer 'for investigation and report'. This power is quite widely used (perhaps about 15% of cases). The welfare officer will usually interview all the parties and report on their proposals for the future of the children. If the children are old enough he will find out their views. He will obtain any reports on the family or the children by such people as doctors or school teachers. The welfare officer's primary duty is to assist the Court and he will usually make a recommendation to it. This recommendation will not necessarily be accepted but a Court which does not accept the welfare officer's report is supposed to explain to the parties why it is not doing so.

Unlike the Magistrates' Court, the Divorce Court can award custody jointly to both parties and this is now more commonly done than was once the case where the parties are likely to co-operate with each other over the upbringing of the children. It is more common to give custody to one of the parents with access to the other. In the simplest form of order the Court will simply provide that the parent who is not to have custody should have 'reasonable access' and leave the details to the parents. This is the most satisfactory arrangement if both parents are willing to co-operate. Unfortunately this is not in practice always the case. The Court can, if necessary, make very detailed orders as to the frequency, time, place and other conditions of access. The Court may impose conditions (see below). In practice, if the party with custody is really determined to frustrate the other parent's visits, he can do a good deal to do so.

In exceptional circumstances the Court may commit the child to the care of a local authority.

Transexual father

In *G v G* (1981) the father was a transexual and the Court ordered that on access should not be accompanied by his male 'friend'. He was also warned as to the danger of confusing the child by wearing aggressively female clothing.

(E) Custodianship. Custodianship is a completely new institution, introduced into English law by the Children Act 1975, the relevant provisions of which have only recently been brought into force. Its purpose is to give foster parents and other persons who have long-term care of a child, formal legal recognition of their relationship with the child falling short of adoption.

A custodianship order vests legal custody of the child in the applicant or applicants but does not terminate the legal relationship with the natural parents who retain the right to withhold agreement to the child's adoption; to administer the child's property; to arrange for the child's emigration from the United Kingdom; to change the child's name and to change the child's religion.

The mother and father of the child cannot apply. Application may be made either by a person with whom a child has had his home for a total of three years (or twelve months if the person or persons having legal custody of the child consents) including the three months immediately before the application or by a relative or step parent with whom the child has had its home for the three months preceeding the application, provided that a person with legal custody of the child consents. Notice of an application for custodianship must be given to the local authority, which will make a report to the Court.

(F) Child care and the welfare services. The provisions so far considered, although complicated, are all primarily concerned with children in the family context, giving the word family a wide meaning. In modern conditions, though this covers many cases, there are a large group of children whose families are unable or unwilling to look after them or, worse, are actually a threat to them. There have been a number of horrific cases which have received widespread public attention where young children have been systematically tortured and eventually killed by their own families. It seems, unfortunately, only too likely that this is simply the tip of the iceberg. The modern position therefore is that in addition to the specific cases already noted where a Court has power to commit a child to the care of a local authority there is a general power in local authorities to take steps for the compulsory transfer of the care of the child to themselves. These procedures are considered below (on page 315: Child Care). In addition it should be noted that many children are voluntarily entrusted to the care of local authorities by their parents, often for short periods of emergency but sometimes for long and indefinite periods. The rules governing this institution of 'voluntary care' are also discussed below (see page 316).

(G) Adoption. Under English law adoption can only take place by Court order. Its effect is basically to transfer a child from his natural parents to his adoptive parents. It is therefore the most final form of Court order for the transfer of parental rights. The institution of adoption is considered on the next page.

Principles governing the Court's exercise of its powers under these procedures. Over the last 60 years English law has adopted the principle that the paramount consideration in the application of the various different jurisdictions which we have just discussed is the welfare of the child. In some cases this principle is explicitly stated in the relevant statute (for example, section 1 of the Guardianship of Minors Act 1971) but in other cases (for example, the wardship jurisdiction) the courts have developed the principle by themselves.

The view that the child's welfare is paramount is relevant not only to disputes between mother and father but also to disputes between the natural parents on one side and others (for example foster parents) on the other.

> **Natural parents versus foster parents**
> In *J v C* (1970) the question was whether the child should be restored to his natural parents, who were Spanish nationals living in Spain, or left with his English foster parents. The child was ten years old and had lived with his foster parents for eight and a half out of those ten years. The House of Lords held that the child should stay with his foster parents. Nothing was said against the natural parents but the view was taken that to move the child which had naturally developed strong bonds with its foster parents might present formidable problems of adjustment and was therefore an unacceptable risk.

At one time it was said that the child's benefit was the most important consideration but that other factors could be taken into account. Today, however, it seems that the child's welfare is the only consideration so that such factors as the parent's wishes or their behaviour are relevant only in so far as they can be shown to affect the child's welfare. The fact that the marriage has broken up because of one party's adultery is irrelevant unless it can be shown that this behaviour is relevant to the child's welfare, for example, because the mother has been staying out all night with her lover and neglecting the child.

Of course, what is for the benefit of the child is very much a matter of opinion and judgment and in deciding what is for the child's benefit the Courts will take account of various factors. These factors will change from time to time as will the weight to be accorded to them. For instance, in the nineteenth century mothers who had been divorced because of their adultery were regularly deprived of their children. That approach is now regarded as clearly wrong on the grounds that an adulterous wife may well be a good mother. In extreme cases this can appear very hard on the father (see box opposite).

The Court would usually start from the basis that very young children should go with their mother but there is no rule to this effect. There will be mothers with whom it would not be for the benefit of the child to stay. Similarly it is usually for the benefit of a number of children to be kept together but this is not always the case.

The Courts have adopted the modern psychological theory that stability is vital to children

> **Children's spiritual welfare**
> In *Re K (Minors) (Children's Care and Control)* (1977) the wife of a clergyman in the Church of England formed an adulterous relationship with a member of the church youth group. An attempted reconciliation did not succeed and she decided to set up home with her lover. She started proceedings seeking custody of the two children, a boy aged five and a girl aged two and succeeded. The Court thought that it was for the benefit of the two year old girl to stay with her mother and for the benefit of the children to stay together. The father argued that it would be harmful for the children's spiritual welfare to be brought up in the home of an adulterous couple. This argument cannot be dismissed out of hand, but it could not be given much weight in the circumstances, since even if the father had been given custody, the Court would have given the mother wide access to the children and they could hardly have failed to discover her true position.

1982 over 25% of those adopted were over ten years of age).

(i) Adoption Services

Although the final formal decision is made by the Court, much in practice turns on the work of the adoption services which are provided in part by the voluntary agencies and in part by local authorities. There is a long tradition of work by voluntary organisations in this field. Today they must be non-profit making organisations approved by the Secretary of State for Social Services. Most local authorities have adoption services and when the relevant provisions of the Children Act 1975 come into force local authorities will be obliged to ensure that an adoption service is provided. Since 1982 it is a criminal offence for anyone, other than an adoption agency, to make arrangements for the adoption of a child unless the proposed adopter is a relative. It is worth noting, however, that it is not a crime for such a person to arrange the fostering of a child and long term fostering in practice may be a prelude to adoption.

and are therefore reluctant to order a transfer of custody unless there are very strong grounds for it. In practice this notion is very important since it means that if one party has had the children for a period, the Court will be increasingly reluctant to order a transfer to the other party.

3. ADOPTION

In English law an effective adoption requires a Court order. Informal arrangements to transfer parental rights and duties from one set of parents to another have no legal effect. Adoption was introduced into English law by the Adoption Act 1926 largely to regulate the practices which had previously been carried on for trafficking in unwanted children (particularly the illegitimate children of unmarried mothers) and also to offer measures of security to *de facto* adopters who under the previous law were exposed to the risk of the natural parents returning to claim a child years later. Between 1926 and the 1950s the majority of children placed for adoption were illegitimate. Since the 1950s the number of illegitimate children adopted has got smaller but there has been a substantial increase in adoption by step-parents and relatives. There has also been a substantial increase in the proportion of older children being adopted (for instance in

(ii) Who May Be Adopted?

The person to be adopted must be under 18 and never have been married. This represents a marked difference between English law and many other systems which permit adult adoption. This reflects the fact that in England adoption has been seen primarily as a question of transferring the bringing up of children, whereas in other systems it has been concerned largely with succession rights. So it was common practice for the Roman Emperors to adopt their successors.

It is permissible to adopt someone who has been adopted before.

(iii) Who May Adopt?

Adoptors must be over 21. There is no legal maximum age but it is understood that for a first adoption many agencies are unwilling to consider couples where the wife is aged over 40 or even younger.

Adoption orders may be made in favour of married couples but otherwise only in favour of one person. An unmarried couple who are living together cannot therefore adopt jointly though an adoption order may be made in favour of one unmarried applicant. In the case of married couples, one partner may apply where the other has disappeared or is too ill to apply, or the parties are living apart and are likely to continue to do so.

There are some very complex provisions designed to limit adoption by relatives and step-parents. These provisions are not only difficult to understand but also controversial. They seem to be based on a desire to prevent the cutting of all ties with natural parents whose marriage break-up has taken the child into a new family group-ing. On the other hand, there is clearly considerable demand for a formal means of completing the integration of the child into its new family.

If an application is made by one parent of a child alone, it must be dismissed unless the other parent is dead or lost or there are other special circumstances which justify the exclusion of the other parent. If an application is made by a step-parent either alone or jointly with a natural parent, the application should be dismissed if the Court thinks the child's custody would be better dealt with under the divorce jurisdiction. The Courts have vacillated in their application of this provision (see below). Where the applicant is a relative of the child or the husband or wife of the child's mother or father, the Court will treat the adoption application as an application for cus-todianship if it is satisfied that the child's welfare would not be better safeguarded by making an adoption order.

Step-parent adoptions

In *Re S* (1977) the Court refused to make an adoption order in favour of a stepfather of three children aged between six and eleven though the natural father showed little inter-est in them and the stepfather had formed a close relationship with them and treated them as his sons. This result was approved by the Court of Appeal on the grounds that the rule required it to be shown that adoption was better for the children than any of the arrangements which could be made under the divorce jurisdiction.

However, in *Re D* (1980) the Court of Appeal said that the test was whether a custody order could be shown to be better than an adoption. In that case weight was attached to the fact that the children (three teenagers) were anxious for the adoption to go ahead so as to make their stepfather their 'proper dad'.

(iv) Other Legal Requirements

(A) Living with the applicants. The child must be at least nineteen weeks old and have had his home with the applicants (or one of them) at all times during the preceeding thirteen weeks. If the child has not been placed by an adoption agency the period is twelve months unless the applicant is a parent, step-parent or relative.

(B) Informing the local authority. The local authority must be informed where the child is not placed with the applicant by an adoption agency. The local authority will be required to investigate the matter and report to the Court.

(C) Appointment of a guardian *ad litem*. The Court must appoint a guardian *ad litem* if it appears that a parent or guardian is unwilling to consent to the adoption order but the Court may appoint such a guardian at any time if it con-siders that the welfare of the child requires it. The duty of the guardian is to see that the interests of the child are represented.

(D) Consent of parents and guardians. In principle the consent of parents or guardians is necessary before the Court will make an adoption order. In this respect adoption is different from the proceedings considered on page 307. There the welfare of the child is paramount. In adoption the welfare of the child is very important but it does not necessarily prevail over all other con-siderations. A Court will not make an adoption order which it does not consider to be for the child's benefit but the fact that the adoption is for the child's benefit is not itself a sufficient reason for making an order without the consent of the natural parents.

The natural parent could attend the Court hearing for the purpose of giving consent but this would be unusual and agreement may be given in writing. However, the agreement can be revoked at any time before the hearing. An agreement by the mother is invalid if given within the six weeks following the birth. The natural parents some-times wish to attach conditions to their consent, for example, as to the religion in which the child is to be brought up. This is not now permitted but the adoption agency is required to take the natu-ral parents wishes as to religious upbringing into account. The natural father of an illegitmate child is not a 'parent' for the purpose of this requirement. His consent would be required if he has become a 'guardian' by obtaining a custody order under the Guardianship of Minors Act 1971.

The vast majority of adoptions are made with parental consent. (In 1978, for instance, it was over 95%.) The Court is, however, empowered to dispense with parental consent in certain closely defined circumstances. Until recently these rules could only be brought into operation when the court was considering a specific application for adoption. Under the Children Act 1975, however, a new procedure was introduced under which the child could be 'freed for adoption' in advance of a specific application for adoption. This is very important because there has always been a small number of cases where the natural parents have agreed to the adoption and then changed their minds after the child has gone to live with the prospective adopters. This causes great stress to the adoptive parents even if, at the end of the day, the court dispenses with the natural parents' consent.

(v) Legal Effects of Adoption

The basic effect of an adoption order is to sever the child's links with its natural family and make it a legitimate child of its adoptive family. In general therefore adoptive children have exactly the same rights of succession as natural born legitimate children. There are, however, special provisions about gifts in wills which depend on the age and/or seniority of children.

If an order authorising the adoption of a child who is not a British citizen is made by a Court in the United Kingdom, the child will become a British citizen from the date of the adoption if the adopter is a British citizen. So, too, in the case of a joint adoption if the adopters are British citizens. A child who is a British citizen does not lose British citizenship by virtue of being adopted by a foreigner.

One respect in which adoption does not sever ties with the natural family is the prohibited degrees of marriage. So if a man who has been adopted marries the daughter of his natural parents the marriage will be void even though neither party knows of the relationship. An adopted person cannot marry an adoptive parent

---

Freeing a child for adoption

This procedure introduced by the Children Act 1975 and in operation since 27 May 1984 enables an adoption agency to apply to the Court for an order declaring a child 'free for adoption'. If such an order is made, an adoption order can later be made without parental consent. Such an order can only be made either if the Court is satisfied that the natural parents consent or on the ground that their consent should be dispensed with on one of the grounds set out below.

Dispensing with parent's consent to adoption

If the Court is asked to dispense with the parents' consent there must be a formal Court hearing and the applicants must show that the case falls within one of the grounds laid down in the Act.

These grounds are that the parent or guardian (a) cannot be found or is incapable of giving agreement; (b) is withholding agreement unreasonably; (c) has persistently failed without reasonable cause to discharge the parental duties in relation to the child; (d) has abandoned or neglected the child; (e) has persistently ill-treated the child; (f) has seriously ill-treated the child and (whether because of the ill-treatment or for other reasons) the rehabilitation of the child within the household of the parent or guardian is unlikely.

It will be seen that grounds (c) to (f) involves serious criticism of the natural parents. In practice few applications are made under these grounds as the Courts have taken a narrow view of their scope. Most applications are therefore under

grounds (a) and (b) and it is clearly critical to consider on what grounds a parent will be treated as unreasonably withholding consent. It is clear that it is not necessarily unreasonable for a parent to withhold consent even though a reasonable person might think that the child would be better off with the potential adopters. In theory the question the Court will ask itself is whether a hypothetical reasonable parent would consent, taking into account all the relevant circumstances such as the child's prospects if adopted. The ability of the prospective adopters to offer the child a financially secure and emotionally stable home will be very important. Since the effect of the adoption will be to cut the remaining ties with the natural parent, the existing strengths of these links will be crucial since the reasonable parent will take into account the real chance of re-establishing these links.

The certificate that confirms the new parent's status and provides the child with his proof of identity.

Only the new name of the child is given on the short adoption certificate and on the birth certificate. The place and date of birth remain unchanged, however. The short form of birth certificate does not give the names of either the child's natural parents or its new ones. The adopting couple are named in the full one

Only the names and occupations of the new parents are given on the adoption certificate. The natural parents are not mentioned. The court order, containing details of the natural parents and the child's original name, is kept by the General Register Office in Titchfield. Information can be obtained from it only by order of a court, or by the child itself at the age of 18

Application No. 728

QHA 007502

CAUTION:—Any person who (1) falsifies any of the particulars on this certificate, or (2) uses a falsified certificate as true, knowing it to be false, is liable to prosecution.

CERTIFIED COPY OF AN ENTRY

1. No. of entry **849**

2. Date **Sixth January 1974**
   and country of birth of child **England**

   Registration District **Bromley**
   Sub-district **Beckenham**

3. Name and surname of child **Emma Mary Lacey**

4. Sex of child **Female**

5. Name and surname **James Edward Lacey, 4 Sunnington Road,**
   address **Upper Edmonton, N18 Member of**
   and **Parliament and his wife Pamela Winifred**
   occupation of adopter or adopters **Lacey of the same address.**

6. Date of adoption order **Twenty sixth November 1974**
   and description of court by which made **Edmonton County Court**

7. Date of entry **Third December 1974**

8. Signature of officer deputed by Registrar General to attest the entry **K. V. Jones**

...y in the Adopted Children Register maintained at the ...d, Fareham, Hants., England. Given at the General ...ce.

...on **Fourth December** 19**74**

...Section 20. This Act provides that the particulars in spaces 2, 3, 4, 5 and 6 ...doption Order.

...Adopted Children Register, if purporting to be sealed or stamped with the ...r or other proof of the entry, be received as evidence of the adoption to

---

XC 586001

1 & 2 ELIZ. 2 CH. 20

CERTIFICATE **OF BIRTH**

728|74

Name and Surname **Emma Mary Lacey**
Sex **Female**
Date of Birth **Sixth January 1974**
Place { Registration District **Bromley**
of
Birth { Sub-district **Beckenham**

Certified to have been compiled from records in the custody of the Registrar General. Given at the General Register Office, London, under the Seal of the said Office, the **4th** day of **December** 19**74**

CAUTION:—Any person who (1) falsifies any of the particulars on this certificate, or (2) uses a falsified certificate as true, knowing it to be false, is liable to prosecution.

849|82

but otherwise there is no prohibition on marrying within the adoptive family.

(vi) Registration

The Registrar General maintains an adopted children's register. Entries are made whenever an adoption order is made by an English Court. A certified copy of any entry will give the child's names and the surname of the adopting parent. The Registrar General can also issue a short form of birth certificate which will not reveal that the child has been adopted. The register is open to public scrutiny.

The Registrar keeps further records which enables the natural parents of an adoptive child to be traced. However, these records are not open to public search. This used to mean that an adopted child could not trace his natural parents but the Children Act 1975 now confers on an adopted child who has reached the age of eighteen the right to the information necessary to enable him to obtain his original birth certificate. This provision applies to any person adopted since 1926 but in the case of a person adopted before 12 November 1975 only if the enquirer has been interviewed by a counsellor.

4. CHILD CARE

The twentieth century has seen an enormous increase in the scope of State action to look after the welfare of children. This expansion has a number of different roots. One is the desire to control child delinquency and a belief that the criminal law cannot be applied in the same way to children and to adults. This has resulted in different procedures for dealing with children accused of crime and a different range of punishments which has a markedly greater reformative emphasis. A quite different element is the paternalism of the modern welfare state. This touches on deeply sensitive issues. When parents systematically maltreat their children even to the point of death an outraged public tends to blame not only the parents but also social workers who have failed to take the child away from the parents. On the other hand, the same social worker may in different circumstances be accused of intruding on the proper scope of parental responsibility. The balance is not easy to strike.

Before the Second World War provision for needy children was largely in the hands of voluntary agencies, of which Dr Barnardo's Homes was perhaps the best known example. Since the Children Act 1948 local authorities have been under a duty to provide care for those children deprived of a normal home life. It is an important feature of the system that this duty falls on local authorities. Since 1970, following the report of the Seebohm Committee, local authorities have been required to have integrated teams of social workers, acting under a director of social services who is responsible for many but not all, of the social services affecting the family. Education, however, falls under the director of education and the education committee (see below under 6. Education) and most matters affecting health are the responsibility of regional health authorities. Council help with housing is also usually the responsibility of a housing department, whose welfare activities are outside the control of the Social Services Department. Central government also has an important role particularly through its operation of the supplementary benefit system. One of the major problems in this area is the difficulty which large bureaucracies have in communicating with each other, so that a family's problems may be divided between a range of agencies of central and local government pursuing divergent policies.

(i) Help Falling Short of Care

As we have seen, the duty to provide care for children deprived of a normal home life was originally imposed by the Children Act 1948. Once this Act was in operation it became apparent that local authorities needed to be able to take steps which would reduce or eliminate the need to take children into care. Not only is it desirable for psychological reasons to keep the family together in most cases but it is also much cheaper and therefore a proper use for public money. Under the Children and Young Persons Act 1963 local authorities are required 'to make available such advice, guidance and assistance as may promote the welfare of children by diminishing the need to receive children into or keep them in care'. The powers of local authorities under this Act are very wide though the practice of local authorities no doubt varies a good deal. A local authority may provide services which help parents having difficulty in coping such as day care. It may also provide financial assistance, for example, the payment of rent and rates arrears or fuel bills.

315

(ii) 'Voluntary' Care

It is common to distinguish between 'voluntary' and compulsory care. Under the voluntary system the local authority's duty is not to *take* the child into care but to *receive* it.

The circumstances in which the local authority is under a duty to receive the child into care are set out in the Child Care Act 1980.

Taking into care by local authority

The local authority should take the child into care (i) *either* if he has no parents or guardians or has been (and remains) abandoned by his parents *or* his parents or guardians are incapacitated from providing for his proper accommodation, maintenance and upbringing; and (ii) it is necessary to act in the interests of the welfare of the child.

Some 30,000 children are received into care under this legislation each year. Some of these cases are for short term reasons, such as the illness of one parent, but the majority are for continuing reasons. Under the 1948 Act the parents were in principle entitled to ask for the return of the child at any time but this right has been substantially qualified by the Children Act 1975. That Act provides:

(a) Once the child has been in care for six months a parent or guardian commits a criminal offence by removing the child without giving 28 days notice.

(b) If the child has been boarded out with foster parents for three years, the foster parents will be entitled to apply to the Court for a custodianship order.

(c) If the child has been in care of a local authority for three years that in itself is ground for the local authority to make a parental rights resolution (see above).

Further, once the child is in care of a local authority, it is open to the authority to pass a resolution by which the authority assumes parental rights and duties. This is an administrative power vested in the council or the authority but in practice delegated to the council social services committee or perhaps a sub committee of that committee. Certain grounds must be present before such a resolution can properly be passed (see opposite). Such a resolution passes to the local authority most of the powers and duties which the parent has in relation to a child but it does not pass the right to agree to an adoption order or to choose the child's religious upbringing nor does it extinguish the natural parents' obligation to maintain the child (though in practice local authorities recover little of the cost of maintaining children in care from the natural parents). If a parent objects to the parental rights resolution, the resolution will lapse unless the authority within fourteen days of receiving the objection makes a complaint to the Juvenile Court. The authority must inform parents of their right to object if they know of the parents' whereabouts. The Court should allow the resolution to lapse unless it is satisfied (a) that the authority had grounds at the time of the resolution was passed; and (b) that there continue to be grounds; and (c) that it is in the interests of the child for the resolution to remain in force.

(iii) Care Proceedings

The Children and Young Persons Act of 1969 requires local authorities to make enquiries into any case where they have received information, which suggests that there are grounds for bring-

---

Grounds on which a parental rights resolution may be passed

1. The child's parents are dead and he has no guardian or custodian
2. The child has throughout the three years preceeding the passing of the resolution been in the care of a local authority.
3. One of the child's parents is incapable or unfit to have the care of the child. Inability or unfitness must fall within one of the five specified grounds which are: (a) that the parent has abandoned the child; (b) that the parent suffers from permanent disability rendering him incapable of caring for the child; (c) that the parent suffers from a mental disorder rendering him unfit to have the care of the child; (d) that the parent is of such habits or mode of life as to be unfit to have the care of the child; (e) that the parents have so consistently failed without reasonable cause to discharge the obligations of a parent as to be unfit to have the care of the child.
4. That a parental rights resolution has been passed in relation to one parent and that parent is or is likely to become a member of the household comprising the child and the other parent.

---

ing care proceedings, and, if it then appears that there are such grounds, to bring care proceedings unless they consider that not to be either in the interests of the child or in the public interest. Historically much such information has come from the National Society for the Prevention of Cruelty to Children (NSPCC) which itself receives much information on a confidential basis about children in need; today local authorities have elaborate procedures for identifying 'children at risk' though even so the procedures are not wholly effective.

Proceedings may be started by a local authority, by a constable or by an 'authorised person' (only the NSPCC and its officers have been authorised). The Court has power to make an order in respect of a child aged seventeen (but not in respect of a married child aged sixteen) if one of a number of conditions is satisfied (see below) and if the court considers that the child 'is in need of care and control which he is unlikely to receive unless the Court makes an order'.

Conditions for making a care order
1. The child's proper development is being avoidably prevented or neglected or his health is being avoidably impaired or neglected or he is being ill-treated.
2. It is likely that condition 1. will be satisfied because it is or has been satisfied in relation to another member of the household to which the child belongs. In other words if condition 1. could be established in relation to one child in the family, then this condition operates if it can be shown that there was a risk that another child would be ill-treated.
3. It is probable that condition 1. will be satisfied because a person who has been convicted of certain serious offences against children is, or may become, a member of the same household as the child.
4. The child is exposed to moral danger.
5. The child is beyond the control of his parent or guardian.
6. The child is of compulsory school age and is not receiving sufficient full time education suitable to his age, ability and aptitude.
7. The child has been guilty of an offence (other than homicide). (In practice children are nearly always prosecuted for criminal offences rather than care proceedings being brought.)

(iv) Place of Safety Orders

In cases of child abuse it may be necessary to act very quickly. A magistrate can on the application of any person make a 'place of safety order'. This authorises the child's detention in a place of safety for up to 28 days. The magistrate need only be satisfied that the applicant has reasonable cause to believe that either one of the first five conditions set out in the box below is satisfied or that a Court would find the second condition satisfied or that the child is about to leave the United Kingdom in contravention of legislation regulating the sending abroad of juvenile entertainers. There is no appeal against an order which cannot be renewed. In practice the local authority may use the 28 days to start care proceedings.

(v) Appeals Against Local Authority Decisions

Many parents may acquiesce in the local authority effectively taking over their children but there will always be a significant group who do not. How can they challenge local authority decision? In practice the quickest and most effective way may be to seek to persuade the local authority to change its mind. A good local authority should have its own procedures for internal review and a local councillor should be able to offer guidance.

There is now a right to appeal to a Juvenile Court where the local authority terminates access to the child. It is important to note that this right only applies where access is terminated and not where it is restricted. There is now a code of practice which sets out basic principles on how local authorities should act in handling decisions as to access. This code emphasises, amongst other things, the need to set up proper procedures to enable parents to pursue complaints and to ask for decisions about access to be reviewed. Failure, without good reason, to follow the code may be treated by the Courts as evidence of unreasonableness (see page 318).

One way of challenging a local authority decision would be to make the child a ward of Court and seek to persuade the Court that the local authority's decision was not in the best interests of the child. However, the House of Lords has held that the Courts should not allow the wardship jurisdiction to be used as a routine way of challenging local authority decisions. The Courts will only intervene if it can be shown that the local authority is acting outside its powers or is acting unreasonably or in some exceptional cases, where the Court's inherent powers fill some gap in the local authority's power to deal with the situation.

Access to child restricted by local authority

In *A v Liverpool City Council* (1982) a local authority had restricted a mother's access to her two and a half year old son to a monthly supervised visit to the day nursery where he was being accommodated. The House of Lords held that this decision should not be reviewed by the Court in the exercise of its wardship jurisdiction.

---

5. FOSTERING

Where a local authority has taken a child into care it can provide for him either by placing him in a residential home or by boarding him out to foster parents. Rather more than a third of children in care are boarded out.

In practice local authorities distinguish between short term fostering, long term fostering and fostering with a view to adoption and the government has laid down detailed regulations as to the selection of foster parents. Foster parents are required to sign an undertaking. In this they promise to look after the child as if it were their own and to allow the child to be removed from their care when required. In practice it is very difficult to find suitable foster homes and research suggests that perhaps as many as half of the fosterings break down.

Boarding out allowances are paid for by the local authority. Local authorities fix their own rates and there are apparently wide variations. Several local authorities pay special rates to attract foster parents for particularly difficult or handicapped children.

Fostering can also be arranged privately but any person who looks after a child to whom he or she is not related for more than 27 days must notify the local authority. Failure to give notification is a criminal offence. Those who are fostering a series of children on a continuous basis need only notify the local authority in relation to the first child.

6. EDUCATION

(i) Introduction

The Education Act 1944 provides that it is 'the duty of parents of every child of compulsory school age to cause him to receive efficient full time education suitable to his age, ability and apititude either by regular attendance at school or otherwise.'

Compulsory school age is from the first day of the school term following the child's fifth birthday. It is the policy of some education authorities for children to start at school in the term (or even the academic year) in which their fifth birthday falls ('rising fives'). It is not compulsory to take up such a place.

Compulsory education continues until the age of sixteen. It would, of course, be very disruptive if all children left school on their sixteenth birthday. There are therefore only two school-leaving dates in the year. For children whose sixteenth birthday falls between 1 September and 31 January the leaving date is the last day of the spring term at their school. If the child's sixteenth birthday falls between 1 February and 31 August, then the leaving date is the 'May school leaving date' which is the Friday before the last Monday in May.

A substantial number of parents satisfy their duty by sending their children to independent schools. A small, but apparently growing number, do so by educating their children at home. This is perfectly permissible provided that the child is receiving efficient full time education. 'Education Otherwise' (25 Common Lane, Hemmingford Abbots, Cambs TE18 9AN) is an organisation formed in 1977 to provide advice and information on how children may be removed from State education.

Possible reasons for non-attendance at school
1. Illness or unavoidable cause. The cause must relate to the child and therefore this ground is not satisfied where the mother was a chronic invalid and the child stayed at home to run the house.
2. For days of religious observance by the religious group to which the parent belongs.
3. Where the school is not within walking distance (usually treated as not more than three miles by a safe route) and the local authority has not arranged either for transport between home and school or boarding accommodation or registration at a school nearer home.

318

However, once the child has been registered at school the parent has a duty to ensure that the child attends regularly subject to certain narrow exceptions (see above). If the education authority is not satisfied with the child's attendance it can serve a school attendance order on the parent. Failure to comply with such a notice is a criminal offence. It is no defence that the parent did not know of the child's absence or was doing his best to ensure that the child attended school. If the parent considers that the child is receiving satisfactory education he should ask the local education authority to revoke the attendance order. When a local education authority decides that the child is not receiving efficient education, the parent may appeal to the Secretary of State.

(ii) Religious Education

The 1944 Education Act required religious instruction to be provided in every county school (that is in schools wholly funded by the county) according to an agreed syllabus. The Act does not define religious education and it is not confined to Christianity. For historical reasons many schools before 1944 had strong ties with particular religions, particularly the Church of England and the Roman Catholic Church. Most of these schools continued their denominational link after 1944 as either voluntary aided or voluntary controlled schools (in both the buildings are provided by the voluntary agency but in controlled schools all other costs are met by the local education authority (LEA) whereas in aided schools some of the running costs are not met by the LEA). Religious education at such schools will have a denominational element which will be absent at county schools, although many children at these schools may not come from families which adhere to that denomination.

The 1944 Act also required that the school day begin both in county and voluntary schools with corporate worship. In county schools this must not be distinctive of any particular denomination. The Act does not say that worship shall be Christian worship.

A parent may request that his child, whether attending a county or a voluntary school be wholly or partly excused from attendance at religious education or religious worship or both. It is probably prudent to put such a request in writing as the right is the parents' and not the child's and a letter from the parent will serve to authenticate the request. Normally this request does not involve absence from school and schools

should supervise those who are withdrawn. However, in certain circumstances a parent may withdraw a child from school to take part in an act of worship outside.

(iii) Choice of School

The Education Act 1944 stated that so far as possible the Secretary of State and the LEA must try to educate a child in accordance with the parents' wishes. In practice this is more a state of hope than commitment since the LEA can often put forward plausible grounds of efficiency for not falling in with the parents' wishes.

It certainly does not mean that parents have a free choice of which school their child should attend. One of the problems in this area is that in practice not all schools run by local authorities are equally good or, perhaps just as important, are not thought by parents to be equally good. Local authorities are understandably reluctant to admit this and will naturally resist the overcrowding of popular schools. In practice however, many schools, as a result of falling birth rates, are not full and head teachers commonly enjoy considerable freedom to admit extra children up to a maximum fixed by the LEA. An informal approach to the head teacher can often therefore be a useful step. If the head teacher will accept a child it does not matter that the child lives outside the normal catchment area for the school though the LEA will not normally accept responsibility for the travel costs. There is no prohibition on child going to school in another LEA, though the receiving LEA may wish to levy a 'transfer fee' from the exporting LEA. (This can be a perfectly sensible step where the child's home is close to the LEA boundary or where the child has moved home at a critical point in its education and it is still practical to travel to the old school).

The Education Act 1980 was designed to improve the parents' chances of effectively influencing the choice of schools. Under this Act the LEA must give each parent a chance to express a preference. The LEA is required to give information to parents to help them and the parent must give reasons for the preference (see boxes on page 320). The LEA may refuse to accept the parental preference on the ground that this would prejudice the provision of efficient education or the efficient use of resources. Refusal may also be justified in those areas where selection is still used by failure in the examination or if the school is an aided or special agreement

319

Information which the Local Education Authority must provide

The information must be available in advance of the school year to which it relates. Normally the LEA will ask for the parents' preference by a given date and the information must be available at least six weeks before that date. The information must be available at LEA offices and schools. In practice most LEAs distribute an information sheet to parents of children who are inside their system and known to be about to change school.

The information must include:

1. The addresses and telephone numbers of LEA offices where enquiries may be made.
2. Details where information may be obtained about particular schools.
3. Names, addresses and telephone numbers of all maintained schools and expected numbers of pupils and age range. Religious connection, if any, should be indicated.
4. LEA policy on transfer between schools other than at normal admission age.
5. LEA arrangements for transport.
6. LEA policy on milk, meals and any arrangements for remission of charges.
7. LEA policy on school clothing and arrangements for grants.
8. LEA policy on entry to public examinations (e g CSE, O Level and A Level).
9. LEA provision for special educational needs.
10. Any changes to the above expected to be made after the start of the school year.
11. In Wales information about teaching of Welsh and instruction in the Welsh language.

Information must also be provided at each individual school about the school. This is often provided in the form of a printed or duplicated brochure which parents can take away. This must include details of subjects taught and the level to which they are taught; subject choices available; details of how teaching is organised and arrangements for homework; information about school discipline and pastoral care and in the case of schools with children over fifteen details of the school's policy for public examinations and an analysis of the results in the last available year.

---

school because admission would be in conflict with the arrangements made between the LEA and the governors.

The LEA must set up an appeal committee so that parents may appeal. The parent must appeal in writing giving grounds and must be given an opportunity to appear before the committee to be heard. Parents may be accompanied by a friend or be represented. A parent who is dissatisfied with the decision of the appeal committee may appeal to the Secretary of State.

Parental preference

Parents must give reasons when stating a preference. Reasons which are often given include:

1. The child has an elder brother or sister at the school;
2. The child has an appropriate religious affiliation;
3. The school is single sex (or coeducational) and the parents prefer single sex (or coeducational) schools;
4. The school offers teaching in subjects which are not available in other schools;
5. The school is the most accessible. (This will usually mean nearest but it might be the journey to the nearest school is particularly dangerous and there is an alternative which can be more safely reached by a child.);
6. In Wales, a preference for instruction in the Welsh language or for a school which teaches Welsh.

---

7. UNMARRIED PARENTS AND THEIR CHILDREN

Historically English law attached great importance to the status of legitimacy and made many significant distinctions in its treatment of those who were characterised as legitimate or illegitimate. The tendency has been to move away from this position but there are still significant differences. Further legislation designed to bring the position of legitimate and illegitimate children even closer seems probable. In the past illegitimate children also suffered from serious social disabilities. Today the children of stable unmarried relationships may be at little or no social disadvantage although this is not necessarily true of children being brought up in a single parent family.

(i) Who Is Illegitimate?

The common law rule was that the child was legitimate if its parents were validly married to each other either at the time of conception or at the time of birth. So a child would be legitimate if the parents were married when it was conceived even if they were divorced by the time of its birth. Similarly if the father died before birth. Much more common in practice, of course, were the so-called 'shot-gun weddings' where the parents married between conception and birth.

Of course this discussion assumes that the identity of the father is known since the husband of the wife may not be the father. The common law, however, had a very strong presumption that a child born 'in lawful wedlock' was legitimate. It was quite insufficient therefore to show that the mother had committed adultery at the relevant time. It was necessary to prove beyond reasonable doubt that the husband could not be the father. Since the husband and wife could not themselves give evidence as to whether intercourse had taken place if the result would be to bastardise the child this would often be impossible unless the husband had been out of the country at the relevant time or could prove that he was sterile or impotent.

These common law rules have been substantially amended by statute. Since 1949 spouses have been able to give evidence that marital intercourse has not taken place and since 1969 it has been sufficient to prove that it is more probable than not that the child is illegitimate.

Further the common law restriction to the children of a valid marriage has been qualified in a number of ways. In 1926 English law adopted the rule which had already been adopted in most other countries that the child could be legitimated by its parents' marriage after its birth. Under the Legitimacy Act 1926 this was only possible if both parties were unmarried when the child was born but this restriction was removed by the Legitimacy Act 1959. Where the child was legitimated in this way the birth must be re-registered to show this.

At common law children born to a voidable marriage were made illegitimate if the marriage was annulled. This was a logical but harsh deduction from the rule that a voidable marriage once annulled was to be treated as if it never was. However since 1971 nullity decrees no longer have retrospective effect so that this rule has disappeared.

The common law similarly treated the children of void marriages as illegitimate. Again this rule was harsh, particularly where the marriage was void but the parties were blithely unaware of the fact. Under the Legitimacy Act 1959 the children of a void marriage are legitimate where one or both of the parents reasonably believed the marriage was valid. An example would be a marriage which was void because one of the parties was already married. Obviously the other party might not know this; indeed the married party might think he was single and that his former spouse who had long since disappeared was dead. In both cases the children of such a marriage would be legitimate.

Finally an adopted child is treated as the child of its adoptive parents and the Children Act 1975 provides that this prevents him from being illegitimate.

(ii) Proving Parentage

As we have seen (above) the common law imposed artificial restraints on the process of establishing parentage by excluding evidence from husband and wife as to marital intercourse and requiring proof beyond reasonable doubt. These obstacles have been removed but some difficulties remain. It may be alleged or indeed proved that the mother was having sexual intercourse with two men at the relevant times (an extreme example being the German lady who had twins which were established to have different fathers!). Here the most helpful evidence will be provided by blood tests, which the Court has power to order under the Family Law Reform Act 1969 in the course of any civil procedings in which paternity is in issue. (Blood will not actually be taken by force but the court may make an adverse inference from refusal to provide a sample.) Blood tests cannot conclusively prove that a man is the father but they can establish that the man could not possibly be the father. It is important to see that the tests may establish that as much as 90% of the male population, or even more, could not possibly be the father. So if a mother has been sleeping with two men, X and Y, and blood tests show that X could be the father and Y could not, then a Court may well infer that X is the father unless it accepts the hypothesis of a third lover, Z, with genetic characteristics shared by only a small proportion of the population.

Under the Civil Evidence Act 1968 entry of the name of a man as the father of a child in the register of births constitutes *prima facie* evidence that he is the father. In practice this means that anyone who wishes to show that the man registered as father is not the natural father will have to bear the burden of proof. In a way this is perhaps surprising since the register is simply an administrative matter but it has considerable practical importance and it is worth saying a little more about the process of registering the birth.

The Births and Deaths Registration Act 1953 provides that the father and mother of every child born in this country must give the Registrar of Births the required particulars of a child's birth within 42 days of the birth. The vast majority of children are now born in hospital and in some cases the Registrar may send officials to the hospital to complete the relevant form. In other cases it will be necessary to call at the Register Office. Hospitals appear to provide the Registrar with details of birth so that he will know that a birth has not been registered. The father of an illegitimate child is not under an obligation to register.

Regulations lay down the information to be provided and the relevant official will normally go through the standard questions and record the answers in the register. The practice is to enter the name given as that of the father unless it appears that the father is not the husband of the mother. In that case the name of the father is normally left blank (with two exceptions discussed below). In other words if the father and mother are living at the same address and using the same surname, the father's name is likely to be recorded without question even though he is not the husband of the mother. On the other hand, if the parties are married but the mother is continuing to use her maiden name, she may have to persuade the official that the father is her husband. The standard form of birth certificate is simply a copy of the entries in the register. So if the name of the father is blank in the register, it will be blank on the certificate. This will inevitably reveal that the child is illegitimate. This could cause considerable embarrassment to the child and since 1947 it has been possible to obtain a short form which does not contain any details of parentage or adoption. Of course, if such forms were only issued to illegitimate or adopted children this would itself arouse suspicion, but they are in fact widely used, especially since they are issued free by the Register Office and full certificates are issued only if asked for.

Under the Births and Deaths Registration Act 1953, the name of the father of an illegitimate child could be registered at the joint request of the mother and the man acknowledging himself to be the father. He had to attend personally at the Register Office and both he and the mother had to sign the register. This method is still possible but the father instead of attending personally may make a statutory declaration. Further, the father's name may be entered at the mother's request if she has obtained an affiliation order against the father. It is also possible to add the father's name at a later date at the mother's request either by producing a statutory declaration by the father or by producing a certified copy of an affiliation order. It should be noted, however, that all the procedures described in this paragraph can only be employed if the mother agrees. The father of an illegitimate child cannot insist against the mother's wishes on his name being registered.

(iii) The Legal Consequences of Illegitimacy

The basic attitude of the common law was to treat illegitimate children as if they did not exist. In the usual way of English law this barbaric attitude was made more respectable by converting it into Latin and describing the child as *filius nullius* (the child of no one). This approach is no longer respectable and there have been a number of statutory changes which have diminished, but not removed, the differences in the legal treatment of legitimate and illegitimate children. Another important point is that the father of an illegitimate child is seriously disadvantaged in his legal rights in relation to the child as compared with the father of a legitimate child. This is a matter of increasing practical importance as more and more couples set up long term unmarried relationships.

There are still important differences in the treatment of illegitimate children in the areas of maintenance, inheritance, citizenship and custody. We will now discuss each of these matters in turn.

(A) Obligation to support an illegitimate child. If the mother and father are living together in a stable relationship they will normally support the child in exactly the same way as if it were legitimate and no problem will arise. However there may be no such relationship or the relationship may break down. In that case the mother may look to the father for help in supporting the child. In practice in such cases the mother often applies for supplementary benefit and the Department of Health and Social Security (DHSS) may seek to pass part of the burden to the father. A significant number of

No fee is chargeable for this certificate

GC 403017

1 & 2 ELIZ. 2 CH. 20

CERTIFICATE

OF BIRTH

Name and Surname *Graham Templar Howard*

Sex *Male*

Date of Birth *Sixth June 1971*

Place Registration District *ALDERSHOT*

of

Birth Sub-district *FARNBOROUGH AND HARTLEY WINTNEY*

I, *Helen A Lay* Registrar of Births and Deaths

for the sub-district of *FARNBOROUGH AND HARTLEY WINTNEY* in the

Registration District of *ALDERSHOT* do hereby

certify that the above particulars have been compiled from an entry in

a register in my custody.

Date *5th June 1971.*

N P C G S *496*

Registrar of Births and Deaths.

CAUTION:—*Any person who (1) falsifies any of the particulars on this certificate, or (2) uses a falsified certificate as true, knowing it to be false, is liable to prosecution.*

such children are taken into care and again the local authority may seek a personal contribution from the father. In practice it seems that the sums recovered are not large since those parents who are most irresponsible in looking after their children are likely on the whole to be those who have fewest resources available for contribution.

The most satisfactory arrangement for the mother, and indeed for the father in many cases, is for the father to agree privately to support the child. Such agreements are enforceable by the mother. If significant sums of money are involved, it is probably prudent for the mother to take legal advice as to the drawing up of the agreement.

If the father will not agree, or indeed denies that he is the father, the mother may apply to the Magistrates' Court for an affiliation order. If the Court finds that the defendant is the father it may order him to make periodic payments and a lump sum not exceeding £500. There is no limit on the amount of the periodic payments but it appears the amounts ordered are usually not large.

Where the mother has been in receipt of supplementary benefit the DHSS may apply, if the mother has obtained an affiliation order, to

LONG FORM BIRTH CERTIFICATE (FOR SHORT FORM CERTIFICATE SEE PREVIOUS PAGE)

DB 846370

[Printed by Authority of the Registrar-General.]

B. Cert.
R.B.D.

CERTIFIED COPY of an ENTRY OF BIRTH.

Pursuant to the Births and Deaths Registration Acts, 1836 to 1929.

Registration District   CROYDON

Birth in the Sub-District of   CROYDON NORTH   In the   COUNTY BOROUGH OF CROYDON

No.	When and Where Born	Name if any	Sex	Name and Surname of Father	Name and Maiden Surname of Mother	Rank or Profession of Father	Signature, Description and Residence of Informant	When Registered	Signature of Registrar	Baptismal Name, if added after Registration of Birth
90	First October 1942 2, Canterbell Road N.9.	John Vernon	Boy		Phyllis May Marsh formerly Curtis	Police Constable	T.P. Howard, Father 1, Lakehall Road Thornton Heath.	Twenty Fifth October 1942.	F.Barth.	

Deputy Registrar

I, **FRED. W. BARTH** Registrar of Births and Deaths for the Sub-District of **CROYDON NORTH**, in the
do hereby certify that this is a true copy of the Entry No. 90 in the Register Book of Births for the said Sub-District, and that such Register Book is now legally in my custody.

Witness my hand this 25th day of OCTOBER 19 42.

Registrar of Births and Deaths

CAUTION.—Any person who (1) falsifies any of the particulars on this Certificate, or (2) uses it as true, knowing it to be falsified, is liable to Prosecution.

The Statutory Fee for this Certificate is 3s. 7d.
If required subsequently to registration, a Search Fee is payable in addition.

have it varied so as to direct payment to the DHSS, or, if no order has been made, may itself apply for one. A local authority which has taken the child into custody has similar powers.

(B) Succession rights. At common law illegitimate relationships did not exist at all for the purposes of intestate succession. So if the father died intestate, an illegitimate son would get nothing. Similarly the father and mother would get nothing if the son predeceased them intestate. This rule was altered by the Family Law Reform Act 1969 to the extent that an illegitimate child has now the same succession rights to its parents as a legitimate child and similarly the parents have the same succession rights on the death intestate of the child. However, the reform only applies to the parent/child relationship and does not extend to other blood relationships like brother and sister, grandparent and grandchild or uncle/aunt and nephew/niece. This will produce results which many people will consider bizarre (see box below).

At common law a testator could make a gift to an illegitimate child but in practice such gifts were often defeated by the ways in which courts interpreted wills. Thus there was a rule that if a gift was made to 'all my children' or to the 'children of A', the word 'children' was to be treated as meaning legitimate children. A testator might meet this by indicating the beneficiary by name or by a gift to 'all my children whether legitimate or illegitimate' but in the latter case the Courts excluded illegitimate children conceived between the making of the will and the testator's death on the grounds that to do otherwise would encourage immorality! These rules have been abolished by the Family Law Reform Act 1969 and the presumption now is that (unless some contrary intention appears) a testator who refers to 'children' means to include those both legitimate and illegitimate.

(C) Citizenship. Illegitimate children are seriously discriminated against in respect of citizenship since they cannot acquire citizenship rights through their father. So, for instance, a child born abroad to a British father and a foreign mother would acquire British citizenship if its parents were married but not if they were not married.

(D) Custody. The basic principle laid down by the Children Act 1975 is that the mother of an illegitimate child is the person entitled to custody and that the father has no parental rights. For this purpose it makes no difference that the relationship between father and mother is a stable one. The father can apply for custody under the Guardianship of Minors Act 1971 (see page 308) but the decisive question here will be what is in the best interests of the child. In some cases, no doubt, the father may be able to persuade the Court that he has established such a relationship with the child, that it is in the child's best interests for him to be given custody.

8. COMING OF AGE

Historically children were regarded as coming of age at 21. This age was changed by the Family Law Reform Act 1969 to 18 though many families continue to celebrate the 21st rather than the 18th birthday of their children. In fact however there is no one single age at which a child's capacity to do things changes. It is much more accurate to think of the period between birth and the age of 21 as a ladder with many steps, each of which involves some legal consequence.

The following table (on page 326), by no means exhaustive, sets out some of the most important results which the law attaches to the achievement of a given age.

Succession rights of illegitimate children

Suppose A and B, a man and woman living together in a stable unmarried relationship have two children X and Y. All the family are involved in a car accident and A, B and X die but Y survives. If the three deceased die in the order A, B, X (or are presumed to do so because of the presumption that in the case of simultaneous deaths the oldest dies first) then the estates of A and B will be divided between X and Y, but X's share will not pass to Y. On the other hand, if the order of death was A, X, B or B, X, A the whole of the family assets would pass to Y.

Birth	Liable to tax Entitled to personal tax allowance Can hold Premium Bonds Can have deposit or current account with bank or building society	**Fourteen years**	Go into bar with adult (but not buy or drink alcohol) Pay full fare on British Rail Boy can be convicted of rape or unlawful sexual intercourse
Six weeks	Must have had birth registered	**Sixteen years**	Marry (with parental consent) Apply for supplementary benefit Leave school Consent to medical treatment (If girl) consent to lawful sexual intercourse (but note that if a girl under sixteen in fact consents, the intercourse though unlawful is not rape)
Nineteen weeks	Can be adopted		
Two years	Pay child's air fare		
Three years	Must be paid for on public transport (some areas may not require payment until five)		
Five years	Must start school Can drink alcohol in private		
Seven years	Can operate bank account or building society account on own signature	**Seventeen years**	Hold driving licence Put name on electoral register
Ten years	This is the minimum age at which a child can be convicted of a crime. This depends on proof that the child can tell the difference between right and wrong. Once the child has reached fourteen this will be presumed.	**Eighteen years**	Vote Marry without parents' consent Own land Enter into binding contracts Buy drinks in bar of pub Make a will
		Twenty-one years	Stand as a candidate for Parliament or local council Drive a lorry or bus (If male) consent to homosexual acts in private
Twelve years	Child can buy a pet Pay full air fare		
Thirteen years	Can have a part-time job		

1. PROPERTY RIGHTS

Many countries have a system of community property under which the property of husband and wife becomes their joint property. There are many different systems: for instance, in some countries only assets acquired after marriage are commonly owned while in others common ownership extends to the separate property of the parties before marriage. In some countries a single system is mandatory, while in others the parties are free to choose from among a number of alternatives. English law has no such systems. In principle marriage has no effect on the property rights of the parties except such as they choose to make for themselves. Since 1970 the Court has had wide power to order one partner to transfer property to the other when granting a decree of divorce or nullity. These powers are discussed on page 177. Since disputes about property most commonly occur when the marriage collapses these statutory powers reduce the extent to which the strict legal position is important. However, there are still a number of situations where the legal position is important. These include disputes arising upon the death or bankruptcy of one of the parties; the situation where one of the parties to the marriage has remarried before seeking the Court's assistance and the increasingly common cases where the parties have never been married at all. Such disputes turn on the legal position. Unfortunately between 1945 and 1970 the Courts had stretched the rules a long way in order to give themselves room to manoeuvre of the kind which they were given by statute in 1970. This has made the law less clear and more difficult to explain than is desirable.

(i) Historical Background

The common law position was well summarised in the aphorism that 'husband and wife are one and the husband is that one.' On marriage all the wife's property and her income became her husband's. The major qualification on this was that any interest the wife had in land only passed to the husband for the duration of the marriage and would therefore revert to the wife or her family at the latest on the husband's death. This rule reflects a wider concern. Wealthy fathers with daughters might be content for some part of the family estate to pass to their grandchildren but not for it to enrich the husband's wider family, nor to be dissipated by the husband himself if he turned out to be an extravagant adventurer. The lawyers also developed techniques to keep other forms of wealth out of the husband's hands. So money was commonly transferred to trustees to hold to the wife's 'separate use.' This did not become the husband's as the trustees were the legal owners of the property and had not married the husband! This device left the wife free to dispose of the capital as she wished. The husband might, of course, 'persuade' her to make a disposition in his favour but this possibility could be excluded by imposing a 'restraint upon anticipation.' This prevented the wife getting hold of anything more than the current income of the fund.

These devices operated quite effectively to protect the *capital* of rich wives. They did not protect at all the earnings and savings of those less rich. This proved less and less acceptable as more and more women entered the wage economy during the nineteenth century. The result was a campaign for the abolition of the rule that all the matrimonial assets belonged to the husband and its replacement by a system of separation of property under which husbands and wives are placed in property terms in exactly the same position as those who are not married. This was brought about by the Married Womens' Property Act 1882.

This Act was undoubtedly a great step forward. However, in the last 50 years it has been subjected to pressures which were barely conceivable in 1882. The last 100 years have seen a shift from a population nearly all of which lived in rented accommodation to one in which well over half live in owner-occupied accommodation. Over the last 50 years this has been accompanied by rises in house prices which have run ahead of, and quite often far ahead of, inflation. This has meant that families of quite modest incomes who have bought and lived in their own home for a number of years have found themselves with a significant capital asset – well worth fighting over if the marriage collapses, as marriages increasingly have.

(ii) The Family Home

If the family has bought a house or apartment, it will in the vast majority of cases be the family's most valuable asset. It is not surprising therefore that most property questions which come before the Court concern the family home. The legal position is, unfortunately, complex. This is partly because of the general complexity of the rules of English law about the ownership of land and partly because of different views among the judges about how far it is permissible to stretch the law to adapt it to changing social conditions. The first question to ask is in whose name the house was bought. Fifty years ago virtually all houses were bought in the husband's name. Today the majority of purchases of houses are in the joint names of husband and wife. (Surveys have shown that whereas in 1960 some 51% of matrimonial homes bought in that year were bought in joint names, by 1970 the figure was as high as 74%. It would be surprising if this proportion has not continued to rise.) This increase in joint ownership is natural where the house has been bought with a mortgage raised against the income of both parties, but it is also increasingly done where the transaction is financed by one partner. There is no doubt that the wife is much better protected where the house is bought in joint names, though, as we shall see, she is by no means without protection where the husband is the sole legal owner.

(A) The house is bought in the husband's name. English law requires transfers (conveyances) of land to be made by deed (that is, by a document under seal) (the details are discussed in Section 2 The Law and Your Home). Thus it will always be clear who is the *legal* owner of the land. However, English law recognises also the possibility of *equitable* ownership of land. The most important example is where A, the legal owner, holds land on trust for B. Although the creation and transfer of some kinds of equitable ownership requires to be in writing, this rule does not apply to 'resulting, implied or constructive trusts.' The practical question therefore is in what circumstances the law will hold that, although the husband is the legal owner of the house, he holds it on trust for his wife – or more commonly, for himself and the wife. (In exceptional cases the husband may have contracted to transfer a share in the house to his wife or declared himself a trustee for her. This would

need to be evidenced in writing signed by the husband.)

The simplest (though hardly the most usual) case would be where the wife provided the whole of the purchase price in cash. Here it is clear that there is a presumption that the house is held on resulting trust for her. This could in principle be rebutted by showing that the wife intended to make a gift of the money to the husband but clear evidence of this would be required. Similarly if the house was bought in the husband's name but the husband and wife contributed equal shares to the price, then the presumption would be that the house was held on trust for the husband and wife in equal shares and if in different shares then in proportion to their contributions. However, in each case the presumption can be rebutted by showing that the parties' intention was different.

Outright purchases of houses for cash are rare. Usually the house will be bought with the aid of a substantial mortgage. In this case the primary test is said to be what the parties intended. If there is clear evidence of what the parties did intend this would present no problem. In practice, however, the parties have often not said what they intended or indeed have never formulated any clear intention. Sometimes the Courts appear to be deciding what they think the parties would have intended if they had thought about it, though the House of Lords has twice said that this is not the law! Another difficulty is that in theory the question is what the parties intended *at the time that they acquired the house*, but in practice the question does not arise until later and often much later. This means that one or both of the parties will seek to rely on events which happened after the house was acquired and in practice the Courts take such events into account.

The clearest case is where the wife has contributed in cash towards that part of the price which the parties paid themselves. In that case the Courts have consistently held that the wife was intended to be joint owner. The same result has normally followed where the wife has regularly paid mortgage instalments out of her own money.

The position is more difficult where the wife's contribution to payment for the house is indirect. Suppose for instance that both husband and wife are employed. They may adopt all sorts of different schemes for sharing household expenses. These schemes will often be devised without any consideration of their effect on property rights but in practice it may make a considerable difference what scheme is adopted even though, as would usually be the case, the scheme was not legally binding between the parties. So the wife will normally get an interest if it is agreed that she will pay the mortgage instalments and the husband will meet the household bills but her claim seems to be weaker if the arrangement is that she will meet the household bills and the husband will pay the mortgage. To many people these distinctions do not appear sensible and the attitude of the Courts has fluctuated. The two leading cases in this area are the decisions of the House of Lords in *Pettitt v Pettitt* (below) and *Gissing v Gissing* (right). These cases seem to show that it is not enough that the wife has made a contribution to the family fortunes by staying at home and looking after the home and children. On the other hand, if the husband and wife have pooled their incomes by putting them into a joint account and then paying their various expenses out of such a joint account the inference would be strong that they intended to share the ownership of the house even though it was the husband who arranged the mortgage payments. There would also be an inference that joint ownership was intended when it was clear that it was only the wife's financial contributions which enabled the family to afford so expensive a house. On the other hand, where the husband's income was sufficient to meet the mortgage and normal outgoings and the wife's income was used to pay for something which the family might otherwise not have done like sending the children to fee paying

---

Husband's entitlement to share in wife's house on marriage break-up

In *Pettitt v Pettitt* (1970) the parties were married in 1952 and lived in a house which belonged to the wife, who had inherited it, until 1961. During this time the husband did a good deal of redecoration and some other improvements. In 1961 they moved to another house which was also bought in the wife's name with the proceeds of the sale of the first house and lived there for about four years before the marriage collapsed. The husband claimed that during those four years he had carried out many improvements in the house and garden and that the total value of the work and materials was £723. He claimed to be entitled to a share in the house. The House of Lords held that he was not so entitled.

Wife's interest in house on break-up of marriage

In *Gissing v Gissing* (1971) the parties were married in 1935. They bought a house in 1951 for £2,695 which was conveyed into the sole name of the husband. They raised a mortgage for £2,150 and a loan of £500 by the husband from his employers. The husband paid the balance of £45 and the legal charges from his own money. Both parties were working for the same employer. In 1951 the husband was earning £1,000 and the wife £500. By 1961, when the marriage broke down, the husband was earning £3,000 a year and the wife £500. The husband repaid the loan from the employer and paid the mortgage instalments. He also paid the outgoings on the house, gave his wife a housekeeping allowance and paid for the holidays. The wife bought her own clothes and those of the son of the marriage. Each party had a separate bank account and separate savings and there was no joint account or joint savings. The House of Lords held that the wife was not entitled to any interest in the house.

---

schools, or going on more expensive holidays, the inference that the parties intended joint ownership of the family home is not strong.

(B) The house is bought in the wife's name. The position here is for the most part the same as where the house is bought in the husband's name. There is however one difference. Historically as we have seen where land is bought in A's name with the money of B there was a presumption of a resulting trust in favour of B. However, where A is the wife of B there is a presumption of advancement, that is a presumption that the husband intended to make a gift to the wife. This presumption again is refutable by proof of a contrary intention and the modern tendency is not to give much weight to the presumptions of advancement and resulting trust. There are certain kinds of argument which the husband cannot legitimately make about intentions. He cannot say that he put the house in his wife's name so as to keep it out of the hands of his creditors, because it could only properly be kept away from the creditors if the transfer was genuine.

(C) The size of the share. Once the Court has decided that though the house has been bought in the name of one party, it was intended that both parties should have rights in it, it has to decide in what proportions the parties' shares should be. In simple cases this would be proportionate to the contribution to the purchase price. So if a husband and wife buy a house for cash for £60,000 and the husband contributes £40,000 and the wife £20,000 the usual inference would be that the wife was entitled to a third. This would mean that if the house was worth £90,000 by the time that the dispute arose the husband's share would now be £60,000 and the wife's £30,000. In practice this clear cut type of case is very rare. Indeed in many cases the parties will be unable to say with any great precision what their contributions have been. However, the Court will take a broad view and decide what seems fair in all the circumstances.

Normally it is contributions between marriage and separation that have to be taken into accunt. However, if one party stays in the family home after separation and keeps up the mortgage payments these ought to be taken into account so far as they affect the capital position. Interest payments should normally be disregarded, however, since they are in effect the equivalent of rent for the continued use of the house.

(D) The house is bought in the names of both husband and wife. It is probably the case that if the parties have decided to convey the house into their joint names, they intend to take equal shares. However, this does not follow automatically. The simplest course is for the conveyance to say expressly that the parties are to take in equal shares or in other proportions if that is intended. If the conveyance says nothing about this, then it is open to one party to argue for a larger share because of larger contributions.

There is also a very important technical question. Are the parties 'joint tenants' or 'tenants in common'. The practical effect of this mysterious lawyer-like distinction is that if the parties are joint tenants the interest of the one that dies first automatically passes to the survivor. If the parties hold their beneficial interests as tenants in common, then the share of the deceased passes under his will or, if there is no will, under the rules as to intestacy. It is quite likely that either husband or wife will wish to be able to dispose of their share by will. If the parties are 'joint tenants' either of them can 'sever' the joint tenancy which converts it into a tenancy in common. Severance can take place by notice in writing to the other party; by agreement; by seek-

ing to dispose of one's own share, for example, by selling or mortgaging it or by acts showing that the parties intended to treat their interest as being as tenants in common.

(iii) Joint Bank Accounts
It is now extremely common for married couples to have joint bank accounts. It is important to see that these create relationships between husband and/or wife on the one hand and the bank on the other and between the husband and wife.

(A) Position with the bank. As far as the bank is concerned, this is basically just another account governed by the usual rules which affect the relationship between banker and customer. The bank is entitled to honour any cheques which comply with the mandate given to the bank by the customers. In business accounts it is common to provide that cheques (or cheques above a given value) must bear two signatures. This appears to be very unusual with husband and wife joint accounts. It does mean, however, that normally either party can withdraw the entire contents of the account without there being any recourse against the bank. Indeed it would normally mean that if either party overdrew the account the bank could claim repayment from either of the parties and not only from the one who overdrew.

(B) Position between husband and wife. It has sometimes been held that although there is a joint account, one party is merely a nominee and has no beneficial interest in the credit balance in the account. This was held in a number of cases in the 1914–1918 war where the husband opened a joint account so that the wife would have access to money while he was away at the war. This sort of inference would less easily be drawn today but it is still possible, where the account is fed entirely by funds supplied by one party, that it will be held that the beneficial interest is entirely in that party.

In many cases, particularly where the account is being fed with money from both partners, the inference will inevitably be that they intend to share equally in any credit balance that exists and this will mean that if one dies, the balance will automatically pass to the survivor.

A potentially important question concerns the ownership of articles bought with cheques drawn on the joint account. The cases appear to say that ownership goes to the party who signs the cheque. It is hard, however, to believe that this is true without qualification. It is, no doubt, very likely that if the husband buys a suit or the wife a dress with a cheque drawn on the joint account and signed by the husband or wife respectively, then the suit belongs to the husband and the dress to the wife. It is much more doubtful whether the same principle applies to an article which is clearly intended for common use, such as a drawing room carpet.

(iv) The Position of Unmarried Partners

Since, as we have seen, the basic principle of English law is that there are no special rules about property rights as between husband and wife, it should follow that the rules which we have just described should apply equally to other situations where two or more people are living together. These situations would include not only the so-called cases of 'common law marriage' but also cases where a house was being shared by partners of the same sex or indeed asexual sharing by partners of different sexes.

One clear qualification on this is that, since the operation of the rules depends so much on the inferences which the Court will draw from the facts, similar facts occurring between husband and wife and between other partners may be the subject of different inferences. One reason for this is that marriage is supposed to be, and usually is, a long term relationship whereas a good many of the other relationships mentioned above are of a short-term nature. Another reason is that married partners owe each other legal obligations

which unmarried partners do not. In some cases this can affect the natural interpretation to be put upon the partners' behaviour.

One result of this difference is that the Courts have been significantly more willing to treat the conduct of unmarried parties as amounting to a binding contract than in the case of married couples (see below). It is sometimes said that contracts which promote sexual immorality are contrary to public policy. This is no doubt true, even today, of the straightforward sale of sex as in the agreements made by prostitutes with their clients, but it seems extremely unlikely that it applies to agreements made between two unmarried partners in a long term relationship. Certainly in all recent cases the possibility has been studiously ignored by all concerned.

(v) Position Where Family Home Is Sold or Mortgaged

If the house has been bought in the joint names of the parties, each of the parties will need to agree to any sale or mortgage and will have to sign the appropriate documents. This requirement will usually operate to protect one party from the other dealing with the property behind his/her back, though it will not do so if one partner simply signs without reading the documents which the other party puts forward. This is because the purchaser or mortgagee will usually be entitled to assume that all the parties who have signed the documents have agreed to them. It is undoubtedly prudent therefore for each partner to read the documents carefully. If you

---

Rights of unmarried partners

In *Tanner v Tanner* (1975) the female partner gave up her rent-controlled flat and went to live in a house which the male partner had acquired for them and their two children. When the relationship broke down it was held that she had a contractual right to stay in the house so long as the children were of school age. Clearly an important factors here was that she had given up a secure home of her own.

In *Horrocks v Foray* (1976) the defendant had been for 17 years the mistress of a married man; he continued to live with his wife, who was unaware of the relationship. In 1973 he bought a house in Kensington where the defendant lived with her child. In 1974 the man was killed in an accident. The Court of Appeal refused to hold that the

defendant had any contractual rights in the house. Here the analysis was that the man was primarily motivated by generosity rather than by a desire to confer any legal rights on the woman.

In *Chandler v Kerley* (1978) the man bought the woman's former matrimonial home for £10,000 after her marriage had broken down. At the time of the purchase the parties intended to live in the house together as man and wife. The woman had asked what would happen if the relationship came to an end and he had said 'he would not put her out'. Six weeks after the purchase he brought the relationship to an end and sought to turn her out. In this case the Court of Appeal held that she was entitled to twelve months' notice.

Wife's recovery of loss

In *Cornish v Midland Bank* (1985) the husband and wife were married in 1972. In 1973 they bought a house in their joint names for £10,000 with the help of a building society mortgage for £9,000. In 1975 they decided to buy another property for £16,000 in their joint names with a building society mortgage for £10,000. The house needed considerable renovation estimated to cost about £2,000. The husband arranged with the manager of a local branch of the bank to borrow £2,000 for renovation and to have an overdraft on his current account of £200. These advances were to be repaid from the proceeds of the first house when it was sold and the bank was to have a second mortgage on the new house. This second mortgage required the wife's signature. The bank's second mortgage was on a standard bank form which gave the bank security not only in respect of the £2,000 lent for the renovation but also for any other lending made to the husband. When the wife went to the bank to sign the document its effect was explained by the clerk who was in charge of the transaction. His account was honest but misleading. He said that it was like a building society mortgage. This was untrue since building society mortgages do not usually cover future lending. Shortly after signing the mortgage the wife left the husband. Over the next few years the bank allowed the husband's borrowing on his current account to rise to over £9,000 and on the house loan account to over £6,000. In due course the second house was sold for £27,000 but all that was left after paying the first and second mortgages was £748. The Court of Appeal held that the wife had suffered serious loss (calculated at £7,034) as a result of signing the mortgage documents, which she would not have done but for the bank's mispresentation and that she could recover this loss from the bank.

are selling you house, your solicitor should be willing as part of the service to explain the legal effects of the mysterious language employed. If you are signing a mortgage it is worth asking the bank or building society to explain its effects. You will have a remedy if they explain it incorrectly.

The position is more complicated where the house has been bought in the name of one partner but the other partner has a beneficial interest in the house. In this case the partner in whose name the house is can carry out all the legal formalities necessary to sell or mortgage the property in his own name. How will this affect the rights of the other partner?

The answer to the question depends on whether the house is registered land or unregistered land (explained in The Law and Your Home, page 37). Where the land is registered the matter is governed by the Land Registration Act 1925. Under this Act purchasers and mortgagees are not bound by interests in the land which are not registered unless they are 'overriding interests' within section 70(1) of the Act. Overriding interests include 'the rights of every person in actual occupation of the land or in receipt of the rents and profits thereof, save where enquiry is made of such persons and the rights are not disclosed.' In the leading case (see box opposite) it was held that the beneficial interest of the wife who had no legal title to the house was such an 'overriding interest.' However, the case does not decide that the wife's interest is always protected. First, the purchaser or mortgagee may have asked the wife what her rights, if any, are. Since it is extremely likely that many wives do not understand the differences between legal and beneficial ownership, such an enquiry might well receive an incautious response which prejudiced the position. (Note, however, that replies by the husband would not appear to prejudice the position of the wife. In practice it appears that sometimes questions are only addressed to the husband.) Secondly, the wife is probably not protected if she is not in occupation at the time of the transaction, for instance, because she has left the husband before he sells the house. (Occupation is not limited, however, to physical presence in the narrowest sense. A wife who goes away for the weekend, leaving her possessions in the house is certainly in occupation of it.)

If the house is unregistered land a purchaser or mortgagee will be bound by the wife's rights if he has notice of them. Notice for this purpose is of two kinds, actual and constructive. Actual notice is what you actually know. Constructive notice is what you ought to know. The critical question, therefore, is what enquiries a purchaser or mortgagee ought to make. Unfortunately it is not possible to make a completely confident answer to this question! It is certainly highly arguable that someone who makes no enquiries at all is bound by the wife's rights.

Wife's proprietary interest in house

In *Williams and Glyn's Bank Limited v Boland* (1981) the husband was the sole registered proprietor of the family home but it was accepted on all sides that Mrs Boland was entitled to a proprietary interest in the house as she had contributed financially to the purchase. Mr Boland borrowed money from the bank for his business and gave them a mortgage. The business collapsed and the bank sought to enforce the mortgage. It was held by the House of Lords that they were bound by the wife's rights. The bank argued that the words 'in actual occupation' were only applicable to someone who had a legal title to the land and was in possession of it. It is fair to say that many expert conveyancers would have thought that that was what the words meant but the House of Lords held that they must be given a common sense natural interpretation and therefore meant simply someone who was physically present.

It will be seen from this discussion that a wife who has contributed to the purchase of the family home and is entitled *as against the husband* to a share in it, will not always be protected where the property is sold or mortgaged. There is no doubt therefore that it is much safer for both partners to be named in the conveyance.

(vi) Position Where the Family Home Is Rented

It is certainly desirable to persuade the landlord to grant a tenancy to both partners. There would then be no doubt that if one leaves, the other is entitled to remain, pay the rent and enjoy the various protections given to tenants (discussed in The Law and Your Home, page 37).

In practice, however, the tenancy is often given only to one partner, usually the husband. It used to be the case that if he left and stopped paying the rent, the landlord could evict the wife. However the Matrimonial Homes Act 1983 provides that the spouse left behind is entitled to remain in occupation as tenant and to pay the rent and the landlord must accept it. This protection is only available, however, to spouses and not to other partners nor to children.

A Court granting a decree of divorce or nullity has wide powers to order the transfer of a tenancy from one party to the other.

Under the Rent Act 1977 a surviving spouse of the original tenant is entitled to become the statutory tenant and therefore receive the statutory security of tenure if he/she was residing in the house immediately before the spouse's death. If there is no succession to a surviving spouse, then the tenancy will pass to any 'member of the original tenant's family' who was residing with the tenant at the time of his death and for the six months immediately preceding his death. In a case in 1950 the Court of Appeal held that a woman who had lived with a man for twenty years without marrying him was not a member of his family but the opposite view was taken in a case in 1976.

(vii) The Wife's Rights in the Housekeeping Allowance

A wide variety of arrangements exist for managing the family's finances. One traditional arrangement where the husband was the sole wage earner was for him to give the wife money for the 'housekeeping.' The classic form of this arrangement would arise where the husband was paid in cash each week and gave his wife the 'housekeeping' in cash each week – the assumption being that she would meet the household expenses in cash. This arrangement can never have been universal; for instance, it was apparently not uncommon for the husband to give the wife his wage packet unopened and for her then to give him his 'beer money'.

Under the classical arrangement the Courts held that the 'housekeeping money' was still the husband's and that any savings the wife made from it therefore belonged to him. Similarly it was held that anything bought by the wife with savings from the housekeeping belonged to the husband. This rule has long since ceased to seem attractive and the Married Womens' Property Act 1964 provided that 'if any question arises as to the right of the husband or wife to money derived from any allowance made by the husband for the expenses of the matrimonial home or for similar purposes, or to any property acquired out of such money, the money or property shall, in the absence of any agreement between them to the contrary, be treated as belonging to the husband and wife in equal shares.'

This provision undoubtedly has its heart in the right place but it is unfortunately not very easy to apply to many of the arrangements which modern families make for organising their finances. If the family income (whether from one partner or both) is paid into a joint account out of which all the expenses are met, it would seem to be governed by the rules discussed in section (iii) on page 330.

(viii) Contributions to the Improvement of Property

The decision of the House of Lords in *Pettitt v Pettitt* (see box on page 329) was widely thought to be harsh and was followed by the enactment of section 37 of the Matrimonial Proceedings and Property Act 1970. Under this section a husband or wife who makes a substantial contribution to the improvement of the house will be entitled, in the absence of agreement between husband and wife, to such share or enlarged share in the beneficial interest in the house as the Court may think just. It should be emphasised that the Act only applies to husbands and wives and not to other partners. The section applies both to a spouse who does the improvements personally and to one who pays for the improvements.

2. POSITION ON DEATH OF ONE PARTNER

Even today more marriages end by death than by divorce. The effect of death on the property rights of the surviving spouse therefore raises very important practical questions. Two important preliminary points should be made. The first is that it is essential to see what property already belongs to the surviving spouse. This property will be unaffected by the death. The second is to see what property, such as the house and the joint bank account, belonged jointly to the husband and wife. Joint property passes automatically to the survivor. The rules relevant to these questions have just been discussed above.

What happens to the deceased's property depends on whether he has left a valid will or whether he died intestate (that is, without having made a valid will). A person may die intestate because he has never got around to making a will or because he knows what the laws of intestacy are and, being content with the results for his property, deliberately decides not to make a will. Even when you are content with the rules of intestacy, there can be good reasons for making a will – for instance, that you want to appoint guardians for your children or that you want a particular person to look after your estate (to be your executor).

Many systems of law impose restrictions on the freedom of a testator to dispose of his property by will by insisting that a certain proportion of it is reserved for his wife and/or children. English law historically had no such rules but in the last fifty years restrictions have been imposed on the ability of a testator to leave his family destitute.

(i) The Deceased Made a Will

(A) Requirements of a valid will

(a) The testator must be of sound mind. If the testator is obviously demented at the time of making the will it is clear that the will is invalid. A more difficult situation is where it is alleged that the testator was suffering from senile dementia and did not know what he was doing. This kind of allegation is quite often made when an elderly testator suddenly makes a new will and does not leave his property to those who consider themselves the obvious beneficiaries. The critical question is whether the testator knew what he was doing. It is, unfortunately, quite often the case that testators know quite well what they are doing and enjoy changing their will and teasing their relatives. This does not make the will invalid. In cases of this kind it is sometimes alleged that a beneficiary has exerted *undue influence*. Where the beneficiary stands in a special relationship to the testator (for instance, his solicitor or doctor or nurse) it will be for him to prove that there was no undue influence. Where there was no such relationship it is for the person making the allegation to prove it.

(b) The will must be in writing.

(c) The will must be witnessed. There must be at least two witnesses to the will. The purpose of the witnesses is to authenticate the testator's signature and they must therefore see the testator sign and sign the will afterwards. It is not necessary for them to see the contents of the will. Any adult who is not blind can be a witness. Someone who is a beneficiary under the will should not be a witness since this will invalidate the gift to him and for the same reasons the spouse of a beneficiary should not be a witness. If, however, the witness happens to marry the beneficiary later this does not invalidate the gift.

There is a special exception permitting soldiers and sailors on active service to make valid wills which are unwitnessed.

(B) Is it safe to make your own will? After buying and selling houses the making of wills is probably one of the most common reasons for

---

Inheritance Tax (formerly Capital Transfer Tax)

Capital Transfer Tax (CTT) was the successor to a tax which was correctly called estate duty but commonly referred to as death duties. Estate duty was payable only on death whereas CTT was payable on gifts both during your life and on your death.

Major changes were introduced in the 1986 Budget. These abolished the tax on transfers during the lifetime of the transferors. The tax was renamed Inheritence Tax. There would be tax, however, on transfers within seven years of death on a sliding scale, running from 20% of the full rate where the transfer was in the seventh year before death to 100% of the full rate where it was within three years of death. The starting point for tax was raised to £71,000 and the highest rate became payable on estates over £317,000.

---

visiting a solicitor. Making a will is much less complicated than buying a house. Anyone who feels confident in their own ability to express themselves clearly and accurately on paper should be able to manage. One situation where professional advice is certainly needed is where the testator owns enough property to make significant sums of Inheritance Tax (formerly Capital Transfer Tax) payable. For very wealthy testators there are a number of ingenious schemes which reduce the amount of this tax payable very substantially. These schemes work best if you plan far ahead and it is certainly worth while taking first class professional advice.

You will not save a great deal of money by making your own will. You should certainly ask a solicitor for an estimate. For a fairly straight-forward will £30.00 might be a reasonable figure. For this the solicitor should steer you away from the errors which previous generations of testators have made. The classic example is the testator who in his homemade will leaves 'everything to my wife, Victoria, and after her death to my children Albert and Edward'. He probably means to leave everything outright to Victoria in the hope that she will leave what is left over to Albert and Edward. The Court is likely however to treat it as simply a gift of a life interest to Victoria, that is, that she receive the interest on the testator's property, the capital going to Albert and Edward after her death.

Apart from thinking out clearly what you want to do, perhaps the most important general advice is to remember that things change. You will not want to make a new will every six months and therefore it is very desireable to formulate the gifts in a way which will make sense in five or ten years time. To take a simple example, suppose you think that you are worth £5,000 now and have four children, three boys and a girl. You might decide to give £1,000 to each of the boys and the balance to your daughter. If you die in ten years time worth £50,000 this will mean that your daughter will get £47,000, whereas if you had given one-fifth to each of the boys and two-fifths to her, the result would have been very different. Some of the things you may want to think about are set out on page 336.

(ii) The Deceased Died Intestate

The deceased's property is distributed under the Administration of Estates Act 1925 as amended in 1952. The rules are based on a survey of the provisions people made in their wills. However, there have been dramatic changes in family arrangements since 1952, particularly with the numbers of divorces, second marriages and families with step-parents and step-children. It is doubtful whether the rules adequately take account of this. The distribution depends on whether the deceased leaves a spouse and/or issue (that is children, grandchildren, great grandchildren and so on, whether legitimate or illegitimate).

(A) Deceased leaves a spouse but no issue. If the deceased also leaves a parent or a brother or sister the spouse takes all the personal chattels, a statutory legacy of £85,000 and one half of the balance. If the deceased leaves a parent or parents they take the balance (in equal shares if both parents survive). If there is a surviving brother or sister or issue of a predeceased sister or brother they take on the 'statutory trusts'. (Basically the income until the age of eighteen and then their share of the capital.) If the deceased leaves no parents, brothers or sisters the spouse takes the whole estate.

A short check list for testators

1. Executors. One of the advantages of a will is that you can chose executors. The choice is basically between friends and relations who may be expected to do the work for nothing and professional executors like solicitors, banks and the Public Trustee. It is worth investigating carefully how much they would charge. It is widely believed, for instance, that bank charges for work as executors are high, particularly for small estates. Whatever you decide to do, you should ask the executors if they are willing to act as they are not obliged to do so. If you are choosing friends, it may be sensible to have two executors rather than one.

2. Revoke any previous wills. Wills are automatically revoked by marriage except when made 'in contemplation of marriage'. If you are making a will shortly before getting married you should state that the will is made in contemplation of marriage. Divorce does not revoke a will but under the Administration of Justice Act 1982 a divorced spouse is treated for the purpose of the will as having died before the testator. This means that a gift to an ex spouse lapses but that the will is otherwise valid. It is sensible expressly to state that the will revokes previous wills and to destroy earlier wills.

3. Put the will somewhere safe but not so safe that no one can find it.

4. Remember that people can die in unexpected orders. It is natural to analyse what you want to do on the basis that people who are younger than you will die after you. This will not necessarily happen! You may die before your parents and/or after your children. This is important because usually if you have made a gift to someone in the will who dies before you the gift will lapse. If you make a gift for your children and they die first it will pass to their children.

Similarly you should think what you want to happen if you and your wife are killed simultaneously in a car accident. If there are no children you would probably not want all of your property to go to your wife's family but this is what will happen if she is younger than you and you have made a will simply leaving everything to her.

5. Specific gifts. If you are making specific gifts to people or to charities make sure the donee is clearly and correctly identified. It can do no harm to give the full name and address. It is best to avoid descriptions like 'my sister-in-law' since your brother may have remarried before your death. If you are making gifts by a class description such as 'to my brother's children' this will include illegitimate or adopted children but it will not include his second wife's children by her first marriage. It is worth spending some time thinking exactly whom you wish to benefit. If you make a series of specific gifts you should also make a gift of what is left over (that is technically called the residue). It is extremely unlikely that you will succeed in making a series of pecuniary legacies which will exactly equal the amount of your estate.

6. Alterations. It is sensible to make sure that there are no corrections in the text of the will as originally signed and witnessed. This may require a little extra effort but it will avoid any argument that the will was altered after it had been executed. It is permissible to make minor amendments to wills by codicil. This must refer to the original will, confirm the unaltered parts, state exactly the change and be signed and witnessed by two witnesses. Do *not* write on the text of the original will!

It is sensible to take steps to make it difficult for some dishonest person to add clauses to the will. So a line should be drawn across any areas of blank space at the bottom of the page or on the reverse side. If the will runs to more than one page, it is sensible to number the pages; to indicate the total number of pages; to sign each page with the witnesses witnessing each signature. These are not legal requirements, simply common sense precautions.

(B) Deceased leaves a spouse and issue. The spouse gets the personal chattels, a statutory legacy of £40,000 and a life interest in half the balance. The balance of the estate is held on the statutory trusts for the issue.

(C) Deceased leaves no spouse. If he leaves no issue but a parent or parents they take absolutely.

If he leaves neither issue nor parents then the following relations take in this order: (i) brothers and sisters of the whole blood (the issue of any predeceased brother or sister taking their share); (ii) brothers and sisters of the half blood (and issue as above); (iii) grandparents; (iv) uncles and aunts – that is brothers and sisters of the whole blood of a parent of the intestate; (v) uncles

SPECIMEN WILL

I   *SEPTIMUS HARDING*

of   *THE ALMSHOUSE, BARCHESTER*

HEREBY REVOKE all Wills and Testamentary Dispositions
heretofore made by me and declare this to be my last Will

1.   I WISH to be cremated

2.   I APPOINT my wife/~~husband~~ *ELEANOR*

and *MY SON FREDERICK*

to be the EXECUTORS AND TRUSTEES of this my Will   (and
they and the Trustee or Trustees for the time being hereof
are hereinafter called "my Trustees")

3.   I BEQUEATH free of all duties and taxes payable on or by
reference to my death:-
*MY BOOKS TO THE LIBRARY OF ALL SOULS
COLLEGE, OXFORD*

4.   I DIRECT that all income of my estate during the period of
thirty days from the date of my death shall be accumulated

5.   IF my said wife/~~husband~~ shall survive me by not less
than thirty days as aforesaid I DEVISE AND BEQUEATH all
(the remainder of) my property of whatsoever nature and
wheresoever situate unto my said wife/~~husband~~ absolutely

6.   IF my said wife/~~husband~~ shall predecease me or fail to
survive me as aforesaid then I DIRECT as follows:-

A.   I DEVISE AND BEQUEATH all the real and personal
property whatsoever and wheresoever of or to which I shall
be possessed or entitled at my death or over which I shall

Name and address of
testator to be inserted

To be deleted if not
applicable

Fill in name of
executors. It is prudent
to ask them if they will
serve

Details of special gifts

then have a general power of appointment or disposition by
Will except property otherwise disposed of by this my Will
or any Codicil hereto unto my Trustees UPON TRUST to sell
call in and convert the same into money with power at
their absolute discretion to postpone such sale calling in
or conversion without being liable for loss. And after
payment thereout of my funeral and testamentary expenses
and debts and any legacies bequeathed by this my Will or
any Codicil hereto (and so that all legacies shall be paid
primarily out of my personal estate) and all duties and
taxes thereon my Trustees shall at their discretion invest
the residue of the said moneys in or upon any of the
investments hereby authorised with power to vary or
transpose such investments for or into others of a like
nature and shall stand possessed of the residue of the
said moneys and the investments for the time being representing
the same and of such parts of my said estate as shall for the
time being remain unsold and unconverted all of which premises
are hereinafter called "my Residuary Estate" UPON the following
trusts hereinafter declared

B. MY TRUSTEES shall stand possessed of my Residuary
Estate Upon Trust as to capital and income for such one or
more of my children as shall be living at my death and
shall attain the age of eighteen/~~twenty one~~ years and if
more than one in equal shares absolutely. Provided always
that if any child of mine shall predecease me or fail to
attain the age of eighteen/~~twenty one~~ years leaving a
child or children such child or children shall take and if
more than one equally between them on attaining the age of
eighteen/~~twenty one~~ years the interest which such child of
mine would have taken had he or she survived me and
attained the age of eighteen/~~twenty one~~ years

C.   MY TRUSTEES shall have the following powers:-

(i)   To invest or apply trust moneys in the purchase
or by way of contribution to the purchase of or at
interest upon the security of such stocks funds
shares securities or other investments or property of
whatsoever nature and wheresoever situate and whether
involving liability or not and whether producing
income or not or upon such personal credit with or
without security and whether or not subject to
payment of interest as my Trustees shall in their
absolute discretion think fit including (but without
prejudice to the generality of the foregoing):-

(a)   the purchase upon trust for sale (with power to
       postpone sale) repair decoration and improvement
       of any freehold or leasehold property as a
       residence for any beneficiary of my Residuary
       Estate

(b)   the purchase of chattels whether for the use or
       enjoyment of such beneficiaries or otherwise

(c)   in effecting maintaining exchanging converting
       surrendering or otherwise dealing with any
       policy or policies of insurance or assurance
       whatsoever

To the intent that my Trustees shall have the same
full and unrestricted powers of investing and
transposing investments and laying out money in all
respects as if they were absolutely entitled thereto
beneficially

(ii) To insure against loss or damage by fire or from any other risk any property for the time being comprised in my Residuary Estate to any amount and even though a person is absolutely entitled to the property and to pay the premiums for such insurance out of the income or capital of my Residuary Estate or the property itself and any money received by my Trustees under such a policy shall be treated as if it were proceeds of sale of the property insured

(iii) To exercise the power of appropriation given them by Section 41 of the Administration of Estates Act 1925 without obtaining any of the consents required by that Section and even though one or more of them may be beneficially interested

(iv) Power to sell all or any part of my Residuary Estate to any one or more of their own number by private treaty or public auction. Provided that the price paid on any sale by private treaty shall be such as may be agreed between the purchasing Trustee or Trustees and my other Trustee or Trustees and in default of agreement shall not be less than what shall be certified in writing to be a fair price by the company's auditor in the case of a sale of shares in a company not listed on a recognised Stock Exchange and by an independent duly qualified valuer in the case of a sale of any other asset

(v) At any time or times to borrow any moneys required for the purposes hereof upon such terms as to repayment of principal and payment of interest as they shall in their absolute discretion think fit and they may for this purpose mortgage or charge in favour of the lender the whole or any part of my real or personal estate or any interest therein

D.   SECTION 31 (relating to maintenance and
accumulation) and Section 32 (relating to
advancement), of the Trustee Act 1925 shall
apply hereto with the following variations:-

(i) Section 31 shall have effect as if the words "the
Trustees think fit" were substituted in sub-section
(1) (i) for the words "may in all the circumstances
be reasonable" and as if the proviso at the end of
sub-section (1) commencing with the words "Provided
that in deciding" and ending with the words "the
income of each fund shall be so paid or applied" were
omitted

(ii) Section 32 shall have effect as if the words
"one half of" were omitted from proviso (a) to
sub-section (1) thereof

7.   ANY EXECUTOR OR TRUSTEE of this my Will being a
solicitor or other person engaged in any profession or business
may be so employed or act and shall be entitled to charge and
be paid all professional or other charges for any business or
act done by him or his firm in connection with the
administration of the trusts hereof including acts which an
executor or trustee could have done personally

    I N   W I T N E S S   whereof I have hereunto set my hand
this *first* day of *May*   One thousand nine hundred and
eighty *six*

SIGNED by the above named   ) *Septimus Harding*
)
as h.. last Will in the presence of us)
both present at the same time who at h..)
request in h.. presence and in the   )
presence of each other have hereunto   ) *Tom Brown*
subscribed our names as witnesses:-   ) *Jane Smith*

Insert his or her

Insert his or her

Signatures of two
witnesses. Note:
witnesses should
witness the signature of
testator. They do not
read the will

341

and aunts of the half blood. If none of these potential beneficiaries exist the estate passes to the Crown as *bona vacantia*. The Crown may make *ex gratia* gifts to anyone for whom the intestate might have been expected to provide.

It will be seen that the rules make no provision at all for an unmarried partner. Such a person might well apply to the Crown for an *ex gratia* payment. In addition the unmarried partner will often be entitled to apply under the Inheritance (Provision for Family and Dependants) Act 1975 (see section (iii) below).

(D) Altering the Intestacy Rules by will!

In *Re Wynn* (1984) the testator's husband asked her to make a will making it clear that he was to have no entitlement to her estates. She made a will which provided simply for the revocation of all previous wills and stated 'I wish that all I possess is not given to my husband'. It was held that the effect of this was to exclude the husband from his ordinary rights on intestacy.

(iii) Claims by Dependants That They Have Been Inadequately Provided For

Until 1938 English law, unlike many other systems, imposed no limits as to how a testator might dispose of his property. If the will was formally valid he might cut off his wife or children without even the proverbial shilling. This was changed for the first time by the Inheritance (Family Provision) Act 1938, which introduced the notion that the Court should have a discretion to overturn the will to ensure that certain kinds of dependant were adequately provided for. The present law is contained in the Inheritance (Provision for Family and Dependants) Act 1975. The Act is a considerable extension on the previous law but it remains based on the notion of dependency. It is not a vehicle for attacking wills on the grounds that they are unfair.

(A) Who may apply.

(a) *The wife or husband of the deceased.* This includes a person whose 'marriage' is void, provided that they entered into the marriage in good faith, did not obtain a decree of divorce or annulment and did not remarry during the deceased's life time. It covers therefore those who go through a ceremony of marriage with a spouse who neglects to mention an existing marriage.

(b) *A former wife or former husband of the deceased who has not remarried.* The Divorce Court has extensive powers to order property transfers at the time of the divorce and in most cases this will render application under the 1975 Act inappropriate. The Divorce Court has power actually to provide that a former spouse shall not be entitled to apply under the Act. This could be part of a provision for a 'clean break'. (The powers of Divorce Court are discussed on page 353.)

(c) *The child of the deceased.* This includes illegitimate, adopted and posthumous children. Under the 1938 Act a daughter could only apply if unmarried and a son only if under 21. These restrictions have now been removed.

(d) *Any person (not being a child of the deceased) who, in the case of any marriage to which the deceased was at any time a party, was treated by the deceased as a child of the family in relation to that marriage.*

(e) *Any person, not in the classes above, who immediately before the death of the deceased was being maintained, either wholly or partly by the deceased.* This category was introduced by the 1975 Act and is a major expansion of the scheme. The principal qualifier under this scheme is obviously the unmarried partner but the section is by no means confined to such partners. It includes friends or relations who were being supported by the deceased. The key word is 'maintained' which is defined to be that 'the deceased, otherwise than for full valuable consideration, was making a substantial contribution in money or money's worth towards the reasonable needs of that person.' The Courts have held that if the deceased and the applicant were living in a joint household then the contribution of each must be measured and balanced against that of the other. If the contributions are roughly equal then the applicant was not being maintained by the deceased. To put it another way, for the purpose of the Act the applicant is better off if he is a sponger than if he pulls his weight. This unattractive conclusion perhaps shows the logic of the dependency principle being carried too far.

(B) What the applicant must prove.

The Act says that the Court must be satisfied 'that the disposition of the deceased's estate effected by his will or the law relating to intestacy or the combination of his will and that law, is not such as to make reasonable financial provision for the applicant.'

It will be seen that the Act applies not only to wills that do not make reasonable provision, but also where the law of intestacy does not do so. At first sight this seems odd since the rules of intestacy were laid down by Parliament. The point is that these rules are not sufficiently flexible to cover every eventuality. In particular they exclude altogether unmarried partners and there are cases in which they may be thought over-generous to the spouse as opposed to the children (which is particularly important where the children are by a former marriage as is increasingly often the case).

In deciding whether there has been 'reasonable financial provision' the Act draws a distinction between the surviving spouse and other applicants.

In the case of a surviving spouse the Court should consider what provision a surviving husband or wife should receive, whether or not that provision is required for his or her maintenance. The Court is also required to take into account what provision the spouse would have received if the marriage had ended by divorce and not by death. (This is discussed below.) For an example of the Court's operation of the Act see the box below.

For all other applicants the question is whether the provision is such as it would be reasonable for the applicant to receive for his maintenance. That is a distinctly less generous test, but, even so, maintenance is not limited to the bare necessities of life.

Provision for wife

In *Re Besterman* (1981) the testator Dr Theodore Besterman died in 1976 aged 71. He had devoted his life to the study of Voltaire and left most of his fortune worth £1,300,000 to the Taylorian Institute at Oxford so that his work on Voltaire's manuscripts could be continued. He had left his wife chattels worth £790 and a life interest in War Loan producing a pre-tax income of £3,500. Mrs Besterman was then 65 and had been married to Dr Besterman for eighteen years. The trial judge awarded Mrs Besterman sums which would make the total provision for her some £259,250. The Court of Appeal increased this to £378,000. The principal reason for this was if the marriage had ended in divorce she could have expected to get about one-third of the estate.

(C) What the Court can do. The Court can make an order for payment of a lump sum. It can also make an order for periodical payments and such orders may be varied and in the case of orders in favour of the former spouse must end on remarriage. The Court can also make a wide variety of other orders, for example, that the deceased's house is transfered to the applicant or that the applicant be allowed to live in it for the rest of her life.

(iv) How the Deceased's Estate Is Handled

In many systems of law property passes directly from the deceased to his heir(s). This is not the English system which involves an intermediate stage in which the estate is gathered in and then distributed. This is done by the *personal representatives* of the deceased who are either the executors, if appointed by the will or the administrators, if no executors were appointed or accepted appointment.

One of the big advantages of appointing executors is that it avoids disputes about who is to be the administrator. It is obviously sensible if possible for the family to agree as to who is to administer the estate but there are rules as to who is entitled to be the administrator. This is basically in ranking order; surviving spouse; issue (i.e. children, grandchildren etc); parents; brothers or sisters of the whole blood; Treasury Solicitor unless there is no surviving spouse in which case brothers and sisters of the half blood (or their issue); grandparents; uncles and aunts of the whole blood (or their issue); uncles and aunts of the half blood (or their issue); Treasury Solicitor.

It should be noted that this is the order which determines which of the competing applicants shall be appointed. No one is required to apply.

Appointment is by the Court and so the personal representatives must apply to the Probate Registry. They will receive a certificate which in the case of executors is called a grant of probate and in the case of administrators a grant of administration. This vests the assets and liabilities of the deceased in the hands of the personal representatives as from the date of death and provides proof that this has happened.

The executors or administrators may administer the estate themselves or they may employ a solicitor to do it for them. The solicitor will of course expect to be paid and the personal representatives are entitled to pay reasonable fees out of the estate. There is much to be said for this course unless the estate is very straightforward. The main disadvantage is that the fees may be quite substantial though probably not as large as those of banks who also take on such work.

If you are an executor or administrator and wish to administer the estate yourself, you can certainly read with advantage *Wills and Probate* (published by the Consumer's Association) which explains very clearly the steps you would have to take.

3. INSURANCE AND PENSIONS

Nowadays much of a family's wealth consists in expectations of receipts from insurance policies and pensions. Enormous sums of money are generated for this purpose and put in the hands of insurance companies and pension funds for investment. As a result these bodies, often collectively referred to as the institutions, have come to be the owners of large shareholdings in most important British companies. In effect we have moved from a society in which a small number of people owned shares to one in which a much larger group of people have an indirect interest but in a way which is so oblique that it is difficult for them to understand. In this section we shall say something therefore about life insurance and pensions. We shall also touch on property insurances, since adequate insurance of the family assets is essential for their preservation.

It is important to remember that the insurance policy is basically a contract and that therefore the insurance company is only bound to pay up if the event which has happened is one which they agreed to cover. It is essential therefore to read the policy. Unfortunately, insurance companies often use long winded lawyer's language in their policies, which sometimes conceals the meaning from the ordinary reader! However, it is perfectly reasonable to ask the insurance company to explain anything you do not understand. It would be prudent to do this in a letter and to keep the reply in a safe place.

The law of contract regards insurance contracts as special in one respect. Normally a contracting party is not required actually to provide the other party with information which will affect his decision to enter the contract. He is only required to answer truthfully the questions that he is asked. However, in the case of insurance the law requires the insured voluntarily to tell the insurance company any material fact known to

him. A material fact is defined as one which would lead a reasonable insurance company either to decline a policy or to accept it only at a higher premium. So if you had a heart attack last year you are bound to tell the insurance company even if they don't ask. A more practical example is in the field of motor insurance. It is not unknown for a father to take out a policy on a car to cover himself and anyone driving with his consent, well knowing that the car will be driven most of the time by his eighteen year old son. Failure to tell the insurance company this, even if they do not ask, makes the policy void. Of course the insurance company will often ask you to complete a proposal form, which asks a lot of questions. You must answer these questions *honestly* of course but you may find that the proposal form contains some small print which amounts to an undertaking by you to answer them *accurately*, that is to give the right answer even if you do not know it. This is deeply unsatisfactory, of course, even though a respectable insurance company would be reluctant to take advantage of this if it thought that the insured had acted honestly.

(i) Life Insurance

The golden rule for life insurance is that one should have enough but not too much. Unfortunately this rule is easier to state than to apply! The situation is complicated by the fact that people buy life insurance not only to obtain protection against death but also as a form of saving. Until the 1984 budget life insurance had tax advantages as a form of saving. These advantages do not apply to new policies but insurance companies do sell much life insurance on a savings basis. The advantage of this from the point of view of the insured is that it is a simple and relatively cheap way of taking advantage of the experience of life insurance companies in managing investments. A major disadvantage is lack of flexibility. Once you have started a policy you can usually not stop without some disadvantage. This is particularly so in the first two or three years. The reason for this is that you have contracted to go on with the policy for the agreed term. In practice most insurance companies will accept a surrender of the policy, that is they will agree to cancel the policy, and pay you a cash sum. However, if you surrender within the first two years of taking out the policy, you are unlikely to get back as much as you have paid in. This is because the setting up cost of the policy is high; in many policies the first year's premium may effectively go on commission to the agent who has sold you the policy. You should not therefore take out life insurance as a form of medium or long term saving until you have made adequate arrangements for saving for short term crises.

This leaves life insurance as a form of protection. The need for protection will obviously vary greatly with the personal circumstances of the insured. A bachelor of 21 with no dependants; a married man of 40 with four young children and a married woman of 55 whose children have grown up, can stand in quite a different position. It is essential to analyse carefully your own precise needs. The father with young children will want to provide for their upbringing but this is not a need that will continue for ever. If he survives until they are grown up, all will be well, and, even if he dies before that, he only needs to ensure that money will be available until they are grown up. It is also desirable to think the unthinkable. Husbands tend to take if for granted that their wives will survive them but obviously this does not always happen. A father with young children whose wife dies will usually need substantial sums to hire help for the children. Many do not insure against this risk.

Different types of policy are available to meet different needs. *Whole life* policies are payable only on death. *Endowment* policies are payable at the end of an agreed term, say ten, twenty or thirty years or on your earlier death. For the same amount of cover a whole life policy will usually be significantly cheaper because of the chance that you will survive the term and go on paying premiums to a ripe old age. Both whole life and endowment policies are sold on a *without profits* and *with profits* basis. In a without profits policy the amount insured is fixed at the time of contract. In a with profits policy the minimum is fixed but a policy holder will share in the profits which the insurers earn by investing the premiums. Insurers declare the profits (usually called bonuses) at regular intervals (sometimes annually, sometimes after three or five years). Once the bonuses are declared the insurers are obliged to pay them. Usually the insurers also pay a terminal bonus at the end of the policy.

Again, for any amount of insurance, the premiums on without profit policies will be lower than for with profits policies. If you simply want to make sure that a fixed risk is covered at the least cost, then a without profits policy may be attractive. However, in the last thirty years with profits policies have usually seemed more attractive most of the time. It is important to realise however that profits are not guaranteed. Insurance companies produce diagrams and figures showing you what you would receive in ten or twenty years time if the future was like the past. Of course it is extremely unlikely that the future will be the same as the past. Nevertheless the company's past record is a guide to the skill of its investment management.

Another form of life policy is a *term* policy. Under such a policy the insurer pays if you die within the term but the insured gets nothing if he survives until the end of the term. This is a cheap form of policy because there is a good chance that the insurance company will not have to pay out. It is very suitable therefore for a specific need which will disappear at the end of the term if you survive – for example, to pay off your mortgage. Instead of having a lump sum you might arrange periodical payments to your family for the rest of the term. This is a relatively cheap way of providing money to bring up your children if you die, because again the chances are you may very likely survive.

One of the problems about life insurance is to get reliable objective advice. Most people who sell life insurance do so on a commission basis. This applies not only to full time salesmen but also to those such as accountants, solicitors and bank managers who sell insurance as a sideline. There are two dangers here. One is that many agents are tied to a particular company and can only sell that company's policies. With such agents you are unlikely to hear much about other company's policies. A perhaps less obvious danger is that the amount of commission an agent gets varies quite widely according to the policy sold. There is therefore a serious danger that he will try to sell you a policy which earns him a bigger commission even though it is not the most suitable for your needs.

Insurance salesmen call themselves by all sorts of fancy names. However, they can only call themselves insurance brokers if they have registered with the Insurance Brokers Registration Council. They must have agreed to follow a statutory code of conduct and persuade the Registration Council that they are not unduly dependent on one company. Many brokers are also members of the British Insurance Brokers Association which lays down further guidelines to its members.

345

(ii) Property Insurance

You need to have an insurance on the contents of your house and on the house itself. This is usually done by two policies though the policies can be with the same company. In fact this avoids arguments about whether things like shelves are contents or fabric.

With a contents policy you may have a choice between an *indemnity* policy and a *new for old* policy. The first will pay you enough to enable you to replace an article in the condition it was whereas the latter pays you enough to enable you to buy a new one. Since in most cases you are likely to replace at new rather than second hand prices, the latter policy is generally preferable though premiums on this basis are likely to be somewhat higher. Most insurance companies now offer index linked policies, under which the value of the contents is automatically uprated each year. However, this increase is on the basic figure you set when you originally took out the policy. If this figure was too low, indexing will still leave it too low. Experience suggests that most people seriously underestimate the value of the contents of their house. You really need therefore to go carefully around your house with pencil and paper working out how much it will cost you to replace the contents.

If the contents of your house are worth £20,000 and you have only insured for £10,000 it is obviously a disaster if the house burns down. However, you will also suffer if burglars get in and remove your video recorder. This is because of the principle of *average*. Under this principle if you only insure for half the value of the contents, you will only recover half of the value of what is stolen.

The normal contents insurance will only cover the contents while they are in your house, but obviously some of your possessions, such as jewellery, cameras and the like, you will want to take out of the house. Under most policies it is possible to list a number of items of this kind which will be covered wherever they are.

If you have a mortgage your mortgagee will insist on your insuring the fabric of the house but this is obviously a sensible thing to do in any case. Building societies used to insist that mortgagors took out fabric policies through them so as to collect the commission. Most building societies should now give you some choice and some will permit you a free choice.

Again you need to decide how much to insure the house for. This might seem straightforward if you have just bought it but most insurance companies now require insurance on a rebuilding cost basis. This means that you need to work out the cost of rebuilding the house. Unless the house is brand new the rebuilding price is likely to be significantly higher than the purchase price. This might seem odd since if you have bought a £75,000 house and insured it for £125,000, it is unlikely that you would rebuild the house if it burned down. The reason is that the vast majority of fabric claims are for partial damage where the cost of rebuilding is usually very relevant. If you are underinsured the principle of average may again operate to reduce the amount you recover and this makes the initial valuation of the property vital. Most policies are now index linked so that the valuation is increased year by year by an appropriate amount.

(iii) Pensions

Pensions may be provided either by the State or privately. Nearly everyone has a right to a State pension. Private pensions may be provided by employers or, if you are self employed, you can make your own arrangements. There is a major difference between public and private pensions. Money put aside for private pensions by employers and employees is normally paid into a separately managed fund so that one could realistically say such pensions are the product of the pensioner's own efforts (the employer's contributions being a form of deferred salary). In the case of State pensions, although there are contributions, it cannot be said that there is any realistic connection between the contributions paid and the pension received. In effect 1986 pensions are being paid out of 1986 contributions and 1986 tax. The future therefore of State pensions depends on the willingness of future generations to pay tax at appropriate rates.

(A) State pensions. The State scheme is complicated by the fact that it comes in a number of different elements.

(a) Flat-rate pension. This is what most people are usually referring to when they talk about the State scheme. Everyone is entitled to this at the pensionable age (65 for men and 60 for women) provided that they have paid an average of 50 contributions a year between the age of sixteen and retirement. If you did not pay contributions because you stayed in full-time education after sixteen or were ill or unemployed you will have

HOME SECURITY PLUS POLICY
MASTER SCHEDULE I

THE COMPANY	PEARL ASSURANCE PUBLIC LIMITED COMPANY				

POLICY NUMBER	3|8 **6753177**	AGENCY	DIV	DIST	AGENT

THE INSURED	A BROWN

OPERATIVE SECTIONS	The operative sections (or items thereof) are those against which a premium is shown below.

THE SECTIONS	RENEWAL PREMIUM* £	FIRST PREMIUM £	SUM INSURED £
1. Contents of the Home			9000
2. Compensation for death	3575	3575	See Policy
3. Home and Personal Liabilities			See Policy
4. Personal All Risks			
B1 Clothing and Personal Effects	1875	1875	1250
B2 Valuables			
B3 Personal Money and Credit Cards	200	200	250
B4 Articles specified in Master Schedule II			
5. Frozen Food			
6. Jury Service			See Policy
7. Personal Accident			See Policy
TOTAL	5650	5650	

*RENEWAL PREMIUM	The renewal premium shown hereon may be subject to alteration and the actual premium required for the renewal on expiry of each period of insurance will be shown on the renewal notice.
COVER	For full details of the cover provided under any of the above sections (or items thereof) see the Policy.
DECLARATION	The Insured has declared that the Sums Insured under Sections 1 and 4 of this Policy in total represent and will be maintained at not less than the full value of the contents of the Home.

PERIOD OF INSURANCE	FROM	Day 19	Mth 5	Year 83	TO	Day 18	Mth 5	Year 84	and any subsequent period for which the Company may accept a Renewal Premium

DATE OF POLICY		Day 19	Mth 5	Year 83	OPERATIVE CLAUSES (to which the policy is subject)	NONE		

	POLICY HEREBY CANCELLED	POLICY NUMBER		Renewal Debit Due		
		Code	Number	Day	Mth	Year

In consideration of the payment of the first premium the Company will provide insurance in the terms of this Policy.

In witness whereof this Policy has been signed on behalf and with the authority of the Company on the date of Policy mentioned in the Master Schedule I.

Director

F 3462 1/83 190-8

received a 'credit'. A single person currently receives a pension of £38.70 a week and a married couple £61.95 a week. A married women who did not work or who opted to pay the lower rate of National Insurance Contributions, (which is no longer possible except for those who were paying the lower rate in 1978) will receive no pension in her own right. A married woman who has worked and paid contributions at the full rate will earn her own pension. Where a person has a less than 100% contribution record – for example because of working abroad, then the pension will be proportionately reduced.

A widow is entitled to a pension when her husband dies. If she is over 50 she will receive the full widow's pension; if she is between 40 and 50 she will receive a smaller pension unless she has dependent children in which case she will receive the full pension. For the first six months after she is widowed, she will receive the widow's allowance which is higher than the State pension.

The pension is payable from the age of 65 for men and 60 for women but it is not compulsory to retire at that age. Indeed in the light of a recent decision of the European Court of Justice it is very doubtful whether it is legitimate for employers to have a different retiring age for men and women. It is anticipated that the Government will soon introduce legislation explicitly to forbid this. You can carry on at work after pensionable age and then choose either to receive the pension or to delay receiving it until you actually stop work. If you carry on working full time it will nearly always be worth delaying the pension because the pension is subject to an earnings rule which reduces the pension in line with your earnings.

(b) Graduated pensions. This was a scheme which existed from 1961–1975. Anyone who paid contributions on this scheme during these years will receive an extra pension based on those contributions. The sums involved are not likely to be large.

(c) State earnings related pensions. This is a scheme introduced in 1978 which provides an extra pension calculated on the amount you earned while contributing. The scheme will not be fully operational until 1998 when women who were aged 40 in 1978 and men who were aged 45 reach pensionable age. Those who were over these ages in 1978 will receive reduced benefits which reflect the number of years they have paid contributions.

Basically the scheme involves taking a slice of your earnings between a lower figure (about the current single person's pension) and a higher figure (about seven times the current single person's pension) and paying a pension of about 25% of the difference between the lower figure and the higher figure (or your actual earnings if less than the higher figure). Further contributions are of course levied to pay this pension.

Self-employed workers are outside this scheme. In addition those who are in occupational pensions schemes may have been contracted out of the scheme by their employers. An employer cannot do this unless his scheme provides benefits at least as good as the State scheme but many occupational schemes provide better benefits and many employees have therefore been contracted out.

The future of this scheme must be regarded as in some doubt. In the recent review of the social security system the Minister, Norman Fowler, seemed at one stage about to suggest its abolition. He appears to have retreated from this position but there remain fears, at least in the Conservative Party, that the scheme will prove too expensive when it is fully operational.

(d) Supplementary benefit. Anyone who is living on the basic State pension alone is hard up. In principle such a person is entitled to apply for supplementary benefit, though savings over £3,000 will be taken into account in calculating entitlement to benefit.

(B) Private pensions

(a) Company pensions. Many employers now provide pension schemes. Many employees simply close their eyes to pension questions. This is a mistake as the pension is one of the most important parts of the remuneration package. The schemes vary widely in detail and you should obtain a copy of your employer's scheme and study it carefully. If you do not understand it, it is certainly worth trying to find someone who does and to discuss it with him. (Your union, if you belong to one, may be able to help with this.) However, the following are among the most important questions you should ask.

(1) Who can join? Most employers make the scheme compulsory but there is quite often a waiting period, so that only those who have worked for the company for six months or a year can join. Part time employees are often excluded.

(2) Contributions. Some schemes are non-

contributory, that is the employee pays nothing. This is not necessarily as good a deal as it sounds, since this depends on the level of benefits. It will be better to be in a scheme where you pay 5% and the employer pays 10% than in a scheme where you pay nothing and the employer pays 8%. If your employer's scheme is approved by the Inland Revenue as most are, this advantage will be increased by the fact that contributions enjoy tax relief. So if you pay tax at the basic rate of 29% it will cost you only £71 to make a £100's worth of contributions. Your employer's contributions are tax free too and where the money is invested in a tax free fund then the proceeds of the fund are free from income tax and capital gains tax. This means that you get better value for money than in almost any other form of private saving.

Most contributory schemes require the employee to pay about 5% to 6% of his income. The employer has to pay enough into the fund to enable the fund to pay the benefits promised. The fund should be reviewed periodically by an actuary to see that it is adequate to meet its obligations. (This is a complex question because it depends on what assumptions it is reasonable to make about future rates of inflation and salaries and so on.) In a reasonably generous scheme one would expect the employer to be paying in about 10–12% of his wage bill.

(3) Calculation of pensions. The most common system is the *final salaries* scheme. Under this the pension paid is calculated on some fraction of the final salary. It is important to see how final salary is defined for your scheme. Does it for instance include overtime or commission or is it based on basic salary? Many schemes take figures over the last few years of employment rather than the final years. Some good schemes will take the salary paid in past years and notionally increase it by the use of the retail price index so as to calculate its real worth. This helps to protect those whose wage increases have been less than the going rate of inflation.

The fraction of final salary will usually be based on years of service for the employer. Most commonly one gets either ⅟₆₀th or ⅟₈₀th of final salary for each year of service. So if you have worked for one employer for 40 years you would get respectively ⁴⁰⁄₆₀ths or ⁴⁰⁄₈₀ths of your final salary.

Some employers operate instead a *money purchase* scheme. In such a scheme you get the pension which is actually earned by the money which you and your employer's contributions have produced. This is attractive to employers, as it means the fund cannot become actuarially unsound as might happen in a small company with a number of centenarian pensioners. As far as any pensioner is concerned it will reflect life time earnings rather than final salary and would favour one who reached a high salary at an early age over one who reached the same salary only a few years before retirement. In recent years higher rates of inflation and large increases in money wages have tended to erode this distinction.

(4) Death benefits. Most schemes will make payments to widows if an employee dies in service. This commonly takes the form of a lump sum (perhaps between one and four times current salary) plus a pension (commonly half the pension you would have received if you had retired on the day of your death.) Where a pensioner dies after retirement, it is common for his widow to receive a fraction, often a half, of his pension. It is unusual for widowers to receive similar benefits except perhaps where they are financially dependent on their wife. Since pensions are a form of deferred pay, it is doubtful whether this form of discrimination against women employees can be justified and it is beginning to be abandoned in the better schemes.

(5) Lump sums. Most schemes provide for part of the pension to be taken in a lump sum, in return for a reduction in pension. The lump sum cannot normally exceed 1½ times your final salary. Such lump sums are tax free.

(6) Inflation after retirement. Traditionally pensions were fixed at retirement. With modern rates of inflation this has caused great hardship to those pensioners who long survive retirement. Many schemes now provide for some increases. Often however the increases are discretionary. Public sector pensions however are usually index linked so that they are protected against inflation. The Government set up a committee to enquire into this some years ago. It is widely believed that the Government hoped that the committee would recommend the abolition of index linking. Instead it proposed its expansion to the private sector. Little has been heard of this question since.

(7) Portability. The traditional employer's scheme favours those who work with one employer all their life. Under such schemes changing jobs even at a considerably higher salary has a very bad effect on your ultimate pen-

sion. This is because your final employer will only pay you a pension based on your years of service with him. It is a great advantage therefore to be in a pension scheme which allows you to move job without adverse effects. For instance school teachers are employed by a local education authority but the pension scheme is common to all teachers so that a teacher can move from one authority to another without suffering a loss of pension. This is also in the public interest as it removes a disincentive to accepting promotion.

The Government is very concerned about the unfairness caused by lack of portability in the private sector and legislation is likely to improve the position. At the moment the options are less attractive. You may be entitled to the return of your own contributions (but not those of your employer). Alternatively you may be entitled to a pension based on a fraction of your leaving salary. So if you worked for an employer for 10 years from the age of 20 to 30 and left when you were earning £10,000 you may be entitled on retirement to $^{10}\!/\!_{60}$ths of £10,000. But this will obviously be a lot less than $^{10}\!/\!_{60}$ths of your retirement salary 30 years later, and with modern rates of inflation it may be almost worthless. A better deal, if you can get it, is to transfer the money from your old scheme into your new scheme. You can only do this if both schemes agree. In most cases it is unlikely that you will receive the full value of the contributions to the old scheme. The one exception is between different pension schemes in the public sector when transfers are often permitted allowing full credit for the years already worked.

(b) Self employed pensions. If you are self employed you will have to provide your own pension above the State basic pension. However, you should undoubtedly do so as a pension is much the most tax effective way of saving. A self-employed person may put up to 17½% of his income into a personal pension plan or more if he was born before 1934.

If you are employed but have freelance work, then you are self-employed as far as this work is concerned and can put 17½% of these earnings into a pension plan. Again this is usually an excellent course.

Many insurance companies offer pension schemes designed for the self-employed. Most of the schemes have the features which we have just discussed in relation to employers' schemes.

Many of these schemes can be used in conjuction with a mortgage so that you will pay back the mortgage out of the lump sum provided by the pension. This will usually be the best way for a self-employed person to buy a house.

One of the problems with being self-employed is that it is very difficult to predict one's income from year to year. However, most schemes offer flexibility in how much you must pay each year. Further there are arrangements under which if you do not use the whole 17½% of your permitted maximum contribution in one year, you can make payments in subsequent years to use up this surplus.

(C) Pensions and unmarried partners. One of the principal features of both the State and private pension schemes is that they make no provision at all for unmarried partners or for former spouses. In the case of former spouses, the Divorce Court is entitled to take loss of pension rights into account in the property adjustment it makes on divorce. There is no similar power in the case of partners who have never been married. In financial terms this is one of the major disadvantages of not getting married.

4. COVENANTS

'Covenant' is basically a lawyer's word for promise. It has however come to be used primarily to mean a special kind of promise – one made under seal. This is an historical survival. In the middle ages contracts were normally made under seal and informal arrangements were not usually binding. English law had abandoned this position by 1600 by which date it was possible to make completely binding agreements not only without the seal but without any writing at all. However the old possibility of making an agreement binding because the seal was attached to it survived, and it was useful where a party wished to make a binding gratuitous promise. In English contract law a promise to make a gift is not ordinarily binding but it can be made so by making it under seal.

This possibility has assumed added importance in recent years because in certain circumstances there are tax advantages arising out of making binding promises in this way. If A, a taxpayer, covenants to pay money to B, a non-tax payer, then in certain circumstances B can recover the tax which A has paid in respect of income used to make the payment. The two main classes of non-tax payer who benefit from this are charities and dependent children. Benefits to charities are outside the scope of this chapter but we must say a little about the position of children.

This is perhaps best explained by an example. Let us suppose that A is the father of B, an eighteen year old student, and pays income tax at the standard rate, currently 29%. A covenants to pay B £1,000 for seven years. He in fact pays B £710 and B collects the balance of £290 from the Inland Revenue. It will be seen that A can pass quite a large part of the cost of supporting B on to the tax payer and it is not surprising that such covenants have grown in popularity over the last few years. It would perhaps not be surprising if the Chancellor of the Exchequer were to seek to restrict this but so far he has not done so – perhaps conscious that the majority of those making covenants are likely to be Conservative voters.

What Are the Limits of the Device?
(1) A must be a tax payer. Since the scheme depends on claiming the tax which A has notionally paid it will not work if A does not pay tax.

(2) B must not have too much other income. The money will not be taxable in B's hands if B's total income is below the single person's allowance. The scheme depends on the fact that everyone, even a new born child, is entitled to this allowance (currently £2,335). There is no point therefore in covenating to pay an amount in excess of this allowance and if the recipient has other income, say from savings or from part-time work, then the amount that can be covenanted with advantage is reduced by the amount of that income. However grants and scholarships do not count as income for this purpose.

(3) Parents cannot make tax effective covenants to children under eighteen. However, grandparents and other relatives can do so. Grandparents who wish to help with the cost of sending children to fee-paying schools should certainly consider doing so in this way. (Of course the fees at most such schools are now well above the single person's allowance.)

(4) The covenant has to be in the form approved by the Inland Revenue. There is no great mumbo-jumbo about the form. The Inland Revenue produces its own form of covenant, IR 47. You also need forms R 185 (AP) and R 40. The document must be sealed but all that this

now means is that a small red disc of paper must be attached to it.

(5) The covenant must run for seven years. Strictly speaking it has to run for more than six years, so that the minimum period is six years and one day, which is why seven annual payments is just right! If you are a parent and are thinking of making a covenant in favour of your daughter to help pay the cost of her going to university, you may say the course is unlikely to last seven years. This is true but there is nothing to stop you and your daughter agreeing to tear up the covenant after she has got her degree. Strictly speaking you should not agree to do this in advance.

5. BANKRUPTCY

Bankruptcy is the condition which overtakes someone who is unable to meet his debts as they fall due. It often means that you do not have enough assets to pay the debts but this is not always so since it may be that you cannot convert the assets into cash quickly enough to pay the bills. In legal terminology individuals become bankrupt and companies go into liquidation. The general name for bankruptcy and liquidation is insolvency. The law is complex and has just been the subject of a major reforming statute – the Insolvency Act 1985 (now incorporated in the Insolvency Act 1986).

The details of bankruptcy are outside the scope of this chapter but we should briefly notice the effect that the bankruptcy of one member of the family may have on the family assets. This is most likely to arise when one member of the family has been trading as a sole trader or partner (see 'The Law and Your Business', page 217) though it can arise simply from the inability of a non-trading family to manage its finances.

If the husband becomes bankrupt, a trustee in bankruptcy will be appointed whose task will be to gather in the husband's assets, convert them into cash and distribute them among the creditors. For this purpose the property of the wife, or indeed the children, is not the property of the husband and is therefore not available for the creditors, though, as we shall see, this will be the subject of some qualification.

The first task therefore is to discover what property is owned by the wife and what by the husband. We have already discussed this in relation to the house. In the case of chattels, such as furniture or jewellery, this may depend on whether the husband has made an effective gift to the wife. Gifts of chattels require a physical delivery. This is easily and naturally achieved in the case of jewellery but in *Re Cole* (1964) the Court took a very strict view in relation to furniture. In this case the husband bought a new house in 1946, filled it with expensive furniture, took the wife to the house and led her from room to room, showing her the furniture and saying 'it's all yours.' When the husband became bankrupt many years later it was held that the furniture belonged to him.

Even when there has been a transfer which is effective between husband and wife, it may be possible for the creditors to set it aside in the following circumstances:

1. A transaction entered into for the purpose of putting assets out of the reach of creditors by transferring property at an undervalue (this includes giving it away) can be set aside under sections 423–5 of the Insolvency Act 1986.

2. Transactions at undervalue may also be set aside under sections 339–342 of the Insolvency Act 1986, as may be the giving of a preference (that is treating one of the creditors better than the others, for example by paying him). Under these sections transactions at an undervalue may be upset if they took place within a period of five years before the presentation of the petition or, in the case of a preference, within two years of that day.

Even if the wife has a secure half share in the house the trustee in bankruptcy may apply to the Court to order a sale so as to convert the husband's share into cash. Under section 171 of the Insolvency Act 1985 the Court has a discretion whether to order such a sale, but if the application to sell is made by the trustee in bankruptcy more than one year after his appointment, the Court is directed to treat the interest of the bankrupt's creditors as outweighing other considerations unless the circumstances are exceptional. In practice this seems likely to mean that the trustee in bankruptcy will usually not seek an order for sale for twelve months.

1. INTRODUCTION

A marriage may be brought to an end either by a decree of nullity or by a divorce. The grounds upon which a decree of nullity may be granted have been discussed earlier and this discussion will therefore be concerned with divorce. We need to consider the grounds upon which a divorce may be obtained but in practice today disputes arising out of divorce proceedings are much less often about whether the marriage should come to an end than about the provision for the children and the financial results of the divorce.

2. DIVORCE

(i) The History of Divorce

As is so often the case in English society the present position can only be understood in the light of the past. Although the English Church broke with Rome because of Henry VIII's determination to nullify his marriage with his first wife, Catherine of Aragon, divorce did not thereafter become generally available. The Ecclesiastical Courts had power to order what we would now call a decree of judicial separation, which relieved the parties of their duty to live together but did not enable them to remarry. It was only possible to obtain a divorce by Act of Parliament. This involved a complex and expensive procedure which involved proof that the other party to the marriage had committed adultery and that the person seeking the divorce had not.

Judicial divorce was introduced in England in 1857 when a Court for Divorce and Matrimonial Causes was set up with power to grant divorces, but again only if the respondent had committed adultery and the petitioner had not. Indeed the law discriminated between husbands and wives since it was not sufficient for a wife petitioner to show that her husband had committed adultery. She had to show either that the adultery was incestuous or that it was combined with bigamy, rape, sodomy, bestiality, cruelty or desertion for at least two years. Although this discrimination against the wife was removed in 1923, adultery remained the only ground until 1937 when cruelty, desertion for three or more years and incurable insanity were made grounds for divorce.

Even after 1937 English law remained firmly wedded to the notion of the matrimonial offence, that is, that a partner could only be divorced for having done something seriously wrong. This doctrine had numerous corollaries, for instance that the petitioner must not have committed an offence, must not have agreed to the respondent committing the offence (collusion) or have forgiven it (condonation). The most obvious consequence was that if both parties had committed adultery neither was entitled to a divorce.

Although the principle of basing divorce law on the matrimonial offence was reaffirmed by a Royal Commission appointed in 1951, it came under increasing challenge from the notion that divorces should be granted where the marriage had broken down. A number of changes in the law were made which reflected this view; for instance, the petitioner who had himself/herself committed adultery could obtain a divorce provided there was full disclosure of that adultery in 'a discretion statement.' Eventually Parliament by the Divorce Reform Act 1969 accepted the principle that the basis for divorce should be that the marriage had broken down, but in a typically murky compromise retained the matrimonial offences as amongst the principal ways of proving that breakdown.

(ii) The Ground(s) for Divorce

Section 1 of the Divorce Reform Act 1969 said that 'the sole ground on which a petition for divorce may be presented to the Court by either party to a marriage shall be that the marriage has broken down irretrievably.' There is no doubt that this represented a massive conceptual change but the practical effect was more restricted because the Act required the petitioner to prove one or more of five 'facts' in order to establish breakdown. It is not enough therefore for a petitioner to establish that the marriage has broken down unless he can establish one of the 'facts'. So a petitioner husband who has left his wife and set up home with another woman might well persuade the Court that his marriage had broken down but this by itself would not entitle him to a divorce. It is true that since one of the grounds is five years separation, he can be sure that he will get a divorce in the end but experience shows that in such circumstances petitioners (and their new partners) often do not want to wait so long. In principle where a petitioner has established one of the 'facts' the Court may still hold that the marriage has not broken down. In practice however it seems that it will only do so in wholly exceptional circumstances (see the box below). The result of this is that in practice the 'facts' by which breakdown has to be established come to look like grounds and they are often so described though this is clearly theoretically wrong. We will now consider each of the 'facts' in turn.

(A) That the respondent has committed adultery and the petitioner finds it intolerable to live with the respondent. Adultery consists of consensual sexual intercourse with someone who is not your spouse. So a wife who has been raped has not committed adultery. 'Heavy petting' will not amount to adultery since some element of penetration, however transitory, is required. As we have seen, adultery has long been the classic matrimonial offence. The 1969 Act made a major change by requiring that the petitioner should find it intolerable to live with the respondent. This requirement was seen as a logical consequence of the breakdown principle.

'Irretrievable breakdown'
In *Le Marchant v Le Marchant* [1977] the petitioner husband established that the parties had been living separately for five years. The wife gave evidence she still loved her husband and wanted him back. The Court held that the marriage had irretrievably broken down.

In *Biggs v Biggs* [1977] the wife was granted a decree *nisi* of divorce in 1973 because of her husband's adultery. He was then in prison but was released in 1974 and returned to his wife. She applied to have the decree made absolute (apparently because she thought this would restrain his activities with other women). The Court held that the marriage had not broken down because the parties were living together and having sexual intercourse. This appears to be the only reported case since 1969 where a petition was rejected because there was no irretrievable breakdown.

It was thought that many marriages survive isolated acts of adultery by one or both parties and that the old rule that a single act of adultery was sufficient should not survive unaltered. However, cases where isolated acts of adultery take place and are forgiven do not usually come before the Courts. In practice this requirement has not proved much of a barrier to divorce because the Courts have held that the critical question is whether the petitioner finds it intolerable and not whether a reasonable petitioner would do so. Further, Courts have held (though the matter is not free from controversy) that the petitioner does not have to show that it is because of the adultery that he finds it intolerable. However, it should be noted that if the parties have lived together for a period exceeding six months or for periods which combined exceed six months after the petitioner knew that the respondent had committed adultery, the petitioner cannot rely on that act of adultery.

(B) That the respondent has behaved in such a way that the petitioner cannot reasonably be expected to live with the respondent. 'Cruelty' was made a ground for divorce in 1937 and had been a ground for judicial separation before that. Over the years the Courts built up a complex body of case law on what constituted cruelty. It would seem that the present head embraces anything that was cruelty before 1969 but is rather wider in scope. It appears that the petitioner has to show that the respondent has behaved in a particular way and that in the light of that behaviour the petitioner cannot reasonably be expected to go on living with the respondent. This requirement of reasonableness excludes behaviour which the petitioner finds intolerable for wholly idiosyncratic reasons. On the other hand, the Court is certainly entitled to look at the whole personality and behaviour of each of the parties before deciding (box at top of page 355).

There can be few marriages in which one partner is not at some time guilty of behaviour which the other party finds unreasonable. But this is not the test. The question is whether the petitioner cannot be expected to go on living with the respondent. The answer to this question clearly depends on one's view of how tolerant spouses should be expected to be of each other's failings. The statute gives no guidance on this other than reasonableness. It is very doubtful whether there are any community wide values which can be

---

'Unreasonable behaviour'

In *Archard v Archard* [1972] both parties had been practising Roman Catholics. The wife for medical reasons wished to avoid pregnancy and to use contraceptives. The husband refused to have intercourse if the wife used contraceptives. Refusal to have sexual intercourse could certainly constitute unreasonable behaviour but the Court held that in the light of the parties' religious beliefs it was not such behaviour that the wife could not reasonably be expected to live with the husband.

In *Pheasant v Pheasant* [1972] Mr Justice Ormrod said that 'a petitioner who is addicted to drink can reasonably be expected to live with a respondent similarly addicted.'

In *Thurlow v Thurlow* [1976] the wife suffered from epilepsy and had become a bedridden invalid in need of full-time institutional care. She threw things at her husband's mother and wandered the streets causing alarm to her husband and those looking after her. A decree was granted.

---

applied to this question. Inevitably therefore much will turn on how the question appears to the individual judge. The problem is particularly difficult when considering how far one spouse should be expected to accept the consequence of the physical or mental illness of the other (see above).

(C) That the respondent has deserted the petitioner for a continuous period of at least two years immediately preceding the presentation of the petition. Desertion was a ground of divorce under the 1937 Act though it had to last for three years. Again the Courts developed a complex body of rules which were carried forward into the 1969 Act. Fortunately, however, the complexities do not now have too much practical importance as where the parties have lived apart for two years the petitioner will usually rely on Ground (D) below.

Desertion requires both separation and an intention to desert. Factual separation is essential though it can take place within a single

house if the parties genuinely lead separate lives. A wife who locks her husband out of the bedroom but continues to cook his meals is not separated from him. In order for separation to be desertion it must be accompanied by an intention to desert. It follows that there is no desertion if the separation is by agreement (though it is still desertion if, after the husband has left, the wife is happy to see the back of him) or there is a good cause for separation as where the husband is sent to prison. It is not necessary that the separation and the intention to desert start at the same time. So if the husband is sent to Hong Kong by his firm and after six months announces that he does not intend to return home he will be in desertion.

It does not necessarily follow that the party who leaves is the deserting party. It may be that in effect he was driven out. This is said to be 'constructive' desertion. Obvious examples are where the husband physically expels the wife or orders her to leave, but the doctrine also embraces conduct, such as installing his mistress in the house, which no reasonable wife could be expected to put up with. There is obviously a potential overlap here with conduct under (B) above. The difference is that conduct which makes it unreasonable to expect the petitioner to live with the respondent is an immediate ground for divorce whereas desertion is only a ground if it is continuous for two years.

The desertion has to continue for two years. It is provided however that a period of less than six months during which the parties resumed living together or a number of periods not exceeding six months in total do not prevent the desertion being continuous though they do not count towards the two years. So if H deserts W in January 1983, but comes back for five months from January to May 1984, he will have completed two years 'continuous' desertion at the end of May 1985. In principle desertion comes to an end if the deserting party makes a *bona fide* offer to return which is refused. This used to be of considerable practical importance but now the party who has been deserted can shift ground to separation under (D) or (E) below.

(D) That the parties to the marriage have lived apart for a continuous period of at least two years immediately preceding the presentation of the petition and the respondent consents to a decree being granted.

355

(E) That the parties to the marriage have lived apart for a continous period of at least five years immediately preceding the presentation of the petition. These two grounds were wholly new when they were introduced in 1969 and marked the major shift of approach in the Act since they are completely independent of any notion of fault on the part of either partner. Since they substantially overlap it is more convenient to consider them together.

The fact of separation is treated in much the same way as the separation element in desertion just discussed, so the parties can be living separately even though they live in the same house provided that they lead separate existences. Sharing meals or watching television together would be inconsistent with separation. There can be wholly exceptional cases where separation is consistent with the provision of services, provided that the services are not provided as a spouse (see the box below).

The converse problem arises where one of the partners is away from home for reasons which are perfectly consistent with an intention to return, for instance, because he is a soldier serving in Northern Ireland. The Court of Appeal has held that the parties are not living apart unless at least one of them regards the marriage as at an end. The Court also held that the separation was effective from that moment even though the other partner has not been told.

The great difference between the two year separation and five year separation grounds is that the former is dependent on the respondent's consent. There are procedural steps designed to ensure that the respondent understands the effect of giving consent. In addition the Court has power to revoke a decree before it is made absolute if the petitioner misled the respondent about any matter that the respondent took into account in deciding whether to give consent.

Husband and wife not living together
In *Fuller v Fuller* [1973] the husband and wife separated in 1964 and the wife went to live with another man. In 1968 the husband had a serious heart attack and it was arranged that he would move into a room in the house in which the wife was living with her new partner. He was provided with food by the wife for a weekly payment. It was held that the husband and wife were not living together.

(iii) Other Limits on Divorce
Even if the petitioner is able to establish one of the 'facts' just discussed it does not inevitably follow that a divorce will be granted.

(A) No divorce proceedings can be started within one year of marriage. Until 1984 divorce proceedings could not be started within three years of the marriage unless the Court gave its permission on the grounds either that the petitioner would suffer grave hardship or that the respondent had displayed exceptional depravity. Section 47(1)(a) of the Matrimonial and Family Proceedings Act 1984 has replaced this with a simple provision that no proceedings may be started within a year of marriage. Of course events within the first year of marriage may constitute 'facts' for a petition presented after one year has elapsed.

(B) The marriage has not irretrievably broken down. This is discussed above (see box on page 354).

(C) Grave hardship to the respondent divorced under the five year separation ground. In the debate which preceded the 1969 Act considerable concern was expressed about the unilateral divorce of an 'innocent' respondent, that is one who had committed no matrimonial offence. Some were of course wholly opposed to permitting this but eventually a compromise was struck which is now embodied in section 5 of the Matrimonial Causes Act 1973. Under this section, if the Court would otherwise grant a divorce on the five year separation ground, it may refuse to do so if it thinks that the divorce would cause grave financial or other hardship to the respondent and if having considered all the circumstances it thinks it would be wrong to grant the divorce.

In practice this defence has not been of great assistance to respondents because it is usually very difficult for the respondent to show that the divorce causes great hardship. This is because the alternative to divorce is not the continuance of the marriage as a going concern but separation and it is the *de facto* collapse of the marriage rather than the divorce which causes the greatest hardship. Usually the divorce does not add to the hardship caused by the collapse of the marriage especially in view of the wide power of the Court to make financial orders.

The most likely example of hardship is loss by

the respondent of potential pension rights (either public or private) to which she will only be entitled if she survives the petitioner as his widow. The Court has little power to reallocate such rights in divorce. If the husband has other resources the Court can order a transfer of these resources to compensate the wife for the loss of pension rights. A sufficiently wealthy husband could take out an insurance policy or buy an annuity for his wife to cover the risk. Conversely if the wife is sufficiently impoverished she would be eligible for supplementary benefit and it might make no difference that she did not receive a widow's pension, since she would receive the same amount of money from a different part of the public purse. Nevertheless between those extremes there may be cases where the wife will suffer grave hardship by being divorced. Even if the Court concludes that there would be grave hardship it has still to consider whether in all the circumstances it would be wrong to grant the divorce. It appears that few divorces have been refused under this ground (see box below).

(D) Financial provisions in divorces for two or five year separations. Section 10 of the Matrimonial Causes Act 1973 enables the respondent in a separation case to apply to the Courts after the granting of the decree *nisi* not to make the decree absolute unless it is satisfied either that the petitioner should not be required to make any financial provision for the respondent or the provision actually made is reasonable and fair or at least the best that can be made in the circumstances. This power is quite separate from the Court's general power to make financial orders which is discussed in Property and Financial Questions, on page 360. Usually the Court by exercising these powers will make a provision that is fair or reasonable or the best that

---

Refusal to grant decree

In *Julian v Julian* [1972] the husband was 61 and the wife 58. Neither was in good health. If the divorce was granted the wife would lose her right to a police pension of £790 a year. The only provision the husband could make for the wife after his death was an annuity of £215. The Court refused to grant a decree. It was said that it was not hard on the husband to deprive him of the possibility of another marriage, granted his age and health.

---

can be made in the circumstances. But there may be cases where the Court lacks the power to make a direct order but can say to a petitioner that it will not grant a decree absolute unless he takes some step which it cannot directly compel him to take. So the Court may be able to do indirectly what it cannot do directly. Again loss of potential pension rights would be a good example of such a case.

(iv) The Procedure for Obtaining a Divorce

Normally in a book such as this one would say little about the detailed procedure of the Courts but in the case of divorce the procedure is in practice usually more important than the substantive legal position which we have just discussed.

In 1857 Parliament set up the Divorce Court and thence forward took the view that divorce was a matter of such importance that it always required the attention of a High Court Judge and this continued to be the view until relatively recently. This decision was eventually perceived, however, to have some serious disadvantages. In the vast majority of cases the petition for divorce was not defended and this meant that the parties had to incur the not inconsiderable cost of engaging a solicitor and counsel in order to appear in court for a few minutes. Research suggested strongly that this had an alienating effect on many parties. In the small fraction of cases which were defended, the procedure encouraged the minute analysis of the behaviour of the parties over many years. This often served primarily to exacerbate the parties' mutual dislike. In addition the marked increase in the number of divorces involved substantial cost to the taxpayer since the hearings consumed the time of many highly paid judges and one or both of the parties might be in receipt of legal aid.

In 1973 a major change was made by the introduction of the so called 'special procedure' which is in fact the ordinary procedure for undefended divorces. Legal aid is no longer available for undefended divorces, though if the petitioner is within the financial limits, legal advice may be obtained under the 'Green Form' scheme to help with the completion of the formalities. Forms for the petition and subsequent documents are available from the Divorce Court offices (look in the telephone directory under Courts for your local County Court. Not all County Courts are Divorce Courts but your local County Court will be able to tell you which is the nearest Divorce

Court. Alternatively you can apply to the Divorce Registry, Somerset House, Strand, London WC2R 1LP). You can also obtain a free booklet – *Undefended Divorce – a guide for the petitioner acting without a solicitor*.

The first step is to complete the petition. There are standard forms of petition for each of the 'facts.' (You can of course allege more than one 'fact'.) The petition also contains spaces for the petitioner to apply for the custody of the children and for 'ancillary relief' (that is, orders as to financial and property questions, discussed in Property and Financial Questions, page 360). The petition must contain the address of the respondent and, if adultery with a named person is alleged, the name and address of the co-respondent. The Court will send to the respondent a copy of the petition (and also to the co-respondent if there is one). That will be accompanied by an 'acknowledgement of service' form which should be returned within seven days. This also asks various questions about the respondent's intentions, for example does he intend to seek custody of the children. If the respondent wishes to defend the divorce he needs to decide so quickly at this stage (see (v) Defended Divorces below).

The Court will send a copy of the respondent's acknowledgement of service to the petitioner who can then apply for 'directions for trial.' This involves completing another form which will be supplied by the Court and the completion of an affidavit. An affidavit is a statement sworn under oath. The swearing can be done be taking it to the Court office, which will not charge or by taking it to a solicitor or commissioner for oaths (but not your own solicitor) who will make a small charge. The affidavit serves as evidence in support of the petition. Completion of the affidavit can normally be effected by answering the questions in the form supplied by the Court (a different form for each 'fact').

The registrar will read the papers and decide whether the affidavit contains sufficient evidence to support the petition. If, as in the vast majority of cases he will, he thinks so, he will issue a certificate to that effect. The actual granting of the decree *nisi* takes place in Court but this is simply an empty formality to retain a vestigial judicial element.

If the registrar does not consider the affidavit evidence sufficient he may invite the petitioner to file a further affidavit or provide further information. If he is still not satisfied he may remove the case from the special procedure list. This will mean that it will then be heard in open Court before a judge.

The granting of the decree comes in two stages – the decree *nisi* and decree absolute. The petitioner can normally obtain a decree absolute six weeks after the grant of the decree *nisi*. If the petitioner has some special reason for wishing to have a decree absolute earlier, for instance in order to get married before a child is born, application can be made to the judge at the time when the decree *nisi* is granted explaining the reasons. If the petitioner does not apply to have the decree made absolute, the respondent may do so nineteen weeks after the granting of the decree *nisi*. In the normal case the gap between decree *nisi* and decree absolute is used to resolve any disputes about the children or financial and property matters. It is these questions which in practice usually give rise to difficulty.

It will be seen that where this procedure is employed the critical question is what must be said in the affidavit to satisfy the registrar. In practice many of the theoretically difficult problems which the law presents will not arise because there will be nothing in the affidavit to alert the registrar to their existence.

(v) Defended Divorces

In 1969 it may have seemed likely that divorce on the grounds of separation would gradually oust divorce based on conduct which had previously been classified as a matrimonial offence. In practice this has not happened. In 1984 there were 178,940 petitions of which

50,720	were based on adultery	(28.34%)
73,340	were based on behaviour	(40.98%)
3,060	were based on desertion	(1.71%)
38,950	were based on two year separation	(21.76%)
10,780	were based on five year separation	(6.02%)

(The balance were based on more than one ground.)

There are major differences between husbands and wives in the use of the various grounds so that whereas some 40% of petitions based on adultery are brought by husbands, only a little over 10% of petitions based on behaviour are so brought. Recent research also suggests that there are considerable class and age differences in the use of the various grounds.

It will be seen that although separation has largely extinguished desertion as a separate 'fact' the majority of petitions are still brought on the old-fashioned matrimonial offence grounds of adultery and behaviour. The reason for this appears to be that in many cases one at least of the parties is not prepared to wait the two years needed to get a divorce on separation grounds. This can present a problem for a respondent who is prepared to acquiesce in the marriage being brought to an end but finds the allegation as to adultery or behaviour unacceptable. While there is no doubt that in theory such a respondent is entitled to defend the petition, there is equally no doubt that in practice there are formidable disincentives to doing so. One is the cost which is likely to be very considerable; another is that your lawyer and the registrar may be anxious to encourage you to abandon your defence. What is certain however is that if you want to defend you must act quickly since if you fail to make it clear to the Court that you are going to defend, the registrar may continue to operate the special procedure. You should certainly not attempt to defend yourself so that you should go to a solicitor as quickly as possible after receiving the petition. You are perfectly free to withdraw your defence at a later stage and this is in practice often done.

(vi) Conciliation

Starting divorce proceedings does not impose any obligation on the petitioner to carry them through to the decree. The petitioner is perfectly free to abandon the proceedings and in fact each year a significant number appear to do so. (The number of decrees *nisi* granted each year is significantly less than the number of petitions and the number of decrees absolute is less than the number of decrees *nisi*.) It is often suggested that the divorce law should provide institutional encouragement to reconciliation between divorcing spouses. At the time of the 1969 Act much was made of this, but in fact the relevant provisions of the Act appear to be a dead letter. Effective steps at reconciliation need to come earlier in the day than the start of proceedings.

If reconciliation is now thought to be a matter best attempted earlier, there has been great interest in the last few years in attempts at 'conciliation'. This word is, because of its similarity to reconciliation, misleading and it is perhaps unfortunate that some other word such as mediation is not used. What is envisaged is not steps to mend the marriage but steps to get the parties through the divorce process with the minimum of

bitterness. In practice the steps taken have focussed primarily on helping the parties to agree as to the arrangements to be made for the children of the marriage.

The whole question is in a state of flux and rapid development. Who should conciliate, when they should conciliate and whether conciliation should be publicly funded are current questions of debate. It is very likely therefore that there will be further changes in the next few years. Any explanation of the current position has to take note of the distinction which has been drawn between 'in Court' conciliation and 'out of Court' conciliation.

There appears much to be said for the view that, if conciliation is to be effective, the sooner it takes place the better. At the moment there is no general scheme which operates throughout the country but there are a variety of local schemes often set up by the voluntary efforts of professional workers in the family law field. It is obviously worth finding out whether there is such a scheme in your neighbourhood. A well known example is the Bristol Courts Family Conciliation Service. Referrals may be made to the service by the parties themselves or through solicitors or such bodies as the Citizens Advice Bureaux. Such schemes usually involve meetings with the parties, in some cases separately and in other cases together. The conciliator is usually a social worker and the aim of the exercise is to help the parties to reach an agreement on the issue in dispute. It is of the essence of such a scheme that the conciliator has no authority to impose a solution; the solution, if there is one, is that of the parties.

'In Court' conciliation centres on the pre-trial review conducted by the registrar. This was used first in the case of defended divorces. In principle the pre-trial review was designed to elicit the real issues in dispute between the parties; in practice some registrars have seen it as an opportunity to convert the case into an undefended one (see (v) Defended Divorces above). More recently there have been experiments by which a conciliation appointment is made when there are contested applications over custody and/or access. The husband and wife and every child over ten must attend and the registrar aided by a welfare officer will seek to help the parties to reach an agreed solution. If the parties do agree the registrar will embody their agreement in an order; if they do not any subsequent appointment will be with a different registrar and welfare officer.

3. JUDICIAL SEPARATION

Instead of seeking a divorce a petitioner may seek an order for judicial separation. If one of the 'facts' is proved the Court must make such an order provided that it has satisfied itself as to the arrangements for the children.

The effect of such a decree is to relieve the petitioner from any obligation to cohabit with the respondent and to terminate each party's rights on the intestacy of the other. When granting the decree the Court has all the powers as to custody and financial matters that it has in the case of a divorce.

4. DISPUTES ABOUT CHILDREN

In practice once one party has reached the stage of starting divorce proceedings it is very likely that a divorce will follow. The respondent may regret this, put up with it or actively welcome it, but in most cases there will not be a fight in Court about the divorce. The disputes, if there are any, are nearly always about the children or about financial and property questions. The law regulating disputes about children has already been discussed in Chapter 2 – see particularly p 309.

5. PROPERTY AND FINANCIAL QUESTIONS

If the parties are young, have no children and are both working, the divorce may be relatively free from financial difficulties. If the wife is not working and there are young children, the divorce will add substantially to the family's burdens without adding at all to its income. There will have to be two houses and this will usually mean that extra furniture and household equipment is needed. If the husband remarries, his second family will also make demands on his income. In such circumstances it is likely that some, and perhaps all, of the parties will suffer hardship. Reluctance to accept this may produce bitter disputes in which each of the parties seek to shift the greater part of the hardship on to the other's shoulders. We have already considered in Family Assets the rules which determine who owns what within the family. In the context of divorce, however, they are just a starting point as the Court has very wide powers to order transfers of property. To start with we will consider disputes about who is entitled to live in the family home as this is often the problem which arises

first. We will then consider the powers which the Court has to provide for the income and capital needs of the parties and the children.

(i) The Right to Live in the Family Home

During the 1950s the Court of Appeal held in a number of cases that where a husband, who owned the family home, deserted the wife leaving her in the house, he could not turn her out. However, it was an open question for some time whether someone who bought the house could evict the wife. Eventually the House of Lords held in 1965 that the wife's right to stay was a purely personal right which she enjoyed against the husband and which did not bind purchasers even if they knew of her rights. This decision was widely thought to be technically correct but to produce unsatisfactory results and it was followed by the Matrimonial Homes Act 1967. This Act reaffirmed the right of a spouse who was in occupation of the family home not to be evicted during marriage except by Court order. Strictly speaking if the deserted spouse has a share in the legal ownership then he or she cannot be turned out anyway. The Act was primarily aimed therefore at spouses who had no property rights in the house but in 1970 it was extended to cases where one spouse had a beneficial interest in the house but no legal title and in 1976 to the case where both parties have a legal interest in the house.

The right to remain is void against the husband's trustee in bankruptcy but it can be made effective against purchasers of the house if it has been purchased after the right has been registered in the Land Registry. Since a potential purchaser searches the Land Registry as a standard part of the procedure for buying a house he will readily discover the existence of the wife's right. An important point to note however is that a purchaser for this purpose includes a mortgagee. In the normal case where the husband has bought the house with the aid of a mortgage, that mortgage will prevail over the wife's right since that will not have been registered at the time the mortgage was granted. The wife's rights would be best protected by routine registration of the right at the time the house was bought, although this might perhaps be regarded by some husbands as an unfriendly act, and it would in practice make it very difficult for the family to raise money later by a second mortgage.

It nowadays not uncommonly happens that, although the marriage has collapsed, both parties continue to live in the house because neither can afford alternative accommodation. This situation is likely to lead to considerable tension and not infrequently to violence. What remedies can the law afford in this situation? The most effective remedy is likely in many cases to be an injunction, that is an order of the Court to do or not to do something enforceable in the event of disobedience, by committal to prison for contempt. Such injunctions in this field take two forms: non-molestation orders and ouster orders.

A non-molestation order is designed to stop the husband 'assaulting, molesting, annoying or otherwise interfering with' the wife. These are wide words and the Courts have taken a wide view of their content. An ouster order directs one party (usually the husband) to leave the matrimonial home forthwith. The rules under which such injuctions can be granted are complex, being based on a number of overlapping statutes. The Matrimonial Homes Act 1983 enables a spouse to apply to the Court for orders concerning the occupation of the matrimonial home. This Act does not apply to unmarried couples. The Domestic Violence and Matrimonial Proceedings Act 1976, which applies to both married and unmarried couples empowers the County Court to grant both non-molestation and ouster orders in respect of the family home. The Court also has a general jurisdiction to grant injunctions under the Supreme Court Act 1981, but the House of Lords has said that this should not be used in areas which are covered by the two more specific statutes. It may be useful however where the remedy falls outside those statutes, for instance, because the position of the children is involved. A spouse would be rash to attempt to negotiate through this maze without the help of a solicitor but the procedure does have the great advantage of speed. In cases of great emergency it has been known for orders to be obtained on the same day that the solicitor was consulted.

(ii) Financial Adjustments
(A) Financial powers of the High Court and Divorce County Court.
Where the Court is granting a decree of divorce or nullity or ordering a judicial separation it has wide powers to make orders as to financial matters. Orders can be against either husband or wife but in practice the vast majority of orders are made against the husband. It will be convenient therefore to talk of orders against the husband.

The Court may order the husband to pay maintenance to the wife pending suit, that is to enable her to maintain herself until the hearing of the suit. Thereafter it can order the husband to make periodical money payments. The Court has power to vary such an order later, upwards or downwards. It is common therefore where the wife has no immediate income needs to make a nominal order so as to keep open the possibility of making a substantial order later. Of course the making of the order does not always ensure that the husband pays the money. In appropriate Court cases the Court can provide against this possibility in advance by securing the order against some property of the husband so that if he does not make the payment, his property can be used. Such an order can only sensibly be made if the husband has significant assets and in some cases the family home will be such an asset. The Court may make an order for any period it thinks appropriate or for an indefinite period. Such orders, however, terminate automatically on remarriage of the wife.

The Court also has power to make orders for the transfer of capital. So it may order the husband to make a lump sum payment to his wife (in appropriate cases in instalments); to transfer property to her (such as the family home); to settle property (so, for instance, the family home might be settled on the wife for her life and then go to the children) or to vary existing settlements. The Court also has power to order the sale of an asset, for example the family home.

It will be seen that the Court has very wide powers. The powers are not without limit however. The Court cannot dispose of the contingent rights which the parties have to pensions nor can it order the husband to take out an insurance policy to protect the wife against loss of pension rights. On the other hand it can certainly take loss of pension rights into account in deciding what to do and in many cases the husband may be persuaded to offer voluntarily what cannot be ordered, lest the Court should order something else which he would find unacceptable.

It is possible, though not now very common, for a party to apply to the Court for a financial order without seeking divorce, nullity or judicial separation on the grounds that the other party was failing to provide reasonable maintenance for the applicant or any child of the family. The Court can make an order for periodical payments or a lump sum order.

(B) Principles upon which the Court exercises its powers. The Court receives guidance from the Matrimonial Causes Act 1973 which was subject to a major amendment in 1984.

(a) The Court must consider all the circumstances. The Court is directed to have particular regard to a number of matters (see below). This list is not exhaustive and the Court must always take into account any other circumstances drawn to its attention which seem relevant.

Section 25A of the Matrimonial Causes Act 1973

Under section 25A of the Matrimonial Causes Act 1973 the Court should have regard in particular to the following matters

(a) the income, earning capacity, property and other financial resources which each of the parties to the marriage has or is likely to have in the foreseeable future, including, in the case of earning capacity, any increase in that capacity which it would in the opinion of the Court be reasonable to expect a party to the marriage to take steps to acquire;

(b) the financial needs, obligations and responsibilities which each of the parties to the marriage has or is likely to have in the foreseeable future;

(c) the standard of living enjoyed by the family before the breakdown of the marriage;

(d) the age of each party to the marriage and the duration of the marriage;

(e) any physical or mental disability of either of the parties to the marriage;

(f) the contributions which each of the parties has made or is likely in the foreseeable future to make to the welfare of the family, including any contribution by looking after the home or caring for the family;

(g) the conduct of each of the parties, if that conduct is such that it would in the opinion of the Court be inequitable to disregard it;

(h) in the case of proceedings for divorce or nullity of marriage, the value to each of the parties to the marriage of any benefit (for example, a pension) which, by reason of the dissolution or annulment of the marriage that party will lose the chance of acquiring.

Although the current list was drawn up in 1984 most of the heads were originally contained in legislation in 1970 and there was a vast body of case law which it is impossible to consider here. We may make some general observations, however. It is clear that the Court cannot satisfactorily perform its function if the parties do not make a full and frank account of their financial affairs. The wife should therefore spend some time making a careful statement of her own income and outgoings. If she suspects that the husband is concealing assets or income it is obviously well worth while trying to remember investments, bank accounts, building society deposits and the like which were revealed during the marriage. The Court can compel her husband to reveal his income tax accounts, bank statements, credit card accounts and the like. If there are large sums at stake, it will probably be worthwhile hiring an accountant to analyse the husband's figures.

If the husband remarries the assets of his second wife should not be taken directly into account. However, if he argues that he cannot pay his first wife as much as she needs because he has a second family to support, the second wife's financial position will then become indirectly relevant. There is obviously some danger that some second wives will feel that they are working to support the first wife.

If the husband has a low income, divorce and remarriage may take both families into the supplementary benefit zone. In such cases it may make little difference to the wife how much she receives from the husband, since the balance will be made up by supplementary benefit. However it is not in general right for the husband to shift the burden of supporting his wife on to the State. It is proper therefore for the Court to take into account the cost to the tax payer of adopting such a solution.

There is, however, one way in which the wife is worse off, if she is being supported partly by her ex husband and partly by supplementary benefit than she would be if she were being supported entirely by supplementary benefit. This is that she is exposed to the risk that the husband will not keep up the payments. This risk is substantial. However, there is now an important administrative procedure which protects the wife against this risk. If the wife qualifies for supplementary benefit and has an order for maintenance which is for no more than the scale rate for supplementary benefit then the DHSS will pay her the full supplementary benefit rates in return for her authorising the Court to pay over any maintenance payments to the DHSS. In 1981 nearly 80% of wives with maintenance orders, who were on supplementary benefit, were using the diversion procedure. Apparently the DHSS are more reluctant to employ this procedure where the wife's order is for more than the scale rate of supplementary benefit.

Just as the supplementary benefit system is of critical importance where the divorced partners are poor, so the tax system is central to the financial arrangements of those who are better off. The Court will expect to be told what is the post tax as well as the pre-tax position of the parties. If there is enough money available there are significant possibilities for minimising tax. So, once divorced, both the husband and the wife are entitled to relief on interest paid on a mortgage up to £30,000. So, if the wife is left in possession of the family home which has an outstanding mortgage of £30,000, money paid to the wife by the husband can be used to pay the mortgage interest and enjoy tax relief, while the husband can enjoy tax relief on the mortgage on his new house. Indeed once the decree absolute has been granted, the parties, if reconciled, can enjoy £60,000 worth of mortgage interest tax relief on one house so long as they do not remarry!

A further important point is that if payments are made by the husband to the wife or the children under a Court order they cease for tax purposes to be income of the husband and become the income of the wife or child respectively. If the husband's tax rate in relation to the payment is higher than that of the wife or the child, then tax will be saved. So, if the child has no other income, the father can pay the full amount of the single person's allowance to the child (currently £2,335) without the child having to pay any tax on it and without having to pay tax on this sum himself. The way this operates is that the father deducts the relevant amount of tax and pays the net sum to the child, who then recovers the balance from the Inland Revenue. So if the father had been ordered to pay £1,000 a year and was paying tax at the standard rate of 29%, he would pay £710 to the child and the child would collect £290 from the Inland Revenue. If the father was a very rich man and his highest rate of tax was 60% then he would pay only £400, and £600 would be recovered from the Inland Revenue. The same financial system applies in the case of payments to the wife.

From a tax angle therefore it will often be sensible to make a payment both to the wife and the children rather than all the money to the wife as at first sight it would be natural to do when the children were young. Of course there is some danger that a precocious fourteen year old will claim to be able to spend the money; there is also some danger that the husband may try to keep the smaller payments to the wife when the children are grown up. Of course the wife's needs will usually be smaller once the children are grown up but not necessarily by the artificial amounts that may have been agreed for tax purposes. It is prudent to reach agreement if possible on this at the time of divorce.

One disadvantage for the wife of all of this is that she may suffer an initial cash flow problem since the husband will pay the ordered sum net of tax and she will have to wait for the Inland Revenue to refund the balance. It would certainly be sensible to ask your local tax office how they handle such problems, since practice does not appear to be uniform. If small sums are involved there is a procedure for 'small maintenance payments' under which the husband pays the gross sum to the wife and gets the money back through an alteration in his coding. This will improve the wife's cash flow though it does not affect the ultimate tax position of either party. It should be noted that there is also a special allowance for single parent families (the figure is currently £1,320).

(b) The relevance of conduct. Historically a wife who had committed adultery could find herself cut off without support. In more recent years it has come to seem more and more unacceptable to make so much turn on what may be an isolated lapse. Indeed many have felt that in most cases both parties must take some share of the blame for the collapse of the marriage. Furthermore to attach financial consequences to the conduct of the parties invites them to rake over the marriage for examples of bad behaviour. In most cases this simply wastes time and generates bitterness and it is very doubtful whether traditional methods of trial are suited to decide the question of which party is more to blame for the failure of the marriage.

These considerations undoubtedly lead to paying less attention to conduct than in the past but the Act clearly does not direct the Court to disregard conduct altogether. Indeed it clearly recognises that there will be some cases where it will be unfair to ignore the conduct of the parties.

These cases are undoubtedly to be regarded, however, as very much the exception.

(c) First consideration should be given to the welfare, while a minor, of any child of the family who has not attained the age of eighteen. We saw in 'Parents and Children' that in relation to many of the questions considered there the welfare of the child was paramount. The language used here is not so strong and no doubt in appropriate cases the welfare of the child might be outweighed by other circumstances. It is 'children of the family' to whose welfare primary consideration should be given. This will include not only the children of the husband and wife but also other children who have been treated by both husband and wife as belonging to the family. If both husband and wife have been married twice, this could for example, exclude the husband's children by his first marriage if they were living with his first wife. The Court is not forbidden to take their welfare into account but it is not required to give it priority. In the same way the Court may consider the needs of the child over eighteen for support while at university but this is not a priority case. It has, indeed, been held that such a child may intervene in divorce proceedings to seek financial support for a university education. This is paradoxical because the child of a happily married couple who think a university education is a waste of money has no such rights.

The direction to give priority to the interests of the child does not simply mean that the child's financial needs come first. The Court might decide, for instance, that it was in the child's best interests that the mother stays at home to look after it and this would effect the appropriate order in favour of the mother.

(d) The 'clean break' principle. Much modern thinking about divorce has suggested that there are a significant group of cases where it would be good for both parties if there was a 'clean break', that is, there should be no long term financial dependency of one party on the other. This will of course usually be impossible where there are young children and it would only be possible in the case of an older wife who could not reasonably be expected to go out to work where the husband had sufficient capital. However, it may be appropriate where both parties are young, as where if the husband supported the wife for two or three years she could retrain and equip herself for a well-paid job. The Court is therefore required to consider whether financial payments should be made for a limited term and it has the power to dismiss an application for periodical payments with a direction that no further application should be made.

(e) Changes made by the Matrimonial and Family Proceedings Act 1984. Under the Matrimonial Causes Act 1973 the Court, after being directed to consider all the circumstances, was then told to exercise its powers so as to put the parties so far as possible in the same position as they would have been in if the marriage had not broken down. Between 1973 and 1984 it became apparent that in most cases this objective simply could not be achieved and it was removed by the 1984 Act. This does leave the Court's discretion more unfettered than before which makes it difficult to say with any confidence how the Court will act in any given case. The nearest thing to a general guide is the so-called one-third principle which was approved by the Court of Appeal in *Wachtel v Wachtel* [1973] as a convenient starting point. When this principle is applied the wife should get one-third of the joint post divorce incomes of the parties (together with appropriate provision for the children). It cannot be too much emphasised that this is not a rule but simply a starting point for calculation. In particular cases there may be plausible reasons for arguing for more or for less but the solicitors acting for the parties have to have some idea of the sort of figure the Court may order since otherwise effective negotiation will be impossible.

(f) Housing needs of the parties. Clearly housing will usually be one of the major problems for the now divorced family. Both husband and wife will need accommodation. It may be that the family home will be too large or expensive for either partner so that it should be sold and each partner should find new housing. Alternatively, it may be convenient for one partner to live in the house but it does not follow that that partner should simply be given the house. There may well be a need to release part of the equity of the house to go towards the housing costs of the other partner.

The Court now enjoys very wide powers in this area. It may order the immediate sale of the house and division of the proceeds (after repayment of the mortgage) in whatever shares seem to it fair. Alternatively it may make an order to sell but postpone its operation until the children are grown up. The Court may order one partner to transfer his/her share to the other and, if appropriate, order the transferee to compensate the transferor. So the matrimonial home may be transferred to the wife but she may receive smaller income payments or conversely the matrimonial home may be transferred to the husband in return for a lump sum payment to the wife.

In the case of rented accommodation the Court has power to order the transfer of tenancies.

(g) Change of circumstances. It may be that in the years after the Court's financial order events take place which make the order seem inappropriate at least to one of the parties. The husband may achieve promotion with a substantially increased income; the wife may remarry. In almost all cases inflation will erode the value of periodic payments. In general if there was an order for periodic payments, the Court has power to vary it. This is why it is common to make a nominal order in favour of the wife in order to maintain the Court's jurisdiction. The one exception is where the earlier Court has expressly ordered that there should be no entitlement to apply for an extension of the order. (Such orders are sometimes made in support of the 'clean-break' principle.) On the other hand, lump sum orders cannot normally be varied as the object of making them is to reach a definitive solution to the capital question. This could mean that a wife with a wealthy husband, who thought she had good chances of remarriage, could be better off to take a lump sum rather than periodic payments. It appears that she is not required spontaneously to reveal plans to remarry although, of course, she must not tell lies if she is explicitly asked.

make proper contribution towards, reasonable maintenance for any child of the family.

(c) That the respondent has behaved in such a way that the applicant cannot reasonably be expected to live with the respondent.

(d) The respondent has deserted the applicant.

Magistrates' Courts have usually ordered the respondent to pay so much a week for an indefinite period. However, an order for periodic payments may be made for a fixed term and the Court may also make a lump sum order. Such orders must not be made for more than £500 but a number of such orders may be made over a period of time.

A new power granted to the Court by legislation in 1978 provides that the Court may make a periodical payments order if (a) the parties to a marriage have been living apart for a continuous period exceeding three months; and (b) either party has deserted the other; and (c) one party has during the period of three months preceding the application been making periodic payments for the benefit of the other.

The classic situation at which this provision is aimed arises when the parties agree to live apart, the husband has been paying sums to support his wife but the wife does not feel confident that the husband will continue with the payments. Under the previous law the wife would have had to wait until the husband stopped making payments before she could apply.

(C) Financial powers of the domestic Court. One of the curious features of English family law is the existance of two parallel Courts. Quite separate from the jurisdiction of the High Court/ Divorce County Court is the domestic jurisdiction of the magistrates which goes back to 1868. This jurisdiction is convenient in that it is local and relatively cheap but modern research suggests strongly that in the eyes of many users, Magistrates Courts are regarded as primarily criminal in function. A curious feature of the system is that the law administered is not exactly the same as that applied in the higher Court.

The jurisdiction is primarily concerned with the making of orders for financial provision. This can be done on one or more of the following grounds:

(a) The respondent has failed to provide reasonable maintenance for the applicant.

(b) The respondent has failed to provide or

(D) Agreements between the parties as to financial questions. English law normally encourages parties to settle their disputes out of Court and, indeed, the legal system would not operate if most disputes were not so settled. To promote out of Court compromises the usual rule is that such compromises are binding even though one party can later show that he would have done better if the case had been fought to a finish. This view has not been applied in matrimonial disputes for at least two reasons. One is a degree of paternalism; the parties and especially the wife are likely to be under such pressure immediately after the collapse of the marriage that they are liable to agree to proposals which are clearly not in their best interests. The other reason is that there is a public interest in seeing that so far as possible the burden of supporting the parties or either of them does not fall on the State.

These considerations still carry force but on the other hand it has come to be realised that to encourage the parties to make sensible agreements will both reduce bitterness and lessen the pressure on the Courts. In practice then the parties or their solicitors often negotiate before the hearing before the registrar and they often present an agreed proposal to the registrar. It is quite clear that the registrar is not bound to accept the parties' proposal but it seems that in practice many such proposals are accepted.

The parties may of course make an agreement about financial matters without going to Court at all. If such an agreement contains a promise by the wife not to apply to the Court for maintenance, that promise is void but the husband's promise to pay maintenance is binding. However, there is a very wide power introduced by the Maintenance Agreements Act 1957 for the Court to vary such an agreement because of a later change of circumstances.

Some Useful Addresses

Registers

Adoption. There are two registers. The Registrar-General has kept the Adopted Children Register since January 1927 and a copy certificate (showing date and Court of adoption, child's adopted name, names and addresses of adopting parents) can be supplied to any applicant. The second register cross-references the entry in the Adopted Children Register to the Births Register and enables the child's parent(s) to be identified. The cross-reference register is not open to the public although the adopted person may be able to make a search in it.

Certificates from the Adopted Children Register can be obtained either in person (from the Registrar-General's office – see address in 'Births, marriages and deaths') or by post from the General Register Office, Registration Division, Titchfield, Fareham, Hants.

Births, marriages and deaths. Copy certificates are available from the Registrar-General, General Register Office, St Catherine's House, 10 Kingsway, London WC2 (01-242 0262). Personal searches can be made on weekdays between 8.30 a m and 4.30 p m. Search can also be made by post, either using the free application form or by sending a letter stating (at least) the date and place of the event and the full names.

Generally, the registers only date back to 1 July 1837; where the event occurred abroad, registers were only kept from July 1849.

Divorce. Anyone can apply for a copy of a decree nisi or decree absolute. The decree will show the name of the parties to whom the decree was granted, the grounds, and the date.

Personal application is made to the Principal Registry, Family Division, Room 44, Somerset House, London WC2 (01-405 7641). Once the applicant has found the entry in the index he can ask for a copy.

Parish Records. Records of burials, marriages, and baptisms are kept in many parish churches, but the extent and completeness of the records varies considerably.

Anyone can apply to inspect the records. Application is made to the incumbent, but if he does not have the records, or does not know where they are, application is made to the Diocesan Record Office or the County Record Office.

Many nonconformist registers are now in the Public Record Office.

Probate and letters of administration. Records are kept of every grant, including the name and address of the deceased and the personal representatives, and the value of the estate. Postal or personal application should be made to the Principal Registry, Family Division, Somerset House, Strand, London WC2 (01-405 7641).

Wards of Court. A Ward Book is kept of all infants who have been made Wards of Court. Application for information can only be made by a person with a legitimate interest.

Apply in person to Room 169, Royal Courts of Justice, Strand, London WC2. There is no fee.

Wills. Copies of wills lodged when probate or letters of administration were taken out can be obtained by any applicant.

A personal search is first made at the Principal Family Registry, Family Division, Strand, London WC2 (01-405 7641), for the reference number of the will. A copy can then be inspected. Application can also be made by post.

Adoption Resource Exchange
40 Brunswick Square
London WC1N 1AZ

Advisory Centre for Education
18 Victoria Park Square
London E2 9PB
(01-980 4596 2 p m–5.30 p m)

British Agencies for Adoption and Fostering
11 Southwark Street
London SE1

Child Poverty Action Group
1 Macklin Street
London B5 NOH
(01-242 3225)
Citizens Rights Office
(01-405 5942 2–4 p m)

Families Need Fathers
Elfrida Hall
Campshill Road
London SE13
(01-852 7123)

Gingerbread
35 Wellington Street
London WC2
(01-734 9014 or 01-240 0953)
(Help for one parent families)

National Council for One Parent Families
255 Kentish Town Road
London NW5 2LX
(01-267 1361)

National Foster Care Association
Francis House
Francis Street
London SW1 PDE
(01-828 6266)

National Marriage Guidance Council
76A New Cavendish Street
London W1
(01-580 1087)

National Society for the Prevention of Cruelty to
    Children
1 Riding Street
London W1 8AA
(01-580 8812)

National Women's Aid Federation
51 Chalcot Road
London NW1
(01-586 5192)

Women's National Commission (Formally
    Women's Forum)
Government Offices
Great George Street
London SW1P 3AQ
(01-233 4208)

Women's Liberation Workshop
38 Earlham Street
London WC2

SECTION 7
MOTORING AND THE LAW

Highways have always been hazardous. Technology has increased the risks. There are more motor vehicles on the roads and they are capable of going faster, carrying or pulling more weight and causing more damage than ever before. The modern motor car is a potentially lethal weapon. If badly driven or badly maintained, these vehicles and their drivers are like accidents looking for somewhere to happen.

In an attempt to control the risks, if not to eliminate them, a complex array of laws has been developed. These regulate every aspect of motoring on public highways. There are rules governing who may drive, what they may drive, what they may carry or tow and how, the condition of their vehicles, insurance, the manner of driving and what happens if things go wrong.

(i) The Highway Code
As well as the rules of law derived from Acts of Parliament, Regulations made by the Secretary of State for Transport and decisions of the Courts, the Department of Transport publishes the Highway Code. This is a summary of good practice for road users of all sorts. It does not itself have the force of law (although much of it reproduces the effect of legal requirements contained in the Road Traffic Acts, for example in relation to road signs, obstruction of the highway and speed limits). However, the Code can be used as evidence of what is good driving practice in any legal proceedings where the question is relevant. For example, the Highway Code recommends minimum distances to be left by a driver between his car and the one in front, based on estimated stopping distances at different speeds. If a driver runs into the back of another car, the distances given in the Code may be useful to help the Court decide whether he was driving negligently so as to be liable to compensate the owner of the other car. The Code may also be used in criminal proceedings arising out of road incidents.

All drivers should have a copy of the Highway Code, which costs only 50 pence, and be familiar with it. Another helpful publication, though one that has no special legal status, is the manual *Driving*, published by the Department of Transport at £3.95.

(ii) Other Useful Sources of Information
The Automobile Association (AA) and Royal Automobile Club (RAC) provide a mass of information for their members about all aspects of motoring law and practice. They also provide legal advice if necessary. Many insurers provide advice for policyholders about what to do in the event of accidents. The Department of Transport provides a number of helpful leaflets giving information about what is required of drivers and their vehicles, and many of these are available from Post Offices, Traffic Area Offices or local vehicle licensing centres. An example is leaflet D100, giving information about applying for driving licences, available from Post Offices. A useful book, especially on motoring offences and prosecutions, is James Mathers, *The Motorist's Guide to the Law* (London, Fourmat Publishing, 1986, price £3.95).

(iii) Matters Dealt with by This Section
The section deals mainly with the law relating to drivers of motor vehicles which are used or kept on the road. It does not cover pedestrians, pedal cyclists or commercial vehicles.

(iv) What Is a Motor Vehicle?
A motor vehicle is defined, unsurprisingly, as a mechanically propelled vehicle intended or adapted for use on roads. A car is a motor vehicle, but a caravan or trailer is not: they are separate for motoring law purposes, even when hitched together. A car or motorcycle is always a motor vehicle, even if the motor is temporarily out of order. However, a car without an engine would not be a motor vehicle. A moped is normally a motor vehicle, but in one case, *Lawrence v Howlett* in 1952, essential parts had been removed from the motor of a moped so that it could only be used as a pedal cycle. Even though there was still petrol in the tank, it was decided that it was no longer a motor vehicle and so did not require to be insured as one.

(v) What Is a Road?

The Road Traffic Act 1972 defines 'road' as meaning any highway and any other road to which the public has access. A highway is a road over which there is a public right of way. A road need not be metalled: footpaths and bridleways are roads for this purpose even if not made up. Private roads may be 'roads' for our purposes if, for example, they lead to buildings and are accessible to the public. 'Road' includes a lay-by, and a hotel's private forecourt which was used by the public both to get to the hotel and as a short cut between adjacent highways. On the other hand, a forecourt belonging to a shop used by the public only to get to the shop is not a road; nor is a private courtyard opening off a road by a narrow entrance, or a road open to a restricted class of people with a sign up forbidding access by trespassers.

Before a motor vehicle, trailer or caravan can be driven on a public road, four requirements must be satisfied. First, the driver must be entitled to drive. This means that he must hold an appropriate licence and must not be disqualified or disabled from driving. Secondly, the vehicle must be covered by an appropriate motor insurance policy. Thirdly, vehicle excise duty must be paid and an appropriate tax disc displayed. Fourthly, the vehicle must comply with the law's requirements as to its condition and roadworthiness.

1. THE DRIVER: LICENSING AND LEARNING

(i) Who May Drive?

The first requirement for drivers is that they must be old enough to drive the type of vehicle concerned.

It is a criminal offence to drive a motor vehicle while under the permitted age on a public road. It is also an offence for any person to cause or to permit an under-age person so to drive. On conviction the Court may impose a fine, together with disqualification from driving for such period as the Court thinks fit, and endorse the convict's driving licence if he has one.

These age limits do not apply to places which are not roads, so under-age drivers can practice or take part in competitions so long as they do not drive in public places.

(ii) Applying For a Licence

Anyone who wants to drive a motor vehicle on the road must have a valid current driving licence.

(A) Application procedure. An applicant for a licence to drive ordinary private vehicles need only fill in an application form (available from a Post Office) and send it, together with the appropriate fee, to the Driver and Vehicle Licensing Centre (DVLC, Swansea, SA99 1AB).

(B) Disabled drivers. Among other things, the applicant must declare on section 6 of the form whether he suffers, or has ever suffered, from any of the following disabilities (a term which includes diseases): epilepsy; certain types of mental disorder, subnormality or deficiency; sudden attacks of disabling giddiness or fainting, including attacks brought on as a result of a heart defect for which the applicant has been fitted with a heart pacemaker; inability to read a car registration plate (with glasses if worn) at a dis-

---

Minimum ages for driving different types of vehicles

16: mopeds; invalid carriages; agricultural tractors taxed as agricultural machines no more than eight feet wide drawing only a two wheeled or close-coupled four wheeled trailer not exceeding eight feet in width; mowing machines; pedestrian controlled vehicles such as petrol-driven hand mowers.

17: motorcycles; small passenger vehicles (which for this purpose means vehicles constructed to carry only passengers and their effects, and not adapted to carry more than nine people including the driver); small goods vehicles (i e vehicles constructed or adapted to carry or haul goods and not more than nine people including the driver, which has a maximum permissible weight not exceeding 3.5 tonnes); any agricultural tractor; road rollers under 11½ tons unladen weight which are not steam driven and do not have soft tyres; any other

motor vehicle driven by a member of the armed forced doing urgent work of national importance in accordance with an order of the Defence Council.

18: medium sized goods vehicles (i e a goods vehicle with a maximum permissible weight of over 3.5 tonnes but not more than 7.5 tonnes); large passenger vehicles where the driver is not carrying passengers and he either holds a public service vehicle driving licence or is under the supervision of a PSV licence holder or is undergoing a PSV driving test; large passenger vehicles if the driver holds a PSV licence and is either driving on a regular service on a route not exceeding 50 km or is driving on a national transport operation in a vehicle not adapted to carry more than 15 passengers.

21: any other motor vehicle.

tance of 75 feet if the letters are 3½ inches high or 67 feet if they are only 3⅛ inches high (as on the old-fashioned registration plates). These must be declared even if the questions on the form do not specifically mention them by name.

An applicant must also declare any disability which is likely to cause his driving to be a source of danger to the public. In *Woodward v Dykes* (1968) it was held that deafness is such a disability: hearing is an important asset to a driver in anticipating traffic movements.

In addition, an applicant must declare any disability which may become such a disability as is mentioned above. These prospective disabilities may arise, for example, where a person is suffering from a progressive disease or one in which the symptoms occur at intervals or undergo remissions.

It is a criminal offence knowingly to make a false statement for the purpose of obtaining a licence.

A full licence lasting to the age of 70 will not normally be granted to a person who is suffering from a disability such as those mentioned above. However, a provisional licence may be granted, and an applicant may even be granted a full licence (though only for a limited period or subject to conditions, for example about the types of vehicles that may be driven or adaptations that must be made to them) if he has at some time passed a driving test and the disability has not become worse since the test, or if the disability can be shown to have been appropriately controlled. Examples of the latter are where an epileptic has had no attacks while awake within the last three years and his driving is unlikely to be a danger, or where a person with a heart pacemaker is under medical supervision by a cardiologist and his driving will not cause a danger.

Once an application has been made to drive vehicles of a particular class, a licence *must* be issued unless (1) the applicant is too young to drive vehicles of that class (note that you can apply for a licence up to two months before the date when it is to take effect), (2) he already holds a licence for vehicles of that class, even if the other licence has been suspended (for example, following a disqualification for a traffic offence), or (3) he is subject to a disqualification by order of a Court following conviction for an offence or as a result of disability.

If a person discovers during the currency of a driving licence that he is suffering from a disability of one of the kinds described above, he

must inform the Secretary of State, who may revoke the licence.

(iii) Types of Licences and Their Effects

There are several sorts of driving licences. Of greatest interest to ordinary motorists are provisional licences, and full licences.

(A) A provisional licence. A provisional licence is issued to someone who has not yet passed a driving test entitling him to drive the class of vehicles he wishes to drive. A provisional licence holder is entitled to drive on the road, subject to a number of conditions.

Conditions to be observed by provisional licence holders
1. An 'L' plate must be clearly displayed at the front and rear of the vehicle.
2. When driving cars, goods vehicles and large passenger vehicles, the licence holder must be supervised (not merely accompanied) by a full licence holder.
3. A person holding a provisional licence to drive a motorcycle must not ride motorcycles over 125 cc engine capacity unless it is permanently attached to a sidecar.
4. When riding a motorcycle, a provisional licence holder must not carry a pillion passenger unless the passenger holds a full motorcycle licence and is supervising the rider.
5. A provisional licence holder may not draw a trailer or caravan, except when driving an agricultural tractor or articulated vehicle.
6. No provisional licence holder may drive on motorways.

Provisional licences are issued by the DVLC on behalf of the Department of Transport. They are mostly valid until the holder's seventieth birthday, and cost £10. Renewals are free if the first provisional licence was granted after 30 September 1982. There is one exception to all this. To prevent motorcyclists riding solo all their lives on a provisional licence without ever taking a driving test, it is now provided that a provisional licence to drive only motorcycles is valid for just two years, and cannot be renewed within twelve months of the date when it expires. This means that motorcyclists can only drive for two years without passing a test, and then are off the road for at least a year.

This is an application by a person with one endorsement in the last four years and a minor health problem for a full duplicate licence to replace one destroyed.

This form only covers applications for licences to drive light vehicles and motorcycles privately. HGV and PSV licences are granted by a separate procedure (see page 376).

Permanent address in Great Britain. If your permanent address is outside Great Britain, or you have no permanent address, give the name of someone who has a permanent address in Great Britain and can contact you at any time.

First five letters probably PUGWA as in surname.

If you will want to drive a motorcycle on a provisional licence, tick here.

Note that the reason for needing a new licence will affect the type of licence you need and the fee payable.

A full licence is normally granted to expire when the driver reaches the age of seventy.

DVLC

Application for Your Driving Licence
D1 Rev. June/86

Please do not write above this line

For DVLC use

Please complete this form in BLACK INK and BLOCK LETTERS

1 About yourself

a. Surname **PUGWASH**

Christian or forenames **HORATIO**

Please tick box or state other title such as Dr. Rev.

b. Mr | Mrs 2 | Miss 3

Other title **CAPTAIN**

Your full permanent address in Great Britain (see note on left)

c. Number and Road **THE BLACK PIG INN**

District or Village **BORCHESTER -ON- SEA**

Post Town **BORSETSHIRE**

Postcode (Your licence may be delayed if the postcode is not quoted) **BRI 1BR**

d. Please tick box — Male ✓ 1 — Female 2

e. Please give your date of birth — Day **0 1** Month **04** Year **2 5**

f. Have you ever held a British licence (full or provisional)? Answer YES or NO **YES**

If YES please enter your Driver Number (if known) in the box below (and make a separate note of it).

NOT KNOWN

2 What licence do you want?

a. Please tick the type of licence you want (see note 'Types of Licence' on left, especially the one headed IMPORTANT under Provisional licence)

1 Provisional WITHOUT motorcycle entitlement | 2 Provisional WITH motorcycle entitlement

3 Full | 4 Duplicate ✓ | 5 Exchange

b. When do you want your new licence to begin? A licence cannot be backdated. You can apply during the 2 months before you want your licence to begin.
Day **0 7** Month **01** Year **8 6**

c. If you have passed a driving test since the issue of your last licence write the new Group passed here and enclose the pass certificate.

3 What was on your last licence?

Please ENCLOSE and give details of your last GB licence or any foreign licence you wish to exchange. All EEC licences will be returned to the issuing authority.

a. If your last licence was surrendered on disqualification write S/D or if you have not previously held a GB licence, write NONE

b. Type of licence i.e. Provisional or Full **FULL**

c. Expiry date **3/4/95**

d. If your last licence has been lost, stolen, destroyed or defaced please tick the appropriate box below. If a lost licence is later found and is still current you must return it to DVLC.

Lost or stolen | Destroyed ✓ | Defaced and I enclose it

e. Name and/or address on licence if different from that at 1 above

Surname

Christian or forenames

Address

Postcode (please quote)

Now please turn over

If you need more information before you fill in this form please ask at your post office for leaflet D100.

To drive a Heavy Goods Vehicle or a Public Service Vehicle you need an additional licence. Consult a Traffic Area Office.

Address
You must give an address in England, Scotland or Wales where you live permanently. If you cannot do this, give the name and address of a person who does live there and through whom we may contact you at any time.

Types of Licence

● Provisional licence (1 and 2)
This allows you to drive motor vehicles with a view to passing a driving test. You will not need a provisional licence if you hold a full licence which gives cover to drive, as a learner, other groups of vehicles.
If you are applying for your first provisional licence do not drive until you receive it.
IMPORTANT
If you wish to ride a MOTORCYCLE as a learner now or when you reach age 17 you MUST tick the Provisional Box 2. The term motorcycle includes scooters but does not include mopeds. If you are under 17 and ask for motorcycle entitlement it will start from your 17th birthday.

● Full licence (3)
You may apply for a full licence if during the last 10 years you have:
● passed the British driving test; or
● held a British full licence; or
● held a full licence issued in Northern Ireland, the Channel Islands or the Isle of Man
or if you hold:
● a valid licence issued by a country recognised for exchange purposes (this covers all member states of the European Economic Community including a British Forces Germany licence) and you apply within one year of becoming resident in the United Kingdom.
Otherwise you may only apply for a provisional licence.

● Duplicate licence (4)
To replace a lost, stolen, destroyed or defaced licence.

● Exchange licence (5)
For a driver:
● who holds a current full GB licence and wants new group(s) added to it; or
● whose existing licence is running out of date endorsements (see leaflet D100); or
● who wants provisional motorcycle entitlement added to the licence (see leaflet D100); or
● who wishes to 'give up' provisional motorcycle entitlement—(see leaflet D100).
An exchange licence will normally expire on the same date as the licence being exchanged.

Department of Transport

Provisional-1 Full-2 | Rec. type | 2
Cont. No. | 3
4
5
6
7
8
9
10
11
12
MC | 13
DRE | 14 | 15 | End | 16
TPC | 17
18
Ent. | 19
20 MP | RE | VDOB
21 | 22 | 23 | 24
MIM | Amount
25 | 26
DAM
27 | 28

374

List for question 4b

- Driving or attempting to drive while under the influence of drink or drugs.
- Driving or attempting to drive with an excess of alcohol in the body.
- Failure to provide a specimen of breath, blood or urine at a police station after driving or attempting to drive a motor vehicle.
- Aiding or abetting one of the above offences.

Health

See also section on Physical and Mental Fitness in leaflet D100. Among the reasons for answering YES to 6e and for giving details are:

- that you have been treated for drug addiction in the last three years; or
- that you have diabetes; or
- that you have a heart condition or are fitted with a cardiac pacemaker.

If you have or have had epilepsy, you may still be considered for a licence if you have been free from attacks for two years; or if you have attacks only while asleep, you must have established a pattern of such attacks over a period of more than three years.

Payment

There is to be a change in the payment due for licences commencing on or after 1.9.86. The revised amounts are shown in the right-hand column.

	Before 1.9.86	On or after 1.9.86
First GB licence		
Renewing a provisional licence issued before 1.10.82	£10	£15
Changing a provisional to a full licence after passing a driving test	FREE	FREE
Renewing any licence issued after 30.9.82		
Duplicate licence		
Removing endorsements		
Adding or removing the provisional motor cycle group D	£3	£5
Adding new groups to a full licence		

The table above covers most licences. See leaflet D100 for the complete fee table.

How to pay

Please do not send cash or banknotes unless you have to and then only use Registered Post.

Cheques or postal orders should be made payable to 'Department of Transport' and crossed 'Motor Tax Account'. Post-dated cheques cannot be accepted. Please write your name and address on the back of any cheque. If you are paying by National Girobank transfer write 'Driving Licence Account' in the space provided for the number of the account to be credited. The transfer form must be sent to the Driver and Vehicle Licensing Centre with the application.

IMPORTANT NOTES

Driving without a licence
The law allows you to drive even if you do not actually have a licence provided that:

- you have held a licence before and are still entitled to obtain one (that is you are not disqualified or the licence would not be or has not been refused on medical grounds; and
- a valid application for a licence has been received at the Driver and Vehicle Licensing Centre; and
- you can meet any conditions which apply when using that licence, such as those applicable to provisional licence holders.

You can drive without actually holding a licence for only one year from the date of receipt of the application by the DVLC.

Enquiries about your licence
To allow for time in the post to and from the Centre, please allow at least 3 weeks for your licence to arrive. If you do not receive it by then, please contact the Driver Enquiry Unit, DVLC, Swansea SA6 7JL, or telephone: 0792-72151 quoting your Driver Number or your full names and date of birth.

Your licence may be delayed if you do not answer ALL the questions

4 Driving offences

a. Are you disqualified by a Court from holding or obtaining a driving licence?

Answer YES or NO [NO] If YES give name of Court _____

Date and period of disqualification _____

b. Has a Court ordered you to be disqualified or your licence to be endorsed for **ANY** offence in the last 4 years (or in the last 11 years for any offence in the list on the left)?

Answer YES or NO [YES] If YES give details of all disqualifications and endorsements
- Date of conviction 10/5/83 Court BORCHESTER MAGISTRATES
- Date of conviction _____ Court _____

Give details of any other disqualifications, endorsements or successful appeals on a separate sheet; date it, sign it and enclose it with this application.

If you enclose a separate sheet please tick box [ ]

5 Your eyesight

a. Can you read a vehicle number plate in good daylight (with glasses if worn), at 67 feet for figures 3½" high?

Answer YES or NO [YES] (If NO you may still be able to obtain a licence for a pedestrian controlled vehicle or a mowing machine – see leaflet D100).

b. Have you any uncorrected defect of vision which might affect safe driving? (for example: double vision, tunnel vision, partial loss of sight or night blindness).

Answer YES or NO [NO] If YES give details

6 Your health

Questions 6a–6e MUST be answered (Please do not use a tick or dash)

a. Have you ever had a licence refused or revoked for medical reasons?

Answer YES or NO [NO] If YES give date and reasons

If you are in doubt about your answers to 6b, 6c, 6d or 6e consult your doctor

b. Has a doctor ever advised you not to drive?

Answer YES or NO [NO] If YES give details

c. Are you without hand or foot or have you any defect in limb movement or power?

Answer YES or NO [NO] If YES give details

If the answer is YES and you have held a licence before
(i) was this limb disability mentioned in your previous application? Answer YES or NO – [ ]
(ii) If so, has it got worse since then? Answer YES or NO [ ]

d. Have you now or have you ever had epilepsy or fits or sudden attacks of disabling giddiness or fainting or any mental illness or defect?

Answer YES or NO [YES] If YES give details WHEN UNDER ATTACK ON HIGH SEAS

e. Have you now or have you ever had any other disability or medical condition which could affect your fitness as a driver either now or in the future? (see 'Health' note on the left)

Answer YES or NO [NO] If YES give details

7 Your declaration

Warning: If you or anyone else knowingly gives false information to help you obtain this licence, you and they are liable to prosecution.

I apply for a driving licence
I enclose the fee of £ 3 (if applicable, see notes on the left) ~~Postal Order~~/Cheque no. OOO 175
I declare that I have checked the details I have given and that to the best of my knowledge they are correct, and that I am entitled to the licence for which I am applying.

Your Signature H. Pugwash Date 1st September 1986.

If you are enclosing an EEC licence which entitles you to drive heavy goods (HGV) or public service (PSV) vehicles and you wish to drive any such vehicles in Great Britain you will need a GB HGV or PSV licence. Please tick this box [ ] and make a separate application as soon as possible to the Traffic Area Office in which area you live.

If you are applying for your FIRST British licence, please send this form to:– First Application Section, DVLC, SWANSEA, SA99 1AD	RENEWAL, Duplicate and Exchange applications should be sent to:– Driver Licence Section, DVLC, SWANSEA, SA99 1AB

Please remember to enclose your last licence [ ] fee [ ] test pass certificate [ ]

Printed in the UK for HMSO by R.P.W. Ltd. Dd. 8800410. 4/88.

(margin note) REMEMBER: it is a criminal offence knowingly to give false information in answering questions on the form. Failing to declare a conviction leading to endorsement or disqualification, a health problem etc. is the same as giving false information for this purpose.

(margin note) The applicant is right to declare this, even though it will probably not make him ineligible to hold a licence.

A provisional licence is intended to permit the holder to drive while he is learning. Once a provisional licence holder takes and passes a driving test, he is entitled to a full licence, as long as there are no other reasons for refusing to grant one to him.

(B) A full licence. A full licence may be issued to a person who has passed a driving test and entitles the driver to drive vehicles of the class in which the test was taken on any road without supervision. It relieves the driver of the restrictions imposed on those with only a provisional licence. It is issued by the DVLC on behalf of the Department of Transport, and costs £10. (Renewals will in future be free, though a charge of £3 is made for issuing a duplicate or exchange licence.)

A full licence remains in force until the driver's seventieth birthday, unless it is revoked or suspended as a result of a Court order or for some other reason (for instance, because of the driver's ill health). A new licence which is granted on or after, or up to three years before, the applicant's seventieth birthday will remain in force for only three years, and will then need to be renewed. It is an offence to fail to inform DVLC of a change of name or address.

(C) What vehicles does a licence entitle you to drive? Motor vehicles are divided into groups for licensing purposes. A driving licence will specify the groups which the holder is entitled to drive.

A **provisional licence** only entitles a person to drive, subject to the usual restrictions, vehicles in the class shown on the licence. A **full licence** only covers vehicles in the class specified, but also acts as a provisional licence, subject to the usual restrictions attaching to provisional licence holders, to drive a vehicle in one of the other groups. It is important to note that a licence for Group B does not entitle the holder to drive vehicles in Group A, so passing a driving test on a car with automatic transmission will not entitle the driver to a licence to drive cars with manual transmission, i e a gear lever. On the other hand, a Group A licence covers both manual and automatic transmission vehicles.

(D) Heavy Goods Vehicles (HGV) and Public Service Vehicles (PSV). An ordinary driving licence does not entitle the holder to drive a heavy goods vehicle (HGV) or a public service vehicle (PSV), nor does it operate as a provisional licence to drive them. A separate licence must be obtained. HGV licences are normally obtained from the licensing authority of the traffic area where the person resides. In London in the Metropolitan Police District, PSV licences are obtained from the Commissioner of Police at the Public Carriage Office. Elsewhere they are issued by the traffic commissioner for the traffic area in which the applicant resides.

An **HGV** is any vehicle constructed or adapted to carry or haul goods which is either an articulated vehicle or has a maximum permissible weight in excess of 7.5 tonnes. A **PSV** is a motor vehicle other than a tramcar, which is *either* made or adapted to carry more than eight passengers and is used to carry passengers for hire or reward, *or*, if made or adapted to carry eight or fewer passengers, is used in the course of a business for carrying passengers for hire or reward at separate fares.

(E) International driving permits. Anyone who is resident in the United Kingdom aged 18 or over and who has passed a driving test or holds a full licence can obtain an international driving permit from the Automobile Association, the

---

Vehicle groups for driving licence purposes

A. Any vehicle except one in group D, E, G, H or J;

B. Any vehicle with automatic transmission, except one in group C, D, E, G H or J;

C. Any motor tricycle (other than an invalid carriage) weighing up to 425 kg unladen;

D. Any motor bicycle, with or without a sidecar;

E. A moped;

F. An agricultural tractor mounted on wheels;

G. A road roller;

H. A track laying vehicle steered by its tracks;

J. An invalid carriage;

K. A mowing machine or pedestrian controlled vehicle;

L. An electrically controlled vehicle other than an invalid carriage or a motor bicycle;

N. A vehicle exempted from duty under the Vehicles (Excise) Act 1971, i e one used entirely on private roads, some invalid carriages, vehicles acquired by overseas residents for use abroad, and various public service vehicles.

[There is no group I or M.]

Royal Automobile Club or the Royal Scottish Automobile Club. These permits are issued on behalf of the Secretary of State, and entitle the holder to drive abroad: they are internationally recognised as a certificate of competence to drive under the International Convention on Motor Traffic, which was signed at Paris as long ago as 1926. They do not normally allow a United Kingdom resident to drive within the UK: an ordinary licence is needed for that. However, if the holder is residing outside the United Kingdom and is only temporarily in Great Britain he does not need a domestic licence during the period of twelve months following his most recent entry into Great Britain. (The same applies to holders of foreign driving licences and British Forces driving licences.)

(iv) Learning to Drive

A learner driver must hold a provisional licence, or a full licence having the effect of a provisional licence, for the class of vehicles on which he wants to learn. He must ensure that any vehicle he drives on a road carries red-letter 'L' plates front and rear. He must not drive on motorways. Unless he is taking a driving test or is driving a motorcycle or a vehicle of a type not made or adapted to carry passengers besides the driver, he must always be supervised by a full licence holder.

A person who supervises a learner driver has a legal duty to do just that. He is not there merely to accompany the learner. It was even decided in *Rubie v Faulkner* (1940) that if the learner commits a moving traffic offence and the supervisor makes no attempt to stop him or stop the car, the supervisor may be guilty of the offence of aiding and abetting the learner driver's offence. Were the supervisor not responsible for directing the efforts of the learner, there would be little point in him being there at all. It would seem to follow that the supervisor may be liable, jointly with the learner, to compensate anyone who suffers loss, damage or injury from the learner's negligent driving.

Driving lessons. There is no legal requirement that a person should take lessons before presenting himself for a driving test. Nor is there any requirement that lessons must only be given by qualified, trained instructors. In this Great Britain lags behind many other countries. The only legal regulation of driving tuition is that anyone who gives instruction for payment must be registered as an approved instructor by the Department of Transport. One can, therefore, take lessons from a friend, relation or total stranger, as long as they are free.

(v) The Driving Test

The driving test is a test of competence to drive. It is conducted (in the case of motor cars and motorcycles) by a Department of Transport examiner, who must be satisfied that the driver is capable of controlling the vehicle and driving safely and with due consideration to other road users and has the requisite knowledge of the Highway Code. On passing the test, the much desired pink form stating that the driver has passed immediately takes effect, in combination with the driver's provisional licence, as a full licence and the successful learner can 'go solo' for the first time. He can then apply for a full licence to drive that class of vehicles. If the candidate fails the test, the examiner provides a list of the points on which he failed. The driver can continue to use the provisional licence subject to the usual restrictions, renewing it if it becomes out of date, until retaking the test.

(vi) The Driving Licence

When a driving licence is received, it must be signed in ink by the licence holder. It is an offence not to be able to produce a signed licence if requested to do so by a constable while driving. The details on the licence must be checked, and any changes in the name or address notified to DVLC.

2. MOTOR INSURANCE

(i) Compulsory Motor Insurance

As noted above, motor vehicles create hazards to people besides the driver and owner of the vehicle. The law therefore requires a person using a vehicle to take certain steps to protect those who may suffer injury, by making arrangements to ensure that compensation is available. Normally, the protection takes the form of compulsory third party insurance.

It is a criminal offence to use a motor vehicle on a road, or cause or permit a motor vehicle to be used, unless there is in force in relation to that use of the vehicle a policy of insurance covering certain third party risks. Third party risks are risks to people other than the owner or user of the vehicle and the insurance company arising out of the use of the vehicle. A policy only takes effect when the insurer issues a certificate of insurance. The certificate must be kept and produced at the request of a constable when the vehicle is being driven on a road or after an accident or traffic offence. You must also give details of your insurance to anyone reasonably asking for them after an accident if someone is injured (see section 7.4 on page 398).

Motor insurance policies cover vehicles. It does not necessarily follow that you are insured to drive a friend's car just because you are insured to drive your own or your spouse's car. It depends on whether the policy on your friend's car covers 'any driver' or named drivers only, and whether you are one of the named drivers. Alternatively, your own policy may insure you to drive any vehicle. In short, some policy must be in force covering (a) the particular vehicle (b) for the particular use (c) by the particular driver.

The policy must cover the person insured against legal liability to pay damages in respect of the death of, or personal injury to, or emergency treatment of, any person, which may be caused by or arise out of the use of the vehicle on a road. The only exception to this requirement that may apply to a private motorist is a rather curious one: the motorist need not insure if he has deposited £15,000 with the Supreme Court. This amount is intended to perform a similar function to an insurance policy by providing security for any damages the driver may become liable to pay as a result of negligent driving. However, with six-figure awards for personal injuries becoming more common, £15,000 is grossly inadequate security, and this exception (in section 144 of the Road Traffic Act 1972) ought to be repealed.

The limitations of compulsory cover. A policy which merely satisfied the legal requirements for third party personal injury and death insurance would confer very limited benefits. For example, it would *not* cover the following risks: injury to, or death of, the person insured; damage to, or destruction or theft of, the insured's own car or other property; damage to, or destruction of, the property of third parties for which the insured may be legally liable; any death, personal injury or property damage or loss for which the insured is not legally liable to compensate another person.

The hypothetical example below gives some idea of the limited protection given by a policy which does no more than the minimum required by law. The way the system works also encourages litigation by insurers, as they are not liable to pay out anything unless it can be shown that the injury was caused by the negligence of the insured. Many serious injuries go uncompensated because of the need to prove negligence before compensation can be obtained. This has led to suggestions that the law should effectively withdraw from accident compensation, and injuries should be compensated out of a national insurance fund specially set up for the purpose, without the need to prove any fault. This happens in New Zealand, and has been recommended by a Royal Commission in Great Britain, so far without effect.

Limitations of third party policies: a hypothetical example

In order to save money, Fred took out a policy covering only what the Road Traffic Act specifically requires. Shortly afterwards, he failed to take reasonable care while overtaking a lorry and collided with a car coming in the other direction. The driver of the other car, Denise, was killed, Fred was injured and off work for ten months, both cars were write-offs and a wall belonging to an adjoining landowner was damaged. Denise's family claim £100,000 damages for Denise's death, plus the cost of replacing the car (£6,000). The landowner claims £1,000 for damage to the wall. Fred loses £12,000 income while he cannot work. Fred has to replace his own car at a cost of £7,000. How much of the cost of all this will ulti-mately fall on Fred personally, and how much will be covered by his insurance policy?

The policy only covers death and personal injury, so Fred will have to find the money to buy a new car for Denise's family and repair the landowner's wall. What is more, the insurance company is only required by the policy to pay those sums for which Fred would be liable in damages if sued. As he cannot sue himself, Fred will have to bear the entire cost of the injuries to himself, his loss of income and the replacement of his car. He will therefore have to find £14,000 out of his own pocket at a time when he is losing £12,000 income. The insurance company will however pay the £100,000 damages in respect of Denise's death.

(ii) More Extensive Policies

Because of the limitations of the compulsory cover, most drivers take out policies offering wider protection. These add extra options to the compulsory third party insurance, such as: insuring against the risk of damage to the property of a third party, or damage to or loss of the insured vehicle as a result of fire or theft (the 'third party, fire and theft policy'); insuring against the risk of liability for damage to property arising out of the use of the vehicle, which may include risk of damage to the insured vehicle, in addition to the risks already mentioned (the 'comprehensive policy').

Of course, the precise details of each extension of cover varies from company to company and policy to policy. The policy document you get will have full details of the protection offered by the company, and will contain a schedule setting out which particular bits of the policy document apply to your own policy. This affects what you will be entitled to claim for in the event of an accident or theft involving the vehicle, so it is important to make sure that your insurance broker, insurance company or other adviser explains exactly what you are covered for when you take out the policy. It will be too late to change your policy when you want to claim on it if you turn out to have the wrong sort of policy.

Own damage excess. The insurer may make it a condition of the policy that the insured pays for the first £25, £50 or some other sum of a claim in respect of damage to the insured vehicle, and the insurer will only be liable for the excess. These compulsory excess provisions are common where one of the named drivers, or someone who is likely to drive the vehicle, is young (usually under 25). In other cases, the proposer (the applicant for insurance cover) may volunteer to accept such an excess provision, which will have the effect of reducing the number of claims it will be worth making and so will reduce the cost of the insurance.

(iii) Applying for Insurance Cover

When you apply for cover, you will have to complete an application form (see page 380). This will ask you questions about yourself, where you live, what sort of vehicle you want covered, your health, who else is likely to drive the vehicle, whether you will use it for any purposes other than domestic and pleasure, whether you have had any accidents within a stated period,

whether you have been convicted of any offences or have any prosecutions pending against you, and perhaps other questions as well. You will be asked whether any insurer has refused to provide insurance, or provided it subject to conditions. There will also be a section asking you to provide any information which may affect the company's decision whether to give you cover.

It is *extremely important* that you should answer all these questions fully and absolutely truthfully. The law expects the 'proposer', as an applicant for insurance is known, to show the utmost good faith in answering questions put to him by the insurer. (Lawyers use a Latin phrase, *uberrima fides*, to described this duty.) If any material detail is withheld by the proposer, or if the vehicle is later used for a purpose or in a way different from that which the proposer said it would be, the insurer is not bound by the agreement to insure, and can refuse to pay out on any claim under the policy. When filling in a proposal form, then, the watchword must always be:

DECLARE ABSOLUTELY EVERYTHING YOU CAN THINK OF THAT MIGHT CONCEIVABLY BE RELEVANT, EVEN IF YOU DO NOT THINK IT WILL BE SIGNIFICANT.

Similarly, once you are insured:

(A) TELL THE INSURERS AT ONCE OF ANY CHANGE CONCERNING YOUR DRIVING, THE VEHICLE, THE PURPOSES FOR WHICH YOU WILL BE USING THE VEHICLE OR THE PEOPLE WHO WILL BE DRIVING IT; and

(B) MAKE ABSOLUTELY CERTAIN THAT YOU ALWAYS ABIDE BY THE LETTER OF YOUR POLICY, OBSERVING ANY CONDITIONS OR RESTRICTIONS THAT MAY BE ATTACHED TO IT.

If you fail to do so, you may well find that you are not insured.

This can happen very easily. For instance, in various cases misrepresentations about the age of any person likely to drive the vehicle, non-disclosure of previous convictions even if occurring more than fifteen years before, and failing to disclose the fact that a previous insurer had indicated that the proposer would not be invited to renew the policy, have all been held to be material non-disclosures, or misrepresentations

This is an application by Capt. Pugwash for motor insurance. We have already seen his application for a duplicate driving licence. This application is through a well-known broker. REMEMBER: Any material misrepresentation may lead to the policy being avoided by the insurer.

It will be surprising if his proposal is accepted in its present form. Using the vehicle for an illegal purpose is almost certain to be an excepted risk, not covered by the policy. Innkeeping is legitimate; piracy (or burglary) is out.

Oh dear – clearly an illegal use, and won't be covered by the policy.

This minimal cover will satisfy the law's demands.

On types of policy, see text. Ask the broker or insurer exactly what is covered.

On own damage excess and no claims discount protection, see text.

AA Enquiry/Proposal for Private Car Insurance

Underwritten by:

PLEASE WRITE IN BLOCK CAPITALS WITH A BALLPOINT PEN. *This paper copies automatically.*

AGENT: Name .... Staff No: ....

Region: ....

POLICY NUMBER

Please answer all questions. Tick (✓) the appropriate box.

About yourself

Mr/Mrs/Miss CAPT Forenames HORATIO Surname PUGWASH

AA MEMBERSHIP No. N/A

Address THE BLACK PIG INN
BORCHESTER - ON - SEA
BORSETSHIRE

Telephone No. BORCHESTER 99000

Post Code BRI IRB

COVER REQUIRED FOR ONE YEAR FROM: 16 , 10 , 19 86

Occupation(s) Full Time and Part Time INN KEEPER AND PIRATE

Employers Business(es) N/A

Date of Birth 01 , 04 , 25

About your car

Make of vehicle	Precise model	Engine cc	Type of body No. of seats	Year of first registration	Present value £	Date of purchase	Is the vehicle right hand drive	Reg. mark
FORD	SIERRA 1.6L	1595	SALOON 5	19 82	3,000	12/7/85	NO / YES ✓	ABC I 23Z

1 Has the vehicle been modified from the makers standard specifications. If 'YES' give details including any adaption for disability. NO / YES ☐ *Please tick (✓) the appropriate box.*

2 Is the vehicle owned or registered in the name of another person or company. If 'YES' give name and address of the owner and/or registration details. NO / YES ☐

3 Is the vehicle left at a different address to the above? If 'YES' give address at which it is usually kept. NO / YES ☐

When do you use your car?

4 In addition to social, domestic and pleasure use will the vehicle be used for: If 'YES' give details below.

(a) Business purposes for yourself in person only. * NO / YES TRANSPORTING, BOOTY AND CANNON BALLS

(b) Business purposes by any person other than Yourself in person. If 'YES' give name of person and details. * NO / YES TON (THE CABIN BOY) : SEE BELOW. S.

(c) Commercial travelling. * NO / YES

NB. All policies exclude use for carriage of passengers for reward. * *Please delete answer that does not apply.*

What cover do you want? See prospectus

Comprehensive ☐   Third Party, Fire & Theft ☐   Third Party only ☐

Do you wish to have a 'no claims discount' protection, if so tick box ✓

Options

5 Do you wish to bear part of the cost of any damage claim to you own vehicle. NO ☐ YES ✓

NB. Young and/or inexperienced drivers are subject to compulsory excesses (see prospectus) in addition to above.

A specimen of the insurers' policy form is available on request.

If yes indicate amount £50 ✓ £75 ☐ £100 ☐

About the drivers Include you own personal details where appropriate

6 Do you require driving to be restricted.
Please tick (✓) the appropriate drivers box required.
Yourself only [ ]   Yourself and spouse only [ ]   Yourself and one other driver [✓]   Any authorised driver [ ]

7 Who will be the main driver of the vehicle ....

8 Give details below of YOURSELF and ALL OTHERS particularly those under 25, who you know will drive the vehicle.

FULL NAME Forenames	Surname	Occupation	Age	Length of regular car driving experience	No. of years full UK Driving licence held	No. of years resident in UK
1 TOM	PUGWASH	CABIN BOY	17	1/2 yrs	1/2 yrs	17 yrs
2				yrs	yrs	yrs
3				yrs	yrs	yrs
4				yrs	yrs	yrs

Think who might need to drive, for instance in an emergency. The policy will only cover those whom you ask for it to cover.

Inexperienced driver: might be expensive to get a policy to insure him as a driver.

History

9 Have you or any person who will drive:

If any part s answered 'YES' give name of driver concerned, and details. Where a conviction is involved state date, type of conviction and sentence imposed (Licencing Authority offence code should also be quoted, if known).

(a) been convicted and/or have pending any prosecution(s) for a motoring offence.   NO [ ]   YES [✓]

(b) at any time been refused motor vehicle insurance or renewal and/or had a policy cancelled and/or been asked to agree to special terms or premium.   NO [ ]   YES [✓]

(c) ever suffered from defective vision and/or hearing (not corrected by spectacles, contact lenses or hearing aid), heart condition, epilepsy, diabetes, loss of use of a limb, arthritic condition and/or any other disease, disorder, illness or physical infirmity which could affect the driving of a motor vehicle.   NO [ ]   YES [✓]

10 Have there been any accidents or losses regardless of blame during the past 5 years in connection with any vehicle owned or driven by you or any of those named above.   NO [ ]   YES [✓]   If 'YES' give details in space provided.

Date	Own damage cost £	Third Party cost £	Name of Driver concerned and brief details of occurrence
1/7/85	£3000	—	CAPT. H. PUGWASH, DRIVING INTO PORCHESTER DOCK YARD WHEN VEHICLE TOTALLY DESTROYED BY CANNONBALL FIRED ACCIDENTALLY FROM SHIP BY MR. MATE

Note that this specifies 'motoring offence', so Capt. Pugwash's 1959 conviction for piracy on the high seas is not relevant. However, it may well be worth disclosing it anyway. The same applies to the Captain's habit of fainting when under attack (see Driving Licence Application, page 374).

Unfortunate incident. Clearly the ship's insurance didn't cover this risk, so the claim cost Capt. Pugwash his no claim discount. He isn't goint to risk that again: see the section on 'What cover do you want?'

No claim discount?

11 Are you claiming a no claim discount.   NO [✓]   YES [ ]   If 'YES' attach your last renewal notice and state number of years entitlement [ ] years

12 State policy number and name of insurers with whom you are now, or have been, insured in respect of any motor vehicle.   MARINE AND TRANSPORT INSURANCE OF LIBERIA p/c

13 If no previous insurance state how driving experience, if any, was gained.

DECLARATION Please read carefully before signing

I/we declare that the above statements and particulars whether written by me/us or others on my/our behalf are true and complete to the best of my/our knowledge and belief and that I/we have not withheld any material fact and that the Vehicle(s) to be insured is/are and will be kept in good condition and I/we agree that this proposal and declaration is promissory and shall be the basis of the contract between me/us and the Insurers (and of any renewal of it which may be agreed) and I/we agree to accept the Insurers' policy subject to its terms, exceptions and conditions.
Failure to disclose material facts could result in the Insurer refusing to deal with a claim under your policy. Material facts are those which the Insurer would regard as likely to influence the acceptance and assessment of the Proposal. If you are in doubt as to whether or not certain information is material then it should be disclosed.

PROPOSER'S SIGNATURE   H. Pugwash
Date   15 OCTOBER   19 86

INS 618(1/85)

NOTE: No cover attaches until the Insurer has accepted this proposal and has issued a Certificate of Insurance or Cover Note. The Insurer reserves the right to decline any proposal or to modify terms.

MOTOR INSURANCE COVER NOTE

This is a temporary cover note issued on acceptance of an insurance proposal. It takes effect as a certificate of insurance, satisfying the law's demands for motor insurance during the period it remains in force. In due course the insured will receive a policy document and certificate of insurance (see page 384). It is completed by the insurer or broker.

Read this form carefully. It tells you what you are insured for, and for how long. There may be notes attached, in which case you should read those too. If the details do not reflect the agreement made with the insurer or broker, point it out at once.

As was envisaged (see page 381), the insurer was not willing to cover Tom the Cabin Boy to drive the car (or perhaps the price of a policy to cover Tom was too high, so Captain Pugwash settled for this one). Only the Captain is insured to drive.

Although this says it is comprehensive and covers use for business purposes other than commercial travelling, it will not cover Captain Pugwash's piracy business, as that is an illegal use.

Motor Insurance Cover Note

Particulars of motor vehicle insured   No._____/EIS

Make and Model	Type of body	c.c.	Year of make	Estimated value	Registration No.	Number of seats
FORD SIERRA	SALOON 5	1600	19 85	£ 3,000	ABC 123Z	5

Persons or classes of persons entitled to drive
(Delete paragraphs inapplicable)
A The insured only
B ~~The insured and spouse only~~
C ~~The insured or any person who is driving on the order or with the permission of the insured~~
D _____
   _____
   _____

Provided always that the person driving holds a licence to drive the vehicle or has held and is not disqualified from holding or obtaining such a licence.

Cover
Comprehensive ☑   Third Party Fire and Theft ☐
Third Party only ☐   ☐
Excess   £   50
(in addition to any standard Policy excess)
Special Conditions   PROTECTED NO CLAIMS BONUS

Classes of use – see next page for details use in accordance with category
☐ SDP   ☐ SDX   ☑ CL1   ☐ CL2
☐ CL3   ☐ BU1   ☐ BU2   ☐ BU3

Effective date of commencement of insurance for the
purpose of the Act ___OOO I___ am/pm
to the same time on the ~~thirtieth~~ day after. 16·10·86

Name of Insured	CAPT. H. PUGWASH
Address	THE BLACK PIG INN
	BORCHESTER-ON-SEA
	BORSETSHIRE
	BR1 1BR

Cover is hereby provisionally granted (subject to the terms and conditions of the Policy issued by the Authorised Insurers named below applicable to such form of insurance) and to the terms and conditions shown hereon to the undernamed insured in respect of the above specified vehicle against the risks shown above until notice is given that the insurance is declined, but in no case for a longer period than that mentioned.

Form C
Certificate of Motor Insurance
I hereby certify that this covering note satisfies the requirements of the relevant law applicable in Great Britain, Northern Ireland, the Isle of Man, and the Islands of Guernsey, Jersey and Alderney.

Authorised Insurer

Source No. _____
Time and date of issue _____
Examined _____
Reason for issue _____
Policy/Client Number _____

THIS COVER NOTE IS NOT VALID UNLESS BEARING THE STAMP OF THE AUTHORISED INSURER

Captain Pugwash agrees to pay the first £50 of any damage to his own vehicle. This will have reduced the cost of the cover.

Protected no claims bonus. This is useful in case of future mishaps (with cannonballs). However, certain situations may not be covered, for example in times of war or civil unrest – check the list of exceptions in the policy.

Expiry time and date. If you have not received another cover note or a certificate of insurance by then, you may not be insured. Do not drive after this date without checking. You will need a cover note to produce when lawfully required to do so.

382

MOTOR INSURANCE COVER NOTE – *continued*

SDP	Use for Social Domestic and Pleasure Purposes including travel by the Insured to his or her permanent place of business or study.
SDX	Use for Social Domestic and Pleasure Purposes excluding use by any permitted driver for travel to or from his or her place of business or study.
CL1	Use for Social Domestic and Pleasure Purposes and by the Insured in person in connection with his business excluding commercial travelling.
CL2	Use for Social Domestic and Pleasure Purposes and business of the Insured excluding commercial travelling.
CL3	Use for Social Domestic and Pleasure Purposes and for the business of the Insured.
BU1	Use for Social Domestic and Pleasure Purposes and by the person named under "Special conditions" overleaf in connection with his or her business, excluding commercial travelling.
BU2	Use for Social Domestic and Pleasure Purposes and by the Insured in person in connection with the Insured's business and by the person named under "Special conditions" overleaf in connection with his or her business excluding commercial travelling.
BU3	Use for Social Domestic and Pleasure Purposes and for the business of the person named under "Special conditions" overleaf.

EXCLUDING IN ALL CASES

Racing, rallies, trials, pacemaking or speed testing, carriage of passengers for hire or reward, hiring, any use in connection with motor trade, message despatch or courier services.

which led to the insurer not being liable to pay out under the policy. The same result follows where the insured drives a different vehicle from the one covered by the policy, unless he is specifically covered to drive other vehicles; or where a vehicle insured for 'social, domestic and pleasure purposes' was used on a single occasion in connection with the driver's business; or where the insured under a policy which restricted driving to the owner only became ill while driving, and a friend took over.

(A) Insurance premiums. As with other forms of insurance, the insurer sets the premium partly according to actuarial calculations of the likelihood that a typical person showing the characteristics of the person insured will make a claim during the period for which the policy is to run. The weight given to different factors may vary from company to company, as will the incidental costs the company has to cover. This leads to different companies offering similar policies at different prices, and makes it worth shopping around. The AA and RAC offer instant computerised quotes for insurance, and insurance brokers also offer advice. Brokers are particularly useful if you have unusual insurance needs, or are in a position which might make it difficult to persuade an insurer to accept you.

Typical factors affecting the level of premiums for individuals include:

(1) **age** (on the whole, young drivers are a worse risk than older drivers and pay higher premiums);

(2) **location** (large cities are more expensive areas than the countryside);

(3) the **type of car** being insured (foreign cars tend to be more expensive to repair than smaller cars or those where parts are more readily available, and more powerful cars are more likely to be involved in accidents);

(4) the **driving record** of the insured, previous claims and any convictions, especially for motoring offences;

(5) the **sex** of the person insured (women have fewer accidents than men, so some companies charge them lower premiums);

(6) the **purposes** for which vehicles will be used.

(B) No claim discounts and protected policies. When a policy is renewed after a year in which the person insured has not made any claims under the policy, the renewal premium may be reduced by a percentage (the 'no claim discount'). The discounts may be built up from year to year, until after six years without a claim the discount may reach 60% or 65% of the premium. This is usually the maximum permitted discount, and means that the person insured is paying only two-fifths or seven-twentieths of the premium which would be required of a new

This Certificate must be produced on request to a police officer. The Certificate is a Schedule to the Policy, which contains all the details about what the rights and duties of the Insured are. The Certificate and Policy should therefore be read together.

Tom the Cabin Boy is not insured. Nor are other authorised drivers, unless they have their own comprehensive insurance policies.

Expiry date. The insurer may well send a reminder shortly before the renewal premium is due, but it is *your* responsibility to ensure that you are covered. Make a note of the date prominently in your diary.

This covers Capt. Pugwash to drive (a) his own car(s), and (b) cars he is buying on hire purchase. It would not, without more money, cover him to drive ordinary hire cars (a separate policy will be needed) or cars belonging to anyone else. If he drives cars belonging to other people, he will be uninsured (a criminal offence) unless the owners have a policy covering any authorised or named driver and they have authorised him to drive or named him as a driver on their insurance proposals.

However, there is in this case an extension to the policy, because it is a comprehensive policy, allowing him cover to drive other cars or motor cycles. There will certainly be a condition that he is driving lawfully, i e not stealing the car etc.

This is limited to *lawful* business. It does not include piracy, burglary etc, which will certainly be excepted risks.

The policy also does not cover use for the purposes listed.

Certificate of Motor Insurance

B02 /W

Certificate No.   KP455/F6763149

1. DESCRIPTION OF VEHICLES
   ANY MOTOR CAR THE PROPERTY OF THE POLICY HOLDER OR HIRED TO HIM UNDER A HIRE PURCHASE AGREEMENT

2. Name of policy holder.   H.PUGWASH

3. Effective date of the commencement of insurance for the purpose of the relevant law.   15.27HRS 14th NOVEMBER 1986

4. Date of expiry of insurance.   15th OCTOBER 1987

5. Persons or classes of persons entitled to drive.

   (A) THE POLICY HOLDER
   THE POLICY HOLDER MAY ALSO DRIVE A MOTOR CAR OR MOTOR CYCLE NOT BELONGING TO HIM AND NOT HIRED TO HIM UNDER A HIRE PURCHASE AGREEMENT

   Provided that the person driving holds a licence to drive such vehicle or has held and is not disqualified for holding or obtaining such a licence.

6. Limitations as to use.

   (1) USE FOR SOCIAL DOMESTIC AND PLEASURE PURPOSES

   (2) USE BY THE POLICY HOLDER IN PERSON IN CONNECTION WITH HIS BUSINESS

   The policy does not cover

   (A) USE FOR HIRING COMMERCIAL TRAVELLING OR FOR ANY PURPOSE IN CONNECTION WITH THE MOTOR TRADE

   (B) USE FOR RACING PACE-MAKING OR SPEED TESTING

   I hereby Certify that the policy to which this certificate relates satisfies the requirements of the relevant law applicable in Great Britain, Northern Ireland, the Isle of Man, the Island of Guernsey, the Island of Jersey and the Island of Alderney.

   GUARDIAN ROYAL EXCHANGE ASSURANCE plc
   (Authorised Insurers).

   General Manager

   NOTE: For full details of the insurance cover reference should be made to the policy.
   Any termination of the insurance to which the Company may on request agree will operate only from the return of this certificate.

   ZR 289 (7/84)   *(SEE OVER)*

   AA /AM

driver. However, if the driver then makes a claim and the insurance company cannot recover the money from another driver or insurance company, he will lose all or part of the no claim discount. This may happen, for example, if the damage was caused by the person insured rather than by another driver, or if the driver who caused the damage cannot be traced. The effect will be to put up the premiums he has to pay the next year and perhaps for several years afterwards. Because of this, the long-term cost of making an insurance claim may sometimes outweigh the short-term benefit of having a damaged car repaired at the insurer's expense, especially if there is an excess provision in the policy.

This can be very frustrating for drivers, and a type of policy is available which, for a relatively small additional premium, gives a protected no claim discount. Typically, these policies allow you to make up to two claims in a three-year period without losing your no claim discount. Information about this can be obtained from your insurer or broker.

(iv) Policy Documents and Certificates of Insurance

When you take out a policy, you will be provided with a cover note, which has the effect of a temporary certificate of insurance. Until that is issued, the policy is not operational. In due course you will be provided with a copy of the policy, and a full certificate of insurance. Your policy document will probably have within it details of all the policies and restrictions on them which the insurer offers. The policy should be read together with the schedule to the policy which tells you which bits of the policy you have actually bought. You are not entitled to any of the benefits of the policy except those specified in the schedule.

The certificate of insurance will need to be produced (1) to obtain a tax disc for the vehicle and (2) when it is requested by a police constable.

(v) When Does the Policy Become Inoperative?

Policies cease to operate entirely, and leave you completely uninsured, in any of the following circumstances: if the vehicle covered by the policy is sold or given away; if the period for which insurance was granted has expired and the policy has not been renewed; if the insurer revokes the policy because of some material misrepre-

sentation or non-disclosure on the part of the person insured at the time of the proposal for insurance.

Policies do not operate during the period that the vehicle insured is being used by a person who is not insured to use it (for example, where a policy is for named drivers only and a friend of a named driver is driving) or by anyone for a purpose not covered by the policy (such as where a car insured for social, domestic and pleasure purposes only is used for commercial travelling).

3. VEHICLE LICENSING AND REGISTRATION

The DVLC operates a comprehensive system of vehicle licensing and registration. The aim is to make is possible to know who is responsible for each of the vehicles on the road and ensure that vehicle excise duty (or car tax, as it is sometimes known) is paid. The system also makes it easier to trace the owners of vehicles which are suspected of being involved in criminal offences or road accidents.

(i) Registration

When a new vehicle is put on the road, it will need to be licensed. The first time that a licence is applied for, the vehicle will automatically be registered and a registration mark assigned to it. The registration mark consists of letters and numbers which are unique to that vehicle, such as WXY 789 Z, or A 123 BCD. These are called the registration mark.

(A) **The form of registration marks.** The law requires that the registration mark must be displayed on the front and rear of a vehicle. It must be on a flat rectangular plate or flat rectangular unbroken surface forming part of the vehicle. The letters and numbers must be indelibly inscribed, or attached in such a way that they cannot be readily removed. They must either be white, silver or light grey on a black background, or be on one of the more modern reflecting type of number plates (usually black on a white background at the front of the vehicle and black on a yellow background at the rear). They must be easily legible at a distance of 75 feet in normal daylight (or 60 feet in the case of motor cycles, pedestrian-controlled vehicles and invalid carriages). At night, the rear registration plate must be easily legible from a distance of 60 feet (or 50 feet in the case of motor cycles, pedestrian-controlled vehicles and invalid carriages) and must be lit so as to make this possible.

The driver is responsible for ensuring that the registration marks are easily legible at the required distances. This means that regular cleaning of the plates is necessary.

(B) Personalised registration marks. For a (substantial) fee, the owner will be allowed to choose a registration mark for his vehicle as long as it has not already been allocated and the DVLC approves. Alternatively, one can transfer a registration mark from another car. Registration marks are regularly advertised in the press at extraordinarily high prices: some marks are worth more than the cars they are attached to, and firms specialise in arranging their transfers. The DVLC charges the transferee £80 for registering the change. This is great for egomaniacs with plenty of spare cash.

(C) Vehicle registration documents. The Secretary of State issues a vehicle registration document for the vehicle, setting out the information necessary to identify the vehicle and its registered keeper. This used to be known as the 'log book', but it is no longer a book. The registered keeper is not necessarily the owner, so the document does not establish title to the vehicle. However, it is essential to have it in order to register a change of keeper, so it will not be possible to sell the vehicle without it. It is an offence to deface or alter the document, except to fill in and return the document or the relevant parts of it to the DVLC to inform them about any change in the particulars relating to the vehicle or the registered keeper of the vehicle.

It is also an offence to fail to notify the DVLC of any change of keeper, keeper's name and address or vehicle particulars, or of the fact that a vehicle has been scrapped or permanently exported. When the vehicle is sold or transferred, the previous keeper must fill in the tear-off notification of sale or transfer from the foot of the document, and return it to the DVLC. The new keeper must then complete the notification of changes on the reverse of the document, and return the document to the DVLC.

The registration document must be kept in a safe place, and must be produced if requested at any reasonable time by a police constable or an official of the Department of Transport.

(ii) Vehicle Excise Duty
Vehicle excise duty is the tax which is charged on any vehicle which is used or kept on a road. When the tax is paid, either to DVLC, a Post Office or a local licensing office, a tax disc is issued, which licenses the vehicle to be used or kept on a road. It is an offence to use or keep a motor vehicle on a road without a valid licence disc.

The disc sets out the registration mark of the car, the make and model, the duty paid and the period for which the licence is valid. Licences may be obtained for six or twelve months. At the moment a twelve month licence costs £100 and a six month licence costs £55, but the amount tends to change from year to year as it is a favourite way of increasing revenue at budget time.

The disc must be in a holder to protect it from the weather, and must be displayed on the nearside of the windscreen of a car or on the nearside of any other vehicle in front of the driver's seat. It must not be placed on the offside or in the middle of the windscreen of a vehicle if it has a windscreen which extends to the nearside, nor may it be placed on the dashboard or anywhere else in or on the car.

It is an offence to alter, mutilate, deface or add anything to a licence disc, or to display a disc so dealt with. It is also an offence to display a disc which has become illegible or on which the colours have altered by fading. It is a serious offence to forge or fraudulently alter a disc, registration mark or registration document, or to lend or allow to be used any disc, registration mark or registration document.

4. THE CONDITION OF THE VEHICLE

The law imposes a minimum standard of roadworthiness on any vehicle which is taken on the road. First, there are many detailed provisions governing the condition of vital parts of the car, such as brakes, tyres and lights. Authorised police officers, authorised Department of the Environment examiners and other authorised examiners can test any vehicle on a road to see whether these provisions are complied with, and a constable can stop a vehicle on the road to allow a check to be conducted. Secondly, an annual check is imposed to see whether cars over three years old satisfy a minimal set of safety requirements: the so-called MOT test.

(i) Parts of the Car and their Condition
The rules governing the condition and use of parts of the vehicle are the Motor Vehicle (Construction and Use) Regulations 1978 and the

Road Vehicles Lighting Regulations 1984. It is an offence punishable by a fine to use a motor vehicle, or cause or permit one to be used, in contravention of the Regulations. Under the Regulations, every motor vehicle and trailer, all parts and accessories, and the condition, weight distribution and packing of loads, must be in such a condition that no danger is caused to any person in or on the vehicle or on the road. It has been held that this covers the efficiency of mechanical parts, so that it is an offence (for instance) to use a vehicle in which there is excessive play in the steering.

It is therefore wise to observe the following two general rules.

(1) Follow the manufacturer's advice about regular maintenance and servicing: have services carried out at the recommended intervals by a competent motor mechanic, following the manufacturer's maintenance schedules.

(2) If there appears to be a problem with the car, have it checked and, if necessary, repaired, by a competent mechanic at once: do not drive a potential death-trap round the streets.

The Regulations deal in some detail with various parts of the car. What follows is a summary of the main provisions.

(A) Audible warning. Motor vehicles other than works trucks and pedestrian-controlled vehicles must have some instrument, such as a horn, with which sufficient audible warning can be given of its position or its approach. Where the vehicle was first used on or after 1 August 1973, the horn's sound must be continuous, uniform and not strident. Two-tone horns, gongs, bells and sirens are absolutely prohibited except on emergency vehicles. However, mobile shops are allowed to have an instrument to let customers know that they are there, such as the ubiquitous and often annoying chimes on ice-cream and hot dog vans.

Horns must not be sounded in the following situations:

(1) when the vehicle is stationary on a road, unless it is used as a theft alarm or to get help or is used when danger arises because of another moving vehicle on the road;

(2) on roads with restricted speed limits where there are street lights at intervals of not more than 200 yards, between the hours of 11.30 pm and 7 am.

(B) Brakes. Every motor vehicle first used on or after 1 October 1937 must have two independent braking systems capable of stopping the vehicle within a reasonable distance under the most adverse conditions. They must be capable of being applied manually, and on vehicles first used on or after 1 April 1938 must not depend on the engine turning. On vehicles first used on or after 1 January 1968, one of the systems must allow the vehicle to be held stationary when parked on a gradient of at least 1 in 6.25.

(C) Direction indicators. These must be fitted to cars, and may be of two kinds. The old-fashioned illuminated indicator arms show a steady or flashing light, and stick out from the side of the vehicle. They must project at least six inches beyond the widest point of the vehicle, changing the outline of the vehicle by at least six inches measured horizontally, and must be no more than six feet behind the base of the windscreen. When extended, it must remain steady and must be illuminated, being clearly visible at a reasonable distance in front and behind.

The more modern amber flashing indicator lights are on the front and rear of the car, with optional extra lights at the sides. They must be clearly visible from a reasonable distance, and be optically separated from other lights on the vehicle. They must flash not less than 60 times a minute and not more than 120 times a minute (beware if your battery is running down).

Another kind of indicator is the flashing lamp situated not more than six feet behind the base of the windscreen, showing an illuminated area of at least 3½ square inches to both front and rear. It may show in amber or white to the front and amber or red to the rear, but must be amber if it shows both to front and rear.

The driver must be aware when the indicators are on, either from a warning signal in the vehicle or by being able to see at least one of the indicators on each side of the vehicle. All the indicators, including indicators on a trailer being pulled by a car, must be operated by the same switch in the car.

(D) Exhaust system. Every internal combustion engine on a vehicle must be fitted with a silencer or some other efficient method of reducing the noise from escaping gases. The vehicle must also be constructed so that no visible vapour or avoidable smoke escapes from the vehicle while it is running.

(E) Lighting. Lights on vehicles fulfil two purposes: to see and be seen. To avoid confusing other traffic, no vehicle may ever show a red light to the front.

(a) Being seen: sidelights. A vehicle on a road during the 'hours of darkness' (defined as the period from half an hour after sunset to half an hour before sunrise) must carry two lamps showing a white light to the front (or a yellow light if they are incorporated in headlamps which only show a yellow light), and two lamps showing a red light to the rear, each visible at a reasonable distance. When the vehicle is on a road during the hours of darkness, these side-lights must:

(i) be kept lit, except when the vehicle is parked on a road where a speed limit of no more than 30 mph is in force, the vehicle is parked at least 10 metres (11 yards) from the nearest junction on either side of the road and the nearside of the vehicle is parallel to, and as close as possible to, the left-hand kerb (or, in a one-way street, nearside or offside of the vehicle is parallel to and as close as possible to either kerb);

(ii) be kept properly trimmed (a reminder of the days when cars had candle- or oil-powered lamps with wicks) and in a clean and efficient condition;

(iii) be attached to the vehicle in the prescribed manner and positions.

Vehicles must also carry efficient reflectors, showing up red to the rear.

One or two rear fog lamps may be fitted, and must be fitted to vehicles made on or after 1 October 1979 and first used on or after 1 April 1980. The lamps must show red. They must only be used during adverse weather conditions when the vehicle is moving or is temporarily forced to stop. (There are special exceptions for vehicles made or adapted to carry seven or more passengers, and for vehicles used for the purposes of the police, fire brigade or ambulance.)

(b) Seeing: headlamps and front foglamps. Two obligatory front headlamps must be fitted to most motor vehicles first used on or after 1 January 1937. The lamps must emit a white or yellow beam of light, with a rated wattage of at least 30 W. The lamps must be designed to emit a dipped beam, or be capable of being controlled by the driver to emit a dipped beam, so as to avoid dazzling other road users.

Obligatory headlamps must be turned on when the vehicle is in motion during the hours of darkness on a road which does not have street lights at intervals of not more than 200 yards, or where the street lights are not on. They must also be lit at other times in conditions of poor visibility. 'Poor visibility conditions' are any conditions (including smoke, fog, rain, etc) which seriously reduce the driver's ability to see or to be seen on the road. However, they need not be lit in poor visibility conditions if front foglamps are lit.

Up to two front foglamps may be fitted. If two are fitted, they may be used instead of headlamps during the hours of darkness on unlit roads in fog or falling snow, or during the daytime in conditions of poor visibility.

Front foglamps, headlights and other front lamps with a wattage over 7 W (the standard wattage for sidelights) must be switched off if the vehicle is stationary on a road, unless the stoppage is enforced. (There are exceptions for certain large passenger vehicles picking up or setting down passengers, rescue vehicles etc.)

(c) Reversing lights. One or two reversing lights may be attached to the back of a vehicle.

(d) Hazard warning lights. Hazard warning lights are devices by which all the flashing indicator lights can be activated at the same time. They may be used to warn other road users when the road is temporarily obstructed, but only while the vehicle is stationary because of a breakdown, accident or emergency. They must never be used on a moving vehicle.

(e) Red stop lamps. Red stop lamps linked to the brakes are required on the rear of most vehicles and trailers, including caravans. There must be two of them, or one if the vehicle was first used, or trailer manufactured, before 1 January 1971.

(f) Other lights or beacons. No other lamp or beacon may be fitted to a vehicle unless it is one authorised to carry a beacon for police, ambulance, fire brigade, breakdown or other emergency purposes.

(F) Seat belts. Seat belts must be fitted to the driver's seat and front passenger seat in motor cars manufactured on or after 1 July 1964 and first registered on or after 1 January 1965, and to motor tricycles over 255 kg unladen weight manufactured on or after 1 March 1970 and first used on or after 1 September 1970. The driver and front seat passenger must use the seat belts when the vehicle is in motion, unless it is operating under trade plates, the person concerned is suffering from certain disabilities or the driver is reversing.

(G) Speedometer. Every motor vehicle must be fitted with an efficient speedometer enabling the vehicle's speed to be read at any time. A rev counter is not sufficient.

(H) Springs. Every motor car and trailer must be suitably and sufficiently sprung.

(I) Tyres. Motor cars must in general be fitted with suitable pneumatic tyres. A radial tyre must not be fitted to a wheel on the same axle as one with a cross-ply tyre: follow manufacturers' directions carefully, and take advice if in doubt. Tyres must be correctly inflated according to the manufacturer's directions: the vehicle handbook will give the correct tyre pressures. The depth of the tyre tread must be at least 1 mm all round the circumference of the tyre and across at least three-quarters of its breadth. The base of the grooves forming the tread must be clearly visible on all parts of the tyre originally covered by the tread pattern. No tyre may be used if it has a bulge in the structure, visible ply or cord structure exposed, or a cut which is 25 mm long (or, if longer, 10% of the width of the tyre).

(J) Windows and visibility. All windows in motor vehicles first used on or after 1 January 1959 must be made of safety glass. Vehicles must be constructed to allow the driver a full view of the road and traffic ahead. Windscreen wipers and washers must be fitted to the front windscreen of cars and other vehicles if the driver cannot obtain a clear view ahead without looking through the windscreen. They must be properly maintained and adjusted and in working order.

Private cars must be fitted with at least one internal or external mirror to help the driver to see traffic conditions behind the car. The car must not be loaded with passengers or goods in such a way as to obstruct the drivers view to the rear in the mirror.

(ii) The MOT Test and Certificate

Every motor vehicle must be submitted to an approved examiner for a test if it is to be used on a road more than three years after the date of first registration (or first use if earlier). The registration document, or other evidence of the date of first registration, must be produced on request. An examiner need not carry out the test if the vehicle is in such a dirty condition that it makes the examination unreasonably difficult. The examiner tests the vehicle to ensure that the legal requirements for the condition of the car are complied with, and that the essential parts are in efficient working order. If the vehicle passes, a certificate is issued which is valid for a year, at the end of which time the vehicle must be retested. If the vehicle fails, a notice giving the grounds of failure is issued.

It is an offence to use on the road a vehicle which requires a test certificate and does not have one. However, there are exceptions, of which the most important are: vehicles being taken to a previously arranged test, being taken away from one, or during one; vehicles being tested *by a motor trader* during or after repairs to it; vehicles detained or seized by the police or under the customs and excise Acts.

The test certificate will be needed in order to obtain a vehicle excise licence for the vehicle.

1. OFFENCES CONNECTED WITH MOTORING

(i) The Condition of the Vehicle

As noted in the preceding section, it is an offence to use a car on a road in contravention of the Regulations governing construction and use. The vehicle and all parts and accessories must be properly maintained.

(ii) Loads and Numbers of Passengers

A vehicle must not carry more passengers or a heavier load than it is entitled to do. If in doubt about this, consult the vehicle's registration document and handbook.

Loads must be secured in such a way that they do not cause a danger or nuisance to anyone else or to property. The Department of the Environment publishes a code of practice, *Safety of Loads on Vehicles*, which is available through HMSO. When a load projects over the end of a vehicle, special provisions apply which are set out in the box below.

Children in cars should always be suitably restrained, whether in the back or the front seat. Children who are free to move around in the car cause danger to themselves in the event of an accident and are also likely to cause an accident by distracting the driver or other road users. The law requires that children under the age of one year, if in the front seat, must be in an approved child restraint specifically designed for a child of that age and weight. Children between the ages of one and fourteen must wear either an approved child restraint or adult seat-belt. The driver, not the child, will be criminally responsible for breaches of these requirements. In the latter case, the seat should be adapted for the size of the child in accordance with manufacturer's recommendations to prevent a child being seriously injured by the belt in the event of an accident.

All drivers, and front seat passengers over the age of fourteen, must wear an approved seat-belt unless specifically exempted. Grounds of exemption are: holding a medical exemption

---

Requirements in respect of projecting loads on motor vehicles

1. Loads projecting sideways from the vehicle.

No load may be carried if: (a) it projects over the side of a vehicle by more than 305 mm (approximately 1 foot); or (b) its total width exceeds 2.9 metres (approximately 9 feet 6 inches).

However, there are exceptions where: (i) the load consists of loose agricultural produce; or (ii) the load is indivisible, it is not reasonably practicable to comply with the width limits and the police have been given two clear days' notice that the load is going to be used. In addition, an attendant must be employed for the load, in addition to the driver, if it is over 3.5 metres (about 11 feet 6 inches) wide. No load over 4.3 metres wide is allowed.

2. Loads projecting over the back of the vehicle.

(a) If a load projects more than 1.07 metres (about 3 feet 6 inches) beyond the back of the vehicle, steps must be taken to make it visible to other road users. For example, a coloured cloth could be attached to the end of the projection. (b) If a load projects more than 1.83 metres (about 6 feet) beyond the back of the vehicle, an end marker board, consisting of an isosceles triangle at least 610 mm (2 feet) high with alternate red and white stripes, must be attached to the load not more than 2 feet from the end of the projection. (c) If a load projects more than 3.05 metres (about 10 feet) beyond the back of the vehicle, marker boards must be fitted, notice must be given to the police and an attendant must be employed in addition to the driver.

3. Loads projecting over the front of the vehicle.

(a) If the load projects more than 1.83 metres (about 6 feet) over the front of the vehicle, an attendant must be employed for the load, in addition to the driver, and marker boards must be fitted to the projection. (b) If the load projects forwards by more than 3.05 metres (about 10 feet) notice must be given to the police, marker boards must be fitted and an attendant must be employed.

---

certificate (which may be given, for example, to pregnant women who have difficulty with seat-belts because of the women's shapes or conditions); drivers who are reversing; those local rounds of deliveries or collections in a vehicle specially constructed or adapted for the purpose. (This covers people such as milkmen and postmen.)

Motorcyclists may not carry more than one pillion passenger, and the passenger must be provided with adequate foot supports. Motorcyclists and passengers must wear approved crash helmets, unless exempted from this requirement on religious grounds by reason of being Sikhs. Learner drivers on motorcycles must not carry pillion passengers.

(iii) Driving

The driver of a vehicle on the road must be in a position in which he can have proper control of the vehicle and a full view of the road. This means that, for example, the driver must not be obstructed by parcels restricting the range of movement or ability to see out or reach the controls. Holding a dog on the driver's lap is definitely unlawful.

It is an offence to fail to give precedence to pedestrians at pedestrian crossings, or to overtake in the area before a crossing marked with zig-zag white lines.

Nobody may use a television set in a vehicle in a position where it can be seen, either directly or by way of reflection, by the driver or where it might distract the drivers of other vehicles.

Further moving traffic offences are explained under sections 2 opposite and 3 on page 395.

(iv) Speed Limits

For ordinary motorists, leaving aside goods vehicles and large passenger vehicles to which special rules apply, the maximum permitted speed depends on the type of road that is being driven on. For speed limit purposes, there are three types of roads.

(1) **Restricted roads** are those, usually though not exclusively in built-up areas, where there are lamp posts at intervals of not more than 200 yards. The speed limit here is **30 miles per hour**, unless there are round speed limit signs showing a lower or higher limit.

(2) **Motorways and dual carriageways** have a limit of **70 miles per hour**, unless there are signs which indicate a lower limit.

(3) **Other roads** are subject to a speed limit of **60 miles per hour**, unless there are signs indicating a lower limit.

For additional restrictions affecting vehicles drawing trailers or caravans, see section 7.6 on page 402.

The police sometimes operate radar speed tests at points on the road where there is thought to be a particular likelihood that drivers are exceeding the speed limit, or wait in cars and follow and stop drivers who are clearly going too fast. The common practice among drivers who notice a speed trap in operation of flashing their lights at cars approaching the area to warn them is not lawful: drivers who do that are committing the offence of wilfully obstructing the constables in the execution of their duty.

(v) Complying with Directions

Every driver of a vehicle, and every pedestrian, must comply with the directions of a constable in uniform or a traffic warden in uniform on traffic duty. This includes obeying instructions as to lanes that vehicles should be in.

Every driver of a vehicle must stop when required to do so by a constable in uniform.

The requirements for drivers and vehicles to be licensed and to be covered by insurance are explained in section 7.2 (see page 372).

(vi) Producing Documents

If a driver is asked by a constable in uniform to produce his driving licence, insurance certificate and, where applicable, MOT test certificate he must do so. Failure to do so is an offence. However, few people carry all their documentation around. The law therefore provides that it is not an offence if the documents are produced within seven days. The constable will ask what police station the driver wants to produce his documents at, and then give the driver a copy of a notice (known as HORT 1), on which will be written the papers that are required, the address of the police station where they are to be produced and the date by which they must be produced. If they are not produced by that date, there is still a defence to a criminal charge if it can be shown that it was not reasonably practicable to produce them, for example, because a driving licence was away at DVLC being amended or an insurance certificate was lost and could not be replaced in time.

(vii) Parking

It is an offence for a person in charge of a vehicle or trailer to cause or permit it to be stationary in a road in a position, condition or circumstances where it is likely to be a danger to other road users. This offence covers, for example, leaving a car parked without applying the handbrake. It also covers leaving a vehicle or trailer where it would narrow the road and make it difficult for other traffic to pass (eg by an island or where another car is parked on the other side of a narrow road), leaving it close to a junction or anywhere else that might make it difficult for people to see the road, and leaving it where it causes danger to pedestrians, such as by school crossing patrols, on a footpath or bridleway or near a bus stop.

There are specific prohibitions on parking on the zig-zag white lines at zebra crossings, on a clearway except in an emergency, on an urban clearway during restricted times except to allow passengers to board or disembark, on a motorway except on the hard shoulder in an emergency, in a bus lane, on any part of the road with a double white line in the middle except to allow passengers to embark or disembark, where there are yellow lines restricting parking or 'No Loading' plates by the side of the road, in a 'Disc Zone' without a parking disc, or in an area where parking is restricted to certain classes of people (such as disabled drivers or residents) unless one is a member of the class. For a full list, see the Highway Code (1978 edition, revised 1985) rule 115.

Some exemptions from the parking restrictions are given for drivers of disabled people over two years of age who receive mobility allowance, or have a DHSS vehicle, or are registered blind, or suffer from a permanent and substantial disability causing an inability to walk or very substantial difficulty in walking. These people can obtain an orange badge from their local authorities which will allow them to park in certain places not normally permitted. If the local authority refuses a badge, there is an appeal to the Department of Transport in England, the Welsh Office in Wales and the Scottish Development Department in Scotland. It is an offence for someone to use a badge when not entitled to it. It is also an offence for a disabled person to allow his badge to be displayed on another person's vehicle, and may lead to the badge being withdrawn from the disabled person.

No motor vehicle or trailer must be allowed to stand on the road so as to cause an unnecessary obstruction. As well as its being an offence, the police or local authority may remove such a vehicle, and also any vehicle which has been abandoned on the road without authority. It does not matter whether anyone has actually been obstructed: it is enough if the ability of other road users to pass and repass on the road would be unnecessarily restricted.

Vehicles must not be left with their engines running. Stationary vehicles must have their parking brakes applied.

In the hours of darkness, parking is only allowed if the nearside of the car is parallel, and as close as possible, to the left side of the road, or, if it is a one-way street, to the right- or left-hand side of the road: i e the car must be parked facing in the same direction as traffic using that side of the road. This avoids confusing other drivers with the colour of lights and reflectors.

(viii) Doors

Nobody must open, or cause or permit to be opened, a door of a vehicle or trailer so as to cause injury or danger to other road users.

(ix) Failure to Report an Accident

The requirements in respect of reporting accidents to the police are explained in 7.4 (see page 397).

2. OFFENCES AND POLICE POWERS IN RELATION TO DRINK AND DRUGS

Anyone who has been in a hospital casualty department after 11 o'clock at night, especially on a Saturday, knows how much misery to innocent road users results when normally competent drivers pour out of pubs and take to their cars and motorcycles. Alcohol, even in small quantities, reduces one's sensitivity to, and inhibitions about, danger and also one's ability to cope with it when it arises. Because of this, responsible drivers do not drink and drive. Parliament, the police and the Courts try to ensure that the irresponsible ones have a hard time. Conviction on a drink-drive or drugs-drive charge leads to automatic disqualification, which may go together with imprisonment for a period of up to two years and/or a fine. Many otherwise good and public-spirited people have very properly lost their livelihoods as a result.

(i) The Offences

(a) It is an offence to drive or attempt to drive a motor vehicle on a road or other public place when the alcohol in one's body is in excess of prescribed limits, set out below.

(b) It is an offence to be in charge of a motor vehicle on a road or other public place with alcohol in excess of the prescribed limits in one's body.

(c) It is an offence to drive or attempt to drive a motor vehicle on a road or other public place while unfit to drive through drink or drugs.

(d) It is an offence to be in charge of a motor vehicle on a road or other public place while unfit to drive through drink or drugs.

Excess of alcohol. A person has an excess of alcohol if tests on his breath, blood or urine show that he had an unlawful level of alcohol in his body. The prescribed limits are:

breath tests: 35 microgrammes of alcohol per 100 millilitres of breath;

blood tests: 80 milligrammes of alcohol per 100 millilitres of blood;

urine samples: 107 milligrammes of alcohol per 100 millilitres of urine.

The way in which the tests are conducted is explained below.

Driving. Anyone who attempts to control the vehicle can be said to be driving it: the Courts have refused to limit the offence to people sitting in the driver's seat, so a drunk person reaching over to try to steer a runaway vehicle is driving.

'In charge of' a vehicle. This is much wider than driving. It covers being in charge of a parked vehicle: the person who lies down in the car to sleep off the effects of drink may be in charge of it for the purposes of the criminal law. A driver who left his car double-parked with the door open and made off across fields when he saw the police was still held to be in charge of the car when he was caught some distance away. There is a defence to a charge of being in charge if the accused can prove that there was no likelihood of him actually driving while under the influence. However, the accused is not allowed to use the fact that he was injured, or that the car was damaged, in proving it, so the usefulness of the defence is much reduced.

'Unfit to drive'. This means that the person's ability to drive *properly* is, at that particular time, impaired. He need not be shown to be incapable of driving at all: if he were, he would actually be rather less dangerous.

Unfit to drive through drugs. All drugs have an effect on one's metabolism. That is why people take them, whether for medical reasons or for pleasure. If drugs are prescribed by a doctor, or provided by a pharmacist, ask whether it would be wise not to drive and abide by the advice. If drugs are not provided by a doctor, it is unwise to drive at all. (Of course if they are controlled drugs and have not been obtained on prescription, possession of them is illegal anyway.) Ultimately the question whether a particular driver was fit to drive will turn to a great extent on the way he was behaving, and the question whether that unfitness was caused by drugs will be decided by medical evidence.

Unfit to drive through drink. Evidence from analysis of a breath, blood or urine sample can be used to support other evidence relating to unfitness to drive.

(ii) Police Powers in Respect of Drink and Drugs

(A) Breathalysing drivers. Police officers in uniform are allowed to require a breath specimen, and stop a vehicle if necessary to get one, whenever they have reasonable cause to suspect (usually because of the manner of driving) one of three things:

(i) that a person is driving, attempting to drive or in charge of a vehicle on a road or in a public place with excess alcohol in his body or while unfit to drive through drink or drugs;

(ii) that a person has been doing one of the things set out in (i) and still has alcohol in his body;

(iii) that a person has committed a moving traffic offence, such as speeding, going through a red traffic light or driving carelessly.

A constable need not form the suspicion while the car is being driven. He can ask for a breath specimen if, for example, he stops a car because of defective lights and then notices a smell of alcohol in the car, or the car has been involved in a minor collision.

The person will be asked to breathe into a breathalyser device. These devices look a bit like a balloon. They consist of a plastic bag with a tube sticking out. The tube contains crystals which react chemically to alcohol. A mouthpiece is attached to the end of the tube. The driver will be asked to take a deep breath and blow firmly through the mouthpiece until the bag is filled. This must be done with one breath: a person who takes two puffs has failed to provide a valid specimen, which is an offence for which he can be arrested. If there is alcohol on his breath, it will react with the crystals in the tube, which will get warm. If the concentration of alcohol is above the permitted level, it will be enough to make the crystals change colour.

If the crystals change colour, or the person refuses or fails to provide a proper specimen, the police will arrest him. They will also take steps to ensure that the vehicle does not cause an obstruction. If there is no passenger in the car, or any passengers appear to have been drinking or cannot drive, the police can take the car keys and arrange for it to be driven away.

It used to be popular to try to have another drink before the police arrived, or before providing a specimen, then argue that it was the drink taken after stopping driving that had put the driver over the limit (the 'hip-flask defence'). This is no longer likely to work, because the law now puts the onus on the driver to prove that he was not over the limit while he was driving. This would be very difficult, requiring complicated calculations to work out the speed at which alcohol is taken up by the blood to work back to the level that would have been found had the driver been tested while driving. This sort of 'back calculation' evidence is very uncertain, as was pointed out by the British Medical Association in 1965, and is unlikely to carry much weight in Court. Anyway, the 'hip-flask defence' has the other drawback that it leaves the driver exposed to a prosecution for the offence, admittedly less serious, of wilfully obstructing the constables in the execution of their duty.

(B) Entry to premises. The police have no general power to enter or remain on the driver's own premises in order to administer a breathalyser test. However, the driver probably cannot escape by going onto anyone else's premises. Even his own home provides no protection if the police have reasonable cause to suspect him of having been involved in an accident in which another person was injured: in that case they can enter, using reasonable force if necessary, to breathalyse him. They can also enter by force if necessary to arrest him for refusing a proper request for a breath specimen or after a test which gave a positive result.

(C) At the police station. At the police station or, if he ends up there, at a hospital the arrested person will be required to provide two specimens of breath for a breath testing machine. These automatically analyse a sample of breath and provide a visual display and a print-out showing the concentration of alcohol. The best-known of the machines are the Lion Intoximeters. It is an offence to refuse to provide specimens unless a doctor says it would interfere with the patient's treatment to provide them. Refusal to give specimens tends to be severely dealt with by Courts, for the excellent reason that the Courts know that the usual reason for refusing a specimen is that the person knows or suspects he is over the limit.

(D) Blood and urine samples. If there are medical reasons for refusing a breath specimen or the machine is unreliable, the police may require the person to provide a sample of blood or urine for analysis. If a blood sample is required, it will probably be taken by the police surgeon. It is an offence to refuse to give a sample without good cause.

If the lower of the two readings given by an Intoximeter is over the prescribed limit but under 50 microgrammes of alcohol per 100 millilitres of breath, i e less than 15 microgrammes over, the person will be given the chance to provide a specimen of blood or urine for analysis. If he agrees, the result of the analysis will be used in evidence instead of the reading from the Intoximeter.

Where the police require or allow a person to give a blood or urine sample, it is for them, not for him, to choose whether to take blood or urine. However, if the person has a sound medical objection to giving blood, such as a phobia or haemophilia (it is for a doctor, not the police, to judge whether this is so), he can insist on giving a urine sample. Refusal to give a blood sample after a valid request without a proper excuse is an offence.

If a sample of blood or urine is given, it will be divided into two parts. One will be kept by the police and sent for analysis. The other will be given to the accused so that he can send it for independent analysis. If he is not given part of the sample, the results of the police analysis cannot be used in evidence against him.

(E) Prosecutions based on 'back calculation' evidence. Following a successful prosecution before magistrates in 1986, moves are afoot to prosecute some drivers even if their test results are below the permitted maximum. This is because the test only measures the alcohol which is present in the driver's system at the time of the test. If the police have reason to think that the alcohol level when the driver was actually driving must have been above the limit, but enough alcohol had been broken down by the driver's metabolism before the test to give a result below the limit, they may prosecute. To succeed, the police will need to convince the Court that the driver's metabolism worked to break down the alcohol at a sufficient rate to explain the gap between the legal limit and the test result. The police will use the sort of 'back calculation' evidence referred to in (A) on page 393.

This sort of evidence is usually unreliable, for a very simple reason. Most 'back calculations' are based on statistical tables showing average metabolic rates for people of certain sizes. The actual metabolic rates of individuals vary widely, and can be affected by various factors, including one's state of health. Therefore to prove a case beyond reasonable doubt the police should have to show that the particular defendant's metabolic rate was average at that time, or that the particular defendant (rather than an average person) would almost certainly have broken down alcohol at no less a rate than that on which the calculations are based. A statistical, or balance of probabilities, approach is not a sufficient basis for a criminal conviction. Accordingly it can only be done, scientifically speaking, by testing the particular defendant to establish the rate at which his system absorbs and disposes of a known quantity of alcohol. Such tests would require the active co-operation of the defendant, and the police have no power to compel defendants to co-operate in such tests even if the personnel with the expertise needed to perform them were generally available.

Therefore such prosecutions ought to succeed only in relatively few, very clear, cases.

3. OTHER SPECIFIC MOVING TRAFFIC OFFENCES

(i) Driving Without Reasonable Consideration for Other Road Users
This can include driving that is too slow for the road conditions. The person who thinks he is driving safely by crawling along at 15 mph on the crown of the road in clear visibility is actually annoying all those behind him, especially if the road is one where they cannot pass. Drivers then get frustrated and take risks to pass, making accidents more likely.

(ii) Driving Without Due Care and Attention
The standard of due care and attention is that of the reasonably prudent and skilful driver. This is the commonest of moving traffic charges.

(iii) Reckless Driving and Causing Death by Reckless Driving
Reckless driving is a serious crime, and carries penalties to match. The only difference between it and causing death by reckless driving lies in the consequences: if some person is unfortunate enough to be killed as a result of the driver's gross deviation from normal standards of care, the latter, even more serious, charge will be brought.

Two elements of the offence of reckless driving must be proved to get a conviction. First, the defendant must have been driving in a way which a reasonably prudent person, realising that it created a real risk of serious harmful consequences, would have avoided. Secondly, the defendant must either have failed to consider that very real risk at all, or have thought about it but decided to go ahead regardless.

Conviction is likely to lead to a long period of disqualification and a large fine, or if death or serious injury to anyone results a term of imprisonment is likely.

4. PENALTIES

Fines are a general method of penalising breaches of the criminal law, in motoring cases as in other areas. Another general method, imprisonment, is used only in relation to the more serious motoring crimes: reckless driving, causing death by reckless driving and drink-drive offences. However, there are certain penalties which are peculiar to driving offences and which merit a brief description.

(i) Disqualification
Disqualification can be imposed for a number of offences, including most moving traffic offences. It is mandatory in drink-drive cases, though the Court has a discretion, very rarely exercised, not to order disqualification if there are exceptional circumstances. The circumstances must relate to the circumstances in which the offence was committed, not to any hardship the accused will

suffer from disqualification. If the Court thinks that the accused knew or ought to have known that he had drunk too much, or ought to have been able to avoid driving while affected by drink (for example, by planning ahead or ordering a taxi or an ambulance) they will certainly disqualify the driver. Disqualification is also more or less certain to follow conviction for reckless driving or driving without insurance, and is a distinct possibility for failing to stop after an accident if the driver also fails to report it to the police.

If the Court orders disqualification, the driver will have to surrender his driving licence, which will be returned when the period of disqualification ends. Driving while disqualified is a serious offence, equivalent to driving without a licence.

(ii) Penalty Points
Penalty points are awarded by Courts after conviction for moving traffic offences, unless there are exceptional circumstances relating to the offence which can mitigate its seriousness. No such circumstances are recognised in relation to careless or reckless driving. Penalty points accumulate in the same way as those awarded to footballers. If a driver accumulates twelve points in any three year period, he is automatically disqualified from driving, usually for six months but sometimes for longer. Disqualification can only be avoided by convincing the Court that exceptional hardship exists, for instance because it would lead automatically to the loss of one's job. (However, it could be argued that a person with such a bad driving record ought not to be doing a job that requires him to drive.) To give an idea of the points given for different offences, speeding carries three points, careless driving between two and five depending on the seriousness of the offence, failing to stop after an accident between five and nine and driving without insurance between four and eight.

(iii) Endorsement
After each conviction, the driver's licence is taken away and endorsed by DVLC with the nature of the offence and the number of penalty points

awarded. After four years (a year after the offence ceases to count towards the driver's current total) the offence can be cleaned off one's licence by surrendering it to DVLC and applying for an exchange licence (for a fee of £3). Of course, later convictions will still be shown on the new licence.

If one is disqualified, usually a clean licence is returned when the disqualification ends. However, some endorsements do not get removed: reckless driving offences must remain on the licence for four years, and drink-drive offences and failure to provide a specimen for eleven years from the date of the conviction. If two drink-drive offences are committed within ten years of each other, the offender might not get the licence back at the end of the period of disqualification: in some circumstances he may be required first to undergo a medical examination to see if he has an alcoholism problem.

(iv) Fixed Penalties
Fixed penalties have long been familiar for overstaying one's welcome at a parking meter. Since 1 October 1986, they have been extended to a wide range of offences, including some traffic offences, where the offender admits his guilt and, if the offence carries penalty points, surrenders his licence to be endorsed. Where the offence does not carry penalty points, the sum payable is £12; in other cases it is £24. In each case it is less than the fine would be if the case was contested in Court and ended in conviction. It is wise to pay a fixed penalty promptly on receiving the notice: if the police have to go to Court to collect it, it will be replaced by a fine of 1½ times the amount of the fixed penalty.

The registered keeper of the vehicle is the person principally responsible for paying the fixed penalty. He will be liable, even if he was not driving when the alleged offence took place, unless he completes and returns a statement of ownership and a statement of facts on the notice which the police will send him. He can defend himself in court against liability to pay if he was no longer the owner of the vehicle at the time of the offence, or if he did not commit the offence (either because it was committed by someone else or because no offence was really committed).

1. WHAT TO DO IN THE EVENT OF A BREAKDOWN

Every driver at some time faces the frustration of being in charge of a vehicle which is not working properly. If there is a doubt about whether the vehicle is working properly, get it seen to by a mechanic before using it. The AA and the RAC used not to deal with breakdowns at the member's home, but now they offer a home call-out service in addition to their other services.

Inevitably, though, some breakdowns occur on the road. When that happens, there are a number of points to bear in mind from the legal angle.

(i) Keep the Carriageway Clear

Is the vehicle causing an obstruction or a danger to other road users? If possible, the vehicle must be removed from any place where it does so. At the very least, it should be pushed to the side of the road. If the breakdown occurs on a motorway, you may use the hard shoulder (the extreme left-hand part of the carriageway not used by traffic) if there is one.

(ii) Give Warning

If the vehicle presents a danger and you can do nothing about it, you should take steps to warn approaching traffic. You are permitted to use a red reflective warning triangle to warn other road users. This must be placed at least 50 yards before the obstruction (150 yards if it is on the hard shoulder of a motorway), and should be placed so that it can be seen by drivers before they see the obstruction. For instance, if the breakdown occurs just after a bend, the triangle should be placed before the bend. If the vehicle is fitted with hazard warning lights, switch them on. (Remember to switch them off again when you start moving.)

(iii) Call for Assistance

The horn may be used if necessary to summon assistance. On motorways, telephones are placed at one mile intervals, and posts at the side of the motorway have arrows on them pointing in the direction of the nearest telephone. From there you can call the AA or RAC if you are a member.

If you are not, you can summon the motorway breakdown service, which will make a fairly hefty charge. On other roads, find the nearest telephone. Do not abandon the vehicle overnight or for any extended period without telling the police: they, or the local authority, can tow away a vehicle which is causing an obstruction or appears to have been abandoned, and may charge you for the cost of recovering it.

(iv) Keep Off the Carriageway

It is particularly important to keep passengers, children and animals from wandering on the highway. On motorways, remember that the hard shoulder is part of the road: it is not safe to let anyone wander or stand on it.

2. WHAT TO DO IN THE EVENT OF AN ACCIDENT

There are several desirable steps which are not legal requirements. It is a good idea to have a first aid kit in the car. It is also a good idea to take a first aid course to equip you to deal with accidents: the St John Ambulance Brigade runs courses, and local branches can be contacted through Yellow Pages. The Highway Code has basic tips, as do other publications.

The law requires a number of steps to be taken in the event of an accident.

(i) What Do We Mean By 'Accident'?

An accident here means an event where a motor vehicle is present on a road and the consequences include any of the following:

(a) personal injury is caused to a person other than the driver of that vehicle; this includes injury to drivers or passengers of other vehicles, or passengers in one's own vehicle;

(b) damage is caused to another motor vehicle or a trailer drawn by another motor vehicle, whether it is moving or parked;

(c) damage is caused to an animal in another motor vehicle or trailer; 'animal' for this purpose includes any horse, cattle, ass, mule, sheep, pig, goat or dog. It does not include cats, a matter of great concern to the cat lobby;

(d) damage is caused to any other roadside property, that is anything constructed on, fixed to, growing in or otherwise forming part of the land on or adjacent to which the road is situated.

(ii) What Steps Are Required?

First, *you must stop.* Secondly, there are stipulations about the information that must be given to other people at the scene of the accident, to enable insurers to be contacted and compensation obtained. Thirdly, there are requirements about reporting to the police, and providing them with documents or information. This is both to enable them to establish whether there is any criminal liability arising out of the accident and to help in settling civil claims for compensation.

(A) Stopping. It is a very serious offence not to stop, or to stop and then drive off again, after an accident of the sort described above, and may lead to disqualification.

(B) Information to be given to others at the scene or to the police. There is some information you must provide to anyone at the scene with reasonable grounds for asking for it. Such people obviously include police officers and the drivers of other cars which are involved in the accident, but may also include witnesses. To be safe, you should give the information to anyone who asks for it at the scene: your name and address; the name and address of the owner of the vehicle, if different. If for any reason you do not give your name and address to such a person, for example because nobody is around when you have a collision with a parked car or a goat, you must report the accident in person to the police as soon as practicable, and must in any case report it within 24 hours.

If anyone is injured, you must also produce a certificate of insurance to a police officer and to anyone else who requires to see it and has reasonable cause for doing so. If you are unable to do so, you commit an offence unless you report the accident in person to the police as soon as possible, and in any case within 24 hours, and produce your certificate of insurance either when you report the accident or to any police station within five days of making the report. It is a serious offence to drive without insurance, and the certificate of insurance is your evidence that you are insured.

Even if you are not strictly required to do so, it is wise to inform the police whenever you think that somebody might have been injured by an accident.

(a) Giving other information. It is a condition of insurance policies that the insured neither admits liability nor offers compensation without the consent of the insurance company. This is to prevent the company being saddled with a liability which they would not otherwise have had to bear. There is a risk that an insured person could collude with someone to defraud the company by accepting liability for an accident which he was not really responsible for, in order to get money out of the company which is not really due. It is therefore important not to say anything which could be construed as an admission of liability or an offer of compensation. Your insurer should be informed of anything you or anyone else says at the scene of the accident.

The effect of admitting liability after an accident without the insurer's consent is as follows. The insurance company will still be liable to pay out any damages the victim can claim against you as a result of the accident, but will then be able to reclaim the amount paid out from you. This is in effect a breach of contract action: you broke your contract with the insurer by improperly admitting liability without the insurer's consent. Your policy will then have benefited the victim, who will have his damages, but will not have helped you: you may well end up being driven into bankruptcy by your own insurance company.

(b) Informing your insurer. You should inform your insurer of anything that happens that might lead to a claim being made. Many insurance companies provide with the policy documents a form with a check list of questions, answers to which may be noted down at the time. This serves as an *aide-mémoire* and, if kept in the car, is useful for drawing a sketch map of the area, noting who said and did what, listing the names and addresses of other drivers and their insurers and of witnesses, and the registration marks of the vehicles involved. You should also make a note of the name, number and police station of any police officer who is at the scene.

It is a condition of insurance policies that the insurer must be informed *immediately* of any accident, claim or proceedings against the insured. The effect of failure to do so is the same as the effect of an unauthorised admission of liability, on which see above. Further information about insurance is provided in 7.5, opposite.

This section deals with civil (i e non-criminal) liability to compensate victims of accidents for damage or injuries received. It is a general principle of English law that fault must be proved, in the form of negligence, before any person (or any insurer) can be made liable for injury to another person.

1. LIABILITY FOR PERSONAL INJURY

(i) Negligence

The law requires all road users to observe a certain standard of care. The duty to observe that standard is owed to all those who it could reasonably be foreseen might be injured in the event of an accident caused by lack of care. That means that road users owe duties to each other, and to those whose property adjoins the road. If someone fails to observe the proper standard of care, and one of the people to whom the duty is owed suffers injury or damage to property as a reasonably foreseeable consequence of that failure, the person who fell below the required standard is said by lawyers to have been 'negligent'. He (and through him, his insurers) are then liable to compensate the victim for the reasonably forseeable loss or damage.

The standard of care that is expected of road users is a commonsense standard. All road users, and particularly drivers, are expected to exercise reasonable care. This is in some ways a flexible standard. Drivers must act in the way that a reasonably careful driver would behave in all the circumstances. They are not expected to be infallible. A momentary error of judgment in a crisis will not be negligent, if any reasonable driver could have done what the defendant did. It depends on the circumstances, and the driver is not expected to do what only an unusually skilful driver could have done.

On the other hand, the standard of conduct does not vary with the ability of the particular driver. The Highway Code is evidence of what a reasonably careful and skilful driver can be expected to do, in the absence of extraordinary circumstances. Thus a driver who crashes in icy conditions is negligent if at the time he was going faster than was wise in the conditions; a learner driver is subject to the same standards as reasonably experienced drivers for the purpose of liability; someone who is driving badly because he is ill cannot use his illness as an excuse (indeed it might be negligent to drive while ill). It is what lawyers refer to as an 'objective' standard, i e one that is not moulded to the individual defendant but is set by reference to road users as a group. There is no reason why someone knocked down on the road should fail to get compensation just because the person responsible was and had always been unusually incompetent.

A breach of one of the statutory duties imposed on a driver, for example exceeding the speed limit or driving while under the influence of drink or drugs, does not necessarily lead to liability if someone happens to be injured while the driver is speeding or drunk. The question will still be (i) whether the driver was negligent (failing to observe an ordinary standard of care) and if so (ii) did the negligence cause the injury? However, breach of a statutory duty, like breach of a Highway Code rule, is evidence, and sometimes strong evidence, in relation to (i).

Where the defendant was driving with proper care, but the condition of the vehicle was defective and that caused the accident, the driver may be liable if it can be shown that a reasonably careful driver would have checked for and corrected the defect. For example, a driver towing a caravan who failed to lock the caravan properly on to the towing mechanism will be held to be negligent if the caravan escapes and causes damage or injury. However, if the defect was one which only an expert mechanic could reasonably have discovered, the driver probably will not be liable. If the vehicle had just been serviced and was returned with a defect which the mechanic ought to have discovered and corrected during the service, the mechanic may be liable in negligence if the defect was the cause of the accident.

(ii) Contributory Negligence

Even if the defendant can be shown to have caused the accident by failure to take reasonable care, he may argue that the damage was partly the result of the plaintiff's failure to take proper care for himself. This is called 'contributory negligence.' If that is established, the judge will work out (on a fairly rough and ready basis) what proportion of the blame for the particular injuries suffered is attributable to the plaintiff himself, and will reduce the damages accordingly.

For example, it has been well established that wearing seatbelts substantially reduces the risk of death or serious injury in an accident. Where a front seat passenger in a car is thrown through the windscreen and sustains injuries as the result of the driver's negligence, his compensation will be reduced by 25% if a seatbelt was fitted and he was not wearing it. On the other hand, if a motorcyclist is not wearing a crash helmet when he is knocked off his motorcycle and breaks a leg, the failure to wear a helmet will not affect his damages, as he would have broken a leg even if he had worn one.

(iii) Plaintiff's Duty to Limit His Loss

As well as contributory negligence, the plaintiff may not recover all his losses after the accident if he has not acted as a reasonably prudent person would have done in order to limit the extent of his loss. He cannot expect to be compensated for losses, even if they flow more or less directly from the accident, if he could reasonably have prevented them. He has what lawyers refer to as a 'duty to mitigate the damage'. For example, a person will be expected to consent to ordinary medical treatment which is available to improve his condition. On the other hand, he is not expected to accept any treatment whatever that might conceivably help. He would not act unreasonably, for instance, if he refused to consent to potentially hazardous surgery where the chances of benefit did not clearly outweigh the risks. Nobody is expected to put his life at risk to reduce the plaintiff's (or the insurer's) bill.

(iv) Negligence of Several Defendants

Where damage or injury is caused to X by reason of the combined negligence of Y and Z, X can claim from Y and Z, who are what are called 'joint tortfeasors'. X can collect his damages from either Y or Z, but if X sues Y, then Y can bring in Z as a co-defendant. In that case, the judge will decide on the damages to be paid to X, and Y and Z will be required to contribute according to the proportion of the blame that each is held to bear.

2. LIABILITY FOR DAMAGE TO PROPERTY

Liability for damage to property is decided in exactly the same way as that for personal injury,

on general principles of the law of negligence, tempered by the rules on contributory negligence and mitigation of damage. In relation to mitigation, it should be noted that it will not usually be considered reasonable to repair an article if it would be cheaper to write it off and replace it. However, there are circumstances where it will be considered reasonable to repair even then, and full compensation will be payable by the defendant. Examples are where a unique car is badly damaged, so that it could not be properly replaced, or where a family pet is injured and the veterinary bills exceed the market value of the pet. English law has too much feeling for animals to require a pet owner to have his dog destroyed when it could be saved at a price. As long as the plaintiff acts reasonably he can hire a car to replace the damaged one while it is being repaired; he can reclaim as damages from the defendant the reasonable cost of hiring for a reasonable time. If the plaintiff's car is a 'right-off', he will normally be able to recover the value of the car from the defendant.

3. LIABILITY OF HIGHWAY AUTHORITIES

Highway authorities are under a statutory duty to maintain roads. If damage results to a road user from the authority's failure to maintain them in a proper condition, damages can be recovered from the authority.

Highway authorities are liable to be sued for negligence in their provisions for road safety. However, their duty is not very extensive: it amounts to a duty give proper consideration to dangers and decide what can reasonably be done to alleviate them.

Three examples will illustrate the effect of this. In one case, *Allison v Corby District Council* (1979), a motorcyclist was killed when five uncontrolled dogs ran into the road in front of him. The judge decided that the authority had taken reasonable steps to prevent this, by appointing a dog-catcher, requiring all dogs on roads to be kept on leashes and putting up signs telling owners to keep dogs on leashes. They were therefore not negligent; neither were they in breach of their duty to maintain the road, because the danger caused by dogs was transient and did not amount to a failure to maintain the road. In *Bartlett v Department of Transport* (1985) it was decided that the Department was not in breach of its duty to maintain the road when a strike of workmen meant that an icy stretch on the A34 could not be gritted or salted and a fatal accident resulted. In *West v Buckinghamshire County Council* (1984) someone was killed while overtaking on a road where the council had decided not to put down double white lines. The Court decided that the council was not liable to pay compensation for the accident, because road markings were a matter for the council's discretion, and it owed no duty to any particular plaintiff.

It would seem that the position might be different if the highway authority actually creates a danger by negligent design of a road or junction system. However, no authority appears yet to have been successfully sued in England for negligence in road design.

4. MAKING CLAIMS ON THE INSURER

If there is an accident, the insurer must be informed at once. A motorist's insurer is acting for itself, not solely for the motorist. Of course, the interests of the insurer will usually overlap those of the insured motorist: if the motorist is held liable to pay damages to somebody else, the damages will actually be paid by the insurer, so it is in the insurer's interest to contest the motorist's liability. Because of this, the insurer is likely to pay for legal advice, and may well be obliged to do so under the policy. If the insurer pays for the defence, it effectively runs the defence. It can dictate to the motorist whether to fight or settle. This can impose quite a burden on the motorist, who may well want to settle the matter as quickly as possible and forget about it but be forced to go through lengthy litigation. Insurers are not benevolence institutions: they are there to pay out on legal liabilities, but owe duties to shareholders and other policyholders not to pay out unnecessarily.

If one insured motorist makes a claim against another arising from an accident, the insurance companies fight it out. However, where there are not vast sums involved and it would be expensive for the companies to dispute liability, insurance companies operate what are known as 'knock for knock' agreements, under which each company pays for the damage sustained by its own insured and does not try to establish that the other party is liable. This can present a number of problems for the insured motorists. The main problem is that each will be treated as having made a claim

on his own insurers for his damage. He will therefore be liable to lose his no claim discount and have no control over the insurer's decision.

A further problem in that situation relates to the motorist's own damage excess. If he has agreed with the insurer to pay the first £50, say, of the damage to his own vehicle, the money he receives from his own company acting under a knock for knock agreement will not cover that first £50. If he thinks the other driver was responsible, he will have to claim the money directly from the other driver without his insurer's assistance. A motorist may face a similar problem in deciding whether to try to recover damages from an uninsured person such as a pedal cyclist or a dog owner who causes an accident. The motoring organisations offer their members legal advice but in difficult cases, it is usually worth taking legal advice from a solicitor.

5. UNINSURED DRIVERS

Where damage is caused by a driver who has a legal obligation to take out third party insurance but is actually not insured for some reason, the Motor Insurers Bureau has an agreement with the Secretary of State for the Environment to satisfy any unsatisfied judgment given against the uninsured driver. This is done out of a fund maintained by the MIB with funds provided by its members, the insurance companies. Often the MIB will settle the claim to keep costs down. They may then try to reimburse themselves from the guilty driver. The advantage for the victim is that he knows he will be paid out of the fund, when the individual defendant might not have enough money to pay damages. Unfortunately the MIB has no role where the person responsible for a road accident had no legal obligation to be insured, as where the accident was caused by a negligent dog owner, pedal cyclist or pedestrian. In such cases it is usually not worth suing, unless the defendant is wealthy enough to pay up.

6. DISPUTES WITH INSURERS

Insurance policies often contain an arbitration clause, requiring any dispute between the insurer and the insured to be submitted to arbitration rather than to the Courts. Where there is a dispute with the insurers, it is usually worth obtaining advice from a solicitor, as insurance law is very complicated.

7.6 SPECIAL RULES RELATING TO CARAVANS AND TRAILERS

Caravans, or living vans, designed to be drawn behind a car are particular examples of trailers and are generally subject to the same rules as trailers.

All trailers must have pneumatic tyres which comply with the usual tyre requirements. They must carry a registration plate of the usual sort, which must have the same registration mark as the drawing vehicle. They must have rear lights which satisfy the requirements for the rear lights of a motor car (stop lights, indicators, reversing lights, fog lights, reflectors). They must work directly off the lighting system of the drawing vehicle, so that the indicators on the trailer flash at exactly the same time as those on the car. Trailers must also have a braking system connected to the car's braking system (virtually always the footbrake) if the trailer has a maximum design gross weight (i e it was designed to weigh when fully laden to the manufacturer's specification over 750 kilograms, about 1654 lbs). Trailers over 5 metres long must have side-facing amber reflectors on each side, according to an internationally approved design.

Trailers over 1020 kilograms undergo a plating examination, where the vehicle is weighed and its weight recorded on a metal plate, and a roadworthiness inspection. The weight plate is then attached to the nearside of the trailer, and a certificate of roadworthiness is issued if appropriate. This happens twelve months after being supplied by the retailer, and the roadworthiness test must be repeated every twelve months.

Special speed limits apply to trailers, more restrictive than those which apply to cars or motorcycles. The maximum speed that a vehicle and trailer, including a caravan, can do on any road, including motorways, is 40 mph, unless it complies with four conditions. They are:

(i) the kerbside (unladen) weight of the drawing vehicle is marked either on the inside or the outside nearside of the vehicle;

(ii) the maximum gross weight of the trailer or caravan is marked on its nearside;

(iii) the trailer or caravan carries a '50' plate on the rear;

(iv) if the trailer or caravan has brakes linked to the footbrake on the drawing vehicle, the maximum gross weight of the trailer or caravan does not exceed the kerbside weight of the drawing vehicle; or if it is an unbraked goods trailer, its laden weight, or, in the case of any other unbraked trailer, its maximum design gross weight, does not exceed 60% of the kerbside weight of the drawing vehicle.

If all four of those conditions are met, the maximum speed on any road is 50 mph.

Nobody may be carried in a caravan in motion which has less than four wheels.

When travelling abroad with a motor vehicle it is important to bear in mind that motoring law in the country you are visiting is likely to be different in many respects from English law. Very often they have more stringent requirements about the state of the vehicle and drivers' ages. It is important to establish well in advance what these are, and whether they apply to visiting vehicles and drivers.

Find out about rules of the road and road signs in the countries you are visiting and familiarise yourself with them. Some may seem very strange: for instance, in some countries like France there are roads where priority is given not to vehicles already on the road but to vehicles joining the road at junctions. Not knowing what is expected can cause chaos, be very embarrassing and, more seriously still, land one in very serious trouble, especially with the authorities.

Vehicles going abroad must carry 'GB' plates on the rear of the vehicle. These can be obtained from the motoring organisations, ferry companies and elsewhere.

There are four matters which need to be thought about well in advance, because they can take some time to organise.

(i) Insurance

Most insurance policies cover vehicles for use in the United Kingdom and Republic of Ireland. If you are going elsewhere you will need to get extended cover, for which you will have to pay. You must be insured to comply with the requirements of the country you are visiting. Under international agreements, a Green Card, issued by the Motor Insurers Bureau through your own insurance company, is accepted as evidence that you are insured to meet the requirements of host countries. The Green Card is, in effect, a valid certificate of third party insurance in the countries for which it is issued.

To obtain one, complete an application form and sent it to your insurer. You will be informed of the premium payable, and on payment the Green Card will be issued to you. You should allow at least a month for the card to reach you. Carry it with you when you go.

An application for a Green Card is an insurance proposal, and the duty of full disclosure of all material facts applies to it as to any other insurance proposal: see under heading Motor Insurance, in 7.2, on page 377.

(ii) Bail Bonds

Everyone hopes to have a trouble free holiday, and the vast majority of travellers do. However, if you do get into difficulties you may find it more difficult to get out of the country than to get in. A motor accident may lead to you and your vehicle being detained, either to face criminal charges or as security for damages or costs that may be awarded against you in civil proceedings. This may happen even if you were not at fault. This is particularly likely in Spain.

Because of this, to motor in Spain you are required to be in possession of a bail bond as well as a Green Card. The bail bond is a letter from your insurance company guaranteeing that it will be responsible for payments up to a stated sum (usually £1,000) to enable you and your vehicle to be released and return home. You will then be able to provide security for your bail without having to produce the cash there and then. Insurance companies sometimes require an undertaking by you to indemnify the company for any amounts it has to pay out.

You should arrange a bail bond well before you leave England.

(iii) Tyres and Lights

Check well in advance that your tyres and lights satisfy the local requirements of your destination, so that you can have them adjusted if necessary. Any country where traffic drives on the right will require you to have your headlights adjusted, as a normal UK dipping mechanism will only serve to shine the headlights into the eyes of oncoming drivers there. Special covers are available to correct this: consult your motoring organisation, dealer or mechanic for details.

(iv) International Driving Permits

International driving permits have been described on page 376. They are useful for a driver who has passed a test but does not hold a current UK licence and who wants to drive while abroad for a limited time without obtaining a full UK licence.

SECTION 8
THE LAW AND YOUR LEISURE

1. INTRODUCTION

Historians have traced the habit of gambling back to the dawn of human history. The desire to stake money on the uncertain outcome of a future event beyond the participant's direct control is clearly a deep-rooted one. What is also clear is that laws to restrict control or even prohibit forms of gambling have an equally ancient lineage.

The justifications put forward for some legal limitations on gambling activity vary from the moral, through the practical, to social and economic reasons. Despite the absence of any Biblical injunction against gambling, the Church has always regarded the idea of making profit out of the inevitable loss and suffering to others as the antithesis of love of one's neighbour. Even putting aside religious considerations, political leaders usually speak of gambling in disapproving tones – like Disraeli's description of it as 'a vast engine of demoralization', or the young Harold Wilson's description of Premium Bonds as a 'squalid raffle'. More practical reasons motivated the Unlawful Games Act 1541 – there the object was to enable archery to be practised more regularly.

The present legal rules relating to betting, gaming and lotteries no longer seek to direct potential gamblers towards alternative pursuits. Though some would still detect in the legal rules some elements of moral disapproval of the activity, the aim of the law today (it is said) is to interfere as little as possible with individual liberty to take part in the various forms of gambling, but to impose some restrictions to discourage excess, and to ensure that the participants in gambling, (be it football pools, betting, gaming or lotteries) are not defrauded. Regulation of gambling also assists in the task of ensuring that gambling does not become an inordinate source of profit for criminal elements in society; the cynic would add that such regulation also allows the State to take its share of the profit in the form of taxes or duties.

2. SOME BASIC PRINCIPLES

(i) Gambling Activities Which Are Subject to Control

Gambling may be taken to mean betting on a future event or the placing of stakes in money on such future event the outcome of which is uncertain and beyond the direct power or control of the person making the bet. Such a wide definition might include investment on the Stock Exchange or certain items of insurance – but in such circumstances any gambling element is marginal and subsidiary to the activity's main aims. The law is also not concerned with private domestic gambling: it is when a commercial operator is involved seeking to make a profit from the activity that the law steps in to control and regulate.

There are three main activities subject to control and the rules regulating each differ.

(A) Gaming: This is now defined as 'the playing of a game of chance for winnings in money or money's worth' and will include games such as poker and pontoon, roulette and baccarat. There are special rules for some games, such as bingo, and lotteries and football pools are excluded from gaming control and also have separate regulation.

(B) Betting: A bet is the staking of money (or other value) on an event of a doubtful issue and, for the present law, includes:–

(a) Betting on horse or dog races, including totalisator transactions;

(b) A bet with a registered pool promoter;

(c) A wager, which is a contract between two people on the outcome of a future uncertain event (or on a past event the result of which is not known). A wager will therefore include a bet on the result of the next General Election, whether it is with your friend or at your local bookmakers. The essential feature of a wager is that either side may either win or lose.

(C) Lotteries: A lottery is the distribution of prizes by lot or chance *and* the chance of winning must be secured by a payment by the participant. All such lotteries are unlawful unless conducted under the provisions of the relevant Act.

Although it will be convenient to look at each area of gambling activity in turn, it is important to note that the legal definitions are not precise. As a judge once remarked, Parliament has found it impossible to keep up with the enormous variety of gambling activities which has arisen from the ingenuity of gamblers and those who try to exploit them. Consequently, the legislation gives a general indication of the activity that is controlled and leaves detailed interpretation to the courts, often in the guise of local magistrates. There is also overlap between the three main areas set out above – for example, certain pool promoters, although their activity is deemed to be the taking of bets, can acquire licences from the Gaming Board of Great Britain.

(ii) Illegality and Unenforceability

The distinction between *illegality* and *unenforceability* also needs to be stressed. Some forms of

---

Premium Bonds

Premiums Bonds are the closest thing that we have to a national lottery at present. Few people would regard it as gambling, let alone a leisure activity, yet it is undoubtedly a flutter with the interest you would otherwise earn on your investment.

The sale of premium bonds is one way that the Government borrows money. The capital which you put in is safe; £5 of bonds can be cashed at any time for £5. In effect, however, the interest is gambled; all the interest earned by these bonds goes into regular draws for prizes. The chance of winning is over 100,000 to 1 against. At present:

(1) The minimum purchase is £10, and in £5 units thereafter.

(2) Bonds must be held for three months before inclusion in a draw.

(3) There are weekly draws for prizes up to £100,000; and a monthly draw including a £250,000 prize. Currently, about £11 million is paid in total prizes each month.

(4) The maximum bond holding is £10,000 for each person.

---

gambling are inherently unlawful and penalties may be applied if they occur: lotteries which fall outside the statutory scheme and unlicensed gaming will be illegal in this sense. By way of contrast, most bets and wagers are not illegal, but the contract of gaming or wagering which comes into being when two parties agree on a bet is, and has been since 1845, void and unenforceable. Thus you can quite lawfully bet with your friend or bookmaker, but you cannot sue in a Court to recover the winnings due to you if he fails to pay up. Not all betting comes within this definition of a 'wagering contract'; bets with a totalisator or on the football pools are different because the tote or pools promoter cannot lose but will take a specified proportion of the monies received as expenses or profit. In this case, therefore, the activity is both legal, and enforceable. This means that if the Totalisator Board allow you to have a credit account and you fail to pay the bill, they can bring a legal action to recover the money due.

In practice, the wagering contract principle is not a problem, and failure to pay by a bookmaker is unlikely to occur on a valid bet (though the validity of the bet may be disputed!). A bookie who did fail to pay might well be expelled from the National Association of Bookmakers and would find renewal of his licence to operate virtually impossible.

(iii) The Systems of Control

The principal system of control is by means of licensing. *Licences* will be necessary for betting shops and to permit gaming in clubs, and are also required for all racing tracks except horse racecourses with a certificate of approval from the Horserace Betting Levy Board. Where the gambling is not done at particular premises, *registration* is usually required. Pools promoters and societies promoting public lotteries must be registered with the appropriate local authorities.

Detailed *Regulations* and *Rules*, some contained in Acts of Parliament, others in secondary legislation made by a Minister, provide the framework within which the various gambling activities operate. The result is a system of some complexity, notwithstanding the attempts to rationalize and liberalize the law in 1960. It is only possible to give a general outline of the regime to which the different gambling activities are subject. Persons seeking to apply for any licence would be well advised to seek legal advice at an early stage.

3. BETTING

(i) Off Course Betting

(A) Some prohibitions. Off course betting has been permitted in licensed betting offices since 1960, but outside betting shops clear prohibitions remain. Thus:

(1) It is an offence to use any premises for the purposes of betting unless the premises are licensed, or are an approved horse racecourse or licensed track – maximum fine on 'standard scale' 3, currently £400.

(2) It is an offence to use any street or public place, or to loiter in streets, for the purposes of betting, book making or receiving or settling bets. Maximum fine here not exceeding standard scale 4, currently £1,000. 'Street or public place' will include any place to which the public has access and will include, for example, subways, alleys, even a railway carriage while being used for carrying passengers. Doorways and entrances of premises are included too if they abut onto a street.

(3) Betting with a person under the age of 18 continues to be prohibited, provided the young person is 'apparently' under 18 or the offender knows or ought to know that person is under age. Maximum penalty here is on the level of standard scale 5, currently £2,000.

These restrictions mean that, effectively, the only legal off course betting allowed is either in or through licensed betting shops, or by post, since the sending of ready money bets in the mail has been lawful since 1960.

(B) Betting shop licensing. A betting shop can only operate lawfully if it is granted a betting office licence, which is subject to annual renewal. Application is made to the betting licensing committee of the local magistrates; and only the Totalisator Board, the holder of a bookmakers permit, or a person accredited by a bookmaker and the holder of a betting agency permit can apply for a licence. Application must be in a specified form with notice being given to the chief officer of police, the local authority and the local Customs and Excise Office. The application must be advertised in a local newspaper allowing fourteen days for objections to be sent to the clerk to the justices. Notices must be posted outside the proposed premises for the two week minimum period.

At the hearing of the licensing application objectors may be heard; the license can be granted or refused after the hearing of the evidence. In a few circumstances the application must be refused (for example, if the premises are not enclosed; there are more general grounds of 'Unsuitability of the premises' or 'inexpediency' on which the licence may, in the magistrate's discretion, be refused. If, for example, the magistrates consider that there are already sufficient betting shops to meet the demand, they could decline to grant a licence. It should be noted that planning permission for a betting shop will be required before an application for a licence can proceed.

There is a right of appeal against the refusal to grant a licence. The reasons for which a renewal of a licence can be refused are the same as those which apply to the original grant of a licence.

(C) Management of betting shops. Since their establishment in 1960, there have always been rules regulating the internal management of betting shops. Until recently, the prohibition of advertising outside a betting shop and restrictions on the provision of television broadcasts and refreshments meant the betting shop was an austere place. As a judge remarked, the clear intention of Parliament was that these establishments should be difficult to find and, when found, should be internally as dreary as possible. Recently however, (1984) the statute was amended to allow the Secretary of State to make regulations permitting the provision of refreshments (but no alcoholic liquor) and allow the broadcasting of live sound and television transmissions or video recordings. These fresh regulations were brought into force in early 1986. Detailed restrictions still remain however. A betting shop cannot open on Sundays, Good Friday or Christmas Day and on other days cannot open before 7 a m and must close before 6.30 p m. The proprietor's betting office licence, his rules of betting and a notice prohibiting the admission of persons under the age of eighteen must all be clearly displayed. There are still strict limits on advertising the business outside the premises, though the latest regulations give a slightly greater degree of freedom and the old prohibition on the display of other written advertisements and signs no longer applies. Patrons of a betting office cannot be encouraged to bet either by the proprietor or any one acting on his behalf.

(ii) On Course Betting – Horseracing

On course betting, which in terms of money

staked means mainly horseracing and dogtracks, has a long social history. Such activity (especially in the case of horseracing) has not attracted the same opposition or restriction in the past as other forms of gambling. This may in part be due to the participation by all sections of society. Certainly the breeding and training of good horses was once a vital military and economic activity to which horse racing – and consequent betting – was a logical consequence. Now horse racing is a premier sporting activity despite the demise of the horse in a mechanised and technological society, and the patronage of racing by the Royal Family by the training of horses and attendance, ensures a status for horse racing unequalled for other forms of gambling.

When the law relating to betting and gaming was radically overhauled in 1960, organised horse racing was largely excluded from the provisions of the legislation relating to betting. This does not mean, however, that there is no control – quite the contrary.

First, though any horserace is lawful in itself, the legal restrictions preventing the use of premises for betting or bookmaking on racecourses will apply *unless* the racecourse is an 'approved race course' used on the day in question solely for horseracing. Such approval is only given if a certificate is issued by the Horserace Betting Levy Board (The 'HBLB'). Secondly, in practice all such approved race courses are under the effective control of the Jockey Club, which has been incorporated by royal charter. Exclusion from the more general rules of control was therefore allowed because it was thought that the control which the Jockey Club has long exercised (formerly in association with the National Hunt Committee) was adequate to ensure the good management of racecourses.

A further reason that horse racing and its attendant gambling has always escaped from close restriction is that it is, by its nature, an occasional rather than a regular activity. In its detailed rules for the management of courses, the Jockey Club does have powers to limit the number of race meetings – and bookmakers and the public makers of bets are both subject to the discipline of the club and what is called the 'Committee of Tattersalls'. This is a semi-official body dealing with betting disputes. Its decisions are invariably observed, even though not enforceable by Court action.

A punter at a racecourse will have the choice of two main forms of betting, (i) with a bookmaker offering known odds; or (ii) with the 'tote' – the totalisator pool organised by the Horserace Totalisator Board (the 'HTB'). A bookie's odds will, of course, fluctuate from time to time in response to the support – or lack of it – for a particular runner. The punter will know in advance from the odds offered and accepted the amount he can expect in the event of a win.

The tote is a form of pool betting (see below) under the exclusive control of the HTB in which all money staked on the various chances is accumulated; and after the race there will be a specified deduction for expenses and the levy and the balance is shared among the winning tickets. The punter will not know the final odds until the time for bets to close. On the face of it, the tote looks 'safer' in that it does not qualify as a 'gaming contract', discussed above, and is therefore enforceable. In practice, all bookies will also pay up, for if they fail to do so they may well find themselves excluded from all racecourses under Jockey Club rules for failing to pay or settle betting losses.

The Horserace Betting Levy Board imposes a levy on bookmakers and the tote (via the HTB): and the money so collected is devoted to the advancement and improvement of horse breeding and racing. Through this levy, the HBLB has a measure of control over horseracing in general.

(iii) On Course Betting – Dog Racing and Other Licensed Tracks

Apart from horseracing, on course betting can only take place at a 'licensed track': though this will include both betting at donkey derbies and (at the other end of social acceptability) hare coursing, in practice the rules are only relevant to dog tracks. Indeed, when compared with horseracing, (in terms of money staked on off course betting, if not in television coverage) greyhound racing might claim to be the premier sport.

The licensing of dog tracks is a function of the relevant local authority; and the exact procedure is a complex one which need not concern us, save to note that, like application for a betting shop licence, plenty of time and a considerable number of notices and advertisements are required and there are provisions for objections to be heard. The licensing authority, in this case, usually a committee of the local council, has a discretion to refuse a licence which is requested. The acquisition of a track licence is likely to be a major undertaking, invariably requiring legal advice and representation; but once granted it remains in force for seven years, unless revoked.

The law prohibits racing on a licensed track on Sundays, Good Friday and Christmas Day; and the former '104 days in the year' limit was raised in 1971 for dog tracks to 130 days in any year. Gambling at such tracks will, as in the case of horseracing be either by a totalisator pool or with a bookmaker:

(1) The licensed dog track operator has the right to install his own tote – a right which is always exercised. The establishment and operation of such a tote is subject to detailed rules; so an accountant and mechanician (this is the word that the statute uses for a technical adviser!) must be appointed to inspect and examine the machine and the accounts to ensure punters are paid their due. In particular, a track operator cannot maximise his tote taking by excluding bookmakers; indeed he is under a duty to admit them and provide space for them to operate. However, the bookmaker's right of entry is not absolute or unlimited. Thus, in one case, the track operator limited the number of bookmakers he would admit to 5 to ensure the economic viability of the track and the Court upheld this limitation.

(2) The track bookmakers must be independent of the track operator – it is an offence for the operator to engage in bookmaking on his own track, and he is limited in the admission charge he can make to such bookies (5 times the charge for public admission).

It follows from the above that betting at the fighting or baiting of any animal (dogs, badgers, bears, cocks or whatever) is unlawful. It may also be an offence of cruelty: badgers are especially protected under the Badgers Act. There are additional offences of holding or attending events where animals are fought or baited.

(iv) Pool Betting, Especially Football Pools

Pool betting has similarities to both bets at fixed odds and lotteries and it is lawful if conducted by registered pools promoters. In commercial terms, pool betting is in practice almost exclusively confined to football pools, but the legislation makes provision for pools betting on other events in addition to football.

The meaning of pool betting can be seen by comparison with betting at fixed odds on the one hand and lotteries on the other:

(A) Any bet which is not a bet at fixed odds will be by way of pool betting. When a bet at fixed odds is made, the punter can know at the time the amount he will win if the bet succeeds (except where the bet is linked, for example, to the odds later offered just before the race begins). In pool betting, however, his winnings (if any) will be a share of the stake money paid and will often be divisible with other persons similarly entitled as winners. Thus eight scoring draws on the pools may produce a jackpot payout for one person: a dozen such draws will see the pool shared among many more winners.

(B) Like a lottery, pool betting is based on the principle that a number of entrants make a stipulated payment in advance. A lottery, however, occurs when the winners are determined by lot or chance, as is the case when a 'Prize Draw' is made. In the case of pools betting, entries comprise a forecast as to the result of sporting or other events. This involves the *possibility* of the exercise of a certain element of skill in forecasting. It is enough that there is that possibility: the fact that many pools entrants have a fixed forecast each week, or choose their numbers in a random way does not invalidate a pool or turn it into a lottery.

The law requires a commercial pools promoter to be registered with the local authority of the area where the business is situated; and the following requirements must be complied with:

(a) The business must be in the form of competitions for prizes for making forecasts as to sporting or other events. 'Other events' might include the movement of stocks and shares, and at the time of writing an organisation called 'City pools' has achieved registration in East Yorkshire for such forecasts.

(b) Each bet must be an entry into a particular competition.

(c) The stakes and the winnings must be paid wholly in money.

(d) In each competition, the prizes must be equally available for all the bets, so that the question of which bet qualifies for the prize or prizes shall be determined solely by the relative success and accuracy of the forecast made. An entrant who wins but stakes twice as much as a similar winner will achieve twice as much by way of winnings.

(e) The total amount payable by way of

winnings shall be the total amount of the stakes in that competition, less only pool betting duty and a percentage previously determined (and notified to the accountant) which is the same for all the competitions on the same day.

Notwithstanding these basic principles, the rules of any competition may provide for slight variations, so it is wise to check the rules applicable to any competition you enter. In particular rules can provide:

(i) that winnings shall not, in the case of any bet, exceed a stated amount with the excess being shared for bets qualifying in other prizes;

(ii) that in specified circumstances one or more of the prizes shall not be paid and the amount that would have been payable to be applied to increasing the amount payable to winning bets qualifying for another prize and other prizes in that competition;

(iii) for the winnings of winning bets to be increased or decreased by not more than three pence provided this is with a view to facilitating payment;

(iv) most importantly, a rule of a pools competition which completely excludes legal liability on behalf of the pools promoter has been upheld in an old case and this rule is accepted as applying to current legislation. This means, of course, that where such a rule applies you cannot sue your pools promoter in a Court for winnings you allege to be due to you. All football pools contain this 'honour clause' (which states that the transaction is binding in honour only); but the Pools Promoters Association have a procedure to investigate any claim of failure to pay or alleged irregularities: a successful complainant will be paid what he should have won.

The law requires the appointment of an independent qualified accountant which helps to ensure equitable distribution and to minimise any possibility of the insertion or substitution of coupons after the results have been made known.

If you are sending in a pools coupon, first make sure that:

1. You complete the form clearly and correctly;
2. You sign it;
3. You post it in good time. Late entries will be rejected. The Post Office is protected against claims for delayed delivery and it is no use proving you posted it. Delivery is required.

4. The alternative to posting is the collection system used by 90% of entrants. The use of collectors is supervised by the pools companies. The coupons state that the collectors are the agents of the punters, not the companies. This means that you cannot sue the company if the collector fails to ensure that your entry arrives in time. You could sue the collector if he has deprived you of a win, but he may not have the means to pay. This 'agency' clause has not been tested in the Courts; if it were, it seems likely to be upheld.

Two other forms of pool betting may be encountered:

(1) Pool betting may be conducted on race days by the Horserace Totalisator Board or by their authority at horseracing, or by the occupier of a track on a dog racecourse.

(2) Charity Pool Competitions: a registered pools promoter who obtains a certificate from the Gaming Board (he must satisfy them that he has held at least nine competitions for the financial benefit of a charitable, cultural, sporting or non commercial society), may be licensed by the board to hold pool competitions for prizes. This provision was passed to cover competitions where the vast majority of the entrants do not make forecasts of their own. A Court decision in 1971 held such pool betting to be a lottery, and therefore subject to lottery rules; this provision allows such licensed competition to continue as pool betting.

4. GAMING

(i) General Principles

Gaming is the staking of money in a game of chance with other players. Since 1960, the playing of any such game is not in itself unlawful, but three types of game can only be played in licensed or registered premises. They are games:

(1) which involve playing or staking against a bank (whether or not the bank is held by one of the players); or
(2) where the chances in the game are not equally favourable to all players; or
(3) where the chances lie between the player or players and some other person who is not playing, and the chances between the players and the outsider are unequal.

411

These rules mean that games such as whist and bridge are quite lawful, since all players have an equal chance; but pontoon or roulette are only lawful in licensed premises.

Generally, outside licensed premises:

It is unlawful to take part in any gaming in a street or public place;

It is unlawful to make a charge for participation in a game, whether by way of a levy on the stakes or the winnings. Club subscriptions are excluded.

Two important principles maintain and uphold social tradition, so that gaming in your own home (defined as 'taking place on a domestic occasion in a private dwelling') or hostel or hall of residence is lawful – but don't charge for entry! The second exception maintains an ancient practice, so that the playing of dominoes or cribbage in public houses is permitted provided all participants are over eighteen; and gambling linked to games of skill (darts or shove ha'penny) is not caught by the legislation.

(ii) Gaming in a Casino

Casinos were permitted in 1960, and the next eight years saw an uncontrolled expansion of the activity; in 1968, a further Gaming Act sought to prevent exploitation and provide a framework for gaming in an orderly manner free from intrusion from undesirable elements. The work of the Gaming Board since 1968 has largely achieved those objectives. The number of casinos and gaming clubs is small, 121 in 1976 and 115 on 1 January 1986, compared to over 1,200 in the mid 1960s, and less than one person in every thousand will visit a casino regularly. In 1985, 1.6 billion pounds was taken as 'Drop money' (money exchanged for chips) in casinos; though much of this will be returned as winnings, it is instructive to compare this figure with the £496 million staked at bingo. It is therefore by far and away the most expensive form of gambling in which to participate because a roulette table can turn nearly every minute, perhaps with a minimum £5 (or more) stake each time.

The operation, management and profits of casino operators are closely controlled by both the law and the Gaming Board.

Gaming licences must be obtained – these are granted by local licencing magistrates on an annual basis. For both first applications and renewals, notices must be served with advertisements in the local press. Objections can be sent to the justices clerk and objectors have a right to be heard when the application is considered. Until recently, gaming licence applications were heard only in May of each year; now they can be heard at any time of the year. There are many grounds on which a gaming licence can be refused – particularly, the licencing justices must be satisfied there is substantial unsatisfied demand; the premises must be suitable; and noise, nuisance, lack of parking facilities or inadequate fire precautions are all reasons which might be used to reject an application. If a licence is granted, conditions or restrictions can be imposed.

Obtaining a licence is insufficient in itself – the *Gaming Board* has concurrent powers. So before application for a licence can be made, a certificate from the Gaming Board is required. Such certificates are only given if the board approves. Though the board has to act fairly, it does not have to give reasons for refusing consent. The board will retain oversight of a casino which has been granted its certificate and licence through its full time inspectors (paid out of a levy on the casinos) who have wide powers of entry and inspection. The certificate can be withdrawn by the board but only on specified grounds, e g it finds it was given wrong information. If the board is dissatisfied on other grounds, it can object to renewal of the licence.

In general, the principle underlying these rules is that facilities should be sufficient to satisfy unstimulated demand for gaming – but no more. Various rules buttress this idea:

(a) *Permitted areas:* Casinos cannot get a certificate or licence for a location outside a permitted area – largely big towns or holiday resorts.

(b) *The 48 hour rule:* Members of a casino can only take part in gaming if they were admitted to membership more than 48 hours previously after a personal application. The idea is to prevent entry on an impulse – personal application and a two day wait are needed. *Bona fide* guests of existing members are however allowed to participate.

(c) *Live entertainment* in the form of musicians, cabaret or dancing is prohibited – as it might be an attraction to take part in gaming.

(d) *Advertisements* of a casino are prohibited except for a sign on the premises, a single notice in a newspaper to state a licence has been granted or advertisements in overseas newspapers. Artificial stimulation of demand is again prevented.

(e) *Hours for gaming* are limited but not ungenerous. Play on Sunday is allowed, but hours are limited to afternoons and evenings through to the early hours (up to 4 a m most nights)

(f) *No credit rule:* It is an offence for a casino operator (or his staff) to allow any credit for gaming, whether by funding in advance or allowing credit in order to gamble or to cover losses. The idea is to prevent a gambler playing beyond his means on easy credit. (Of course, anyone else can advance on credit.) The only exception to this 'chips for cash' rule is that a player's cheque will be accepted; but it cannot be backdated and must be presented within two days. If the gambler's cheque 'bounces' (i e it is dishonoured by his bank) the casino can sue for the sum due because 'gaming' is not a wagering contract. A successful player can likewise sue for winnings due.

The *games* played in a casino are of two types, and regulations exist under the statute law to regulate each.

(A) Conventional banker's games

(A) Conventional banker's games are games of unequal chance of which roulette is the most popular, but also include blackjack, baccarat banque, punto banco and chemin de fer. In each case, the existence of the bank gives the casino its edge and secures its profit. The regulations ensure that the gambler is not 'taken for a ride'. They forbid, for example, two zeros on roulette wheels or the more extreme 'mug options' at blackjack.

(B) Card-room games are games of equal chance such as backgammon, poker and dice. Here the casino takes its profit by a commission on winnings or a participation fee. It is cheaper, of course, to play in private.

(iii) Gaming in Proprietary Clubs

Where genuine members' clubs, miners' welfare institutes and the like wish to provide gaming facilities as a purely incidental activity, without a profit motive but perhaps benefiting club funds in a minor way, the law allows a registration procedure to make such activities lawful.

Such a members' club does not require a certificate from the Gaming Board, but regis-

tration is by the local gaming licencing justices and the procedure is similar to that for a full casino licence. The club must satisfy the justices that it is a permanent members' club with over 25 members and that the principle purpose for which the club is established is not gaming. Registration procedure therefore is quite elaborate but once achieved the club can make charges for gaming sufficient for a modest profit to benefit general funds. Regulations allow the non banker games and some of the banker games such as pontoon and chemin-de-fer. Few clubs now bother to register and content themselves with gaming machines and bingo.

(iv) Gaming Machines

A gaming machine is constructed for playing a game of chance, with a slot for the insertion of coins or tokens. This wide definition not only includes fruit machines but also 'amusement only' machines where the player can (at best) hope for his money back.

Three main types of machine exist – each with different rules.

(A) 'Jackpot machines': These offer large cash prizes and are usually of the fruit machine variety. To operate these, premises are required with either (a) a casino licence, or (b) a bingo club licence, or (c) being a members' club, registration with the licensing authority.

In all cases: no more than two machines are allowed; a single play must not exceed a statutory figure, recently increased to 20 pence; prizes must be in cash, not tokens. There is no limit on the amount of the jackpot, but giving the prize in cash by the machine imposes some practical limit and is rarely more than £100.

(B) 'Amusement with prizes' machines: These machines, sometimes of the fruit machine variety can be installed in public places which have a permit – granted by the local authority or, in the case of a pub, by the licensing justices. The authority can limit the number of machines. These machines are widely found, in pubs, cafés, arcades and shops. For such machines: the maximum charge for play must not exceed 10 pence; the maximum cash prize is fixed by law – currently it is £1.50, but a non-monetary prize can be of a value of up to £3; if the prize is in the form of tokens a player must be able to exchange his tokens for goods or non-cash prizes. Travelling showmen and travelling fairground operators do not require a permit.

(C) Games without prizes: if no prize is offered a permit is not required. These machines are usually found in fairgrounds and amusement arcades.

The only exception to the above rules are for persons or organisations holding bazaars, fêtes, sporting meets or indeed any charity or other non- commercial entertainments. If (and only if) gaming is incidental to the main purpose, gaming machines (including jackpot machines) can be provided, but none of the proceeds can be taken for private gain.

(v) Bingo

Bingo is a lottery played as a game and whenever it is played for money stakes it is a form of gaming, but specific rules apply to relax the full rigour of the law. Bingo can lawfully be played: (i) in licensed clubs; (ii) in members' clubs.

(A) Commercial Clubs (1,270 clubs were licenced in 1985) dominate organised bingo and operators who have a magistrates' licence limited to bingo operate under relaxed rules:

(1) To participate, a person only has to apply for membership 24 hours in advance – and usually a very nominal fee is payable.
(2) Licences are available in all parts of the country.
(3) Shows and entertainment, forbidden in gaming establishments, are allowed. This allows provision of up to two gaming machines.
(4) Limited 'Linked' Bingo is allowed, providing for simultaneous games on more than one premises, but with a weekly prize limit of £3,000. The Gaming (Bingo) Act 1985, which came into force on 9 June 1986, allows multiple bingo by licensed bingo clubs for maximum prizes of £50,000.
(5) The proprietors can enhance the prizes by up to £1,250, but otherwise they must not exceed the total amount staked.

In bingo, unlike the football pools, the total stake is redistributed as winnings. The promoter makes his profit from the entrance fee (about 20–25p a session) and a participation fee for each game or series of games. There is then an enforceable legal contract between player and promoter, and either can sue in a dispute. The only sum deducted from the stakes is bingo duty.

Despite these relaxations, operators require the usual certificate from the Gaming Board and a magistrates' licence, which requires annual renewal.

(B) Prize bingo, where the winnings are not in money but goods, is not gaming but an amusement with prizes and is therefore found on fairgrounds and the like, with a local authority permit. It is also used in commercial bingo clubs, who require no extra permit to play this game, often during the 'interval'; the promoter can take a cut of the stakes. Stakes are limited to 10 pence.

(vi) Bridge and Whist Clubs

Bridge and whist, despite the degree of skill that is involved, involve an element of equal chance and are covered by gaming legislation – though as 'non-banker' games, they can be played without licence or registration provided the limits on permissable entry charges are observed. Special provision has been made here and bridge and whist clubs can charge £6 per person per day compared to 15 pence for all other games.

5. LOTTERIES

A lottery is a distribution of prizes by lot or pure chance. No skill is involved; if there is a degree of skill, it is not a lottery.

Lotteries are illegal unless they come within one of the exceptions set out below. All lotteries for private gain are unlawful. It may appear paradoxical that lotteries (which appear relatively harmless compared to other forms of gambling) are strictly controlled: the reason is that they present the greatest possibility for fraud: the punter does not see what is happening to his money. There is also the risk of inducing people to spend more than they can afford.

The following lotteries, in 'ascending' order of scope, are lawful. A promoter of a lottery must ensure that the types are not mixed:

(i) Small Lotteries

These are lotteries incidental to entertainments and activities such as bazaars, fêtes, dinners, sales of work or sporting events (and those of similar character); they are lawful, whether they are for a single day, or longer, provided:
(a) The lottery is not the main purpose or inducement of the event
(b) Tickets are sold only at the event
(c) No more than £50 can be taken from the proceeds for prizes
(d) Cash prizes are prohibited
(e) All proceeds, after deduction of expenses and

up to £50 for prizes, must be devoted to purposes other than private gain

(f) The result must be declared during the event. Small lotteries require no registration or special tickets and are common.

(ii) Private Lotteries

Private lotteries are those organised exclusively among a group of people who either work together, are all members of one society or club (but *not* a gaming club) or who are all resident on the same premises (e g students in a hall of residence).

Again, no registration is required, but stricter rules must be kept.

(a) Printing expenses can be deducted; otherwise the whole proceeds must go on prizes, or if a club or society, part on prizes and part to the purposes of the society.

(b) No advertisements of the lottery are allowed – except a notice on the premises.

(c) The price of every ticket must be the same – and stated on the ticket.

(d) Each ticket must include on its face the name and address of the promoters, a description of the persons to whom sale is restricted and a statement that prizes can only be delivered to the person to whom the ticket was sold.

(e) Cash or value must be paid for each ticket.

(f) Tickets cannot go on general sale or be sent through the post.

Though no registration is required, private lotteries do need specially printed or prepared tickets.

(iii) Public Lotteries

Public lotteries are also known as *Society lotteries* and are the ones perhaps most frequently encountered. Registration (on payment of a fee, currently £25) with the local authority is required; once so registered a charitable, sporting, cultural or other society not established for commercial activity can conduct up to 52 lotteries in any one year with a seven-day minimum gap between each. Registration can only be refused on the grounds that one of the organisers has been convicted of fraud or a lotteries offence or that the club or society is not run on non-profit lines. The rules for society lotteries are detailed and must be strictly observed. Persons organising such lotteries must take care that they have obtained a copy of those rules, understand them, and observe them. They are, in outline, as follows.

(1) The promoter must be a member of the society and authorized by the society to act on their behalf.

(2) Tickets must not exceed a specified sum,

currently 50p; their total value must be limited; the present maximum is £10,000.

(3) Tickets must not be sold to a person under the age of 16.

(4) Tickets must not be sent through the post except to society members.

(5) Tickets must show the price, the name and address of the organisers and the date of the draw.

(6) Expenses must not exceed whichever is the lesser of (i) the actual expenses; (ii) 25% of the lottery proceeds (15% if the total proceeds exceed £10,000).

(7) There are limits as to the size of individual prizes; lotteries registered with the Gaming Board can give higher prizes but the current basic limit is £2,000. Total prizes must not exceed half the whole proceeds.

(8) The total amount raised after deduction of expenses and provision of prizes must be applied for the purposes of the society.

(9) The lottery cannot be advertised except to members or by a notice on the society premises.

(10) A return must be made to the local authority showing details of money raised, expenses deducted and the way the money raised is to be spent. Lotteries registered with the Gaming Board are allowed higher limits on both the maximum value of tickets sold and the maximum value of prizes.

Breach of these rules is a criminal offence with maximum penalties of either a £400 fine or up to two years imprisonment.

(iv) Local Authority Lotteries

Local Councils are now permitted to raise money from lotteries, but must register with the Gaming Board. There are restrictions similar to those imposed on society lotteries, e g a maximum of 52 in any one year. The purpose and object of the lottery must be publicised and proceeds can only be applied for that object. Tickets can be sold publicly, through shops, kiosks or other outlets.

All other lotteries, except for a quaint 1846 exemption given to art unions, are illegal. No national lottery is now allowed, though many were held in earlier centuries, particularly in the eighteenth century. The last was in 1826. Many are held in other countries; and the 1978 Royal Commission recommended a United Kingdom

Prize Competitions

Prize competitions have flourished in recent years, almost exclusively to promote sales of beer, newspapers, petrol and other goods. Readers will be familiar with newspaper bingo (top people call it Portfolio), petrol station treasure hunts and the chance of a holiday of a lifetime with nearly everything that you buy. These competitions can flourish because they are *not* subject to legal control provided the promoter ensures that:

(1) If it is a competition of pure chance, it does not fall into the definition of an illegal lottery.

(2) If it is a competition involving a degree of skill, it does not fall into the definition of an illegal prize competition.

A competition of pure chance (e g newspaper bingo or petrol station game) is *not an illegal lottery* provided *no payment* is necessary for the opportunity to take part. Thus if a prize card is included in a cigarette packet for instance, that is an illegal lottery, because you can only take part by buying the cigarettes. If, on the other hand, you can win a newspaper competition without buying the paper, that is not a lottery. So also with the petrol station or pub games – the tickets will state 'No purchase necessary' and you can call to collect a card every day without buying the product.

If success in the competition depends on the exercise of a degree of skill, it is *not an illegal lottery* because the result does not depend solely on chance. Payments can be required for entry into these competitions; but even then they will be unlawful as 'illegal prize competitions' when published in newspapers or in connection with a trade or business if:

(1) prizes are offered on the forecast of a future event, or on a past event whose result is not generally known, or

(2) it is any other competition which does not involve a *substantial* degree of skill.

Spot-the-Ball competitions have been upheld as involving a sufficient degree of skill; but in many competitions, the degree of skill appears very small; and the Royal Commission's view in 1978 was that the test of skill was unworkable.

The rules in this area are hard to defend. It is anomalous that prize competitions can be run for private gain without legal control, while lotteries for good causes are subject to strict limits. The Royal Commission's recommendation – to make unlawful prize competitions with an entry charge – has not been implemented.

National Lottery for good causes: to date, this recommendation has not been acted upon.

6. TAXATION ON GAMBLING

Once the gambling activities described above became accepted, it was natural that they should be taxed. The principal taxes and duties are:

(A) General betting duty on bets with a bookmaker or on the Tote at horseraces or racing tracks. The duty is currently levied at 4% for on course betting and 8% off course.

(B) Pool betting duty is charged on all bets by way of pool betting, particularly on football pools. The amount of that duty is now a staggering 42½%. Thus, for every £1 you stake on the pools, 42½p is paid to the Exchequer.

(C) Gaming Machine licence duty is paid when licences for machines are given. The rates vary according to both the type of machine ('small prize' machines pay less) and to the number of machines authorised. The lowest duty levied is £120 per annum per machine; the highest £750.

(D) Gaming licence duty is a licence duty of £250 is payable on application. Further duties are payable on the gross gaming yield, beginning at a rate of 2½% and rising in stages to 33%; the greater the profit, the higher the duty.

(E) Bingo duty is charged at 10% of the money taken per week as charged for cards, plus one ninth of the net profit thereafter. Domestic or small scale play of bingo is exempt from duty.

(F) Income tax. In addition to the above duties, all profits from gambling activities are subject to income tax – even if they arise from illegal betting or gaming! Winnings to punters, however, are exempt from capital gains tax; and income tax will not be charged unless the punter is so successful that he makes his living from gambling.

Holidays can give rise to a number of legal difficulties. We will first look at the legal implications of travelling by train, coach and air. After that, passports and foreign travel will be examined, and then problems with travel agents and tour operators. Finally, we will look at related questions concerning hotels, restaurants and public houses.

1. TRAVELLING BY TRAIN

When a passenger buys a ticket he makes a contract with British Rail (or with whoever operates the railway). That contract will be subject to standard conditions; in the case of British Rail, these are published in their booklet 'Conditions of Carriage of Passengers and their Luggage'. Below are some of the matters that are dealt with in the Conditions.

(i) Unavailability of Seats

Buying a ticket does not entitle a passenger to a seat and a second class passenger has no right to sit in first class when all second class seats are taken, unless invited by the guard or on payment of the difference between the first and second class fare. If a seat has been reserved, the conditions state that the reservation fee is refundable if no seat is available, but that no additional compensation will be payable. It is likely that a Court would consider this to be unreasonable and therefore not allow British Rail to rely on it.

(ii) Timetables and Train Services

Trains are not guaranteed to start or arrive on time, or indeed to run at all, and liability for any loss which a passenger may suffer as a result is excluded. It is possible that a Court would consider this provision to be unreasonable, and therefore order compensation to be paid where a loss is suffered.

(iii) Loss of, or Damage to, Luggage

British Rail are not liable for loss of or damage to a passenger's luggage unless it can be proved that the loss or damage resulted from British Rail's negligence. If, however, the luggage is carried in the guard's van, the onus is on British Rail to show that the loss or damage was not caused by

their negligence. Liability is limited to £500 per passenger; whether this limit applies will depend on whether the Court considers it to be reasonable. It should be noted that the conditions do not, and cannot, exclude liability for death or personal injury caused by British Rail's negligence.

(iv) Complaints

Complaints about rail travel should be addressed in the first instance to the area manager. If satisfaction is not obtained, the Area Transport Users Consultative Committee should be approached.

2. TRAVELLING BY COACH

(i) Bookings

A passenger who has booked a seat on a coach has a contract with the operator. That contract will be breached if no seat is available, thereby preventing the passenger from travelling or forcing him to travel on a later coach or by different means. In these circumstances the passenger will be entitled to compensation for such expense as he might have been put to, for example, the additional cost of travelling by rail or the price of overnight accommodation. If the booking conditions contain a provision excluding or limiting the operator's liability, the conditions must have been sufficiently drawn to the passenger's attention, and the provision must be reasonable if it is to be effective.

(ii) Delays

If a coach is seriously delayed, and this is the fault of the operator (for example, the coach breaks down because it has been inadequately maintained), it may be possible for a passenger to claim compensation. Booking conditions excluding liability for delay will only be effective if the Court considers them to be reasonable.

(iii) Accidents

If a coach is involved in an accident and this is a result of the driver's negligence or results from inadequate maintenance, a passenger can recover compensation from the operator for any physical injuries or damage to his property that may have been caused. Liability for personal injury cannot be excluded in the booking conditions and a clause excluding liability for property damage must be reasonable. If the accident is caused by another road user, it will be possible to sue that person if he was negligent.

(iv) Complaints

As well as seeking legal redress in appropriate circumstances, a complaint can be made to the Traffic Commissioners for the relevant area about dangerous or inadequate service. The Commissioners will investigate the matter and in extreme cases can revoke a coach operator's licence.

3. TRAVELLING BY AIR

(i) Terms of Travel

The terms on which a flight between two or more countries is made are governed by an international agreement called the Warsaw Convention. This regulates the conditions which can be contained in the contract between the carrier and the passenger. These conditions will be referred to in the ticket issued to the passenger.

(ii) Personal Injury

The carrier will be liable for the death of a passenger or personal injury which occurs on board the aircraft or in the process of getting on or off the aircraft. The carrier will not be liable if it can show that it took all necessary measures to avoid the injury or that it was impossible to take such measures, unless the flight involves a stop in the United States, in which case this defence will not be available to the carrier. Where the carrier is liable, the Warsaw Convention limits the amount of compensation payable; the maximum amount in most cases at the moment is about £7,000, which means that it is sensible for a person travelling by air to take out appropriate insurance.

(iii) Loss of, and Damage to, Baggage

The carrier will be liable for lost or damaged luggage, unless it can show that all necessary measures were taken to avoid the loss or damage. Liability is limited, however, to about £12 per kilo unless the value of the baggage is declared in advance and the appropriate supplementary charge paid. It is important to report any loss or damage immediately as very short time-limts are imposed for claiming compensation.

(iv) Delay

A carrier is liable to pay compensation if passengers or baggage are delayed beyond what is reasonable, except where the delay is due to factors beyond the carrier's control. An airline might be required to compensate a passenger for an over-night stay at a hotel, for instance, where the unavailability of a plane has made this necessary. Damages might also be payable for causing a passenger to lose part of his holiday.

(v) Over-booking

If the plane has been over-booked and a passenger is denied a seat, the airline will be liable to the passenger for breach of contract. Many airlines now operate a scheme whereby they offer compensation in accordance with a fixed scale in the event of over-booking. It will usually be advisable to accept the compensation offered unless the passenger's loss is significantly greater, rather than take legal action against the airline.

(vi) Complaints

The Air Transport Users' Committee will investigate complaints made by passengers about problems arising out of air travel, for example, with respect to lost luggage or overbooking. The committee will give advice but cannot award compensation.

NOTE. For motoring abroad, see Section 7 'Motoring and the Law' (page 403).

4. PASSPORTS AND TRAVELLING ABROAD

(i) Types of Passport

It is necessary to have a passport in order to enter another country. There are two types of British passport – the standard passport and the visitor's passport. The standard passport is valid for use in all countries and lasts for ten years. The visitor's passport may be used in most West European countries and in a number of countries outside Europe, including Canada. It is only valid for one year. The holder's husband or wife and children under sixteen can be included on either type of passport, but they can only travel with the passport holder. If they wish to travel alone, they must obtain a separate passport. Children over five are entitled to a passport in their own name, for which parents or guardians must apply.

(ii) How to Obtain a Passport

Application forms for either type of passport are available at Post Offices. A visitor's passport can be issued at the Post Office, but it will be necessary to have the application form signed first by a minister of religion, doctor, teacher or person of similar standing. The current fee is £7.50, or £11.25 if the husband/wife of the holder is to be included. In the case of a standard passport, the completed application form must be sent to the appropriate regional passport office, together with the fee of £15, or £22.50 where the husband/wife of the holder is included. The application should be sent at least four weeks before the planned journey. It may be sensible for someone who travels abroad frequently to apply for a passport which contains 94 pages for visas and entry stamps, rather than the usual 30. These cost twice as much as the 30 page passport, but when the latter is full a new passport, at the full fee, must be obtained.

(iii) Visas

Some countries will only allow admission to persons to whom a visa has been issued. Travel agents or the consulate of the country to be visited will give information about this.

(iv) Health Care Abroad

Visitors from the United Kingdom are entitled to receive immediate necessary medical treatment in countries which are members of the EEC. In most cases, however, it is necessary to obtain a Form E111 from the Department of Health and Social Security before travelling. The UK has reciprocal health arrangements with a number of other countries, in which emergency treatment can be obtained free or at reduced rates. Information about these can be obtained from the leaflet SA 30, obtainable from the DHSS. In countries with which there are no health agreements, persons needing treatment will have to pay the full cost, which means that adequate health and accident insurance cover is desirable if these countries are to be visited.

(v) Criminal Offences Abroad

A visitor to a foreign country will be subject to the local law, which may well be different from English law. If an offence is committed, it is no excuse that the offender did not know that what he was doing was illegal. If a traveller is arrested he should ask the police to contact the British Consulate immediately.

5. PROBLEMS WITH TRAVEL AGENTS AND TOUR OPERATORS

A number of problems can arise with holidays booked through travel agents. The travel agent might go bankrupt before the holiday takes place, the trip might be cancelled, a different date or hotel might be substituted at the last minute, or the hotel facilities might be very disappointing. If these things occur the holiday-maker may be entitled to compensation. In the case of a package holiday, the contract will usually be with a tour operator rather than with the agent through whom the holiday-maker books, and so generally it is the tour operator who should be pursued if things go wrong.

(i) Booking Conditions

Many travel agents and tour operators are members of the Association of British Travel Agents (ABTA). Brochures and booking conditions used by members must comply with the minimum standards laid down by ABTA. These help to ensure that the conditions are fair and clearly set out the respective rights and obligations of the holiday-maker and the provider of the holiday. For example, booking conditions may not give the operator the right to cancel a holiday after the date on which payment of the balance of the price of the holiday becomes due, except when forced to do so by hostilities, political unrest or other such circumstances beyond the operator's control. Where an operator does cancel a holiday, he is required by the ABTA rules to offer the holiday-maker a choice of a comparable holiday or a full refund. It may be noted that if an operator cancels a holiday otherwise than as a result of factors which are beyond his control, the holiday-maker has a right under the general law to compensation, but acceptance of a comparable holiday will often be a more appropriate solution.

Booking conditions are also likely to contain provisions relating to variations in the holiday booked and surcharges. The ABTA rules require prompt notification of alterations and insist that if a major alteration is made (for example, delayed departure or change in hotel), the holiday-maker shall be given the option either to cancel the holiday and receive a full refund, or to accept the new arrangements which must be of at least a comparable standard. Booking conditions which purport to give the tour operator the right to change the holiday details without paying compensation or giving the holiday-maker the option to cancel are likely to be legally ineffective. A tour operator can only make a surcharge (that is, increase the cost of the holiday beyond the price at which it was booked) if the booking conditions allow this. Provisions are often included which permit the price of a holiday to be increased as a result of currency movements or other increases in costs which are beyond the tour operator's control.

(ii) Cancellation by the Holiday-maker

Once a firm booking has been made, the holiday-maker does not in normal circumstances have the right to cancel the holiday. If he does, the tour operator will usually be allowed to retain the whole of the deposit which the holiday-maker has paid. Since cancellation will constitute a breach of contract, the tour operator will also be entitled to damages for his loss of profit if he is not able to sell the holiday to someone else. Booking conditions often specify that a certain percentage of the cost of the holiday may be retained by the operator, in excess of the deposit. The nearer the cancellation of the holiday to the date that it is due to take place, the higher the percentage will be. If booking conditions provide for a large retention even where ample notice of cancellation

Jarvis v Swans Tours Ltd

In *Jarvis v Swans Tours Ltd*, decided in 1972, Mr Jarvis booked a 'houseparty' holiday for two weeks in Switzerland with Swans Tours. Mr Jarvis was to take the holiday on his own, and the brochure promised the following arrangements: 'Welcome party on arrival. Afternoon tea and cake . . . Swiss Dinner by candlelight. *Fondue* party. Yodler evening . . . farewell party.' The brochure also said that the resident host spoke English, that there were ski runs nearby and that skis would be available. The total cost of the holiday was just over £63. The holiday turned out to be very disappointing. In the first week the houseparty consisted of only thirteen people. During the second week Mr Jarvis was the only person staying, and as the host did not speak English, he had no one to talk to. There was no welcome party; the cake for tea consisted of potato crisps and dry nut-cake and the yodler evening was no more than a local man in his working clothes who sang four or five songs very quickly. The ski-runs were some distance away and in the first week there were only mini-skis available. These rubbed Mr Jarvis's feet which meant that he could not ski at all in the second week. When he got home Mr Jarvis sued Swans tours and he was awarded £125 damages. Mr Jarvis was entitled to have the benefit of the features mentioned in the brochure and the Court could order a tour operator to pay in damages a sum greater than the cost of the holiday. People go on holiday to enjoy themselves and where a holiday is ruined because of the absence of the advertised facilities the damages should reflect this fact.

Jackson v Horizon Holidays

In this case, decided in 1974, Mr Jackson booked a four week holiday for himself, his wife and their two young children at a hotel in Sri Lanka. The total cost was £1,200. Mr Jackson requested, when he booked, that there should be a connecting door between his and his wife's room and the children's room. Horizon's brochure stated that the hotel had excellent facilities, including mini-golf, a high-class restaurant, swimming pool, and beauty and hairdressing salons. The bedrooms were described as being well-furnished, each having a private bath, shower and wc. As it turned out, there was no connecting door between the two rooms, but in any case the children's room was unusable because of mildew and fungus on the walls. There was no private bath and the shower and wc were dirty. The food was unpleasant, and there was no mini-golf, no swimming pool and no beauty or hairdressing salons. After two weeks Mr Jackson and his family moved to another hotel; this was better than the first one, apart from the fact that building work was still taking place. Mr Jackson sued Horizon for breach of contract. The facilities which Horizon had promised either did not exist or were inadequate and the Court awarded him compensation of £1,100. The Court held that it was permissible to award him damages which included compensation for the disappointment and inconvenience suffered by his family as well as by himself. It may also be noted that Horizon did not own the hotel and so did not have direct control over the availability and standard of its facilities, but nonetheless they were held responsible for them.

is given, someone cancelling a holiday should consider challenging this.

(iii) Disappointing Holidays

The facilities promised in the brochure should be available on the holiday, and the accommodation and service should be of a standard commensurate with the price paid. The two cases on the previous page illustrate in what circumstances a tour operator will be liable to pay compensation when a holiday does not live up to the expectations that the brochure creates.

(iv) Conciliation and Arbitration Scheme

If something goes wrong on a holiday booked with an ABTA member, ABTA offer a conciliation service and an arbitration scheme. As regards the former, a conciliator studies the complaint made by the holiday-maker and any correspondence between him and the tour operator, and suggests terms on which the dispute might be settled. The tour operator cannot, however, be compelled to accept the terms put forward. If a complaint about a package tour cannot be satisfactorily resolved, the holiday-maker may make use of the arbitration scheme which is operated on behalf of ABTA by the Chartered Institute of Arbitrators. An application, on the prescribed form, must normally be made within 9 months of returning from the holiday, and can be made by anyone mentioned in the booking form. The scheme does not apply where a claim is made for more than £1,000 per person or £5,000 per booking form, or where the claim is very complicated or largely in respect of physical injury or illness. Disputes are decided purely on the basis of written submissions – there is no oral hearing. A fee of £17.25 for a single claimant (there is a small additional charge for further claimants) is made for this service. The decision of the arbitrator will be binding on both the holiday-maker and the tour operator. Instead of using the arbitration scheme, or where the tour operator is not an ABTA member, a holiday-maker can seek redress in the Courts. This will involve a more formal procedure and may be more expensive.

(v) Bankruptcy of Travel Agent or Tour Operator

ABTA members are required to provide financial bonds or guarantees. This means that monies paid to a travel agent or tour operator in advance of a holiday will be reimbursed if they become insolvent. ABTA also has an insurance indemnity scheme in respect of insolvent travel agents. In certain cases, there is protection even where a tour operator is not an ABTA member. Operators who are required to take out an Air Travel Organisers Licence, for instance, must give a financial bond, as must members of certain other travel organisations, for example, the Bus and Coach Council.

(vi) Holiday Insurance

Given the various things that can go wrong with a holiday, insurance cover is a sensible precaution. Some tour operators insist that their own policy be used; where this is so the policy should be carefully checked to make sure that it is adequate. The following risks should be covered:

(a) Cancellation. This should provide for reimbursement of all amounts payable in respect of the holiday which are not recoverable from the tour operator, if the holiday has to be cancelled by the holiday maker as a result of some unforeseen event;

(b) Delay. Compensation for delay will not be payable by the tour operator if this is caused by adverse weather conditions or strikes, and hence insurance cover is advisable to pay for an overnight stay at a hotel or similar expenses which stem from the delay;

(c) Medical expenses. The amount of cover required depends on the country to be visited. For EEC countries it should be at least £25,000. For the United States a minimum of £500,000 would be appropriate;

(d) Accident. Death and personal injury should be covered, including the cost of the journey home, where appropriate; *personal liability* covers damages that may have to be paid by the insured person as a result of causing injury or property damage to a third person;

(e) Luggage and personal property. The policy should cover the full replacement value of all property taken on holiday; most policies limit the amount payable in respect of an individual item and in respect of money carried abroad.

422

6. HOTELS

(i) The Duty to Supply Food and Accommodation

If an establishment is a 'hotel' as defined by the Hotel Proprietors Act 1956, the owner is under a duty to provide accommodation and supply food and drink to all travellers unless he has a reasonable ground for refusal. Premises will be a hotel within the definition in the Act where the proprietor holds the premises out as offering food and accommodation on these terms. Where the proprietor does not represent that he is willing to take all-comers, therefore, the establishment will not fall within the provisions of the Act. This will be so, for instance, in the case of a 'private hotel' or 'residential hotel', or private house offering bed and breakfast. A public house may often include the word 'hotel' within its name, but if no accommodation is provided, it will not be within the Act either.

As well as being under a duty to accommodate a traveller, a hotel-keeper must also store his luggage, and, if he has space, the traveller's car. A hotel-keeper is even obliged to take in a guest's dog, unless, as observed in *R v Rymer* in 1877, the dog is dangerous or unclean! The proprietor is discharged from his obligation to provide accommodation if the hotel is full, and, if food and drink have run out he is not liable for failing to provide it. Facilities may be denied to travellers who are drunk or are otherwise in an objectionable state. The proprietor may also demand payment of a reasonable sum in advance, and if this is not forthcoming, or the traveller otherwise appears unable to pay, he may refuse accommodation. A hotel keeper who wrongfully denies facilities to a traveller is liable to prosecution, and the traveller may sue him for damages.

If premises are not a hotel within the meaning of the Act, the proprietor may, subject to what follows, deny accommodation or refreshment to a person who requests it without giving any reason. The landlord of a public house, for instance, may, at his discretion, refuse to serve a customer. Even where the premises are not a hotel, however, but are a boarding house or similar establishment, it is an offence to refuse to provide accommodation, or to refuse to provide accommodation of similar quality and on similar terms to those normally offered by the proprietor to the public at large, on grounds of colour, race, nationality, ethnic or national origin (Race Relations Act 1976) or on grounds of sex (Sex Discrimination Act 1975).

Where a traveller has booked a room in any type of accommodation but, when the time comes, there is no room available, the proprietor will be in breach of contract and will be liable to compensate the traveller for any losses he may have suffered. This might include the additional cost of staying in a more expensive hotel, for example.

(ii) Display of Prices

All hotels, as defined above, which have four or more rooms or eight or more beds must display a notice setting out information about the prices of rooms. The notice must be placed in a prominent position in the reception area, or if there isn't one, at the entrance, where it can be easily read by anyone seeking sleeping accommodation at the hotel. The notice must state the current price (including any service charge payable) per night of:

(1) a bedroom for occupation by one adult;
(2) a bedroom for occupation by two adults; and
(3) a bed other than one situated in a room for one or two persons; in this case it must be stated whether the bed is in a dormitory or a room to be shared with other guests.

Where rooms within a category have different prices, it is sufficient to state the highest and lowest prices within the category.

The notice must also state whether the prices include value added tax; if they do not, the amount of tax payable must be expressed as a monetary amount. If the room charge includes meals, which meals are being paid for must be indicated.

A hotel which does not display the above information will be liable to prosecution under the Tourism (Sleeping Accommodation Price Display) Order 1977. A guest who is dissatisfied should complain to the local trading standards department.

(iii) Responsibility for Guests' Safety

Anyone providing accommodation, whether it technically constitutes a hotel or not, must take reasonable care to see that guests are not injured as a result of the condition of the premises. Where a passage is insufficiently lit, for example, and it ought to be anticipated that guests will use it at night, the proprietor will be liable to pay damages to a guest who is injured. The proprietor cannot exclude his liability for causing death or personal injury as a result of his negligence by putting up a notice, since the Unfair Contract Terms Act 1977 makes such provisions ineffective.

(iv) Responsibility for Guests' Property

The proprietor of a hotel, as defined above, will generally be liable to a guest whose property is lost, stolen or damaged. Subject to what will be said below, the hotel-keeper's liability is strict, which means that he is liable even though the loss or damage is not a result of his negligence or that of his employees. This rule applies where the property was situated within the hotel buildings at the time of the loss or damage, or in a place so closely connected with the buildings as to be treated as part of them. For liability to be strict, it is not necessary for the hotel-keeper to take the goods into his custody for safe-keeping. The hotel-keeper is not liable, however, for loss or damage to vehicles, or property contained in them, unless it can be proved that he or his employees were negligent.

The hotel-keeper's liability will only be strict, as opposed to depending on proof of negligence, where: (1) at the time of the loss or damage sleeping accommodation at the hotel had been engaged for the traveller who owns the property in question and (2) the loss or damage occurred during the period commencing with the midnight immediately preceding, and ending with the midnight immediately following, a period for which the traveller was a guest at the hotel and entitled to use the accommodation so engaged.

The hotel-keeper will not be strictly liable if the loss or damage results from the negligence of the guest himself. It may amount to negligence for a guest to leave his door unlocked, but this is not necessarily so and will depend on the particular circumstances of the case.

A hotel-keeper can limit the amount of his strict liability by displaying a notice in the form prescribed by the Hotel Proprietors Act 1956. The notice is shown below.

In order to be effective, the notice, printed in plain type, must have been conspicuously displayed in a place where it could conveniently be read by guests at or near the reception office or desk or, where there is no such office or desk, at or near the main entrance. Assuming that these requirements are satisfied, the notice will be effective in accordance with its terms, that is, the hotel will not be liable for more than £50 per article, and a total of £100 to any one guest. If the notice is misprinted, however, it will not operate at all.

Where a notice of the kind set out above is properly displayed, the hotel will still be liable if the guest's property was lost or stolen as a result of the negligence of the proprietor or of his employees. In the case of an establishment providing accommodation which is not a 'hotel' for the purpose of the Act, negligence will be the only basis for the proprietor's liability. Liability for negligence which causes loss or damage to property can only be avoided by the proprietor if there is an effective exclusion clause in the contract between himself and the guest. This involves three things: the exclusion clause must be a part of the contract entered into when it is agreed that the guest shall be allowed to stay; its wording must exclude liability for what has happened, and the clause must be a reasonable one. If the latter requirement is not satisfied the clause will be made ineffective by the Unfair Contract Terms Act 1977. The reasonableness requirement will generally be difficult to satisfy. The case of *Olley v Marlborough Court Ltd* (opposite), decided in 1948, illustrates when an exclusion clause will be treated as being part of a contract for accommodation in a hotel.

NOTICE

Loss of or Damage to Guests' Property

Under the Hotel Proprietors Act 1956, an hotel proprietor may in certain circumstances be liable to make good any loss of or damage to a guest's property even though it was not due to any fault of the proprietor or staff of the hotel.

This liability however –

(a) extends only to the property of guests who have engaged sleeping accommodation at the hotel;

(b) is limited to £50 for any one article and a total of £100 in the case of any one guest, except in the case of property that has been deposited, or offered for deposit, for safe custody;

(c) does not cover motor-cars or other vehicles of any kind or any property left in them, or horses or other live animals.

This notice does not constitute an admission either that the Act applies to this hotel or that liability thereunder attaches to the proprietor of this hotel in any particular case.

Olley v Marlborough Court Ltd

Mr and Mrs Olley were guests in the defendant's private residential hotel. (It was not a 'hotel' for the purposes of what is now the Hotel Proprietors Act 1956 and hence the proprietor would only be liable for loss or damage to guests' property if negligent.) The contract to stay at the hotel was entered into at the reception desk when the Olleys first arrived – the proprietor agreed to let them stay in return for payment in accordance with the hotel's usual rates. The Olleys then went up to their room; there was a notice on the bedroom wall to the following effect:

'The proprietors will not hold themselves responsible for articles lost or stolen, unless handed to the manageress for safe custody. Valuables should be deposited for safe custody in a sealed package and a receipt obtained.'

Sometime later Mrs Olley went out and placed her room key, as requested, on a board in the reception office. During her absence an unknown person removed the key from the board, entered her room and stole a fur coat and other valuable property. It was held that the hotel had been negligent. They had not taken reasonable care to ensure that unauthorised persons did not take the key and thereby gain access to the Olleys' room. It was also held by the Court that the hotel could not rely on the exclusion notice on the wall of the Olleys' bedroom because it was not a part of the contract – this had been formed at the reception desk and any notice that could only be seen subsequently came too late to be incorporated into the contract.

(v) Hotel's Right to Detain Guests' Property

If a guest is unable to pay the bill when he leaves, the hotel is entitled to detain the guest's luggage or other property brought into the hotel (not a guest's car) as security for payment. The proprietor may ultimately sell the property if the bill is not paid.

7. RESTAURANTS

(i) Bookings

A firm booking of a table constitutes a contract between the customer and the restaurant and so if a table is not available within a reasonable time after the time for which it is booked the restaurant will be in breach of contract. The customer will be entitled to damages if he can show that he has suffered a loss – for example, the cost of travelling to and from the restaurant or to an alternative restaurant. By the same token, if the customer does not turn up the restaurant will be able to sue him for any profit they may have lost. It will probably be otherwise, however, if plenty of notice of cancellation is given; the restaurant may then be able to use the table for another customer and so will not suffer a loss of profit.

(ii) Prices

By regulations made under the Prices Act 1974, a restaurant must display a menu and wine list with prices at or near the entrance of the eating area, which will normally mean outside or just inside the door. In a self-service restaurant, prices must be visible at the place where food is chosen. If the restaurant serves more than 30 different items, the prices of only 30 items need be quoted. Where the restaurant is licensed, the prices of at least six different wines must be given, or if fewer than six are offered, of all of them. The price list must be in an obvious position and be easy to read. The prices quoted must include value added tax. If there is a service charge, or a minimum charge, information concerning these must be displayed at least as prominently as the price of the food.

If this information is not displayed the restaurant will be committing a criminal offence. Also, if it has not been made reasonably clear before the meal is ordered that there is a service charge, or that the meal is subject to a minimum charge, the customer is entitled to refuse to pay it.

(iii) Quantity of Food and Drink

The law does not lay down minimum quantities of food to be served, but if quantities or weights are indicated in the menu, these must be complied with. If wine is sold in a carafe, the amount contained must be indicated.

(iv) Quality of Food

The rules about hygiene in restaurants, and in premises selling food generally, are strict. These are contained in the Food Act 1984 and regulations made under it. Premises must be clean and sanitary, and there must be adequate lavatory and washing facilities for staff, for example. Non-compliance with the regulations is a criminal offence and the Court can make a compensation order in favour of a customer who has suffered as a result of poor hygiene standards. The Court can also close down an unhygienic restaurant. If a customer thinks that a restaurant's standards of hygiene are unsatisfactory, a complaint should be made to the local environmental health officer.

Food and drink must be fit for human consumption. The sale of items which do not satisfy this requirement is a criminal offence even if the restaurant did not know that the food was defective and even though there has been no negligence. It is also an offence to sell food and drink which is not of the nature, substance and quality demanded. If bread is stated on the menu as being baked with wholemeal flour, for instance, this must be the case. As well as imposing a criminal penalty for breach of these requirements, the Court can also award compensation to the customer. An extreme illustration of selling 'food' which was not fit for human consumption, and which was not of the nature demanded, is *Meah v Roberts*, decided in 1977 (see below).

A customer can also bring civil proceedings in respect of food poisoning which results from food eaten in a restaurant. The person who pays for the meal can bring an action under the Sale of Goods Act 1979 and does not have to prove negligence on the part of the restaurant. Whether other members of a party can sue without proving negligence depends on whether they have a contract with the restaurant. In *Lockett v A & M Charles Ltd*, decided in 1938, a husband and wife had a meal in a restaurant and the wife subsequently became ill. There was no evidence as to who actually ordered the meal, but it was paid for by the husband. It was held by the Court that there was a contract between the restaurant and the wife: unless one member of the party is obviously 'in charge of proceedings' each customer is liable to the restaurant to pay for the meal and hence if the meal is defective each customer can sue the restaurant for breach of contract. Where the contract is only with one member of the party, a guest can only sue the restaurant if there has been negligence on its part. The restaurant would not be liable to the guest, for instance, if it sold food which was infected when they received it, and there were no means of detecting that there was something wrong with it and all proper cooking and serving procedures had been followed.

If the food or drink served is not what was ordered, or is substandard, the customer is entitled to reject it. Where a meal is very poor, the customer might decide not to pay for it or to pay only such amount as he considers it was worth. If he does this, he should give his name and address to the proprietor. It is a criminal offence under the Theft Acts 1968 and 1978 to leave a restaurant with a dishonest intention of avoiding payment. If the customer gives his name and address this will enable the restaurant proprietor to sue him if he wants to (he will fail if the meal was seriously substandard), but the matter will not be of interest to the police unless there is a risk that a breach of the peace might ensue!

(v) Damage to Customers' Property and Loss of Property

If a waiter spills food onto a customer, the restaurant will be liable to reimburse the customer the cost of having affected items of clothing cleaned, or the cost of a replacement if a garment is damaged beyond repair, providing the waiter was negligent. This will be so, for instance, where he was not paying proper attention to what he was doing. A restaurant is responsible for taking reasonable care of customers' property that is under its control. If a coat is handed in to a cloakroom attendant, or the waiter takes it away, for example, the restaurant must take reasonable steps to make sure that it is safe from theft or damage. If a customer hangs his coat up in the eating area, however, it is his own responsibility to protect it. Where a restaurant has failed in its

Meah v Roberts

In this case, a husband and wife took their two children to a restaurant and ordered lemonade for them. A colourless liquid, resembling lemonade, was poured from a lemonade bottle and the children started to drink it. The bottle did not contain lemonade but a strong solution of caustic soda which was used for cleaning the pipes of the equipment from which lager was served. One of the children was seriously injured as a result. The caustic soda had been put in the bottle and left behind the bar by a brewery representative. He had explained to one of the waiters what the liquid was for, but the waiter did not speak much English and did not understand. Both the restaurant and the brewery, as employer of the representative, were prosecuted, and compensation was ordered to be paid to the children.

duty to safeguard a customer's property, but tries to rely on a notice excluding liability, the notice will only be effective if it is clear and sited in a prominent position, and if its terms are reasonable.

(vi) Alcoholic Drinks in Restaurants

A restaurant must have a licence if it serves alcoholic drinks and drinks may only be supplied to persons who are taking a meal. The restaurant will be bound by the local licensing hours (the same as those applying to public houses), though many restaurants will have a supper hour certificate, which allows them to serve alcohol up to 3 p m in respect of the lunchtime session, and for an hour after the usual public house closing time in the evening.

8. PUBLIC HOUSES

(i) Right to be Served

There is no right to be served in a public house, though an offence is committed if the reason for refusal is the race or sex of the customer.

(ii) Who May Enter and Be Served in a Public House

The Licensing Act 1964 imposes restrictions on who may enter licensed premises, and on the consumption and sale of alcohol to young persons.

(1) An alcoholic drink may not be sold in the bar for consumption by a person under the age of eighteen. An offence is committed by the landlord if this restriction is knowingly breached. An offence is also committed by the young person if he buys or attempts to buy an alcoholic drink, or if he consumes alcohol in the bar, with the exception of certain drinks taken with meals (see (2) below). A person who buys or attempts to buy a drink *for* a person under eighteen for consumption in the bar can also be prosecuted.
(2) A person under eighteen but over sixteen can be served with beer, porter, cider or perry for consumption with a meal, in a part of the premises usually set aside for the service of meals which is not a bar.
(3) Persons under eighteen but over fourteen are allowed into a bar, but must not consume or buy alcohol. Children under fourteen are not permitted to go into the bar at all (except to pass through, e g to the toilet, where there is no other convenient route).

For the purpose of these rules, a 'bar' is defined as including 'any place exclusively or mainly used for the sale and consumption of intoxicating liquor'. This rather vague definition can give rise to problems in certain cases, but it is generally safe to assume that children under fourteen are allowed to be present in a pub garden or 'children's room', since these are unlikely to be classified as being part of the bar.

(iii) Opening Hours

Opening hours vary in different parts of the country. The general rule is that public houses can open from 11 a m to 3 p m and from 5.30 p m to 10.30 p m from Monday to Saturday, and from 12 noon to 2 p m and 7 p m to 10.30 p m on Sundays, Christmas Day and Good Friday. Licensing magistrates may extend the evening opening hours until 11 p m, and this is frequently done in respect of Fridays and Saturdays. Extensions can be obtained for special occasions and where meals are served or there is permitted music and dancing.

A customer is allowed ten minutes drinking-up time after closing time is called. Once that time has expired the drink must be left (it must not be taken from the premises) and no drinks may be served during drinking-up time. Drinking-up time is 30 minutes if the drink is served with a meal.

(iv) Quantities Sold

Alcoholic drinks may only be sold in public houses in recognised quantities. These are stipulated by the Weights and Measures Act 1963. Draught beer and cider can only be served in quantities of one-third of a pint, one half pint or multiples of a half-pint. The drink must be served in a glass which has its capacity marked on it or from an instrument which dispenses a measured quantity. Gin, rum, vodka and whisky can only be sold in quantities of one-quarter, one-fifth or one-sixth of a gill, or multiples of these. Wine sold for consumption on the premises must be sold in quantities of 25cl, 50cl, 1 litre, 10 fl oz or 20 fl oz, unless it is served in a closed bottle or by the glass. There are no stipulations as to how much a glass must contain. A notice must be displayed stating what measure is used for the spirits mentioned above and in what quantities wine is sold. A customer who thinks that he has been given short measure should complain to the local trading standards officer.

It is an offence for a public house to serve a

larger measure – known as a 'long pull' – than was asked for, though few customers are inclined to complain! It is also illegal to supply drinks on credit in a public house.

(v) Display of Prices

The prices of drinks (and of any food being offered) must be displayed in a prominent position near where they are served. Where there are not more than 30 different items for sale, the price of each item must be given; where there are more than 30, the prices of at least 30 must be quoted. The price given must be for a drink of a stated measure.

(vi) Drunkenness

It is an offence under the Licensing Act 1964 for a licensee to permit drunkenness or 'violent, quarrelsome or riotous conduct' on licensed premises. A person who is drunk or is engaging in conduct of this kind can be prosecuted for refusing a request of the licensee for him to leave the premises. It is an offence to sell liquour to a drunken person. If the companions of someone who is drunk 'procure or attempt to procure' liquor for him, they too will be committing an offence.

1. INTRODUCTION

Many sports entail some element of danger. This varies from the obvious potential risk to health in boxing to the danger to limbs on the football field or even nowadays on the cricket field. The risk is not confined to participants. Officials, spectators or even passers-by may be injured; such accidents are infrequent but they certainly happen. Sporting activity may also disturb the peace of a locality. Furthermore, tempers are often raised during sport and this may lead individuals to harm others in a manner which would be unthinkable in a different context.

These issues form the bulk of the current discussion. We will not consider the special problems of professional sportsmen or professional clubs. We will emphasise the law as it affects participants and organisers of sporting activity. The latter raises problems such as dangerous equipment or buildings, inadequate supervision and inadequate fencing of activities. The insurance position both of individuals and of clubs is of great importance. This chapter will not deal with questions of licensing, lotteries and other revenue-raising activities.

2. THE CRIMINAL LIABILITY OF PARTICIPANTS

A person playing games or being on property where games are being played is subject to the ordinary criminal law of the land. There are no special rules if the belongings of other players are stolen from a changing room or if another player is assaulted after an argument in the bar after the game. The same is true if the referee or umpire is deliberately struck. There are, however, special rules applying to injuries caused by one player to another. This is because the normal criminal law makes it a crime to injure someone deliberately or recklessly. In some sports deliberate injury is the objective while in others it is known to be possible. If all injuries inflicted in the course of games were crimes it would of course not be possible for those games to be played; sports like boxing and rugby would take on the illegal status of bear-baiting or cock-fighting.

The Defence of Consent

The law regulates such injuries through the defence of consent. It is possible to consent to being injured if that is the likely or possible outcome of a game. So in a game such as boxing, wrestling or judo, where physical contact is the objective, there is no criminal liability if the fighters stay within the rules. This is the law even in those sad cases where death follows a boxing or other match. The law, however, does not allow a person to consent to the deliberate causing of his own death, a rule which leads to the prohibition of euthanasia. It is different if the death is an accidental, unforeseen result of a deliberate punch or series of punches. Outside boxing, etc a deliberate punch leading to an unexpected death will usually amount to the crime of manslaughter.

The rule that there is no liability for injuries inflicted in boxing and like sports only applies where the game in question is properly organised. There is no special rule for playground fights, for privately organised fights, and probably not for prize-fights, with or without gloves, arranged outside the control of the British Boxing Board of Control or equivalent governing body. In one case decided in 1980 two youths decided to settle their differences in a fight. The injuries sustained were no worse than a bleeding nose and bruising. Although they were acquitted of assault occasioning actual bodily harm, the case was referred to a higher court to enable the law to be clarified. The Court of Appeal said that people may only cause each other deliberate harm in the course of properly conducted games and that most private fights will be illegal even if the participants consent. It makes no difference whether the fight takes place in public or on private property. The effect of this decision is that some relatively normal behaviour in sport is held to be criminal, though the Court said that prosecutions should not be brought in minor cases.

The criminal law has not been used to challenge or outlaw new and potentially dangerous sports such as martial arts and kick-boxing. Some are regulated by official governing bodies and would therefore probably come within the Court's idea of 'properly conducted games.' Others may be run much less formally and there must be a risk that injury to a participant might lead to a prosecution and conviction.

The defence of consent may also be excluded if the injury results from action outside the rules of even a properly organised game. This is true both of games where injury is the objective and those where it is an inherent risk. The law is uncertain, because some activity outside the rules is so likely to cause some injury that it is sensible to say that those taking part accept that risk. It would be strange if the law were that an ordinary soccer foul constituted a crime. The line between legal and illegal behaviour must be socially acceptable. The reason there have been few cases is that traditionally few people injured by opponents have brought a prosecution. In 1978, for example, J. P. R. Williams, the Welsh rugby player, suffered serious facial injuries and the identity of his assailant was known, yet he refused to press charges. That this is a matter of practice, not law, was shown by the important case of *R v Billinghurst*, decided the same year. Again Welsh rugby was involved; here the defendant punched the opposing scrum-half in an off-the-ball incident, fracturing his jaw. The defence argued that the injured person must have consented to being injured in this way as in modern rugby punching

is the rule rather than the exception. The judge directed the jury that the test was whether the injury was one 'which could reasonably be expected to happen during a game' and the defendant was convicted and sentenced to nine months' imprisonment suspended for two years. A recent trend suggests a greater willingness to use the law. In one case David Bishop, a Welsh Rugby International, was sentenced to one month's imprisonment after a serious attack on a player well away from the ball. However, on appeal the sentence was suspended. In another case, a Welsh policeman was jailed for six months for biting off part of an opponent's ear during an inter-force rugby match. The law at present is only *used* in the most severe or blatant cases, but any deliberate assault which is clearly abnormal, such as an off-the-ball kick or punch, is a crime; so are things which happen quite frequently, such as punches in a rugby scrum. It is probable, though, that most 'ordinary' soccer fouls will not be crimes unless it can be proved that the motive was to injure; the further away the ball was at the time, the easier it will be to show. Finally, the law holds that a player consents to the risk of injury from a normal rugby tackle, soccer shoulder charge, cricket bouncer and so on.

Possible crimes

There are various offences which can be committed in these circumstances. Manslaughter is the most serious. In *R v Bradshaw* (1898) the accused, in the course of a football match, charged a defender and struck him in the stomach with his knee, causing fatal injuries. He was charged with manslaughter. While the jury acquitted him this does not mean that a sportsman could never be convicted. If a crime has been committed within the principles laid down in *Billinghurst* and the victim happens to die then that crime will be manslaughter and the attacker could expect a substantial prison sentence. Normally of course death will not result, and the crime committed will be within one of the sections of the Offences Against the Person Act, 1861. These are, starting with the most serious, intentionally causing grievous bodily harm, malicious wounding and assault occasioning actual bodily harm. The former is unlikely to have been committed as it requires the intentional causing of really serious injury. The second, which was the charge brought in *Billinghurst*, requires that the defendant foresaw that some injury was likely while the last only

requires that some injury happened whether or not the accused expected it.

The reason so few cases are brought is that people choose not to prosecute. While the decision whether or not to bring a prosecution is normally that of the Crown Prosecution Service, in this type of case it has been the practice to charge only where the injured party wishes it. There may be good reasons for not wishing to, particularly if the injury is relatively minor. Obviously bad feeling may result from charges being pressed and by the time of the hearing tempers may have cooled. Furthermore, it may be financially better for those who have been injured to bring a civil claim rather than a criminal charge.

The sporting context makes no difference to the normal right of self-defence. If a player is attacked there is a right to defend oneself so long as no more force is used than is reasonably necessary in the circumstances. It is surely only when the control of the referee and indeed of the other players has broken down that the right of self-defence is likely to be of much relevance.

Children and the Criminal Law

The position of child participants depends on whether they are attackers or attacked. No child under ten can be prosecuted for a crime, and those between ten and fourteen can only be convicted if it can be shown that they knew that what they were doing was clearly wrong. A child victim, on the other hand, is taken to consent to the risk of injury on the same basis as an adult. This is true of junior boxing clubs as well as football and rugby etc; were the law otherwise much physical contact in junior sport would be criminal. As long as the child is aware that some risk is involved parental consent is probably not necessary, though obtaining it is a sensible precaution. Consent applies not just to organised games but also to normal casual play. The principle that consent is only a defence where the game is properly conducted is only applicable to games such as boxing and wrestling where the attack is the essence of the game. In other games it is probable that the law treats casual games, whether involving children or adults, in the same way as more formal games, so that a player is held to consent to the risk of injuries normally resulting. The player who causes such an injury cannot be prosecuted for any offence.

Football Hooliganism

The most obvious examples of hooliganism, whether inside or outside the ground, involve the crimes of assault, theft and criminal damage. For the details reference should be made to the chapter on criminal law. If no individual suffers any damage from the behaviour it is still possible that crimes have been committed. These are the public order offences, and include possessing an offensive weapon, threatening behaviour, obstructing a policeman (usually by refusing to obey his orders) and the new offence of disorderly conduct.

Clubs also have the right to refuse entry to a ground for whatever reason, and police have the right to search people before they are allowed to enter. Ejection is also permissible if either the conditions of entry or the criminal law are broken. It follows that clubs may try to prevent the consumption of alcohol on their premises, whether bought there or brought in by spectators. It will be negligence if clubs fail to take reasonable steps to protect members of the public from the consequences of hooliganism: the stewarding and the barricades must be adequate.

3. THE CIVIL LIABILITY OF PARTICIPANTS

The relevant branch of civil law is the law of tort, which is an old word simply meaning 'wrong.' The basis of tort is a claim by one individual against another, unlike crime where the case is brought in the name of the Crown on behalf of the state. The remedy is also different; the claim is that the defendant should compensate the victim (or in some cases stop the offending behaviour) rather than be punished by fine or imprisonment. It is possible for both criminal and civil proceedings to be brought in respect of the same event.

There are two possible relevant torts, battery and negligence. The definition of battery is an intentional hostile touching by one individual of another; negligence is the careless infliction of harm. The latter cannot usually lead to criminal proceedings as they normally require that the defendant was aware that his behaviour might cause harm. The defence of consent will always be a defence to the tort of battery if it would have been a defence had criminal charges been brought. Every case where a sportsman commits a crime on the field of play also constitutes the tort of battery and gives rise to a claim for compensation. The same is true of crimes committed in unlawful boxing or wrestling matches or assaults on participants or officials unconnected with the actual play. On the other hand there may be cases where a tort is committed but the behaviour is not also a crime.

The Sportsman's Standard of Care

The other relevant tort is negligence, which usually applies where the harm was not caused intentionally or recklessly but carelessly. Not all carelessly caused harm is a tort; there must be a duty to take care owed by one person to another, a breach of that duty which is defined as the failure to take such care as would have been taken by a hypothetical reasonable person, and finally damage resulting from the breach of duty. There are also certain defences available; no damages are awarded if the injured party accepted the risk

431

of being injured in the way in which he was in fact injured, and damages can be reduced if the injured person was partly to blame for his injuries.

The law is clear that people participating in sport owe a duty of care to anyone who may be affected by their activities, whether other players, spectators or anyone else in the vicinity. The most important question is the test for deciding when that duty has been broken. Here there is a special rule: there is no breach of duty if the player is simply doing his best. If a cricketer hits a six and injures a spectator he is not liable; the same is true if his shot injures a close-in fielder. An example of someone doing his incompetent best is a golfer whose sliced shot injures someone on the next fairway; again, no liability. If a soccer or rugby player slides off the field into a spectator the same rule applies. The principle has even been applied to motor sport. In *Wilks v Cheltenham Home Guard Motor Cycle and Light Car Club* (1971) a motorcycle scrambler left the track and injured a spectator and was found not liable as he was only doing his best; errors of judgment are occasionally bound to happen in racing. For the same reason a rally car which left the road would probably not expose the driver to a negligence claim, though it is absolutely certain that a similar error on an ordinary road would be negligent. There is a possible negligence claim against the organisers if they should not have allowed such an incompetent or inexperienced driver to take part.

The reason for the rule is that a sportsman is often acting in the heat of the moment. If that is not the case then ordinary negligence principles apply. In *Harrison v Vincent* (1981) a racing motor cycle left the course and caused injury. The driver was held negligent as the cause of the accident was careless adjustment of the brakes *before* the race. Again in *Cleghorn v Oldham* (1927) the defendant struck an observer while demonstrating how to play a golf stroke, and was held liable for negligence. Golf is not a game where the heat of the moment principle could ever apply; neither are demonstrations rather than actual play, for example, of hockey or lacrosse techniques. The rule depends on whether it was necessary to take time to reflect on whether it was safe to carry on. If it were, it is still the case that there is normally no liability if a participant has merely done his incompetent best.

The most important case on the issue is *Wooldridge v Sumner* (1963). The accident occurred at a horse show where a rider was galloping his horse along the side of the open-air arena. He took a corner too quickly and the horse veered to the left, injuring a cameraman. The Court of Appeal held that this was a mere error of judgment which was bound to happen sometimes; only if it was such a serious error of judgment that it would be fair to regard it as having been reckless would the rider be liable for negligence.

It is important that the Court concluded that the rider's standard of care was not broken. This is because it would be unfair to say that the cameraman consented to the risk of being injured as he had no knowledge that horses were liable to behave in such a way. Furthermore, while someone in the front row at Lord's might accept the risk of being injured by a cricket ball, the law holds that young children can never consent to negligence, nor can their parents, so to speak, give consent on their behalf. The rule is different in the case of a child participating in a game which has an unavoidable and obvious risk of injury. The reason why the child in the front row cannot claim damages from the batsman is not that he has consented to run the risk of injury but that the batsman has not been negligent even though he almost certainly appreciates the risk, slight as it is, that his batting may injure someone.

The most difficult question is whether every breach of rules gives rise to a tort claim. The recent case of *Condon v Basi* concerned a claim for damages for a broken leg suffered as a result of a very dangerous but hardly unusual late tackle on the football field. The financial significance of cases like this is shown in that the successful claimant was awarded damages of £4,900. The footballer was held liable because he failed to exercise the degree of care to be expected of a footballer in his position; a player only consents to the risk of injuries which occur as a result of the exercise of proper reasonable care. In this case it was held that there was shown a 'reckless disregard' of safety. It may well now be the law that any breach of the rules leading to injury is a tort; this statement is almost certainly true of rules designed to promote safety and may be true of other rules as well. The law has not yet reached that position, as this case was a flagrant violation, but it is likely to do so soon. On the other hand it is not clear that a Criminal Court would decide that this late tackle was a crime. A different result to *Condon* was reached in a karate case only reported in a Cornish local paper. A 'roundhouse' kick, described as one of the commonest moves in karate, caused a ruptured spleen, but there was no evidence that the blow was in excess of what could reasonably have been expected to be used, particularly as accidents such as teeth being knocked out and noses broken were said to be not uncommon. Unlike *Condon*, there was no breach of the rules in this case.

A warning of danger may avoid liability for negligence, but only if sufficient to enable the person warned to avoid the danger. In one case a golfer lost his ball in the rough and indicated to his playing partners that they should complete the hole without him. When they had reached the green he found his ball and played another shot. A partner was hit despite the golfer's cry of 'Fore!' The warning was clearly inadequate to enable evasive action to be taken. It is hard to see that a warning by a participant can ever be sufficient, because events will usually be happening very quickly. Warnings are much more likely to be effective in relation to a danger-ous state of affairs than a dangerous activity.

4. THE CRIMINAL LIABILITY OF ORGANISERS

The position of participants and organisers is clearly distinct. If the rally-car is liable to leave the road the question is whether the organisers have a responsibility to prevent injuries occur-ring. The same is true if golf balls are likely to be hit outside the boundaries of the golf-course. It is easy to think of other examples. The responsi-bilities of organisers, both in criminal law and in civil law, may arise to both participants, especi-ally children, and to spectators and those off the premises.

Criminal liability will only arise in extreme cases, as the majority of serious criminal offences require either intention or recklessness, and an organiser is unlikely to have shown more than carelessness. An organiser may be liable in the same way as an ordinary individual if he assaults someone, but that depends on the normal law and not on the fact that he is the organiser.

Manslaughter is the only serious crime which can be committed if the state of mind which law-yers call 'gross negligence' is present. This could apply to organisers, but there appear to be no cases where such a charge has been brought. Imagine, though, a rifle-range; if a participant fired before the all-clear had been given and killed someone it is possible that he could be con-victed of manslaughter by gross negligence; if an organiser gave the all-clear at an inopportune moment and the same thing happened he might be liable rather than the marksman. Permitting children to play unsupervised with equipment or machinery known to be extremely dangerous is another possible example. While not a case involving sport, the events where children were swept off the rocks near Land's End demonstrate the importance of proper supervision. There was no criminal negligence in this case, but those teaching climbing, sailing, caving, etc could con-ceivably find themselves charged with man-slaughter if a child or indeed an adult dies as a result of their grossly negligent conduct. There is a major peculiarity in the criminal law relevant here. While it is a crime to cause *death* in a grossly negligent manner, it is not a crime to cause non-fatal injuries through gross negligence, although it is a tort.

There are many other ways in which the criminal law is relevant, especially to sports clubs. Clubs are subject to building and planning regulations in the same way as other owners; licensing and gambling law includes some criminal offences; the Health and Safety at Work Act applies if a club employs staff; food hygiene rules may apply; tax and national insurance may be payable. These issues relate to the organ-isation and administration of a sports club as opposed to the activities for which the club is in existence. They apply to all clubs, sporting or otherwise, and are not discussed here.

5. THE CIVIL LIABILITY OF ORGANISERS

It is here that sports clubs and sporting activity are most likely to fall foul of the law. Damage may be suffered by participants, by spectators, by those on the premises for some other purpose, and by those not on the premises. The question is always whether reasonable care has been taken to ensure that injury does not occur. The law of negligence does not require that organisers *guar-antee* that accidents will not happen, merely that reasonable steps are taken to prevent them. Because the concept of reasonableness is flexible and applies to a whole variety of different situations it is often impossible to state the law with certainty; all that can be done is to mention factors which courts take into consideration. It is also important that the law holds an employer liable for the torts of his employees committed while they were at work; so if a player is injured as a result of the negligent maintenance of club equipment by a groundsman the club will be liable as well as the individual, and the realities of insurance are such that the club may be able to pay damages whereas the employee may not. The club will also be liable for torts committed by members acting as such, for example if the equipment were negligently serviced by a club member on a Sunday morning.

(i) Safe Premises

The first duty of a club is to ensure that the club property is reasonably safe, including club buildings where this applies. The duty here is similar to that of an ordinary householder to maintain his property. If someone is injured by a falling tile or a defective floor the occupier of the building is extremely likely to be held liable. This includes making adequate arrangements to have the property repaired. So in *Brown v Lewis* (1896) committee members were held personally liable after an incompetent person had been hired to repair a stand. Similarly in *Francis v Cockrell* (1870) a club was held liable for the collapse of a grandstand. It makes no difference whether or not the injured person has paid to come in; if he has not the case is one of tort and depends on whether the occupier had fulfilled the general duty to take reasonable care, while if he has paid to come in that creates a contract between him and the club. That contract will be held to include a term requiring the occupier to take reasonable steps to ensure that the property is safe for the entrant's purpose, and this imposes the same standard as the tort test. So the same standard is owed by both professional and amateur clubs. In some situations, though, the occupier of the defective building will not be the club but, for example, the local council from whom the club hired the property. If so the council, not the club, should be sued unless the damage was caused by the activities of a club member.

It may not affect the club's responsibility that the accident happened in a somewhat unexpected way. The principle is that so long as the end result was a reasonably foreseeable consequence of the original act of negligence the club will still be liable. In *Hosie v Arbroath Football Club* (1978) the club knew that a gate was corroded and dangerous. The actual accident happened when spectators charged the gate and it collapsed. While the club was not legally responsible for the activities of spectators, whether on or off club premises, it was foreseeable that this kind of behaviour might occur and that the gate might collapse in consequence. An ordinary amateur club which never sees more than a handful of spectators would probably not be liable if this happened, as it would not be foreseeable. They would be liable, however, if, for instance, a cricketer trying to stop the ball going over the boundary collided with a fence or a pavillion, which then collapsed on him. While that kind of thing only happens very rarely, if ever, it is foreseeable as a possible consequence of negligent maintenance of a sports ground.

(ii) Safe Equipment

The next duty is that owed by organisers to participants. This sub-divides into the duty to ensure that equipment is reasonably safe and the duty to provide adequate supervision. The idea of equipment needs to be interpreted widely. In *Gillmore v LCC* (1938) a gym activity was taking place on a highly polished floor when one of the participants slipped and was injured. The Court held that the floor was unsuitable and that to maximise safety an unpolished floor should have been used. This principle could apply to the use of dangerous cricket nets or a decision to sail in weather unsuitable for the size of yacht, as well as more obvious examples such as defective gymnasium equipment. There is unlikely to be liability, however, if it is apparent to the participants that the organisers or the club have no greater expertise than they do, for the law would then conclude that the former took the risk of injury upon themselves. There is a difference between the provision of defective equipment where the danger is not apparent, such as a yacht whose rudder is broken, and the decision to engage in an activity with some obvious degree of risk. The law recognises that some sports and pastimes carry an obvious and inevitable risk; negligence arises where, through the fault of the organisers, there is a greater risk than is normally present. It would therefore be negligent for an organiser to give the impression of having greater skill and experience than was in fact the case. This principle was illustrated in *Simms v Leigh RFC* (1969) when a Rugby League player suffered a broken leg as a result either of a legal tackle or of colliding with the boundary wall. The evidence was unclear but on either view the claim failed. If the tackle caused the injury no-one was to blame as players consent to the risk of being injured in the normal course of the game; if the collision was the cause the club was not to blame as the wall was the regulation distance from the touch-line, such an accident was not known to have happened before and so the player must be taken to have accepted the risk of this injury which did not occur through negligence.

(iii) Adequate Supervision

The duty to provide adequate equipment and facilities overlaps with the duty to provide proper supervision, for the reasonableness of a decision to proceed will often depend on the experience of the participants and the amount of available supervision. Whether it is negligent to take a party of schoolchildren hill walking in the Lake District when heavy rain is forecast will depend on a number of variables, such as the age of the children, their experience and that of their leader, and how well-equipped they are. This kind of case has reached court so rarely that it is impossible to be dogmatic in advance as to the outcome; two cases are never identical. *Jones v LCC* (1932) shows that it can be reasonable to engage in, or even require participation in, activities with a degree of risk. Unemployed young people 17 years old attended a training centre the activities of which included compulsory physical education. The instructor ordered them to participate in a 'piggy-back fight' in the course of which an injury occurred. It was held not to be negligent to require them to participate in activity with a clear though small risk of injury; the instructor gave evidence that he had seen the game played for twenty years without serious accident. It might be different if, for example, one pair was very much heavier and stronger than another pair.

The law recognises that supervision cannot prevent all accidents. *Clarke v Bethnal Green BC* (1939) concerned an accident at a swimming pool which occurred when a swimmer let go of the springboard from underneath and catapulted off the person waiting to dive. There were unproved allegations that the attendant was not paying proper attention, but the Court considered that even if this were true the accident could not have been avoided. It was not a risk of which a reasonable swimming-pool attendant should have been specifically aware, and she could not be everywhere at once. Note that the person actually responsible for the accident may have been liable for the damages. It is probable that the responsibility of supervisors is less in individual pastimes, such as riding and beach or pool swimming, than when competitive games are taking place, particularly where adults are taking part.

(iv) Injuries to Spectators

The next question is when organisers are liable for injuries to spectators. We saw that, for example, a cricketer is not liable if his shot hits a spectator; this is true for golfers using proper care but hitting a bad shot, for hockey players and so on. The issue is whether the organisers have a legal duty to protect spectators by fencing or other means. This will depend on numerous factors, such as how likely injury was to occur, how serious any resulting injury was liable to be, and how easy it would be to stop it. A difficulty with explaining the law is that the two most relevant cases might well be decided differently today if the same thing happened. In *Hall v Brooklands Auto Racing Club* (1933) two cars collided and hit the barrier railing, which broke leading to the deaths of spectators. The Court held that reasonable care did not require the strenthening of the barrier as no such accident had occurred in 23 years. Since then speeds have increased enormously, more than 80 people were killed in a similar accident at Le Mans in 1955 and, to give them credit, race organisers now take far greater precautions. In fact the failure to take such precautions as are now normally taken by others would probably be sufficient by itself to show negligence. The problem arises where the circuit is very long, as in the Isle of Man TT or where there is no circuit as in the RAC Rally. Clearly in such cases fencing is impracticable; it is suggested that the duty would be satisfied if the organisers kept spectators away from the points on the course where they knew from experience that accidents were most likely and perhaps also provided barriers in such places if possible. In *Hall* the Court also said that any reasonable spectator accepted the risk of being injured in such a way. This reasoning is dubious as it is wrong to suggest that spectators accept the risk of being injured in a *negligent* manner; furthermore children may be injured and it can never be said that they consent to being injured. In *White v Blackmore* (1972) a spectator at a jalopy race was killed owing to the negligent erection of barrier ropes such that when a car collided with the ropes a main stake was lifted from the ground with great force. The spectator did not consent to the risk because he was unaware that the ropes had been tethered incorrectly; although, as we will see later, his claim failed for a separate reason.

The other case, *Murray v Harringay Arena* (1951), concerned a six-year-old hit in the eye by a puck at an ice-hockey match. He failed in his claim on the ground that there was no duty to guard against a danger which was inherent in the game. This principle seems unnecessarily wide. Pucks are highly dangerous and very likely to be hit above the edge of the rink. It is suggested that there must be a duty to provide fencing high enough to prevent most shots from getting into the crowd. Compared with cricket this would happen far more frequently and be liable to cause far more damage. Of course for most amateur sports clubs the lack of spectators means that injury is less likely and therefore the duty is not as stringent.

For amateurs it is the passer-by who is more at risk: the sliced golf shot hits a pedestrian, the football goes into the road and causes a car-crash and so on. Again basic principles of negligence law apply and various factors must be weighed. In *Lamond v Glasgow Corporation* (1968) a pedestrian was hit while walking along a lane adjacent to a golf-course. The evidence was that some 6,000 balls per year came over the fence; there was also evidence from golf-course architects that it would be possible to redesign the course at no great cost to reduce that figure. On these facts it was easy to hold the club liable and they would probably have been liable even if redesign had not been possible given the high risk of injury. On the other hand, in *Bolton v Stone* (1951) a passer-by outside a cricket field failed to recover compensation after being hit on the head by a ball. The club had erected a high fence and the evidence was that this was an exceptional hit, balls having cleared the fence only a handful of times in 30 years. The club had taken all reason-

Nuisance

Clubs may also be liable for the tort of nuisance. This is concerned not so much with actual damage to person or property but with interference with one's right to enjoy one's property. In such a case the remedy which is sought will usually be an injunction, which is a Court order that the nuisance should cease. Failure to comply may constitute a contempt of Court.

Typical examples of nuisances are extreme noise or extreme smells. So if a sports club created unusually pungent smells or organised discos which frequently went on late into the night, adjoining property owners could seek an injunction. Whether one would be issued depends on how frequently it happens, how close the neighbouring properties are and how many of them are affected. A Court may grant a compromise order, for example, that no music shall be played later than midnight. Obviously it is cheaper and more neighbourly to attempt to resolve these cases without going to Court; it is only if the situation is very bad that it would be advisable to seek an injunction.

In some cases the actual playing of the game may be the alleged nuisance, and in a serious case the injunction will require the activity to cease altogether. In *Stretch v Romford FC* (1971) the club were required to cease permitting speedway meetings to take place in their stadium. In such a case the nuisance must relate to the actual playing of the game rather than any inconvenience caused by large numbers of spectators with consequent possible parking problems and even vandalism or hooliganism. For these the club is not responsible; were the law otherwise almost every large stadium would have to be shut.

Stretch was a clear case; two other recent cases were less certain. *Miller v Jackson* concerned cricket balls being hit into the gardens of adjoining houses, causing minor damage and preventing the Millers using their garden while cricket was in progress. Despite the undeniable interference, the Court refused an injunction to stop cricket being played. There was no other available pitch in the village and the club was said to be one of the focal points of village life. In other words, the public interest prevailed over the private though the club would have had to pay compensation for any future damage caused by cricket balls. A different result was reached in *Kennaway v Thompson* (1980), where an injunction was sought to restrain power-boat racing on a lake adjoining Mrs Kennaway's house. The judge was able to compromise, so that the club were permitted to continue organising racing, but only on a limited number of weekends during the year and operating under a maximum decibel limit. It will only be in very unusual situations that a sporting activity will cause interference to an extent that a judge will grant an injunction. Residents are expected to put up with the minor inconvenience which is all that will occur in most cases.

able steps to prevent injury. It is clear, though, from *Miller v Jackson* (1972) that if property damage is unavoidable (in this case to a greenhouse with the possibility of damaging houses) the club will have to pay compensation; this would also be true in the unlucky event of injury to people in the house or garden. If it is likely that at some time someone outside the club will suffer damage to his person or his property then it is only in very exceptional cases like *Bolton v Stone* that the club will not be held negligent. If the ball causes a driver to swerve to take evasive action and an accident results a Court would probably hold that to be a reasonably foreseeable consequence of a failure to contain balls within the ground and so the club or the occupier would be liable. Of course in many situations fencing would either be impractical or very unsightly (planning permission may be unobtainable) so in theory the club is in an impossible situation, but in practice the risk seems less severe than one might imagine and adequate insurance should be obtainable.

(v) Defences to Negligence

In some situations a club may have been negligent, but yet will not be liable to pay damages because it has a defence. If something is dangerous a warning may avoid liability if people can avoid the danger as a result; such a warning can be either verbal or by a notice. To fix a notice telling people not to use the cricket nets or to skate on a pond will probably be enough, although even then, if the club knows that young children are in the habit of using the facilities, it may have to go further and actually prevent their use. But a warning will be insufficient if the people on one's property have no alternative. To warn about the state of an unlit pathway or drive will not necessarily mean that an injured person cannot sue the occupier. The warning may be inadequate for the same reason that 'Beware. Falling Rocks' is inadequate.

The defence of consent has already been mentioned. It is this which prevents the tort of battery being committed in any contact sport. Children are held to consent by themselves or through their parents, teachers or guardian. But consent is only given to risks normally incident to the game; for this reason there was no defence to the bad foul in *Condon v Basi*. Equally it is virtually impossible to give consent to a negligent act, for consent requires awareness of the risk. Most of the cases where courts have said that participants or spectators consented to the risk turn out to be cases where neither the participant nor the organisers were negligent; examples are the cases of *Wooldridge v Sumner* and *Murray v Harringay Arena* discussed earlier. To summarise, the defence of consent, both for children and adults, applies to normal, inevitable risks but not to additional risks which are the result of negligence by either participant or organiser.

The defence of contributory negligence is much commoner than that of consent; this applies where, although negligence caused the injury, the victim was partly to blame through lack of care for his own safety. He still gets some compensation though; the Court decides by what percentage he was to blame and reduces by that percentage the amount of compensation it would have awarded had he been blameless.

One frequently sees on notice-boards, tickets or programmes a statement that the occupier or organiser is not liable for any injury howsoever caused. This is an attempt to avoid having to pay compensation even if an injury is caused through negligence. The Unfair Contract Terms Act 1977 restricts occupiers of *business* premises from relying on such clauses. If personal injury is suffered the attempted exclusion is completely ineffective; the case proceeds as if it were not there, though occupiers have not been stopped from putting them up. If the damage is only to property the defendant may rely on the exclusion if it is reasonable to allow him to do so. Professional sports clubs are business premises and local authorities are specifically included in the definition of business. Amateur clubs are not businesses even if they seek to make money through bar sales, social activities etc. They are therefore permitted to rely on such notices. To do so reasonable steps must be taken to draw people's attention to them. In *White v Blackmore* the claim by the deceased's widow failed because of such a clause inside the programme he was given when he entered the course. The most likely use of such a notice is to try to exclude liability if belongings are stolen from club property. This may happen without any negligence by club members or officials; if so, the notice is unnecessary. But if there is negligence, such as forgetting to lock a door, the notice will mean that the club will not be liable. It must cover what happened; so, if it excludes liability for damage or loss to belongings, it will not work to exclude liability if someone suffers personal injury through negligence.

6. THE NEED FOR INSURANCE

Any sports club which fails to take out adequate insurance is extremely foolish. It is exposing itself to the slight but definite possibility of having to pay large damages. Equally important, it is leaving open the possibility that a member may receive no compensation for a serious injury for which no-one is to blame.

The relevant insurance is of two main kinds, first party and third party. Under the former, payment is received simply upon proof that the loss has occurred. The question of who, if anyone, was to blame is irrelevant. The commonest examples of this form of insurance are household contents policies and that part of a comprehensive motoring policy dealing with accidental damage to the vehicle. A club needs to ensure that its own buildings and property are adequately insured. It may also be possible to take out a policy covering the property of private individuals while on club premises and the property of club members while elsewhere but representing the club. This may be expensive and it is reasonable to expect individuals to insure their own property against loss.

We are accustomed to thinking about first-party insurance as dealing with property, but it is possible to insure people as well. Most sports injuries will not be the result of any tort and there will in all probability be no legal right to damages. Yet each year a number of rugby players are paralysed for life, and serious injuries may occur in most sports. There is no legal obligation on sports clubs to insure their members, and policies can be taken out by individuals, yet very few do so. It is suggested that there is a moral responsibility to protect the interests of members in this way; this is even more true where children are involved who cannot be expected to protect their own interests.

Third-party insurance provides protection not against being injured but against being held liable to pay damages for someone else's injury. Without legal liability no payment is due. There are, as we have seen, many situations in which such a liability can arise, situations where there may have been no more than momentary carelessness. If a club is not insured and is not set up as a limited company any such damages will have to be paid by the club or even in exceptional cases by members of the committee or the individual who was negligent. Most awards of damages are less than £1,000, but in the rare cases of lifetime paralysis or brain damage they can exceed £300,000. The public liability part of a contents policy may or may not cover an individual, but it cannot apply to the liability of his club. The need for and the provision of sports insurance is growing, and clubs should find no difficulty in arranging cover. The potential gap concerns injuries suffered in casual games in the park or on the beach. Here there is no question of club liability; individuals will almost certainly be uninsured in respect of their own injuries and, unless their public liability policy provides cover, in respect of injuries to others. The possibility of an uninsured catastrophic loss is unavoidable.

7. CLUBS AND THEIR MEMBERS

(i) Discrimination Law

While clubs are in theory private bodies, there are controls on the way membership is regulated. It used to be the law that anyone could be rejected for membership for whatever reason, but the coming of controls on discriminatory behaviour has changed that. Racial discrimination is nearly always unlawful; if a club has less than twenty-five members it may discriminate on racial grounds in respect of who is admitted to membership or the terms of such membership. Also, a club is permitted to discriminate if its purpose is to provide recreational and social benefits to people of a particular nationality, such as London Welsh or Indian Gymkhana, though this exception does not apply to discrimination on ground of colour rather than nationality. The law does not prevent refusal of membership for an adequate reason such as that the club is full or the person has been expelled from a similar club. Clubs with less than twenty-five members are *not* permitted to discriminate in the employment of staff.

The Sex Discrimination Act 1975 also applies to clubs. In this case there is a much wider exception, as non-profit clubs may be restricted to men or women only or have different classes of membership for women or for men. It is also unlawful to discriminate on grounds of sex or against a married person in the employment of staff. At present this prohibition does not apply if less than five employees are employed, which probably includes most clubs, but legislation going through Parliament in 1986 will remove this 'small firms' exception.

Discrimination law applies to participation in sport as well as club membership. The only permitted instances of race discrimination are where teams are selected on the basis of nationality. Those few clubs permitted to discriminate in team selection are not allowed to discriminate as regards who they will play against or access to club facilities after a game. In other words no club may restrict use of bar facilities to whites only or Indians only. The small clubs exception applies only to membership and not to other facilities which may be offered.

Sex discrimination against participants is a different problem as it is the average lower strength and height of women which puts them at a disadvantage in certain sports, though this difference only appears in the teenage years. The Act provides that sports can be restricted to one sex only where the average women is at a disadvantage compared with the average man. This permits discrimination in most adult sport. *Bennett v Football Association* (1978) concerned a ban on a twelve-year-old girl from playing in league matches. The ban was upheld by the Court on the ground that the Act looks to the average woman and not to the average girl. It might be possible to argue that such a blanket ban is contrary to European Community Law, but no-one has yet brought an action. There is room for disagreement about whether in a particular case the average woman is at a disadvantage (snooker, darts, bowls?) and it is surprising that more cases have not been brought. Of course the law only *permits* such discrimination; it does not *require* it, so if the sport's governing body agrees, mixed sports are always lawful at whatever age.

(ii) Disciplinary Action

Sometimes a club may wish to discipline or even expel a member. While the Courts are unwilling to intervene very often, there are certain minimum standards with which clubs must comply. Disciplinary action can only be taken if the club is given power to do so by its rules, and then only for reasons specifically stated in the rules. The proper procedures must be followed, so that if, for instance, the rules say that the club secretary must be a member of any disciplinary committee, any decision without his presence will be null and void. The basic rule is simply that the club rules must be strictly complied with. If not, a Court ruling may be sought that the discipline was invalid; this does not prevent the club starting again and carrying out the procedure properly if possible. The club must also comply with the rules of natural justice. There are two. No-one shall be a judge when he has an interest in the matter; for example, if the case arose out of a disagreement between a committee member and an ordinary member, it would be wrong for the committee member to sit on the disciplinary committee. The second rule is that everyone has the right to state his case. This means a right to know in advance of a discipline hearing why the club wants to impose discipline and a chance to speak in one's own defence.

In the sporting context discipline is more likely to be imposed by the sport's governing body; suspensions are the most common cases. Again the Courts are reluctant to intervene. The same principles apply however: the disciplinary body must comply both with its own rules and with the rules of natural justice. As long as the procedure is basically fair there is no right to be represented by a lawyer, although the particular procedure may allow it. There is no right actually to appear before a tribunal, merely an opportunity to put one's defence either orally or in writing. The Courts consider such bodies to be expert and therefore do not encourage what are in effect appeals to the Courts unless there has been basic unfairness in the procedure.

Every inch of the countryside is owned by some-one. It is trespass to go onto someone's land without authority – which means either their permission or some legal right. But the public are able to use large parts of the countryside, including some commons, and all public rights of way and country parks.

1. RIGHTS OF WAY

The commonest way to get out and enjoy the countryside is by using part of the 120,000 miles of public rights of way. A public right of way is a route which any member of the public can use, for a journey, or simply for recreation.

There are three categories of public right of way:

Footpaths which can be used on foot, with a dog or with other things such as prams which a pedestrian may have.

Bridleways which can be similarly used by pedestrians and also by persons with horses, animals driven in a pack and by pedal cyclists.

Byways open to all traffic which can be used by all these, and vehicles.

Maps also sometimes refer to **RUPP**s: roads used as a public path. All RUPPs are gradually being converted into one of the other classes of right of way – usually a bridleway or byway. Until they are converted the public can certainly walk, ride a horse or bicycle along them and may be able to drive a motor vehicle depending on the particular path. The County Council should be able to advise on each path.

Long distance routes, heritage walks, recreation paths and coastal paths have no special legal status, they are simply a series of paths which have been joined together into a longer route. However, canal-side towpaths are special. In law they are provided by canal owners for use by people towing boats on the canal. In some places the canal owner has also given the public a right to use the towpath for walking or riding. When the public are allowed to use a towpath, users must give way to people using the canal. A sign on the towpath will indicate the conditions on which the public may use it. 'Green lanes' have no legal status. There may be no public right to use them at all, although many are byways.

The public only have the right to pass and repass along a right of way. There is no right to wander off the path onto adjoining land – unless the path is so muddy or obstructed it cannot be used, in which case a user can go onto nearby land just as far as is needed to get round the obstruction. The public can stop for a rest, and generally picnicking is accepted, but camping on the path or its verge is not lawful. The person becomes a trespasser and may be guilty of obstruction.

(i) How to Find Rights of Way

The easiest way to find out where there are rights of way is by looking at an Ordnance Survey Map – notably the 1:25,000 Pathfinder Series – but the Ordnance Survey do not guarantee that any routes shown on the map are actually public rights of way. Most of the time these maps are accurate enough, but if there is any doubt the county council or (borough) should be consulted, for they are required to maintain an up to date 'Definitive Map' – which is just what it says it is. In law, that is the correct statement of public rights of way. If a way is on the map that right along that route exists. The map is conclusive evidence that the rights shown do exist, but it does not prove that rights not on the map do not exist – only that nobody has put them on the map yet, so if people are sure of their facts, they may use a public right of way which is not on the Map. Details of the procedure for getting the Definitive Map altered may be obtained from county councils. The process of updating the maps is time consuming so most are out of date with a backlog of claims. Nonetheless, a claim should be made as soon as an error is discovered, if only to reserve a place in the queue!

The Definitive Map not only contains the route of a right of way, it also has notes concerning some rights of way, for example, details of their width. Otherwise it is difficult to find out how wide a right of way should be, as there is no legally prescribed width. In the absence of any other evidence, if a way is enclosed on both sides it is reasonable to assume the entire space between each hedge or fence is part of the right of way. Although the width of the right of way itself is not fixed by law, any gates on a bridleway must be at least 1.5 metres (5 ft) wide.

The county council must ensure there is a sign wherever a footpath, bridleway or byway leaves a metalled road, giving details of the class of route, its destination and its distance. Any council or the landowner may waymark routes, by putting small markers along the route, to ensure users can find the way. The landowner's consent is needed to install them. Detailed advice, including the standard colour codes for waymarking arrows and the legal requirements can be obtained from the Countryside Commission. Any member of the public may take the county council to Court to enforce their obligations.

(ii) Maintenance

For most public rights of way, if the landowner declines to take action, the highway authority (the county council, metropolitan district council or London borough council) has an obligation to keep them maintained, and district and parish councils have a range of powers to assist. This means keeping the surface of the path in good order, as long as the path exists, but where a path ceases to exist, such as a cliff path collapsing into the sea, the council is not obliged to restore it. The standard of maintenance varies according to the use of the path. As a judge said in one case, you cannot expect the same standard for a family walking to church on Sunday and someone out for a rural ramble. Department of Environment guidelines state that:

'where paths are used mainly for pleasure by ramblers, it will no doubt generally be sufficient that they should be free from obstructions or impassable water or mud. . . . The main requirement is clearly that they should serve their purpose, whether business or pleasure, and not that they should conform to some arbitrary standard of construction.'

(iii) Obstructions on the Way

The commonest complaint when using a right of way is to find it obstructed by an overgrown hedge, wired up gates or ploughing. It is an offence for anyone wilfully to obstruct a right of way, including the landowner, even if the obstruction does not totally block the way, as long as part of the path is interfered with. If a right of way is obstructed, details should be given to the county council.

If the obstruction has a natural cause, such as a rock fall, the county council itself must clear the path as quickly as possible. Otherwise the landowner is legally responsible for maintaining things like gates and fences, keeping hedges trimmed and so on. If he declines to take action, the county council may, on due notice, remove the obstruction and recover their costs from the person responsible for the obstruction. In addition anyone can prosecute a person for obstruction or can take the county council to Court for an order requiring them to carry out their duty to keep the way free from obstructions. A Court cannot compel an offender to remove an obstruction, but it may be able to fine the person a continuing sum per day until the obstruction is removed. A person using a path can only remove just so much of the obstruction as is necessary to allow him to continue his journey, for example, by untying a gate. If he can get round without removing the obstruction, he cannot interfere with the obstruction. Deliberate parties of people going out to remove obstructions are unlawful, unless they are doing so with the consent of the highway authority or landowner, and they could be sued for trespass or prosecuted for criminal damage.

Gates are allowed on all rights of way, but stiles are only permitted on footpaths. The landowner must maintain them in a safe condition. If he fails to do so the county council can carry out the repairs and send him the bill or obtain a Court order requiring him to carry out repairs. If a landowner voluntarily maintains stiles or gates on public rights of way on his land, he can claim 25% of the costs from the county. The consent of the county council is needed to erect a new stile or gate across a right of way.

The biggest cause of obstructions is ploughing. The occupier of farm land is entitled to plough up a footpath or bridleway which crosses a field, but not one which runs round the edge of a field, but he must restore the surface so as to make it reasonably convenient for the public to use the path within two weeks from the time when he began to plough. If he is prevented from doing so by exceptional weather conditions, he must make the path useable as soon as practicable. Not to do so is an offence for which continuing fines may be imposed for every day the obstruction continues after conviction. Again the county council must enforce this law, but district and parish councils also have powers to do so. A Code of Practice giving guidance to farmers has just been published by the Countryside Commission.

441

(iv) Interference and Intimidation

Any unreasonable interference with the use of rights of way may lead to prosecution or a civil action, by the landowner or a user. If anyone threatens, intimidates or harasses someone using a right of way, for example by ordering the user to leave or by keeping a fierce dog beside the path, this is an offence which should be reported to the county council. An individual may also be entitled to bring a private prosecution. Misleading signs, which are likely to deter people from using a public right of way are also unlawful, again the county council should be informed.

(v) Injury

A landowner, across whose land a right of way runs is not liable for injury to people using the right of way unless he has done something to cause the injury. If he has merely failed to maintain his land he may not be liable. A user of a right of way can sue his fellow users, if they negligently cause him injury. If a person is injured because of the state of the surface of the way, the county council may be liable if it has failed to take reasonable care to ensure the highway is safe. That does not mean the path must be absolutely safe, but that the council must have a system of inspecting paths regularly (how often a path should be inspected depends on the money the county has available, and the importance of the path). But it is rare for people to succeed in getting compensation for injuries on footpaths in the countryside, because the courts do not expect councils to carry out frequent inspections.

(vi) Acquiring Public Rights of Way

Public rights of way can arise in a number of ways. In most cases a right of way is dedicated by the owner of the land it crosses. Sometimes the landowner may sign a statutory declaration saying the way has been created or otherwise expressly declare he is creating a path, but more usually he simply lets use begin. After twenty years of use by the public, as of right, the path becomes a public right of way and cannot be lost by disuse. Extra rights on public paths can also be acquired in the same way, so if a footpath is used by horses without challenge for twenty years the footpath will become a bridleway. To establish a public right of way, there must be evidence that the way has been used by the public, not just a small group – such as the landowners staff or friends – and the use must be open, that is people must have used it believing they had a right to the land without challenge. If the public are using a path which a landowner does not want to become a public right of way and 20 years use has not yet passed, the landowner must take steps to show he is not intending to create a public right of way and does not want the public to use the land. The safest way to do that is to deposit a formal notice with the local authority stating he is not dedicating a highway, together with a 6″ to the mile map showing the routes accepted as public rights of way, declaring that no others are intended. Such a statement lasts for five years.

Alternatively, he can take steps to interrupt use. Whether any steps are sufficient to stop a right of way being created is a difficult question and depends on its own facts. Putting up a notice prohibiting the public is probably not enough, unless the public obey it and stop using the way. Traditionally landowners have closed paths for one day a year, but that is a far from certain way of preventing dedication – indeed the Courts have said it may not be effective in some cases, nevertheless people still continue to do it. Even putting up a 1.5 metres (5 ft) fence across the way may not be enough – it will depend on the reason for the fence.

(vii) Closing or Diverting Rights of Way

Rights of way cannot cease to exist through disuse – once a highway always a highway. They can only be closed or diverted if the way is not needed or there is a more convenient route. In most cases closure or diversion orders are made by the county or district council. Notices must be placed in the local press, and on the paths affected, with a plan showing the effect of the order. These signs have to be legible but are not always large. The notice specifies the closing date for objections, which must be at least 28 days away. If there are no objections the county or district council which made the order may confirm the order, but if there are objections the order together with the objections are sent to the Secretary of State for the Environment, who may hold a public inquiry before reaching a decision. As an alternative a right of way may be closed by a Magistrates' Court, on application from a county council.

There are special rules for closing rights of way when someone is going to build on the land. If there are any objections a public inquiry is held. There are also special powers to close rights of way temporarily or permanently for defence purposes.

(viii) Temporary Closure

Rights of way and other public land may be closed during outbreaks of diseases such as foot and mouth. In addition there are a number of powers in local Acts of Parliament to close land in certain circumstances. In each case, a sign will be put up. Local authorities will have details of what is happening. It is a criminal offence to disobey these restrictions. Traffic Regulation Orders, issued by a county council, can restrict or prohibit all, or some use of a public right of way – either on a temporary or permanent basis. Notices of orders must be published in a local newspaper, and a sign must be maintained on the site as long as the Order applies. It is an offence to disobey an order. They are commonly used to prohibit all traffic for roadworks, or major sport events, or to control one type of user such as motorcyclists.

2. OTHER PLACES TO USE IN THE COUNTRYSIDE

(i) Commons

There is widespread misunderstanding about what a common is. In law, a common is any piece of land registered under the Commons Registration Act 1965, as being land over which commoners have certain agricultural rights such as grazing cattle or taking wood. In this legal sense, large tracts of uplands, urban commons, and many village greens, heaths and recreation areas may be commons. The common is owned by someone – usually the Lord of the Manor, a company or a local authority. As such it is private land, like any other; the difference is that some people called 'commoners' have extra rights over the land. To be a commoner, the person's rights must have been registered with the county council prior to 1970. The extent of those rights depends on local history.

There is no automatic right of the public to use commons for recreation, although that right does exist on many commons, particularly those in built-up areas. Where the public do have a right to use some commons for recreation, there are normally bye-laws controlling that use. Although the laws giving the public the right to use commons for recreation are all over 60 years old, there are still many uncertainties in the law; for example, lawyers are still disputing whether horses may be ridden on commons, except on defined bridleways. The county council maintains a register of commons listing existing commoners rights and the name of the owner and will also know the extent of any general public rights to use the common for recreation. Landowners cannot built on commons, without consent from the Department of the Environment, even for recreation. An application to build has to be advertised in a local newspaper and at least 28 days allowed for comments. The prime factor is whether the building will be of benefit to the whole neighbourhood, not just a limited number of people – so public sports fields and pavilions will generally be allowed, private houses will not.

(ii) Parks, Country Parks and Open Spaces

Many areas of unbuilt land are owned by local authorities for the public to use, and are often said to be 'publically owned land', or 'public open space'. Nonetheless this does not give the public unlimited rights to use the land. If the land was purchased as a park or open space any member of the public may use it for recreation, subject to any bye-laws or regulations restricting activities. These will be displayed at the entrance to the land. It is an offence to disobey bye-laws. Charges can be made for facilities such as boating, bowls or picnicking. A country park is simply a park in the countryside, and is subject to the same sorts of legal controls as other parks.

(iii) National Parks

The ten National Parks cover 13,600 square kilometres of land, mainly in the mountains and moorlands. There are special laws which protect the landscape, but there is no general right of public access to land in National Parks. Exactly the same rules about access apply in National Parks as anywhere else.

(iv) Nature Reserves

Nature reserves are designed to assist in conservation. Some are therefore not open to the public, although others allow the public to visit the reserve, on conditions. The first step is to find out who owns the Nature Reserve, and approach the owner for permission to use it. The owner will give details of the special rules which apply to the site.

(v) Permitted Access

In addition to these general legal rights to use the countryside, there are many places the public can use, with the consent of the owner. If an owner is allowing the general public to use his land, the public must obey the conditions he imposes. Some landowners do this by entering an access agreement with the council. This guarantees the public use of the land for a longish period, but in return the landowner can obtain bye-laws to help regulate what people do on his land. Breach of a bye-law is an offence.

What are bye-laws?

These are made by local authorities and other public bodies, confirmed by the Home Office. It is an offence to break them, for which a person can be prosecuted and fined – although the fines are generally very low. If a person persistently disobeys a bye-law a High Court injunction could be obtained, breach of which could result in imprisonment, so indirectly bye-laws do have some teeth. An authority can change bye-laws with the consent of the Secretary of State.

---

3. WHAT CAN BE DONE IN THE COUNTRYSIDE

(i) Vehicles

It is an offence to drive a vehicle on a footpath and driving on a bridleway is trespass, unless the landowner has given his consent. Vehicles, including motorcycles and cars can use any byways, although great care must be taken as other users may not be expecting vehicles.

A motor vehicle cannot be driven onto a field, common or open land, even to park, whether or not the public is allowed to use the land for walking, unless the landowner has given permission. It is a criminal offence to do so. It is sometimes said the public can park anywhere within 14 metres of a road. This is not true, although it is not a criminal offence, it is still trespass. However people can park on verges, providing they do not obstruct gates or other road users.

People often think motorcycles have no place in the countryside, but many grassed rights of way are, in fact, ancient roads, which cars and motorcycles may use. In Wiltshire, for example, the old main road from London is now a muddy right of way in places because when the road was surfaced at the turn of the century a new route was chosen. People out for a quiet day in the country often complain about motorcyclists – but they may have as much right as anyone else to be

there. In extreme cases a Traffic Regulation Order can be used to ban motor vehicles from a particular right of way or the right of vehicular use can be extinguished.

(ii) Animals

It is an offence to keep any dangerous animal in such a way as to endanger members of the public. But even normally harmless animals can sometimes cause injury or damage. An owner is responsible for what his dogs or livestock do, including any injury or damage caused by the animal, if the owner has been negligent in some way. For example if a cow strays onto the road and damages a car, the owner will be liable if the cow escaped because he had not maintained fences, but he will not be liable if it escaped because a rambler left a gate open. Anyone taking an animal onto a right of way or other public place must similarly take reasonable care, and should be suitably insured.

Bulls are a special case. It is an offence to keep a bull in a field or enclosure crossed by a public right of way unless (a) the bull is under eleven months old or (b) is not from the following breeds: Ayrshire, British Fresian, British Holstein, Dairy Shorthorn, Guernsey, Jersey and Kerry and is accompanied by cows or heifers. Even if a bull falls within one of these two categories, its owner can be liable for any injury it causes, if the owner knew it to be dangerous.

Dogs are also subject to special controls. First, local authorities can designate particular roads as requiring any dogs to be kept on a lead and may have byelaws prohibiting dogs from fouling footpaths. Secondly, dogs in any public place must have a collar, stating the owner's name and address. Thirdly, if a dog is a danger to people or other animals and not kept under proper control, the police or local authority can take action, or an individual can bring a private prosecution. One complaint will seldom be sufficient to prove the dog is dangerous, hence the comment that dogs are allowed two bites. Certainly the police are reluctant to take action on only one incident; nonetheless serious incidents should be reported in case of further incidents. A Court can require the owner to keep the dog under control, or order the dog to be destroyed. It is an offence for a dog to 'worry' livestock on agricultural land if it could reasonably be expected to cause injury or suffering to the livestock. If the dog actually injures cattle or poultry, or chases sheep, action can be taken in the Courts, as if it were a dangerous dog.

A farmer can only shoot a trespassing dog where there is no other way to prevent serious injury to a person or animal.

(iii) Horses

No licence is needed to keep or ride a horse. Many of the laws concerning traffic do not apply to horses, but there are additional restrictions on horses. The highway code should be obeyed. Councils may prohibit horses using particular grass verges along the roadside. It would be an assault to ride a horse so as to injure someone, and indeed, to ride a horse furiously, so as to obstruct, annoy or endanger the public is an offence. Riding schools require licensing from the local authority, and must comply with stringent regulations concerning insurance.

(iv) Metal Detecting

The public may carry and use a metal detector in the countryside, but must not disturb the ground surface to remove anything discovered. To do so is trespass, and may also be a criminal offence.

(v) Litter

It is an offence to drop any litter in a public place, including streets, parks and on rights of way. Local bye-laws may also make it an offence to drop litter in other places. It is also an offence to dump larger items, such as furniture or garden refuse anywhere except in an authorised dump.

(vi) Boating

The public can boat and sail on the sea, and on all tidal rivers, up to the top point at which it is tidal. Local bye-laws can regulate boating close to the shore. This is commonly done at popular seaside resorts. Such rules should be displayed somewhere along the shore line, but the sign may not be easily visible. To be sure, check with the local authority.

On all other waterways – other parts of rivers, canals, lakes – people may only boat if there is a public right of navigation (like a right of way, but on water), or the owner of the land adjoining the river gives consent. Launching, mooring and landing boats also requires the consent of the owner of the bank, unless the public have acquired rights to do so.

When the waterway is owned by a public body the terms on which the public may use the waterway will be displayed at the site as regulations or bye-laws. If you are in doubt, the local authority should know where to find them. Canals are subject to regulations laid down by the British Waterways Board, which require a licence obtainable from the Board for sailing pleasure boats on canals.

Local navigation rules apply in many places in addition to the normal rules for sailing. Just as with driving a car, a person will be liable for any damage he causes negligently whilst sailing. Insurance is not compulsory, but is therefore highly advisable.

4. AT THE SEASIDE

The area between high and low water marks, the foreshore, is owned by the Crown, but is usually administered by a local council. The foreshore can be used by anyone for recreation, although bye-laws may regulate what can be done on the foreshore, and the water out to 1,000 metres from low water; for example, swimming may be restricted for safety or conservation. The public may be excluded from foreshores used by bodies such as the Ministry of Defence, but it is safe to presume the foreshore is public, unless a sign says otherwise. A local authority will confirm whether the sign is correct.

The land above high water mark is often owned by the local authority at popular seaside resorts, but some beaches are owned by other people, who may, or may not choose to allow the public to use their beach, just as they can choose to let the public use any other land they own. They cannot prevent the public from using the foreshore, between their land and the sea, but can prevent the public crossing their private land to get to the foreshore or sea, unless there is a public right of way.

Everything on a beach is owned by the landowner. In some cases there are customary rights for local residents to remove sand, gravel or other substances from the beach, but in most places removing shells or pebbles is unlawful, and could be theft as well as trespass – although the landowner would be hard put to show he had suffered damage as a result. Abandoned or unidentifiable objects found loose on the beach may be taken, although they should be reported to the police. When objects apparently from a wreck are found, they must be handed to the local Receiver of Wrecks. Unclaimed material from wrecks belongs to the Crown.

5. PROTECTING THE COUNTRYSIDE

Many laws seek to protect the countryside. Users of the countryside are affected by some, notably the laws protecting wild birds, animals and plants. When animals, birds or plants are protected it is an offence to destroy or interfere with them, even if the person does not realise they are protected, although, if a motorist accidentally kills a protected bird or animal, it is not an offence – but it is an offence to take the bird or animal home if it is game, unless the driver has a game licence.

(i) Birds

All wild birds, except game birds, and those regarded by law as pests are protected. It is a criminal offence to kill or injure them, or interfere with their nests or eggs. But damaging any bird, nest or egg from the list of specially protected birds is a particularly serious offence.

Apart from the black-headed gull and common gull (and the lapwing if the eggs are taken between 1 January and 15 April), wild birds eggs cannot be sold without the consent of the Department of the Environment (Countryside and Recreation Division), the Nature Conservancy Council or the Ministry of Agriculture.

There are few exceptions to these controls though even a protected bird can be destroyed on humane grounds. Landowners can kill birds, except protected birds, if they are interfering with crops. Species regarded as pests may be killed and their nests and eggs destroyed, but only by the landowner or someone acting for him. If the birds are on publically owned land someone authorised by a local council, a water board or the Nature Conservancy Council can act.

Specially protected birds

Avocet	Merlin
Bee-eater	Osprey
Beswick's swan	Owl, barn and snowy
Bittern and little Bittern	Peregrine
Black redstart	Plover, Kentish and little-ringed
Black-tailed godwit	Purple heron
Black-winged stilt	Red kite
Bluethroat	Red-backed shrike
Brambling	Red-necked phalarope
Bunting, cirl, Lapland and snow	Redwing
Chough	Ruff
Common quail	Sandpiper, green, purple and wood
Corncrake	Scarlet rosefinch
Crossbill	Scaup
Diver	Scoter, common and velvet
Dotterel	Serin
Eagle, white and golden	Shorelark
Fieldfare	Short-toed treecreeper
Firecrest	Spoonbill
Garganey	Spotted crake
Golden oriole	Stone curlew
Goshawk	Temminck's stint
Grebe, black-necked and Slavonian	Tern, black, little and roseate
Greenshank	Tit, bearded and crested
Gull, little and Mediterranean	Warbler, Cetti's, Dartford, marsh and Savi's
Gyr falcon	Whimbrel
Harrier	Whooper swan
Hobby	Woodlark
Honey buzzard	Wryneck
Hoopoe	From 21 February to 31 August at sea or on the
Kingfisher	seashore, and from 1 February to 31 August
Leach's petrel	elsewhere Goldeneye ducks, Pintail ducks, Grey-
Long-tailed duck	lag Goose (in some places) are also protected.

Birds considered as pests are: collared dove; crow; domestic pigeon now wild; gulls, lesser and greater, black-backed, herring; house sparrow; jackdaw; jay; magpie; rook; starling; wood-pigeon.

(ii) Animals

Unlike birds, many animals receive no protection. The only protected animals are otters, bats, sand lizards, great crested or warty newts, smooth snakes, red squirrels, natterjack toads, badgers and seals. It is an offence to interfere with these animals, or their nests or shelters except to prevent serious damage to property or with the permission of the Ministry of Agriculture or Nature Conservancy Council. Licences can be obtained to control badgers or seals. In all cases involving rare species, advice should be sought from the local authority before taking action.

It is an offence to possess or to sell any of the protected animals or an adder, common frog, viviparous lizard, palmate newt, smooth newt, slow worm, grass snake, common toad. Animals which are considered pests, such as foxes, rats and coypu may be killed.

It is an offence to release into the wild any animal which is not normally resident or visitor here, because they can damage the ecological balance. It is also an offence to release animals which exist in the wild, but are unwelcome: coypu, prairie dog, fat dormouse, mongolian gerbil, mink, black rat, grey squirrel and some reptiles. These offences both are subject to unlimited fines.

No animals, even pests can be killed by inhumane means such as snares, explosives or decoys, and for some species the restrictions on methods of killing are even tighter, such as badgers, bats, dormice, hedgehogs, shrews, red squirrels and seals. Nor can automatic weapons, bows, explosives or light be used to help kill or catch wild mammals, except under licence. Only pests can be killed by poisoning.

(iii) Insects

The protecting of endangered species extends as far as insects. It is an offence to kill, injure, catch or possess any protected insect, or disturb its nest or home, except to protect property. But the spider in the bath can still be washed away, providing he does not feature on the list.

Protected insects
Beetles – Rainbow leaf
Butterflies – Chequered skipper
    Heath fritillary
    Large blue
Dragonflies – Norfolk Aeschna
Grasshoppers – Field cricket
    Mole cricket
    Wart-biter
Molluscs – Carthusian snail
    Glutinous snail
    Sandbowl Snail
Moths – Barberry Carpet
    Black veined
    Essex Emerald
    New Forest burnet
    Reddish-buff
Spiders – Fen raft spider
    Ladybird spider

(iv) Trees

Tree Preservation Orders impose severe penalties on anyone who cuts down, uproots or destroys any tree subject to such an order, or damages, tops or lops it in such a way that he is likely to destroy it, even if the person does not know of the TPO. A Crown Court can impose unlimited fines. Once the order is made, it is only lawful to interfere with the tree with the consent of the district council, or if the tree is dead, diseased or dangerous. The order can cover a single tree, an entire wood, or all the larger trees in an area. If an order is made in respect of a tree on someone's land he may appeal against the order within 28 days of its being made. Anyone can ask a district council to make a tree preservation order. Department of the Environment guidelines advise authorities to agree to them where the tree is enjoyed by the public and there is a risk of damage to it. The district council keeps a list of trees which are covered by orders; it is open to the public. If it is feared a landowner may fell a tree before an order is imposed, it is possible to get the council to take emergency action in secret. Bushes, hedgerows and young trees fall outside this protection, and have no special status, unless they belong to a rare species or form part of a Site of Special Scientific Interest (SSSI).

Quite apart from TPOs, if a landowner wishes to fell trees on his land, even if it is a solitary tree, he may need a licence from the Forestry Commission. The Commission should be consulted, as it is an offence to fell a tree without a licence where one is needed. There may also be additional local restrictions, for example in conservation areas. Details of these may be obtained from the local authority.

(v) Flowers and Plants

The casual user of the countryside has seldom been known to try to take an entire tree home in his pockets, but may be tempted to pick an attractive flower, or dig up a root which would look just right in the garden.

Plants belong to the landowner, who can sue others for removing a plant, although he would have to show actual damage – this would be easy in cases such as taking potatoes. It is also a criminal offence to pick or uproot wild plants (except mushrooms and fungi) without the land-owner's consent. If the plants are cultivated, or wild plants are picked for sale it may also be theft.

Certain plants are protected even from action by their owner, because of their rarity. The only people who can authorise their picking or uproot-ing is the Nature Conservancy Council. It is not an offence to destroy even the rarest of plants if it is an incidental effect of proper farming or for-estry, such as the destruction of ancient meadows by modern chemicals. In such cases the only pro-tection is to designate the land a Site of Special Scientific Interest, when the landowner receives compensation in exchange for restrictions on what he may do on the land.

In a nature reserve, it is an offence to pick or uproot any plant, even a common one, with the same penalty as if it were a protected plant. Local authorities and the Nature Conservancy Council can designate nature reserves, but these will normally be clearly signposted. If they are not, it may be possible to avoid conviction.

Protected flowers and plants
(Not to be picked or uprooted)

Adder's-tongue spearwort	Monkey orchid
Alpine catchfly	Norwegian sandwort
Alpine gentian	Oblong woodsia
Alpine sow-thistle	Oxtongue broomrape
Alpine woodsia	Perennial knawel
Bedstraw broomrape	Plymouth pear
Blue heath	Purple spurge
Brown galingale	Red helleborine
Cheddar pink	Ribbon-leaved water plantain
Childing pink	Rock cinquefoil
Diapensia	Rough marsh-mallow
Dickie's bladder fern	Round-headed leek
Downy woundwort	Sea knotgrass
Drooping saxifrage	Sea lavender
Early spider orchid	Sickle-leaved hare's ear
Fen orchid	Small alison
Fen violet	Small hare's ear
Field cow-wheat	Snowdon lily
Field eryngo	Spiked speedwell
Field wormwood	Spring gentian
Ghost orchid	Starfruit
Greater yellow rattle	Starved woodsedge
Jersey cudweed	Teesdale sandwort
Killarney fern	Thistle broomrape
Lady's-slipper orchid	Triangular club-rush
Late spider orchid	Tufted saxifrage
Least lettuce	Water germander
Limestone woundwort	Whorled solomon's seal
Lizard orchid	Wild cotoneaster
Military orchid	Wild gladiolus
	Wood calamint

(vi) Hunting

The laws concerning hunting are complex. A licence may be needed, but additionally there are restrictions on when hunting can occur and how it may be carried out.

A game licence is needed before it is lawful to hunt for rabbits and 'game birds' i e pheasant, partridge, grouse, snipe, woodcock and capercaille, but a licence is not required to hunt foxes. A licence is needed to hunt deer, unless the hunting is with hounds, or on enclosed land. No licence is needed for hare coursing – that is using greyhounds to pursue hares. A licence is also needed to sell game. Game licences can be obtained from Post Offices, or local councils. There are three types:

(a) Red licence – lasts for a year from 31 July;
(b) Green licence – from 1 August to 31 October;
(c) Blue licence – from 1 November to 31 July.
Special fourteen day licences can also be obtained.

Anyone found on land with a gun or dog, if he is thought to be hunting, can be asked to produce a game licence by the owner or occupier of the land, a gamekeeper, the police, an official from the local authority or even by anyone who has a game licence. If the person does not have a licence with him he must give his name and address and details of where the licence was obtained, so that this can be checked.

In addition to a licence, the consent of a landowner is always needed to hunt on his land, or it will amount to trespass and possibly also theft. If a hunt enters land without permission, the occupier can sue the Master of the Hunt and any huntsmen he can identify for trespass, and for any injury or damage caused by the hunt. Anyone can prosecute a huntsman who causes an animal unnecessary suffering. It is also possible to obtain an injunction, preventing the hunt from entering land in the future, although many Courts seem reluctant to grant such injunctions.

The law imposes limits as to when hunting for

When hunting is unlawful – close seasons

Close season for birds
1 Feb to 11 Aug
Common snipe

1 Feb to 31 Aug
Common redshank
Coot
Curlew (not stone curlew)
Godwit, bartailed
Golden Plover
Moorhen
Widgeon

1 Feb to 31 Aug (inland)
(starts 21 Feb at sea or on foreshore)
Common pochard
Gadwall
Goldeneye
Goose, Canada, greylag, pink-footed, white-fronted
Mallard
Pintail
Scaup
Shoveler
Teal
Tufted duck

1 Feb to 30 Sept
Capercaillie
Woodcock

Close season for hares and rabbits
Hares cannot be sold between 1 March and 31 July.
Anyone who owns or rents enclosed arable land can kill rabbits or hares at any time of year, except hares cannot be killed on Christmas Day or Sundays. But someone who owns or rents land which is NOT enclosed cannot kill rabbits or hares between 1 April and 31 August, and in addition cannot shoot them between 1 September and 10 December.

Close season for deer
Red and Sika deer stags and fallow deer bucks – 1 May to 31 July.
Red and Sika deer hinds and Roe deer does 1 March to 31 October.
Roe deer bucks 1 November to 31 March.

some creatures can take place, even if the animal is bred for hunting. No bird or animal can be hunted between one hour after sunset and one hour before dawn, except on a person's own land. In addition there are close seasons for many birds and animals during which time they must not be hunted at all. Some are related to breeding seasons, but others have no apparent *rationale* – such as the law that hares must not be killed on Sundays or Christmas Day.

During close seasons it is an offence to kill the species, except to protect crops, or with the consent of the Ministry of Agriculture.

(vii) Poaching

Poaching is hunting on someone's land without their permission or in breach of the law, at the wrong time or without a licence. Whilst people are no longer transported for poaching, it remains a criminal offence even if the person catches nothing. A person may be convicted even if he has not fired a shot, but appears to be intending to poach. If a person fires at a bird from land he is authorised to be on, it is nonetheless poaching to move onto neighbouring land without authority to collect the kill. It is a more serious offence to poach at night. Substantial fines are possible, and the poaching equipment may be confiscated by the Court.

(viii) Fishing

There are no general protections for fish, unlike birds. Fishing in the sea and tidal waters is lawful at all times, unless local bye-laws prohibit it. Tidal waters extend up stream on rivers to the point where fresh water begins, or the tidal effect is no longer noticeable – which can be tens of miles.

The rights to fish in a river or lake belong to the person who owns the banks, unless he has sold it to someone else. The owner of the bank of a river generally owns the river bed, and the fishing rights to the mid point in the river. To fish in a river, pond, lake or canal without permission from the owner of the fishing rights is trespass, and theft, so a person risks prosecution and the confiscation of tackle and catch. However, landowners frequently lease out fishing rights, to individuals or clubs. In that case the people who have rented the fishing rights have exclusive use of them, and can take action against trespassers. This means the easiest way to fish lawfully is to join an angling club or obtain a licence from a landowner to fish a particular stretch of water.

As well as getting permission from the landowner, an angler may also need a licence from the fisheries officers of the water authority, or from Post Offices and fishing tackle shops in areas where fishing is popular. The fee varies from area to area. Although the law does not require licences everywhere a licence is needed in most parts of the country. The terms of licences vary and must be read carefully, but most licence one person to use one rod, and cover a particular type of fishing, although if someone owns fishing rights along a stretch, a licence can be obtained from him which covers anyone using the stretch with his consent in writing. Fishing without a licence where one is required is an offence, but if a fish which falls outside the licence is caught accidentally, that is not an offence providing the fish is returned to the water immediately.

As with other hunting, there is a close season for some species, and burbot, dolphins and porpoises cannot be caught or killed without a special licence.

> **Close season for fish**
> Salmon 1 Nov to 31 Jan.
> Trout 1 Oct to last day of Feb.
> Coarse fish 15 March to 15 June.
> These can all be varied by local bye-laws. Bye-laws also regulate rainbow trout fishing in some places. Before fishing, variations should be checked locally. The dates are different for Scotland.

The use of explosives, poisons and electrical devices, as well as being dangerous, is illegal inland or at sea, as is ensnaring fish by lights, fish roe bait, firearms, gaff, spear, wire or snares.

SECTION 9
CRIMINAL LAW AND YOU

9.1 INTRODUCTION

In the other sections of this book we have considered the importance of the law in your everyday activities – your home, your job, your money and your leisure time. In this section we shall consider something which you may not encounter on an everyday basis – crime. Despite the impression given in several popular newspapers, being a victim of crime – especially serious crime – is not an inevitability or even a serious likelihood. The British Crime Survey in 1981 showed that the average adult can expect to be the victim of a robbery once every five centuries, an assault resulting in injury once every century and a burglary in the home once every 40 years! Nevertheless, other less serious crimes are more common and it is not much comfort to the victim of a burglary to be told that he has been unlucky. Being a victim of a crime can be a traumatic event, and once the initial shock has worn off, the victim is likely to wonder where he stands in law. We shall consider this in the first part of the section. In the second part we shall consider what can happen to another kind of victim; the victim who is wrongly accused of having committed a criminal offence.

9.2 THE LAW AND THE VICTIM OF CRIME

In many cases it will be obvious if you have been the victim of a criminal offence; for example, if someone attacks you in the street or if you come home and discover your house has been ransacked. But sometimes it will not be so clear. Criminal law is complex: behaviour that you think *ought* to be illegal could turn out not to be, and on other occasions you could be the victim of a criminal offence without being aware of it at all. Determining whether or not an offence has been committed could be important. As we shall see below, victims of some crimes could have greater scope to obtain compensation and reparation than victims of accidents or mistakes. Moreover, many insurance companies require that the police are notified before payments can be made to victims of crime.

1. HAS A CRIME BEEN COMMITTED?

(i) Attacks

The 'mildest' forms of attack in the criminal law are assault and battery. Although many people use the term 'assault' to refer to both of these, there is an important difference between them. An assault occurs if the offender intentionally causes his victim to fear the immediate application of force against him. Like many criminal offences, assault is also constituted if the offender has acted *recklessly* – where he saw the risk that his behaviour might cause such fear, but still continued to behave in that way. The typical situations found in decided cases include the clenched fist, the raised arm, and the menacing approach. Remarkably, the law is unclear as to whether the use of threatening words unaccompanied by any menacing gesture can amount to an assault. A cry such as 'Let's get him, lads' is surely just as frightening as a raised fist. Many writers, however, think that if the point were to be raised in one of the higher Courts, the use of words alone would be held to be a sufficient threat.

If the circumstances are such that there is no possibility of the threat being immediately carried out, then there is no assault. If an offender, while being taken away from the scene of a crime by the police or taken to the cells below

a court, were to shout threats at his victim, there would be no assault. However, in one recent case, *Smith v Chief Superintendent, Woking Police Station* (1983), the Court of Appeal gave a fairly liberal interpretation to the word 'immediate'.

> **Smith v Chief Superintendent, Woking Police Station**
> At about 11 p m one evening a woman was in her bed-sitting room when she suddenly noticed Smith staring at her through the window. He admitted that he had intended to frighten her. The Court of Appeal decided that he could be found guilty of an assault, even though he would have been unable to get anywhere near the woman without breaking into the building.

A battery occurs if the offender intentionally or recklessly applies force to his victim. Only the slightest degree of force, such as touching, is necessary. The force can be applied directly, such as hitting the victim, throwing something at him, spitting at him, turning a hosepipe on him or standing on his foot; or indirectly, as by placing some obstruction in front of him which he falls over. If the resultant harm is more serious, such as bruising, the offender could be guilty of the offence 'assault [which here means battery] occasioning actual bodily harm' under section 47 of the Offences against the Person Act 1861. This offence is punishable with a higher maximum penalty than battery. If the harm is even more serious, offences involving wounding or grievous bodily harm, under sections 18 and 20 of the 1861 Act, will become relevant. Section 18 states that it is an offence to unlawfully and maliciously wound or cause grievous bodily harm to any person by any means whatsoever with intent to do grievous bodily harm, or with intent to resist or prevent the lawful apprehension or detainer of any person. For a wounding, the skin must be broken and grievous bodily harm has been defined as meaning 'really serious harm'. Section 20 states that it is an offence unlawfully and maliciously to wound or inflict any grievous bodily harm upon any person. This is a considerably less serious offence than the one provided by

453

section 18; the fundamental difference is that the prohibited harm in section 20 can be caused recklessly whereas, for liability under section 18, nothing less than an intention to bring about the forbidden consequences will suffice. In addition, the word 'inflict' in section 20 has been interpreted more narrowly than the word 'cause' in section 18, possibly because the latter is followed by the words 'by any means whatsoever' whereas the former is not. The precise meaning of 'inflict' was in some doubt until the recent House of Lords decision in *R v Wilson* (1983) which stated that there is no need for a battery to be proved if the accused's act, although not in itself a direct application of force to the victim's body, directly resulted in force being applied to the body. This ruling supports the decision in *R v Lewis* (1970).

R v Lewis

Lewis became involved in an argument with his wife, who locked a door between them. He threatened to kill her and, although she was in another room, she became so scared that she jumped out of a window of their third floor flat and broke both her legs. The Court of Appeal upheld Lewis's conviction under section 20.

Apart from the argument that the harm (or threat of harm) caused was accidental, a possible defence to a charge of assault, battery, wounding or grievous bodily harm is that the victim consented. The law, however, has imposed restrictions on this. It is now established that consent can generally not be a defence if actual bodily harm is intended and/or results. As actual bodily harm has been defined as 'any hurt or injury calculated to interfere with the health or comfort of the victim', it is clear that this includes a hysterical or nervous condition. But this rule has important exceptions. Harm resulting from properly conducted games and sports, reasonable surgical interference and dangerous exhibitions will not result in criminal liability as it is in the public interest that these activities should take place. A technical infringement of the rules in a body-contact sport will not automatically constitute a battery as the participants will be taken to consent impliedly to such an occurrence. However, in the case *R v Billinghurst* (1978) a Circuit Judge ruled that a punch thrown in a rugby game which broke the victim's jaw could amount to an assault

occasioning actual bodily harm. Such an incident is completely outside the normal course of the game. It is not clear what the notion of 'public interest' will cover; this could change from time to time. It is unlikely that it would include sexual flagellation so, if this results in 'actual bodily harm', the consent of the parties would be no defence to a criminal charge. 'Consent' for this purpose must be voluntary and not obtained by fear or coercion.

In some other cases, especially those not resulting in any harm, consent can be implied. In our day-to-day activities, such as walking down a busy street, or queuing to get on to a bus, a certain amount of bodily contact is inevitable. Even if this is not strictly accidental, it is inconceivable that a Court would find that a battery had been committed in situations of this sort, as a person would be taken to consent to the possibility of such contact by setting foot outside his front door!

There are two situations where a certain amount of force is permitted in law even in the absence of consent. A person is allowed to use reasonable force in self-defence, the prevention of crime or in carrying out a lawful arrest. The accused himself must produce evidence to support his claim. There may be difficulty in determining whether the force used was 'reasonable'. This is always a question for the jury and not for the judge. The test is whether a reasonable man, with knowledge of the circumstances of the case that were known to the accused, and with the same amount of time as he had to reflect on them, would have acted in the same way. This may seem rather harsh, but as Lord Morris said in the case *Palmer v R* (1971):

'If there has been attack so that defence is reasonably necessary it will be recognised that a person defending himself cannot weigh to a nicety the exact measure of his necessary defensive action. If a jury thought that in a moment of unexpected anguish a person attacked had only done what he honestly and instinctively thought was necessary that would be most potent evidence that only reasonable defensive action had been taken.'

In addition, a parent, teacher or person *'in loco parentis'* can apply reasonable force to their children or pupils for disciplinary purposes. The right of a person other than a parent to use such force is currently under discussion. Many local authorities now prohibit their teachers from using corporal punishment and, if parents are in any doubt about the rules that apply to their children, they are advised to contact the appropriate education authority.

(ii) Sexual Assaults

This area provides a particularly good example of how the popular press, through its banner headlines and typification of the unusual, can make the public think that there has been a massive increase in criminal offences. In fact, the increase in recorded sexual offences has for some years been far less than for many other types of crime and the 1984 Criminal Statistics actually show a fall of 1% from the 1983 figure. This is even more significant when it is realised that victims of sexual attacks are increasingly more likely to report their experiences to the police. This is probably because the police, in response to public criticism, are taking steps to deal with victims more sympathetically than in the past.

(A) Rape. The crime of rape is now defined in section 1 of the Sexual Offences (Amendment) Act 1976. It is committed where a man has sexual intercourse *per vaginam* with a woman, either knowing that she does not consent or being reckless (in the sense that he is aware of the possibility, but ignores it) whether she consents or not. Boys under fourteen are legally presumed to be incapable of sexual intercourse and so cannot be guilty of rape. The age of the woman is irrelevant. Consent must be genuine and not obtained through violence, threats, fraud or coercion. One case that involved fraud was *R v Williams* (1923).

> **R v Williams**
> Williams, who taught singing, had sexual intercourse with a sixteen year old pupil by claiming that it would help to train her voice. The girl believed this and offered no resistance; indeed she was unaware that she was engaging in sexual intercourse. The Court of Criminal Appeal held that Williams had rightly been convicted for rape.

It can also be rape to have intercourse with a woman who is unconscious or asleep; or when the rapist impersonates the woman's husband; or where the woman is not in a position to consent on the grounds of being mentally deficient, too young or drunk. The slightest penetration of the penis into the vagina is sufficient; there is no

requirement for the hymen to be broken nor for any emission of seed. To the annoyance of many women, the law provides that a husband cannot rape his wife unless there is a decree *nisi* of divorce or nullity; or the parties are separated by a Court order or separation agreement; or the husband has been ordered by a Court not to interfere with his wife.

One of the reasons why rape victims have often been unwilling to report their experience to the police is the fear of the publicity that would occur if the case went to Court. This situation was improved by the Sexual Offences (Amendment) Act 1976 which provided that complainants in rape cases (and, indeed, accused persons) are, save in exceptional circumstances, to be anonymous. Nevertheless, if the accused pleads not guilty, it is almost certain that the victim will be required to appear in the witness box and this itself can provide a strong disincentive for some women to complain. In December 1985 a report was published by the Women's National Commission, a body which advises the government, claiming that many women are still unwilling to report sexual attacks because of the treatment they fear they will receive from both the police and the Courts. The report also claimed that the provision for the victim's anonymity in the Sexual Offences (Amendment) Act 1976 is sometimes disregarded by judges.

(B) Indecent assault. An indecent assault is an assault or battery accompanied by circumstances of indecency. It can be committed by a man or woman including a boy under fourteen. What 'circumstances of indecency' means has never been defined but seems to refer to any overtly sexual conduct, including kissing. An act which, in itself, is not overtly sexual cannot be indecent simply because of the unrevealed motive of the actor. This is illustrated in the case *R v George* (1956). George attempted to remove a shoe from the foot of a girl because it gave him sexual satisfaction. The trial judge refused to let the case go to the jury as there was no evidence of indecency.

The question of consent is crucial. As in the case of ordinary assaults and batteries, the victim's consent is not valid if actual bodily harm was intended and/or caused, nor if the apparent consent was obtained by fear and coercion. For indecent assault, however, there are further restrictions; a person who is mentally defective or under sixteen cannot give a valid consent. If the accused thought the other party was over sixteen, it is no defence even if the mistake was a reasonable one. On the other hand, in the case of a mental defective who has apparently consented, the accused will not be guilty unless he knew, or had reason to suspect that the person was a defective.

The problem of indecent photography of children, which itself would not amount to an indecent assault, is dealt with in the Protection of Children Act 1978. Section 1 provides that it is an offence for a person to take an indecent photograph or film of a child under sixteen, or to distribute or show the photograph or film, or to possess a photograph or film with a view to distributing it or showing it (whether or not for a commercial purpose). There is a defence to distributing or showing the photograph or film, or possession with a view to distributing or showing it, if a person can show (a) he had a legitimate reason for doing so, or (b) he had not seen it and did not know, or had no reason to suspect, that it was indecent.

(C) Indecency with children. The requirement of an assault prevents a mere invitation to a child to commit an indecent act from being an indecent assault. Clearly, the use or threat of force would be a different matter but sexual advances to children are often made in a very gentle way. Such advances are not covered by the Indecency with Children Act 1960 which makes it an offence for a man or a woman to commit an act of gross indecency with or toward a child under fourteen or to incite a child to engage in such an act. 'Gross indecency' must be stronger than the level of indecency required to constitute indecent assault. Indecent contact with the genitals would be the usual sort of conduct giving rise to this offence; this would also include contact through clothing.

(D) Indecent exposure. The criminal law contains two offences dealing with indecent exposure. There is a very old-established offence of committing an act outraging public decency in public in such a way that more than one person can see it. This offence, which applies to both males and females, would certainly include indecent exposure of the body. It is not necessary to prove that anyone was actually annoyed by the act. This offence is rarely prosecuted, however, and reliance is usually made on the quaintly-worded section 4 of the Vagrancy Act 1824 which provides '. . . every person wilfully, openly, lewdly and obscenely exposing his person with intent to insult any female . . . shall be deemed a rogue and a vagabond . . .' (There is also a more telling punishment of a fine and a prison sentence.) As the word 'person' has been held by a Court to mean 'penis', it is clear that the offence can only be committed by males. Presumably, the practice of 'mooning' (exposing the buttocks) is not covered by this offence. The difficulty for the prosecution in proving that the accused intended to insult the victim results in a sizeable number of 'flashers' being acquitted. Indecent exposure is also prohibited under a number of local bye-laws.

Undoubtedly, many instances of this offence occur which are never reported to the police. In many cases the exposer will be a harmless, inadequate individual who succeeds in causing no more than annoyance (or even amusement) to his victims. Indeed, the evidence suggests that such a practice is highly unlikely to cause any psychological harm, even to children. Nevertheless, the offender is likely to be in need of help which he is unlikely to receive unless his activities are brought to the attention of the authorities.

(E) Soliciting and 'kerb-crawling'. In some respects it is inaccurate to include this sort of behaviour under 'Sexual Assaults' because it is not so much the sexual nature of the behaviour that is offensive but more the nuisance value. Section 1 of the Street Offences Act 1959 provides that it is an offence for a prostitute to loiter or solicit in a street or public place for the purpose of prostitution. It is not only men but also other women who find this practice annoying. A prostitute in English law has always been assumed to be female. Perhaps not surprisingly, in recent years there has been a growing demand that action be taken to deal with the practice of 'kerb-crawling' whereby men, usually driving slowly in cars, make sexual propositions to women in the street. Recently a new law has been introduced to deal with this. Under section 1 of the Sexual Offences Act 1985, it is an offence if a man, for the purpose of prostitution, solicits a woman in a public place from a motor vehicle, or if he has just got out of a motor vehicle, if he acts persistently or in such a manner as is likely to cause annoyance to the woman or a nuisance to other persons in the neighbourhood. Section 2 provides that a man commits an offence if he persistently solicits a woman in a public place for the purposes of prostitution. Some women may be annoyed to notice that a man's behaviour in this respect is only illegal if it is 'persistent' – a requirement not necessary in the case of a prostitute.

(iii) Interference with Your Possessions

Although having one's personal belongings stolen or otherwise interfered with is less dramatic than being the victim of an attack, the inconvenience – and, indeed, financial loss – caused can be very great. As we shall see below, the hardship can sometimes be reduced by insurance but this is not always the case.

(A) Theft. Section 1 of the Theft Act 1968 states that 'a person is guilty of theft if he dishonestly appropriates property belonging to another with the intention of permanently depriving the other of it'. For the scope of the offence to be properly understood, it is necessary to consider the meaning of some of the words in the definition.

Section 3 of the Theft Act 1968 provides that 'any assumption by a person of the rights of an owner amounts to an appropriation, and this includes, where he has come by the property (innocently or not) without stealing it, any later assumption of a right to it by keeping or dealing with it as owner'. Under this definition a thief can assume the rights of the owner even if he does not succeed in escaping with the stolen goods. This point is illustrated in the case *Corcoran v Anderton* (1980).

Corcoran v Anderton

Partington intended to steal Mrs Hall's handbag. He struck her on the back and pulled at the handbag, causing it to fall to the ground. Corcoran, an accomplice, was convicted of robbery (the commission of a theft is an essential element in robbery). The Divisional Court upheld Corcoran's conviction; there had been an appropriation of the handbag as Corcoran had assumed the rights of an owner.

Goods can be appropriated without the thief ever laying his hands on them if he assumes the rights of the owner. This point was discussed in *R v Pitham and Hehl* (1976).

R v Pitham and Hehl

Millman, a burglar, took Pitham and Hehl to his victim's house and offered to sell them the furniture. They paid Millman and took it away. They subsequently appealed against their conviction for handling stolen goods on the ground that the handling was not 'otherwise than in the course of stealing' which is a requirement of that offence. The Court of Appeal, dismissing their appeal, held that Millman committed an act of appropriation when he offered to sell them the furniture.

The definition in section 3 allows for an appropriation even where the original possession or control was not inconsistent with the rights of the owner. If someone takes a book from your shelf intending to return it, he is not guilty of theft because, although there is an appropriation, there is no intention permanently to deprive. If, however, the person then decides to keep the book, he is guilty of theft because he has assumed a right to it by keeping or dealing with it as owner, and he intends to deprive the owner of it permanently.

'Property' is defined in section 4 of the Theft Act 1968 as including money and all other property, real or personal. A person cannot steal land (real property) itself but it is possible in certain circumstances to steal things growing on land. It is not an offence to pick wild flowers (unless they are a protected species) or mushrooms growing wild on any land for private use or to give away to people. However, under section 4 it is an offence to do so 'for reward or for sale' and it is also an offence to take cultivated flowers or mushrooms either from a private garden or a market garden. Domestic animals or wild animals which have been tamed or are ordinarily kept in captivity (such as zoo animals) are capable of being stolen. Electricity does not come within the scope of section 4, but it is an offence under section 13 of the Theft Act 1968 to dishonestly use without due authority, or dishonestly cause to be wasted or diverted, any electricity. This provision is obviously intended to cover people who dishonestly re-connect electricity supplies that have been cut off, but it is capable of less serious applications. It would, for example, be an offence for someone to dishonestly use another person's transistor radio (whether mains or battery) or private telephone. The dishonest use of a public telephone would also seem to come under this provision but this is now covered by section 48 of the British Telecommunications Act 1981.

The phrase 'belonging to another' has a wider application under the Theft Act 1968 than it would in normal usage. Section 5(1) states that property shall be regarded as belonging to any person having possession or control of it. The word 'control' can be useful to deal with situations where the question of possession may be debatable, as is shown in the case below.

R v Woodman (1974)

Woodman went on to land owned by English China Clays and took some scrap metal. The right to collect the scrap metal had been sold to another company who had taken most of it, but had left some pieces on the site. English China Clays, who were unaware that any metal had been left there at all, put up a barbed wire fence around the site, together with notices telling trespassers to keep out. The Court of Appeal dismissed Woodman's appeal against his conviction for theft, commenting that there was plenty of evidence that English China Clays intended to control the site, which must include anything on it.

It is possible in law for one spouse to steal property belonging to the other, although prosecution in these cases can only take place with the permission of the Director of Public Prosecutions if the parties are living together. It is even possible for a person to steal his own property. The phrase 'belonging to another' is defined as covering any person having possession or control of the property. This point is illustrated in the case *R v Turner* (1971).

R v Turner

Mr Turner took his car to a garage to be repaired. When the work was finished he told the garage owner he would return the next day to pay for the repairs and collect the car. In fact, he returned a few hours later and took the car without telling the garage owner. The Court of Appeal decided that Mr Turner had rightly been convicted of theft of the car as the garage owner had 'possession or control' of it.

Section 5 of the Theft Act 1968 deals with three special situations where, were it not for the provisions in the section, the property might belong to a dishonest person rather than the honest victim. The first of these deals with trust property. If property is transferred to a trustee to keep for the benefit of a third party, the trustee receives legal ownership of it and, apart from this provision, could not be guilty of stealing it. However, under section 5(2) it is provided that 'where property is subject to a trust, the persons to whom it belongs shall be regarded as including any person having a right to enforce the trust, and an intention to defeat the trust shall be regarded accordingly as an intention to deprive of the property any person having that right'.

The second of these situations is where B receives property from A and is under an obligation to retain and deal with it in a certain way. Section 5(3) provides that, where this is the case, the property shall be regarded as belonging to A. The word 'obligation' has been held to refer to a legal obligation, not a moral one. It is important to distinguish between, for example, giving a workman £50 in advance to carry out repairs in your house, and £50 to go out and buy certain tools which he needs to carry out the repairs. The former situation is not covered by section 5(3), as the money was not handed over *for him to deal with in a certain way*; but the latter situation is covered, and the workman could be guilty of theft if, rather than buying the tools, he kept the money. One case which illustrates the difficulties that can arise is *R v Hall* (1972). Presumably, the decision in this case would have been different if the arrangements with the clients had made it clear that Hall was to use each separate sum advanced to purchase the required ticket(s).

R v Hall

Hall was a travel agent who received deposits from various clients for flights to the USA. Some clients even payed in full. None of the flights took place and Hall did not refund any of the sums paid. He argued that all the money had been paid into his firm's account and that section 5(3) did not apply. He was convicted but the Court of Appeal allowed his appeal on the grounds that there was no evidence that he was required to deal with the money in any particular way.

The third of these special situations covered by section 5 is the most complicated one. This deals with situations where B obtains property from A as a result of a mistake. Section 5(4) provides that, if B is also under a legal obligation to restore the property or its proceeds to A, the property is to be considered as belonging to A. Consideration of when such a legal obligation arises is too complicated to deal with here; but perhaps the commonest situation would involve a mistake of fact such as an employee, who had been given a 'sub' the previous week, receiving a full week's pay in his next pay packet. As the employee would be under a legal obligation to pay the excess amount to his employer, that amount, under section 5(4), would be regarded as belonging to the employer and an intention not to make repayment could amount to theft. One common situation where there would not be a legal obligation to make restoration would be where the mistake related to the motive of the person who transferred the property. If A gave B his stereo cassette player because he mistakenly thought that B did not have one, B would not be under any legal obligation to give it back and, as the ownership would have passed to him, he could not be guilty of stealing it.

A person who, on the face of it, appears to have committed theft cannot be guilty if it is determined that he did not act dishonestly. Section 2(1) of the Theft Act 1968 indicates three situations where a person would not have acted dishonestly: (a) if he thought he had a legal right to deprive the other person of the property; or (b) if he appropriated the property in the belief that the other person would have agreed if he had known of the circumstances; or (c) if he believed that the owner of the property could not be discovered by taking reasonable steps. In (a), it is important to emphasise that the belief must involve a *legal* right; a belief that it is right to 'bash the rich' would not be sufficient. Situations covered by (b) would include someone helping themselves to a spoonful of your coffee at work in the belief that you would not object. If you discovered a 10p coin in the middle of a field (or maybe anywhere) most magistrates or juries would believe you if you claimed to be covered by (c).

The definition of 'dishonest' in section 2 is not a complete one, and it is open to an accused person to claim he had acted honestly in situations other than the ones set out there. The test to be applied in these cases was laid down by the Court of Appeal in the case *R v Ghosh* (1982). First, the magistrates or jury must consider if the accused's conduct was dishonest according to the standards of reasonable and honest people. If, on this test, the accused was not dishonest, he is not guilty. However, if he was dishonest according to this test, the magistrates or jury must consider a second question; did the accused realise that he was acting dishonestly according to the standards of reasonable and honest people? If he did not, then he did not act dishonestly.

The final requirement of the definition of theft in section 1 of the Theft Act 1968 which we must consider is that the accused, to be found guilty, must have intended to permanently deprive the owner of his property. An actual deprivation is not necessary in that an accused is still guilty if, on his apprehension, the stolen property is returned to the owner. This is the provision that ensures that, in most cases, borrowing does not amount to theft. However, section 6 of the Theft Act 1968 provides two situations where an intention to permanently deprive will be assumed by the law, even if the taker did not specifically have that intention. Section 6(1) states that this will be the case where the accused has the intention to treat the thing as his own to dispose of regardless of the other's rights. If someone borrowed a book from you but, having read it, became fed up with carrying it around and left it on a railway station two hundred miles away, that could be treated as an intention to permanently deprive under this section because it is almost inconceivable that you would ever be able to recover the book. On the other hand, if the person left the book in another friend's house, this would probably not amount to an intention to permanently deprive under section 6(1). The section also states that a borrowing or lending of property may amount to treating it as the accused's own, if the borrowing is for a period and in circumstances making it equivalent to an outright taking or disposal. Suppose that you lend your football season ticket to a person, intending that he uses it for one game. In fact, he keeps the ticket until the end of the season and then returns it to you. Although you have regained your property (the ticket), it is now of no use whatsoever. This can amount to an intention to permanently deprive under section 6(1).

What is the situation if you suspect or discover that items you have recently acquired are stolen goods? The answer depends on whether or not you have paid for them:

(1) If you have paid for them, you cannot be guilty of stealing them owing to section 3(2) of the Theft Act 1968 which covers this situation. Nor can you be guilty of the offence of handling stolen goods unless you 'undertake their disposal for the benefit of another'. The House of Lords in the case *R v Bloxham* (1982) ruled that money obtained from selling such items is not 'for the benefit of another'.

R v Bloxham

Bloxham bought a car which, unknown to him, had been stolen. Some time later he decided that it must have been stolen because the seller failed to produce the registration documents. He then sold the car to a man he did not know who agreed to buy it without the registration documents. The House of Lords, allowing Bloxham's appeal, said that the man had not obtained a benefit in this sense just because he had obtained the car.

---

(2) If you have not paid for the items, you could be guilty of theft by either keeping them or selling them, as you are not covered by section 3(2). The situation concerning the offence of handling stolen goods is the same as discussed in (1).

The best course of action is to contact the police immediately if you suspect you are in possession of stolen goods.

(B) Robbery. Robbery can loosely be defined as theft accompanied by the use or threat of force. More precisely, section 8 of the Theft Act 1968 states 'a person is guilty of robbery if he steals and, immediately before or at the time of doing so, and in order to do so, he uses force on any person or puts or seeks to put any person in fear of being then and there subjected to force'. There are several important requirements before guilt can be established. Theft must be proved, so if any of the conditions preventing this mentioned above apply, there can be no robbery. The use or threat of force must be immediately before or at the time of the theft. If a victim of a simple theft chased after a thief, who eventually turned round and attacked him, this would not be robbery. However, the Courts seem prepared to interpret the words 'at the time of' fairly widely, as can be seen in the case *R v Hale* (1978).

R v Hale

Hale and McGuire went into Mrs Carrett's house. While Hale kept his hand over Mrs Carrett's mouth, McGuire went upstairs and took her jewellery box. The two men then tied her up and told her that her child would be harmed if she called the police during the next five minutes. The Court of Appeal upheld Hale's conviction for robbery saying that, in practical terms, they were still in the course of stealing when they tied her up.

If force is used, it must be 'on' a person. It is insufficient for a robbery conviction if the only force used is against the actual property, for example snatching a handbag. If the owner were to put up any resistance to the snatch it would probably be a different matter. The force used or threatened must also be in order to steal. If a victim were beaten up after an argument and then the assailant as an afterthought were to search his pockets, it would not amount to robbery.

Some of these conditions may appear restrictive but, even in cases where it would be difficult to establish robbery, there would be the likelihood of convictions for theft or an offence against the person.

(C) Burglary. Formerly, the crime of burglary was very complicated, with a number of variations depending on such factors as the type of building involved. It is still common for the layman to talk of 'breaking and entering' although there is no longer any requirement of breaking to constitute burglary. There are in fact two separate offences of burglary provided in section 9 of the Theft Act 1968. The first in section 9(1)(a) is committed when a person enters a building or part of a building without permission with the intention to steal, or inflict serious bodily harm, or commit rape, or cause any damage to the building or its contents. The burglar does not actually have to have done any of these things to be guilty of an offence; it is sufficient if the prosecution can prove that he intended to at the time of the entry. For this purpose a 'building' includes an inhabited vehicle (such as a dormobile or caravan) or a boat. The significance of the phrase 'part of a building' is that a person may have permission to be in one part of a building but no permission to be in another. If he enters the other part with, for example, an intention to steal, he can be guilty of burglary. A 'part of a building' does not need to be a separate room as is shown in the case *R v Walkington* (1979).

R v Walkington

Walkington went into a department store. He then entered an area bounded by a three-sided moveable counter where he opened the till. The Court of Appeal decided that there was evidence on which a jury could find that the area behind the counter was a separate part of the building and find Walkington guilty of burglary.

Permission to enter a building can be express or implied. Obviously there is an implied permission for people to enter shops to look around or make purchases. However, if a person entered a shop with the intention to steal, the implied permission would be effectively withdrawn as it can hardly be argued that a shopkeeper would give permission to people to enter and commit theft! A person will not be considered to have entered without permission if he wrongly thought he had permission, or was 'reckless' (see the definition above) as to whether he had permission. Permission can be given by an owner or someone else lawfully in the building. These points were illustrated in the unusual case of *R v Collins* (1972).

R v Collins

Collins, who was desirous of sexual intercourse, found a step-ladder leaning against the wall of a house leading to an open bedroom window. He took off all his clothes except his socks, climbed up the ladder and perched on the window ledge. He observed a naked girl lying on a bed. She woke up, and thinking Collins was her boyfriend, beckoned him into her room. Only after sexual intercourse had taken place did the girl realise that Collins was not her boyfriend. The Court of Appeal, allowing Collins's appeal against his conviction of burglary, said that the judge had not made it clear to the jury that, unless Collins knew that he was a trespasser at the time he entered the house, or was reckless as to that fact, he could not be guilty of burglary. For this purpose the girl, although not the owner of the house, could give him permission to enter.

It is very important to appreciate that a person who enters your home without permission does not automatically become guilty of burglary. He must intend to commit, or, as we shall see in a moment, actually commit an offence. If a tramp enters your home through an unlocked door or open window, falls asleep in your chair (or indeed looks around your house) and then leaves without causing any damage or stealing anything, he is not guilty of burglary, or probably any other offence. Similarly, it must be remembered that certain people, such as police officers, are entitled to enter your home against your wishes when acting under a search warrant (and sometimes when acting without one). If a police officer acts outside the scope of the warrant – for example, if he causes unlawful damage – he will be liable to prosecution just as any other person.

The second offence of burglary in section 9(1)(b) occurs when a person, having entered a building or part of a building without permission, steals or attempts to steal anything in the building or inflicts or attempts to inflict any serious bodily harm. The important distinction between this and the first offence of burglary is that here there is a requirement for conviction that an offence of theft or inflicting serious bodily harm has been committed, or at least attempted. There is no requirement, however, of any intention to commit either of these offences at the time of entry. So, to use the same example, if the tramp who entered your home in search of a warm place to sleep (and nothing else) subsequently decided to steal some food from your fridge, he would be guilty of the second offence of burglary.

There is also an offence of aggravated burglary contained in section 10 of the Theft Act 1968 which occurs where a person commits burglary and at the time has with him any firearm, imitation firearm, weapon of offence or explosive. This offence only exists to render a burglar liable to a more severe penalty if he goes about his business armed.

(iv) Fraud

There is no such criminal offence as fraud although there is an offence of conspiracy to defraud. The term fraud is usually used to describe a collection of criminal offences, most of which involve the practising of some deception on the victim. With the growing use of advanced technology in banking and other financial services, the potential for fraud is rapidly increasing. But even in ordinary day-to-day activities, such as buying second-hand goods, a person may discover that he has been 'swindled' or 'cheated' and it is important to appreciate the situations that are covered by the criminal law.

(A) Obtaining property by deception.

Section 15 of the Theft Act 1968 provides that 'a person who by any deception dishonestly obtains property belonging to another with the intention of permanently depriving the other of it' commits an offence. 'Property' includes both goods and land although it is unlikely that land would feature in this offence. Deception is defined quite widely in the law: it will cover deception by conduct, deception by words and sometimes even deception by silence. An interesting example of deception by silence can be seen in the case *Director of Public Prosecutions v Ray* (1973).

Director of Public Prosecutions v Ray

Ray went into a restaurant with some other students. The others agreed to pay for his meal as he did not have sufficient money with him. After they had finished their meal they decided to leave the restaurant without paying. The House of Lords, in dismissing Ray's appeal against conviction, said that, as there had been an implied representation that the meal would be paid for, there was a deception in the failure to indicate to the waiter that the representation was no longer valid.

A common example of deception by conduct concerns bouncing cheques. The Courts have decided that a person paying by cheque impliedly represents that the cheque will be honoured when presented for payment on or after the date specified on the cheque. This does not apply if the cheque is backed by a cheque card because, provided the conditions on the card have been complied with, the bank is contractually bound to honour the cheque. However, the Courts have held that there is another type of deception here, in that the drawer of the cheque is impliedly representing that he has the bank's permission to use the card, which clearly he does not if he exceeds the amount he is allowed to borrow from the bank by way of overdraft.

Deception by words includes both deception as to fact and deception as to law. Deception as to fact could arise in any situation where the seller of

an article intentionally (or recklessly) misleads his victim about some attribute of an article that it does not have; for example, that a motor car is newer than it is. In certain circumstances, such as when the seller is in business, there could also be criminal liability under the Trade Descriptions Acts. The 'property' which the seller would 'obtain' in these cases would, of course, be the victim's money! However, if the seller acted innocently, or if he offered an opinion about an article which he did not know clearly to be wrong, he would not be guilty of an offence.

Deception as to law does not arise very commonly in practice. Most professional people would not intentionally do this and the layman's view of the law is usually honestly held even though it is often inaccurate.

To what extent can a failure to state the truth amount to a deception? If a person, in the course of buying an article off someone, makes a comment about its condition or value which the seller knows to be inaccurate, does the seller practise a deception by keeping quiet and failing to correct the mistake? Surprisingly, the law is not clear on this point but it is thought that money obtained in such circumstances could be said to have been obtained by deception.

There are several important requirements that must be satisfied before this offence is committed. The accused must have made his deception deliberately or recklessly. In addition, he must have obtained the property dishonestly and intended to permanently deprive the other person of it. So if the accused acted in good faith, or if he intentionally practised a deception to enable himself to borrow something, he is not guilty of an offence. Moreover, there must be some evidence that the victim parted with his goods or money as a result of the deception. If the

---

R v Laverty

Mr Bedborough bought a second-hand car from Laverty, not realising that the number plates had been changed. The Court of Appeal allowed Laverty's appeal against his conviction for obtaining property by deception as it appeared that Mr Bedborough had bought the car from Laverty because he thought Laverty was the owner. There was no evidence that he was at all concerned whether or not the car possessed the original number plates.

---

victim does not hear the deception, or if he does not believe it, or if he would have acted in just the same way had he known the truth, then the offence is not committed. This last point is illustrated in the case *R v Laverty* (1970).

(B) Obtaining services by deception. This offence, contained in section 1 of the Theft Act 1978, is committed where a person by any deception dishonestly obtains services from another. 'Obtains services' is defined in the law as being 'where the other is induced to confer a benefit by doing some act, or causing or permitting some act to be done, on the understanding that the benefit has been or will be paid for'. If, therefore, your neighbour asks you to mow his lawn, or give him a lift to the station, or babysit for him, on the understanding that he will pay you, but all along he is dishonest and has never intended to provide payment, then he is guilty of an offence. In some respects, the criminal law has been extended into areas which might have been better left for the civil Courts to resolve or, in the case of minor domestic disputes, to the common sense of the parties themselves. It is debatable whether the police would take any interest in the more trivial agreements. In any case, there is a requirement that the benefit must have been conferred on the understanding that it has been or will be paid for and that will preclude criminal liability in many of these cases.

(C) Evasion of liability by deception. This heading comprises three separate criminal offences which are contained in section 2 of the Theft Act 1978. They are rather technical in their requirements but are important in that they create liability for people who by deception avoid paying their debts. The first offence concerns the dishonest securing by deception of the remission of the whole or part of an existing liability to make payment. For example, if someone who owes you money persuades you to forget the whole or part of the debt by telling you (wrongly) that he has lost his job, he is guilty of this offence.

The second offence, which is more elaborate, is committed where a person, intending to make permanent default of an existing liability to make payment, deceives the creditor into waiting for payment or forgoing payment. The main difference between this offence and the other two is that it can be committed without the creditor ever having agreed to forgo or wait for payment. So if someone owes you money and you go to his flat only to find a notice saying (wrongly) 'Moved away', the person can be guilty of this offence. This law also provides that a person who is induced to accept a worthless cheque in payment is to be treated not as being paid but as being induced to wait for payment. If the worthless cheque is handed over with the intention to avoid payment altogether, it could amount to this offence.

The third offence is committed where a person dishonestly obtains any exemption from or abatement of liability to make a payment. It is unlikely that an individual, other than perhaps a shopkeeper, could be a victim of this offence, in that the typical situation in which liability is incurred will be that of a person who obtains a free bus pass or a rate rebate by falsely stating he is a senior citizen.

(D) Making off without payment. Section 3 of the Theft Act 1978 provides that 'A person who, knowing that payment on the spot for any goods supplied or service done is required or expected from him, dishonestly makes off without having paid as required or expected and with intent to avoid payment of the amount due shall be guilty of an offence.' This particular offence is stated clearly and succinctly in the criminal law. It is designed to deal with behaviour which is commonly known as 'bilking' – disappearing from a place such as a restaurant or petrol filling station at the moment payment is due. As such, it is only likely to create victims among members of the public who are engaged in such businesses, in addition to taxi-drivers and shopkeepers.

(v) Blackmail

The crime of blackmail has existed for centuries and, owing to its treatment in literature and theatre, has come to acquire a certain romantic aura. This is wholly unjustified; blackmail is a cruel crime, which in a number of cases has led to the victim's suicide, and is treated very seriously by the police. Section 21 of the Theft Act 1968 provides that blackmail is committed where a person, with a view to gain for himself or another or with intent to cause loss to another, makes any unwarranted demand with menaces. A demand is not considered unwarranted where the person making it believes (a) he has reasonable grounds for making the demand, *and* (b) the use of menaces is a proper means of reinforcing the demand.

The actual demand is the essential part of the

definition, so the offence can still be committed even if the blackmailer obtains nothing. Although the demand will usually be for the transfer of money or goods, this is not a requirement of the offence. The term 'menaces', which historically was limited to threats of violence, is now much wider and can include any threats of action detrimental to the person addressed. The menaces do not have to refer to action to be taken by the person making the demand; a threat of violence could typically involve bringing in 'the heavy mob' to carry it out. The requirement of the blackmailer intending gain for himself or another or loss to another is defined in wide terms. The terms 'gain' and 'loss' are to be confined to money and other property. Gain includes a gain by keeping what one has, as well as getting something one does not have; 'loss' includes a loss by not getting what one might get, as well as losing what one already has! This seems rather complicated but, taking these two requirements together, it is possible to envisage a wide range of demands with menaces which do not involve a demand for the transfer of property. For example, a demand may relate to the destruction of incriminating letters (losing what one already has) or cancelling a debt (not getting what one might get).

As stated above, a demand is not unwarranted if the person making it believes he has reasonable grounds for doing so and that the use of menaces is a proper means for reinforcing the demand. If the accused honestly held these beliefs, that should be sufficient to secure his acquittal and it would be legally irrelevant that no reasonable person could possibly have thought the way he did. Legally irrelevant, perhaps – but not totally irrelevant, because, if the accused's beliefs were wholly unreasonable, it is unlikely that a jury would believe him!

It is not uncommon for tardy debtors and other people to be threatened with legal proceedings if they do not pay up. No offence is committed here because, although there is a demand with menaces, it is highly unlikely that any jury would fail to believe a person making such a demand who claimed that going to Court would be a reasonable way of enforcing such a demand.

(vi) Damage to Your Possessions or Your Land

Vandalism, or as the law calls it, criminal damage, is one of the fastest-growing crimes in this country at present. Much of it is committed against public property but individuals' homes and belongings – particularly their cars – are frequently subject to it as well.

There are, in essence, two offences of criminal damage, the second of which is an 'aggravated' form which applies where life is endangered and carries a far more severe penalty. The 'basic' offence contained in section 1(1) of the Criminal Damage Act 1971 is committed where a person without lawful excuse destroys or damages property belonging to another, either intentionally or recklessly. It is necessary to point out immediately that the term 'reckless' when applied to criminal damage has been held by the Courts to have a different meaning than the one given above. In relation to criminal damage, recklessness is established when a person does an act which creates an obvious and serious risk that the property will be destroyed or damaged and either: (i) has not given any thought to the possibility of there being a risk of destruction or damage, or (ii) having recognised that there is some risk involved and having still gone on to do it. If the damage or destruction is caused by fire, the offence is charged as arson.

'Property' can be defined for this purpose as including land (and anything on it) possessions and tame animals. It does not, however, include mushrooms, flowers, fruit or plants growing wild on any land. The property must belong to another person; the basic offence cannot be committed by a person's destruction of or damage to his own property. A Court has decided that property is 'damaged' if it is rendered inoperative or imperfect. A piece of machinery would be rendered inoperative for this purpose if a crucial item were removed, even if neither the item nor the machinery itself suffered any physical injury. Writing or spraying graffiti on buildings amounts to criminal damage, even if the writing or paint would wear off in the course of time. 'Destruction' requires something going beyond this, such as the dismantling of a machine or the knocking down of a wall. The killing of an animal would also be covered by this term.

The requirement that the accused, to be guilty of this offence, must have acted 'without lawful excuse' is elaborated in the law. It is provided that an accused is to be treated as having a lawful excuse if he believed that the person whose property was destroyed or damaged had consented, or would have consented if he had known of the destruction or damage and its circumstances. The provision goes on to state that the accused also had a lawful excuse if he destroyed or damaged property in order to protect property belonging to himself or another, believing that the property was in immediate need of protection and that the means of protection adopted were reasonable in the circumstances. It is irrelevant whether the belief was justified or not as long as the accused held it at the time; but he will obviously have to provide some evidence of this and, if his story sounds implausible, there is a danger that a Court or jury will not believe him. Even a drunken belief is sufficient, however, as is illustrated in the case *Jaggard v Dickinson* (1981).

> **Jaggard v Dickinson**
> Ms Jaggard went to a house late at night. She was drunk and thought it was a house belonging to a friend. She believed, quite correctly, that her friend would not object to her breaking in. Unfortunately, she had chosen the wrong house. The Court of Appeal held that her belief, although caused by drink, that she was entitled to break in provided a sufficient lawful excuse.

The second part of the defence, concerning the protection of one's own property, could arise in a number of ways. For example, there can be no doubt that a farmer who saw a dog worrying his sheep would be able to rely on this defence if he shot the dog. The defence also extends to the protection of a 'right or interest in property', so if someone parked their car on your property (which probably would not include the pavement outside your house) for such a period of time that he was seriously interfering with your use of it, your honest belief that you had to force a door window or lock in order to remove the car would probably be accepted by a Court or jury. Similarly, if your property had been subject to a number of burglaries and you placed barbed wire on top of your high garden wall, it is unlikely you would be found guilty of causing criminal damage to a trespasser's clothing!

The 'aggravated' offence contained in section 1(2) of the Criminal Damage Act 1971 is committed where a person without lawful excuse intentionally or recklessly destroys or damages property, whether belonging to himself or another, intending to endanger the life of another, or being reckless whether the life of another would be endangered. 'Reckless' has the same meaning as in the basic offence. One significant difference, however, from the basic offence is

that here the accused can be liable for destroying his own property. Obviously, if life is endangered, the question of who owns the property should be irrelevant.

(vii) Entering and Remaining on Property

During the early 1970s increasing publicity came to be given to a new social phenomenon – squatting. The only criminal offences existing at the time to deal with this, such as forcible entry and detainer, were archaic and in several respects inadequate to deal with the full implications of the problem. These were abolished and new laws created. Two main offences were created; using or threatening violence for securing entry to any premises, contained in section 6 of the Criminal Law Act 1977, and adverse occupation of residential premises, contained in section 7. The word 'premises' in both these offences means any building, any part of a building under separate occupation (such as flat or bed-sit) and any land ancillary to a building. A 'building' can be any immoveable or moveable structure, such as a caravan. The phrase 'ancillary to a building' means that the land must be adjacent to a building and used in connection with the occupation of a building. A field in the middle of the countryside would obviously not come within the scope of this definition.

The first offence under section 6, concerning the use of violence to secure entry, is committed where a person without lawful authority uses or threatens violence for the purpose of securing entry to premises for himself or any other person where he knows there is someone on those premises who is opposed to the entry. The threat of violence is the important part of this offence; entry itself is not required. The purpose of the intended entry is immaterial. Although the law was aimed at people wishing to take up residence, it would also cover 'gate-crashers' at a party. The violence can be threatened or used against a person or property, and the offence can be committed even if the threat or use occurs outside the building, provided it is made for the purpose of gaining entry to it. The requirement that someone must be present at the premises when the violence is threatened or used is very important. This offence is not committed (although others might be) if someone enters your house and takes up residence when you are on holiday. Even if someone is present at the time of the incident, the offence is not committed unless that person (or someone else on the premises) is opposed to the entry. The accused must intentionally or recklessly use or threaten violence. 'Reckless' in this crime means that the accused realises the possibility that someone might feel threatened, but still continues to act in the same way. No offence is committed in cases where a person has lawful authority to use or threaten violence to secure entry to premises. Policemen have the power to enter premises by force in certain cases in pursuance of their powers of arrest and search. However, lawful authority does not extend to someone such as a landlord who would be guilty of this offence if he were to use or threaten force in order to obtain entry.

The law does provide a defence for a 'displaced residential occupier' of premises who himself uses or threatens force to try to regain possession of his own home. A 'displaced residential occupier' is defined as any person who was occupying the particular premises immediately before being excluded from occupation of them. It seems that this definition would also cover holiday homes. If an occupier or anyone acting on his behalf uses or threatens violence for the purpose of gaining re-entry to premises, it shall be a defence to any criminal charge if the occupier (or person acting on his behalf) can prove that he was a 'displaced residential occupier'. However, occupiers should be very wary of taking this course of action and there is much to be said for contacting the police instead.

The second offence under section 7 concerns adverse occupation of residential premises. Any person who is on any premises as a trespasser, having entered the premises as a trespasser, is guilty of an offence if he fails to leave those premises on being asked to do so by, or on behalf of (a) the 'displaced residential occupier' or (b) an individual who is a 'protected intending occupier' of the premises. We have already seen the definition of a 'displaced residential occupier'; the definition of a 'protected intending occupier' is more complex. There appear to be two types of this sort of occupier. The first has a freehold or leasehold interest with at least 21 years to run which he has purchased; he requires residential occupation of the premises but is excluded by the occupying trespasser; and he, or someone acting on his behalf, holds a written statement signed by him and witnessed by a magistrate or a commissioner for oaths which specifies his interest in the premises and states that he requires them to live in. The second type

is a tenant of the local council, the housing corporation or a housing association; he requires residential occupation but is excluded by the occupying trespasser; and he holds a certificate from the local authority, housing corporation or a housing association stating that he has been authorised to occupy the premises. In both cases, the purpose of the written document is to enable the police to identify easily the lawful claimant in what could be a turbulent situation. It seems unfortunate that these provisions do not apply to people with a lease with less than 21 years to run or a short-term tenancy provided by a private landlord.

This offence was created to give a residential occupier or intending residential occupier of premises who has been excluded by squatters an easier and quicker remedy for recovering possession than having to resort to the civil Courts. He can ask them to leave and, if they refuse, he can call upon a uniformed police officer, who, as in the case of the first offence, can arrest without a warrant anyone who is, or whom he with reasonable cause suspects to be, guilty of the offence. To this end, the officer can enter (by force, if necessary) and search the premises. It appears that neither the police officer nor displaced residential occupier will commit an offence under section 6 if violence is used to secure entry; but a protected intending occupier has no such defence. The fact that liability under section 7 can only arise when the accused has originally entered the premises as a trespasser is important as the person who remains on premises after the expiry or termination of a tenancy or licence cannot be guilty of this offence.

Three defences are provided for an accused under section 7 but, in each case, he has to prove them to the Court. One is that the person requiring him to leave was neither a displaced residential occupier or protected intending occupier of the premises. The second is that the person did not produce a written document complying with the Act when asked to do so by accused. The third defence is that the premises are used mainly for non-residential purposes.

2. REASONS WHY THE OFFENDER MAY NOT BE CONVICTED IN COURT

So far, the discussion has concentrated on the more serious crimes of which a person may find himself to be a victim. However, in some cases, although the incident – for example, an attack or a burglary – may undeniably have taken place and although there may be no dispute that the accused was the perpetrator, the accused may not be convicted in Court. Understandably, this can be particularly galling to the victim, and it is worthwhile pointing out some of the reasons why this happens.

(i) The Accused Did Not Intend to Commit the Crime

In the case of most serious criminal offences, a person cannot be found guilty unless he carried out the conduct or caused the circumstances forbidden in the offence, such as the beating of his victim or the taking of his wallet, and at the same time intended to carry out the conduct or cause the circumstances, or, for some crimes, was reckless as to whether he did so. As we have already seen, the meaning of the word 'reckless' has recently been complicated by the Courts giving it a different meaning for offences involving criminal damage, but otherwise the definition given in relation to offences against the person is to be applied. The importance of this principle is that, for these serious criminal offences, a person cannot be found guilty if he carried out the forbidden conduct accidentally – although care must be taken to distinguish 'accidentally' from 'recklessly'. For example, if a person accidentally bumps into you in a busy street, he is not guilty of a criminal offence. In all the offences discussed above, except criminal damage, he will not even be liable if he should have foreseen that his behaviour would result in the forbidden circumstances (in the sense that most other people would have realised it) but did not.

Many minor criminal offences can be committed simply by the defendant carrying out the conduct or causing the circumstances forbidden in the offence irrespective of his state of mind (as long as he was acting consciously). These offences are known as crimes of 'strict liability' and most of the motoring offences discussed in Section 7 of this book come into this category. For example, it is no defence to a charge of driving with one back light not working to claim that the driver did not know of the defect.

It is very important to notice that, in this country, ignorance of the law cannot be a defence to a criminal charge. Given the vast amount of legislation containing criminal offences (often offences of strict liability) this rule may seem rather harsh, but there would obviously be severe practical difficulties if it did not exist. Not even overseas visitors are exempt from the rule.

(ii) The Accused Was Under the Age of Criminal Liability

A child under the age of 10 years cannot be convicted of a criminal offence. If it were felt that action should be taken in respect of his unlawful activities, the only possibility would be for care proceedings to be brought under section 1 of the Children and Young Persons Act 1969. Children aged ten but under fourteen are presumed incapable of committing an offence but this presumption can be rebutted if 'mischievous discretion' is proved. This has been interpreted by the Courts that the child must have appreciated that what he did was seriously wrong. Evidence of the child's home background, mental state and previous convictions would be relevant in determining this point as, presumably, would be the nature of the offence itself. Police make considerable use of their discretion in deciding whether or not to prosecute juveniles, especially for relatively minor offences.

(iii) The Accused Was Drunk

Evidence suggests that a lot of the offences against the person, burglaries and acts of criminal damage in this country are committed by people who were, to a greater or lesser extent, under the influence of alcohol. Not surprisingly, therefore, the scope of the defence of drunkenness has been considerably influenced by considerations of public policy; the Courts are hardly likely to allow an offender to 'get away with it' just because he has had a few drinks. The first point to appreciate, then, is that drunkenness can never be a defence to a criminal charge unless it prevented the offender being able to form the intention to carry out the prohibited act. Everyone knows that alcohol loosens a person's inhibitions, but that in itself is insufficient to prevent criminal liability. Similarly, it can never be a defence that an offender contemplated the commission of a criminal offence and then made himself drunk to give him sufficient courage to do it. In what situations, therefore, can drunkenness amount to a defence?

This area of the criminal law has not been noted for its clarity or consistency, but in the leading case of *R v Majewski* (1976) the House of Lords decided that drunkenness can only be a defence to offences requiring proof of a 'specific intent'. Unfortunately, the precise meaning of

467

this term is not wholly clear but, with one exception, it seems to refer to criminal offences that cannot be committed recklessly. The exception is section 1(2) of the Criminal Damage Act 1971 which the House of Lords in another case has held to be a crime of specific intent when charged in the form of intention *or recklessness* to destroy or damage property, with an intention to endanger life. A number of cases make clear the crimes which have been held to require specific intent and, therefore, to which drunkenness can be a defence. They include murder, wounding or causing grievous bodily harm with intent, theft, robbery, burglary with intent to steal, handling stolen goods, the form of criminal damage just referred to, and an attempt to commit an offence. It is important to note that, for some of these offences – particularly the offences against the person and the offence of criminal damage – there will still be liability for lesser offences that can be committed recklessly. In addition, although the word 'drunkenness' has been used here, exactly the same rules apply for the use of drugs. However, if drugs are taken for medicinal purposes and the prescribed dosage is adhered to, the accused will have a defence if his intoxicated state prevented his forming the intention to carry out the prohibited act *or being reckless as to whether or not he did so.* (There is no requirement here of specific intent.) This defence also covers the situation where alcohol is secretly added to a non-alcoholic drink.

(iv) The Accused Was Legally Insane or Acted as an Automaton

Although there is a lot of academic discussion about the defence of insanity in the criminal law, it is of virtually no practical importance nowadays and is raised in only a handful of cases each year. This is not so much because the legal test is difficult to satisfy and is completely out of line with contemporary views of mental illness, but that the prospect of being locked up indefinitely in a mental hospital seems worse to most offenders than pleading guilty and facing the possibility of imprisonment. Historically, the defence was important as a way of avoiding the death penalty in murder cases but, even before capital punishment was abolished in 1965, a less strict verdict of 'manslaughter on the grounds of diminished responsibility' had been introduced.

The question of automatism is more relevant. If the act with which the accused is charged was committed involuntarily, he will have a defence.

This would be fairly obvious in a case where a man grabbed the accused's hand, which happened to be holding a kitchen knife, and directed the knife into the victim's back. But the defence of automatism can also apply where the accused's act resulted from an involuntary spasm or reflex action. Not surprisingly, the Courts have been very wary of this defence. In a number of cases it was raised unsuccessfully as an alternative defence to insanity, no doubt in an attempt to avoid the disadvantage of that defence discussed above. In the recent case *R v Bailey* (1983) the question was raised whether a diabetic, who failed to take sufficient food after a dose of insulin and consequently fell into a state of unconsciousness, could rely on the defence of automatism to a charge of wounding or inflicting grievous bodily harm contrary to section 20 of the Offences Against the Person Act 1861 (see above). The Court of Appeal decided that, if the offence charged requires specific intent, automatism can be a defence, whatever its cause. If the offence charged does not require specific intent, automatism can never be a defence if it arises from voluntary intoxication. If the automatism arises from another cause, as in the case of a diabetic like Bailey who had not eaten enough food, automatism can be a defence, unless the accused appreciated the risk he was taking (for example, in not eating enough food) but still proceeded with his course of conduct.

Needless to say, the fact that the accused was feeling unwell or generally 'off-colour' for reasons unrelated to drink or drugs cannot be a defence to a criminal charge.

(v) The Accused Enjoyed Diplomatic Immunity

A victim is not likely to encounter this difficulty unless he lives in the London area. Foreign diplomats are immune from the criminal (and civil) jurisdiction of English Courts. The precise categories of individual who enjoy this position are found in various Acts of Parliament; the Diplomatic Privileges Act 1964 is one example. The privilege from liability is actually vested in the governments which these diplomats represent so it can always be waived by them and, indeed, it often is in serious cases. However, with the behaviour of some foreign Governments becoming increasingly unpredictable, and a growing number of diplomats residing in this country, the significance of diplomatic immunity is likely to increase.

(vi) The Prosecution Was Unable to Prove Its Case

It is a fundamental principle of English criminal law that it is the duty of the prosecution to prove the guilt of the defendant. Since the decision of the House of Lords in the case *Woolmington v Director of Public Prosecutions* (1935), it is clear that the prosecution must convince magistrates or a jury that the defendant is guilty 'beyond a reasonable doubt'. If, for any reason, the prosecution fails to do this, the defendant must be acquitted. Therefore, however certain a victim might be that it was the defendant who attacked him, or burgled his house, this will be of no consequence whatsoever if the prosecution fails to prove its case. The statistics make interesting reading. In 1984, 64% of defendants appearing at the Crown Court pleaded guilty to all charges. However, 51% of those pleading not guilty to all charges were acquitted by the jury either after deliberation or following a formal direction by the judge. There are several possible explanations for this level of acquittals: (a) the accused was genuinely innocent and the victim was mistaken; (b) the accused was guilty and was wrongly acquitted. This could have happened because of any of the following reasons.

(A) The jury made a mistake. This is something which inevitably happens from time to time where there is trial by jury. The jury has come in for a lot of criticism recently for various reasons including methods of selection and inability to understand complicated issues.

(B) The prosecution was incompetent. Research published by McCabe and Purves in 1972 suggested that many of the jury acquittals in their study could be attributed to the failure of the prosecution to present its case properly.

(C) The rules of evidence in criminal cases are too heavily biased in favour of the accused. A lot of information about the accused and the circumstances of the case may never be revealed to the jury. For example, if the accused does not attack the character of a prosecution witness, his own previous convictions may not be disclosed to the jury. Some people think that the pendulum has swung too far in favour of the accused, but it can be argued that the prosecution still has the major advantages in our system of criminal justice.

3. WHAT TO DO IF YOU ARE A VICTIM

Criminal offences and the circumstances in which they are committed vary considerably. So too do the victims of crime. Elderly and nervous people are more likely to be distressed by fairly minor crimes – such as a petty theft – than young people who are usually more resilient. But some crimes could shock even the most phlegmatic person. What should you do if you are the victim of a crime?

One of the first things that should happen is that you or someone else should contact the police immediately. It is in everyone's interests that an offender should be apprehended and the sooner the police know about the crime the more likely it is that they will be able to do this. The police emphasise that even seemingly trivial incidents should be reported to them. Even if there is no apparent likelihood of the offender being traced, knowledge of the crime will help keep their records up to date, and a pattern of criminal offences committed by the same individual may start to emerge. Sympathy for the offender, especially if it is a child, may incline someone towards not reporting a crime; but a relatively trivial offence committed against a young healthy person on one day may be followed by a similar incident causing terror to an elderly person the next. In any case, much deliberation takes place before juvenile offenders are prosecuted, especially for minor crimes. Moreover, many insurance companies now require that victims report their losses or damage to the police before any claims are met.

As far as possible, the victim should take care not to disturb any evidence of the crime that might be of assistance to the police. Obviously, if a person has been viciously attacked, he cannot be expected to stand around until a policeman arrives to look for clues! But the scene of a burglary, however upsetting it might seem to a tidy householder, is best left undisturbed until checks have been made for fingerprints. Even a victim of rape should ideally allow herself to be examined by a police surgeon as soon as possible after the attack but perhaps, in the extremely harrowing circumstances, it would be hardly surprising if many women were reluctant to do this.

A number of voluntary organisations have been set up to help alleviate the distress and suffering experienced by victims of criminal offences. The largest and best-known is the

National Association of Victims Support Schemes which was set up in 1980 and now has about 170 affiliated schemes in the United Kingdom using more than 3,000 volunteers. In 1982 over 41,000 victims were contacted by these schemes. Each local scheme has a co-ordinator who every day telephones the liason police officer. The officer will then tell the co-ordinator the names, ages and addresses of local victims of crime. The co-ordinator will then contact the volunteers and they will visit the victim usually on the same day. Initially they will provide support such as helping to claim insurance; changing a lock; advising on the law; contacting the local housing department to repair damage to property; and even providing small sums of money, sometimes as a short-term loan and on other occasions as a gift from local charitable sources. They will also try to give emotional support to the victim, where necessary. The NAVSS is funded by a central government grant but this is insufficient to pay for the services provided by the local schemes so they have to generate their own additional income. About one third receive financial contributions from local authorities or central government.

Another important service for victims is provided by rape crisis centres, of which nineteen exist in England, four in Scotland, one in Northern Ireland and one in Wales. There is no central organisation. Each of the centres provides a telephone counselling service and deals with any woman or girl who has been raped or sexually assaulted. The centres offer medical and legal advice and, if requested, someone will accompany the victim to see a doctor, or the police, or even to Court. Most of the counselling is carried out by telephone but meetings can be arranged. The victim has to contact the centre herself; this is seen as an important step towards her regaining a measure of self-confidence.

For women victims in need of temporary accommodation, groups affiliated to the National Women's Aid Federation provide over 200 refuges throughout the country. These are available for women and their children who have suffered physical or mental harassment. Support, information and advice are available to any woman even if she is not a resident. Women approach the refuges themselves but referrals also come from such groups as the police, social services and doctors. An 'open door' policy applies throughout the system as a whole; a woman will always be found a place in a refuge even if the one she has applied to happens to be full.

4. ARE YOU ENTITLED TO COMPENSATION?

(i) Compensation and Restitution from the Court Trying the Offender

Under section 1 of the Criminal Justice Act 1972, Courts have the power to order a convicted offender to compensate his victim for any injury, loss or damage resulting from his offence. This can be in addition to any sentence imposed. Magistrates can order compensation of up to £2,000 to be paid. There is no limit in the Crown Court. Orders are far more commonly made by magistrates than Crown Court judges. In 1984, magistrates made 118,682 compensation orders but judges in the Crown Court only made 6,217. In 1984 magistrates imposed compensation orders on 67% of people convicted of criminal damage, on 50% convicted of fraud, 37% convicted of burglary, 28% convicted of robbery, 19% convicted of theft and handling stolen goods, and 20% convicted of violence. The overall figure for Magistrates' Courts is 22%. The figures in the Crown Court are significantly lower: 25% for criminal damage, but only 15% for fraud, 6% for burglary, 4% for robbery, 8% for theft and handling stolen goods, and 12% for violence. The overall figure for the Crown Court is 8%.

These figures are disappointingly low. Courts seem happier making compensation orders in criminal damage cases, where the amounts concerned are easily quantifiable, than in personal injury cases where they feel somewhat out of their depth. There are several problems with compensation orders in criminal Courts: (a) the offender must have been apprehended; (b) the means of the offender may be such that he is unable to pay compensation; (c) the offender may be unwilling to pay compensation, or only to pay it in small amounts over a long period of time. A Home Office Research Study in 1978 showed that a quarter of the offenders in the survey who had been ordered to pay compensation had not completed payment within eighteen months and that a tenth of those ordered to pay had paid nothing at all. In addition, a Court may feel that ordering compensation is inconsistent with the sentence it wishes to pass. Not surprisingly, compensation is not often ordered when a Court has passed a custodial sentence, especially a lengthy one.

Even where compensation is ordered, it can take a while for payments to begin and some considerable time to enforce the sanctions available for non-payment.

Section 28 of the Theft Act 1968 states that, where goods have been stolen and a person has been convicted of an offence relating to the theft, or has had his involvement in the theft reflected in a sentence passed for some other offence, the convicting Court can order that anyone who has possession or control of the goods should restore them to any person entitled to recover them from him. If the goods have been sold or exchanged, any goods which now represent the original goods can be made the subject of the order. Alternatively, the Court can order that any sum of money found on the convicted person at the time of his apprehension can be paid to the person entitled to the goods, provided that the sum does not exceed the value of the goods. If the goods which represent the original goods are of less value than the original goods, a Court can order that the goods and a sum of money found on the offender should be given to the person entitled to restoration provided that the combined value does not exceed that of the original goods.

Section 28(4) places an important restriction on the use of these powers. The subsection provides, in effect, that a Court should only exercise its powers under section 28 where the facts of the case are completely clear and there can be no dispute as to who is entitled to the property. This seems reasonable, as a criminal Court is not a suitable place to decide difficult questions of ownership.

(ii) The Criminal Injuries Compensation Board

The Criminal Injuries Compensation Board (CICB) was set up in 1964 to make payments to people who have suffered personal injury which is directly attributable either to a crime of violence, or to trying to prevent a crime, or apprehend a suspect. Close relatives or dependants of such a person who dies of his injuries may also be entitled to compensation. The payments are 'ex gratia', not as of right, although the CICB report in 1979 stated that 'The Board's view of its legal obligation and duty under the scheme is that, if an applicant's entitlement to compensation is established there is no power to withhold compensation'. The victim must complete a form which requires information about such matters as the nature of the offence, the injuries received

and how they were treated, the victim's financial loss and any other compensation or state benefits received. The CICB, on receiving an application, will acknowledge it and then start to check the information on the form. For example, the police will be asked whether they think the injury was caused by one of the three situations which can lead to an award under the scheme (see above). They will also be asked whether the victim's behaviour contributed in any way to his injuries and whether there has been a prosecution in the case. If the victim has been scarred, or the medical information indicates that he is still suffering from the effects of his injuries, or the victim might be entitled to industrial disablement benefit, another form (CSIA) will be sent to him requesting further details and, in the case of scarring, he might be asked to send black-and-white photographs. If it seems that there could be a lengthy delay before the medical details are fully known, the CICB can make an interim award. Otherwise, the application will be referred to a single member of the CICB who can decide (a) to make an offer for the full amount claimed or a lesser amount; or (b) to make no award at all; or (c) to pass on the application to be considered by a two or three member panel of the CICB. If the applicant wishes to appeal, there will be a hearing at which the applicant is required to appear.

There are a number of points concerning the operation of the CICB which should be noted. The CICB can reduce or even withhold compensation if it considers that the applicant did not inform the police of the attack without delay (but only if criminal proceedings are not brought); or that the applicant has failed to assist the board in its inquiries; or that the conduct and lifestyle of the applicant make an award inappropriate. The CICB has provided some amplification of this. Any person who has a 'record [showing] that he is a man of violence' or is 'a victim who has persistently obtained his living by committing offences of dishonesty and has not made a serious attempt to earn an honest living', is unlikely to receive any compensation. Moreover, compensation will not be paid in any case if the board considers that the total compensation payable after deduction of social security benefits would be less than £400. Formerly, an applicant who lived with the offender as a member of the same family was not eligible for compensation but this rule has been relaxed in certain cases. Legal aid is not available for applications to the CICB but the

471

Green Form Scheme could be used (see section 1 of this book). In 1982–83 there were 29,440 applications to the board and there were 19,773 monetary awards. In the year ending March 1984, compensation totalling £156,825 was paid.

The scheme is open to criticism on a number of grounds. One is that it does not provide compensation for property offences. The Government's view appears to be that this can be adequately provided by private insurance. A study published in 1982 indicated that 30% of the sample who had suffered a burglary in their home were under-insured. Research by Joanna Shapland suggests that ignorance of the CICB is fairly widespread among victims; indeed only 39% in her sample had ever heard of it. The same study indicated that the average period between the application for and receipt of an award was just over nine months. A further criticism is that, even in the cases where the CICB does make awards, the amount of compensation can be very low. This was highlighted in a case in 1985 when it was disclosed that two victims of rape, who were subsequently awarded damages in the High Court of £10,480 and £7,080 against the defendant, had earlier been awarded £3,600 and £1,000 respectively by the CICB for their ordeal.

Perhaps the biggest disadvantage of the scheme is the lower limit to claims of £400. The Government has argued that the cost of processing a claim of less than this amount would exceed the value of the claim itself and there seems little likelihood of any change in its position in the foreseeable future. It has been estimated that in 1983 between 3,000 and 4,000 victims had no entitlement to compensation for this reason alone.

(iii) Civil Proceedings Against the Offender

As an alternative to compensation at the offender's trial or an application to the Criminal Injuries Compensation Board, a victim can always consider suing a victim in a civil Court. He could pursue an action in respect of an offence against the person, or loss of property or damage to property. The relevant area of civil law is the law of 'torts'. There are torts of assault and battery, both of which can be committed in the same way as the corresponding criminal offences. If a Court considers that one of these torts has taken place and damage has resulted, it will award a sum of money (known as damages) as compensation. However, it should be noted that, if criminal proceedings in respect of an assault or

battery take place in a magistrates' Court and an accused obtains a certificate from the magistrates that either the complaint against him was dismissed or sentence has been passed on him, he is released from all other proceedings, civil or criminal, arising out of the incident. This rule would not apply to convictions for assault occasioning actual bodily harm or offences involving wounding or grievous bodily harm.

Concerning loss of property or damage to property, the relevant torts are conversion and trespass to goods respectively. The tort of conversion, broadly speaking, would apply to the common situations covered by the crime of theft. It involves the unjustified interference with and possession of goods that were in someone else's possession. Unlike the provisions for restitution under section 23 of the Theft Act, the victim does not have to have owned the goods to be entitled to legal redress. In some respects, the tort of conversion is even wider than theft in that it could apply to innocent receivers of goods, whether or not they had paid for them. Conversion can also arise if goods are destroyed. If goods are only damaged, however, recourse must be made to the tort of trespass to goods. For both these torts, the normal form of compensation will be an award of damages, but in an action for conversion, restitution can be ordered.

A person who enters on your land and interferes with any buildings on them can be liable for the tort of trespass to land. Although liability in this tort does not depend on the proof of any particular damage resulting, in reality there would be no point in suing in the absence of damage as you would end up in a worse financial position than when you started! As we have seen already, section 7 of the Criminal Law Act 1977 provides a much better remedy for evicting squatters.

The main problems arising from the use of civil remedies have been referred to in Section 1 of this book. Legal Aid can be difficult to obtain in civil cases, especially ones involving small sums of money. In the absence of Legal Aid, costs can be a prohibitive factor. Even if you have been able to identify the offender, he may not have any money to pay the damages awarded against him. In the unusual case referred to above where two rape victims were awarded £10,480 and £7,080 in the High Court against the defendant, the only reason that there was any chance of the compensation being paid was that he himself had been awarded £45,000 in damages in 1984 in respect of a road accident which completely changed his personality and resulted in his committing the attacks. For sums of less than £500 a victim's best course of action is to use the County Court arbitration scheme. This is cheap and relatively informal; legal representation is permitted, but officially discouraged as the winner cannot recover the costs of representation from the loser.

In the first part of this section we considered the situation of the victim of crime; the situations when a criminal offence has actually been committed and leaves a victim; and what the victim can do about his plight. But there can also be another 'victim' – the victim of the wrongful prosecution. Amidst the clamour for a 'tightening-up' of our criminal justice system, so as to restrict trial by jury, interfere with the rules of evidence and generally make it easier for the prosecution to obtain a conviction, there remains one clear fact: an increasing number of wrongful convictions is coming to light every year. This is largely a result of the growing publicity given to these cases by campaigning journalism on television, radio, and to some extent in the press. Indeed, it is ironic that the popular press can, on one page, call for easier convictions and stiffer sentences and then, on the next page, spotlight the case of someone who has spent several years in prison as a result of a wrongful conviction! Many wrongful convictions probably occur each year even for serious offences and the number is undoubtedly far higher for less serious ones.

1. SUMMONS OR ARREST?

There are three different ways that a person suspected of committing a criminal offence can be brought before a Court; by a summons, by a warrant for arrest or by an arrest without a warrant. A summons is issued by a magistrate or his clerk after an application by a police officer. It will require the defendant to turn up at the Magistrates' Court on a specified date (see opposite). A warrant for arrest is also issued by a magistrate on the application of a police officer usually when the offence is a serious one or the address of the suspect is not known. The power to make an arrest without a warrant is now found in section 24 of the Police and Criminal Evidence Act 1984. The power exists for 'arrestable offences' and certain other specified offences. An 'arrestable offence' is basically one which carries a maximum sentence of five years imprisonment or more. The law states that any person may arrest without a warrant anyone who is, or whom he has reasonable grounds for suspecting to be, in the act of committing an arrestable offence.

Where an arrestable offence has been committed, any person can arrest without a warrant anyone who is, or whom he has reasonable grounds for suspecting to be, guilty of the offence. 'Any person' here means what it says – this is the scope of the so-called 'citizen's arrest'. However, there is one important difference between the power of the citizen to arrest and the power of a police officer. If a police officer makes an arrest, he is protected from a civil action for wrongful imprisonment if he had reasonable grounds for suspecting that an offence had been committed, even if the arrested person were subsequently acquitted in Court. Any other person, such as a store detective, who arrests someone he suspects of having committed an arrestable offence is only protected from civil action if it turns out that such an offence was in fact committed (by someone). A police officer (but not an ordinary citizen) can also arrest without a warrant anyone who is, or whom he has reasonable cause for suspecting to be, about to commit an arrestable offence. He also has a common law power to arrest without a warrant where a breach of the peace has been committed and there are reasonable grounds to believe that it will be continued or renewed; or where he has reasonable grounds to suspect that a breach of the peace is about to occur.

Under the Police and Criminal Evidence Act 1984 the police have special powers to arrest without a warrant for non-arrestable offences. Section 25 provides that, where a police officer has reasonable grounds for suspecting that an offence has been, or is being committed (or attempted), he can arrest a suspect without a warrant if he thinks that (a) it would be impracticable or inappropriate to serve a summons, or (b) he cannot ascertain the suspect's correct name and address, or (c) he has reasonable grounds to think an arrest is necessary to prevent the suspect causing harm to himself or someone else; or damage to property; or an offence against public decency; or (d) obstruction to the highway.

Section 30 of the 1984 Act states that an arrested person must be taken to the police station 'as soon as practicable' after the arrest unless his presence is reasonably necessary elsewhere for the purposes of the investigation. On arrival, the custody officer has to consider if there

(1013) BRISTOL MAGISTRATES' COURT
SUMMONS

SPECIMEN

To:

ANDREW THOMAS

2 HIGH STREET
REDLAND
BRISTOL 6

Date of Information/Complaint

| CASE NUMBER |

Date of Summons October 7th 1985

Date of Birth

YOU ARE HEREBY SUMMONED TO APPEAR BEFORE THE MAGISTRATES' COURT SITTING AT

Nelson Street, Bristol 1

ON February 5th 1986
TO ANSWER TO THE FOLLOWING INFORMATION

AT 10.00 am
OF WHICH PARTICULARS ARE GIVEN BELOW

Alleged
Offence: That you, on August 8th 1985, in Hampton Road, Redland,
Bristol 6, did drive a motor vehicle on a road without
due care and attention contrary to section 3 of, and
schedule 4 to, the Road Traffic Act 1972.

Informant: Inspector James Plod

Address: Redland Police Station

Communications relating to this Summons
MUST QUOTE THE CASE NUMBER GIVEN ABOVE
and should be addressed to:

1st White	— Defendant
2nd White	— Parent/Prosecutor
Green	— Service
Pink	— Division
Yellow	— Court

C/8/83/50000

THE CLERK TO THE JUSTICES,
MAGISTRATES' COURT
P.O. BOX 107
NELSON STREET
BRISTOL BS99 7BJ

Gerard Sullivan

Clerk to the Justices

is sufficient evidence to charge him immediately. After being charged, he must be released, with or without bail, unless (a) his name and address have not been ascertained, or (b) the custody officer reasonably thinks he should be detained to prevent his causing harm to himself, or to others, or damage to property, or (c) the custody officer reasonably thinks he should be detained because if released, he would fail to answer to bail, or interfere with witnesses or otherwise obstruct the course of justice. If charged and not released he must be brought before a Magistrates' Court 'as soon as practicable' and not later than the first Court sitting after being charged.

Supposing the arrested person is not charged immediately on arrival at the police station? After six hours, the custody officer has to review the need for detention. Thereafter, he has to make reviews at intervals of not more than nine hours. The police can in the first instance detain a suspect without charge for a maximum period of 24 hours after his arrival at the police station. A senior police officer, at least of the rank of superintendent, can then authorise detention for up to a further twelve hours. If further detention is required beyond this period, there must be an application to a Magistrates' Court, with the suspect present and legally represented if he requires it. The magistrates can authorise up to a further 36 hours detention; if the police wish to detain the suspect further, they must return to the Magistrates' Court. Once again, a maximum of 36 hours detention may be granted, but the overall period of detention without charge at the police station must not exceed 96 hours. However, detention beyond 24 hours is only allowed where the offence concerned is a serious arrestable offence. This category includes, murder, manslaughter, rape, possession of firearms with intent to injure, and any arrestable offence which is likely to cause serious harm to the security of the state, serious interference with the administration of justice or the investigation of offences, death or serious injury, or substantial gain or loss to anyone.

Under section 32 of the 1984 Act, the police are entitled to search an arrested person. The police can also enter his home and search for evidence relating to the alleged offence or to some other offence 'which is connected with or similar to that offence' (section 18), and an officer is also entitled to seize articles in a person's home under a search warrant if he reasonably believes that it is evidence relating to *any* offence, or that it has been obtained through the commission of an offence and it is necessary to seize it to prevent its being hidden, lost or destroyed (section 19).

Does an arrested person have a right to see a solicitor while he is at the police station? Section 58 of the 1984 Act states that 'a person arrested and held in custody in a police station or other premises shall be entitled, if he so requests, to consult a solicitor privately at any time'. Access should be allowed 'as soon as is practicable'; delay is only permitted if the suspect is being detained in connection with a serious arrestable offence. Refusal to let the suspect see his lawyer can only be authorised by a police officer of at least the rank of superintendent when the officer reasonably considers that such permission (a) will interfere with the investigation of a serious arrestable offence or lead to physical injury to other persons; or (b) will lead to other persons suspected of committing such an offence, but not yet arrested, being alerted, or (c) will impede the recovery of property obtained as a result of such an offence. Section 54 of the 1984 Act provides that 'one friend or relative or other person who is known to him or who is likely to take an interest in his welfare' can be notified of his detention. Delay is allowed in the same circumstances as for access to a solicitor.

When the accused person arrives home and contemplates his fate, he is likely – and, at any rate, would be well advised – to contact a solicitor, if he has not seen one at the police station. One question that will arise is whether or not he will be entitled to legal aid or free advice under the Green Form Scheme. These matters are considered in Section 1 of this book. He will then have to decide whether he wants to be tried by magistrates or by a judge and jury at the Crown Court. This choice is not open to everyone charged with a criminal offence. For this purpose, there are three categories of criminal offence: (1) Offences that can only be tried 'summarily' by magistrates. These include many road traffic offences. (2) Offences that can only be tried 'on indictment', by a judge and jury. Serious offences such as murder, manslaughter, rape and robbery come in this category. (3) Offences triable 'either way', in other words offences that can be tried either by magistrates or by a judge and jury. This category includes the crime of theft. When the accused person appears before the magistrates, that Court *can* insist that he be tried on indictment, but they *cannot* insist that he be tried summarily if he objects. In other words,

IN THE INNER LONDON AREA AND IN THE METROPOLITAN POLICE DISTRICT

LIMEHOUSE

Magistrates' Court (Code 7761)

INFORMANT: Police Constable Nick Curry

ADDRESS: Limehouse Police Station

Information is today laid before me the undersigned for:—

Delete as appropriate

{ a warrant to search
{ a warrant *Summons* against

Marie Little

116 Limborough House

Thomas Road

Limehouse

ALLEGED OFFENCE: Driving without due care and attention contrary to section 3 and Schedule 4 to the Road Traffic Act 1972.

This Deponent

on oath *affirmation* says:— that Marie Little on 13th November 1986 at Burdett Road, Limehouse E14 did drive a motor vehicle without due care and attention.

Date 24th December 1986

Taken and sworn *affirmed* before me

Sharon Brown

Sharon Brown

Metropolitan Stipendiary Magistrate
Justice of the Peace for the Inner London Area

M.C.A.1

INFORMATION

The Informant must give particulars in support of the charge—confining himself as far as possible to facts within his own knowledge.

M.P.-78

477

he cannot be denied a trial by judge and jury at the Crown Court, if he wants it.

Before the accused person makes his decision, there are several important factors he should consider. A trial by magistrates is likely to take place sooner than a trial at the Crown Court, and, having started, will not last as long. Trial by magistrates will be cheaper than at the Crown Court, where a defendant is obliged to use a barrister. If an accused were convicted at the Crown Court, he would probably receive a higher sentence than if he were convicted of the same offence by magistrates. On the other hand, it is easier to obtain legal aid at the Crown Court. In addition, the proceedings would be conducted at a 'higher level' at the Crown Court: there would be a greater formality, a higher standard of advocacy, and a more considered application of the law. A Home Office Research and Planning Unit report ('Managing Criminal Justice') published in December 1985 suggests that defendants have a far greater chance of being acquitted by a jury than by magistrates.

Let us assume first that the accused agrees to summary trial by magistrates. The trial is on the 'information', the formal document containing the allegations against the accused. The information is usually brief, and will contain in plain language the basic facts which constitute the alleged offence (see page 477). The information will be read to the accused who will then be asked to plead. The accused obviously needs to be present in Court for this purpose, but it is worth noting that an accused can be tried by magistrates in his absence (a) if he fails to turn up, or (b) if he takes advantage of the option to plead guilty by post. This procedure is available where the offence charged does not carry a sentence of more than three months imprisonment and the accused has been sent a notice containing the prosecution allegations and explaining the relevant procedure. It is most commonly used for motoring offences.

If the accused pleads guilty to the charge, the prosecution will then outline the facts of the case to the magistrates, any further offences that the accused wants taken into consideration, and his antecedents and any previous convictions. The practice of having other offences 'taken into consideration' is useful for both the accused and the police. The accused will have 'his slate wiped clean' without making very much difference to his sentence. The police will be able to have unsolved crimes cleared up. It has been suggested that the police might sometimes apply pressure to an accused to admit to other offences, perhaps with the inducement that they will present the case against him in Court as favourably as possible. Defendants are strongly advised to resist such persuasion. Social enquiry reports might be requested by the magistrates and in certain situations (such as before a community service order can be passed) they are obligatory. If the magistrates require a report, and one has not already been prepared, they would normally adjourn the case. The report itself will deal with the defendant's personal circumstances and probably make a recommendation as to sentence. The accused, or his solicitor, will be entitled to make points concerning mitigation of sentence whether or not a report is presented to the Court. The magistrates will then normally retire to consider their verdict.

If the accused pleads not guilty to the charge, there will probably be an immediate adjournment to enable the prosecution and defence to assemble their witnesses and prepare their cases. On an adjournment, the question of bail will arise. Although this will already have been considered when the accused was at the police station, the granting of bail by a Court is based on different principles. The Bail Act 1976 introduced for the first time in English law a presumption in favour of bail. Section 4 of the Bail Act states that a person *shall* be granted bail subject to certain exceptions. Unfortunately, the width of the exceptions coupled with the way they are interpreted by the Courts results in the apparent right to bail being greatly diminished. The exceptions that apply depend on whether or not the offence charged is punishable with imprisonment. If the accused is charged with an imprisonable offence he need not be granted bail if the Court considers there are substantial grounds for believing that he would, if released on bail, (a) fail to surrender to custody, or (b) commit an offence, or (c) interfere with witnesses or otherwise obstruct the course of justice. In addition, the accused need not be granted bail if the Court considers that it has not been practicable to obtain sufficient information to make a proper decision. In making any decision on bail, the Court is directed to consider a number of factors including (a) the nature and seriousness of the offence and how it is likely to be dealt with, (b) the defendant's character, antecedents, associations and community ties, (c) the defendant's previous record in complying with bail conditions, and (d) the strength of the case against him. If the defendant is charged with a non-imprisonable offence, it is almost inconceivable that he could be refused bail, but the Bail Act states that this is possible if the defendant has failed to surrender to bail for a previous offence and the Court believes that, if released, he would fail to surrender to bail yet again. If bail is refused, or conditions are imposed, the Court must give reasons to enable the accused to make an application to another Court.

An appeal against magistrates' refusal to grant bail can be made to a Crown Court judge, whether or not he has actually been committed to the Crown Court for trial or sentence. Appeal against the refusal of either magistrates or a Crown Court judge to grant bail can be made to a High Court judge in chambers.

At the trial before the magistrates, the prosecution will make an opening speech and then call witnesses to give evidence. Each witness will be examined by the prosecution and then may be cross-examined by the defence. The prosecution will have a right to re-examine but this should be confined to points which arise in the cross-examination. At the end of the prosecution evidence, the defence can make a submission of no case to answer and request the magistrates to acquit the defendant without hearing further evidence. The submission is on the basis that no reasonable tribunal could safely convict on the prosecution evidence because (a) an essential element of the prosecution case has not been proved, or (b) the prosecution evidence has been discredited on cross-examination. If the submission succeeds, which is unusual, the accused will immediately be discharged. If it does not, the defence will then present its case.

The defence will usually call witnesses who will then be cross-examined and possibly re-examined in the same way as the prosecution witnesses were. At the end of the defence case, the defendant or his solicitor is entitled to make a closing speech to the magistrates. The prosecution may exceptionally be allowed to address the Court again but the defence will always be entitled to the last word.

2. TRIAL ON INDICTMENT AT THE CROWN COURT

If the accused decides that he wishes to be tried at the Crown Court, he will inform the magistrates of this and the case will be adjourned until committal proceedings can take place. A trial on indictment before a judge and jury can only take place if magistrates decide in a special hearing – known as committal proceedings – that there is a *prima facie* case made out against the accused. It is important to note that the magistrates in these proceedings are not trying the accused; they are simply attempting to ascertain if, in the words of a 1937 case there is 'such evidence that, if it be uncontradicted at the trial, a reasonably minded jury may convict on it.'

There are two forms of committal proceedings. The 'old style' proceedings consist of a full oral hearing before the Court. The prosecution will call witnesses, who will be subject to cross-examination and possibly re-examination just as at a summary trial, and the whole of their evidence must be written down, read back to them and authenticated. The defence may then make a submission of no case to answer. If that is unsuccessful, the defence must then decide whether or not to submit evidence. If it does, the statements of the witnesses will be treated in exactly the same way as those of the prosecution witnesses, and the magistrates must then make their decision. If it does not, the defendant will be immediately committed for trial.

In certain circumstances the Court will accept written evidence but this does not stop the old style committal proceedings from taking a long time. It was partly for this reason that an alternative procedure was introduced in section 1 of the Criminal Justice Act 1967. (It is now contained in section 6 of the Magistrates' Courts Act 1980.) Magistrates can now commit a case for trial at the Crown Court without any consideration of the evidence provided that all the evidence is in the form of written statements, the accused is legally represented and the accused does not claim that the statements disclose insufficient evidence. The accused cannot demand this quicker form of committal proceedings but he can object if the prosecution wants it. However, most cases nowadays use this form. Defence lawyers realise that their chances of having the case against them stopped by the magistrates are very slim and they generally prefer to hold back their witnesses until the trial and perhaps add an extra element of surprise. Nevertheless, defence lawyers sometimes think they have a realistic chance of succeeding or they may wish to judge the strength of the prosecution case. The question of bail will arise and the principles discussed above will apply.

The order of proceedings at the Crown Court is similar to that at a summary trial. The main differences are caused by the presence of a jury. The accused stands at the bar of the Court and the indictment is read to him. The indictment is a more formal document than a summons and contains the charge(s) against the accused together with a brief statement of the basic facts which constitute the offence (see below). Each separate charge is referred to as a 'count' and the accused is required to plead to each count in turn. A jury of twelve people is then sworn in. The defence is allowed to challenge up to three jurors without giving any reasons; the juror would then be replaced by another one from the panel. In addition, any juror can be challenged for cause; for example, if the defence lawyers happen to know that the juror is disqualified from sitting on a jury. The case will open with counsel for the prosecution addressing the jury. Witnesses will then be called by the prosecution, each one being subject to examination, cross-examination and possibly re-examination. At the end of the prose-cution case, defence counsel can make a submission that there is no case to answer. If this is unsuccessful, the defence presents its case. Defence counsel can make an opening speech to the jury if he is calling at least one witness other than the defendant to testify as to the facts of the case. He will call his witnesses and examine them. They will then be subject to cross-examination and re-examination. At the end of the defence evidence, both counsel may address the jury. The prosecution will speak first and, as usual, the defence will have the last word.

The judge will sum up to the jury which will then retire to consider its verdict. Juries are now permitted to return majority verdicts but not until they have tried to reach a unanimous verdict for at least two hours. The actual amount of time that is then allowed before a judge tells a jury that he will accept a majority verdict is at his discretion. If there are not less than eleven jurors in the case, ten of them must agree on the verdict. If there are ten jurors in the case, nine of them must agree. A jury can be allowed to fall to nine

---

INDICTMENT   No.

The Crown Court at BRISTOL

THE QUEEN -v- PETER JOHNSON

PETER JOHNSON
                is charged as follows:-

COUNT 1   STATEMENT OF OFFENCE
                 Theft contrary to Section 1(1) of the Theft Act 1968.

                 PARTICULARS OF OFFENCE
                 PETER JOHNSON, on the 8th day of November 1985, stole £50 cash
                 belonging to Susan Davies.

COUNT 2   STATEMENT OF OFFENCE
                 Burglary contrary to Section 9(1)(b) of the Tehft Act 1968.

                 PARTICULARS OF OFFENCE
                 PETER JOHNSON, on the 8th day of November 1985, having entered as
                 a trespasser a building known as 85 Green Road, Clifton, Bristol 8,
                 stole two diamond necklaces.
                 Signed

                 S Wilson
                 Officer of the Court   MCR 342261/1/F24341 3m 4/85 TL

Form 5088

members (individuals may be excused through sickness) but in that case a unanimous verdict is required. If the defendant is found guilty, his antecedents and any previous convictions will be read out together with any social enquiry report. His counsel will then make a plea in mitigation. The contents of such a speech are somewhat predictable and it is unfortunate for a defendant with genuine points to raise that the judge will probably have heard hundreds of very similar – and sometimes totally unfounded – arguments before. Ill-health, a lengthy period of unemployment and a recent break-up of marriage are points commonly raised. Great emphasis would be placed on the fact that the defendant had no previous convictions (minor motoring convictions would be ignored); or if he had previous convictions that were of a different nature to the offence charged; or if his last conviction was quite a long time ago. The judge will then pass sentence.

3. SENTENCE

Sentencing law and practice is a vast area which it is not possible to go into in any great detail here. Every criminal offence has a maximum sentence and a Court will impose a sentence somewhere on the scale in accordance with a number of established principles. Most of these principles have been laid down by the Court of Appeal and, although they are intended for general application, they are more consistently applied in the Crown Court than in Magistrates' Courts. Consequently, sentences in Magistrates Courts are more unpredictable and, as we shall see later, there is some danger in appealing against them. We shall now consider the main sentences that can be passed on adults in Magistrates' Courts and the Crown Court and the principles that apply in particular to custodial sentences.

The most common penalty is the fine, particularly in Magistrates' Courts. In 1984, Magistrates Courts imposed fines on 98% of those sentenced for summary motoring offences and 89% of those sentenced for other summary offences. Even more than half the people convicted by magistrates of offences triable either way were fined. The Crown Court can impose an unlimited fine for any offence other than treason or murder, but a fine is rarely used by itself for serious offences. Maximum fines in Magistrates' Courts are limited by the particular statutes creating the offences. There is now a procedure whereby the levels of fines for summary conviction of offences triable either way can be altered by the Home Secretary to keep up with inflation. Theft, for example, is liable to a maximum fine of £2,000.

If a Court decided not to punish the defendant by way of a fine, it might consider making a probation order. This would involve placing him under the supervision of a probation officer for a specified period of not less than six months or more than three years. The Court can impose conditions on the order to secure his good conduct and prevent the commission of any offences. Such conditions could include a requirement to live at a probation hostel, attend a day centre, or undergo psychiatric treatment. The accused must consent to the order, although this is a formality which by no means guarantees that he will co-operate with his probation officer. It is important to note that a probation order does not constitute a sentence, except for any proceedings that arise from it, such as an appeal. Therefore, if an offender were subject to a suspended sentence of imprisonment a probation order would not activate it.

A further alternative open to a Court is to make a community service order. Any offender aged at least sixteen years who has been convicted of an offence punishable with imprisonment can, provided he consents, be required to perform unpaid work for the community for a specified period of between 40 hours and 240 hours (120 hours for a sixteen year old) under the supervision of a probation officer. The work should normally be completed within twelve months. A wide variety of work is carried out, including painting and decorating, outdoor conservation and gardening for elderly people. Some offenders exercise their right of declining to be subject to such an order and they must receive some other sentence, but there is always a veiled threat of it being a custodial one. Indeed, community service was originally introduced as an alternative to imprisonment but evidence now suggests that it is used as an alternative to a number of sentences.

On the other hand, if the Court considers that it is inexpedient to inflict punishment on the defendant and that he is not likely to benefit from a probation order, it might make an order discharging him. There are two types of discharge, absolute and conditional. Absolute discharges involve no punishment being imposed at all. They are used rarely and are usually confined to situations where magistrates consider that an offence was so trivial that a prosecution should not have been brought in the first place. The effect of a conditional discharge is that, if the offender commits a further offence in a stipulated period (which must not exceed three years), he is liable to be punished for the original offence as well. Unlike a suspended sentence, he would not have a specific punishment 'hanging over him' and conditional discharges are usually granted for relatively minor offences, but otherwise the overall effect of the two sentences is similar. A discharge, like a probation order, does not constitute a sentence, except for proceedings that arise from it.

Let us now consider sentences of imprisonment. If a criminal offence is contained in a statute, it is necessary to refer to the statute itself to see the maximum prison sentence provided. Some offences – such as dropping litter or many minor motor vehicle offences – are not punishable by imprisonment. There are still a few common law (not statutory) crimes remaining, such as manslaughter, and for these the length of any period of imprisonment imposed is usually at the discretion of the Court. Murder, also a common law offence, is one exception; it carries a mandatory sentence of life imprisonment. Magistrates are not allowed to impose a sentence of imprisonment exceeding six months for any one offence or twelve months where two or more consecutive sentences (see below) are imposed for offences triable either way. Maximum sentences can vary quite considerably and sometimes seem wholly disproportionate to the gravity of the offence. This is because a number of offences which had their maximum penalties fixed in the nineteenth century are nowadays considered as far less serious than they were then. A good example of this is the offence of bigamy, which under section 57 of the Offences against the Person Act 1861 is punishable with seven years imprisonment. Nowadays, it is unusual for the police to prosecute for this offence. On the other hand, the Theft Act 1968, which provides such maximum sentences as ten years imprisonment for theft, fourteen years for burglary and handling stolen goods, and life imprisonment for robbery, is sufficiently recent to provide a sentencing range which is used to its full extent by judges.

How, then, does a judge, when he thinks imprisonment is appropriate, decide on the length of sentence to pass on an offender? A study of Court of Appeal decisions has suggested that an inital choice has to be made between a sentence calculated to reflect the wrong doing of the offender (a 'tariff' sentence) and a sentence to suit the particular needs of the offender, in that it might help him not to re-offend (an 'indivualised' sentence). The tariff sentence is the more common of the two. There is no tariff in the sense of a published table of different penalties for different factual situations, but is seems that broad guidelines can be established by looking at decided cases. The basic object of the tariff system is to achieve a level of consistency in sentencing while at the same time allowing for possible aggravating or mitigating factors in particular cases. The first step is for the judge to make an initial placement on the scale of imprisonment reflecting the seriousness of the offence. For this purpose, the maximum permitted sentence is to be reserved for the most serious example of the offence which is possible (This would not apply to outdated provisions such as the maximum sentence for bigamy discussed above.) The next stage is for the judge to make allowance for any relevant mitigating factors. Such factors as the age of the offender, the lack of previous convictions, or a significant gap between the last conviction and the present one can be taken into account here and allowance is also made for a guilty plea. On the other hand, adverse factors such as a bad record of previous convictions cannot aggravate the initial placement on the scale; but they can cancel out the whole or part of the allowance made for the mitigating factors. An individualised sentence, on the other hand, frequently involves non-custodial measures but sometimes a sentence of life imprisonment is used for this purpose. This happens particularly when it is felt that the date for the offender's release can best be determined by executive decision at a later date.

Where a person is sentenced to terms of imprisonment for two or more offences, the terms may be ordered to run either consecutively or concurrently; for example, two consecutive sentences of one year would make an effective total of two years imprisonment, whereas two concurrent sentences of one year would run together and make an effective total of one year's imprisonment. The decision which order to make is not entirely at the whim of the judge. For example, if the offences have arisen out of a single event, the sentences should normally be concurrent.

A Court when passing a sentence of imprisonment can decide to suspend it, partly or in full. Any Court passing a sentence of imprisonment for two years or less can suspend it for not less than one year or more than two years. If the offender is then convicted of an offence punishable with imprisonment during the period of suspension, a Court must bring the suspended sentence into effect unless, having regard to all the circumstances, it considers that it would be unjust to do so. A suspended sentence of more than six months can be coupled with a supervision order. The effect of this order is similar to that of probation. Section 22 of the Powers of Criminal Courts Act 1973, which contains the power to suspend a sentence of imprisonment, states that the sentence should only be used where a sentence of imprisonment would have been appropriate in the absence of a power to suspend. However, there is evidence that Courts sometimes overlook this requirement and impose suspended sentences in cases which otherwise would have been dealt with by a fine or a probation order. Partly suspended sentences were provided for in section 47 of the Criminal Law Act 1977 but this section was not brought into force until 1982. The law now states that, where a sentence of imprisonment of not less than three months or more than two years is imposed, the Court may order that only part be served and the remainder held in suspension. The part to be served must be at least 28 days and the part to be held in suspense must be at least a quarter of the whole term. The power to partly suspend should only be used where the Court has considered but rejected the possibility of passing a wholly suspended sentence.

Once a person has started to serve a sentence of imprisonment, the question of the date of release becomes very important. Under the Prison Rules a person serving a determinate sentence of imprisonment of more than one month may be awarded remission of one third of his sentence if he behaves well. In practice, prisoners are given this remission as a matter of course unless they behave badly. The other way of obtaining early release is by being granted parole. The Home Secretary may release on licence a prisoner who has served at least a third of his sentence or six months whichever is the greater. The Home Secretary grants parole on the recommendation of the Parole Board which itself looks at reports from the local review committees at the prisons. Parole is officially considered to be a privilege and not a right; one result of this is that prisoners who are refused parole are not given reasons. In 1983 the Home Secretary, Leon Brittan,

announced that he would refuse parole to certain categories of offender (particularly ones convicted of violence) serving sentences of at least five years. This was challenged by some prisoners in the Courts, but without any success. Prisoners who are serving life sentences are not awarded remission for good behaviour or parole; but they can be released on licence by the Home Secretary at any time if there is a recommendation by the Parole Board and after he has consulted the Lord Chief Justice and the trial judge. The period of licence runs for the rest of the offender's life and he will always be liable to be recalled to prison. The average time spent in prison by a person serving a life sentence is ten and a half years.

4. RIGHTS OF APPEAL

A convicted offender may wish to appeal against the conviction itself and/or the sentence. The rules governing appeals vary depending on the Court the offender was convicted in and the Court he wishes to appeal to. If he was convicted by magistrates, he can appeal to the Crown Court against both conviction and sentence, provided, of course, he pleaded not guilty; if he pleaded guilty he can only appeal against sentence (see page 484). Permission is not needed to appeal but there is one important point that should be noted: on an appeal to the Crown Court against sentence, the Court can actually replace the magistrates' sentence with a heavier one. This provides a powerful disincentive to people who feel they have been punished too severely in the Magistrates' Court. The prosecution have no right of appeal by this method. However, the prosecution can appeal under the alternative method of challenging magistrates' decisions. Either the prosecution or the defence can ask the magistrates to state a case for the opinion of a Divisional Court of the Queens Bench Division in the High Court. This has to be either on a question of the meaning of the relevant law (as opposed to a challenge to a finding of fact) or a question of the magistrates' jurisdiction to try the alleged offence. If a case is stated for the consideration of the Divisional Court, the defence loses its right of appeal to the Crown Court. The case stated should include the facts as found by the magistrates, the contentions of the parties, the magistrates' decision and the question of law to be determined. The Divisional Court cannot hear new evidence and must accept the magistrates' findings of fact. The Court may (a) reverse, affirm

Crown Court Rules 1982, r.7.

SUPREME COURT ACT 1981

Section 84(1)

Notice of Appeal to Crown Court

(1) Give full address of Magistrates' Court.

To the Clerk of the Magistrates' Court sitting at (¹)

Nelson Street, Bristol 1.

(2) Insert name and address of other party to appeal, eg. Chief Superintendent.

And to (²)   Inspector James Plod

of   Z Division stationed at Redland Police Station

(3) Insert name and address of appellant.

Take notice that I (³)   Andrew Thomas

of   2 High Street, Redland, Bristol 6

Intend to appeal to the Crown Court at

against [my conviction and] [the sentence passed upon me] [the order imposed upon me]

by the Magistrates' Court aforesaid on the   5th   day of February   19 86

(4) Give nature and length of sentence/order.

when I was sentenced/ordered to (⁴)   5 penalty points and a fine of £150

(5) Give date and short description of offence.

for having on (⁵)   August 8th 1985 in Hampton Road, Redland, Bristol 6,

driven without due care and attention contrary to Section 3 and

Schedule IV of the Road Traffic Act 1972.

(6) Set out grounds of appeal if appeal under an enactment listed in Part III of Schedule 3 of the Crown Court Rules 1982.

The general grounds of such appeal are (⁶):

1. The conviction was contrary to the evidence

2. I am not guilty of the offence

3. The sentence was too severe

Dated the   6th   day of   February   19 86

(Signed)

IMPORTANT

(a) This notice must be completed in triplicate: one copy to be lodged with the Magistrates' Court and one copy to be sent to the other party to the appeal.

(b) This notice must be lodged not later than 21 days after the day on which the decision appealed against is given unless the Crown Court has granted leave to appeal out of time.

© **oyez** The Solicitors' Law Stationery Society plc, Oyez House, 237 Long Lane, London SE1 4PU

F2671 10/82
★ ★ ★ ★

Criminal 8

or amend the magistrates' order; or (b) remit the matter to the magistrates with its opinion; or (c) make such other order as it sees fit, for example an order as to costs (Summary Jurisdiction Act 1857). An application can be made from the Crown Court to the Divisional Court by either side on exactly the same basis in cases where the accused has appealed to the Crown Court from a decision of a Magistrates Court.

What is the situation if the defendant is convicted at a trial on indictment at the Crown Court? The first point to make is that in this country the prosecution has no right of appeal if the defendant is acquitted by a jury. If the defendant is convicted, however, he may appeal to the Court of Appeal (Criminal Division) (see pages 486 and 487). He may appeal without permission on any ground which involves a question of law alone. If he appeals on any ground which involves a question of fact, or a question of mixed law and fact, he can appeal (a) with the permission of the Court of Appeal, or (b) if the trial judge grants a certificate that the case is fit for appeal. In addition, the Court of Appeal can agree to hear an appeal on any other ground it considers could be a sufficient ground for an appeal (section 1 of the Criminal Appeal Act 1968). A defendant can even appeal against conviction following a plea of guilty if he can show he did not understand the nature of the charge; or he did not mean to admit his guilt; or because on the facts as admitted he could not be guilty; or because of a wrong ruling in law. Frivolous applications can be penalised by the Court's using its power to order that time spent on remand in custody awaiting trial, which is normally included in computing the overall time to be spent in prison, should not be counted for this purpose.

The Court of Appeal will usually allow an appeal against conviction if it considers (a) that the verdict of the jury, in all the circumstances of the case, is unsafe or unsatisfactory; or (b) that there was a wrong decision of any question of law; or (c) that there was a material irregularity in the course of the trial (section 2 of the Criminal Appeal Act 1968). However, there is an important proviso to this. Even if the Court of Appeal is satisfied that the point raised in the appeal is valid, it can still dismiss the appeal if it considers that there has been no actual miscarriage of justice in the case. The Court will do this if it considers that the jury would still have convicted the defendant even if the mistakes at the trial had not occurred. The Court of Appeal can also consider fresh evidence although it will look for a reason as to why the evidence was not admitted at the trial. If it considers that the evidence is true and clearly points to the defendant's innocence, it will allow the appeal; if it considers that the evidence is untrue, it will ignore it. In other cases, the Court may exercise its power to order a retrial. The Court can also order another trial where it considers that the first trial was a nullity on the grounds of a serious procedural defect.

The defendant can also appeal against the sentence passed on him at the Crown Court to the Court of Appeal (Criminal Division). (There is no appeal where the sentence is fixed by law, for example, life imprisonment for murder.) However, the permission of the Court of Appeal or the sentencing judge must be obtained in all cases. The Court of Appeal can quash the sentence and replace it with any sentence provided the defendant is not dealt with more severely than he was at the trial. This is an important difference between appealing against a sentence passed by magistrates and appealing against a sentence passed by the Crown Court. The Court of Appeal will normally only interfere with the sentence of the trial judge if it considers that it is wrong in principle, or manifestly excessive or that it fails to reflect the presence of some mitigating factor. The Court may hear fresh evidence in relation to the sentence.

Either the prosecution or the defence can appeal from a decision of the Court of Appeal (Criminal Division) to the House of Lords. There are two main requirements for this: (1) the Court of Appeal must certify that the case involves a point of law of general public importance; (2) either the Court of Appeal or the House of Lords must give permission for the appeal to be heard. In dealing with the appeal, the House of Lords can use any of the powers available to the Court of Appeal (Criminal Division) or it can send the case back to the Court to deal with.

5. DISQUALIFICATIONS

In addition to any sentence it may pass, a Court in certain circumstances can disqualify an offender from engaging in certain activities. For example, Courts can order that convicted persons should not run animal boarding establishments, catering premises or gaming premises. A convicted person may also be disqualified from owning an animal, being a company director, possessing a firearm, being a foster parent,

SEE NOTES ON BACK	**CRIMINAL APPEAL ACT 1968**	(See R2 Form 2)

| COURT OF APPEAL CRIMINAL DIVISION **N** | NOTICE OF APPLICATION FOR LEAVE TO APPEAL AND OF OTHER APPLICATIONS (See Note 7) | To the Registrar, Criminal Appeal Office **REF. No.** Royal Courts of Justice, Strand, LONDON, W.C.2A 2LL |

Write legibly in black

PART 1

Particulars of APPELLANT	FULL NAMES Block letters	FORENAMES PETER	SURNAME JOHNSON	Age on Conviction 22

	ADDRESS If detained give address where detained	H.M. PRISON, BRISTOL	Index number if detained

COURT where tried and/or Sentenced. (see note 3)	DATES of appearances at the Court including dates of conviction (if convicted at the Court) and sentence.	Name of Court	CROWN COURT, BRISTOL
		Name of Judge	HIS HON. JUDGE MAGYAR QC

Particulars of OFFENCES of which convicted. (State whether convicted on indictment or by a magistrates Court) and particulars of SENTENCES and ORDERS.	OFFENCES	Convicted on INDICTMENT or by MAGISTRATES COURT	SENTENCES AND ORDERS
	THEFT	I	6 MONTHS
	BURGLARY	I	ONE YEAR

Offences TAKEN INTO CONSIDERATION when sentenced. NONE	TOTAL SENTENCE 1 YEAR 6 MONTHS

PART 2

The appellant is applying for:— (*Delete if inapplicable)

*EXTENSION of time in which to give notice of application for leave to appeal.

*LEAVE to appeal against CONVICTION.

*LEAVE to appeal against SENTENCE.

*LEGAL AID.

see note 8

*BAIL.

*LEAVE to be present at hearing.

*LEAVE to call WITNESSES.

CHAIN AND SMITH (Signed) (Appellant)	Date 1/10/86	Address of person signing on behalf of Appellant. (See Note 6) QUEENS ROAD BRISTOL

This notice was handed in by the appellant today. (Signed) (Officer)	Date	**N**	Received in the Criminal Appeal Office. FORMS N.G. Date

E.D.R.

CRIMINAL APPEAL ACT, 1968

SEE NOTES ON BACK

(See R2 Form 3)

COURT OF APPEAL CRIMINAL DIVISION **G**

Grounds of Application for
Extension of Time
Leave to Appeal Against Conviction
Leave to Appeal Against Sentence

To the Registrar, Criminal Appeal Office

REF. No.

Royal Courts of Justice, Strand, LONDON, W.C.2A 2LL

Write Legibly in Black

FULL NAMES OF APPELLANT Block letters	FORENAMES	SURNAME
	PETER	JOHNSON

Give the Name and Address of the Solicitor and/or Counsel (if any) who represented the Appellant at the Trial

SOLICITOR	CHAIN AND SMITH QUEENS ROAD BRISTOL	COUNSEL	SIMON POMP TEMPLE LONDON

List of Documents sent with this Form which the Appellant wishes to be returned. Criminal Appeal Forms will **NOT** be returned

THE APPLICATIONS ARE FOR:—

EXTENSION of time in which to give notice of application for leave to appeal against:—

　　　*CONVICTION　and　*SENTENCE
　　　(*Delete if inapplicable)

Delete this section
if
no extension required

LEAVE TO APPEAL AGAINST CONVICTION for the following offences:—

1.　THEFT

2.　BURGLARY

Delete this section
if
there is no application
against conviction

LEAVE TO APPEAL AGAINST THE FOLLOWING SENTENCES OR ORDERS:—

1.　SIX MONTHS IMPRISONMENT ON COUNT 1

2.　ONE YEAR IMPRISONMENT ON COUNT 2

Delete this section
if
there is no application
against sentence

THE GROUNDS ARE AS FOLLOWS:— (Include reasons for delay if extension asked for)

If Grounds of Appeal have been settled and signed by Counsel they should be sent with this Form (see note 14)

　　　　　SETTLED BY COUNSEL

Continue (and sign) on Page 3 if necessary.

I HAVE READ FORM A A CHAIN AND SMITH (Signed)　　　(Appellant)	Date 1/10/86	Address of person signing on behalf of Appellant (See Note 13) QUEENS ROAD BRISTOL

G

FOR USE IN THE CRIMINAL APPEAL OFFICE
Received

Form 1457　31430—4-5-70　XBD

entering licensed premises, being a member of a local authority or holding certain public offices. Disqualification from driving a motor vehicle has been dealt with in section 7 of this book (see page 395). Under the Juries (Disqualification) Act 1984, any person who has served a period of imprisonment during the last ten years is disqualified from jury service. In addition, convicted persons may be disqualified from engaging in certain activities as a result of decisions made otherwise than in Courts. For example, the Secretary of State for Education and Science can exclude certain people from being teachers or youth leaders; and the Law Society can remove the names of solicitors from its roll.

6. CONTROLLING STIGMA

So far, we have discussed the procedures that a person who has been convicted – rightly or wrongly – of a criminal offence will encounter, the possible sentences that can be passed and the rights of appeal against conviction and/or sentence. For a truly innocent person, the ordeal of having to appear in Court will be especially traumatic and possibly far worse than the sentence that is passed on him. Yet when he walks out of the Court (or prison) his problems may be only just beginning. We have seen how a professional man, in addition to any sentence passed on him, may be excluded from his profession. However, any person who has been convicted of a criminal offence may have to cope with the accompanying stigma. The law does go some way towards controlling this, but in the opinion of many people, it could do a great deal more.

The greatest intervention by the law is to be found in Juvenile Court proceedings. Nothing can be reported by the news media that could in any way lead to the identification of a child or young person appearing before a Juvenile Court, or in any appeal from a decision of that Court. The Juvenile Court itself can order that identification be allowed but this happens very rarely. The facts of the case and the decision, however, can be reported. Juvenile Court proceedings are not open to the general public. Paradoxically, the same restrictions do not apply when juveniles appear before the Crown Court. The judge has to make a direction if he wants the identity of the child or young person to be protected and this by no means happens in every case. Adults have far less protection. A Court in general has no power to prohibit the news media from reporting the identity of defendants in criminal cases, whether or not they are convicted. Everyone who reads newspapers, especially provincial evening newspapers, knows that Court reports form a large part of a newspaper's content; indeed, some newspapers would be at a loss as to what to print if they were denied this 'staple diet'. There are, however, two situations where the identities of adult defendants are protected. The first is where an adult is charged together with a juvenile and identification of the adult would inevitably lead to identification of the juvenile. The second is where an adult is charged with rape, attempted rape or aiding and abetting rape. This latter provision, found in section 4 of the Sexual Offences (Amendment) Act 1976, was introduced as a backbench amendment in the House of Commons to a provision which was essentially aimed at providing anonymity for women complainants in rape cases. The protection of the defendant's identity in rape cases seems to cause no problems and there is a good argument for saying that it should be extended to all criminal offences.

As we have already seen, offenders who are placed on probation or granted absolute or conditional discharges are deemed not to have been convicted of an offence for any purpose other than proceedings arising out of the offence, such as an appeal against the order, or the consequences that will follow if the order is breached (section 13 of the Powers of Criminal Courts Act 1973). This means that a probation order or discharge does not have to be disclosed on a job application form. Exceptions are provided under the Road Traffic Act 1972, whereby probation orders and discharges do count as convictions for the purposes of endorsements and disqualifications. In addition, a police officer will mention them to a Court when reading out the defendant's antecedents.

The strongest protection against stigma the law can offer adults convicted of offences is provided by the Rehabilitation of Offenders Act 1974. The effect of this Act is that an offender's conviction is deemed to be 'spent' after a certain period of time, depending on the type of sentence he received. He is then to be treated, as far as the law is concerned, as if he had never committed the offence or been prosecuted for or convicted of it, or received a sentence in respect of it. If he is asked for information about his previous convictions for a job application or in any other situation, he is under no obligation whatsoever to reveal them if they are spent. The subsequent discovery by an employer of a spent conviction cannot in itself be a valid ground to dismiss an employee or for refusing to employ him. The Act applies to convictions imposed before it came into force. This rule applies to Court proceedings in general but it does not apply to criminal proceedings. If the offender is subsequently convicted of another offence, it is in order for any person giving antecedents or presenting a social enquiry report to mention spent convictions. However, if the conviction is recorded as spent on the written record, it will often not be read out in Court. A judge is allowed to take it into account in determining sentence but in many cases he will probably choose not to do so.

The periods of time (referred to in the Act as 'rehabilitation periods') after which a conviction becomes spent include the following (all periods run from the date of conviction):

An absolute discharge: six months.
A conditional discharge, binding over or probation order: one year or the length of the order, whichever is the longer.
A fine or community service order: five years.
A sentence of imprisonment not exceeding six months: seven years.
A sentence of imprisonment or youth custody for more than six months but not more than 30 months: ten years.
A sentence of imprisonment or youth custody for more than 30 months: never.

If the offender is under seventeen when imprisoned, fined or made subject to a community service order, the above periods are halved. No reduction is made, however, if an offender under seventeen is granted a discharge, bound over, or made subject to a probation order.

It will be immediately apparent that the provisions of the Act relating to discharges and probation orders appear to ignore section 13 of the Powers of Criminal Courts Act 1973, discussed above, which provides that, for this purpose, these do not count as convictions. This seems to be an oversight on the part of Parliament, and it is thought that, in any conflict between the two Acts, section 13 would be held to prevail.

Not surprisingly, there are a number of exceptions to the protection offered by the Rehabilitation of Offenders Act 1974. The full list is con-

tained in the Rehabilitation of Offenders Act 1974 (Exceptions) Order 1975 (SI 1975/1023) and is too long to include here (It can be found in some large public libraries or purchased from Her Majesty's Stationery Office). A number of employments, offices and professions are excluded from protection; these include the medical and legal professions, accountants, teachers and jobs involving the enforcement of law, such as the police.

Section 9 of the Act provides that it is an offence for anyone who, in an official capacity, knows of the details of spent convictions to disclose this information to any other person unless the offender is dead or has requested that such disclosure be made. The Home Office has also stated that the provision of information to any other officials acting in the course of their duty (such as Court clerks, police officers, or local authority employees assessing an applicant's suitability to work with children) would not be in contravention of this section.

CCAS (Crisis Counselling for Alleged
  Shoplifters)
c/o National Consumer Protection Council
London NW4 4NY
Telephone 01-202 5787 or 01-958 8859

The Criminal Injuries Compensation Board
10-12 Russell Square
London WC1B 5EN
Telephone 01-636 2812

London Rape Crisis Centre
PO Box 69
London WC1
Telephone (24 hrs) 01-837 1600

National Association of Victims Support
  Schemes
34 Electric Lane
Brixton
London SW9 8JT
Telephone 01-737 2010

National Womens Aid Federation
374 Grays Inn Road
London WC1
Telephone 01-837 9316

BIBLIOGRAPHY

The Law in Action
White, Robin C.A., *The Administration of Justice*. Blackwell, 1985

The Law and Your Home
Consumers' Association, *The Legal Side of Buying a House*. Hodder and Stoughton, 1986
Joseph, *Conveyancing Fraud*. Michael Joseph, 1980
Sar, Elaine, *Buying a Home: a Practical Guide*. SHAC (London Housing Aid Centre), 1986
Steele, *Do it Yourself Conveyancing*. David and Charles, 1984
Tunnard and Whately, *Rights for Home Owners*. SHAC (London Housing Aid Centre), 1985
Vickers, *Buying a House or Flat*. Penguin Books, 1985

The Law and Your Job
Code of Practice on the Elimination of Racial Descrimination and the Promotion of Equality of Opportunity in Employment. Commission for Racial Equality
Code of Practice on the Elimination of Discrimination on the Grounds of Sex and Marriage and the Promotion of Equality of Opportunity in Employment. Equal Opportunities Commission
Department of Employment Leaflets:
  No. 1 Written Statement of Main Terms and Conditions of Employment
  No. 4 Employment Rights for Expectant Mothers
  No. 7 Union Membership Rights and the Closed Shop
  No. 9 Guarantee Payments
  No. 13 Unfairly Dismissed
  No. 14 Rights on Termination
Facilities for Shop Stewards. Trades Union Congress (TUC)
Industrial Tribunals Procedure. Her Majesty's Stationery Office (HMSO)
Know Your Rights – Health and Safety at Work. Trades Union Congress (TUC)
McMullen, J. *Rights at Work*. Pluto Press, 1978

The Law and Your Money
Borrie, G. and Diamond, A.L., *The Consumer, Society and The Law*. Penguin Books, 1981
Cheshire, Fifoot and Furmston, *The Law of Contract*. Butterworths, 1986
Goode, R.M., *Commercial Law*. Penguin Books, 1982

The Law and Your Business
Ballard, R.M. and Chapman, A.L. (eds), *Tolley's Company Law*. Tolley, 1984
Barrow, *The Small Business Guide*. BBC Publications, 1984
Mason and French, *A Practical Guide to Company Law*. Financial Training Publications, 1986
Tax Guide for the Self-Employed. Touche Ross, 1984
Tolley's Tax Guide. Tolley, 1986
Underhill, Sir A., *Principles of the Law of Partnership*. Butterworths, 1986

The Law and Your Family
Bromley, P.M., *Family Law*. Butterworths, 1981
Consumers' Association, *Children, Parents and the Law*. Hodder and Stoughton, 1986
Consumers' Association, *Getting a Divorce*. Hodder and Stoughton, 1976
Consumers' Association, *What to do When Someone Dies*. Hodder and Stoughton, 1978
Consumers' Association, *Wills and Probate*. Hodder and Stoughton, 1983
Cretney, Stephen, *Principles of Family Law*. Sweet and Maxwell, 1984

Motoring and the Law
Driving. Department of Transport
Encyclopedia of Road Traffic Law and Practice. Sweet and Maxwell, 1960
The Highway Code. Her Majesty's Stationery Office (HMSO)
Kitchin, L.D., *Road Transport Law*. Butterworths, 1985
Mathers, J., *The Motorist's Guide to The Law*. Fourmat Publishing, 1986

The Law and Your Leisure
Clayden, P. and Trevelyan, J., *Rights of Way: A Guide to the Law and Practice*. Open Spaces Society, 1983
Countryside Commission: *Out in the Countryside*. One of a wide range of useful Contryside Commission publications
Grayson, E., *Sport and the Law*. Butterworths, 1986
Royal Commission on Gambling, Final Report. Her Majesty's Stationery Office (HMSO)

Criminal Law and You
Seago, Peter, *Criminal Law*. Sweet and Maxwell, 1985
Smith, J.C. and Hogan, B., *Criminal Law*. Butterworths, 1983

INDEX

ABTA (Association of British
  Travel Agents) 420, 422
ACAS (Advisory Conciliation and
  Arbitration Service) 146, 147,
                    151, 156, 168
accidents *see* motor accidents
'acknowledgement of service' 358
Acquisition of Land Act 1981 119
actual bodily harm 454, 455
Administration of Estates Act
  1925 335
Administration of Justice Act
  1985 ....3, 15, 42
administrator 343
Admiralty Court 29
admission, defence and
  counterclaim, form of 25–6
adoption 306, 310, 311–15, 366
Adoption Act 1926 311
Adoption Resource Exchange ...367
adultery 354
advertising 291–3
Advertising Standards
  Authority 186, 293
Advice Centres 5
Advisory Centre for Education ...376
affiliation orders 322
agricultural holdings 77
Agricultural Holdings Act
  1948 ....76, 77
air travel 419
A. Ketley Ltd v Scott 207
*Aldin v Latimer Clark Muirhead
  & Co* 93
Allen v Greenwood 109
Allison v Corby District Council ...400
Andrews v Hopkinson 178–9
animals 113–14, 444, 447, 457
  fights 410
Animals Act 1971 113–14
Annual Percentage Rate 207
appeal 483–5
apprenticeship, contract of 122
appropriations 457
arbitration 31
  County Court 20, 28
Archard v Archard 355
armed forces 133
arrest 454, 474, 476
  see also imprisonment
assault 453, 454
  sexual 455–7
  torts 472
assault and battery 113
Association of Bankrupts 216
Association of Mail Order
  Publishers 186
attacks 453–5
Attorney General v Overton 106
auction sales 184–5

Auctions (Bidding Agreements)
  Acts 1927–69 185
automatons 468
A v Liverpool City Council 318

badgers 447
Badgers Act 410
bail 476, 478, 479
Bail Act 1976 478
ballots, secret 149
bankruptcy 216, 271, 351–2, 360
  employees rights and 152
banks:
  accounts 209–12, 330–1
  conveyancing and 3–4
  customers' duties 210
  loans 208
  mortgages 39, 41, 47, 48, 49
barristers:
  audience, rights of 4
  clerks 5
  complaints against 15–16
  insurance 16
  numbers of 5
  partnerships prohibited 5
Barron v Potter 240
Bartlett v Department of Transport ...400
battery 453, 454
battery, tort of 431, 437, 472
Baxter v Baxter 301
*Bell Houses Ltd v City Wall Properties
  Ltd* 226
Bennett v Football Association 439
Bethiaume v Dastous 303
betting 406–7
  off-course 408
  on-course 408–10
  pool 410–11
betting duty 417
betting shops 408
bigamy 300–1, 482
Biggs v Biggs 354
bingo 414, 416, 417
birds 446–7
*Birmingham District Council v
  Beyer* 145–6
birth certificates ... 322, 323, 324, 366
Births and Deaths Registration Act
  1953 322
Bishop, David 430
blackmail 463–4
blood samples 394
boating 445
Bolton v Stone 436–7
bona vacantia 342
bookmakers 409, 410
borrowing and theft 459
boundaries and fences 115–17
boxing 429, 431

Boxing Board of Control 429
Bradford v Robinson Rentals Ltd 139
'breach of promise' 296
breakdown (vehicular) 397
breaking and entering 460
breathalysing 393–4
bridge 414
*Bridges and Others v Harrow London
  Borough* 113
Bristol Law Society 14
British Agencies for Adoption and
  Fostering 367
*British Aircraft Corporation v
  Austin* 156
British Airways 107
British Airways Board v Taylor 183
British Code of Advertising
  Practice 186
British Insurance Brokers
  Association 345
British Medical Association 314
*British Pharmaceutical Society v Boots
  Cash Chemists Ltd* 178
*British Syphon Co Ltd v
  Homewood* 122
British Telecom 191
British Telecommunications Act
  1981 458
British Waterways Board 445
Brittan, Leon 483
*Broome v Director of Public
  Prosecutions* 146
Brown v Lewis 434
budget accounts 201–2, 212
budget option accounts 202
building regulations 118
buildings, listed 119
building societies:
  cartel abandoned 47, 48
  conveyancing and 3–4
  estate agency and 38
  mortgages and 39, 41, 47, 48,
                                    49
  repossessions 17
Building Societies Bill 1985 3–4
bulls 444
burbot 450
burglary 460–1, 468, 472
Bushell v Faith device 228, 238
business:
  changing hands 130
  financing 264–72
  tax and 273–85
  types 218–70
  see also limited companies;
    partnerships; sole traders
Business Expansion Scheme 264,
                                    267–8
Business Names Act 1985 262
bye-laws 444, 456

Canon Law 297, 301
capercaille 449
capital: raising 264–8
Capital Allowances Act 1968 273
capital gains tax 273, 279–80, 282
Capital Gains Tax Act 1979 280, 281
capital transfer tax 335
caravans 399, 402
care: local authority 308, 309, 310, 315–18, 323
cars: tax and 274
'cash cards' 208
casinos 412
Central Office of Industrial Tribunals 148
Challinor v Taylor 158
Chancery Division 29
Chandler v Kerley 331
change of use 117–18
Chartered Institute of Arbitrators 422
chattels 40
check-trading organisations 205
cheques:
  bouncing 462
  guarantee cards 210, 211, 212, 462
  payment by 210–12
  worthless 463
Child Care Act 1980 316
'child of the family' 308
Child Poverty Action Group 367
children:
  access to, supervised 307
  criminal law and 431
  criminal responsibility 431, 467
  discipline 454
  indecency with 456
  maltreatment of 315
  see also adoption; care, local authority; custody, fostering
Children Act 1948 315, 316
Children Act 1975 309, 311, 313, 316, 321, 325
Children and Young Persons Act 1963 315
Children and Young Persons Act 1969 316, 467
Citizens' Advice Bureau 4, 5, 359
citizen's arrest 474
citizenship 325
'city pools' 410
Civil Aviation Act 1949 106
Civil Evidence Act 1968 321
civil servants 158
Clarke v Bethnal Green BC 435
Clean Air Acts 1956 115
Cleghorn v Oldham 432
'closed shops' 146, 147
'closing order' 95
coach travel 418–19
coal 106
Coal Nationalization Act 1946 106
Collier v Sunday Referee Publishing Co Ltd 124

coming of age 325–6
Commercial Court 29
Commission for Racial Equality 166
committal proceedings 479
'common fund' basis 13
common law:
  dismissal and 151
  health, safety and welfare at work 141–2
  property rights 327
'common law wife' 304
common redshank 449
commons 443
Commons Registration Act 1956 443
community service order 481
companies *see* directors; limited companies; partnerships; sole traders
Companies Act 1985 223, 224, 226, 228, 237, 241, 242, 245, 246, 252
Companies House 225
compensation 470–3
compulsory purchase 119–20
computer agencies 69
Condon v Basi 432, 437
conservation areas 119
Conspiracy and Protection of Property Act 1875 149
Consumer Credit Act 1974 184, 194, 195, 196, 201, 203, 205, 207, 212
Consumer Credit Association: address 182
Consumer Credit Licensing Branch 193
Consumer Credit Trade Association: address 182
consumer protection 178–87
Consumer Protection Act 1961 183–4
Consumer Protection Act 1974 187
Consumer Safety Act 1978 183–4
Consumer Association: address 182
Consumers in the European Community Group: address 182
contempt of court 112
contraceptive advice 306
contract, restricted 73, 77, 79
contractors' obligations 188–9
contractual liability 178–81
'contrary interest' 6
contributary negligence 143, 399–400, 437
'control' 458
Control of Noise (Appeals) Regulations 1975 112
Control of Pollution Act 1974 112, 115
conversion: torts 472
conveyancers, licenced 3, 38, 42
conveyancing:
  do-it-yourself 42–3

conveyancing – *continued*
  solicitors' monopoly ended 3–4, 42
convictions:
  failure of 466–9
  stigma 488–9
  wrongful 474
Cook v Deeks 240
coots 449
copyright 123, 287–8
Copyright Act 1956 123, 287
Corcoran v Anderton 457
Cornish v Midland Bank 332
corporal punishment 31, 454–5
corporation tax 277–9
costs 13, 31–5, 67
Cotman v Brougham 226
Council for Licensed Conveyancers 3
council housing 97–103
  eviction 98
  rent regulation 99
  rights and obligations of parties 99–103
  right to buy 47, 77, 101–3
  tenure, security of 77, 98–9, 100, 103
country parks 443
countryside:
  protecting 446–9
  using 440–9
Countryside Commission 441
County Courts:
  action, types of 17–20
  arbitration scheme 15
  creation of 17
  judgments, enforcement 28–9, 215–16, 269
  procedure 17–28
  proceedings 17, 213–15
  rules 20
  warrant of execution 269–70
County Courts Act 1984 4
Court of Appeal 29, 485
  Criminal Division 30
courts:
  audience, rights of in 4
  civil 17–29
  see also County Courts; Court of Appeal; Crown Courts; Divorce Courts; High Court; House of Lords; Magistrates' Courts
covenants 350–1
  positive 110–11, 116
  restrictive 92, 110, 117
credit:
  discrimination and 206
  extortionate bargains 206–7
  interest, calculating 207
  long-term 194–207
  rating 205–6
  refusal 205–6
  regulation of 205
  see also following entries
credit cards 202–4, 205
credit reference agency 203, 205–6

credit sale agreements 200–1
cribbage 412
cricket 430, 432, 434, 436–7
crime: victims of 453–74
Crime Survey 1981 452
criminal appeal 483–5
Criminal Appeal Act 1968 485
criminal damage 464–5, 470
Criminal Damage Act 1971 464,
                                         465, 468
Criminal Injuries Compensation
   Board 471, 489
Criminal Justice Act 1967 479
Criminal Law Act 1977 ....465, 472
Criminal Legal Aid Committee ...13
criminal offences abroad 420
criminals: civil proceedings ...472–3
Criminal Statistics 1984 455
Crisis Counselling for Alleged
   Shoplifters (CCAS) 489
Crown, lettings by 77
Crown Courts:
   acquittal 478
   choice of 476
   costs 35
   juries 480
   legal aid in 13, 14
   nature of 30
   trial procedure 479–81
Crown v Webb 206
Crowther v Shannon Motor Co 179
Crow v Wood 116
curlews 449
current accounts 208–10
Curtis v Chemical Cleaning and Dyeing
   Co Ltd 189
custody of children 306–11, 312,
                                              325
customers: suing 268
Customs and Excise 216, 282,
                                         283, 284

Dalton v Angus 109
damage, criminal 464–5
Dean v Andrews 40–1
death: property rights and ...334–44
death duties 335
debentures 246
debt collecting agencies 213
debtors 213–22
   bankruptcy 216
   County Court
      proceedings 214–15
   earnings, deductions from 216
   garnishee order 216
   judgment summons 216
   seizing goods 215
   see also bankruptcy
deception 462, 463
deer 449
defamation cases 32
default action 17, 20
   request for entry of judgment 27
default summons 22–3, 214, 215
Definitive Maps 440

Denning, Lord ... 16, 89–90, 206, 211
deposit accounts 212
Designs Registry 289
development 117–18
development plans 117
diabetics 468
diplomatic immunity 468
Diplomatic Privileges Act
   1964 469
'directions for trial' 358
Director of Public
   Prosecutions 457
Director of Public Prosecutions v
   Ray 462
directors:
   alternate 239
   appointment 238
   assets, transfer of 237
   committee of 239
   company debts and 262
   disqualification 238–9
   duty 240–1
   emoluments 255–7
   interests 229
   loans to 262
   pensions 261
   proceedings of 239–40
   register of 249
   removal of 228, 238
   remuneration 261, 265
   report 257, 258
   retirement 238
   service contracts 241, 252
   shares and 241, 252
discharge 481–2
Disciplinary Practice and
   Procedures Code of
   Practice on 151
discoveries 122
'dishonest', definition of 459
dismissal:
   capability 153–4
   common law and 151
   conduct and 154
   constructive ... 152, 158, 162, 174
   criminal record and 155
   definition 151–3
   fair 153
   grounds for 153–6
   notice 137–8
   reasons for, written statement
      of 138
   statutory restriction 155–6
   summary 136
   theft and 154
   unfair 130, 136, 148,
                                  149, 151, 153
   wrongful 151
disqualifications 485, 488
dividends 257, 260, 265
   corporation tax and 277–8
   profits, necessity for 259
Divisional Courts 29, 483
divorce:
   application 366
   children and 360, 364

divorce – continued
   conciliation and 359
   defended actions 358–9
   financial questions 357, 360–6
   grounds for 353–6
   history 353
   home and 360–1, 364–5
   limits on 356–7
   maintenance 303, 361, 363–4
   pensions 361
   proceedings 309, 357–8
   property rights and ...329, 360–6
Divorce Court 309, 357
Divorce Reform Act 1969 353,
                                         355, 356
Divorce Registry: address 358
dockworkers 137, 158
Dr Bernardo's Homes 315
dog racing 406, 409–10
dogs 114, 444
   see also previous entry
dolphins 450
Domestic Violence and
   Matrimonial Proceedings Act
   1976 361
'dominant tenement' 107
dominoes 412
Donaldson, Sir John 29
Donoghue v Stevenson 181–2
doorstep buying 187
Drane v Evengelou 81
driving:
   accidents 397–401
   age and 372
   breakdowns 397
   criminal offences 390–6
   directions, complying with ...391
   disabled people 372–3
   disqualification 395–6
   documents, producing 391
   drink and 392–5
   drugs and 393
   insurance 377–85, 401, 403
   learning 377
   licences 372–7, 396
   loads 390
   offences 390–6
   orange badge 392
   overseas 403
   parking 392
   passengers 390–1
   speed limits 391, 402
   test 377
   see also caravans; vehicles
drugs 468
drunkenness:
   criminal liability 467–9
   vandalism 465
   see also driving: drink and
Dunbar v Ford Motor Company
   Ltd 146–7
duty solicitor schemes 14–15

'easements' 107, 108, 109–10,
                                      111, 116

East Lindsey District Council v Daubrey 154
Eaton Ltd v Nuttall 164
education 318–20
Education Act 1944 ....318, 319
Education Act 1980 319
EEC 30, 164
either-way offences 14, 30, 476
electricity 457–8
employer: change of 128
Employers' Liability (Compulsory Insurance) Act 1969 287
Employers' Liability (Defective Equipment) Act 1969 140
employment:
  appointment, letter of 128–9, 130
  disciplinary rules 136–7, 156–7
  discrimination 163–6
  holidays 133
  hours of work 133
  maternity rights 133–6
  public duties, time off for 133
  redundancy 153, 154–5, 158–62
  segregation 166
  terms and conditions 128–30
  victimisation 166
  see also following entries and dismissal; wages
Employment Act 1980 151
Employment Act 1982 ....148, 151
Employment Appeals Tribunal 146, 148, 151, 154, 156, 164, 173, 174
employment contract:
  employee's duties 122–3
  employer's duties 123–5
  ending 137
  terms and conditions 128–30
  wages 130
  written particulars of 125–8, 130
Employment Protection (Consolidation) Act 1978 ....125, 130, 132, 137, 151
endowment insurance 345
enforcement notice 119
engagement 296
Equal Opportunities Commission 163, 165, 168
equal pay 164–5
Equal Pay Act 1970 ....163, 164
Equal Pay (Amendment) Regulations 164
equity finance 264
Equity Proceedings 17
estate agents 38, 40, 69
estate duty 335
European Commission on Human Rights 30
European Court of Human Rights 30–1
European Court of Justice 31, 164, 348
eviction 71
exclusion clauses 184, 188, 189
executors 336, 343
'existing use value' 120

Faccenda Chicken Co Ltd v Fowler 123
Factories Act 1961 ....139, 143
factoring 267
Fair Trading Act 1973 184
Families Need Fathers 367
Family Division 29
Family Law Reform Act 1969 ....305, 325
Family Legal Benefits Insurance 33–4, 35
Family Legal Expenses Insurance 35
fences 116
Fielding & Platt v Najjar 211
Finance Act 1971 281
Finance Act 1984 ....273, 277
Finance Act 1985 280
finance companies 196, 200, 201, 205
fines 481
Fires Prevention (Metropolis) Act 1774 91
first party insurance 438
Fisher v Bell 178
fishing 450
fitness for purpose 179
fixed charge 246, 271
fixed date action 17, 20
fixed fee scheme 11
fixed penalties 396
fixed-term contracts 138, 153, 158
'fixtures' 40
flagellation 454
'flashers' 456
floating charge 246, 271
flowers 448, 457, 464
Food Act 1984 425
food poisoning 426
football 430, 431
football pools 407, 410–11, 417, 432
Foreign Marriages Act 1892 303
Foreign Marriages Act 1947 303
Forestry Commission 447
fostering 310, 318
Fougere v Phoenix Motor Co Ltd 176
Fowler, Norman 348
foxes 449
France 403
Francis v Cockrell 434
Francis v Cowlcliffe Ltd 95
fraud 461–3
'freehold' 39, 40, 116
Freeman & Lockyer v Buckhurst Park Properties (Mangal) Ltd 254
Fuller v Fuller 356

gadwalls 449
Galt v Philp 149
gambling:
  control of 406–7
  definition 406, 407
  taxation 417
  see also gaming
game birds 449

game licences 449
gaming:
  casinos 412–13
  clubs and 413, 414
  definition 406
  licences 412, 417
  machines 413–14, 417
  principles 411–12
  taxation 417
  see also gambling
Gaming Act 1968 412
Gaming Board 407, 412
garnishee order 216, 270
gas 106
'gate-crashers' 465
Gazette 254
'gazumping' 39
geese 449
General Cleaning Contractors Ltd v Christmas 140
General Rate Act 1967 89
George v Beecham Group Ltd 176
Gibbons v Westminster Bank Ltd 211
Gillick v West Norfolk and Wisbech Area Health Authority 306
Gillmore v LCC 434
Gingerbread 367
giros 212
Gissing v Gissing 329
godwits 449
gold 106
golden plover 449
golf 432, 433
goods:
  buying and selling 178–87
  description 179
graffiti 464
Grainger & Son v Gough 178
grants 267
Green Card 403
Green Form Key Card 9–10
'Green Form Scheme' 6, 7–8, 476
greyhound racing 406, 409–10
grievous bodily harm 453, 454, 468
'gross indecency' 456
'gross negligence' 433
grouse 449
guarantees 180–1
guardians 306–7
Guardianship of Minors Acts 1971 ....306, 308, 310, 325
Guardianship of Minors Act 1973 306
G v G 309

Hall v Brooklands Auto Racing Club 435
Hall v Hall 302
Hanlon v The Law Society 13
Harassment Officer 81
Hardwicke, Lord 297
hare coursing 409, 449
Harrison v Michelin Tyre Co Ltd 124
Harrison v Vincent 432
Harris v Nickerson 184

Hayward v Cammell Laird Shipbuilders Ltd 165
Health and Safety at Work etc Act 1974 139, 140–2, 433
Health and Safety Commission 142
health care abroad 420
Helby v Matthews 194
Help-the-Aged Housing Association (Scotland) Ltd v Vidler 174
Herbert Clayton & Jack Waller Ltd v Oliver 124
HGV licence 376
High Court: divisions of 29
highway authorities 400–1
Highways Act 1959 116
Hillesden Securities Ltd v Ryjack Ltd 192
Hindes v Supersine Ltd 159
'hip flask defence' 394
hire-purchase 191, 194, 195–200
Hire Purchase Act 1964 195
Hire-Purchase Information Ltd 195
hiring goods 191–3
Hivac v Park Royal Scientific Instruments Ltd 122
holiday lettings 76, 79
holidays 133, 418–28
'Homebuyers Report' 42
Homeloan Scheme 50
hooliganism 431
Horrocks v Foray 331
Horserace Betting Levy Board 407, 409
horse racing 406, 408–9
horses 445
Hosie v Arbroath Football Club 434
Hotel Proprietors Act 1956 423, 424
hotels 423–5
housekeeping 333–5
House of Lords 29, 30, 485
house purchase:
  choosing the property 38–45
  completion 58–68
  conveyancing 42–3
  draft contract 45
  Enquiries before Contract 45, 46
  exchanging contracts 52–8
  financing 45, 54
    see also mortgages
  legal charge 62, 63, 66
  local search 43, 44
  mortgages 39, 45–54
  publications on 68
  requisitions on title 58, 62
  surveys 39, 41–2
  transfer document 60–1, 62
  see also rented accommodation; solicitors; conveyancing
houses:
  insuring 68–9, 346
  property rights 328–30, 360–1
  selling 69–70
  see also previous entry

Housing Act 1957 93, 94, 96
Housing Act 1961 84, 91, 94, 98, 99
Housing Act 1974 95
Housing Act 1980 47, 76, 77, 79, 80–1, 83, 84, 91, 98, 100, 101
Housing Act 1985 95, 96, 98, 100, 102, 103
Housing and Building Control Act 1984 101, 103
Housing Association Act 1985 96
housing associations:
  tenancies 96–7
Housing Corporation 96
Housing Defects Act 1984 102
Housing Defects (Expenditure Limit) Order 103
Housing (Right to Buy) (Maximum Discount) Order 1980 101
Housing (Right to Buy) (Mortgage Limit) Regulations 1980 102
hunting 449

ice-hockey 436
illegitimacy 297, 302, 306, 308, 320–5
imprisonment 474, 482–3
  see also arrest
Income and Corporation Taxes Act 1970 273, 278
income tax 273–7, 280, 417
indecent assault 455–6
indecent exposure 456
indemnity basis 32
indictable offences 30
indictment 480
indoor management rule 254
Industrial and Provident Societies Act 1965 96
Industrial Relations Act 1971 151
Industrial Relations Code of Practice 155
industrial tribunals:
  addresses 167
  unfair dismissal 130, 136, 148, 149, 151, 167–76
  wages 132
inertia selling 186
'inflict' 454
Inheritance (Family Provision) Act 1938 342
Inheritance (Provision for Family and Dependants) Act 1975 342
inheritance tax 280–2, 282, 335
Inland Revenue:
  covenants and 351
  divorce and 363
  mortgage tax relief and 49
insanity 468
insects 447
Insolvency Act 1985 216, 270
Institute of Consumer Advisers 182
insurance:
  applying for 379–85

insurance – *continued*
  brokers 345
  business 286–7
  certificates 384, 385
  life 344–5
  material facts 344
  motor accidents and 401
  own damage excess 379
  property 346
  rented accommodation and 91
  travelling abroad 403
  utmost good faith 379
Insurance Brokers Registration Council 345
International Convention on Motor Traffic 377
international driving permits 376–7, 403
International Sports Ltd v Thompson 154
intestacy 334, 335, 342
intoximeters 394
inventions 123
investment funds 268
invitation to treat 178

Jackson v Horizon Holidays 421
Jackson v Watson 179, 180
Jaggard v Dickenson 465
jalopy racing 435
Jarvis v Swans Tours Ltd 421
Jeune v Queen's Cross Properties Ltd 95
Jockey Club 409
'joint tenants' 330
'joint tortfeasors' 400
Jones v LCC 435
'judicial review' 118
'judicial separation' 353, 360
judo 429
Juhan v Juhan 357
'juniors' 5
Juries (Disqualification) Act 1984 488
jury service 488
Juvenile Courts 317, 488
J v C 310

karate 432–3
Kaur v Singh 301
Kennaway v Thompson 111, 115, 436
Kenny v Preen 92
kerb-crawling 456–7
'key money' 84
kick-boxing 429
Kilshaw, Mr 106

Lamond v Glasgow Corporation 436
land:
  ownership of 328
  registered 42, 43, 67
  three-dimensional aspect 106–7
  unregistered 42, 58, 67
Land Charges Register 58

Land Compensation Act
  1961 119–20
Landlord and Tenant Act
  1927 ....90, 91
Landlord and Tenant Act
  1957 ....76, 77, 104, 105
Landlord and Tenant Act
  1985 ....84, 91, 94, 95, 99
landlord's notice proposing a
  statutory tenancy 104
landlord's notice to resume
  possession 104
Land Registration Act 1925 332
Land Registry 62, 67, 102, 115
Lands Tribunal ... 105, 109, 110, 120
Latimer v AEC Ltd 140
law centres 5
Law Commission 111
Law of Property Act 1925 ...... 73, 90,
                                        110, 116
Law Reform (Contributory
  Negligence) Act 1945 143
Law Reform (Miscellaneous
  Provisions) Act 1970 296–7
Law Society:
  address 15
  advertising 4
  complaints 15
  Contract for Sale 45, 53–6
  conveyancing 3
  costs and 31, 35
  Council 15
  legal aid and 11, 12
  Legal Aid Office 6
  Notes for Guidance 11
  Lay Observer 15
League Against Cruel Sports v Scott ...113
'leasehold' 39, 40, 116
'leasehold enfranchisement' 104,
                                        105
Leasehold Property (Repairs) Act
  1938 90
Leasehold Reform Act 1967 ...104–5
Leasehold Valuation
  Tribunal...104
leases:
  covenants in 84
  example of 85–8
  exclusive possession 72
  forfeiture 73, 89
  long 76, 103–6
leasing 266–7
legal advice:
  funding of 5–10
  sources of 3–5
Legal Advice and Assistance
  Scheme 5–10
legal aid:
  civil cases 11–13, 167–8
  criminal cases 13–14
  divorce and 357
  extension of 5
  means test 11–12, 14
  merits test 11, 13–14
Legal Aid Act 1974 ....11, 13, 15
Legal Aid Act 1982 14

Legal Aid (Duty Solicitor)
  Scheme 14
Legal Aid Office 12, 13
Legal Benefits Ltd 35
Legal Services, Royal Commission
  on 3, 5, 14
Legitimacy Act 1926 321
Legitimacy Act 1959 321
Le Marchant v Le Marchant 354
Lemmon v Webb 112
Lesney Products & Co Ltd v Nolan ...159
'levying a distress' 84
liability:
  contractual 178–81
  exclusion of 180, 188, 189,
                                        427, 437
  in negligence 181
liability insurance 287
licence agreements 71–2, 73,
                                        76, 98
Licensing Act 1964 ....427, 438
life insurance companies:
  mortgages 47
Limitation Act 1980 116
limited companies:
  accounts 255–7
  advantages 222–3
  AGMs 243, 255, 260
  annual returns 258–9
  articles of association ... 227–9, 236,
                                        240, 243, 252
  audit and auditors 257–8
  boards 229, 236, 240, 253, 254
  books and records 249–52, 284
  borrowing 245–6, 257, 265–6
  business transfer 280
  capital maintenance 259–60
  capital raising 264–8
  certificate of incorporation 234
  chairman 229, 239
  close 278
  contracts and 252–6
  customers' insolvency 270–2
  EGMs 243, 260
  financial assistance to third
    parties 260
  financing 245–6, 264–8
  formation 224–9
  liability 226
  liquidation 261, 262
  losses, tax and ... 275, 278, 280, 282
  managing director 239, 253
  memorandum of
    association 224–7, 229,
                                        236, 252
  mortgages 245–6, 247–8,
                                        249, 252
  names 224–5, 246–9, 262
  objects 225–6, 236, 252–3
  officers 238–45
  payment by customers 268–72
  profits, retention of 279
  ready-made 224, 234–6
  registering 229–34, 237
  running the business 246–56
  secretary 239, 249, 253

limited companies – *continued*
  share capital 226–7, 236, 245,
                                        249, 264–5
  stationery 246, 249
  transactions with 261
  types 223–4
  winding up 242, 245, 246,
                                        262, 271
  see also directors; shares
Limited Partnership Act 1907 ...219
listed buildings 119
Litigants in Person (Cost and
  Expenses) Act 1975 32
litter 445
Liverpool City Council v Irwin 94
livestock 114
loan accounts 212
local authorities:
  lotteries 416
  mortgages 47
  wardships and 307
  see also highway authorities
Lockett v A & M Charles Ltd 426
London Building Acts
  (Amendment) Act 1939 117
London Rape Crisis Centre 489
lost property 107
lotteries 407, 414–17

'McKenzie men' 4, 28
McKenzie v McKenzie 4
madness 468
Magistrates' Courts:
  acquittal 478
  choice of 476
  costs 35
  criminal cases 29–30
  legal aid in 13, 14
  matrimonial proceedings 308
  trials procedure 478–9
Magistrates' Courts Act
  1980 ....4, 479
mail order buying 185–6
Mail Order Traders
  Association 186
maintenance 302
Maintenance Agreements Act
  1957 366
mallard 449
management companies 40
*Mancetter Developments v Garmanson
  and Givertz* 90
manslaughter 429, 430, 437, 482
manufacturers:
  claims against 181
  guarantees 180–1
mariners 137
marriage 296–304
  age 300
  capacity 300
  certificate 299
  Church of England 298
  civil 298
  consent 301–2
  consummation 301

marriage – *continued*
death, property rights
and 334–44
desertion 355
formalities 297–300
homosexual 301
invalid and valid 303
'irretrievable breakdown' 354
Jewish 300
non-Anglican religious 298–300
nullity decree 302–3
overseas 303
parental consent 297
polygamous 303–4
prohibited degrees 300
Quaker 300
valid and invalid 303
void 300, 302, 303
voidable 301–2
see also divorce
Marriage Act 1836 ....297, 298
Marriage Act 1983 298
Married Women's Property Act
1882 327
Married Women's Property Act
1964 333
martial arts 429
Master of the Rolls 29
Maternity Pay Fund 134
maternity rights 133–6
Matrimonial and Family
Proceedings Act 1984 .....356, 364
Matrimonial Causes Act
1973 ....309, 362, 364
Matrimonial Homes Act 1967 ...360
Matrimonial Homes Act
1983 ....333, 361
Matrimonial Proceedings and
Property Act 1970 334
Meah v Roberts 426
members *see* shareholders
Mental Health Review Tribunal ...6
merchantability 179
metal detecting 445
Miller v Jackson 115
MIRAS 49
Mock Auctions Act 1961 185
money purchase scheme 349
Monopolies and Mergers
Commission 5
'mooning' 456
'moonlighting' 122
moorhen 449
Mormons 303
Morris, Lord 454
mortgages 39, 45–54
brokers 47
capital repayment 47–50
constant net repayment 49, 50
deeds 62, 63, 66
endowment 47, 50, 62
gross profile 49, 50
indemnity guarantee 67
kinds of 47–51
pension 50–1
property rights 331–3

mortgages – *continued*
size, determinants of 51–2
tax relief and 45, 47, 48, 49
see also house purchase *and under*
banks; building societies
*Morton Sundour Fabrics Ltd v
Shaw* 159
motor accidents:
liability 399–401
meaning 397–8
procedure after 397–8
reporting 392
motorcyclists 391, 400, 444
motoring *see* breakdowns; driving;
vehicles
Motor Insurers Bureau 401
Motor Vehicle (Construction and
Use) Regulations 1973 387
MOT test 386, 389
Munro v Allied Suppliers 163
murder 468, 482
Murray v Harringay Arena ...436, 437
mushrooms 457, 464

National Association of
Bookmakers 407
National Association of Victims
Support Schemes 470, 489
National Coal Board v Galley ...124
National Conditions of Sale 45
National Council for One Parent
Families 367
National Federation of Consumer
Groups 182
National Foster Care
Association 367
National Hunt Committee 409
National Insurance 284–5, 348
National Lottery 417
National Marriage Guidance
Council 367
National Parks 443
National Society for the Prevention
of Cruelty to Children 317, 367
National Women's Aid
Federation 367, 470, 489
nature reserves 443
negligence 113, 181, 399–400,
431–3, 433–9
contributory 143, 399–400, 437
neighbours 106–17
newspaper bingo 416
Newspaper Proprietors'
Association Scheme 186
noise 11–12, 436
Noise Abatement Officer 112
non-molestation order 361
Norman v Bennett 182
*Nottinghamshire County Council v
Bowley* 154
nuisance, tort of 111, 112, 113,
114, 436
Nullity of Marriage Act 1971 300

'obligation' 458
Occupiers' Liability Act 1957 ...116
Offences Against the Person Act
1861 ....113, 430, 453, 468, 482
offences 'taken into
consideration' 478
Office of Fair Trading 193, 205,
206
Offices, Shops and Railway
Premises Act 1963 139
oil 106
Olley v Marlborough Court Ltd ...90,
424, 425
open spaces 443
ouster order 361
overdrafts 208, 210, 265
overseas workers 137
overtime 135
Owen, Clifford 201
Owen v Gadd 92

Palmer v R 454
parentage, proving 321–2
parental rights 305–11
entitlement to 306–11
parents, unmarried 320–5
parish records 366
Paris v Stepney Borough Council ...139
Parker v British Airways Authority ...107
parking meters 396
parks 443
parole 483
Parole Board 483
'participators' 278
Particulars of Claim ...18–19, 20, 21
Partnership Act 1890 ....218, 220,
221
partnerships:
agreements 219–22
debt liability 219
employees 218
forming 219–22
limited 219
new 219
retiring 219, 222
sole company and 281–2
tax and 275–6
torts and 218
partridge 449
part-time employees 125, 134,
137, 158, 348
party and party basis 13, 32
passing off 262, 290
passports 419–20
Patents Act 1977 ....122, 123,
288, 289
Patent Cooperation Treaty 288
Patent Office 288
address 122
patents 288–9
Patents Court 123
PAYE 282, 285
'payment into court' 20, 32
Pearce v Foster 122
Pearson, Lord Justice 92

pensions:
calculation of 349
contracting out 128
divorce and 361
private 348–50
state 346–8
tax and 282
Pepper v Webb 136
Perera v Vandiyar 92
permissive waste 90
Pettitt v Pettitt 329, 334
pheasants 449
Pheasant v Pheasant 355
Phipps v Pears 110
picketing 146
pintails 449
place of safety orders 317
plaint note 24
planning law 117–19
planning permission 39, 117, 118
plants 448, 464
poaching 450
pochard 449
police:
powers 393–5, 461, 455,
476
service 133
Police and Criminal Evidence Act
1984 ....14, 474, 476
pool betting 407, 410–11, 417
Pools Promoters Association 411
*Porcelli v Strathclyde Regional
Council* 164
porpoises 450
Portfolio 416
Portugal 403
possession 458
Potter v Potter 301
power-boat racing 436
*Power Packing Casemakers Ltd v
Faust* 149
Powers of Criminal Courts Act
1973 ....483, 488
'premium' 84
Premium Bonds 406, 407
Prescription Act 1832 108–9
pre-trial review 20
Price Marketing (Bargain Offers)
Order 1969 183
prices, display of 428
Prices Act 1974 425
pricing offences 292
Prison Rules 483
Privy Council, Judicial Committee
of 31
prize competitions 416
prize-fights 429
Probate Registry 343
address 366
probation 481
'property', definition of 457, 464
*Property Guards Ltd v Taylor and
Kershaw* 155
property rights 327–34, 360–6
property shops 69
prosecution, wrongful 474

'prospective development
value' 120
prostitutes 456
Protection from Eviction Act
1977 ....73, 81, 92
Protection of Children Act
1978 456
PSV licence 376
public decency 456
public duties: time off work for ...135
Public Health Act 1936 ....95, 115
Public Health Act 1961 116
public houses 427
public liability insurance 287

Queen's Bench Division 29, 483
'Queen's Councils' 5
*Quick v Taff-Ely Borough
Council* 94
Quinnen v Howells 163
Quinn v Williams Furniture Ltd 206

rabbits 449
Race Relations Act 1976 .....165, 423
racial discrimination 163, 165–6
rail bonds 403
rallying 433
rape 455, 460, 470, 472, 488
crisis centres 470, 489
rates 89
Raynor v Remploy Ltd 153
Re Besterman 343
receivers 472
'reckless': definition of 453, 461,
464, 465, 467
reckless driving 395
Re D 312
*Re D (A Minor) (Wardship
Sterilisation)* 306
redundancy 153, 154–5, 158–62
Redundancy Fund 161
Re E 307
Regis Property v Dudley 89–90
Registered Designs 289
Registered Designs Acts
1949–1961 289
registration agents 224, 225, 234,
239
rehabilitated persons 155
Rehabilitation of Offenders Act
1974 ....155, 488–9
Rehabilitation of Offenders Act
1974: (Exceptions) Order
1975 489
Re Halt Garage 261
*Re K (Minors) (Children's Care and
Control)* 311
religious education 319
remuneration certificate 31, 67
rent: amount 71
Rent Act legislation 71, 72, 73,
92, 99
see also following entry
Rent Act 1977 .....76, 77, 80, 81, 82,
83, 84, 91, 96, 97, 103, 104, 333

Rent (Agriculture) Act 1976 77
rental agreements 191
Rent Assessment Committee 83,
105
rentcharge 40, 111, 116
rented accommodation:
alterations and
improvements 90–1
assignment and sub-letting 91–2
breach of contract 73
contracts, restricted 73, 77, 79, 83
eviction 71, 79, 81, 98
harassment 71, 81
insurance and 91
landlord's rights 84–92
licence to occupy 71–2, 73, 76
notice to quit 73, 74, 78, 79
private tenancies 72–96
quiet enjoyment 92
rent regulation 81–4, 97, 99
repairs 89, 93–6, 98
rights and obligations of
parties 84–96
rights of entry 91
tenants' rights 92–6
tenure, security 72–81, 92,
96–7, 104
see also tenancies
Rent Officer 72, 82, 97
Rent Tribunal 79, 83
repairs 188–90
repairs and services 188–90
'repairs notice' 95
Re S 312
Research Institute for Consumer
Affairs: address 182
restaurants 425–7
retrial 485
Re Wynn 342
riding schools 445
rifle-ranges 433
Rigden-Murphy v Securicor Ltd 157
rights of light 108–9
Rights of Light Act 1959 109
rights of support 109
rights of way 107–8, 440–3
Rimmer v Liverpool City Council 93
Road Traffic Act 1972 ....378, 488
Road Vehicles Lighting
Regulations 1971 387
robbery 460, 468
Robb v Leon Motor Services Ltd 145
Robophone Facilities Ltd v Blank 191
Rondel v Worsley 16
roulette 412
Royal Commission on Legal
Services *see* Legal Services,
Royal Commission on
rubbish 114
Rubie v Faulkner 377
rugby 429, 430, 431, 434–5, 438
R v Bailey 468
R v Billinghurst 430, 454
R v Bloxham 460
R v Bradshaw 430
R v Collins 461

R v George 455
R v Hale 460
R v Hall 458
R v Laverty 462
R v Lewis 454
R v Majewski 467
R v Pitham and Hehl 457
R v Rymer 423
R v Turner 458
R v Walkington 461
R v Williams 455
R v Wilson 454
R v Woodman 458

Safety Representatives and
   Safety Committee Regulations
   1977 142
Saif Ali v Sydney Mitchell & Co 16
sailors 334
Sale of Goods Act 1979 ..... 178, 179,
         181, 195, 205, 426
sales between private
   individuals 184
Samma v Hazlehurst 72
sample, sales by 180
savings accounts 212
scaups 449
schools: choice of 319
seals 252
search warrant 461, 476
seaside 445
Seebohm Committee 315
self-defence 454
self-employed people:
   mortgages and 52
   pensions 350
   redundancy 158
sentences 481–3
   mitigation of 478
'servient tenement' 107
sex discrimination 163–5, 439
Sex Discrimination Act
   1975 ....163, 423
sexual assaults 455–7, 470
sexual harassment 164
Sexual Offences Act 1985 456
Sexual Offences (Amendment) Act
   1976 ....455, 488
share capital............ 226, 236, 245,
         249, 264–5
shareholders:
   agreement 241–2
   board and 240
   majority 243
   meetings 243–5
   minority 241, 242–3
   number necessary 262
   register of 249
shares:
   allotment of 228
   bonus 259
   capital raising 264–5
   ordinary 264
   partly paid 224, 227, 259
   preference 260, 265

shares – *continued*
   premiums 259, 260
   redeemable 260, 264
   registering 227–8
   transfer 245
Shaw v Shaw 296
Sheffield v Oxford Controls Co Ltd ...151
shipwrecks 45
shoveler 449
sickness pay 132
silver 106
Simms v Leigh RFC 434–5
*Singh v British Rail Engineering
   Ltd* 165
sit ins 149
skating 437
'slander of goods' 291
slot machines 413–14
Small Claims Court 268–9
Small Firms Service 269
*Smith v Chief Superintendent, Woking
   Police Station* 453
snipe 449
soccer 430, 431
   see also football pools
social enquiry reports 478
Social Security Act 1975 304
Social Security Pensions Act
   1975 128
social workers 307, 315
soldiers 334
sole traders 218
   partnerships and 281–2
soliciting 456
solicitor and own client basis 32
solicitors:
   advertising 4
   arrested people and 476
   choosing 43
   complaints against 15
   conveyancing 3–4, 39, 42, 43
   costs 31–5; 67
   courts, rights of audience in 4
   duty solicitor schemes 14–15
   fixed fee scheme 11
   income analysis 3
   insurance 15
   legal advice 3–4
   Legal Advice and Assistance
      Scheme 5–10
   Legal Aid and 5
   monopolies removed 3–4
   negligence, suing for 15
   numbers of 3
   wills and 335, 343–4
Solicitors Act 1974 ....3, 4
Solicitors' Disciplinary
   Tribunal 15
*Solloway v Hampshire County
   Council* 113
Spain 403
sports:
   care, standard of 431–3
   civil liability 431–3, 433–7
   criminal liability 429–31, 433
   insurance and 438

sports – *continued*
   spectators, injuries to 435–7
   sports clubs 433–7, 438–9
   spot-the-ball competitions 416
   squatting 465–6
   'staff associations' 145
   stamp duty 67, 245, 281
   standard basis 32
Starkowski v Attorney General 303
   'statutory charge' 6, 12–13
   'statutory nuisance' 95
   Statutory Sick Pay 132–3, 143
   'statutory trusts' 335, 336
Stennett v Hancock 181
   step-parents 307, 312
Stewart v Western SMT Co 153
   Stock Transfer Act 1963 245
   stolen goods 195, 459–60, 468
   'stop notice' 119
   Street Offences Act 1959 456
Street v Mountford 72
Stretch v Romford FC 436
   strikes 132, 145, 149
   structure plans 117
   students 76
   succession rights 325
   Summary Jurisdiction Aid
      1857 485
   summary offences 30
   summonses 474, 475
   supervision order 483
   supplementary benefit 348, 362,
         363
   Supply of Goods and Services Act
      1982 ....188, 192
   Supreme Court Act 1981 361
   surgical interference 454
   surveyors 39, 41–2
Sweeting v Northern Upholstery Ltd
     183
   swimming 435

Tanner v Tanner 331
Tattersalls, Committee of 409
tax relief:
   Business Expansion Scheme 267
   business property and 280
   covenants and 350
   divorce and 363
   losses and 275, 278
   mortgages and 45, 47, 48,
         49, 50, 363
   pensions and 349
Taylor v National Union of Seamen ...150
*Tayside Regional Council v
   McIntosh* 154
teachers 454–5
teal 449
tenancies:
   assured 73, 77, 79–80, 83
   fixed-term 73
   periodic 73, 90
   regulated 73–7, 80, 82
   restricted contract 73
   'secure' 97

tenancies – *continued*
shorthold 80, 84
'tenants in common' 330
thalidomide 182
theft 457–60, 468, 476
 definiton 459
Theft Act 1968 ... 426, 457, 458, 459,
                460, 463, 471, 482
Theft Act 1978 ....426, 463
third party insurance ... 377, 378, 438
Thomas v National Union of
 Mineworkers 146
Thurlow v Thurlow 355
'title, good root of' 42
torts:
 assault 472
 battery 431, 437, 472
 conversion 472
 negligence 181, 431–3, 433–9
 nuisance 111, 112, 113, 114, 436
 partnerships and 218
 passing off 262
 trespass 472
Torts (Interference with Goods)
 Act 1977 190
totaliser 407, 410
Totalisator Board 408, 409, 411
Tourism (Sleeping Accommodation
 Price Display) Order 1977 423
tour operators 420–2
Tovey v F F Robinson Ltd 133
Town and Country Planning Act
 1947 117
Town and Country Planning Act
 1971 ....117, 119
Town and Country Planning
 General Development Order
 1977 118
Town and Country Planning (Use
 Classes) Order 118
Trade Descriptions Act
 1968 .... 182–3, 290, 291–3, 462
trade directories 186, 187
trade marks 289
Trade Marks Act 1938 289
Trade Union Act 1984 149
Trade Union and Labour Relations
 Act 1974 146
trade unions:
 civil immunity 151
 dismissal and 150
 exclusion 147–8
 expulsion 147–8
 membership rules 149–50
 political fund 150
 recognition 148–9
 right not to join 146–7
 right to join 145–6
 time off for duties 146
trading:
 fraudulent 262
 wrongful 255, 262
Traffic Regulation Order 444
trailers 402
train travel 418
transexual people 301, 309

Transport and General Workers
 Union 145
travel agents 420–2
travelling abroad 403, 419–20
'treasure trove' 106
Treasury Solicitor 343
Tree Preservation Orders 447
trees 112–13, 447–8
Treganowen v Robert Knee & Co
 Ltd 167
trespass 113, 440, 441, 445, 449,
                450, 465, 466, 472
tribunals 31
Truck Acts 1831–1940 130–1
Trust House Forte Hotels Ltd v
 Murphy 154
trust property 458
TUC 148
tufted duck 449
Turner v Pleasurama Casinos Ltd 157
Tutton v A D Walter 114

under-insurance 472
unemployment pay 158
Unfair Contract Terms Act
 1977 ....180, 184, 188, 424, 437
unfair dismissal claims 130, 136,
                148, 149, 151, 167–76
United Dominions Trust Ltd v
 Western 194
Unlawful Games Act 1941 406
unmarried unions 304
unsolicited goods 186–7
Unsolicited Goods and Services
 Acts 1971 & 1975 186
urine samples 394

vandalism 464–5
VAT 281, 282–4, 292
vehicles:
 brakes 387
 condition of 386–9
 direction indicators 387
 doors 392
 exhaust systems 387–8
 horns 387
 indicators 387
 licensing 385, 386
 lighting 388, 403
 registration 385–6
 seat belts 388–9, 390, 400
 speedometer 389
 springs 389
 tyres 389, 403
 visibility 389
 windows 389
 see also driving
victimisation 166
visas 420
'voluntary waste' 90
vouchers 205

Wachtel v Wachtel 364
'wagering contract' 407

wages:
 agreement on 130
 deductions from 131–2
 equal pay 164–5
 guaranteed payments 132
 protection of 130–1
 sickness pay 132–3
Wages Act 1986 131
walls 116
wardship 306, 307
wards of court 317, 366
warrants:
 arrest 474
 execution 215
 search 476
Warren v Keen 90
Warsaw Convention 419
Weights and Measures Act
 1963 427
Western Excavating Co Ltd v Sharp: 152
Westminster City Council v Ray Alan
 (Manshops) Ltd 183
West v Buckinghamshire County
 Council 400
whist 414
White v Blackmore 435–6, 437
whole life insurance 345
widgeon 449
Widgery Committee 13
widows:
 benefits 348, 349
 rights 296
wild flowers 457
Wilks v Cheltenham Home Guard Motor
 Cycle and Light Car Club 432
Williams J.P.R. 430
Williams and Glyn's Bank Limited v
 Boland 333
wills 334–5, 336, 337–41, 366
Wills and Probate 344
Wilson v Underhill House School 156
Wings Ltd v Ellis 183
Women's Forum 367
Women's Liberation
 Workshop 367
Women's National
 Commission 367, 455
woodcock 449
Wooldridge v Sumner 432, 437
Woolmington v Director of Public
 Prosecutions 469
work:
 health, safety and welfare ...139–44
 hours of 133
 see also employment
Worringham and Humphreys v Lloyds
 Bank Ltd 164
wounding 453, 454, 468
wrecks 445
wrestling 429, 431
written particulars of
 employment 125–8, 130

yachts 434
Yeoman Credit Ltd v Latter 201
Yianni v Evans 41–2